Winds of Change

States of Emergency (with Keith Jeffery)

Sources Close to the Prime Minister (with Michael Cockerell and David Walker)

What the Papers Never Said

Cabinet

Ruling Performance (edited with Anthony Seldon)

Whitehall

Never Again: Britain 1945–1951

The Hidden Wiring: Unearthing the British Constitution

Muddling Through: Power, Politics and the Quality of Government in Postwar Britain

The Prime Minister: The Office and Its Holders since 1945

The Secret State: Whitehall and the Cold War

Having It So Good: Britain in the Fifties

The New Protective State: Government, Intelligence and Terrorism (edited)

Cabinets and the Bomb

The Secret State: Preparing for the Worst, 1945–2010

Distilling the Frenzy: Writing the History of One's Own Times

Establishment and Meritocracy

The Kingdom to Come: Thoughts on the Union Before and After the Scottish Referendum

The Silent Deep: The Royal Navy Submarine Service since 1945 (with James Jinks)

Reflections: Conversations with Politicians, volumes 1 and 2 (with Robert Shepherd)

PETER HENNESSY

Winds of Change
Britain in the Early Sixties

ALLEN LANE
an imprint of
PENGUIN BOOKS

ALLEN LANE

UK | USA | Canada | Ireland | Australia
India | New Zealand | South Africa

Allen Lane is part of the Penguin Random House group of companies
whose addresses can be found at global.penguinrandomhouse.com.

First published 2019
001

Copyright © Peter Hennessy, 2019

The moral right of the author has been asserted

Set in 10.5/14 pt Sabon LT Std
Typeset by Jouve (UK), Milton Keynes
Printed and bound in Great Britain by Clays Ltd, Elcograf S.p.A.

A CIP catalogue record for this book is available from the British Library

ISBN: 978–1–846–14110–2

www.greenpenguin.co.uk

Penguin Random House is committed to a
sustainable future for our business, our readers
and our planet. This book is made from Forest
Stewardship Council® certified paper.

For my teachers at St John's College, Cambridge, 1966–69
With gratitude
the late Hugh Brogan, the late Harry Hinsley, Peter Linehan,
the late Henry Pelling and the late Ronald Robinson

Contents

Acknowledgements

My thanks to Matt Lyus, whose careful and discriminating eyes are always the first to read my manuscript; and to that prince among copy-editors, Trevor Horwood.

Huge gratitude to Stuart Proffitt, my editor *sans pareil* at Allen Lane and to the exceptionally helpful team at Penguin: Rosie Glashier, Rebecca Lee, Corina Romonti and Ben Sinyor. Cecilia Mackay is a brilliant picture researcher and a delight to work with.

The staff at the House of Lords Library are one of the glories of Parliament and superb providers of assistance. And thanks to the officials of my favourite government department, The National Archives.

Gratitude to the Trustees of the Harold Macmillan Book Trust for permission to quote from unpublished passages of the Macmillan diaries and to the staff of the Bodleian Library at the University of Oxford, where they are preserved. Thanks also to Faber and Faber Ltd for permission to quote from Philip Larkin's 'Homage to a Government' and 'Annus Mirabilis', both collected in *High Windows*.

List of Illustrations

Prelude: A Tale of Two Cotswolds

The bias of my place and generation.

*Eric Hobsbawm, speaking at his ninetieth birthday
party, 2007, about his childhood and youth in
early 1930s Germany and mid-1930s England*[1]

'My place' in the early 1960s was the Cotswolds, in Nympsfield, 700 feet up between Stroud and Dursley where the great wedge of oolitic limestone, the building material of its exquisite villages, tips its escarpment into the Severn Valley. My family had moved there in the summer of 1959 from Finchley in north London.

It was an even greater contrast than it would be now for a twelve-year-old townie to make such a transition. Nympsfield was and felt remote (the last bus left Stroud at 7.15 in the evening and, initially, we had no car). In winters the snow came often and sometimes lingered long. In 1962–3 it fell on Boxing Day and stayed until March. For two weeks the village was cut off by more than eight feet of snow. The local council paid the men to dig out towards Stroud and Nails-worth and an army lorry with four-wheel drive broke the icy blockade with food for the village shop. Being a swot and in my O-level year at the local grammar school, I was one of the first to trudge out over the drifts down Tinkley Lane with a Marling schoolmate the 2½ miles to Nailsworth in the valley to catch the bus to Stroud. We slithered up the hill again in the late afternoon as the light faded and the bitter east wind whipped the snow off the fields chilling the duffel-coated duo of Hennessy and Wooldridge as they plodded back to the dark, snow-entombed village.

I

Nympsfield looked stunning on cold, bright winter days but it was not classic picture-postcard Cotswolds. It was very much a working community of about 350 people with four farms in the village itself, a small factory producing bacon and another that made parts for the shearing equipment manufactured by Lister's in Dursley. Unusually, it had a Catholic convent, a Catholic orphanage and a small Catholic church as well as the late-fifteenth-century St Bartholomew's for the Anglicans. It was the Catholic connection which partly brought us there. We lived in a late-sixteenth-century coaching inn, Bell Court, with a fine listed ceiling and fierce draughts. It was cold even in summer. And the morning after that first blizzard in December 1962, I went to wake my father in the attic in his huge tester bed (he was a tad eccentric) to find a foot of snow gracefully curled around it on the floor. We rented the place as part of Dad's cunning plan to replace commuting on the Northern Line with the life of a gentleman horticulturalist, rhubarb and potatoes being his specialities. Both failed miserably, so we added hardly a jot to Nympsfield's gross domestic product.

The village lived within an economy of rural deliveries as well as of cereals, cattle, sheep, bacon and machine-parts. The bread came up the hill from Leonard Stanley in a prewar van; Mary Wooldridge from Court Farm brought the milk and the village news; meat and coal arrived from Nailsworth; pink paraffin flowed in in a pink van from Wotton-under-Edge. Electricity had reached the village only the year before we settled in, but, apart from that, Bell Court was almost entirely unmodernized.

On some days Nympsfield could have been prewar rural England. A sighting of Hedley Bishop in the fields, for example, was a timeless scene. Hedley laboured on the farm of our friends Michael and Tessa Watts, wore gaiters and a buff coat, got tight on market days and sang 'Don't Bring Lulu' in his cider cups. Arthur Heaven, whose farm was right in the middle of the village, was sighted, similarly attired to Hedley, driving down Crawley Hill to Uley with a pig in his passenger seat.[2] Their accents, naturally, were deepest Gloucestershire. This early-Sixties mid-Cotswolds world was about to change, indeed almost entirely to disappear. Modernity was creeping in, for example in the form of Bert Court, who would drive up from Dursley in his

Austin A35 van every Saturday evening to collect that week's hire-purchase instalment for Mum's prized Hotpoint washing machine, adding, like the other regular deliverers, to the weekly stock of gossip. A thousand or so miles away, Pope John XXIII was steering through the reforms that were to change what was said in the village's Catholic church and the language in which it was spoken.

Broadcasting was the most powerful transformer. The Beatles began to come through the wireless and changed the nature of the pop music charts while I lived in Nympsfield. We acquired a second-hand television in 1962 just in time for *That Was the Week That Was*, although because the reception was rocky in the dip in which Bell Court hid, David Frost, Millicent Martin and co. performed headless as the picture moved up and down, creating a primitive split-screen effect.

Sex and satire mingled with the normal male adolescent grammar-school banter between readings from *Lady Chatterley's Lover* on the school bus from Nailsworth to Nympsfield via Horsley shortly after it was published in 1960 and the extraordinary late spring and summer of the Profumo affair in 1963, when it was rumoured that Christine Keeler was about to take refuge in Amberley (leading one of my classmates who lived close by, so he told us, to prowl its streets in the warm July evenings in the hope of glimpsing her). She never turned up, but thanks to the lurid scuttlebutt and innuendo about the mighty and the well connected in London, we were much better informed about the ways of the world by the time the Denning Report on the scandal appeared just as we returned to Marling School for our first lower-sixth term that September.[3]

These were the years, too, of the assassination of Jack Kennedy and successive Cold War crises. Berlin peaked and troughed and peaked again between 1959 and late 1961. My younger sister's boyfriend in the Gloucestershire Regiment – the 'Glorious Glosters' of Korean War fame – was sent to reinforce the British Army of the Rhine. The Cuban missile crisis, which came out of the blue in October 1962, looked for a week or so as if it really might reduce Nympsfield and everywhere else to irradiated rubble that, if mankind survived, might be the scene of a future archaeological dig to discover how the early-Sixties rural economy had worked before the bombs fell.

We were naturally archaeologically minded in 'Nympie', as we called the village. There is an ancient burial mound in its centre known as 'The Barrow', and you only had to scratch the thin upland topsoil to find a relic of the Bronze Age or Roman Britain. Dr Glyn Daniel, a Fellow of my soon-to-be college in Cambridge (St John's) who achieved great televisual fame in the Fifties as chairman of the top-rated quiz show *Animal, Vegetable, Mineral?*, had excavated Hetty Pegler's Tump on the ridge above Crawley Hill in the late 1930s.[4] J. V. Smith's gem of a history of Nympsfield describes how the main road from Bath to Gloucester ran through the village with two major Roman villas, at Woodchester and Frocester, 'built within two miles either side' of Nympsfield.[5]

While I lived in the village, increasingly anxious about the course of the Cold War, there took place, unbeknownst to any of us, the excavation of a fort of a new and particularly grim kind inside the Cotswold limestone about twenty-five miles to the south of us down the A46, the Stroud–Bath road, and a few miles east along the A4 between Bath and Corsham. It was the super-secret British War Cabinet bunker to be used in the event of a Third World War. Nympsfield was open, traditional upland Cotswolds; STOCKWELL, as it was codenamed in 1959–60* was clandestine, subterranean, doomsday Cotswolds. Not until the early twenty-first century, forty years on and with the Cold War over, could I piece together its provenance, visit its burial chambers (if the Russians had put an H-bomb on it, nobody would have escaped; 'STUCK HERE 4 ETERNITY' is

---

* In the last years of his second and final premiership, Sir Winston Churchill had authorized a study to be made, in the light of the hydrogen bomb (a thousand times more powerful than the atomic bomb on which previous planning had been based), of the location deep in the countryside 'of a skeleton alternative administration which could carry on if the London one were blotted out and to which any official survivors from London could rally' (TNA, PRO, PREM 11/5222, 'Machinery of government in war: plans for the central nucleus (including SUBTERFUGE/STOCKWELL and MACADAM)', Churchill to Brook, 10 April 1953). As work began in the second half of the Fifties, authorized by Sir Anthony Eden during his brief premiership, the bunker, in the old Bath stone quarry beneath Box Hill, was given the codename SUBTERFUGE (Peter Hennessy, *Having It So Good: Britain in the Fifties* (Penguin, 2007), p. 595). In the early Sixties its codename changed from STOCKWELL to BURLINGTON to TURNSTILE (Peter Hennessy, *The Secret State: Whitehall and the Cold War* (Penguin, 2003), chapter 6, pp. 186–205).

scratched macabrely upon its limestone walls) or sample its artefacts.[6] When, with my research students, I visited most of the bunker in June 2006 (I'd been permitted to see a corner of it in April 2001 before its location and former purpose had been officially disclosed), I was allowed to take home the odd souvenir. One was a dish cloth, white with a green stripe on which is emblazoned ER and the royal crown with '1960' and 'TETW' (could that be for 'The End of the World'? 'Tea Towel' more likely) flanking it, which indicates the year STOCK-WELL was first provisioned.

The bunker was probably not fully ready until late 1961/early 1962. But preparations were made to get what was called the 'central nucleus' of government down there in a hurry if the Berlin crisis turned truly critical in 1959–60.[7] The plans for manning the bunker with 4,000 officials, military, intelligence analysts, communications experts and a handful of ministers and key allied and Commonwealth ambassadors make extraordinary reading now and would have caused a sensation at the time.[8] Harry Chapman Pincher got closest in the *Daily Express* on 28 December 1959 with a scoop which began: 'A chain of underground fortresses from which the Government could control Britain and mount a counteroffensive in the event of an H-bomb attack is being built far outside London.'[9] Pincher's scoop caused a spasm of anxiety within the tiny, end-of-the-world planning community,[10] and within a couple of weeks Whitehall had, under the voluntary system of self-censorship then operated by the bulk of the press, issued a D notice on 'Underground Operational Centres', requesting them 'in the national interest not to publish the location of these sites or information indicating their size, depth or communications'.[11]

A briefing in the autumn of 1960 for the Chiefs of Staff gave some of the details:

The headquarters is about 90 feet underground, and includes about 800 offices, signals areas, dormitories, kitchens, a canteen, a sick bay and a laundry. It has its own emergency water, sewage and power supplies, and a Lamson tube system [for internal communication]. It is designed to provide complete protection against fall-out, but it could not withstand a nuclear explosion in the near vicinity. It will be provisioned to operate for a month. Construction work is for practical purposes complete . . . Communications will not be finished for about another nine months or so.[12]

The plan was to move the bulk of the STOCKWELL 4,000 into the bunker in the 'Precautionary Stage' of a run-up to global war, with Prime Minister Harold Macmillan and about two dozen of his close advisers and key ministers staying in Whitehall to pursue preventive diplomacy until leaving for the Cotswolds at the last minute before the Soviet bombs and missiles fell.

Until Macmillan's party arrived, a small ministerial group under Selwyn Lloyd, Chancellor of the Exchequer, would preside over the secret seat of government.[13] If Macmillan and the others didn't make it, it would fall to Lloyd to decide whether or not to order the RAF's V-bombers to retaliate.[14] (After Lloyd was sacked in the great Cabinet purge of 1962, Rab Butler, Deputy Prime Minister and First Secretary of State, was designated minister-for-the-bunker).[15]

Manning STOCKWELL was an elaborate exercise with secrecy built in at every stage. Special trains would wait at Addison Road Station* (now renamed Olympia after the exhibition centre it nestles beside) to carry the designated staff towards (as a decoy) 'Taunton'. Seven trains would move off at two-hourly intervals, their drivers told only at the last minute that Warminster, on the edge of Salisbury Plain, was their actual destination. British Railways declined to provide packed lunches on the trains: the bunker staff would have to bring their own.[16]

That would be the least of their worries. Only hours earlier would the bunker people have been told of their Third World War duties and given just enough time to go home, tell their families they would be away for at least a month with a British Forces Post Office number (4000) to which letters could be sent as the only means of contact.

With monumental British understatement, the 'information slip' advised the bunkerfolk that the dress code 'may be informal'; they

---

* Churchill had used Addison Road for his clandestine departures in World War II, as when he journeyed to Scapa Flow to board the battleship *Prince of Wales*, which carried him to the waters off Newfoundland to meet President Roosevelt in August 1941. From that encounter the Atlantic Charter emerged.

should take a packed lunch for the journey and that 'Facilities for entertainment will be limited. It is therefore suggested that you take a book or so with you.'[17] Although it was not divulged to them, their spiritual needs had already been taken care of: the military would provide the padres and, in classic forces language, the instruments of devotion were listed thus:[18]

COVERS, Altar, frontal, green/purple, reversible	1
COVERS, Altar, frontal, red/white, reversible	1
CROSSES, altar, brass, 21x W/O figure	1
CANDLESTICKS, altar, brass, 12x hexagonal pairs	1

How many of the 4,000 would have refused to head west to this troglodytic mini-Whitehall and insisted on staying with their families as the international scene darkened is unknowable.

Those who, once the mechanics of doom had been activated in a 'precautionary period', actually turned up at Addison Road would have known only that the train was heading west through Reading towards Wiltshire and Somerset; no more. At Warminster they would have been taken in buses to the garrison outside the town and given a meal of stew in the camp cinema before being put in army trucks and driven up through Westbury, Trowbridge and Bradford on Avon and finally along the B3109 road until turning off a few miles short of Corsham. Once out of the lorry inside the perimeter of the 'communications centre' (the cover story), into the lift and down to the most secret of all government establishments, the condition of their hidey hole would have taken them aback. A senior Cabinet Office civil servant, whose duties in the early 1970s included the care and maintenance of the Central Government War Headquarters (as it was officially known), has never forgotten his first impression of the place: 'Dust. I couldn't believe that such a scruffy place would be the last seat of what government would be left.'[19]

How would Harold Macmillan and the final two dozen have got there as diplomacy failed and the missiles were about to fly? Under Operation VISITATION, RAF helicopters, based at Little Rissington in Gloucestershire, were to fly to RAF Northolt in the north-west suburbs of London, refuel and drop on Horse Guards Parade alongside the back door of No. 10 Downing Street. The PM and his party would then be ferried west to STOCKWELL and swiftly down into the suites of rooms allocated to the central nucleus of a Third World War government.[20]* The Queen would not have flown west to join her Prime Minister: the continuity of the state required them to be kept separate as only the sovereign can appoint a head of government. This she would plainly have been unable to do if both had perished beneath the Cotswolds after the Soviets, alerted by the signals traffic emanating from it, had detonated a thermonuclear weapon over Box Hill. Her Majesty's planned Third World War redoubt was a floating one – the Royal Yacht *Britannia*. Its avowed wartime purpose as a hospital ship was another cover. Its real purpose was to house the Royal Family in the sea lochs of north-west Scotland amid mountains that would conceal its location from prying Russian radar. At night, the vessel was to move quietly from one sea loch to another.[21]

Visiting bunker Cotswolds is an eerie experience, and sampling the secret HQ section of its 240 acres and sixty miles of tunnels burns into the template of memory. The big, early-Sixties style telephone exchange (bizarrely, a copy of the *Sexual Encyclopaedia* remains in the telephonists' area alongside all the UK phone books) has a period feel. So, too, does the canteen, with its standard caff cruets, its urns, its traditional white crockery and enamel camper-style plates plus the pile of 'TETW' tea-towels. The library has atlases, Russian dictionaries, ordnance survey maps, pilots' guides, dentists' registers, Admiralty charts. Perhaps most striking of all is a pile of royal pardons – under emergency wartime legislation, the ministers in the bunkers all had draconian powers over life and property.[22]

The inner sanctum is perhaps the most eerie of all. We know which would have been Macmillan's private accommodation had the Cuban missile crisis continued and thrust the world into war (a subject of recurrent nightmares in his old age[23]): it is the only set of rooms with an en-suite bathroom. It resembles a nuclear *Marie Celeste* in reverse. Its bare limestone and breezeblock walls and concrete floor make a chilly, unfurnished monastic cell awaiting Macmillan's arrival.

* My book *The Secret State* was published long before the VISITATION file was released. In it I wrongly assumed that 'VISITATION' was the code word for nuclear retaliation as it came at the end of the drill for manning the bunker.

Nearby is the Map Room, from where, had they reached Box Hill in time, the nuclear retaliation decision would have been taken – the most thought-provoking part of the vast site. It's about fifty feet long and thirty feet wide, lit with fluorescent tubes and with a large white-board at one end (perhaps the British equivalent of Dr Strangelove's 'Big Board' in the classic 1964 Stanley Kubrick/Peter Sellers film of that name[24]). Overlooking it is a viewing area – a decision-takers' gallery that old Cabinet Office hands believe is where the Prime Minister, advised by the Chief of the Defence Staff, would have made the awe-some decision whether or not to authorize nuclear release.[25]

The nearest I came to this extraordinary place in my Cotswolds years was as the snow melted in March 1963. My friend Lewis Noble and I, fed up with being confined by blizzard and frost for so long, decided to break free at least as far as the Youth Hostel in Marlborough for a weekend's walking on the Downs. In those days, hitch-hiking was the journey-method of choice and a milk lorry hauled us slowly up the A4 as it climbed Box Hill from the Avon Valley. No prime minister ever visited it, but thousands of people passed every day fifty feet or so below the secret bunker as the Great Western Castles and the Kings pulled the express trains between Bristol Temple Meads and Paddington below those spartan rooms and dusty corridors. Many years later, the secret reached the Russians and the last phase of the Cold War saw a Soviet spy satellite make regular passes over Box Hill.[26] The bunker was not stood down until 1991.[27] What Churchill might have called the 'broad, sunlit uplands'[28] of Gloucestershire and Wiltshire concealed a grim and dusty secret in one of the most singular contrasts of Sixties Britain.[29]

Overture: From Romans to Italians

> Altogether it was as if vast and barbaric energies, long held in check, had suddenly burst their bounds. It was a wonderful time to be young, but rather disturbing to be anything else. A sympathetic continental observer, the French philosopher Raymond Aron, remarked that the British seemed to have changed from Romans to Italians in the space of a single generation.
>
> *Professor Sir Michael Howard, 2007*[1]

Raymond Aron was speaking to Michael Howard at a conference in Venice in the early 1970s when he delivered his assessment of the British experience in the 1960s.[2] The very term 'the Sixties' is redolent of an era and an attitude, and anyone returning to gaze upon the alleged Italianization of a once imperial people from the 2010s would instantly pick up on the significance of Aron's quip.

This book covers the early 1960s, the anteroom to what might be called the high Sixties – the transition years from the late Fifties which stand out now, as they did then, as especially nuclear-tinged. This was reflected in another side of Raymond Aron's polymathic range – Aron the nuclear strategist and author of *On War: Atomic Weapons and Global Diplomacy*.[3] In fact, writing in 1960, the theoretical physicist Otto Frisch, Jacksonian Professor of Natural Philosophy at Cambridge, declared: 'Power from atomic nuclei is about to transform our world – and threatens to destroy it.'[4]

Few could have spoken then with an authority to match Frisch's. With his aunt, Lise Meitner, he discovered atomic fission in 1939 – that uranium atoms when bombarded with neutrons split into atoms of lighter elements.[5] With his fellow refugee from Nazi-occupied Europe, Rudolf Peierls, at Birmingham University in early 1940, Frisch's calculations showed that far less enriched uranium was needed to make an atomic bomb than had hitherto been thought. In late 1942 the first atomic pile went critical and produced a chain reaction in Chicago, and in the summer of 1945 a bomb based on these processes was tested in the New Mexico desert.[6]

Frisch's 1960 article captured in the same flight of thought the possibility that the coming decade would mark the beginning of an era of abundance based on cheap, limitless energy and that the world could experience nuclear catastrophe and irretrievable destruction in a Third World War. The Frisch paradox, as one might call it, itself partly explains the explosion of hedonism and individual energies that both fascinated and alarmed Michael Howard. It is easy looking back to understand why life lived in the shadow of the thermonuclear arms race between the United States and the Soviet Union had a touch of Paris, Vienna or London in the years before the First World War about it – especially after we all peered over the rim of the abyss during the Cuban missile crisis in October 1962.

The Frisch paradox felt real enough even though the atom produced neither economic transformation nor nuclear immolation by the end of the decade – or (so far) in any of the decades that have followed. It could be argued that another farsighted scientist with a powerful pen, the biologist Rachel Carson, was the more accurate prophet when she published *Silent Spring* in 1962,[7] which has been described as '[a]rguably the most important book published this century . . .'[8] It was undoubtedly one of the 'touchstone books' of its generation.[9] It began with an unacknowledged whiff of Marx and Engels' opening to their 1848 *Communist Manifesto* ('a spectre is haunting Europe') as Carson warned that '[a] grim spectre has crept upon us almost unnoticed' of a physical landscape polluted by pesticides and the fallout from nuclear weapons tests. In words that instantly impressed President Jack Kennedy in the White House in September 1962, she declared:

> The most alarming of all man's assaults upon the environment is the contamination of air, earth, rivers and sea with dangerous and even lethal materials. This pollution is for the most part irrecoverable; the

chain of evil it initiates not only in the world that must support life but in living tissues is for the most part irreversible. In this now universal contamination of the environment, chemicals are the sinister and little-recognized partners of radiation in changing the very nature of the world – the very nature of its life. Strontium 90, released through nuclear explosions in the air, comes to earth in rain or drifts down as fallout, lodges in soil, enters into the grass or corn or wheat grown there, and in time takes up its abode in the bones of a human being, there to remain until his death.[10]

As what turned out to be a great new global movement fuelled by concern for habitat and the careful stewardship of natural resources flickered into life, kindled by Carson's book, another, also initially resource-driven and world-shaping, entered its terminal ward. For the day of the nineteenth-century territorial empire was over – with the cruel and immensely significant exception of the repressive system operated in eastern and central Europe by the Soviets, which had another thirty years to run and whose peaceful demise was wholly unforeseeable in 1960. As the economist J. K. Galbraith put it, there was by 1960 a 'less recognized and, quite possibly, more decisive factor' at work than an indigenous nationalism whose 'insistent pressure . . . had become too strong, too costly, to be resisted' by the old imperial powers (of which the UK was by far the largest). The colonies, said Galbraith,

> no longer rendered any justifying economic advantage. Once they had. They were a rich source of raw materials and varied consumer products. In return, they were a significant market for elementary manufactured goods. Those who so traded were economically and politically powerful . . . And, with all else, there was the ancient commitment to landed territory as essential to the possession of wealth and power.

This, argued Galbraith,

> was the case no more. The engine of economic well-being was now within and between the advanced industrial countries. Domestic economic growth – as now measured and much discussed – came to be seen as far more important than the erstwhile colonial trade. The colonial world having thus been marginalized, it was to the advantage of all to let it go.[11]

As a political or trading partner, Europe would never – could never – provide a sentimental surrogate for the British Empire for the early postwar generation. The UK has exhibited a deep emotional deficit towards the notion of Britain in Europe since Jean Monnet first turned up in London out of the blue from Paris in the spring of 1950 with the plan for a European Coal and Steel Community in his pocket.[12] This was profoundly true in 1960 but hard-headed, practical considerations caused the Macmillan government and the Whitehall machine that served it to realize that the road to future prosperity led towards Bonn, Paris and Rome rather than the old empire of palm, savannah and pine.

In terms of Britain's place in the world – and the satisfaction of its persistent wish to cut a dash globally out of all proportion to its population size or natural resources – the Sixties were a perpetual anxiety. This was especially true of the first years of the decade when the Cold War reached its most perilous phase as a rolling Berlin crisis morphed into a swift, chilling and potentially terminal Cuban missile crisis, the impulse to shed imperial commitments reached near manic proportions and the desire swelled to strap the faltering British economy to its booming western European neighbours. At the same time, the Macmillan administration clung desperately to the United States as the sustainer of Britain as a nuclear weapons power.

Churchill's old 'geometrical conceit'[13] about Britain's power flowing from its locus at the centre of three interlocking circles (North Atlantic, Empire/Commonwealth and Europe[14]) just about fitted the early Fifties but, a decade later, it looked delusory and was mercilessly exposed as the Sixties deepened. As Douglas Hurd (the future Foreign Secretary and then a young diplomat) put it: 'The trouble lay in mistaking a snapshot for a long-term analysis. The three circles were changing shape and size quite rapidly.'[15]

There was one illusion-stripper in particular throughout the Sixties that made the process of post-great power adjustment all the harder – the poor performance of the UK economy compared with its pacemaking competitors (P. G. Wodehouse called it 'a certain anaemia of the Exchequer').[16] Both main political parties made the halting and then the reversal of Britain's relative economic decline their prime selling point. Each promised economic modernization and the institutional reform that improved economic growth required, albeit via differing policies. Bob Morris, a seasoned Whitehall veteran, has developed the concept of the British 'vampiric' issue – a question the country keeps trying to settle by driving a stake through its heart, to find it only a matter of time before it rises up to bite once more.[17] The economy is *the* 'vampiric' issue of the years since 1945 and the 'stake' each political party sharpened to skewer it in the early Sixties was labelled 'planning'.

There were few who spoke up for the purer versions of the free market. Ralph Harris and Arthur Seldon did so from their perch at the Institute of Economic Affairs.[18] Some younger Conservatives, such as the future Chancellor of the Exchequer Geoffrey Howe, added their voices under the banner of the Bow Group.[19] Inside the Cabinet Room, the Minister of Health, Enoch Powell, was probably the only 22-carat free-market/small-state man, and he held Cabinet rank only from July 1962 to October 1963.[20]

From the perspective of the 2010s, it is temptingly easy to overgild the consensual years as an age of stability and harmony, as *The Economist*'s anonymous reviewer of Tony Judt's *Ill Fares the Land* did in the spring of 2010, when he or she described the thirty years after 1945 as witnessing 'a balance between market and state' which 'oversaw a fruitful truce between business and labour that produced a golden period for capitalism all round'.[21] The Sixties were far from a 'golden period' for either British capitalism or its nationalized industries compared with the UK's competitors, including the nearest neighbours across the Channel. And a decade that began with the trade union militancy of Frank Cousins and ended with the rise of Jack Jones and Hugh Scanlon and their triumphant seeing off of a Labour government on the question of trade union power can hardly be depicted as 'a fruitful truce'. The UK's postwar settlement, which had promised so much, was in all kinds of trouble (strongly reflected in the previous volumes of this series, *Never Again* and *Having It So Good*) in the early 1960s, and economic innovation and growth comprised the key battleground of the 1964 general election with which this book finishes.

One of the understudied elements of the Sixties is the interplay of perceived decline/failure/malaise and the itch for a range of social changes that a stuffy, stagnant, old, backward-looking, economically shuddering, fast-fading imperial country was thought to need by the young beneficiaries of the health, education and welfare the Attleean settlement had pumped into them. Tony Judt, like me a prime beneficiary of all that, reckoned it gave 'our age' an 'overwhelming confidence: we knew just how to fix the world. It was this note of unmerited arrogance that partly accounts for the reactionary backlash that followed it',[22] especially in the 1960s.

Modernization, dashes for growth and catching up with the competitors was the meat-and-potatoes of the early-Sixties generation, and of early-Sixties politics. And, as it became increasingly obvious that both the Conservative and Labour elixirs were failing to work their would-be transformative magics, still greater levels of anxiety ensued about balance-of-payments deficits and comparative-growth statistics. In the middle of the decade, Enoch Powell, in the ringing tones of a classically educated, maverick loner fascinated by the vicissitudes of his country's history, chose an Irish audience before whom to unveil his analysis of Britain's Sixties psychodrama. 'Of course,' he cried in that air-raid siren of a West Midlands accent of his to a no-doubt slightly startled university audience in Dublin in the election autumn of 1964,

> nothing halted, because nothing could halt, the continued decline in the relative size of Britain in the industrial and commercial world; but the longer it continued, the more firmly the British embraced the myth of the world's workshop as a lost Golden Age, and the more they flagellated themselves for the supposed latter-day sins which had earned them expulsion from that economic Garden of Eden. The Americans did not do this; the Dutch and the Belgians did not do this; the Germans did not do this; but the British did. It was our own private hell, as the myth of empire was our own private heaven, and under both hallucinations together two generations have laboured.[23]

If you treat twenty-five years as a generation, two more generations have done so since Powell acted as shrink-in-chief to his nation in 1964.

With those characteristically Enochian strictures ringing in his ears, this is exactly the terrain on which the author of a treatment of early-Sixties Britain must first alight, to try to explain the neuralgia that accompanied perceived decline and contributed so powerfully to the making of the political weather in the first years of the 1960s.

I

The Chipped White Cups of Dover

Everywhere in Europe you can have hot food and cold drinks
in the open air or indoors, in the evening or the day-time, on
Sundays or week-days and usually in a clean café. Whereas
everywhere in Britain . . . well, you only have to observe the
expressions on the faces of incoming tourists: the Frenchman
looking down at his plate of meat and two veg; the German
as he alights from his train in the main station of any British
city; the Italian woman as she sits shivering by the warming
pans hanging *on the walls*; the American as he comes out of
the 'rest room' of a Midlands garage.

Michael Young, 1960[1]

What sort of island do we want to be? This is the question
we always come back to in the end. A lotus island of easy
tolerant ways, bathed in the golden glow of an imperial sunset, shielded from discontent by a threadbare welfare state
and an acceptance of genteel poverty? Or the tough dynamic
race we have been in the past, striving always to better ourselves, seeking new worlds to conquer in place of those we
have lost, ready to accept the growing pains as the price of
growth.

Michael Shanks, 1961[2]

The Victorians were pushed forward by a profound belief in
progress and the imperial mission. In 1940 the applied forces
of war brought together the scattered professions and tribes,
and the common danger produced not only a burning radicalism but, paradoxically and wonderfully, an intense interest

17

in the future . . . [T]he post-war years have had a tragic sense of bathos. Radicalism seems less concerned with changing institutions than with a sense of doom from the H-bomb; the social ferment has subsided, the public schools have prospered as never before, and Oxford and Cambridge have refashioned their gilded cages. The professions have become more separate and self-absorbed.

Anthony Sampson, 1962[3]

A free society is necessarily an untidy, uncomfortable and apparently inefficient affair; and I suspect that one of the troubles with the 'State of England' writers is that they cannot bear the whole anxious process . . . [I]t is the lack of sense of proportion in 'State of England' writing that most depresses me . . . I sometimes have the impression that all their criticism comes from a bad digestion. The thing most likely to set them off is a tasteless *bisque d'homard* in a luxury hotel, or the inability to obtain a meal when they reach Ballachulish after 10 p.m. It is all very affecting. But I do not really think you can begin a reformation by nailing the *Good Food Guide* to the door of a provincial hotel.

Henry Fairlie, 1963[4]

I quite liked living in a ramshackle social democracy.

Paul Addison on the early 1960s in 2005[5]

Michael Young was a sociologist with a genius for sensing the significant in the prosaic. Many years later, he reconstituted for me the 'mental map'[6] in his head in October 1960 when he published his exquisitely titled pamphlet *The Chipped White Cups of Dover*. He had been struck that summer, returning home on a cross-Channel ferry from bustling, modernizing France, how drab Dover was. It hit him forcibly when he and the family parked their car and went for a cup of tea before bashing up the crowded A2 to London. It was served in the ubiquitous chipped white cups associated with British cafédom and works canteens.[7] (There were plenty of these in the Corsham

bunker, too, as I discovered when I first entered part of it in 2001).[8]
In the pamphlet he put it like this:

> [T]he old joke about the Continent being cut off [by fog in the English
> Channel] is too painful to be any longer funny, and any traveller not
> an Empire Loyalist is almost bound to return to the chipped white
> cups of Dover with more of a sense of shame than of relief.[9]

By 1960, Young, draughtsman of the 1945 Labour manifesto *Let
Us Face the Future* ('Beveridge plus Keynes plus socialism' as he
would later distil it),[10] had become disillusioned with the existing
political parties as bringers (real or potential) of an amenity society
at home and a truly post-imperial foreign policy abroad.

His pamphlet was one of the more distinguished contributions to a
critical genre whose shared philosophy was neatly caught in the title
of Penguin's 'What's Wrong With Britain' titles, which ran as part of
a series of Penguin specials between 1955 and 1965, picking up pace
and bite after the Suez crisis of 1956.[11] They were written by men and
women born in the 1920s and 1930s.

The cumulative effect of the 'What's Wrong . . .' literature and
associated journalism was to add to the pangs of Britain's relative
economic decline and to help create the intellectual and analytical
climate that contributed to the political change of the decade which
brought Labour's narrow return to power in October 1964 and its
big majority in March 1966. The 'What's Wrongers' were also among
the more profoundly disillusioned centre-left progressives after successive economic crises had taken the bloom off Harold Wilson's
'purposive' progressive politics later in the decade.

In its way, the 'What's Wrong' phenomenon was the retort of those
who felt shamed and enraged by Suez and baffled and irritated by the
credulous smugness of a British electorate that had fallen for Harold
Macmillan's having-it-so-good politics instead of Hugh Gaitskell's
austere progressivism in the polling booths on 8 October 1959.
Arnold Toynbee talked of 'the stimulus of blows' in human and political affairs.[12] Writers of a left-of-centre inclination, reacting to both
Suez and Macmillan's victory, reached for their pens. The 'What's
Wrong' literature was their catharsis and their revenge. The best
remembered of them is Anthony Sampson's *Anatomy of Britain*,

published in 1962, which became a huge best-seller.[13] Their choicest monument – not least because its first essay by the spirited right-winger and sceptic Henry Fairlie took them and their collective *mentalité* apart – was the special 'Suicide of a Nation?' edition of *Encounter* that appeared under Arthur Koestler's guest editorship at the height of the mania induced by the Profumo affair in July 1963.

Most of the contributors were bored by the British New Deal shaped by Keynes's economics and Beveridge's social policy.[14]* They were completely out of sympathy with Macmillan despite his efforts to lever Britain into the European Economic Community (the prosperity and modernity of whose original six members† shone like a beacon for most of the 'What's Wrongers'). They were by 1963 all too ready to succumb to the shiny promise of Harold Wilson's blend of science and socialism. Fairlie's mockery of their politics, their taste buds and their fondness for a shared linguistic litany of ' "vigour", or "dynamism", or "efficiency", or "greatness" '[15] now seems apt, if prematurely cruel. But although they could be characterized in this way they had a point – and they made much of the political and economic running during the first half of the decade and, as we shall see in chapter 3, contributed to the politics surrounding Macmillan's own attempt at the pursuit of modernity.

What were the fuel rods at the core of the 'What's Wrong' chain reaction? The cluster included rods historical, sociological, class-conscious, industrial, economic and cultural; they combined disquisitions on national character, the country's imperial past and its uncertain future with the hard numbers appearing annually from the Organisation for Economic Co-operation and Development in Paris, which provided comparative statistics of national growth in gross domestic product per head that the press converted into league tables read like runes by the political class and the commentariat.

Arthur Koestler as guest editor of *Encounter* declared: 'We cannot

---

* Though nobody at the time called it 'the British New Deal', I argued in *Having It So Good*, the predecessor volume to this one, that the remaking of the economic and social relationships between the state and the citizen in the years after 1945 amounted to just that, with the creation of a comprehensive welfare state, substantial educational reform and the pursuit of a full-employment policy to which the political parties subscribed.

† France, Germany, Italy, Belgium, the Netherlands and Luxembourg.

evade the economist's drab curves, because they are mirrored in our living standards, the prospects before our children, and the rate at which we develop stomach ulcers.'[16] We have, in varying degrees, lived as a country in the shadow of those 'drab curves' ever since. As the chart shows, the UK was locked in a vortex of relative under-performance in the age of postwar economic miracles the ended only with the oil-price explosion of 1973.

GNP, Annual Rates of Growth 1951–73

Japan	9.5
Germany	5.7
Italy	5.1
France	5.0
Netherlands	5.0
Canada	4.6
Denmark	4.2
Norway	4.2
USA	3.7
UK	2.7

Sources: John Cornwall, *Modern Capitalism* (1977), p. 11; OECD, *Economic Survey* (November 1979). Also Angus Maddison, 'Long Run Dynamics of Productivity Growth', *Banca Nazionale del Lavoro Quarterly Review*, no. 128 (1979), p. 4.

The 'What's Wrongers' attempted to penetrate the compost – cultural and social as well as industrial – which underlay those bleakly depressing growth figures. Michael Shanks, whose 1961 Penguin added the 'stagnant society' to the lexicon of decline, allowed his anxious frenzy to run away with him in Koestler's 1963 *Encounter* special by digging deep into African anthropology to find a parallel that would shock. In his essay on 'The Comforts of Stagnation' he drew on Mary Douglas's newly published study of the Lele tribe of the Congo[17] to help his readers better understand Macmillan's Britain. In a passage born of frustration, Shanks made his point with irony:

The Lele are an amusing, cultivated, intelligent Congolese tribe who have conspicuously failed in recent years to advance their economy as have their neighbouring tribes. Mrs Douglas traces the reason for their stagnation back to their distinctive tribal customs, which are based on avoiding what is felt to be the humiliation of old men losing power and becoming dependent on their juniors. To prevent this, the Lele have built up an immensely complex system of checks and balances, in which the old men are given a virtual monopoly of wives and the right to cultivate the fields. The younger men are kept in a state of what amounts to prolonged idleness and avoidance of responsibility, so that they will not infringe on the prerogatives of the elders. In this way a delicate equilibrium has been achieved, but at an enormous price in efficiency . . .

Shanks argued that the 'British, I am afraid, are in danger of becoming the Lele of Western Europe'.[18]

In a way, the 'What's Wrongers' were a tribe in themselves, with their own shared mantras of decline and overlapping explanations. They were to a man (and occasional woman – Elizabeth Young contributed an essay to the *Encounter* collection on education[19]) patriotic, genuinely concerned that their country should flourish and much exercised by the contrast of late Fifties/early-Sixties Britain with the superb burst of collective energy and purpose under the shared duress of the Second World War when they had been young.

Arthur Koestler, their unofficial ringmaster in 1963, was an exception. He was older than most of them, born in 1905 of Hungarian and Austrian parentage and a late arrival in the UK, having escaped from prison in France to reach Britain in 1940 only to be interned by the Home Office (his recently shed communism made him suspect everywhere).[20] By the early Sixties Koestler was an internationally celebrated author and journalist and it was an article by him on patriotism in the *Observer* which had triggered the formidable decline-spasm in *Encounter*.[21] Both the article and the *Encounter* essay began with the bizarre combination of stoical heroism and immovable stubbornness he encountered working alongside the bizarre Brits (as he saw them) in 1940 in the Army's Pioneer Corps, and the decencies of European tradition – hence his essay's title 'The Lion and the Ostrich' and his observation that '[t]hus Pentonville was my prep school, the Alien's Pioneer Corps my Eton':[22]

My company was employed on a vital defence job, and we were of course 'too keen' as foreigners notoriously are. So we asked our British CO to do away with the ritual tea-breaks – which, what with downing tools, marching fifteen minutes to the cook-hut and back, mornings and afternoons, cost nearly two hours of our working time. The CO appreciated our laudable zeal and explained that we had to have our tea-breaks whether we liked it or not because the British Pioneer Companies, plus the local trade unions, would raise hell if we did not. That was about six months after Dunkirk.[23]

Koestler liked his mates – '[t]he majority were a decent lot, with untapped human potentialities buried under the tribal observances' – '[t]he same bloke who unhesitatingly risked his life at Alamein to "keep Britain free" would not lift a finger at [Fords of] Dagenham to save Britain from bankruptcy'.[24]

If one were to distil the essence of the early-Sixties 'What's Wrong' critique, its ingredients would be a blend of the following:

- The continuing blight of class in schoolroom, university seminar, on the factory floor and in the works canteen and in the ideologies of the two main political parties.
- An 'establishment' dominated by Oxbridge males steeped in the classics and the humanities (rather than practical subjects) and what the Cabinet Office civil servant Clive Priestley would later call the amateurish 'good chap' theory of government,[25] in sharp contrast to the engineers and the financially numerate, *grandes écoles*-trained technocrats in Paris, who were widely thought to be the motive power behind a French growth rate double that of Britain's.
- Imperial and great-power illusions that led to an excess of defence spending and expensive overseas commitments and which also militated against a full-hearted attempt to join the booming European Economic Community and to compete in tough markets as opposed to soft, Commonwealth trade; the related desire to sustain the 'frighteningly insecure'[26] sterling area, which financed half of the world trade, based on the UK's gold and dollar reserves that could meet but a third of its liabilities.
- A trade-union movement obsessed with avoiding a return to the mass unemployment of the 1930s, clinging to rulebooks and inter-union demarcations that put a highly effective brake on technical innovation and economic growth.

The benefits of the British New Deal in terms of a better-fed, healthier and more formally educated full-employment society were assumed – rather than praised – by the 'What's Wrongers'. The contrast between the prewar Britain of 1939 and the mass-consumption society of twenty years on were somewhat discounted. Nor did their critique carry all before it in party-political terms.[27] The Conservatives, under a hereditary Scottish aristocrat in the person of Sir Alec Douglas-Home, very nearly fought the Labour Party, under the gritty more-meritocratic-than-thou Harold Wilson, to a draw in the general election of October 1964 – partly, it could be argued, because Macmillan and Douglas-Home had picked up the modernization theme and run with it themselves.

Those who were squeezed out in the early 1960s were the free-market critics on the right who had severe reservations about the increasingly interventionist economic stances of both the major parties. When the Institute for Economic Affairs was founded in 1957, its self-styled 'full frontal market economists',[28] Ralph Harris and Arthur Seldon, felt immense frustration with what Harris called 'a Tory government with a large chunk of socialism built into a consensus'.[29] The IEA, propelled by the ideas of Friedrich von Hayek and sustained by the broiler-chicken fortune of their patron, Anthony Fisher, found little purchase in the Whitehall of the Keynes-reading Harold Macmillan. Their hour would not come for another quarter of a century.

Journalists sympathetic to them, such as Norman Macrae on *The Economist* (inventor of 'Mr Butskell' in Butler–Gaitskell days, and soon to coin the concept of 'stagflation'[30]), fared no better. In his *Sunshades in October*, Macrae railed against an economic profession and a Treasury high command who were, in Keynes's metaphor, slaves to the thinking of a generation past and 'too much ruled by ideas that were rightly conceived for circumstances ten years back'.[31] Macrae had a nose for what Fernand Braudel called the 'thin wisps' of tomorrow that were barely discernible today[32] – in the Sixties, for example, he was prophetic in foreseeing just how great a manufacturing and trading force Japan was to become. In 1963, he suggested that Whitehall and the economics profession had 'to be pulled round into a stance where they can fight against today's dangers, not against yesterday's ones'.[33] The next stage of mass production, Macrae prophetically suggested, might 'lie in such fields as automated house-building, transport, food production and office employment – with all the attendant problems of driving existing workers in those industries out of a job and existing small-scale firms ... out of business'.[34]

Where the left and right critiques converged was the point at which the British New Deal bore down most firmly and malignly in the early 1960s – the structures, practices and powers of the trade unions – which, in Koestler's words, had become 'an immensely powerful non-competitive enclave in our competitive society'.[35] Some, like him, Harris and Seldon, saw trade unions as excessively influential in British economic life; others, Shanks in particular, saw them as lacking the kind of influence Swedish or West German trade unions rightly enjoyed as well-organized and staffed social partners in a co-operative national enterprise devoted to the maintenance of high-productivity/high-wage economies.[36] The question of trade-union power and the sustenance of the British New Deal was a fundamental Sixties preoccupation which absorbed a great deal of government time and produced successive policy and institutional fixes that, after brief bursts of promise, failed to take.

It was in film form that the trade-union question reached those parts of a wider national consciousness that neither the 'What's Wrongers' nor the 'full-frontal' free marketers could touch. Its impact in 1959–60 was instantaneous, and it added a phrase to the permanent storehouse of the English language. It was called *I'm All Right Jack*.[37] John and Ray Boulting's hilariously biting satire exposed the appalling state of both unions and management in some parts of British industry, brilliantly pitting Peter Sellers, as the communist shop steward Fred Kite, against Terry Thomas as the hapless personnel manager Major Hitchcock, with Ian Carmichael as Stanley Windrush, the well-born innocent, keen to work harder to boost exports who brings the arms manufacturer, Missiles Limited, and, in the end, much of British industry to a standstill.

David Puttnam, a connoisseur of British film as well as one of its most distinguished directors, believes *I'm All Right Jack* 'genuinely defined an era',[38] not least because it tackled a subject that was taboo in film terms – taboo partly because of the appalling labour relations within the UK cinema trade itself. Roy Boulting later revealed that Fred Kite was based on a shop steward at Charter Films' Denham studios.[39] Peter Sellers was very reluctant to take the part not because of any lurking trade union sympathies but because, as he said to Roy Boulting, 'Where are the jokes? Where are the laughs?' He wasn't fully persuaded until the first day of filming when, surrounded by members of the works committee, he swung round a corner with Kite's angular, assertive walk en route to bollocking the management and the film came to an immediate halt. In the language of the acting business, the film crew 'corpsed', overcome by laughter to the point where they couldn't carry on. They had recognized the type immediately.

Kite caught the breed to perfection in dress, attitude and speech. Alan Hackney's script was based on a torrent of stilted Trade Unionese, as spoken in scores of strike news bulletins delivered in a kind of staccato – half aggressive; half insecure with a touch of linguistic grandiosity – as when an interviewer asks Fred how many strikes he had led that year. 'I do not regard that question as being relevant to the immediate issues.'

Bill Morris, the much respected leader of the Transport and General Workers' Union in the 1990s, acknowledged that 'for generations . . . the portrait of Kite was seen to be . . . the reality'.

But the Boultings and Alan Hackney were not bent on producing a monochromatic political rant against excessive trade-union power and utterly absurd restrictive practices. A sleazy and manipulative management (the silky Dennis Price using his nephew Carmichael/Windrush as his stooge), doing corrupt arms deals with Middle East potentates, were pilloried mercilessly and Dickie Attenborough played the spivvy Sydney de Vere Cox to perfection. There are several glancing blows against the nature and consequences of the British New Deal, many of them from the mouth of the extravagantly toff-accented Terry Thomas:

> The Welfare State – I call it the Farewell State . . . They're an absolute shower [pronounced 'sharr']. We've got chaps here [he tells a wonderfully twitching, neurotic time- and-motion expert played by John Le Mesurier] who come out into a muck sweat merely by standing still.

The Macmillan government gets a thumping too with 'Coxy' saying: 'And don't forget all that bunk about "Export or Die!"' As Alan

Hackney said, at least Fred Kite was an 'idealist' reading the works of Lenin and idolizing the Soviet Union ('All them cornfields – and ballet [pronounced 'ball-ette'] in the evening').

For Simon Heffer, a devotee of the Ealing Comedy tradition,[40] *I'm All Right Jack* 'always struck me as one of the great monuments to British cynicism ... The Boulting brothers saying "We're washing our hands of the whole lot of you ..." The message that comes out of it is one of complete hopelessness.'[41] Absolutely true.

As David Puttnam noted, British films were at a low ebb (war movies apart) in the late 1950s.[42] But, as Dominic Sandbrook has described, *I'm All Right Jack* swept all before it in British picture houses during the summer and autumn of 1959:

> In seventeen weeks one British comedy attracted more than two million people to cinemas across the country while in New York it ran at the art-house Guild Theatre for four months and broke the house box-office record. In early September, when Harold Macmillan went up to Balmoral to ask the Queen for a dissolution of Parliament and a general election, she arranged that they should spend the evening watching a special projection of the chart-topping film.[43]

By 1960, when the film toured the provinces (I saw it in Stroud) the phrase 'I'm All Right Jack' had become a staple cliché of Conservative Party meetings and acquired legs that carried it into the permanent political lexicon.

There was another mighty popular conveyor of early-Sixties 'What's Wrongery' on a more individual level of anomie-tinged dissatisfaction – the comedian Tony Hancock, whose solo career peaked on BBC Television when his extraordinarily expressive face met the genius of Ray Galton and Alan Simpson's scripts for *Hancock's Half Hour*. The series is best remembered for the episode 'The Blood Donor' (1961), especially for the opening sequence with the nurse (played by June Whitfield) in the waiting room. Hancock, with his characteristic mix of bravado, self-irony and absurdity tells her he had decided it was time to do something for the country. So it was a matter of

> become a blood donor or join the Young Conservatives. As I'm not looking for a wife and I can't play table tennis, here I am. A body full

of good British blood and raring to go . . . British undiluted for twelve generations. You want to watch who you're giving it to. It's like motor oil. It doesn't mix.

Whitfield points out that blood is the same the world over:

> HANCOCK: I did not come here for a lecture on communism.
> WHITFIELD: In fact I'm a Conservative.
> HANCOCK: Then kindly behave like one, madam!
> WHITFIELD: Have you given blood before?
> HANCOCK: Given, no. Spilt, yes. There's a good few drops lying around the battlefields of Europe.

And he goes on to spin a wildly improbable yarn about getting separated from his battalion in the Battle of the Ardennes and setting off for Berlin.[44]

For me, the episode that took the palm was another 1961 Hancock gem, 'The Bedsitter'. It was chipped-white-cups country with a vengeance – thirty minutes' worth of solo genius; a bored Hancock on a Sunday afternoon in his run-down room in the heart of Earls Court bed-sitterland in west London, with its dreadful floral wallpaper, frilly lampshades and seedy clutter. It opens with Hancock lying on his bed in one of those shapeless knitted jumpers that were such a feature of the postwar years trying to blow the perfect smoke ring from his cigarette. Suddenly, he bursts into an ironic Noel Coward impression:

> A Room with a View, and you – and nothing to worry us.
> Tut. Tut. Ta.

He relapses into tedium with a sigh. (No comedian breathed a sigh to such effect.) Trying to draw the last inch from his roll-your-own cigarette, Hancock burns his lips, leaps up and searches for balm in the medicine cabinet but to no avail:

> Gotta put something on my lip. Might get lock-jaw. I know – butter.
> A touch of the old New Zealand.

He protrudes his lip, applies the butter and erupts into more impressions as he stares into the mirror, lip still extended. First Maurice

Chevalier with heavy French accent ('Every little breeze seems to whisper "Louise"') and then of Archie Andrews and Peter Brough (the radio ventriloquist on the BBC Light Programme's *Educating Archie*).

He returns to his bed of boredom and scans the heavy literature (Karl Marx; Bertrand Russell) on his bedside table – to no avail:

> Too much on me mind. Nuclear warfare. Future of mankind. China. Spurs.* It's hard graft for we intellectuals these days.

Just as Tony Hancock was peaking in appeal (his show reached 30 per cent of the adult population in May 1961[45]), a less gentle form of humour – satire with a dash of acid rather than self-irony – began to trickle into the national consciousness, bringing 'back into English life a strain of public insult and personal vilification which . . . it had not known for many years', as Christopher Booker, one of the founders of *Private Eye* in 1961 and someone who has provided a continuous recitative of satire and the lampooner's art from that day to this, put it as the Sixties drew to a close.[46] The time and place of this re-creation of a national phenomenon is easy to establish. The place was Edinburgh; the time, August 1960; the revue, *Beyond the Fringe*, starring Peter Cook, Jonathan Miller, Alan Bennett and Dudley Moore. It opened on the 22nd in the Lyceum Theatre to a house two-thirds empty.[47] That swiftly changed and the ripple-effect was potent. As the historian of the satire boom, Humphrey Carpenter, wrote of August 1960:

> four young men stepped on to a stage in Edinburgh and changed the face of comedy . . . its arrival in London the following year created a fashion for the satirical, or would-be satirical, that was one of the manifestations of what would soon be called 'The Swinging Sixties'.[48]

The show began at 10.45 p.m. once the stage had been cleared after Chekov's *The Seagull* and the more orthodox festival goers had departed for their hotels. It ran for only a week,[49] but it added a new and distinctive sound to the national cacophony. As Morgan Daniels

---

* The programme was first broadcast on 26 April 1961. If Tottenham Hotspur won the FA Cup the following month on 6 May they would become the first team to win the League and Cup 'double' in the twentieth century. They beat Leicester 2–0 and did.

put it in his study of its impact on successive 1960s government, '[t]he satire movement was the most savage, and often the most eloquent voice of Sixties Britain'.[50]

Young Oxbridge (Cook and Miller from Cambridge; Bennett and Moore from Oxford) sliced into the Establishment writ large – but, above all, Harold Macmillan's Britain. Michael Billington, later a famous *Guardian* critic, was sent to review the show for the National Union of Students' newspaper and asked them:

> 'What are you really attacking, what's your gripe?' And they said, 'Complacency.' It was the complacency of Macmillan's England that they really wanted to get at. And I think it's no accident that *Beyond the Fringe* happened when it did. Because the 1950s (which I was brought up in) had been so complacent, parochial, smug, Little England-ish.[51]

It was Peter Cook's cruelly superb parody of Macmillan (he had the slow, measured, world-weary voice to perfection) that had the most savage bite of any of the show's sketches. It was, in fact, a brilliant send-up of Macmillan's highly praised, globe-twirling party-political broadcast in the run-up to the 1959 general election.[52] Cook added extra bite the following year once Kennedy was in the White House and the show was enjoying its London run:

> 'Good evening. I have recently been travelling round the world on your behalf and at your expense.'
>
> 'I went first to Germany, and there I spoke with the German Foreign Minister, Herr . . . Herr and there, and we exchanged many frank words in our respective languages. So precious little came of that.'

It was the next section playing upon the contrast between the ageing Edwardian in London and the young, energetic, new-world man in Washington, that stayed longest in the memory:

> 'I then went to America, and there I had talks with the young, vigorous President of that great country . . . We talked of many things, including Great Britain's position in the world as some kind of honest broker. I agreed with him when he said that no nation could be more honest. And he agreed with me when I chaffed him and said that no nation could be broker.'[53]

Cook's arresting malice at the Prime Minister's expense was matched only by Malcolm Muggeridge in his contribution to *Encounter*'s 'Suicide of a Nation?' special, in his essay 'England, Whose England?' when he wrote:

> Each time I return to England from abroad, the country seems a little more run down than when I went away; its streets a little shabbier, its railway carriages and restaurants a little dingier; the editorial pretensions of its newspapers a little emptier, and the vainglorious rhetoric of its politicians a little more fatuous.
>
> On one such occasion I happened to turn on the television, and there on the screen was Harold Macmillan blowing through his moustache to the effect that 'Britain has been great, is great, and will continue to be great'. A more ludicrous performance could scarcely be imagined. Macmillan seemed in his very person to embody the national decay he supposed himself to be confronting.
>
> He exuded a flavour of moth balls. His decomposing visage and somehow seedy attire conveyed the impression of an ageing and eccentric clergyman who had been induced to play the part of a Prime Minister in a dramatised version of a [C. P.] Snow novel put on by a village amateur dramatic society.[54]

Muggeridge was a professional sceptic, a social dyspeptic who himself looked and sounded as if he was daily distilled in vats of his own bile. Yet those most affected by *Beyond the Fringe* and its followers were not the ageing and cynical but the young and idealistic, such as my friends Kathleen and Tam Dalyell (Tam would hammer the Conservative vote in the West Lothian by-election in 1962, adding to Macmillan's woes). Kathleen Wheatley, as she then was (daughter of Lord Wheatley, Scotland's Lord Advocate during the Attlee governments), has never forgotten the brio and bite of *Beyond the Fringe* that August in Edinburgh:

> We didn't know it was going to be so good. It had a huge impact on us because it was so critical of the Establishment. I had demonstrated against Suez. But this was different. I'd come from a convent [to Edinburgh University]. Humour was not the strong point of the nuns at all.
>
> *Beyond the Fringe* was very funny and very good. It was the excitement of being able to use your intellect to look at institutions with a

critical eye. You didn't think you were being nihilistic. You thought you were going to get a better world by exposing all this hypocrisy.

It was a class thing, too. – Harold Macmillan, the grouse-moor, privilege and all that ... We were the Butler Act generation coming through. There was a real classlessness about the history group I was in at Edinburgh. I'd just graduated a month before. It was the beginning of all this questioning of the Establishment and it had a great deal to do with the Butler Act.[55]

That Was the Week That Was, presented by David Frost and produced by Ned Sherrin, in its short life on BBC Television (starting in November 1962) reached millions (where *Beyond the Fringe* was seen by thousands) and exercised both the Macmillan and Douglas-Home governments. It had a real capacity to shock. Never before had the BBC come anywhere near the bite of TW3's satire, which sometimes went beyond parody to the edge of character assassination. And *Private Eye* carries on the tradition to this day (infuriating every prime minister on the way). But *Beyond the Fringe* retains the freshness and specialness of the pioneer attack breaking through the crust of conformity for the first time.

The mood among many, though not all, of the university-trained young (a mere 216,000 students attended British universities in 1962 – 148,000 men and 68,000 women[56]) was exactly as Kathleen Dalyell remembers, especially those nurtured by the grammar schools. Macmillan came face to face with this in Oxford in February 1962, as recorded by two diarists. First, Paul Addison, then a first-year undergraduate, later top-flight modern historian and, with *The Road to 1945*, prime begetter of the 'great debate' about postwar consensus:[57]

Pembroke
Feb 2 62
towards ten
Missed dinner this evening so as to get to the Union in time to hear the Prime Minister. When I arrived at around half past seven the floor was almost full ... The gallery filled up. The floor was already packed. Someone shouted 'Ban the bomb England.' ...
    A great hullabaloo outside, and flashes of white light caught on the stained glass indicated Mac's arrival. He walked in at a dignified pace,

carrying a portly front before him as royally as possible. An under-graduate next to the platform balanced a paper dart on the dispatch box. Mac sat down, picked it up, examined it and handed it to an anonymous blue-suited aide ... As Mac uttered his first words the howling outside of the late-comers shut out took on tribal proportions.

Mac, untidily shaped under a dark blue suit which hung loosely over him, sombre scarlet tie, hair in an ample sweep of silver lined with grey, eyebrows falling sleepily like a bloodhound's, a slight droop about the moustache, a fatigued, drawling, lugubrious voice appar-ently proceeding from a cavernous throat, a thickness about his sibilants, a whistle about his 't's', gave us, of course, nothing new. He had a rough ride. It's no use any PM trying to fob off an audience of undergraduates with a few well-chosen bromides.[58]

The head man of the British Lele had plainly lost his rapport with the cleverer younger members of the tribe. And yet, as Paul Addison sensed, there was more in Macmillan that night than a trumpeting of the gold of the postwar years (compared to 1918–45) – there was rec-ognition of a need to quicken the pace of reform and improvement, that his having-it-so-good had mutated into having-it-so-edgy. 'Mac,' Addison continued,

put forward the Conservative Party, amidst a great deal of jeering, as the party of change, the party which adapts itself to a new situation. He dismissed 'orthodox Marxist socialism' and 'orthodox laissez-faire Liberalism' in one breath. 'I am not going to review the record of the past ten years,' he said, provoking cries of 'Suez' which grew to a crescendo.

He ignored them. Then he went on to deal with six major issues. He started off with The Bomb, but the Banners weren't around. Then he made his gaffe of the evening: 'Twice in my lifetime,' he said with gravity '– in the Napoleonic Wars and the Marlborough wars –' and then the place almost fell apart. They roared. Then, just as he had affirmed that Britain would stand by the deterrent, he went on to 'the League of Nations', and although he corrected himself there was another burst of derisive applause and laughter. Mac took no notice.

It's possible the Napoleonic/Marlborough wars reference was deliberate old man's play with the young – Macmillan was not averse to sending himself up. He bashed on regardless:

> After supporting UNO [the United Nations Organization] he backed the Common Market. He stressed the need for European unity against a Communist menace, and there was a weak cry of 'Portugal'.

Portugal, a member of NATO (unlike Spain), was then ruled by a fascist dictator, António Salazar. Could the old man get through to the '[r]ows of sports jackets [which] made a motley colour scheme, all packed together along the benches'? Not while he stuck to economic affairs:

> 'The cause of last year's economic troubles [the 1961 'Pay Pause'] . . .' said the Prime Minister. A smart young man yelled: 'Selwyn Lloyd' [Macmillan's Chancellor of the Exchequer] and got an appreciative round of laughter and applause. Mac indulged in some table-thumping about economic policy. 'I have lived through those times,' he said, 'and that is why I am determined (thump) that such suffering and misery shall not happen again.' Heroics go down badly even with Conservative undergrads . . . Britain was prosperous, said Mac, to a cry of 'old age pensioners'. 'No longer does the insurance man come to take away the furniture . . .' A smart young man chipped in: 'It's the HP [Hire Purchase] man,' and got another big laugh.

But a change of gear and mood drawing on Macmillan's High Anglican side left Paul Addison 'surprised . . . a little. He turned to "the deeper spiritual needs"':

> Wealth was a wonderful thing, but it was not enough. Old standards were being questioned (a shout of 'A good job too'). 'The false gods of cynicism, materialism and atheism (derisive moan) are strong,' he said in a memorable phrase. Conservatives must have faith, though he never said what in.
>
> 'I wish you the best of good fortune. And may God bless you in your work.'
>
> This produced a mixed reception. The cynical murmured a moan. The sceptical, including myself, didn't know quite what reaction we felt . . .

Back in his room at Pembroke, Paul Addison mused about the moments Macmillan had quelled the rumbustiousness of the meeting in the university of which he was the proud Chancellor:

It's always worth noting what impresses and touches an audience. Twice in his speech he indulged in a little corn – or rather it was just that he put it cornily – but there was a stillness and silence while he spoke. The first was when he said that Britain had twice (and this came after his great gaffe) in this century fought for the freedom of the world, 'and I hope no one here is ashamed of it'. The second was when he said that in 1945 the electorate dismissed [Churchill] 'the greatest Englishman of this or any other age'.

The more unruly young members of the tribe plainly realized that the bequest and memory of war was beyond mockery. (It's interesting that the send-up of the Battle of Britain and 'the Few' in 'The After-myth of War' sketch of *Beyond the Fringe* caused the cast anxiety; Peter Cook considered dropping it before the London run.)[59]

What did Macmillan himself make of his brush with sports-jacketed Oxford at the Union? His account is rather different from Addison's:

An amusing meeting at Oxford. It was organised by the University Conservative Association and took place in the Union. The hall was packed, with a good sprinkling of Liberals and Socialists. Outside there were 500 or 600 more – who had come to listen. There were loudspeakers. Mixed with them was a band of 'Anti-Bomb' demon-strators. I had some difficulty getting into the hall, but once in it was a splendid meeting. I abandoned most of my prepared speech and I had a very good and attractive audience, with plenty of heckling and interruption. Of course the press today completely misrepresent what happened.[60]

Macmillan seems to have seen the meeting as an example of youthful high spirits, as to be expected from undergraduates. To be fair to him, he always rather relished hecklers and a touch of the rough-house that characterized old-fashioned political meetings.

Much more worrying for him was the degree of griping within his own party and from the press in early 1962 when he motored

35

to Oxford that winter Friday evening. His Press Secretary, Harold
Evans, mused on it in his diary the following Sunday:

> The Sunday commentators inevitably take their cue from the Legge-
> Bourke speech [the somewhat 'crazy', as Macmillan called him, Tory
> MP for Ely had 'made a speech full of praise of me, but saying I should
> retire, exhausted, in favour of a younger man'[61]] and spread them-
> selves in analysing where the PM stands with the Party. Peregrine
> Worsthorne [in *The Sunday Telegraph*] says that the PM's perfor-
> mance at the University Conservative Association's meeting at Oxford
> was lamentable . . .[62]

Worsthorne's and Addison's assessments ring truer than those of
Macmillan himself. Yet even though the opinion polls were moving
against him and the Conservatives and the gilt had gone off the surface of 'having-it-so-good', there was life in the old performer yet.

A sense of both fragility and pleasure jostled uneasily in early-
Sixties Britain, and yet, as Paul Addison would say over forty years
later, there was pleasure in living in a 'ramshackle social democracy'.[63] Macmillan was governing in a strange political climate in
which gusts of contentment vied with a drizzle of complaint to
become the dominant weather pattern.

What the sports-jacketed youth of Oxford and the platoon of liter-
ary 'What's Wrongers' – without access to his diaries or the minutes
he was penning for his ministers – did not know was that Macmillan
himself was suffering a degree of divine discontent similar to theirs,
and had been for some time. Between 1960 and 1962 he dreamt up
and developed a series of interlocking plans – parts of a 'Grand
Design' – to reposition the country geopolitically and economically.
As the glow of his 1959 election triumph faded with many a back-
ward glance towards the ramshackle Edwardian Whiggery for which
he pined,[64] Macmillan-the-modernizer realized that Churchill's geo-
metric comfort blanket, quilted with a mix of US, Commonwealth
and European patches, could no longer provide either economic or
political warmth. And a re-stitch here and there would no longer be
enough. The tired old Balliol-trained brain would have to be tuned
up once more in the service of country and party and, as Macmillan
himself conceived it, for the benefit of the free world.

2

Grand Design

As he grew older, and into the part, [Macmillan's] gestures became more eccentric: the shake of the head, the dropping of the mouth, the baring of the teeth, the pulling-in of the cheeks, the wobbling of the hand, the comedian's sense of timing – the whole bag of tricks seemed in danger of taking over, so that his intellectual originality was constantly surprising. He had a series of set pieces of tragic roles which he would constantly repeat to his colleagues, often with tears in his eyes – the veteran of Passchendaele,* the champion of Stockton's unemployed, the trustee of future generations of children and grandchildren.

Anthony Sampson, 1967[1]

With the Labour Party . . . stricken, and his own Party girding itself to meet the country's long-term problems on a radical and dramatic scale, it might have seemed in that autumn of 1960 that, despite his setbacks earlier in the year, Harold Macmillan was still riding high. It was nevertheless at this moment the first portent appeared that the increasingly aggressive hunger of a certain type of young politician and journalist for 'change', 'action' and political excitement was turning into something that could not be met just by measures alone, however radical. It was becoming a need which went much deeper – for something that no 'Edwardian' father-time figure in his sixties could provide, however imaginative or shrewd.

Christopher Booker, 1969[2]

---

* In fact, he was a veteran of the Somme and it was the battle of September 1916, in which he was seriously wounded, that particularly haunted him.

December 30 [1960]

Motored to Chequers – where I shall stay for a few days alone. I want to try to think out some of these terrible problems wh face us.

January 4 [1961]

... worked all the afternoon on my memorandum ... It must of course be kept *absolutely* secret within a small circle, for much in it is dynamite.

January 6 [1961]

... it is a grand design to deal with the economic, political and defence problems of the Free World!

Harold Macmillan's diary[3]

Harold Macmillan was a month short of his sixty-seventh birthday when he wrote those words. A broody man at the best of times, he was feeling his age and staggered towards the Christmas and New Year break 'quite exhausted'[4] by his 'wind-of-change in Africa' year following his speech to the South African parliament in February 1960, the collapse of the East–West summit in Paris after the Russians had shot down a CIA U-2 spy plane and, before that, a long, sloggy (if mightily successful) election campaign for the Conservative Party. His mood was not lightened by the 'strict diet' on which his doctor had put him.[5] Just as he had thought (wrongly, as it turned out) that the summer of 1960 might ape the summer of 1914 and tip the world unexpectedly and accidentally into a global war, he reckoned '1961 is going to be a dramatic year, for good or ill'[6] and that the Soviet leader, Nikita Khrushchev, 'means to press the German question' with still more pressure on Berlin.[7]

The rise-and-fall-of-civilizations side of Macmillan* began to take over as his tummy emptied and his brain picked up thanks to Dr Richardson's diet over that solitary Chequers New Year. Out of his

---

* He was a keen student of Arnold Toynbee and re-read him in the summer of 1961 as the Berlin crisis worsened, finding it 'soothing, in a curious way, to learn about so many civilizations wh have "risen and fallen"' (Macmillan diaries (unpublished), entry for 8 July 1961; Toynbee is best consulted in the abridged version).

physical and intellectual rumblings came his thirty-two-page 'Grand Design' or 'Memorandum by the Prime Minister' as the draft circulated to an intimate Whitehall few was rather prosaically entitled.[8] Much of it written in bed, the paper was an attempt to combat drift at home and abroad, to concentrate on the weaknesses of a precarious domestic economy, a bloated set of commitments overseas and to give his government a sense of direction now that, as he had confided in his diary at the end of November 1960, '[t]he popular press (tired of Gaitskell and Labour Party disputes) has started to attack me violently and "below the belt"'.[9]

Perhaps, above all, it was his first proper attempt to find a way of 'influencing' the new, about-to-be-inaugurated President John Kennedy in Washington, and working

> out a method of influencing him and working with him. With Eisenhower there was the link of memories and a long friendship. I will have to base myself now on trying to win him by *ideas*.[10]

Macmillan had taken a stab at doing this in a letter to the President-elect in mid-December 1960. It mixed flattery ('as I have just read the collection of your speeches called *The Strategy of Peace* I am looking forward with special pleasure to discussion of some of these things') with Toynbeean grand-sweep ('what is going to happen to us unless we can show that our modern free society – the new form of capitalism – can make the fullest use of our resources and results in a steady expansion of our economic strength'). He rounded it off with a touch of faux deference – 'I am so sorry to inflict this on you when you have so much to think about . . . I await our first meeting with great eagerness'.[11]

Macmillan's first letter to Kennedy was the seed from which the 'Grand Design' grew, nurtured by what he called 'that fatal itch for composition which is the outcome of a classical education'.[12] It turned out to form the blueprint for the middle phase of his premiership, from the election victory of 1959 until de Gaulle's veto of the first UK application for EEC membership wrecked it in January 1963.

Macmillan took immense pains over the document and steered it carefully through small groups of ministers and officials before taking it to the full Cabinet in April 1961. His official biographer, Alistair Horne, reckoned the 'Grand Design showed Macmillan at

the peak of his powers on the wider canvas'.[13] This might be going a
tad far, given his exhaustion at the turn of 1960–61. Certainly, it
showed his intellectual fires were not banked – and it is hard to think
of any subsequent premier who could have ranged so widely and
thoughtfully with his or her own mind and pen.

His 'Introduction' opened in Toynbee mode:

> The Free World cannot, on a realistic assessment, enter on 1961 with
> any great degree of satisfaction.
>
> In the struggle against Communism, there have been few successes
> and some losses over the past decade.
>
> In the military sphere, the overwhelming nuclear superiority of the
> West has been replaced by a balance of destructive power.
>
> In the economic field, the strength and growth of Communist pro-
> duction and technology has been formidable. (Indeed, it ought to be,
> for that after all is what Communism is for.)[14]

To early twenty-first century eyes, after the discrediting and collapse of the Soviet Union, this passage reads oddly. But to early-Sixties
eyes, Soviet industrial advance over the previous thirty years (not just
since 1950) *had* been spectacular and other analysts had yet to appreciate the degree to which a superpower could sustain a first-world
military capacity with a second-world economy and, in some areas, a
third-world agricultural one.

His access to secret sources left Macmillan in no doubt, too, of the
vigorous political intelligence combat that pockmarked the Cold War:

> In the political and propaganda field, Russian (and to a lesser extent
> Chinese) subversion, blackmail, seduction and threats, as well as the
> glamour of what seems a growing and dynamic system, have impressed
> hesitant and neutral countries, and are proving especially dangerous
> among the newly independent nations of Africa and Asia. Against this
> background the long predominance of European culture, civilisation,
> wealth and power may be drawing to its end.[15]

Yet, all was not lost. Since 1945 the United States had not returned
to 'isolationism' and western Europe had 'made a remarkable recovery from the calamitous destruction of the Second World War'. But
'great weaknesses remained' and there was insufficient Western

solidarity in the face of East–West, Middle Eastern and Far Eastern problems.

His specifically British section shows Macmillan had fully absorbed the conclusions of the highly secret 'Future Policy Study' that officials had presented to him ten months earlier on where Britain would most likely be in 1970 if current policies and relative economic performance remained:[16]

> Britain – with all her experience – has neither the economic nor the military power to take the leading role. We are harassed with countless problems – the narrow knife-edge on which our own economy is balanced; the difficult task of changing an Empire into a Commonwealth (with the special problem of colonies inhabited by European as well as native populations); the uncertainty about our relations to the new economic, and perhaps political, state which is being created by the Six countries of continental Western Europe; and the uncertainty of American policies towards us – treated now as just another country, now as an ally in a special and unique category.[17]

Macmillan, despite the weaknesses of the UK's position, craved boldness:

> These problems are all intermingled. It is difficult to deal with them separately. Yet it is a tremendous task to attack them as a whole. So we are in danger of drift. Yet, if we are to influence events, we must not shrink from strong, and sometimes dramatic, action.[18]

Interestingly, given the overwhelming place the politico-military threat posed by the Soviet Union had in his mind over that Christmas and New Year, Macmillan thought that Western economic collaboration offered the best prospect of progress in the West's struggle against what he saw as a monolithic communist bloc. 'I am,' he reminded himself, 'an unrepentant believer in "interdependence". The Communist danger – in its various forms – is so great, and so powerfully directed that it cannot be met without the maximum achievable unity of purpose and direction.'[19] Macmillan, like the British intelligence community that contributed to his picture of the world, was slow to pick up the width and magnitude of the developing Sino-Soviet split until Khrushchev denounced the Albanians, 'the recognized surrogates for the Chinese',[20] at the Twenty-Second Soviet Party Congress in October 1961.

'It is,' Macmillan judged, 'no longer a question of Europe or the Commonwealth or America – we need a united Free World. Of course, we can't get it – in the sense of a politically federal or unitary state. We cannot altogether get it in the sense of a military alliance which can really work as a single team. We could perhaps get nearer to it in a monetary and economic policy.'[21] This argument would feature strongly in Macmillan's dealings with the Americans, the French and the Germans in the coming months.

Before turning to the ways in which such enhanced economic co-operation might be constructed, Macmillan told his select readership that as they had 'read and written so much about our own economy' he did not propose to elaborate in this paper. A touch hubristically, he told them:

> We all know, more or less, what we have to do. We have to *expand*, without inflation. We have to meet increasing Government and local expenditure on things necessary to our economic future – roads, schools, technical colleges, health services – without (if possible) increases of taxation, and even (if we can) with some reduction or at least rearrangement in order to stimulate effort.
>
> We must control – if possible reduce – military expenditure.
>
> We must deal with our balance of payments problems by reducing overseas expenditure (military and other) to the minimum, and above all, by *expanding exports*.[22]

This, to use Macmillan's own heading, was 'The Economic Problem', give or take minor fluctuations, that had faced every set of British ministers since 1945 – the 'New Deal' plus the residual empire plus the Cold War and how to pay for it all with a sluggish economy, a relatively immobile labour market and a set of competitor nations (especially, after 1958, the EEC 'Six').

Macmillan feared his hope for 'real export drive' would be blocked if 'other countries pursue policies which are restrictive or entirely self-protective', in which case 'we shall be driven inevitably to measures of defence' leading to 'economic war between nations of the Free World from which the only beneficiaries will be the Communists'. If

Macmillan could not entice his fellow Western leaders into a kind of global Keynesianism – 'namely, expanding world trade' – Britain 'must be ready for the worst. We must not be caught unawares.' If Kennedy, de Gaulle and the German Chancellor Konrad Adenauer proved difficult and 'chose the path of restriction', the UK would have to retaliate with 'import controls, reduction of oversea [sic] expenditure, (including our troops in Europe), increased control over movement of capital, and external monetary measures'.[23] Such rudiments of a siege economy – which would cut against the grain of the International Monetary Fund, the General Agreement on Tariffs and Trade and, via the British Army of the Rhine, NATO, too – were presumably what Macmillan had in mind when he wrote of 'The Grand Design' in his diary that 'much in it is dynamite'.

Kennedy would be the key. Would he go protectionist, or would he be prepared 'to broaden the base of credit' and lean on the West Germans to revalue the mark to ease pressure on sterling and the dollar? 'He may prove to have the courage and political finesse of F.D.R. [Franklin Delano Roosevelt], the genius of Keynes, and the determination of Churchill. Let us hope so.'[24] If Kennedy proved resistant, Macmillan had the slightly extraordinary idea that Britain could reverse roles within the 'special relationship' and put pressure on *him*:

> I have thought of the possibility of issuing an open challenge to the world on this issue. I might propose an Economic Conference of leading nations of the Free World, to face this problem and to solve it. I could make it clear that this lies at the basis of all co-operation in every other field – defence included. I might be able to force the new President's hand – especially if he would rather like it to be forced.

This was Britain as 'awkward squad' among the Western bloc; Macmillan as a British de Gaulle. Reason began to reassert itself:

> Alternatively, I might try to get him to call such a conference, and put up this policy and get the credit for himself (and his country).

Such 'economic summits', in fact, became a feature of regular Western diplomacy in the mid-1970s and eventually mutated into the G7, and, later, G8 meetings. However, over Christmas/New Year 1960–61, Macmillan was convinced he had to do something. 'In any event, we must not (as we so often do) leave the Americans in any doubt as to the drastic steps we (with our precarious economy) may have to take to defend ourselves, and the consequential tragic results on the whole struggle against Communism.'[25]

Khrushchev and Kennedy and the great East–West struggle were one thing; the constant and growing threat to the UK from the EEC 'Six' was really the driving force of Macmillan's 'Grand Design'. If the EFTA* countries could not reach an accommodation with the Common Market nations, '[t]he economic consequences to Britain may be grave. However bold a face it may suit us to put on the situation, exclusion from the strongest economic group in the civilised world *must* injure us.'

He reckoned the Germans and the Italians would be amenable to reducing, maybe ending, 'the economic split in Europe . . . The French will not. The French means de Gaulle.'[26]

The General would dominate all the Sixties' British premierships to a remarkable degree. He became a constant – and, very often, a malign – presence in the UK's Cabinet Room, a one-man roadblock to Europe. In British eyes he may have been negativism-made-flesh radiating from the Élysée Palace; but what a glorious negativism – such pomp, such circumstance, such style. Macmillan, no slouch himself when it came to this trio of attributes, spent a great deal of his last three years in No. 10 plotting how to handle the General as British entry to the EEC became the great prize of his remaining premiership.

Macmillan did not wish an early retirement to his country home at Colombey-les-Deux-Églises upon his great rival. Quite the reverse, as

> by a strange paradox, if de Gaulle were to disappear, an accommodation might be still more difficult. Whatever happened in France, there would be great confusion, perhaps even disintegration. French Federalist opinion would be strengthened (Monnet and all that)† and timid Frenchmen would seek a refuge in a European Federal State. Difficult

---

* The seven EFTA countries from its creation in January 1959 were the UK, Austria, Denmark, Norway, Portugal, Sweden and Switzerland.

† Jean Monnet, French public servant and original begetter of the idea of a European Coal and Steel Community from which the idea of a wider Common Market developed. Jean Monnet, *Memoirs* (Collins, 1978).

as de Gaulle is, his view of the proper *political* structure (Confederation not Federation) is really nearer to ours. If he wished us to join the political institutions it would be easier for us to do so if they took the form which he favours.

Macmillan was convinced that, should the 'extreme Federalists' 'triumph' in Europe, sooner or later it would mean 'the triumph of the [nuclear] unilateralists and neutralists [as between NATO and the Warsaw Pact] here'.[27] This was an anxious old man whipping himself up into a degree of flappability to which Macmillan *was* prone despite the public mask of world-weary near insouciance. But in terms of de Gaulle as the crux to any 'deal' in Europe, and that such a question 'is now not primarily an economic but a political problem', Macmillan was absolutely right.

So how on earth to deal with the General? Before turning to the answer, Macmillan indulged himself in one of the private anti-German outbursts that punctuated his premiership. He really could not stand the Germans. It was as if that piece of Krupp steel in his pelvis – his daily reminder of the Great War – fed straight into his pen:

> German policy is short-sighted and selfish, and in the long run will prove as disastrous to Germany as to the rest of the world. The Germans secretly enjoy their power, and the feeling that 15 years after defeat they are threatening both the dollar and the pound. They will not organise a proper capital market. They will not lend abroad. They will not reduce their interest rates to a nominal figure. They will not up-value the mark.
>
> They would probably agree to an accommodation on Sixes [EEC] and Sevens [EFTA] but they will not bring effective pressure on the French . . .
>
> Germans, in particular, never yield to the force of argument, but only to the argument of force.[28]

He had clearly not seen the degree to which Germany had changed, was changing, so fundamentally. It riled Macmillan deeply that the EEC was constructed around a Franco-German axis. Why, he wondered, had France and Germany become 'so indispensable to each other'? 'They cannot live apart: they do not find it easy to live together.'[29]

45

This question brought on another attack of the Toynbees at Chequers. It was, no doubt, a good thing Macmillan was lying down in bed in his old brown cardigan as his pen moved into *Völkerwanderung* mode (he called it a 'Digression on the State of Western Europe'):

> Since the Second World War, the movement for a permanent reconciliation between Gaul and Teuton has been based partly on genuine and respectable sentiment and partly on fear of the Slav. It has passed through different phases. The political phase – the European Movement, the Council of Europe – was quickly followed by the first economic moves – Schuman plan [for a European Coal and Steel Community], etc. This grew into the Treaty of Rome and the EEC.[30]

Macmillan knew he had at the very least to weaken the Franco-German spine of the EEC if he was to ease Britain into the Common Market. Why had Adenauer, the German Chancellor, been so accommodating to French needs (including France's imperial possessions) in the making of the Treaty of Rome? Macmillan had two explanations of Adenauer's 'motives' (a man to whom he never warmed, unlike de Gaulle, whom he admired[31]):

> First, fear of France's weakness and eventual neutralism or semi-Communism. Secondly, fear of the kind of Germany that may follow him and a desire to tie his country firmly with its Western neighbours.[32]

In fact, Adenauer had told him as much in a private chat after dinner in the British Embassy in Bonn during Macmillan's first visit to the West German capital after becoming Prime Minister. He noted in his diary for 8 May 1957 (the twelfth anniversary of VE Day) Adenauer's view

> that no one who had lived through the years of Hitler could fail to believe in the Devil. [Adenauer was a devout Roman Catholic whom, as Mayor of Cologne, the Nazis had imprisoned.] He said, 'I tell you, what I could not say to any German, no one realises the harm that Nazism has done to the German soul. It is by no means cured yet. We have got rich again too quickly. I don't want us to get strong again too quickly. I hate uniforms, the curse of Germany. You will see that our Generals in conference are like yours, in civil clothes. I see great

46

dangers ahead. That is why I yearn so for European unity and (in view of France's weakness [this was France pre-de Gaulle]) for British participation.'[33]

De Gaulle's assumption of power in Paris on 1 June 1958 pleased Adenauer, who soon lost his fear of what he had heard of the General's Germanophobia.[34] Looking back from his Chequers bed three and a half years later, Macmillan noted that

> Adenauer certainly welcomed de Gaulle's return to power – Catholic, anti-Communist, patriot. Recently, however, Adenauer's feelings towards de Gaulle and France have not been so friendly. He may have heard reports of de Gaulle's contemptuous references to 'Les petits gens de Bonn' ... He may be genuinely alarmed at the effect on Britain of France's rigid attitude on EEC and fear that Britain may not be so anxious to join in defence of the 'Empire of Charlemagne' and its outpost, Berlin. All the same I would judge that, unless very extreme pressures are put on him, Adenauer will do nothing effective to carry out his promises to us or be prepared to risk a quarrel with France.[35]

So the crux of the 'Grand Design' was to move France towards an accommodation with any UK application for EEC membership, which meant, in effect, shifting de Gaulle. If this could not be engineered, the rest (including the wider world economic aspirations embedded in the Christmas/New Year memorandum) would not fall into place and the master plan of Macmillan's second premiership would fail. How profoundly irritating it must have been, for all Macmillan's championing of de Gaulle during the war (when he was Minister Resident in the Mediterranean[36]) that the terms of mendicancy had swivelled right round. But swivelled they had, and Britain rather than France was now the supplicant. How profoundly gratifying that must have been for de Gaulle, for all the courtesy he sustained in his relationship with the UK premier.

Might events – or anticipated events – soften de Gaulle up? Maybe the Germanophobia Adenauer sensed in him could help? Recently, Macmillan thought,

> there has been a change in the French attitude towards Germany. It is no longer so patronising. There is a note of alarm.

What may follow Adenauer? Will it be [Ludwig] Erhard [prime author of the postwar German economic miracle] and Liberalism? Will it be [Franz Josef] Strauss [of Bavaria] and a new militarism? Will it be something worse? Might there be a lurking danger of a complete reversal – neutralism in exchange for *some* degree of German reunification? Perhaps even a Stalin-Ribbentrop pact brought up to date.

In rising Franco-German anxiety might lie Britain's chance as in

this mood the French may wish to draw closer to Britain (always a loyal ally in the end) and build up a special position within the [NATO] Alliance with Britain and – if they can get it – with the United States. Under the influence of a growing fear of Germany's wealth and strength, the French might be persuaded to accept an agreement between EEC and EFTA and a political structure in Europe which brought Britain in as a balance.

Meanwhile, Macmillan concluded, the 'love/hate complex between France and Germany will continue'.[37]

Macmillan couldn't wait for the moment to ripen within the Paris–Bonn axis. The booming Six stealing the markets from the very much second-division European Free Trade Area was pushing him on. What he really wanted was an end to the

economic split and discrimination in Europe by measures of amalgamation or accommodation between EEC and EFTA. Both these are urgent. Failure to realise this may produce a rapid crisis and drive Britain back to defensive measures.[38]

De Gaulle had written to Macmillan on Boxing Day 1960, inviting him to spend the weekend with him in the country at Rambouillet at the end of January to contemplate the 'difficult problems' looming in 1961. He told Macmillan, 'Like you, I feel the need to reinforce the cohesion of the West' ('Comme vous, il me semble que nous devons renforcer la cohesion de notre Occident').[39] Macmillan's section on how to play the General in his 'Grand Design' paper began with this:

Whether 'Occident' in his mind includes or excludes America, I am not sure. But in any event it must include Europe. I could therefore take him up at once on the Unity of Europe and the New World which is symbolised by NATO . . .

What do we want? What does de Gaulle want? How far can we agree to help him if he will help us?[40]

To 'make it clear to the French that we mean what we say', Macmillan suggested the guarantee of British troops on the Continent, on which France was so keen in the late 1940s when 'France did *not* discriminate against British trade', might be re-examined.

Perhaps inducement rather than threat might be the instrument of persuasion at Rambouillet, as

De Gaulle wants the recognition of France as a Great Power, at least equal to Britain.

He suspects the Anglo-Saxons.

So long as the 'Anglo-Saxon domination' continues, he will not treat Britain as European, but as American – a junior partner of America, but a partner.[41]

This was spot on. To the last days of his life, de Gaulle felt exactly this. As he told his old comrade, André Malraux, at La Boisserie, his country home at Colombey-les-Deux-Églises near Clairvaux, during one bleak day of shared reminiscence in December 1969 (he died on 9 November 1970 in his study there): 'England's tragedy is to be compelled to choose between the remnants of the empire at the cost of American supremacy, and fair play towards the Continent of Europe. As she very well knows!'[42] This after he had rejected *two* UK applications to join the EEC – Macmillan's in 1961–3 and Wilson's in 1967.

Macmillan was also right in the 'Grand Design' to think that de Gaulle felt excluded from the Anglo-American relationship that determined so many of the key decisions in NATO. In September 1958, de Gaulle had asked General Lauris Norstad, the top American soldier in Paris as Supreme Allied Commander Europe of NATO (then based just outside the French capital) to brief him on the locations of US NATO-allocated nuclear weapons in France and their targets east of the Iron Curtain.

'I'm afraid I cannot answer those questions unless we are alone,' said Norstad. 'Very well,' said de Gaulle. The entourages of the two generals left. 'Well?' 'Well, General, I'm afraid I can't answer your questions.'

'General,' de Gaulle concluded, 'this is the last time, I am telling you, that a French leader will hear such an answer.'[43]

De Gaulle, Macmillan continued, 'feels that he is *excluded* from this [Anglo-American] club or partnership'. Hence

(a) his persistent efforts towards 'Tripartitism' – which the Americans and the British have accepted 'en principe' to a limited extent, but have never really operated;

(b) his determination – whatever the cost – that France should become a *nuclear* power. For it is France's *exclusion* from the nuclear club that is the measure of France's inferior status. It is particularly galling for him that Britain should have an independent nuclear capacity; he accepts that the United States is in a different category.[44]

Here, too, Macmillan knew his de Gaulle. From the moment of his return to power, de Gaulle had constantly sought to quicken the pace of France's military nuclear weapons programme. And once they had achieved atomic capacity (the first French atomic test, in the Algerian desert, was on 13 February 1960) he pressed hard for thermonuclear status – determined to ensure it was achieved before he left the Élysée Palace for Colombey-les-Deux-Églises (it was).[45] In fact once his atomic-capable Mirage bombers were operational, de Gaulle had the French launch codes with him night and day (he wrote the numbers down on a tiny 'piece of white card carried inside a medal that he wore in his waistcoat pocket linked by a chain to his buttonhole and which he kept by him during the night').[46] This was in stark contrast to Harold Macmillan, as we shall see in chapter 5.

British and American intelligence took a very close interest in the French nuclear weapons programme.[47] The secret feed was, no doubt, of value to Macmillan on the *pace* of France's progress towards the Bomb; but the degree of *priority* the General gave it did not need the special operations of the CIA and MI6 to disclose it. De Gaulle did it himself in November 1959 first to the officers of the École Militaire and then in one of his theatrical performances before his ministers and the world's press beneath the vast chandeliers of the Élysée Palace. At the Élysée, on 10 November, the General fretted about a time when 'the political *données* having completely changed, those powers possessing the nuclear monopoly come to an agreement to carve up the world', or, agreeing to spare each other, agree 'to crush the others'. So France, 'by giving herself nuclear weapons, is rendering a service to the balance of the world'. And, the General believed, by reaching atomic status without help from the US or the UK, France showed the world 'that she had indubitably recovered her independence'.[48]

So, despite the French test, was 'there a basis for a deal', Macmillan wondered, between Britain and France? A place in the sun, with the USA and the UK, in directing NATO? The Bomb? Might the British nuclear sword be turned into not a ploughshare but a key that would unlock the door to Europe?

> Britain wants to join the European concern; France wants to join the Anglo-American concern. Can terms be arranged? Would de Gaulle be ready to withdraw the French veto* which alone prevents a settlement of Europe's economic problem in return for politico-military arrangements which he would accept as a recognition of France as a first-class world power? What he would want is something on Tripartitism and something on the nuclear. Are there offers which we could afford to make? And could we persuade the Americans to agree?

Of course, a Franco-Anglo-American condominium couldn't be like 'our *special* position with the United States, which we should certainly seek to preserve'. Why not? Because

> that special position is much more a matter of experience of working together. It is based on history. It is confirmed by daily contacts at every level. We have some 'agreements' – but not many.† It can really only work if – at all levels – the personalities, 'click'. At any rate, like Topsy, it has just growed.

This would not suit de Gaulle. He 'would want . . . something much *more formal*, more *organized*, more *institutionalized*. But just for this reason, it would be less *intimate*. It would therefore *not* necessarily

---

* De Gaulle had yet to veto. Macmillan was anticipating the possibility.
† The most notable being that on Communications Intelligence, which dates from 1946, and the mutual agreement of 1958, which restored nuclear weapons collaboration. They both remain current in the twenty-first century.

impinge upon the wider and more special relations between us and the Americans in many spheres.'[49]

Whether this play would run at Rambouillet and after depended on the attitude of the incoming Kennedy administration in Washington. So, too, did what Macmillan liked to call 'the nuclear'. Yet if the British Prime Minister had a card that might trump the French President's doubts about the European credentials of the UK government, Macmillan thought the Bomb, that most political of armaments, was it. Macmillan knew that a bomb 'with a bloody Tricolour on it', to adapt Bevin's famous words about the first British one,[50] was de Gaulle's 'vital . . . ambition',[51] far more important to him than a tripartite arrangement with the US and the UK:

> Can we give him our techniques, or our bombs, or any share of *our* nuclear power on any terms which
>
> (i) are prudent and publicly defensible to us, at home, in the Commonwealth, and generally;
> (ii) the United States will agree to?
>
> At first this seems hopeless. But since I think it is the one thing which will persuade de Gaulle to accept a European settlement – not merely in the economic field of sixes and sevens (which is vital), but in the general association of the British, with other governments, in a confederal system – I think it is worth serious examination.[52]

Was Macmillan cocooning himself in a nuclear delusion at Chequers in late December 1960? Not really. The previous March, the last time he had seen de Gaulle *á deux* at Rambouillet, de Gaulle, even though the Tricolour Bomb had exploded the month before, asked Macmillan for help with his nuclear weapons programme. As the minute by Philip de Zulueta (who, as Macmillan's foreign affairs Private Secretary, recorded the Macmillan–de Gaulle conversations) put it:

> The Americans had refused to give any help. He would be glad if it was possible for the United Kingdom to assist even with the means of delivery only. The Prime Minister explained the complications of the [1958] United Kingdom arrangement with the United States. General de Gaulle understood this.[53]

So why did Macmillan think that what was impossible in March 1960 might be possible in January 1961? Because de Gaulle was now in a position to *'wreck'* the nuclear test ban talks underway at Geneva. Without the Western nuclear powers acting as one, it would be impossible to put pressure on China, the next most likely atomic power (which indeed China was, carrying out its first nuclear test in October 1964).

Macmillan thought that

> [t]his argument could be pressed strongly on the new President. On the other hand, can the United States Government (within their law) agree to our giving information – or weapons – to France *without conditions*. I think the [US Atomic Energy] Act is widely drawn; it is a *permissive* Act, allowing agreements to be made with Powers that have 'nuclear capacity'.[54]

As Macmillan well knew, the restoration of Anglo-American nuclear collaboration in 1958 required an amendment of the US Atomic Energy Act 1954. The 1958 alterations ensured 'that only nations that had made "substantial progress" in the nuclear weapons field could be given atomic weapons data. At the time this description could apply only to Britain, and the British had already, by spring 1958, made considerable thermonuclear progress.'[55] In December/January 1960–61, France was a long way from designing an H-bomb with the Tricolour on top.

Nevertheless, Macmillan was optimistic. 'My experience of Americans – in private as in public affairs – is this. If they *want* to do a thing, they find a way round. If they *don't* the laws offer an insuperable obstacle.' Here, as wishful thinking intruded, came a touch of almost lightheartedness as well, perhaps brought on by Dr Richardson's strict health cure:

> It might, however, be easier both for America and for us to avoid a straight deal with the French by which we just 'gave' them the nuclear weapon.
>
> Could we make it more respectable (and more acceptable to general public opinion) in some other way?
>
> Could Britain and France form a nuclear force – sharing the cost, production, etc. – as European trustees for NATO?

Could we devise a formula for joint political control by us both? Failing that, could we at least have some arrangement for consultation about its use, on the analogy of President Eisenhower's *private* understanding with me? Either of these arrangements could extend, not only to the NATO area, but throughout the world.

Could we thus give France the satisfaction of a nominally 'independent nuclear force' while subjecting them to at least the same kind of moral restraints which the Americans have accepted on their understanding with us?[56]

This extraordinary wave of speculation illustrates three things: Macmillan's desperation about the need for Britain to get access to the markets of the Six and to prevent the EEC from further sapping the UK's wider trading prospects; the salience of nuclear weapons to inter-allied diplomacy in the early 1960s; and the overwhelming importance Macmillan placed on Britain remaining a nuclear power. All this end-of-year ratiocination was devoted to the Bomb not as a deterrer of Khrushchev but as a means of Macmillan getting his and – as he saw it – Britain's way with both de Gaulle and Kennedy.

'I think,' he told the select few who were to read the unexpurgated 'Grand Design', 'we should give urgent study to this and see if we can devise a workable plan – which (at the right moment) we could get the United States to accept and which we could then use to win de Gaulle over.'[57] Macmillan really did believe that, for all his anxieties about the UK as a trader and a producer ('all our economic difficulties, which are endemic to a small and highly populated island'), Britain was still in a position to move the world. The purpose of his 'Grand Design', he wrote, was 'to call attention to the need to organize the great forces of the Free World – USA, Britain, and Europe – economically, politically, and militarily in a coherent effort to withstand the Communist tide all over the world'.[58]

In what might strike subsequent generations as a bout of admittedly high-class and history-fuelled hubris, could Macmillan really have convinced himself that he may have created a winning hand to deploy? The cards to play with Kennedy were not only the need to get France alongside on nuclear testing, but 'only if he can help me to do

a deal with de Gaulle, can we keep Britain in Europe and relieve the
United States of some of their burden'. As for de Gaulle,

> also it would be a deal – but quite an honourable one. It would be the
> reconstructing of a fully united Europe – united economically, politi-
> cally and militarily, and at the same time securing for France (through
> Tripartitism) an equal place with Britain in discussing *world* affairs
> with our American friends. It would also, by bringing in France to the
> trusteeship of the nuclear, give her the position which her greatness
> and her history justify.[59]

He went on: 'Of course, how to play the hand is another matter.
But it is difficult to play any hand blind. One must at least have some
idea of what cards one has to play.'[60]

The 'Grand Design' was an extraordinary document – perhaps the
most remarkable drafted by Macmillan during his premiership. The
stakes were high and the strategy freighted with peril. Not only did it
depend on the forbearance of a new and untried President across the
Atlantic, it turned, above all, on that brilliant, difficult, history-saturated
curmudgeon across the Channel. At the same time at home, the most
pressing politico-economic problem of all – levering the UK into the
EEC – depended, before there were any proposals on which the General could pour Gallic acid, upon Cabinet approval with several of
Macmillan's senior colleagues (Rab Butler and Reggie Maudling
especially) far from convinced about the allure of the Common
Market Six. And rather too much depended upon the British Bomb
being able to earn its political keep.

Before he went off to see de Gaulle, Macmillan decided to try out the
'Grand Design' on a meeting of a small group of his senior ministers
(Alec Home, Foreign Secretary; Selwyn Lloyd, Chancellor of the
Exchequer; Harold Watkinson, Minister of Defence) at Chequers over
the weekend of 21–22 January 1961. Before he did so, inner Whitehall
had a crack at it and, through the grand Cabinet Office co-ordinator
Norman Brook, decorously doused some of the more wishful parts of
the Prime Minister's thinking. On Europe, particularly, the greatest
prize of the 'Grand Design', Brook noted in his 20 January brief for
Macmillan that '[i]n your talks with the Chancellor of the Exchequer
[Selwyn Lloyd] last week-end you concluded that the balance of

economic advantage lay in favour of our drawing closer to Europe'. The Foreign Office believed 'that the balance of *political* advantage lies the same way'. But, was Britain 'prepared to make the sacrifices which this would entail?' Namely:

(i) some shock to other Commonwealth countries and some risk of damage to our relations with them;

(ii) something more than inconvenience, but less than hardship, for our own agriculture and (even more) horticulture. Here the economic sacrifice may not be great, but the political difficulties are, no doubt, substantial. (I believe you have it in mind to discuss all this with the Home Secretary [Butler] fairly soon).[61]

Brook discreetly piled up Whitehall's caveats to the grand scheme inside Macmillan's head: the Foreign Office thought it most unlikely the Americans would grant de Gaulle the degree of tripartite consultation he might want; and would the UK Bomb become a 'wasting asset' in political terms as the Sixties progressed? Would 'British public opinion' be happy if the country seemed

to be stepping down to the position of a European power ... surrendering too much of our 'special relationship' with the United States and our special position as leader of the Commonwealth, which are the main marks of our standing as a world power?

... a bilateral arrangement with France, if we could get it, on the basis of something less than full involvement in Europe on equal terms, would offer us a better prospect of sustaining our special position in world affairs outside Europe and our special relationship with the Commonwealth and the United States.[62]

That, I suspect, was the private Norman Brook talking rather than the Cabinet Secretary as purveyor of the collective wisdom of Whitehall.

Chequers, however, went exactly as Macmillan wished. He told his diary on 23 January:

Left Chequers at lunch time. We had a really splendid talk – Saturday evening and all Sunday. To my surprise, my plan has won general support from all ministers and departments, altho' all realise its extreme difficulty in execution. We must now work to reduce all these ideas to short talking points for the de Gaulle discussions.[63]

Would these ideas run the following weekend in a very different style of country house in the French countryside? Perhaps the most prescient section of Brook's brief for Chequers was the passage that wondered:

Would de Gaulle's aspirations be satisfied by the kind of offer which we could make; and would he be willing, in return, to facilitate our entry into Europe? If it is his aim that France should continue to play the leading part in Europe, on what terms could he afford to have us there?[64]

Macmillan absorbed this fully. In a note he sent his Chequers group the day before he set off for France, the Prime Minister portrayed the forthcoming conversations with de Gaulle as 'a reconnaissance' cocooned in delicacies. 'The French cannot be relied upon,' he wrote, 'not to leak an *ex parte* version of what has been discussed.' So it must not appear to either Khrushchev or Kennedy or Adenauer that the British and the French were concocting a joint plan behind their backs.[65]

Macmillan anticipated de Gaulle's possible ripostes to the ideas of the 'Grand Design', however delicately he floated them at Rambouillet:

(a) The Treaty of Rome is primarily an economic arrangement with little political content. It will not harm the United Kingdom.
(b) The French are not interested in the Nuclear Tests Agreement because they have been denied any help by the Anglo-Saxons in developing their nuclear armament.
(c) The present NATO military organisation is militarily absurd and politically harmful.
(d) The political cohesion of the West suffers because France has been denied her rightful place as one of its three leaders.[66]

Had he read the General right and the latest version of de Gaulle's 'certain idea of France'?

One instrument of the General's projection of his country's specialness to visiting foreigners was the Château of Rambouillet itself. 'I had,' he later wrote, 'developed a liking for ... [Rambouillet] ... as a site for such meetings, Versailles, Compiègne and Fontainebleau, by reason of their size, being unsuitable for restricted gatherings.' Every stone, every room had a story to tell:

> Housed in the medieval tower where so many of our kings had stayed, passing through the apartments once occupied by our Valois, our Bourbons, our emperors, our presidents, deliberating in the ancient hall of marble with the French Head of State and his ministers, admiring the grandeur of the ornamental lakes stretched out before their eyes, strolling through the park and the forest in which for ten centuries the rites of official shooting and hunting parties had been performed, our guests were made to feel the nobility behind the geniality, the permanence beyond the vicissitudes, of the nation which was their host.[67]*

'Uncle Harold' was already quite a connoisseur of life inside the walls of Rambouillet. When he and Lady Dorothy arrived just after noon on Saturday 28 January 1961, after greeting the General and his wife, 'Tante Yvonne', they sorted themselves out in that same kingly medieval tower: 'We were in the same rather romantic suite [as in 1960] in the François Premier tower. But this time the creature comforts were better. The rooms were heated; the bathwater was hot; and there were sufficient bedclothes.'[68]

It did not take long for the grand sweeps of history to swish through the château. After lunch the two swordsmen had a ten-minute chat on Algeria, which de Gaulle had persuaded the French, through the medium of a referendum, to abandon as a colonial possession. Negotiations would now start and de Gaulle expected them to succeed. The General, Macmillan noted, declared,

> 'We had learnt that you could increase your standard of living by internal trade without bothering about colonies at all.' (I felt that this was a reference to the Six.) In any case, it was a period in the world that was over. France had now recognised it and although it was in a sense sad from a sentimental point of view it was best to accept the facts.[69]

Having duly disposed of centuries of the 'expansion' of England and France, as J. R. Seeley famously described the age of British

---

* Macmillan's retaliation was droller, terser and sharper. When a grand Frenchman was to lunch or dine at No. 10, he took care to have a portrait of either Wellington or Nelson over the door to the dining room.

empire[70]* (in common with my imperial history course at Cambridge in 1967–8), with the merest whiff of regret, the President and the Prime Minister got down to the contraction of Europe into the EEC Six and the EFTA Seven. It swiftly became apparent that de Gaulle had a grand design for France and the rest of the world that did not fit Macmillan's for Britain. What the two men did share was the hubristic hope that each could somehow engineer events and the rest of the world to meet their individual countries' requirements. This had not been true of France since 1815 or of Britain since at least 1914. The territorial map of empire may have been fast disappearing from both their considerable minds but the appetite for great power-dom most certainly was not. It was, to borrow the phrase of a particularly thoughtful former officer of Her Majesty's Secret Intelligence Service, a case of 'the itch after the amputation'.[71]

Shrewdly, Macmillan opened the first session that Saturday afternoon in the Marble Room of Rambouillet by asking de Gaulle what he had in mind when, in his 26 December letter, he had suggested discussing the unity of the West? De Gaulle said the 'real centre' of the West was the US, UK and France ('the Germans could also be depended upon to some extent but they were less certain'). Then came a glimmer of hope for Macmillan:

> Broadly speaking, the General continued, France and Britain realised this and there were no serious difficulties between them in spite of the complications about the Six and the Seven: these, however, were not mortal. The United States was now an uncertain quantity. With President Eisenhower there had been special relations particularly on the British side. With the new President there would be a time of uncertainty. Perhaps the United States Government would go more their own way. If so, it was all the more important that Anglo-French relations should be very close.[72]

---

* This hugely influential book by the Regius Professor of Modern History at Cambridge remained in print for seventy-three years until, appropriately enough, the year of Suez (1956) (William Roger Louis, 'The Historiography of the British Empire' (1999), reproduced in William Roger Louis, *Ends of British Imperialism: The Scramble for Empire, Suez and Decolonisation. Collected Essays* (I. B. Tauris, 2006), pp. 955–98. The longevity of Seeley's book is dealt with on pp. 962–3).

Briefly, Macmillan's 'Grand Design' flickered into life. Within seconds, de Gaulle extinguished it:

> While he would like an arrangement in Europe he felt there were great difficulties at the present time. The United Kingdom rightly did not want to harm the Commonwealth. Then there was the difficulty of agriculture. De Gaulle himself wanted the Common Market for economic reasons not only in order to develop French industry and draw it out of its protectionist shell but also so as to hold Germany which in 10 years' time might be different from what it was now. The idea was not at all to upset the United Kingdom and he hoped that England and France could still stay together in world affairs. Any political arrangements would not be directed against the United Kingdom whose island position and Commonwealth naturally made her look outwards across the oceans.[73]

How the General must have savoured those sentences: he was throwing back at a British Prime Minister the very words Winston Churchill had directed furiously at him aboard the prime ministerial train parked 'somewhere near Portsmouth' as the Allied armies prepared to launch D-Day in June 1944. Churchill, enraged by de Gaulle's attitude towards Roosevelt and the Americans, delivered what de Gaulle, in his war memoirs, called his 'outburst':

> 'And you!' Churchill cried. 'How do you expect that the British should take a position separate from that of the United States?' Then, with a passion which I sensed was destined more for his British colleagues than for myself he said: 'We are going to liberate Europe, but it is because the Americans are in agreement with us that we do so. There is something you ought to know: each time we have to choose between Europe and the open sea, we shall always choose the open sea. Each time I have to choose between you and Roosevelt, I shall always choose Roosevelt.'[74]

It was as if, briefly, the unmistakable shadow of Churchill was with them in the Marble Room. Thanks to their open sea/Commonwealth bias, de Gaulle concluded,

> the United Kingdom could not see the Common Market as France did. Nevertheless, Britain and France should hold together in world

affairs if only because united they would have a much better chance of influencing the United States [on such matters as] the colonial question, world security, including atomic security, and how to deal with Mr Khrushchev and later with the Chinese.[75]

De Gaulle's was as 'grand' a 'design' as Macmillan's. But if differed crucially on the most urgent and anxious element of the Prime Minister's – the need to engineer swiftly an entry for the faltering British economy into the booming sextet of the EEC.

It would be excessively teleological to trace a straight, direct line from that moment at Rambouillet with the light fading across the park to the moment, just under two years later, at the Élysée press conference when de Gaulle finally and brutally dashed the European cup from Macmillan's lips – but not entirely so. For the private de Gaulle was convinced in 1961 when, as he put it later, 'the British returned to the offensive on Europe', that he knew exactly what Macmillan was up to – 'Having failed from without to prevent the birth of the Community, they now planned to paralyse it from within.'[76]

Macmillan tried another tack. He now believed 'a good working arrangement' could be negotiated between the EEC Six and as many of the EFTA Seven as possible:

> This was not a question of minor importance but an essential one for the unity of the West because unless it was solved political divisions would inevitably follow economic rivalry . . . At the last Rambouillet meeting President de Gaulle said that England ought to choose between Europe and the United States. But this was really a choice which France would have to make just as much. It was not a choice which either country should try to make. Both of them had world interests as well as European ones.[77]

Macmillan then played the 'tripartite' card to get de Gaulle off the narrow Britain-and-the-EEC point. De Gaulle brought him straight back. Unless Britain abandoned its Commonwealth/Empire trading preferences 'he did not see how an arrangement between the Six and the United Kingdom and some of the Seven was possible'. In time they might disappear, Macmillan countered, before playing his British Army of the Rhine card: 'What he feared was that if no arrangement was made the two parts of Europe would drift apart. It would be very difficult, for example, for the United Kingdom to spend so much money defending Europe.'

De Gaulle did not budge, asserting that 'one day, perhaps in three years, there would be great advantage in having one economic system for Europe. He still wondered if it was possible yet and he did not believe that a way had been found.'[78]

This came nowhere near to meeting Macmillan's aspirations so he now played the nuclear card. Would the Market be worth the Bomb? With the Western unity, tripartite and BAOR cards played, this was something of a last resort (which, after all, is what deterrents are for). New possibilities, Macmillan said, would open up if a nuclear test agreement was reached. De Gaulle pointed out that France 'was not at the [Test Ban Treaty] conference because she had not the same capacity as the other three powers' (his Prime Minister, Michel Debré, later told Macmillan that 'France would be a nuclear power by the end of 1961', by which he presumably meant a weaponized bomb with Mirage aircraft adapted to carry it).

Macmillan, after some general digressions about the condition of NATO, slipped the Bomb in again, as Philip de Zulueta's note records:

> *The Prime Minister* asked what President de Gaulle's views were about nuclear arms in NATO.
>
> *President de Gaulle* said that the idea of NATO as a nuclear force had no reality. The nuclear forces were American and the Americans would use them or not as they wished.
>
> *The Prime Minister* suggested that it was paradoxical that in England many people were frightened that the Americans would use their nuclear power rashly whereas in Europe people feared that they would not use it at all. His view was that the United States was full of good intentions and that many people there realised their terrible responsibility for the nuclear deterrent. Perhaps it might be possible to make some arrangement by which the United States, the United Kingdom and France became trustees of nuclear weapons for the Free World. Possibly some part of the French *force de frappe* need not be under NATO command and there could be a system of allocation

together with a tripartite arrangement on consultation. This could probably not take a definite juridical form. But nevertheless any arrangement of this sort would have to be agreed first with the United States. His own view, however, was that Western unity demanded a close working arrangement with the Alliance so as to make a better Western system.[79]

The General did not bite:

France was beginning to manufacture atomic bombs, but needed further tests for H bombs . . . France could only join a Nuclear Tests Agreement without a disarmament treaty when she had an atomic armoury equal to that possessed by other countries.[80]

As they broke up for dinner followed by a film ('a good one – of exploration in New Guinea'[81]), it is plain from de Zulueta's note that de Gaulle was going it alone on the Bomb; he had not swallowed Macmillan's nuclear bait.

The following day, the historic divide between the two leaders yawned once again as they summed up their positions after Sunday lunch. As Professor Sir Michael Howard expressed it in a lecture in Paris many years later, the difference in historical experience of the two countries since the Counter-Reformation meant British 'history is an obstacle rather than a bridge to our entry into any kind of European Union',[82] despite the shared intensity of seeing off the Germans twice in the twentieth century, especially after the new 'era' that opened up with US entry into the Second World War and the Cold War that followed.[83]

De Gaulle seemed to recognize these two approaches to history were talking past each other that Sunday at Rambouillet. As so often, he gave Macmillan a glimmer of hope. After suggesting pointedly in the morning session that the UK should appreciate 'it might not in future always be necessary to follow exactly in the wake of the Americans', de Gaulle said he 'quite realised that there could be no Europe without England'.[84]

In the final afternoon session in the Marble Room, de Gaulle used history, or, rather, the competing histories of Britain and France, as his alibi for frustrating the number one priority of Macmillan's

'Grand Design'. The General opened with what he must have known was at least a deliberate distortion on his own part, claiming 'that he understood Mr Macmillan's position':

> The United Kingdom had decided to come nearer to Europe. They were prepared to open a new chapter. France and Britain had once been rivals; they had been brought together by the German danger at the beginning of the 20th century. Then between the wars there had been differences between French and British policy, but they had fought side by side even so. He recognised that Great Britain had played a major part in securing victory in the Second World War and that the American intervention had been decisive. At that time power had passed to the United States and Britain had very reasonably decided to align herself with the Americans in the belief that she could in this way best influence United States policy. He quite saw that the United Kingdom had not entirely abandoned hope that this policy might still be successful.[85]

Here de Gaulle *did* show a fine understanding of Macmillan's mind. He went on, with a dash of clairvoyance, to reveal a remarkable insight into the early twenty-first century:

> At first the United Kingdom had favoured European Unity [he was probably referring to Churchill's speeches in the late 1940s] for political reasons, but had then become alarmed at the prospect of being swallowed up in an integrated and denationalised Europe.

Neither Britain nor France 'could regard themselves as purely European powers; this was certainly true although France was less maritime and more European than the United Kingdom'.

De Gaulle then deliberately misunderstood Macmillan:

> As regards the economic arrangements in Europe the United Kingdom was not in a hurry ... He would advise the United Kingdom to take her time and to move little by little.

The Six, the General concluded, would not always remain the Six – 'in time it might expand'. As the weekend drew to a close, Macmillan courteously – if a touch desperately – contradicted his host:

He would only like to add his conviction that there was no time to lose. He felt that he and President de Gaulle should try to achieve something while they still could. Their two countries had, over the centuries, accumulated much wisdom and suffered a good deal. Perhaps this experience gave Britain and France something special to contribute to the benefit of the whole world.[86]

The two grand incarnations of their respective histories, who liked each other a great deal,* had spent the weekend reprising their versions of their countries stories; the difference being that Macmillan's grand sweeps reflected the urgency of a mendicant and de Gaulle's did not.

Somehow the PM contrived to persuade himself that things had gone well and the 'Grand Design' was airborne; in reality, its condition was as 'bumpy' as the flight home to Gatwick in his small plane.[87] On reaching Birch Grove, his Sussex country house, that evening he wrote a short entry in his diary:

Since the full records exist – almost word for word – it is not worth trying to summarise them. Broadly speaking, I think we made good progress, De G was relaxed; friendly and seemed genuinely attracted by my themes – Europe to be united, politically and economically; but France and G Britain to be something more than European powers, and to be so recognised by US. I think everything now depends on

(a) whether we can really put forward a formula for 6s and 7s wh both Commonwealth and British agriculture will wear

(b) whether the Americans can be got to accept France's nuclear achievements and ambitions.[88]

In his own mind, he was still the political orchestrator-cum-shaper of the old man in the Élysée and the young man in the White House. A great deal of his remaining premiership rested on this belief.

---

* De Gaulle: 'We were, of course, old friends ... These [wartime] memories, combined with the respect which I had for his character, and the interest and enjoyment which I derived from his company, caused me to listen to him with confidence and speak to him with sincerity' (Charles de Gaulle, *Memoirs of Hope: Renewal 1958–62* (Weidenfeld & Nicolson, 1971), pp. 216–17). Macmillan: 'A great man and I had a great affection for him, and I think I helped him a lot in Algiers, for which he had an affection for me' (Michael Charlton, *The Price of Victory* (BBC Books, 1983), p. 261).

Macmillan felt a sense of urgency about his next steps. To ensure the curmudgeon of Rambouillet did not get his version of the weekend to Washington and Bonn first, Macmillan sent Kennedy and Adenauer his account over the next three days. On the Sixes and Sevens, he told the German Chancellor: 'While expressing some doubt about the possibility of an accommodation, President de Gaulle, I think, agreed that this was desirable and accepted that fresh bilateral discussions should take place at the official level.' He urged Adenauer to press de Gaulle on the need to achieve economic unity in Europe.[89] Macmillan told Kennedy of de Gaulle's views about France's inability to participate in the nuclear test talks and how, in the General's view, none 'of the plans so far canvassed for NATO control of nuclear weapons would meet the problems of political control'.[90] Kennedy wrote a jolly letter back 'looking forward with keen anticipation to our meeting and the opportunity to initiate what I am confident will be a pleasant and fruitful personal relationship with you'.[91] Here, at least, reality and aspiration were to meet for Macmillan.

In fact, the ingredients for it were put in place sooner than either had anticipated. At the end of March, ahead of their planned first meeting in Washington, Kennedy asked Macmillan to fly to Key West Naval Base in Florida from Trinidad (where he and Lady Dorothy were paying a visit to the West Indies Federation) for a crash meeting on the looming crisis in Laos, which the Americans were striving through all means short of military intervention to keep from falling into communist hands.

Macmillan seized his chance. Though as he noted in his diary for 26 March 1961: 'The journey is going to take 4¾ hours – not 2 hours as President Kennedy seemed to think. He had forgotten Cuba.'[92] Not for long, one is tempted to add. Macmillan was intrigued by the prospect of seeing the tyro President in the flesh. He had watched him carefully during the previous year's election campaign, including at least one of the Kennedy–Nixon televised debates while in New York for a meeting of the United Nations. (He told Eisenhower 'One of them [Nixon] looked like a convicted criminal and the other looked like a rather engaging young undergraduate.')[93]

Macmillan, understandably, was anxious. Over a decade later, in one of the BBC television interviews at which he excelled, dripping with self-irony, he painted the scene in the 'sort of board room' in the

Florida Naval Base – 'this young man, the hope of the youth of this world, and here was an ageing reactionary Prime Minister bringing ten or eleven years of Tory misrule to its end . . .'[94] In the event, Key West went remarkably well. Dennis Greenhill, a senior diplomat in the Washington Embassy, who flew down for the meeting with the Ambassador, Sir Harold Caccia, told me that both the principals acted out their required role to perfection: 'Harold played "The Veteran of the Somme" and Jack Kennedy played "The Boy Wonder".'[95]

Macmillan described it as 'quite an event for me – and perhaps for him. He struck me as a curious mixture of qualities – courteous, quiet, quick, decisive – and tough.' They had a picnic lunch and talked for three hours, mainly about Laos, but also about the succession to Caccia in the Washington Embassy. The outcome was to be crucial for both of them and a key ingredient in what became one of the high-water-mark periods of the US/UK relationship:

He was emphatic for David Gore [currently Minister of State in the Foreign Office and Conservative MP for Oswestry]. 'He is my brother [Bobby's] most intimate friend.' (And, of course, 'my brother' is thought by many to be the Grey Eminence').

Ormsby-Gore was also Macmillan's nephew by marriage. 'Quite a day,' Macmillan concluded on the plane back to Trinidad. 'I have never before been 1800 miles to luncheon – 3600 miles in all.'[96] And lunch was hamburgers; not the kind of London clubland fare one associates with 'Uncle Harold'.

A few days later, the slightly incongruous pair met once more in Washington as part of Macmillan's long-planned five-day visit from 4 to 9 April. The State Department briefing for Kennedy on the Macmillan style might have been a touch superfluous after the session over Navy hamburgers, but it was well judged nonetheless:

The Prime Minister is an exponent of the art of personal diplomacy and likes to think that 'jowl to jowl' he is able to resolve difficult issues. He also has a penchant for soliloquizing in broad and bold historical terms which sometimes turn out to have little bearing on his attitude or that of HMG on specific issues. These monologues can be quite disconcerting if taken too seriously.[97]

Macmillan's version of this would have been (as we have seen) trying to win over the President by ideas.

Macmillan had still not shown his full Cabinet the essential contents of the 'Grand Design' ahead of his Washington talks with Kennedy. Only on 17 April, when they were over and ahead of a pair of Cabinet meetings to discuss the outcome of them *and* Britain in Europe, did he instruct Norman Brook to send them a 'Top Secret and Personal' summary of the document giving no indication of its provenance.

'The attached paper,' Brook wrote, 'was written at an early stage of the preparations for the Prime Minister's talks with President Kennedy. It does, however, examine some of the main issues which were covered in those talks viz. the complex of problems connected with our political and economic relations with Europe and with the future control of nuclear weapons.' The document was of such sensitivity that Brook wanted their copies back straight after the Cabinet meeting.[98] Unusually, too, the Cabinet, ahead of 20 April meeting, were given a copy, as a Cabinet paper,[99] of Brook's record of Macmillan's conversations in Washington.

Primarily, Macmillan wished to convert the Kennedy administration's enthusiasm for British membership of the EEC into real political capital for himself inside his own Cabinet Room. But the *degree* of that enthusiasm in Washington was tricky for Macmillan. This reflected the near-evangelism of Kennedy's principal adviser on Europe, George Ball of the State Department, a long-time associate of Jean Monnet and a staunch friend of European integration. Ball had been visiting Whitehall in March 1961 when Sir Frank Lee, Permanent Secretary to the Treasury, and Ted Heath, Home's number two in the Foreign Office, took him aback with the directness of their question, 'How would the United States react if Britain should make the decision to apply for membership in the European Community?' Ball recalled:

> Both Frank Lee and Ted Heath made it quite clear what the motivating reasons were; and, as I remember them, perhaps the dominant one was the feeling that Britain could simply not afford to be outside the new dynamism that Europe was achieving through the building of the Community. If it did, there would be a certain atrophying of the

industrial strength of Britain – and American investment would come to the Community, it wouldn't come to Britain. It would be, in other words, outside the mainstream of policy.[100]

Ball was in a quandary 'because I had never discussed this matter with President Kennedy except in a very generalised way'. Nonetheless, Ball conveyed America's keenness for a Britain in Europe: 'I was quite prepared to give them an answer because I felt there was only one policy for the United States – and I must say that the President supported me fully.'[101]

So Macmillan arrived in Washington knowing that this piece of his 'Grand Design' was in the bag. And when the question duly arose in the discussions, Kennedy asked Ball to reply: 'I think he left Macmillan in *no* doubt [that he was a supporter]; and I think Macmillan himself felt enormously pleased by this.'[102]

Norman Brook's minute of the morning meeting in the White House on 5 April 1961 suggests that Ball did the talking for the American side on the question of Europe. 'The US,' he said, 'attached more weight to the political than to the economic objectives' of an expanded EEC. When EFTA was created, America

> had feared that the United Kingdom, acting as a pole of attraction, might weaken the forces for unity among the six. But if the United Kingdom became a member of the six and brought her political genius to bear within it, she would provide an element of stability in the period of uncertainty which was likely to follow the departure of the present leaders of France and Germany. Such a decision on the part of the United Kingdom would also confirm even more closely the special relationship of confidence between the United States and United Kingdom Governments. In short, the interests of all parties, on both sides of the Atlantic, would be advanced if the United Kingdom could see her way clear to become a member of the six.[103]

Thus did this huge piece of Macmillan's 'Grand Design' fall into place; no doubt to the immense gratification of its architect. There was, however, a part of it that snagged. George Ball wanted a British application for EEC membership that was wholehearted and without caveat. He was not Monnet's friend for nothing. He had briefed

Kennedy that, if Macmillan put the question to him, it should be made plain that the UK must recognize

> that the Rome Treaty was not a static document but indeed was a process leading towards greater and greater unity, including political unity, and might even ultimately lead to some kind of confederal or federal system for Europe ... we would not favour any British move if the intention of that move was to water down the Treaty of Rome, or to try to transform the Community into anything that would be simply a loose consultative arrangement.[104]

Ball was almost writing the history of the UK and Europe for the next half century and more in that briefing for Kennedy. It was made plain to Macmillan in the White House during that Washington spring that the support of the US for a British application would require the UK to 'fully accept political and institutional obligations of the Rome Treaties', as the rather staccato American note of the discussion on 12 April 1961 put it.[105] Macmillan was well satisfied with his talks with Kennedy: 'He seemed to understand and sympathise with most of the plans wh form what I call "The Grand Design". How far he will be able to go with de Gaulle to help me, I do not know. But he will try.'[106]

Ball remained critical of Macmillan and his government for, as he told Kennedy at the time, trying 'to move crabwise into the Common Market'.[107] To be fair to Macmillan, this was almost certainly the best approach to handling both his own Cabinet and de Gaulle. Ball fully understood, however, the difference between Macmillan the veteran of the Somme and Macmillan the Prime Minister. Looking back in the early 1980s, Ball said:

> I still believe that he believed in Europe, because the one thing I always found with Prime Minister Macmillan was that, in private conversation, he was very moving and eloquent about the need for unity, based on his war experience. His buddies had all been killed, he had a decimated unit he was leading, and the old rivalries had to be put to an end, and there *had* to be the building of a real European structure.

Yet, Ball recognized, in the spring and summer of 1961, 'he had to manage the thing from a tactical point of view and this was his decision'.[108]

Indeed it was. Macmillan had a Cabinet, a party, a Parliament and a people to persuade *and* a British Commonwealth to square. However, it was unjust of Ball to say 'Mr Macmillan gave simply a kind of tradesman's view of the Community' in 1961–3.[109] When he reported on the Washington talks and unveiled the ingredients of the 'Grand Design' to his Cabinet in Admiralty House on the morning of 20 April 1961, Macmillan began in grand sweep/cohesion of the West and noticeably *non*-tradesman mode:

> *The Prime Minister* said that these discussions had strengthened his view that far-reaching decisions would have to be taken soon about the United Kingdom's relations with Europe. In recent years the Communist *bloc* had been gaining ground at the expense of the West and, if this was to be checked, the leading countries of the Western world would need to draw more closely together.
>
> There was, however, a risk that current developments in Europe would tend in the opposite direction; for, if the countries of the Common Market formed a close political association under French leadership, this would create a further political division in Europe and would also have a disruptive influence within the Atlantic Community. This might be averted if the United Kingdom, together with some of the Seven, could join the political association of the Six and help to build in Europe a stable political structure which would prevent France now, and Germany later, from attaining a too dominant position.[110]

Macmillan had finally shown his hand. It was nearly a year since his own tilt to Europe had taken place in the days of depression and disappointment that followed the ruin of the May 1960 East–West summit in Paris.[111] All his colleagues had now heard from his own lips his intention to engineer this great geopolitical shift for his country.

The 20 April Cabinet and the follow-up discussion six days later were the key Cabinet meetings on Britain and Europe – even though the final full Cabinet decision to apply was not taken until 21 July 1961.[112]* On the morning on 20 April, Macmillan eased his policy

---

* We had to wait until January 1992 before we could read the minutes of those pivotal Cabinet meetings. Ten years later we were given a little more detail by Alan Milward, the Cabinet Office's official historian of the UK and the European

forward. 'Cabinet – 11–1 – on Europe and the Future', he jauntily noted in his diary that evening. 'I gave them the outlines of the Grand Design. An excellent discussion – no conclusions. Adjourned till Wednesday.'[113] But caveats and anxieties had emerged, one of them of great and enduring significance.

Macmillan had followed his grand vista opening with a recognition of problems ahead. 'Difficult economic adjustments would be involved,' Macmillan began,

> both for the United Kingdom and for other Commonwealth countries; but it was arguable that both we and the other Commonwealth countries would in the long run gain greater economic advantage from access to a wider market in Europe.

Macmillan, no doubt at his most solemn, indicated to his Cabinet that a decision could no longer be delayed:

> The Cabinet must now weigh all the relevant considerations and determine its future course. If they decided it was right, on balance, to draw closer to Europe, they would have to consider what economic price might have to be paid and what were the tactics by which this objective could be attained. Nothing would now be gained by delaying a decision. And, if the decision went in favour of closer union with Europe, the practical steps to that end would have to be taken before the end of the present Parliament [i.e., by the summer of 1964 at the latest].[114]

It was an extraordinary moment. Britain – or England, if one looks back before the 1707 union with Scotland – had never taken a formal decision to become an imperial power any more than a post-1945 Cabinet took a formal decision to get out of empire as a whole – to deimperialize, as it were. Instead the most extensive territorial empire the world has ever known grew out of a series of ad hoc decisions just as it shrivelled because of individual ones that, cumulatively, though never completely, withdrew dominion back to the home islands.

Community with his publication of *The United Kingdom and the European Community*, vol. 1: *The Rise and Fall of a National Strategy 1945–1963* (Frank Cass, 2002). Milward had access to the Cabinet Secretaries' Notebooks, which, unlike the finished Cabinet minutes, enabled their readers to determine who actually said what.

Yet here, in the spring and summer of 1961, a British Cabinet really was engaged, as Gaitskell put it to the Labour Party Conference in 1962, in going back on 'a thousand years of history'[115] and, at the very least, modifying Churchill's determination in his June 1944 outburst to de Gaulle to always choose the open sea before Europe. And yet, for all the historical and personal impulses of the private Macmillan, the bulk of the discussion in the Cabinet Room on 20 April was about tariffs and foodstuffs and farm produce – grocery mingling with grand strategy.

When Macmillan 'invited his colleagues to express their general views on this issue', Reggie Maudling, President of the Board of Trade and chief British negotiator of EFTA in the late 1950s (and one of only three ministers, in addition to Macmillan, to have their views personally attributed in the Cabinet minutes), expressed his doubts about the acceptability of a UK EEC application to the French.[116] Maudling fully admitted to his colleagues that

> in 1954 we had under-estimated the strength of the forces working for unity between the countries of the Six. The Common Market was now firmly established and, as it developed, our economic interests would be gravely prejudiced if we remained outside it. We should be excluded from one of the largest and most dynamic markets in the world, and, as time went on, the trade and investment of the United States would be drawn increasingly towards Europe. Our attempt to form a European Free Trade Area had failed largely because the French opposed it. The French would also be reluctant to accept our participation in the Six – partly no doubt because they wished to retain its political leadership. We should have therefore to fashion a line which the French would find it difficult to resist.

Maudling anticipated the greatest problem for the UK as an EEC member would not be the external common tariff 'but the concept of a single commercial policy. For this we should need to obtain some derogation, if our special relations with other Commonwealth countries were to be preserved.' Maudling reckoned that in terms of foodstuffs, 'the main burden was likely to fall on consumers, than on farmers, in this country – though British horticulture was bound to suffer . . . British industry was increasingly aware of the advantages which it would gain from our association with the Six.'[117]

Duncan Sandys spoke next. As a lifelong Europeanist by temperament, he played a pivotal role as Commonwealth Secretary in the 1961 EEC Cabinets; not for nothing had Macmillan given him this crucial portfolio in the July 1960 Cabinet reshuffle. He outlined the arguments that would later be the core of the case Macmillan and his ministers put to the Commonwealth heads of government for a Britain fully in Europe. Commonwealth sentiment was of a strength in both the Cabinet Room and the country generally which it is difficult for twenty-first century readers to recall or to appreciate if they did not live through the twilight of empire.

Sandys opened by acknowledging that if the UK joined the EEC, 'awkward adjustments would have to be made in our economic relations with other Commonwealth countries'. Canada as an exporter of manufactures 'would be seriously affected' and New Zealand would face 'special difficulties'. It should be easier to make arrangements for tropical foodstuffs. And here came the crux of what would be the UK's line with the Commonwealth – 'to the extent that our economy was strengthened by our participation in the Six, this would serve the long-term interests of other Commonwealth countries'. Sandys 'believed that if we stood aloof from the Common Market we should get the worst of both worlds; and that the right course on balance was to go fully into partnership with the Six'.

Christopher Soames, moved to Agriculture in July 1960 as another part of Macmillan's grooming of his Cabinet for Europe, buttressed Sandys's emphasis on the long term. British farmers and market gardeners 'would have to be convinced – and this would not be easy – that they would suffer even more serious damage in the long run if we stood aside from the Six. Even so it must be recognised that, if we joined the Six, the net income of British agriculture would be lower than at present [as the UK would have to move over to a continental system of farm support] and our trade with other Commonwealth countries would also be reduced.'[118]

In the general discussion which followed, Lord Kilmuir, the Lord Chancellor, raised the momentous question that has resonated to this day – sovereignty. Kilmuir, the former Sir David Maxwell Fyfe, was another veteran pro-European. With Macmillan and Peter Thorneycroft, he had been seriously disappointed by the Churchill Cabinet's attitude towards the European Coal and Steel Community (from which the EEC emerged) when the Conservatives returned to power in 1951.[119]

Kilmuir warned the Cabinet that April morning in Admiralty House that

> [p]olitical association with the Six might ultimately involve a signifi-
> cant surrender of national sovereignty. Adherence to the Treaty of
> Rome would limit the supremacy of Parliament, which would be
> required to accept decisions taken by the Council of the Community.
> It would restrict the right of the Executive to make treaties. It would
> also involve a final right of appeal from our courts to the Supreme
> Court of the Community. A major effort of presentation would be
> needed to persuade the British public to accept these encroachments
> on national sovereignty.[120]

Though the Cabinet minute does not tell us so, we know from Milward's official history that Kilmuir was nevertheless in favour of
entry.[121]

Kilmuir, in fact, had made this point with clarity and force at the
end of 1960 in an exchange of letters with Ted Heath, the Lord Privy
Seal and Foreign Office Minister for Europe (another careful Macmillan placement in July of that year).*

Kilmuir went to the heart of the constitutional novelty for the UK
in what the Treaty of Rome meant for Britain's treaty-making powers
generally:

> The proposition that every treaty entered into by the United Kingdom
> does to some extent fetter our freedom of action is plainly true ... But
> to transfer to the Council or the Commission the power to make such
> treaties on our behalf and even against our will, is an entirely different
> proposition. There seems to me to be a clear distinction between the

---

* Kilmuir's letter to Heath of 14 December 1960 acquired, for a National Archives
document, a rare political celebrity status during the 1997 general election when 'the
Referendum Party exhumed [it] ... from the files, displaying it as evidence of
the establishment conspiracy of secrecy which Sir James Goldsmith and other RP
zealots believed to have been at the core of Britain's entry into the EEC' (Hugo
Young, *This Blessed Plot: Britain and Europe from Churchill to Blair* (Macmillan,
1998), p. 153).

exercise of sovereignty involved in the conscious acceptance by us of obligations under our treaty-making powers and the total or partial surrender of sovereignty involved [in] cession of these powers to some other body. To confer a sovereign state's treaty-making powers on an international organisation is the first step on the road which leads by way of confederation to the fully federal state. I do not suggest that what is involved would necessarily carry us very far in this direction, but it would be a most significant step and one for which there is no precedent in our case.[122]

That was not quite true. The most dramatic – and, in my view, necessary – cession of sovereignty of the postwar years was Article 5 of the North Atlantic Treaty of 1949 whereby the signatory nations

agree that an armed attack against one or more of them in Europe or North America shall be considered an attack against them all; and consequently they agree that, if such an armed attack occurs, each of them . . . will assist the Party or Parties so attacked by taking forthwith, individually and in concert with the other Parties, such action as it deems necessary, including the use of armed force, to restore and maintain international peace and security.[123]

In effect, NATO's Article 5 locked Britain into a Third World War had it erupted at any time anywhere from the North Cape of Norway eventually to the Turkish-Soviet border until the end of the Cold War – and it still binds us as I write. Nothing in what Kilmuir was pondering in December 1960 matches what Attlee and Bevin contemplated in the spring of 1949. There was one key difference, however. Article 5 dealt with a remote, albeit catastrophic possibility. Signing the Treaty of Rome would instantly syringe sovereignty from Britain to a degree unprecedented, as Kilmuir indicated, in its history.

Summing up, Kilmuir told Heath:

the surrenders of sovereignty involved are serious ones and I think that, as a matter of practical politics, it will not be easy to persuade Parliament or the public to accept them. I am sure that it would be a great mistake to under-estimate the force of the objections to them. But these objections ought to be brought out into the open now because if we attempt to gloss over them at this stage, those who are opposed to the whole idea of our joining the Community will certainly seize on them with more damaging effect later on.[124]

Kilmuir's letter to Heath was a first-class piece of political prophesy – just as his argument put to the 20 April 1961 Cabinet was well judged, though, as we shall see, Macmillan did not follow his advice that Parliament and the British be spared nothing about the price to be paid in sovereignty for easing Britain into the Common Market.

The anonymous section of the minutes of that occasion contain another, to twenty-first-century eyes, striking contribution. The unattributed Cabinet Conclusions – in fact it was the Minister of Aviation, Peter Thorneycroft – record him as saying:

> The special difficulties in respect of agriculture should not be allowed to obscure the undoubted advantages which British industry would derive from the wider market opened to it by our association with the Six. Modern industry needed to operate in a large economic unit. This was strikingly illustrated by the output per worker in the United States and the Soviet Union, which was far greater than that in the United Kingdom.[125]

This was the era when the West was bedazzled by Soviet military technology into reading its prowess in Sputniks and rocketry into its civilian and agricultural sectors.

But Thorneycroft was doing no more than echoing the arguments of the 'Future Policy Study' of 1960 when he maintained that

> British industry could not afford to miss this opportunity of access to the wider market of the Six. If we stood aside from this we should fall behind industrially: the Common Market and the United States would forge ahead and we should be increasingly excluded from our markets overseas. From this point of view it was gratifying that the new Administration in the United States were in favour of our joining the Six.[126]

Macmillan regarded the follow-up Cabinet meeting on 26 April 1961 as not only '[a]n excellent discussion on Europe' but also the moment at which 'I revealed to all the Cabinet "The Grand Design".

On the whole, approval – tho' of course with reservation.' In fact, the proceedings quite carried him away:

> I was very pleased with the intellectual power of the discussion, as well as the high sense of drama and responsibility. This is a fine set of men – equal in intelligence and energy to any Cabinet of the past.[127]

Macmillan opened by saying

> that the time had not yet come to take a final decision on the question whether the United Kingdom should accede to the Treaty of Rome. Many important aspects of this problem would have to be further considered in detail and full consultations would have to be held with our partners in the Commonwealth and in the European Free Trade Association ... The question to which the Cabinet should address themselves at this stage was whether it was to our advantage to work towards a solution by which the United Kingdom (preferably with some of her partners in EFTA) would join with the countries of the Common Market in forming a wider political and economic association in Europe. The question for discussion now was whether, on a balance of advantage, it was in our interests to try and bring this about.[128]

For all his careful words about no final decision, it would have been plain that morning in Admiralty House that Macmillan was nudging, if not shoving, his Cabinet towards Europe. It is clear from the minutes that the bulk of his senior ministers were willing enough to be so nudged but not all and the Cabinet Secretary's minute 'of the main points made' reflects that.

- Under French leadership, the EEC (without the UK as a member) could become a political and economic force able to exercise greater influence than the United Kingdom, both with the United States and possibly with some of the independent countries of the Commonwealth. This development was therefore a threat to the political position of the United Kingdom as a world power. It would be consistent with our traditional policy to seek to prevent the concentration of undue strength in a single political unit on the continent of Europe.

- The EEC, with a market of 160 million people, posed 'a serious economic threat to the UK'. If Britain remained outside and stood aloof from the Six, we should find ourselves in a position of growing economic weakness.
- An 'economic settlement' between the EEC and EFTA countries would no longer be 'practicable' or 'sufficient'. Moreover, the United States Government would not lend their support to a purely economic settlement . . . In these circumstances a political initiative was required.
- Public opinion was shifting towards Europe. Many of the leaders of British industry were in favour of our joining the Six; indeed, there was now some risk that the difficulties would be under-estimated. In political circles also informed opinion was moving in the same direction. On the other hand, it must be remembered that a great weight of sentiment could easily be aroused against any policy which could be represented as a threat to the Commonwealth and to British agriculture. In the Conservative Party, in particular, this could evoke strong emotional reactions comparable to those which had recently arisen over colonial policy.*
- Could the position of the Commonwealth be safeguarded by deroga-tions from the Treaty of Rome not just in trading matters but in access to the London money markets? If we joined the Six, would European interests come eventually to weigh more with us than Commonwealth interests in formulating our general and political and economic policies? The UK was obliged to consult fully with the Commonwealth on such questions and the timing and the method of such consultation would need careful thought.[129]

The Commonwealth and the British farmers had their man in the Cabinet Room that morning in Rab Butler, Home Secretary, and the number two figure in the government. Macmillan was very wary of Butler on the question of Europe. In fact, he wasn't sure Rab had been persuaded – perhaps reconciled is a better word – until the sum-mer of 1962, by which time Ted Heath had been negotiating vigorously in Brussels for about eight months overseen by a Cabinet Committee

* See chapter 4.

on the Common Market Negotiations of which, shrewdly, Macmillan had made Butler the chair.

Butler told Macmillan of his shift to acquiescence in a characteristically feline fashion over dinner in clubland on 21 August 1962 as the PM's diary recorded:

> Dined with Butler. This was at Buck's, to which he invited me to come as his guest. The engagement was made in July. It was clearly to be an occasion. And it was. He told me that in spite of (a) the farmers; (b) the Commonwealth; (c) the probable break-up of the Conservative Party he had decided to support our joining the Common Market. It was too late to turn back now. It was too big a chance to miss, for Britain's wealth and strength. But we must face the fact that we might share the fate of Sir Robert Peel and his supporters.[130]

The Conservative Party did not sunder in the 1960s as it had in the 1840s over repeal of the Corn Laws, but for many of its natural supporters the European question has created a permanent tension that expresses itself as a political virus, from that day to this.

At the 26 April Cabinet sixteen months earlier, Butler raised caveat after caveat and propped them up against the overall tilt towards Europe, making use of Kilmuir on sovereignty in the process:

- In July 1960, the Cabinet had agreed that there were insuperable difficulties in the way of our accepting membership of the Six under the existing provisions of the Treaty of Rome. The Cabinet had then particularly in mind the difficulties in respect of the Commonwealth.
- On 20 April, surrender of national sovereignty had been raised which would certainly require careful thought . . .
- The National Farmers' Union had come out 'strongly against association with the Six'; and, the Government had undertaken not to change the existing support system for agriculture in the present Parliament and the Government would be in very grave political difficulties if they could be represented as having broken their pledges to the farmers.'[131]*

---

* Butler could, on occasion, take the 'Rab – the Farmers' Friend' ploy a little too far. A few years later when he was Foreign Secretary in the Douglas-Home administration he rang the No. 10 private office from his home in north Essex, asking them to inform

At the 26 April Cabinet, the other farmers' friend in the room, the Minister of Agriculture, Christopher Soames, swung his considerable frame into the argument in an attempt to rebut Butler. The NFU's pamphlet 'was concerned with the results which would follow if the United Kingdom joined the Six without any derogations in respect of agriculture. The Government were not contemplating such a course; and he fully agreed that they must avoid putting forward any new policy proposals which would expose them to the charge of having broken their pledges to the farmers.'[132] In the end, after de Gaulle's veto, there was no agreement for the farmers to pass judgement upon.

Ted Heath, the Lord Privy Seal, for whom Britain in Europe was to be a life's work, spoke ahead of Macmillan's summing-up. He left the grand sweeps to his Prime Minister and stuck to the practicalities and the tactics – for dealing with the French especially. The French government, he said,

> had indicated that they were willing to discuss with us how we could join the Common Market, or enter into a special association with it, so long as we were ready to make some concessions on Commonwealth trade and on British agriculture. They had made it plain that, while it was open to us to consider either course, they would greatly prefer membership to association. Hitherto, we had not been able to tell the French how far we were prepared to go either on Commonwealth trade or agriculture. If we could disclose to the French the sort of conditions which the Cabinet were now considering it was possible that further progress could be made in negotiation.
>
> Even so, it was doubtful whether it would be expedient for us to declare at the outset that we were prepared to accede to the Treaty of Rome before we had negotiated the necessary derogations. Such a declaration would involve us in political difficulties in this country: it would also leave us less room for manoeuvre in negotiation. It would be preferable to make further progress with the detailed negotiation of the derogations before taking any final decisions.[133]

---

the Prime Minister that he had to miss a particular Cabinet meeting 'as it's market day in Saffron Walden [his constituency town] you see' (private information).

Heath had no time for the half-way house of an association with Europe. As he wrote in his memoirs:

> Any such proposal simply encouraged the belief that Britain wanted all of the advantages of the developments in Europe, without undertaking any of the obligations. In any case, no association agreement would grant us the political influence that we sought. The choice, therefore, was between accepting the Treaty of Rome in its entirety, together with the domestic and international problems that would arise as a result, or maintaining the status quo and reconciling ourselves to being stuck in Western Europe's second division.[134]

The words that appeared in Heath's 1998 memoir were more explicit and enthusiastic than those he used in the Cabinet Room on 26 April 1961, though I have no doubt his pro-European sentiments were running just as strongly privately then. He tempered them, like a good politician, to the mood and the moment – though in 1961, as in 1998, he stressed the difficult adjustments full membership implied:

> It was evident that we could not accede to the Treaty of Rome without some economic damage, at least in the short term, both to this country and other countries of the Commonwealth: and before a final decision was taken, the Cabinet should have before them a statement showing the balance of advantage and disadvantage in the course ultimately proposed.[135]

The scene was set for Macmillan to unveil his 'Grand Design'. Though the Cabinet did not *formally* decide to apply to join the EEC until 21 July 1961, that 26 April meeting, for me, is the *real* moment of decision and the grand sweep of Macmillan's long summing up was a tour de force that rose to the level of the event.

The 'question' of Europe, he told his colleagues,

> must be viewed in the wider context of the East–West struggle. In this the Communist *bloc* were gaining ground and the Western countries were in some disarray. It was an article of Communist faith that capitalism would in the end destroy itself; and, given competing currencies and conflicting trade interests, there was a real risk of a growing

economic weakness in the western world unless its countries could find means of drawing more closely together.[136]

Here recent postwar history was prayed in aid by Macmillan the scholar – no longer the swordsman, but the 'gownsman' as he liked to call himself in this mode:[137]

For some time after the war, in her years of political and economic weakness, Europe had been dependent on American aid and content to accept Anglo-Saxon leadership. Europe had now regained her strength, and a new situation had arisen. Different means must now be found for binding Europe within the wider Atlantic Community. The United Kingdom, as the bridge between Europe and North America, had the opportunity to take an initiative in this.

And here he showed his hand: it both took a swipe against the Butler line *and* pointed towards Europe:

We could of course decline that responsibility. It would be easy for us to put forward, as excuses, the need for preserving our special relations with other Commonwealth countries and protecting the interests of British agriculture. But, if we decided to stand aloof from inner Europe at this time, might we not find that the eventual damage to our interests would be even greater in terms of the secular struggle between East and West? We should not forget that in this struggle half of our Commonwealth partners and half of our partners in EFTA were neutral.

He moved here from world struggle to the vulnerability of the British economy and back again, for

as the economic strength of the Six increased, other members of EFTA would certainly be under strong temptation to join it; and, to the extent that this happened, the economic position of the United Kingdom would be progressively undermined. The older members of the Commonwealth, though they would stand with us now, might then be obliged to turn increasingly towards the United States; and new world groupings would arise, as a result of which the United Kingdom would lose much of her influence in world affairs. These considerations suggested that, on a balance of advantage, it was in our interest to join the political and economic association of the Six if we could gain admission on terms which would be tolerable to us.[138]

That passage of Cabinet minute is among the most important of the postwar period. It was a recognition, as Ted Heath acknowledged thirty-seven years later, that the Churchillian notion of the three overlapping circles of post-1945 British influence – the United States and the Commonwealth/Empire with Europe as very much a subsidiary third – had shifted with the European circle taking a strong second place and Commonwealth/Empire relegated to a diminishing third. 'In many ways,' Heath wrote of the announcement in Parliament on 31 July 1961 that an application to join the EEC was to be made, '[this] was of much greater significance than the actual fate of the British application. It signalled the end of a glorious era, that of the British Empire, and the beginning of a whole new chapter of British history.'[139] Heath was right. As would become apparent, Macmillan's statement in the House of Commons was *the* hail-and-farewell moment in early-Sixties Britain.

From the high peaks of history Macmillan quickly turned at the 26 April Cabinet to another phenomenon of nature – Charles de Gaulle, whom, rightly, he sensed would be a greater obstacle to a Britain in Europe than all the Commonwealth heads of government *and* the sceptics in his own Cabinet and party *and* the British farmers put together. To join Europe, Macmillan told the meeting, a 'political initiative would be necessary' – he did not, according to the minutes, designate it a 'Grand Design' – 'and France was certainly the key to the situation'.

The fencing at Rambouillet in January was replayed by Macmillan at this point:

Hitherto, General de Gaulle had not wished us to join the Six – presumably because he wanted France to retain the leadership of inner Europe. But his attitude might be changed if he could be brought to see that the West as a whole could not prevail against the Communists unless its leading countries worked together towards a wider unity in the free world as a whole . . . at the present time France was, in more respects than one, a main obstacle in the way of creating a closer unity in the West.[140]

84

He hoped Kennedy would help as 'General de Gaulle must be brought to see that France must co-operate more fully and effectively with her western partners', accept the interdependence of NATO and see her nuclear force as a contribution to Western deterrence as a whole rather than as a national capability. Only in this way could France 'take her rightful place with the United States and the United Kingdom as one of the pillars of the Western Alliance and thus earn the right to participate in the system of tripartite consultation which General de Gaulle demanded'.

Had de Gaulle's secret service provided him with a copy of these Cabinet minutes (which, of course, they did not), his reaction to words like 'must' and 'earn' would have been a joy to see and hear. De Gaulle, the Cabinet was left in no doubt, was the key: 'If General de Gaulle was willing to consider this problem in the wider framework of the world situation, it should be possible to find a solution of the special economic difficulties which the United Kingdom Government would find in acceding to the Treaty of Rome as it now stood.'

And finally, Macmillan sought and received approval from his Cabinet for the principle of Britain in Europe:

> The conclusion reached by the Cabinet, in the light of this discussion and the earlier discussion on 20th April, was that the right policy for the Government to follow at this stage was to work for a solution by which the United Kingdom (preferably with some of her partners in EFTA) would join with the countries of the Six in forming a wider political and economic association in Europe. It would be necessary, in negotiations with those countries, to secure special arrangements to preserve the main trading interests of the Commonwealth; a satisfactory relation with other members of EFTA; and special provisions for British agriculture to enable it to be brought into harmony with the general agricultural policy of the Six on a basis adequate to support the interests dependent on it. If, however, these points could be covered satisfactorily, either in a protocol to the Treaty or otherwise, there seemed to be no reason of principle why the United Kingdom should not accede to the Treaty of Rome, including its political institutions.[141]

Thus, in that slightly circumlocutory fashion, ended a 'thousand years of history'.

Macmillan had steered his Cabinet to the desired conclusion and he lost no time in writing to Kennedy on 28 April with a letter and a supporting memorandum containing suggestions as to how Kennedy might handle de Gaulle on his forthcoming visit to Paris, letting the US President know that 'this is not a formal statement of the British Government's position, but gives my own ideas, which I believe to be in general accordance with the views of my Cabinet colleagues'.[142]

Kennedy's reply on 8 May was sufficient a blow for it to knock over a significant chunk of Macmillan's 'Grand Design' so recently approved by his Cabinet. He would not allow the British deterrent – or his own – to be used as a nuclear spanner to engineer Britain's entry into Europe:

> After careful review of the problem, I have come to the conclusion it would be undesirable to assist France's efforts to create a nuclear weapons capability. I am most anxious that no erroneous impressions get abroad regarding future US policy in this respect, lest they create unwarranted French expectations and serious divisions in NATO.
>
> If we were to help France acquire a nuclear weapons capability, this could not fail to have a major effect on German attitudes ... The damaging effect of stirring up German interest in acquiring a nuclear weapons capability would not, I believe, be offset by a French agreement to consult about use of French nuclear forces or to commit these forces to NATO, in return for our aid.[143]

Macmillan cabled back:

> I quite agree that the nuclear question is the most difficult part of the French problem. As I see it the object of your talks with de Gaulle will be to persuade the General to modify his rather insular policies and to act more as a good free world European ... [by] ... genuinely seeking a reasonable solution for the economic divisions of Western Europe.[144]

The Kennedy ploy did not work. Macmillan knew it hadn't as soon as Kennedy briefed him when they talked alone in Admiralty House on 11 June as the President made his way home from meeting de Gaulle in Paris and Khrushchev in Vienna. It was clear, Macmillan wrote in his diary, that the President (with the exception of the actual delivery of nuclear information or nuclear weapons) carried out most loyally our arrangement and really did do everything I had asked him to do both in Washington and in the memorandum which I sent him recently. De Gaulle was very avuncular, very gracious, very oracular and very unyielding. He would take all the plums – tripartism, new arrangements in NATO, and help with the technique of missiles and bombs (other than the actual nuclear content) with cavalier profligacy. But when it came to giving anything in return – e.g. Britain's desire to enter Europe on reasonable terms, having regard to Commonwealth and British agricultural structures – then the General was in his most austere and Puritan mood. So far as I can see (unless the General was just playing the hand *very* close to his chest) my great plan has failed – or, at least, failed up to now.[145]

From thinking and writing in his Chequers bed over the 1960/61 New Year to his conversation with Kennedy in Admiralty House was a mere four months – the 'Grand Design' had a short life, in its original purpose at least. But it worked in the sense that it carried Macmillan's Cabinet over the European brink. The parts which depended on the rest of the world – de Gaulle in particular – were another matter. The old man still possessed real power he could exert in Whitehall, but for all his style and persistence it did not flow into the Élysée or the White House.

Macmillan was genuinely aware of this. During the busy first week of August – in which he made his statement to the House of Commons about the EEC application on the Monday, took part in the resultant Commons debate on the Wednesday and broadcast to the nation on the Friday – he found time after briefing the lobby correspondents to take his Press Secretary, Harold Evans, down from the Lobby Room in its Westminster turret to his own room behind the Speaker's Chair 'and there I had a dissertation on European history – how ironical it was that this small peninsula attached to the land mass of Asia, thinking itself the hub of the universe, should now be utterly dependent on all the people it had driven overseas by persecution, punishment or poverty'.[146] And here was Britain, he might have added, reduced to a supplicant of six countries on that same, diminished 'small peninsula'.

Yet there is no evidence that the May–June setbacks to his geopolit-ical plan caused Macmillan to consider for one moment postponing (let alone abandoning) the push for EEC membership until de Gaulle had left the Élysée Palace. Quite the reverse. It was as if the idea of the UK in Europe and its close twin – the modernization of Britain (see chapter 3) – had become *the* governing idea of his premiership and his administration. The next phase was for ministers to be put in planes and despatched to talk to the bigger players in the Commonwealth. Over the weekend of 17–18 June Macmillan took the ministers most closely concerned to Chequers to ponder how this should be done:

> A great number of officials arrived. I think we were 25 or 26 at lunch-eon [on Sunday]. We got somewhere – but not very far really. Like all great issues, it will (in the end) be decided by some quite small events. At any rate, we agreed enough to allow the 'peripatetic' ministers (or perh one shd say the St John the Baptists) to set out on their tour of the Commonwealth countries. This is really quite a good plan. Duncan Sandys will go to Australia, NZ and Canada. Heath will go to Cyprus. Ld Perth [Minister of State, Colonial Office] to W Indies. Peter Thorneycroft [Minister of Aviation] to India, Pakistan, Malaya, Ceylon. John Hare [Minister of Labour] to Ghana, Nigeria, Sierra Leone etc. This makes quite an impressive list.[147]

The full Cabinet the following Thursday listened to Macmillan on the tactics to be pursued by his 'St John the Baptists'.

They were plainly not expected to imitate fully the shining can-dour of the saint. Macmillan said the Chequers meeting

> had led to the conclusion that the approach to the Commonwealth should be on the basis that it was undesirable to leave in suspense for much longer a decision on the question whether the United Kingdom should apply to accede to the Treaty of Rome . . . The . . . Ministers should there-fore inform Commonwealth Governments that we were inclined to think that the right course would be for us to make a formal application to accede to the Treaty of Rome in order to find out whether we could secure acceptable terms and conditions which would safeguard the essential interests of other Commonwealth countries, and also meet our own requirements and those of the European Free Trade Association.[148]

The 26 April meeting had been rather more than merely 'inclined to think' that Britain should join the Six.

So off they went over the following weeks. The 'peripatetic ministers' reported back on their Commonwealth travels on the afternoon of Friday 21 July in the Prime Minister's room in the House of Commons. Sandys talked of anxiety and fears in the old Dominions. New Zealand was the most vulnerable in terms of trade. But they 'now expected us to open negotiations, without further consultation, and would be surprised if we did not do so'. Thorneycroft reported a similar reaction from the Commonwealth countries in Asia. Hare said the West Africans had criticized 'the allegedly neo-colonial character of the EEC' based on 'the controlling influence which France was thought to be able to exercise over her former African dependencies through the close financial and commercial ties which persisted'. Rhodesia and Nyasaland did not see it that way and welcomed the prospect of the economic advantages Britain in Europe might offer.

On the home front, Agriculture Minister Christopher Soames warned that the 'NFU were taking the extreme line that the interests of United Kingdom farmers could be safeguarded only by continuation of the existing system of support' so 'considerable opposition' to a British application must be expected from that quarter.[149]

Macmillan said the Cabinet had to decide whether the government should make a statement of its intentions to Parliament before or after the summer recess. 'Discussion showed that there was general agreement in the Cabinet that the right course was to enter into negotiations with the EEC and to announce at once that we intended to do so.' But how to balance the seeking of safeguards with the need for Britain 'to create the right impression in Europe' by representing the decision to negotiate 'as a purposive one and not as an unwilling surrender to circumstances'?[150]

Macmillan, to use one of his favourite phrases, sought to 'point the way'.[151] Summing up, he said

> it was evidently the view of the Cabinet that we should enter into negotiations with the EEC in order to find out what terms they would agree to our joining the Community. A decision to negotiate was a very different matter from the later and much more critical decision to

join the Community but, since a formal application to accede to the Treaty of Rome was a prerequisite of any negotiations on terms, the distinction might not be easy to make apparent to public opinion in this country and in the Commonwealth. A decision to negotiate might be more acceptable to our own public opinion if the emphasis were not all placed on the practical economic advantages of joining the Community (and the inevitable disadvantages of not doing so) but if some appeal were also made to the idealistic elements in British thinking.

With that in mind, he continued, he would bring to the Cabinet next week a draft statement and a motion to be put before the House of Commons.[152]

So, there it was. Within a year of reshuffling his Cabinet with Europe in mind, he had persuaded them – *all* of them, according to his diary – that the application should be made. The following day, at Chequers, he wrote up the 'unanimous decision in principle that I shd announce on Monday next that HMG wd apply to enter the Common Market'. Did he think it would succeed?

> Whether or not, having taken this momentous decision and communicated it to the Governments of the Six, we shall reach agreement on the vital points of a) Commonwealth b) British agriculture, I cannot tell. I shd judge that the chances are against an agreement, unless – on political grounds – de Gaulle changes his mind. For I feel that he is still hostile and jealous.[153]

Nevertheless, just as he did after the Rambouillet meeting at the end of January, Macmillan persevered – not as if de Gaulle wasn't there, more as if there was no real alternative to making the attempt unless Britain was prepared to settle for a life of fast-waning great powerdom and relative economic decline – a prospect Macmillan could not contemplate, though its application was ultimately successful twelve years later.

Macmillan's next bout with de Gaulle in the European championship took place at Birch Grove, rather than Chequers, in late November 1961. Before that, to understand Britain's subsequent protracted emotional deficit with the idea of a UK fully in Europe, it is important to recapture how Macmillan and his Cabinet decided to present the first application to Parliament and the public, and how he handled the Conservative Party Conference in the autumn.

When the Cabinet met on the morning of Thursday 27 July, they first 'confirmed' the decision taken a week earlier 'that a formal application for accession to the Treaty of Rome should be made without delay'. The discussion turned on the wording of the Prime Minister's statement to the House of Commons the following Monday about the motion to be put to Parliament the following Wednesday and Thursday during the two-day debate on Britain and Europe. The Cabinet was told that already thirty of its supporters in the House of Commons had signed a motion 'expressing opposition to any material derogation of British sovereignty, resulting from the entry of the United Kingdom into the EEC, and urging that an agreement with the EEC should not endanger the future expansion of trade with the Commonwealth and EFTA, or the prosperity of British agriculture'.

The sovereignty condition was impossible to fulfil, as the Cabinet recognized, and it was given but fleeting consideration:

> It was pointed out that the act of joining the EEC would inevitably entail some derogation of sovereignty and that, while this might not be harmful, it might well be represented as material. Nevertheless, the statement to be made by the Prime Minister would make it clear that the Government would not conclude any agreement to enter the EEC without seeking the prior approval of Parliament, and there was accordingly no reason why the signatories of this motion should not also support the proposed Government motion.[154]

The Cabinet minutes record the application decision a touch more specifically than those of the 21 July meeting:

> The Cabinet –
>
> . . . Agreed that a formal application to join the Treaty of Rome should now be made for the purpose of enabling negotiations to take place with a view to ascertaining whether the special needs of the United Kingdom, the other Commonwealth countries and the other members of the European Free Trade Association could be met.[155]

Not a word about loss of sovereignty there. But for all the failure to heed Kilmuir, the parliamentary debate in late July and early August did match the significance of the decision to apply for membership of the EEC. Macmillan used his statement to an expectant House of Commons on the afternoon on Monday 31 July 1961 to give MPs an (unattributed) version of his 'Grand Design'. The UK–EEC–Commonwealth relationships were, he said in a delightfully Edwardian use of language, 'clearly matters of capital importance in the life of our country and, indeed, of all the countries of the free world' as '[t]his is a political as well as an economic issue. Although the Treaty of Rome is concerned with economic matters it has an important political objective, namely, to promote unity and stability in Europe which is so essential a factor in the struggle for freedom and progress throughout the world.'[156]

He talked of Europe offering 'a single market of approaching 300 million people'; not just Britain but the closely consulted Commonwealth, too, would benefit from the boost to world trade and economic expansion EEC membership would bring. The 'standard of living of our agricultural community' would be protected. Article 237 of the Treaty of Rome enabled applicants to negotiate for membership – and that is what Britain would do, with the government bringing a recommendation to the House of Commons when discussions were completed. No agreement would be reached without Commons approval and until there had been 'full consultation with other Commonwealth countries'.[157]

Macmillan spoke of the government's 'long and earnest consideration' which preceded his statement and his equally earnest hope that negotiations would begin and succeed.[158] But of the sovereignty question there was no whiff now either. Hugh Gaitskell, the Leader of the Opposition, who followed him, stuck to procedural matters;[159] Gaitskell's eloquence on history lost awaited a later occasion. It was left to one of Macmillan's own backbenchers, Robin Turton, MP for Thirsk and Malton (who followed Gaitskell), to raise the sovereignty question. Why hadn't the Prime Minister chosen to use Article 238 of the Treaty, which covered association with other trading areas, rather than Article 237 'with all its risk of abrogation of sovereignty and of weakening of the Commonwealth'?[160] For Macmillan, the answer was

> very simple. If we were to apply to be an associate member under Article 238 we should have all the same economic difficulties for the Commonwealth . . . and we would have no influence in Europe.[161]

It was another Conservative backbencher, Anthony Fell, MP for Yarmouth, whose dissent is best remembered from the 31 July exchanges. Fell described Macmillan as 'a national disaster' whose 'decision to gamble with British sovereignty in Europe, when 650 million people of the British Commonwealth depend upon his faith and his leadership, is the most disastrous thing that any Prime Minister has done for many generations past . . . I suggest that the best service that the Prime Minister could do to the country would be to resign'.[162] Sir Derek Walker-Smith, Conservative MP for East Hertfordshire (like Turton, but unlike Fell, a former minister), put the sovereignty question much more politely and effectively to Macmillan, who buried it beneath a mound of 'Grand Designery':

WALKER-SMITH: Is . . . his object in negotiation . . . to get a basic modification of the Treaty so as to remove the possibility of any surrender of sovereignty on a significant scale by this country . . . [as] . . . the wording of that Article [237] appears to contemplate only procedural or consequential adaptations as distinct from basic modification?

Replying later to Manny Shinwell, the veteran Labour MP for Easington, Macmillan said:

All these questions . . . we will discuss in our two-day debate . . . but if right hon. and hon. Members were to face the kind of problems which Her Majesty's Government have to face in Europe and the free world today – the enormous monolithic strength of Soviet power and the divided groups of other countries – I would say that there are great risks from failure and great opportunities to be gained by success.[163]

The Labour MP Frank Bowles had earlier asked the Prime Minister 'to give an undertaking that he will not agree to anything that might prevent a future British Socialist Government from establishing Socialism here'.[164] This was precisely the anxiety of Labour's left in the 1970s and 1980s, when some of their opposition to Britain in Europe verged on the vehement. And, indeed, full membership would have meant – and since 1973 did mean – that anything approaching an economic or industrial version of 'socialism in one country' was impossible for the UK.

Macmillan said that this question was 'the best . . . I have had so far' but didn't answer it either. Indeed, his elegant evasions became too much for the veteran Labour left-winger Sydney Silverman, MP for Nelson and Colne, who, on a point of order, asked the Speaker to require Macmillan to answer his question on Article 237. The Speaker, Sir Harry Hylton-Foster, replied, 'No, I cannot make Ministers answer questions' – thereby outlining one of the permanent truths of the House of Commons.[165]

In private, Macmillan was a touch contemptuous of some of his own party's Euro-critics: '2 of them I had to dismiss [as ministers] for incompetence or idleness – Turton and Walker-Smith.' As for Fell, he 'insulted me on Monday; apologized on Tuesday; but followed His Master's Voice on Thursday. He is a stooge of Lord Beaverbrook [proprietor of the outspokenly anti-Common Market *Daily Express*].' But he noted in that same diary entry for 5 August 1961, 'the Conservative party is, naturally, anxious and rather jumpy'.[166]

In fact, the two-day debate on Britain and Europe of 2–3 August 1961 was of high quality. The House of Commons rose to the occasion. Macmillan opened it by reconfiguring Churchill's post-1945 geometry of Britain's great powerdom – 'what he called the three interlocking groups, Britain and the Commonwealth, Europe, and the New World. He spoke of them, I remember, as three leaves of a piece of clover, or, again, as three intersecting circles. Of course, he was right in his analysis, but ever since then we have been, in one way or another, trying to find a practical solution to the problem of their interconnection' (a remarkably insouciant description of what, certainly since Suez in 1956, had been an increasingly desperate business).*

With a quick glance towards 'the moral side' of European integration – 'the reconciliation of France and Germany'[167] – the Prime Minister began his pitch to Parliament and the British people by depicting the Treaty of Rome in a reassuring fashion. He pretended – as several top British politicians were to do subsequently – that the Treaty of Rome had not declared as its core and cumulative purpose 'to lay the foundation of an ever closer union among the peoples of Europe'. As

---

* Churchill was not an enthusiast for EEC membership. To the dismay of the Churchill family, Field Marshal Lord Montgomery had divulged Churchill's view to the press after visiting the now very aged Prime Minister in hospital (Andrew Roberts, *Churchill: Walking with Destiny* (Allen Lane, 2018), p. 960).

Hugo Young was to write in the late 1990s, 'few of the British, even among the political leadership, properly absorbed this. They never really penetrated the words, and, if they did happen to be vouchsafed a moment of enlightenment, it was to see them as a challenge, rather than a credo that had much to do with the island race.'[168]

Macmillan's tactic that August afternoon in 1961 was to concentrate upon what the EEC was *not* by stressing the second 'E' of the acronym:

> I ask hon. Members to note the word 'economic'. The Treaty of Rome does not deal with defence. It does not deal with foreign policy. It deals with trade and some of the social aspects of human life which are most connected with trade and production.[169]*

Macmillan, in a roundabout way, dealt with power balances when presenting the Cabinet's decision to Parliament, as he did with some of the ingredients of the country's deep past that went into the making of its emotional deficit with Europe, including the essentially Catholic impulses of the Robert Schuman/Konrad Adenauer generation in setting up the European Coal and Steel Community:

> In this country, of course, there is a long tradition of isolation. In this, as in most countries, there is a certain suspicion of foreigners. There is also the additional division between us and Continental Europe of a wholly different development of our legal, administrative and, to some extent, political systems. If we are basically united by our religious faith, even here great divisions have grown up.

---

* It was this Macmillanesque camouflage that gave Enoch Powell, the most eloquent of the anti-EEC protagonists in the 1970s and 1980s, his alibi when Rob Shepherd and I questioned him about it in 1993. Powell was Minister of Health in 1961 but not a member of the Cabinet, in whose private debates, therefore, he did not participate. He had, he said, judged the European question in the early 1960s, only in economic terms:

> I said to myself, 'that's going for free trade. I'm in favour of free trade. That's going for an increase in the volume of trade. I'm in favour of the increases in the volume of trade . . .' I only later came to see that the European Community was a political and not an economic structure . . . my mistake in the early 1960s, which I only recovered and repented of in the late 1960s, was failure to understand the political intent, was failure to understand that it was in a sense a renunciation of a balance of power as the basis of British policy (Robert Shepherd, *Enoch Powell, A Biography* (Hutchinson, 1996), p. 248).

It is, the Prime Minister went on,

> perhaps worth recording that in every period when the world has been
> in danger of tyrants or aggression, Britain has abandoned isolationism.
> It is true that when the immediate danger was removed, we have some-
> times tried to return to an insular policy. In due course we have
> abandoned it. In any case, who could say today that our present danger
> had been removed, or will soon disappear? Who doubts that we have
> to face a long and exhausting struggle over more than one generation
> if the forces of Communistic expansion are to be contained?[170]

The great virtue, he said, of a huge single market in what he called
the age of 'automation production lines' was cheaper unit costs and the
prospect of serious industrial research and development which would
create in Europe an '[economic] unit ... of a size comparable, let us
say, to the United States or Soviet Russia'.[171] It is easily forgotten now
that the first application was conceived and announced by Macmillan
profoundly in the context of the Cold War and global balance of power.

Macmillan attempted to deflect the sovereignty question by admitting that 'every treaty limits a nation's freedom of action to some
extent ... since the war this tendency has grown and our freedom of
action is obviously affected by our obligations in NATO, WEU
[Western European Union], OEEC [Organisation for European Economic Co-operation] and all the rest'. But look at the six countries
who had signed the Treaty of Rome – 'I do not see any signs of the
members of the Community losing their national identity because
they have delegated a measure of their sovereignty. This problem of
sovereignty, to which we must, of course, attach the highest importance is, in the end, perhaps a matter of degree.'[172] This was vintage
Macmillan – not exactly dismissive of a crucial question but skilful in
diminishing its rawness or its centrality.

Here he dismissed those who sought 'a genuine federalist system' in
Europe and neatly slid alongside de Gaulle:

> The alternative concept, the only practical concept, would be a con-
> federation, a commonwealth if hon. Members would like to call it
> that – what I think General de Gaulle has called *Europe des patries* –
> which would retain the great traditions and the pride of individual

nations while working together in clearly defined spheres for their common interest. This seems to me a concept more in tune with the national traditions of European countries and, in particular, of our own. It is one with which we could associate willingly and whole-heartedly. At any rate, there is nothing in the Treaty of Rome which commits the members of the EEC to any kind of federalist solution, nor could such a system be imposed on member countries.[173]

This was essentially delusory: as far as Macmillan appeared to believe, 'ever closer union' might not have featured in the Treaty at all.

Hugh Gaitskell followed for the Opposition. It was a technician's speech rather than an orator's. He was, however, eloquent on one point – 'there is no question whatever of Britain entering into a federal Europe now. British opinion is simply not ripe for this, and in any event it is surely completely incompatible with all the pledges and promises which have been made about the Commonwealth. I am not saying that we have to commit ourselves for all time, for twenty, fifty or a hundred years hence.'[174] As it turned out, Britain never was reconciled to the idea of being part of a federal – or federalizing – Europe.

The Commons had to wait for the speaker who followed Gaitskell, Derek Walker-Smith, to hear the true song of sovereignty sung in a highly accomplished parliamentary performance. Walker-Smith looked to the long-term effect upon British sovereignty and its 'constitutional machinery' of signing the Treaty of Rome as 'for the Community economic union is a prelude to political union'.[175] Britain, he declared, had served Europe and the world well through its 'special and separate position'. Was the time for this past?

> Sovereignty came late to most of the nations of the Six. They were part of the Holy Roman Empire, that physical embodiment of the medieval law of nature which preceded the formalisation of the modern doctrine of sovereignty. Our national sovereignty did not follow that doctrine; it preceded it . . .
>
> The Six share their constitutional outlook and practices with each other, but not with us. Their evolution has been Continental and collective. Ours has been insular and imperial. Therefore, for them political union would be a reunion and a rediscovery, while for us it would be a departure and a divergence.

We must, said Walker-Smith, avoid 'any temptation to blink or to mask the long-term implications of this decision'.[176]

The two-day debate did have the air of a protracted history lesson about it. Harold Wilson, then Shadow Foreign Secretary, opening for Labour on the second day, congratulated Macmillan on his 'deep sense of history' and proceeded to give a little seminar of his own:

> I do not think that he will have missed the parallel between this decision which has now to be taken and that which faced Sir Robert Peel [on the Corn Laws] 115 years ago, though I think that . . . in the sphere of world politics the importance of this issue transcends even that of the Free Trade issue of 1846.[177]

The twin stars of day two were the men who made the political running in the post-Macmillan era – Wilson and Ted Heath – as the old man recognized himself in his diary:

> On the second day (Thursday) Wilson made a brilliant speech, attacking the Common Market but more intent on attacking HMG [Her Majesty's Government]. It was mean – as is his character – but admirably done. Ted Heath (Ld P Seal) answered in a speech mainly addressed to the Conservative doubtfuls (Commonwealth interests; sovereignty etc.) and tried to undo the harm done by a very clever and very hostile speech made on the day before by Sir Derek Walker-Smith. This he did well – quietly and simply.[178]

In fact, both Wilson's and Heath's speeches gave a strong, but, of course, at the time unknowable, foretaste of the priorities of their respective premierships to come.

Wilson saw the EEC as a straightforward threat to Britain's indigenous capacity for economic planning:

> I hope that the Prime Minister will be careful to see how far even the minimal amount of planning which the Government do [sic] would be permitted under the Treaty of Rome – exchange controls, control over capital movements and the import controls which may one day have to be introduced, although we all hope not. Even Bank Rate, on which the Government rely, would be susceptible to challenge in the Commission or in the Council of Ministers under the Treaty of Rome.

Wilson said it could be a 1961 equivalent of the 'central bankers' ramp' which had brought down the second MacDonald government in 1931:

> I hope that the Prime Minister will not think me too hag-ridden by references to 1931 if I conjure up the possibility of a situation in which, perhaps, our exports do not increase as much as it is hoped and we go to Europe in a weak condition, needing economic assistance, and in which the central bankers of Europe tell us that we must change our financial, economic and perhaps social policies before they give the assistance.'[179]*

Heath, for his part, outlined a notion of sovereignty pooling (as distinct from sovereignty loss) to which he stuck throughout the 1961–3 negotiation (which failed), his own 1970–72 negotiation (which succeeded) and, indeed, for the rest of his life.[180]

After congratulating Walker-Smith on a speech that 'was powerful and beautifully phrased', he said that, for all the talk of sovereignty loss over the past twenty-four hours,

> it seems to me that it is a conception much more of pooling sovereignty with others who are occupied in the same joint enterprise. Surrender means the abandonment of sovereignty to others. Pooling seems to me to share sovereignty with other people for a common purpose, and there seems to me to be a firm distinction between those two. It is a pooling of sovereignty over a strictly defined field, and that is laid down in the Treaty itself.[181]

Another future party leader spoke and acted in character that day – Michael Foot, who had succeeded his hero Nye Bevan as MP for Ebbw Vale in 1960. He was as searing of his own side as he was of the Conservatives, of Gaitskell and Wilson especially, for proposing a wait-and-see amendment regretting the economic weakness of

---

* Wilson's innate gift for ambiguity was as great as Macmillan's. I learned many years later from his son, Robin, who had accompanied his father on a speaking and fact-finding tour of the USA in January 1962, that Wilson Sr frequently referred to joining the Common Market as likely to provide a 'cold douche to Britain' – a bracing shower to invigorate British industry (E-mail to the author from Robin Wilson, 22 November 2017).

the UK as a starting point for negotiations with the EEC and declaring that the UK should enter only on terms 'generally acceptable to a Commonwealth Prime Ministers' Conference' and which 'accord with our obligations and pledges to other members of the European Free Trade Association'.[182]

Foot wanted a full-blown Labour amendment rejecting UK entry and deployed his famous powers of ridicule: 'One of my hon. Friends said that he wanted to see our country playing in the European first league. My right hon. Friend the Member for Huyton [Wilson] and the Leader of the Opposition seem to be saying, "Yes, we wish to enter the West European football league as long as we can have full consultations with the MCC so that the rules of the game are so altered that it resembles cricket" '[183] – a point, one suspects, that General de Gaulle, had he read Hansard, would have fully endorsed. And it was Denis Healey, who made a speciality of going to the heart of the matter – as he had over the Suez collusion embracing Britain, France and Israel when he questioned Anthony Eden about it on his final appearance in the House of Commons[184] – who summoned the spectre of the General when interrogating Macmillan during his 31 July statement.

'President de Gaulle,' Healey reminded the Commons, 'has recently said that Britain would be welcome in the Common Market only without conditions. Is it not extremely dangerous for this country to enter formal negotiations with the Six without first having an assurance that this is not the final decision of the French Government?'[185] It was indeed extremely dangerous, as Macmillan well knew, but he comfortably won the vote in the House on the evening of 3 August 1961, 313 to 5 (with Labour abstaining apart from Foot and a scattering of Labour dissenters plus Anthony Fell; just under thirty Conservative backbenchers abstained and no minister resigned[186]). On the road to Brussels that was the first and relatively the easiest step. It would take all of what George Ball called the British 'political genius' – and more – to travel the full distance.

Macmillan had told the Commons that 'the failure of these negotiations would be a tragedy. Of course it would.'[187] Was he right? If the UK had succeeded and found itself a member of the EEC before the election due at the latest in 1964, might the bumpy, scratchy relationship with Europe, which was to burn up so much of the country's political energies over the decades since de Gaulle's veto and which was eventually to lead to Brexit, have settled down and become a natural one? It is comparable to the question raised by Roy Jenkins in his life of Gladstone in the context of the Irish question: had Gladstone's first attempt at Home Rule succeeded in the 1880s might Anglo-Irish politics have taken a very different trajectory with great agony avoided all round?[188]

In fact, I think not. Too much historical freight went then – and still does – into the making of Britain's aggregate emotional deficit with Europe. In 2008 Sir Michael Palliser, former head of the Diplomatic Service, whose long career was entwined with the fronds of Britain in Europe, said after UK entry in 1973 – a decade after de Gaulle's veto – he had hoped it would become a normal and accepted relationship,

> but I doubted that it would because it's not in our DNA. It has to do with our history, geography, language, post-imperial experience and relationship with the United States. (We never compare ourselves with Europe; only with America.) We cannot imagine ourselves *not* being an influence in the world – and we are. The rest of the European Union is often infuriated by us – but they *all* want us to stay in which reinforces our world-influence feeling; it makes us feel superior as people do when they feel wanted.[189]

Sir Michael thought it might have been better if the Kilmuir line on sovereignty had been accepted in 1961, 'but I doubt it would have made any difference. Though I do think it would have been better if the first application had succeeded because we would have been in at an earlier stage of the Community's life and adapted. De Gaulle's keeping us out for ten years resonated pretty bitterly with the British people and affected the way they looked at the European project.'[190]

Even if the sovereignty implications had been admitted fully and *en clair*, it is highly likely that a political class and a political nation traditionally averse to reading the fine-print of international agreements would have found speculations on the exact meaning of 'ever closer union' irredeemably tedious. As another seasoned Whitehall figure, the former Cabinet Secretary Richard Wilson, put it: 'We Brits always go into our big decisions as if under anaesthetic, only waking up many years later and wondering "Did we really mean to do that?" '[191]

In the second half of 1961 the bulk of the Conservative Party seemed perfectly willing to allow Macmillan to anaesthetize them. As he wrote to the Queen on 5 August:

> I was under some apprehension that the Conservative Party would be deeply split by the proposal that we should enter into negotiations with the Six European countries. Naturally sentiment and tradition make many Conservatives unwilling to associate themselves more closely with Europe. These Conservatives, in their attachment to the Commonwealth, I think are often thinking more of the old Commonwealth countries than of the new. Nevertheless they sincerely feel that there is a real conflict of interest between Britain as a Commonwealth and Britain as a European power. But I was gratified to find that the Conservative Party was fluid, ready to move with the times, and, especially among the younger men, anxious to seize new opportunities.[192]

Macmillan knew that nobody was more attached in the kingdom to the Commonwealth than the Queen (this has remained true throughout her reign), and one senses that that paragraph was specially crafted for her. We will have no way of knowing, until the Royal Archives are open for her reign (and perhaps not even then), if she gave a hint of her own views to Macmillan at any of their weekly audiences.

For all his confident words to his sovereign, Macmillan was anxious about how Europe would play at the Conservative Party Conference two months later and was mightily relieved when it played well. Watching events from Chequers (in those days, Tory leaders only turned up at conferences to perform once the debates were over), he wrote:

> the Common Market Debate this morning will be ... difficult. Lord Beaverbrook and the *Daily Express* are making tremendous efforts to get hold of our chaps. Some (I fear) have fallen into the spider's web.[193]

And:

> The Brighton Conference has gone very well so far. Yesterday the 'Common Market' received 'overwhelming' support. Only thirty or forty voted against, in a huge assembly of four thousand or more.[194]

He was, Macmillan wrote in his memoirs, 'on safe ground for the time being'.[195] And, for a time, the wider *national* going was fairly good. In December 1961 the polls showed a narrow majority in favour of UK entry. But the figure of 53 per cent was the peak. By May 1962 it was down to 47 per cent and it fell another 11 per cent within a month.[196]

But, as Macmillan knew full well, his biggest problem was not with 50 million Brits or even 4,000 Conservative Party Conference-goers. It was with one Frenchman, and he was due to come for a weekend at Birch Grove at the end of November. The omens were not encouraging. Ted Heath's team had begun negotiating in Brussels in October but already the French were dragging their feet.[197]

Macmillan was primed by a high-quality brief from the British Ambassador in Paris, Sir Pierson Dixon, a shrewd and experienced de Gaulle watcher. The General, he wrote, 'is part visionary, part calculator', which made him difficult to negotiate with:

> He has a profound and ever-present sense of history and he believes that his vision enables the new France to 'marry her century'. He does not like the Americans or value them highly. Too close an association between Europe and the United States does not form part of his vision. As for us, we do 'not fit easily' into his vision either.
>
> We are in his view a world wide power, more powerful recently than France. He probably thinks that we are in some way trying to bring the Commonwealth (which he may not understand very well) *with us* into Europe, thus diluting or even perhaps destroying the European idea. In any case he sees us as more Anglo-Saxon than European and as likely to stick with the Americans. How can our presence in Europe be reconciled with the idea of a separate and powerful Europe exerting its own influence on the world scene?[198]

Countering these points would be at the heart of Macmillan's pitch to de Gaulle at Birch Grove.

Everyone closely involved knew that de Gaulle was both the opposing side *and* the referee in this and subsequent matches of the 1961–2 championship, but Dixon did not think that the game was over before it started:

> General de Gaulle probably finds our application to join the EEC inconvenient at this moment. Anglo-American relations and the

Commonwealth make it seem difficult to him to conceive of Britain playing a role inside Europe consistent with his vision. On the other hand he recognises that, if we were in, Europe would be stronger and more complete, even if French influence were relatively diminished, and that our application cannot be brushed aside. He has probably not yet made up his mind whether he really wants us in. It is certainly not true that he has made up his mind to exclude us.

What the UK really needed from de Gaulle, Dixon concluded, was a directive to the French negotiators across the table from Heath in Brussels, 'to settle the technical problems as rapidly as possible, consistently with the maintenance of the European idea'.[199]

The de Gaulles flew into Gatwick on the afternoon of Friday 24 November 1961 and made the short journey to Birch Grove in time for tea and a discussion before dinner to which Ted Heath came. As country house parties went, this one was a cracker with a distinct whiff of P. G. Wodehouse about it. First of all, there was the problem of the General's blood (de Gaulle was under constant threat of assassination from those opposed to his policy of withdrawing from Algeria and spare supplies followed him everywhere). Lady Dorothy Macmillan was much put out. The fridge was 'full of haddock and all sorts of things' for the coming lunches and dinners. So another fridge was found and plonked in the coach house, preserving the general's plasma, standing there, as Macmillan put it, like 'an altar to Mithras'.[200] The grounds were swarming with members of the Sussex constabulary (a novelty in 1961) and their dogs plus a few gendarmes. As the Prime Minister recorded with suitable *Schadenfreude* in his diary: 'one Alsatian happily bit the Daily Mail man in the behind. Altogether, a most enjoyable show.'[201]

After a brief discussion on Berlin, Macmillan and de Gaulle, with just their interpreters present in the Prime Minister's bibliophile's library, went straight to the point on Europe. The economics of entry could be easily settled if there was a will, Macmillan opened. Political questions were more important. Neither Britain nor France wanted an integrated federal Europe: both wished to see a confederal, Europe-of-nations. As for the Commonwealth, it 'was not a political organization'. The ties with the old dominions were 'of blood and loyalty'. The newer countries were comparable to France's African territories. Europe was the best way to contain Germany, whom '[w]e had seen . . . attack us twice in 50 years'. So, the UK 'wanted to enter the Community for political reasons. The economic difficulties could be solved and in any case led on to the possibility of a wider European influence through the Commonwealth. Europe could not forever rely on the Americans . . . It was therefore important that Europe's economic power in the world should be as widely extended as possible.'[202]

Macmillan was following Dixon's advice, but, in doing so was putting a complexion upon the British case that, in his attempts to fuse it with the General's view, was seriously stretching his prior Cabinet discussions and equally discordant with his tone in the House of Commons.

De Gaulle was not deceived and the elaborate fencing of the two history-infused old men resumed once more. The General said he 'was against an integrated Europe: this was neither practical, sensible nor desirable, and the result would be a materialist, soulless mass, with no idealism left . . . the national identity of the European nations should be preserved'. The Community had started with economics, because it was the easiest, although 'the Rome Treaty had a political reason . . . Nevertheless, this structure was still new and fragile . . . he had difficulty in seeing how the United Kingdom would fit into this beginning of Europe.'

Accommodating some parts of the Commonwealth was not difficult. Like France's 'client states' in Africa, Britain's 'had had nothing to sell'. Canada and Australia did. Why rush? It might be better to apply later when the Commonwealth had changed: 'How could the United Kingdom join the Common Market if these countries were excluded, and how, if they were included, could the United States be kept out? If the United States were included . . . she would be too strong and Europe would not be re-formed.'[203]

The play had been just as Dixon predicted in his match preview. Overnight, as he told de Gaulle when they resumed in the Birch Grove library on the Saturday morning after posing for pictures, Macmillan 'had reflected deeply on their conversation of the previous day and would like to speak frankly to General de Gaulle'.

Sounding like a combination of Arnold Toynbee and Kenneth Clark, he deployed perhaps the grandest historical sweep of his premiership:

> European civilisation was what we must at all costs preserve. It had survived for 3,000 years, but it was menaced from all quarters, by Africans, Asians and Communists and, in a quite different way, even by our Atlantic friends such as the North Americans, and New Zealanders and Australians.

If this section of Philip de Zulueta's note had leaked, the impact upon the Commonwealth Prime Ministers, whom Macmillan was seeking to carry along with the EEC application, can only be guessed at; the same would have been true of the Conservative Party and the House of Commons. 'When President de Gaulle came to power [in 1958]', the note continues, he, Macmillan,

> realised that his [de Gaulle's] ideas were very close to our own and that progress was possible towards a united Europe based not on integrationist ideas but on confederal ideas. The traditionalists in the United Kingdom were still reserved and were fearful of weakening Commonwealth unity. But the young people, and those who had fought in the war, were determined that Europe should not once again tear itself to bits and wanted to draw closer to Europe ... European countries must think in broader terms than trade in Europe alone, they must look outwards towards their old empires and aim to become the most powerful trading body in the world.[204]

De Gaulle was almost Attlee-like in his powers of deflation. As Macmillan's peroration subsided, he said 'there was no great hurry; if the present negotiation was unsuccessful the matter could be adjourned and another attempt made later, say in 1964 [almost certainly an election year in the UK, as the General well knew]'.

At this, Macmillan took flight once more and the rhetoric soared:

> ... this was a turning point in history and for Europe. If the United Kingdom could not enter the EEC in 1962, the chance would not recur. The circumstances were uniquely favourable; the President was in power in France; Dr Adenauer had been re-elected in Germany

for a further period, and he, the Prime Minister, was in power in the United Kingdom. In a manner of speaking, they were men of destiny.

He then changed his tone. If the negotiations failed over New Zealand or a few thousand tons of wheat, 'people would think that the real cause of failure was that the United Kingdom was not wanted in Europe'. If the idea 'was to set up a new empire of Charlemagne' in a Europe without Britain, the UK would have to defend itself by withdrawing her troops from Europe, currently costing £100 million a year. Alluding to the two world wars, he told de Gaulle the UK 'could not be called upon to help only when times were bad'. Finally, Macmillan turned classical scholar:

> if the solution was not found in 1962 the idea of the restoration of Europe would fail. History would regard it as a repetition of the story of the city states of Greece which could not unite or could only unite occasionally as at Marathon. The dream of French and British leadership of Europe would be gone forever as would all hope of giving Europe a strong and individual personality which would enable it to survive as an independent force in the world.

What a pity these exchanges were not taped in the manner of Nixon's White House. De Gaulle confessed himself 'very impressed' by Macmillan's words. But he countered historian-to-historian. The British, he said,

> had a long history and they were also Europeans in their own special way. They were a part of Europe and at one recent time indeed [1940–44], they alone had been Europe. But Great Britain had many extensions which were of far-reaching importance.

It wasn't just a matter of trade and commerce; it was a question of psychology too:

> Canada, Australia and New Zealand may have been Europeans once but they were no longer Europeans in the same sense as the British. He and the French wanted the British in Europe. But they did not want to change the character of their Europe, and therefore did not want the British to bring their great escort in with them.

India and Africa, the General added for good measure, 'had no part in Europe'.[205] But, he added, there was no need for pessimism; more time was needed.

Macmillan on the other hand felt he did *not* have time – 'he could carry through the present policy [of applying for membership] only if the tide was flowing in his direction. He might be wrong, but he knew his country . . . if present negotiations failed, a reaction against Europe would set in in the United Kingdom and all possibility of agreement might be lost for a generation.'[206]

Macmillan had played his best game, but he hadn't scored and he knew it. He went to bed on the Sunday night after 'a really exhausting, but somewhat fruitless two days' and poured his thoughts into his diary in between consoling himself with Macaulay's *History of England*:

> As regards immediate <u>political</u> results, nothing has really been achieved. We have 'agreed to differ' in a reasonable friendly way. But the differences are there. The Emperor of the French (for he is now an almost complete autocrat, taking no notice of any advice and indeed receiving little of independent value) is older; more isolated; more sententious; and far more <u>royal</u> than when I saw him last [at Rambouillet]. He is well informed, yet remote. His hatred of the 'Anglo-Americans' is as great as ever. While he has extraordinary dignity and charm, 'unbends' delightfully, is nice to servants and children and so forth, he does not apparently listen to argument. I mean this almost literally. Not only is he not convinced; he actually does not listen. He merely repeats over and over again what he has said before. And the doctrine – almost dogma – is based on intuition, not ratiocination. He talks of Europe and means France.

For Macmillan, there were centuries of 'inherited hatred of England (since Joan of Arc)' in the room when he and de Gaulle talked, not just 'his bitter memories of the last war':

> Sometimes, when I am with him, I feel I have overcome it. But he goes back to his distrust and dislike, like a dog to his vomit. I still feel that he has <u>not</u> absolutely decided about our admission to the Economic Community. I am inclined to think he will be more likely to yield to pressure than persuasion.[207]

Exactly. But the pressure was all one way – on the supplicant, the UK. Macmillan knew this – and could not bear it, any more than he could live with the seepage of British power generally. It could, on occasion, lead him to be remarkably indiscreet – albeit within a limited circle. For example, he really let rip to Sir Christopher ('Kit') Steel and his staff in the Bonn Embassy in early January 1962 when he travelled to West Germany to see Konrad Adenauer (whom he did not care for). Sir David Goodall* was Steel's Private Secretary in 1961–2 and met a tired Macmillan and Home as they arrived looking 'totally worn out' late in the evening at the British Ambassador's residence after an exhausting day of meetings in Whitehall. 'As I took him [the PM] upstairs to his room, he stopped on the landing half way up, pulled a large handkerchief from his breast pocket and emitted something between a loud groan, a wheeze and a cough which suggested to me he was about to pass out on the spot,' Sir David recalled.

He made it to the sanctuary of his room, however, and came downstairs to sit

in the middle of a deferential circle of senior officials. I stood at one end of the arc, by the whisky decanter, my role being to fill the Prime Minister's glass and hand it to the nearest official, who handed it down the line until it reached Mr Macmillan, who drained it and handed it to the person on his left. It was then passed down the line and back to me; and the performance was repeated.

It did the trick:

Under the influence of the whisky, the Prime Minister revived visibly, like a drooping flower in water, and embarked on a freewheeling monologue, of which sadly I can remember only snatches: 'I shall tell the old gentleman [Adenauer] . . . We [the British] always get the bloody end of the salient: I remember the Somme . . .' 'The trouble with the Germans is that they don't realise they *lost* the war.' Of Soviet pressure on Berlin: 'How can we defend Berlin? . . . Berlin is indefensible.'

At that, the Ambassador, otherwise silent during the monologue, bravely intervened. 'Prime Minister, that is something you must *not* say.

* Later to run the Cabinet Office's Overseas and Defence Secretariat and to retire as High Commissioner in Delhi.

That is something that can only be decided at the time.' Fresh from trying to negotiate the Partial Test Ban Treaty . . . nuclear deterrence was much on Mr Macmillan's mind: 'We must have the Treaty . . . or our children will say YOU are the people who *destroyed the world.*'

'A classic performance,' Sir David noted.[208]

Macmillan, reminiscent of an aging pro exercising once-supple limbs, liked to warm-up before a negotiation. Not so Ted Heath, who led the line in Brussels. Having done much of the spadework in the Foreign Office as Home's number two, the EEC entry negotiation was the job he craved.[209] Even though the enterprise failed, it was the making of Heath. He excelled at it and became the televisual face of the British push for Europe. All his years in the Whips' Office and barely a year as Minister of Labour left him largely unknown to the British public. All that changed thanks to his impressive if a touch wooden ministerial broadcasts on the negotiations, with those odd vowels stranded somewhere between rural Kent and BBC Home Service pronunciation, which led the then nascent *Private Eye* to dub him 'The Grocer' for evermore. Whitehall gave him an impressive backup. Pierson Dixon led the officials while retaining the Paris Embassy. Eric Roll, veteran of 1940s negotiations, including the Marshall Plan, spoke seven languages and could lip read in French and German.[210] Herbert Andrew from the Board of Trade, who became an Anglican priest in retirement, had a nice line in quoting the recently published New English Bible, reading out, at a particularly tricky moment, an extract from the Book of Revelation about 'The merchants of the earth weeping and mourning' for the fallen city of Rome, no longer able to pay for their once glittering cargoes of eastern finery. The Dutch were particularly impressed.[211]

The Dutch showed their appreciation in other, more private ways. They were the best providers of intelligence on the Six's thinking as the negotiations progressed. The UK intelligence community prides itself on discovering the negotiating hand of other countries ahead of meetings. But, naturally, it is extremely rare to find any EEC-related intelligence material on the files at the National Archives; so-called friend-to-friend intelligence is both highly sensitive and never admitted to. A rare example is a piece of human intelligence in the Prime

Minister's office papers dated 23 July 1961, two days after the crucial Cabinet meeting in Macmillan's room at the House of Commons. It reported on a conversation the previous day in Paris between Olivier Wormser, number two in the French Foreign Office – Maurice Couve de Murville's deputy – with 'a reliable established source'. It was hugely discouraging.

Wormser, said the secret source,

> was expecting Mr MACMILLAN in his forthcoming speech in the House to announce HMG's willingness to initiate negotiations for Britain's entry into the Common Market ... If this was correct in Wormser's opinion there were three French 'hypotheses' as to British intention [sic] namely

1. That HMG intended merely to play for time for internal political reasons, but had no real intention of coming in.
2. HMG would propose joining but only on British terms and would therefore adopt a tough bargaining attitude from the start.
3. The British Government were really sincere and would be prepared to sign the Treaty of Rome on terms put forward by the Six (he would not be drawn as to what these would be).

Wormser, the source reported,

> completely discounted the possibility of 3 [so] he could foresee endless and probably fruitless discussions which would mean arguing with the British over each line and clause of the Rome Treaty, a prospect he personally faced with horror ... In Wormser's view it would be quite impossible for the French to agree to any special concessions in the agricultural field until full agreement had been reached on this subject among the Six themselves ... Finally Wormser said that it was not really in the interests of the UK to try and enter at this stage, unless they were willing to forsake the Commonwealth. Anyhow the Six were getting on quite happily without us.[212]

De Gaulle said something equally troubling to Ted Heath when they first met at the Friday evening dinner in Birch Grove. Heath found the General 'quietly spoken, reserved, almost shy':

After dinner, de Gaulle took me and Julian Amery [Minister of Aviation and Macmillan's son-in-law] to one side. Holding his spectacles in one hand and gently tapping them with the other, he enquired, referring to the negotiations for our entry into the European Community, 'What is this all about? Is it serious or is it just a game?'

He seemed at this point to be assuming that Britain was in the first of the positions Wormser had outlined. Heath's French was legendarily awful. So, with the help of Amery, he did his best to persuade the General of Britain's sincerity.[213] Heath does not say, nor does Macmillan's diary record, whether or not this conversation was reported to the Prime Minister, but it would be strange if it had not been and it may partly explain the passion of Macmillan's opening pitch to de Gaulle on the Saturday morning.

Heath was personally utterly sincere and it showed in his opening statement in the French Foreign Ministry, the Quai d'Orsay, on 10 October 1961 which marked the beginning of the negotiations. As journalists noted at the time, there were none of the caveats with which Macmillan had larded his July statement in the House of Commons.[214] 'We recognize it as a great decision, a turning point in our history, and we take it in all seriousness. In saying that we wish to join the EEC, we mean that we desire to become full, whole-hearted and active members of the European Community in its widest sense and to go forward with you in the building of a new Europe.'[215]

Yet, as always in pursuit of a deal, the broad, sunlit uplands of grand declarations swiftly had to give way to slugging it out in the dark and damp ditches of detail. We have no need to reconstruct the archaeology or anthropology of that trench – but detail-filled it was. From November 1961 to August 1962 it was largely taken up with transitional arrangements for Commonwealth products and Commonwealth access to EEC markets thereafter. As Nora Beloff, who reported the Brussels ups and downs for the *Observer*, put it: 'The results were some quaint-looking compromises: zero duty for tea, cricket bats and polo sticks, but only a suspension of duties for desiccated coconut and no more than a slowing-down of the introduction of a common tariff for pepper.'[216]

The French, through their Foreign Minister, Couve de Murville, were far from malleable and not widely liked by the negotiators of the other five. Heath admired Couve but thought his 'unsympathetic, chilly, ascetic, French Protestant manner made him definitely "not one of the club" '.[217] The French were determined to get the Six's new Common Agricultural Policy, or CAP, in place before serious negotiations began; it was not implemented until mid-January 1962.

At the end of the month, Heath, with some justification and considerable foresight, told Eric Roll that the French had 'three reasons' for dragging out the negotiations as long as possible: they expected 'that opposition would grow in the UK the longer the negotiations progressed; that our own desire to reach an agreement would weaken; and, finally, that something else would turn up to prevent the negotiations from being successfully concluded'.[218] (It did, as we shall see.)

When the arguments resumed in September 1962, after the long continental summer break, it was British, rather than Commonwealth, agriculture that hamstrung them. The French, who had most to gain from the continuance in its existing form of the CAP, were convinced that a long transition period up to 1970 in which British farmers would still get the traditional Whitehall subsidy before moving over to the CAP system of quotas and fixed prices would flood the continent with cheap eggs and bacon,[219] with, no doubt, ruinous effect on the cherished 'continental breakfast'.

Cricket bats, polo sticks and eggs and bacon were somewhat prosaic as talking points at European championship level when the contest resumed in early June 1962 at the Château de Champs near Paris. Once more this was a higher order of combat which, one suspects, de Gaulle enjoyed finding Macmillan a more absorbing swordsman than Adenauer, or perhaps even Kennedy. He seems to have got mildly carried away when the Macmillans arrived late on the Saturday afternoon of 2 June 1962. 'If he had his way they would meet every week,' said the General.[220]

The Champs encounter has taken on a historical life of its own, in that the French Ambassador to London, Geoffroy de Courcel, maintained ever after that Macmillan did there offer de Gaulle an Anglo-French nuclear weapon as a way of buying the UK into Europe.[221] But de Courcel was only present at the final Champs session on the Monday, and de Zulueta's note of the earlier sessions has no trace of such a deal being suggested. De Gaulle talked of building 'a small French deterrent', which would not be committed to NATO, to protect France if Russia threatened it with a nuclear weapon – 'at a certain point the precise size of the nuclear deterrent did not greatly matter since unacceptable damage could be inflicted by a relatively small force'.

For his part, at the same Sunday morning session at which de Courcel was not present, Macmillan confined himself to lofty generalities about 'future defence arrangements' which 'should be based upon the Atlantic Alliance. There might be a European organisation allied to the United States. There would be a plan for the defence of Europe. The nuclear power of European countries would be held as part of this European defence.' Later he added that '[i]f there was an attack against Europe at some future date the United States might perhaps hesitate to use her nuclear forces. Some European deterrent was therefore perhaps necessary.'[222] To have gone further would have been to breach Kennedy's prohibition of nuclear sharing in May 1961 and Macmillan did not do so.

The real significance of Champs is that Macmillan succeeded in persuading de Gaulle that if only France and Britain had co-operated fully pre-1914 and pre-1939, some of the worst catastrophes might have been avoided; but failed to convince him that if the EEC admitted Britain to full membership, 'the Community would then cease to be the empire of Charlemagne and would become the empire of Rome and therefore much stronger. Europe needed to be enlarged to the maximum extent in order to be equal to the United States and the Soviet Union.'[223]

De Gaulle persisted in his familiar Britain-the-unready line – the combination of state of mind, Commonwealth, American relationship, agricultural factors – allied to his conviction that a Britain-enhanced Europe would be an entirely different political and economic entity. Macmillan countered with his rebuttals – the UK was serious, he 'would tell the old Commonwealth to go to France and see the cemeteries filled with their dead'.[224] As for young people in Britain, they 'felt much more European than the older people who had been brought up in the days of Kipling with the idea that their work in the world lay inside the British Empire'.[225]

1. Trying to bridge the class divide: Terry Thomas and Peter Sellers attempt to negotiate in *I'm Alright Jack*.

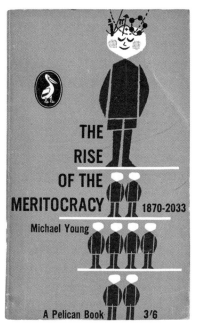

2. 'IQ+Effort=Merit': Michael Young's satire and warning about the excessive pursuit of meritocracy, paperbacked in 1962, was one of the books that defined the era.

3. Tony Hancock in *The Bedsitter*, 1961: Fighting vainly the tedium of a Sunday in bedsit-land.

4. '... trying to win him by *ideas*': Macmillan and Kennedy meet at Key West, Florida, March 1961.

5. (*right*) De Gaulle hosts Macmillan at the Chateau de Rambouillet, December 1962, leaving Macmillan 'astounded and deeply wounded' by the General's attitude towards UK membership of the European Economic Community.

6. The Easter 1961 Campaign for Nuclear Disarmament march from Trafalgar Square to the Atomic Weapons Establishment at Aldermaston leaving Reading on the second day.

7. (*below*) Bertrand Russell, philosopher king of the nuclear demo, sits down in Trafalgar Square, February 1961.

8. Tanganyika looks towards independence as Tanzania: Sir Richard Turnbull, Governor of Tanganyika, leads the Colonial Secretary, Iain Macleod, and the Chief Minister, Julius Nyerere, from the opening session of the Constitutional Conference in Dar es Salaam, 28 March 1961.

9. Last gasp of Empire as the wind of change blows: the Governors of Kenya, Uganda and Tanganyika preside at the commissioning of a new, Clyde-built mail steamer to ply Lake Victoria at the port of Kisumu, 1961. Michael Shaw is to the right of the second pole on the left, wearing a topee, and Richard Turnbull can be seen over the shoulder of the padre in the centre.

"Already, mon general, we've discarded our two-party system and got lots of extra new parties...like France!"

10. The great disruptor: the British party political structure has never been able to cope with the European Question, *Daily Express*, 4 August 1961.

11. 'It means the end of a thousand years of history': Hugh Gaitskell warns the Labour Party Conference in Brighton against UK membership of the EEC, 3 October 1962.

12. Britain's charm offensive: the UK's chief European negotiator, Edward Heath, seeks to smooth the way into the EEC with a beaming Chancellor Ludwig Erhard of West Germany in Bonn, December 1962.

13. (*left*) In the run-up to the Cuban missile crisis, both Kennedy and Macmillan had been reading Barbara Tuchman on how war came in 1914.

14. (*below*) Aircrew practice their nuclear scramble aboard a Vulcan bomber at RAF Scampton, 28 August 1960.

15. The Soviet freighter *Volgoles* carries Russian missiles away from Cuba after the crisis closely monitored by surveillance from *USS Vesole*, an SP-2 Neptune aircraft, 9 November 1962.

16. Selwyn Lloyd and his Treasury Private Secretary, David Hubback, on their way to the first meeting of the National Economic Development Council watched by an unimpressed member of the Westminster Council workforce, 7 March 1962.

17. (*left*) Reginald Maudling, Lloyd's successor as Chancellor, hoping for sustained and accelerated economic growth, 27 August 1963.

Daily Mirror

3d. Saturday, July 14, 1962 ✱ ✱ ✱ ✱ No. 18,217

MAC THE KNIFE..
SACKED—Chancellor Selwyn Lloyd and six other Ministers

.. AND HIS VICTIMS

MACMILLAN'S PANIC PURGE

SACKED
Sir David Eccles, Education Minister.

Government on the run

HAROLD MACMILLAN, Britain's ageing Prime Minister, has faced the truth at last. He is the leader of a Government nobody likes—not even his own Tory Party.

Within a few hours of the disastrous Leicester by-election, he has ruthlessly sacked not only his more inept Ministers, but also some of his friends.

MIRROR PAGE ONE COMMENT

The chief of them was his old faithful, Selwyn Lloyd. The Prime Minister has, at last, come to the conclusion the British people reached several years ago—that Selwyn Lloyd must go.

It has taken twelve by-elections, twelve bad results for the Government to convince the Prime Minister that his economic policies are political poison.

Macmillan has sacked another elderly friend, Lord Mills, who has given him so much advice about industry as it used to be. And he has kissed good-bye to

Continued on Page 2

By **WILLIAM GREIG**

PREMIER **Harold Macmillan** sacked seven of his Ministers last night and brought in fresh faces in a desperate bid to win back the runaway Tory voters.

Chancellor of the Exchequer **Selwyn Lloyd** is one of the men sacrificed in the Premier's dramatic panic purge—which follows a series of staggering by-election defeats for the Tories in recent months.

Here are Mr. Macmillan's changes in the most ruthless Government re-shuffle in Britain for many years:

OUT go:
SELWYN LLOYD, 57, Chancellor of the Exchequer;
VISCOUNT KILMUIR, 62, Lord Chancellor;
HAROLD WATKINSON, 52, Defence Minister;
SIR DAVID ECCLES, 57, Education Minister;
DR. CHARLES HILL, 58, Housing Minister;
LORD MILLS, 72, Minister without Portfolio;
JOHN MACLAY, 56, Secretary of State for Scotland.

IN come:
REGINALD MAUDLING, 45, new Chancellor of the Exchequer;
SIR REGINALD MANNINGHAM-BULLER, 56, Lord Chancellor;
PETER THORNEYCROFT, 52, Defence Minister;
SIR EDWARD BOYLE, 38, Education Minister;
SIR KEITH JOSEPH, 44, Housing Minister;

Continued on Back Page

SACKED
Selwyn Lloyd, with the Budget Box.

SACKED
Dr. Charles Hill, Housing Minister.

SACKED
Viscount Kilmuir, Lord Chancellor

SACKED
Harold Watkinson, Defence Minister

SACKED
Lord Mills,   Maclay

18. 'Mac the Knife': newspaper coverage the day after 'The Night of the Long Knives' saw the purging of a third of Macmillan's Cabinet on 13 July 1962.

In a telegram from Paris, following a conversation of his own with de Gaulle, Dixon had warned Macmillan 'that General de Gaulle does not want the Brussels negotiations to succeed . . . [and] . . . wants to find objections rather than ways of solving the problem'. So why did France agree to take part in the negotiations in the first place? Dixon believed the General 'does not want to be put in the position of appearing too obviously to be responsible for the breakdown of the negotiations. His hope presumably is that we ourselves shall give up trying and that the breakdown will appear as the consequence of our own decision.'[226]

How did Macmillan read de Gaulle post-Champs? Had he lost heart (as before the meeting he believed, not least because of Dixon's message, de Gaulle wished him to)?[227] He penned a very ambivalent reflection in his diary when he reached No. 10 late that Sunday evening:

I find it difficult to be sure about de Gaulle's attitude. My talks with him have certainly convinced him that HMG regard it as, on the whole, a British interest that we shd enter the European Community, if reasonable terms can be made, esp for the old Commonwealth countries. I think he is persuaded that we put as much, perhaps even more, weight on the political as on the economic arguments. He was impressed by my review of this unhappy century, and how a close Anglo-French alliance, really effectively managed from day to day, would have avoided both wars and all that has flowed from them. Nevertheless, I am not at all sure how far de Gaulle and the French really feel it to be in France's interest to have us in . . . it means the end of French hegemony.[228]

For all his awareness of the granitic resistance to the idea of Britain in Europe at de Gaulle's core (which was apparent throughout all their meetings), Macmillan began to stake more and more of his country's future and his own political epitaph on getting in. By the summer of 1962, he certainly had a timetable in mind which neatly coincided with the run-up to a 1964 general election in which, no doubt, had the negotiations succeeded, Britain-in-Europe would have been the centrepiece of the Conservative case for a fourth term of office.

This is revealed in a fascinating exchange in August 1962 with Norman Brook about how best to rearrange Whitehall and the Cabinet structure for a Britain inside the EEC, which, as Brook put it, would 'have a far-reaching effect on the policies and procedures of Whitehall as a whole'.[229] Brook proposed a series of co-ordinating committees in London, a permanent UK delegation in Brussels headed by a senior ambassador and 'a special secretariat' in the Foreign Office as the link between the delegation and the Cabinet committees. Would there be a special Cabinet member for Europe (i.e. Ted Heath by another means) or would the Foreign Secretary be the lead minister?[230]

Macmillan approved the planning process and revealed, in his reply to Brook, the timetable in his head. Final ratification and full membership 'might be at the earliest July, 1963, more likely January, 1964, or perhaps even July, 1964'.[231] The last moment a general election could be held was October 1964 – when it in fact took place, but with Sir Alec Douglas-Home in No. 10 and Harold Wilson as Leader of the Opposition.

If Macmillan's and Dixon's speculation about the true state of de Gaulle's mind was right, might it have been the British Commonwealth that did the General's work for him? For the Commonwealth Prime Ministers' Conference was due in London a month after that very private planning for a Britain-in-Europe machinery of government. The prospect absorbed a good deal of Macmillan's political and emotional energy. (It was at this point, as we have seen, that Butler over dinner with Macmillan at Buck's said he was with him despite the farmers, the Commonwealth and 'the probable break-up of the Conservative Party'.) Macmillan took endless pains on his speech to the Commonwealth premiers, after a burst of slaughtering birds in Yorkshire. He thought the 'conference is going to be terrible – not only all the PMs but most of the opposition leaders. No real discussion; mostly posturing – at least this is what I fear.'[232]

The conference lasted for ten days and it did indeed stir up some genuinely rough and precarious moments for the British government. It began with Macmillan putting all his histrionic talents on full display, including the Balliol philosopher of the rise and fall of empires and nations. Eric Roll watched him with a kind of awe from the officials' seats around the rim of the great conference room in Marl-borough House just off the Mall:

> he started off by talking about 'This great problem of nationality and sovereignty which must be in everybody's mind . . .' – marvellous per-formance it was – and suddenly he seemed to go into a sort of trance! He threw his head back and started to philosophise about what really constituted nationality: and he argued back and forth with himself, aloud. He finally came to the conclusion that 'language' was really the essence of nationality. I can tell you that most of the people around the table . . . did not know what on earth he was talking about![233]

One of the premiers who certainly did understand Macmillan's ploy was Bob Menzies of Australia, who had known him well for years. Menzies was the key to the conference's outcome as Macmillan well knew. They had dined *à deux* on 5 September, five days before the meeting began. Macmillan

> formed the impression that he is going to try to take a constructive line – not break up the conference or appeal to the British people over our heads. I told him that I thought he had the <u>power</u> to prevent Brit-ain joining Europe. But I thought it a terrible responsibility before history.[234]

The British PM was trying to both flatter and warn him, and was shocked, therefore, when Menzies 'wound up the first day with a very able and <u>very</u> damaging speech'.[235]

The line taken by Menzies was similar to the prophecy of Hugh Gaitskell (who had come out against entry just before the premiers met[236]) that it would mean the end of 'a thousand years of history'. The Treaty of Rome meant that British accession would be 'revolu-tionary in its effect and would mark a new era in British history'. What would be the price of entry for the Commonwealth?

Matters improved a little on the second day when Ted Heath, before an admiring Macmillan, gave perhaps the speech of his life, talking from notes for an hour and a half about the negotiations.[237] At their weekly audience the Queen was 'sympathetic' about Macmillan's Commonwealth worries.[238] The question was, would Menzies lead the Commonwealth into a specific rejection of a Britain-in-Europe?

The privately sceptical Rab Butler helped Macmillan steer him away from the brink by walking him round the garden of Marlborough House, as Butler recalled:

> Bob Menzies thought that we were traitors, and New Zealand did too. New Zealand did because of butter and sheep, you see, but Australia did on broader grounds of policy. Bob . . . was half a British statesman really. He was always coming over here! And he was dead against it. He gave great hell, you know, to Harold, and partly to me, and we decided it wasn't much worth going on. But then we persuaded Bob that . . . our Empire was gone, and a lot of our strength was gone, and had we not better join an economic unit where we could be a competitor with the USA and the USSR? And that was the final argument that appealed to Bob. Right up to that morning at Marlborough House, and I walked round that rather dim garden on the Mall with Harold about eight times . . . Bob saw us and joined us. And in the end we all went back into that wonderfully beautiful house – and decided to do it. But it was a very close thing up until the end.[239]

The Commonwealth settled for Britain getting the maximum deal possible for their individual needs and all of them acknowledged the need to win special arrangements for New Zealand.[240]

Within hours, the political electricity switched to domestic channels. Macmillan broadcast to the nation, in a state of real relief, on 20 September 1962. Gaitskell demanded a right of reply, got one and spoke very effectively, as Macmillan privately acknowledged:

> Gaitskell's reply was very <u>clever</u> . . . Whether he was right to move so definitively <u>anti</u> Common Market, time will prove. He went much further than before. He criticised the terms, but he also seemed now to . . . [be] . . . agst going in on <u>any</u> terms. England, he declared, wd be like Texas . . .[241]

In fact, Gaitskell had verged on the poetic. In a phrase he would repeat at his party's conference, he declared:

> It means the end of a thousand years of history; it means the end of the Commonwealth . . . [to become] just a province of Europe . . . I don't think the British people . . . will in a moment of folly, throw away the tremendous heritage of history.[242]

It is possible that, for all Gaitskell's effectiveness on television, a sliver of hubris began to affect Macmillan. His press secretary, Harold Evans, recorded in his diary a sudden surge of euphoria amid the exhaustion when he achieved the communiqué he wanted from the Commonwealth PMs: 'He could scarcely contain his jubilation. It was a miracle, he said, a miracle – with which I agreed but counselled caution.'[243]

The sense of qualified euphoria was heightened when the Conservatives meeting at Llandudno backed Macmillan's line strongly:

OCTOBER 11

The news reached me at lunchtime that the Conservative Conference had rejected the Turton/Walker-Smith amendment on the Common Market by an overwhelming majority – only 50 or so out of 400 voting for it. Butler and Heath seem to have made excellent speeches.[244]

On 14 October in Llandudno Macmillan consolidated his political capital with what Anthony Sampson regarded as the European equivalent of his 'Wind of Change' speech in South Africa in 1960, seeing it as 'Macmillan's last great triumph . . . [He] . . . seemed at the top of his career: he had, in two years, switched his party's foreign policy almost a hundred and eighty degrees.'[245]

The Commonwealth was squared, the Conservative Party prepared, but the world is an unforgiving place. Within days the globe was plunged unexpectedly into the most perilous moment of the Cold War with the Cuban missile crisis and, by the time Macmillan was to joust one last time with de Gaulle, he seemed likely to have to endure another missile crisis all his own because, as he told de Gaulle in their opening session,[246] the Kennedy administration now looked likely to cancel the Skybolt rocket which was to keep the RAF's V-bombers effective into the 1970s. The conferences of the Commonwealth Prime Ministers and the Conservative Party may have failed to do the General's work for him, but in concluding, within a few days of the next de Gaulle–Macmillan joust in December 1962 at Rambouillet, the Nassau deal with Macmillan for the Royal Navy's acquisition of Polaris missiles, President Kennedy certainly did. The Brussels negotiations clanked on, but the final of the European championship would be played out at Rambouillet.

Ahead of Rambouillet, Macmillan's closest advisers, Dixon in Paris and de Zulueta in London, gently prepared him for the possibility of losing. Dixon told him the 'present rhythm of the negotiations is not satisfactory' because the French were 'in the great majority of cases those who object. They rarely make a constructive or helpful suggestion. This is surely a strange way to settle a great issue.' There must now, Dixon concluded, 'be the political will to find solutions'.[247]

De Zulueta tried to turn Macmillan's mind towards planning for failure as well as success. 'Can the French stop our entry into the Six if they wish? I think the answer to this must be "yes" provided that the French do not mind being isolated. And while Dr Adenauer is in power in Germany and President de Gaulle retains his strong connection with him it looks as if the French will never be completely isolated.' As for the Brussels negotiations, 'there must undoubtedly be a crunch before the final success or failure'.[248]

Rambouillet was the 'crunch' over the weekend of 15–16 December 1962. At the end of the Rambouillet weekend Macmillan plainly was close to breaking point. Some reports have him in tears. Couve de Murville says not, though he 'was very sad and he almost broke down'. Asked by Michael Charlton if he could 'confirm one of the myths about the conference, that de Gaulle, when he saw Macmillan so crestfallen, quoted the words of the famous Edith Piaf song, "Ne pleurez pas Milord"?' Couve replied:

> Oh no, no, no, he didn't say that. No. But he used the words when he reported the meeting at our Council of Ministers, the French Cabinet . . . Things were not ended for all time, altogether. And therefore 'ne pleurez pas Milord'![249]

Piaffed or not, Macmillan was under no illusions. When he returned to No. 10 that Sunday night, the ruins of Rambouillet were placed on the pages of his diary:

> . . . de Gaulle was very intransigent . . . [he] . . . took a startlingly cynical line . . . he was quite brutally frank and seemed surprised that we did not accept him in his role as Louis XIV with more enthusiasm.
>
> I thought the discussions about as bad as they cd be from the European pt of view. The only glimmer of hope lies in the French

unwillingness to be held up to all the world as having openly wrecked our entry and having never really tried to negotiate seriously.[250]

As events unfolded, no such glimmer appeared, and the end, when it came, was as brutal as Rambouillet – but this time it would be in public before the world's press and the Corps Diplomatique in Paris at the Élysée Palace on 14 January 1963. We shall return to both dénouements in chapter 6.

3

The Pursuit of Modernity

Selwyn didn't like the subject matter. He didn't like the people. He didn't remotely understand economics.

Tom Caulcott, his number two Private Secretary,
on Selwyn Lloyd's chancellorship[1]

The real trouble about the Chancellor's policy is that (altho' we have all tried to help) he has <u>not</u> been able to put it over. Whether anyone can may be doubted . . . Nevertheless, if (as I must) I decide he must go, <u>when</u> and <u>how</u>? It will be personally terrible and I shrink from it. It will be said to be a 'panic' measure. I will be accused of gross 'disloyalty'.

Harold Macmillan, July 1962[2]

What should be the elements in such a blueprint? Have some ideas of my own, but hope colleagues will contribute. Firstly, basic principles. Do we, or do we not, set out to control the pattern of events, to direct development, to plan growth, to use the instruments of Government to influence or determine private decisions? Believe that this is inevitable. Forces at work now too complicated, risks of setback too great to leave to market forces and laisser faire. Dirigisme. But it must be creative dirigisme. This is the thread which should run through our policy and by which new proposals should be judged.

Harold Macmillan, notes for Cabinet, October 1962[3]

Macmillan wrote those words at the height of the Cuban missile crisis, when it seemed quite possible that British industry might be about to succumb to an extremely violent form of foreign competition. When the Cabinet *did* hear his views on Monday 29 October the imminent danger had passed,[4] leaving him with merely the usual bundles of economic woes to tackle. Essentially, there were three of them – two that would have faced any early 1960s premier; and one personal to him – their effect being that, though a determined modernizer by temperament and conviction, he did not look or sound the part by the autumn of 1962, especially after the 'Night of the Long Knives' the previous July when he sacked a third of his Cabinet, including the hapless Selwyn Lloyd.

The first of the two impersonal intractables was the persistent undertow of the UK's relative economic decline since the mid-nineteenth century. The second was the increasing stress upon the postwar 'British New Deal' built on the combined model of Keynesian full-employment economics and Beveridgite welfare provisions, the twin bibles of the late-1940s settlement.

By 1960 the twinned magic of the incomparable polymath of twentieth-century economics, J. M. Keynes, and its arch social planner, William Beveridge, was plainly not working as intended. The British people *were* fully employed *and* far healthier and better educated than they had ever been, but the great cumulative purpose of that British New Deal – the easing of class antagonisms and industrial tensions in a benign, upward spiral of self-fulfilling economic progress and industrial productivity and growth-funded social peace and justice – was still highly elusive. All this and the relative decline of the country's economic performance, especially in comparison to the EEC 'Six', was becoming ever more widely appreciated.

It was plain to Macmillan and to senior officials in Whitehall's economic ministries that the tussle between the push for economic modernity and the drag of industrial legacy was not being won by the forces of progress. Despite considerable postwar investment in rising industries such as aviation (both civil and military), atomic energy, pharmaceuticals and motor vehicles, at best the position in 1960–61 looked like a dead heat. Mixed-economy business-as-usual would plainly not be enough; nor would the scratchy condition of industrial relations, which the social elements of the postwar settlement were yet (and are still) to transform into sustained and productive harmony.

All advancing industrial countries live with the problem of coping with a mix of sunrise and sunset economic sectors. Keynes in 1945 had, quite rightly, seen Britain as a hard case. In a famous paper on Britain's industrial prospects drafted during the last days of the war in Europe in the spring of 1945 and circulated to the Cabinet in the first days of peace, he noted:

> The hourly wage to-day in this country is (broadly) 2s an hour; in the United States it is 5s per hour (reckoned at an exchange rate of $4). Even the celebrated inefficiency of British manufacturers can scarcely (one hopes) be capable of offsetting over wide ranges of industry the whole of this initial cost-difference in their favour, though, admittedly, they have managed it in some important cases . . . The available statistics suggest that, provided we have never made the product before, we have the rest of the world licked on cost.

Hitler had summoned forth, in Keynes's view, some fine, new and modern industrial sinews in war-stretched Britain:

> For a Mosquito, a Lancaster, Radar, we should have the business at our feet in conditions of free and fair competition. It is when it comes to making a shirt or a steel billet that we have to admit ourselves beaten both by the dear labour of America and by the cheap labour of Asia or Europe. Shipbuilding seems to be the only traditional industry where we fully hold our own.

Then, wielding his verve-filled pen, Keynes crafted one of his best-known lines:

> If by some sad geographical slip the American Air Force (it is too late now to hope for much from the enemy) were to destroy every factory on the North-East Coast and in Lancashire (at an hour when the Directors were sitting there and no one else), we should have nothing to fear. How else are we to regain the exuberant inexperience which is necessary, it seems, for success, I cannot surmise.[5]

If Macmillan had been able to summon his old friend and mentor back from the economists' Valhalla to write a paper for the Conservative Cabinet of 1960, he would scarcely have needed to modify the critique in those last sentences. He could also have done with that most supple of minds to help him with the financial problems created by an overextended defence budget (itself partly the product of resid-ual colonial responsibilities and a string of costly imperial bases still girdling the globe), the burden of sustaining the world's second reserve currency and a sterling area the funding of whose wartime-accumulated sterling balances brought on a perpetual migraine in the Treasury, and the risk of inflation.

Keynes had died at Easter 1946 without leaving any characteristi-cally subtle yet practical plan for dealing with the problems of wages and salaries in a full-employment economy. He had enabled the post-war British government to, as it were, put the Thirties right, but he had not given them a blueprint for the late Fifties and early Sixties, as his colleagues and disciples recognized. One of them, the Cambridge economist Austin Robinson, who had worked in Whitehall's Central Economic Planning Staff in the late 1940s, wrote of Keynes's legacy that the 'problems of preventing inflation in an over-full economy are not those of preventing the cruelties of unemployment in the 1930s. He left us, perhaps, too little precise guidance as to how he would have handled our very different problems.'[6]

That most formidable and forceful of postwar Whitehall intellects, Otto Clarke, sensed this when he heard of Keynes's fatal heart attack on the Sussex Downs. He recorded in his diary the

> [a]ppalling news of the death of Keynes. Felt bereft as at [the] death of Roosevelt and Alekhine (the chess champion). He is the man whose career I would soonest match; I could never hope to match his all round genius, but I might hope to match his type of skill in the field of forensic political economy . . . his death leaves the Treasury in a terrible hole.[7]

It was Clarke who, as Treasury Third Secretary with oversight of expenditure at this time, was instrumental in commissioning a secret internal Treasury history of 'The Government and Wages 1945–1960', covering that crucial Keynesian gap identified by Austin Robinson. The study was completed by A. K. Ogilvy-Webb, a moving spirit of the Treasury's Historical Section, and circulated in July 1962 with a Fore-word drafted by Clarke three months earlier. Clarke declared bluntly that by the summer of 1960, 'existing policies seemed to have come to a dead end: the alternatives did not command ready confidence'.[8] Clarke plainly felt by the end of the 1950s that the Treasury had run out of ideas. Macmillan thought so too, though why he imagined appointing Selwyn Lloyd Chancellor of the Exchequer in July 1960 would put that right remains a mystery – unless one concludes, with Edmund Dell, that 'Macmillan, in reality, wished to remain in charge of economic policy. It was too important politically to be delegated to men like [David] Eccles and [Iain] Macleod who might show too much independence'. I tend to the Dell interpretation that Macmillan knew that 'Lloyd was a staff officer, not a man of ideas', that 'he himself could provide the ideas and the faithful Lloyd would implement them without forcing him to fight too hard to get his way', if necessary.[9]

This is pretty much what happened between July 1960 and July 1962. Poor Selwyn! Eden had wished to be – and acted as if he were – his own Foreign Secretary while Lloyd was at the Foreign Office. On moving from the Foreign Office to Treasury Chambers, Lloyd tried to bargain for a degree of independence by asking Macmillan for, and receiving, an undertaking that he should be allowed to stay three or four years at the Treasury to enable him to control public expenditure and to bring to maturity longer-term policies. He immediately undercut himself with the guileful Macmillan, however, by in effect admitting to a high degree of economic illiteracy: 'I told him he was wrong if he expected any originality. I had v. orthodox ideas about taxation and public expenditure, and knew nothing about the City.'[10]

Macmillan was already sifting in his mind the particles that were to go into the making of what became the first of three successive attempts to breathe new life into the flagging British New Deal. The other two were Harold Wilson's fusing of science with socialism (his 1964–6 'White Heat' of technological revolution ploy, plus a National Plan and industrial reform) and Ted Heath's 'quiet revolution' (a dash of economic liberalism for the private sector, a streamlined public sector and entry into Europe). Wilson and Callaghan's 'social contract' wages policy and 'picking winners' industrial strategy in 1974–6 were such end-game efforts that they don't really qualify, so far had stagflation bitten into Britain's economy and society by the mid-1970s. As for Margaret Thatcher, she was determined to halt and then reverse Britain's relative economic decline after 1979 but definitely *not* in the cause of reviving the postwar settlement. She came to bury it, not to praise it, and saw its Keynesian and Beveridgite motors as the engine rooms of national failure (as we shall see shortly in a fascinating, if courteous, part private/part public showdown with Harold Macmillan in the summer and autumn of 1980).

Macmillan had reshuffled his Cabinet on 27 July 1960. Three days before, at the end of the first parliamentary session since his golden election victory in October 1959, he wrote, as he enjoyed doing, one of his faintly gamey letters to the Queen. Comparing politics to 'boating on a lake. Upon the calmest waters blow down the fiercest storms' (the By-Royal-Appointment version of his famous 'events, dear boy, events'). 'Such popularity', he told his sovereign, 'as we may have been able to obtain among the people is not of our own creation. We owe it to the strange goings-on in the Opposition Parties'[11] (a reference, no doubt, to the post-election Labour Party fight about the future place of nationalization in its programme).

Macmillan then produced an almost Wodehousian account of the UK's economic vicissitudes that might have come from the pen of the profligate Galahad Threepwood, telling the Queen:

> As always, one never seems to have enough money. When one was at a private school or at a public school one felt that ultimately this indigence might rectify itself with reaching manhood or middle age. On the contrary, most individuals have found that as they get older the claims upon them become more and more embarrassing. And so it is with our country. Government expenditure, that is, the demands either of the [Armed] Services, or of the new scientific methods of warfare, or of the social services, education, health and all the rest, or rebuilding Britain and repairing the neglect of many years, all these things together seem to cost more and more. The public want them all, but they do not like the idea of paying for them ... Then there is the problem of foreign trade, European complexities, the balance of payments ...[12]

Plainly those Whitehall studies examining how precariously placed Britain would be by 1970 on present policies,[13] and the need to invigorate the domestic economy if EEC entry were to be secured (and even more so if it were not[14]), which he had absorbed over the course of 1960, were having their effect on Macmillan.

Between July 1960 and his resignation in October 1963, in a somewhat piecemeal fashion, he attempted to tackle that range of interlocking problems he outlined, with more than a touch of eccentricity, for the Queen on 30 July. Together they did amount to a substantial attempt to halt the country's relative decline. It was a political equivalent of the researches of the physician Elisabeth Kübler-Ross, in the USA at this very time, which she later called the 'Five Stages of Grief',[15] the first three of which – 'denial', 'anger' and 'bargaining' – fit Macmillan's premiership rather well ('denial' of the loss of great powerdom post-Suez; late-Fifties 'anger' at de Gaulle's and Adenauer's wrecking of the UK's proposed Free Trade Area instead of an EEC based on a customs union, and attempting to secure a new 'bargain' between capital, labour and government with the creation of a National Economic Development Council in 1961).

In fact, the Macmillanesque ingredients of 'Modernization' went much further than NEDC. As we have already seen, they embraced an attempted accession to the EEC by the time of the next election. They also included modernization of the railways, the motorway programme, the further development of civil nuclear power, an inquiry into the expansion of universities, a renewed effort on incomes policy and an attempt to revive the economic fortunes of north-east England in the short term and to plan and link population growth and industry generally in the longer term. Allied to this were grand, talismanic, prestige projects such as the Anglo-French airliner Concorde and the new Cunard liner (what became the *QE II*).

Planning was to be the instrument for breaking out of the vortex of relative economic decline – first in shaping the way government reached and implemented its spending priorities and then of the economy more generally. Planning became the terrain of choice for 1960s political competition with Labour under both Hugh Gaitskell and Harold Wilson bidding to outdo anything the Conservatives could accomplish because (a) they believed in it and the Conservatives' conversion was skin deep, and (b) they would be better at it because without socialism it would fail and Labour was better placed to inspire and recruit (as voters) the gritty, classless meritocrats in factory and research lab upon whom Britain's industrial future depended. This contest became even more pronounced in the brief era of 'the two Harolds' between Wilson's succeeding Gaitskell (who died in January 1963) and Douglas-Home's replacing Macmillan.

What was it that persuaded Macmillan, over three years into his premiership and a few months after his thumping victory in the autumn of 1959, that a substantial change was needed in his economic policy? His revered friend and mentor J. M. Keynes had given him a benchmark for measuring the degree to which Britain, over what the Annales school of French historians call the *longue durée, was* having it so good. In his celebrated *Essays in Persuasion* (which Macmillan surely read when they first appeared in 1931[16]), Keynes published a lecture he had given in Madrid the previous year when the Depression was biting hard and pessimism was spreading all around. He called it 'Economic Possibilities for Our Grandchildren'. In it he scanned the horizon a hundred years hence and made a prediction that would probably have struck his early-Thirties readers as wildly optimistic.

Assuming 'no important wars and no important increase in population', Keynes wrote, 'I would predict that the standard of life in progressive countries one hundred years hence will be between four and eight times as high as it is today'.[17] In the spring of 2009, Iain de Weymarn, Economic Assistant to the then Governor of the Bank of England, Mervyn King, calculated that by 2008, measured by the growth in productivity, the UK had seen a six-fold increase 'bang in the middle of Keynes' range'.[18] Had Macmillan in the spring of 1960 asked the Bank of England or the Treasury to make a similar calculation for him of progress so far on Keynes's prediction (after one total war and an increase in population from about 45 million to 53 million[19]) it would have shown the UK well on the way to reaching the economic trajectory required for the lower end of Keynes's prediction to be met by 2030 (see table; Iain de Weymarn's calculations are at 2003 prices).[20]

Output per employed head in £, 2003 prices, Keynes's predictions

Date	Data (in £)	Consistent with a four-fold increase by 2030	Consistent with a six-fold increase by 2030	Consistent with an eight-fold increase by 2030
1930	10,046	–	–	–
1940	11,017	11,540	12,018	12,369
1950	11,924	13,256	14,376	15,227
1960	14,523	15,227	17,197	18,747

The rise in living standards in the 1950s had been considerable and electorally advantageous to the Conservatives. Despite this, as we have seen, the old Keynesian in Downing Street knew the UK was increasingly coming off the pace set by its competitors, not least those a few dozen miles across the Channel. In 1960, the private briefs he received, whether it be the final report of the 'Future Policy Study'[21] in February or the document produced in July by a group of officials under Sir Frank Lee, Permanent Secretary to the Treasury, on Britain's economic prospects inside or outside the EEC,[22] spared him nothing about the need for the UK to reach and sustain a new and higher trajectory of economic and industrial performance if increasing budgetary pressure and accelerating relative economic decline were to be avoided.

Macmillan knew, too, that his mentor Keynes had not left a posthumous letter for his friend on how to tackle the problem of wages and salaries in a full-employment society. In the first volume of his memoirs, Macmillan recalled his own efforts in the House of Commons in 1933 to press for the adoption of 'good Keynesian doctrine' on the need for state action and investment to counter the unemployment consequences of economic recession. Writing in the years immediately following his retirement, Macmillan acknowledged:

> As things have turned out, it has not been easy to apply it [Keynesian doctrine], even when its soundness has been generally accepted [as it still was in 1966, when this first instalment of Macmillan's memoirs was published]. For in times of boom, the demand for increasing Government expenditure – roads, schools, universities and the like – becomes very difficult to resist. In other words, we have learnt how to turn the tap on. To turn it off, or even reduce the flow, has not proved so easy.[23]

In fact, Macmillan was temperamentally averse to turning economic taps off. He was a natural expansionist and this most powerful of his governing impulses linked the cluster of remedies he sought to devise and apply over the three years of the second half of his premiership.

He was also a natural dirigiste, as he made plain to his Cabinet in the autumn of 1962.* It was to French planners rather than the social

---

* As illustrated in his speaking notes quoted at the head of this chapter – though his ministerial colleagues would have been remarkably obtuse if they had not realized this long before.

marketeers of West Germany that Macmillan's and Whitehall's eyes turned in 1960–61 when seeking institutional imports to help restructure the economic governance for Britain.[24] On the face of it, this turning to Paris rather than Bonn (to Jean Monnet rather than Ludwig Erhard) is one of the mysteries of economic and industrial policy in the Macmillan years. In terms of compound rates of growth in gross domestic product France had prospered mightily since the late 1940s (4.6 per cent between 1948 and 1963) but West Germany was *the* success story of the postwar boom (7.6 per cent over the same period compared with Britain's relatively meagre 2.5 per cent[25]). West Germany, since its creation as a political entity, had been staunchly Christian Democrat centre-right rather than SPD Social Democrat centre-left. Yet the head of the centre-right government in London since January 1957 found nothing attractive about the combination of Catholic social teaching and free enterprise that shaped the increasingly buoyant and export-led West German economy since Dr Erhard pioneered currency reform in the western zones of occupied Germany in 1948. 'The results were nothing short of miraculous' over the short, medium and long terms, not least because of 'the creation of the social market economy, notably the provision of unemployment insurance and public pensions, which gave workers the security and protection they needed to accept an intensely competitive market environment'.[26]

This particular mix of mixed economy, one might have imagined, could well have appealed to the High Anglican, Keynesian advocate of the 'middle way' in his long hours of reading and reflection at Birch Grove and Chequers. Yet whenever Adenauer or the West Germans crop up in his diaries or remarks there is little else but disdain and dislike. His diary entry for 23 February 1961 is typical (Macmillan was always easily needled by the cost to the UK of stationing the British Army of the Rhine on the territory of a people who, as he had told an 'astonished' Duke of Edinburgh, 'When they are down they crawl under your feet, and when they are up they use their feet to stamp on your face'[27]):

We have had two days of Dr Adenauer and his Germans [on a visit to the UK] – 4 hours talk; dinner; luncheon – and little or no result. Whatever they finally give the Americans [on support costs for the occupying forces], we shall get pari-passu . . . But the large economic issues wh face the world they affect not to understand. In other words, they are rich and selfish – and German.*

He was slightly kinder about Erhard in an earlier volume of memoirs, covering his (Macmillan's) period as Chancellor of the Exchequer in 1955, despite

> Dr Ludwig Erhard – the Finance Minister [of West Germany] – [having] thought fit to state publicly that sterling should and would be devalued [the rate was $2.80 to the pound]. I agreed to the Treasury issuing firm denials, but reluctantly, for I remembered the famous apophthegm: 'No story is worth believing until it has been officially denied.' Dr Erhard, with whom I was to become closely acquainted, was not without charm. He looked like an actor cast for the role of Henry VIII. But he was a brilliant executive in his own field, although as Chancellor of the Reich [Germany had actually ceased to be a 'Reich' in 1945 as Macmillan well knew], after Adenauer's resignation [in 1963], he proved less successful.[28]

Yet the economic and organizational ingredients of the astonishing comeback of West Germany from the rubble of defeat, ruin and territorial dismemberment,[29] seem to have aroused absolutely no interest as a possible exemplar for a Macmillan determined to wrench his country and its productive capacities to a higher level of output and sustained success.†

This is all the more surprising as Harold Macmillan combined intellectual curiosity and a genuinely international cast of mind with the conviction in the early 1960s that, as he put it in his 'modernisation' notes for Cabinet in October 1962 that the 'risks of setback . . . [were] . . .

---

* In the diary extract he published in his memoirs Macmillan omitted 'and German' (Harold Macmillan, *Pointing the Way, 1959–1961* (Macmillan, 1972), p. 327).

† Not all Conservatives were deaf to social market thinking. Younger figures in the Bow Group, such as Geoffrey Howe (who would come into their own during the Thatcher years), were developing ideas along these lines in the late Fifties and early Sixties. Howe's contribution to the Group's 1961 publication, *Principles in Practice*, is especially prophetic on 1980s welfare reform. The idea, as he later put it, was 'to combine One Nation social policies with economic liberalism' (Geoffrey Howe, *Conflict of Loyalty* (Macmillan, 1994), p. 31; James Barr, *The Bow Group: A History* (Politico's, 2001), pp. 60–62).

great'. Some historians have been hard on the interventionist approach that marked the last years of his premiership,[30] or damned him with faint praise,[31] but it was his successor-but-three as Conservative leader, Margaret Thatcher, who put the stiletto heel into the bundle of philosophies, attitudes and experiences he brought to economic discussions around the Cabinet table at about the time (October 1961) when he was giving her her first step up the ministerial ladder as Parliamentary Secretary at the Ministry of Pensions and National Insurance.*

Writing in *The Path to Power* about her pre-prime ministerial days, she was highly revealing of both his and her attitudes towards both history and economic policy:

In both foreign and home policies Macmillan always prided himself on having a sense of history. In his attempts to establish harmony between the two superpowers, as in his fervent belief that Britain's destiny lay in Europe, he was much affected by the experience of two world wars. Indeed, as he would remind us, he was one of the few surviving members of the House who had fought in the Great War. In his preference for economic expansion over financial soundness and his long-standing belief in the virtues of planning, he was reacting

* Their contrasting recollections of her first preferment are fascinating. Macmillan: 'Mrs Thatcher, a clever young woman MP, and Monty Woodhouse are the newcomers' (Peter Catterall (ed.), *The Macmillan Diaries*, vol. 2: *Prime Minister and After, 1957–1966* (Pan Books edition, 2014), p. 417, diary entry for 8 October 1961). Mrs Thatcher (recalling 9 October 1961):

I did not try to conceal my delight when the telephone rang and I was summoned to see the Prime Minister. Harold Macmillan was camping out in some style at Admiralty House while 10 Downing Street was undergoing extensive refurbishment. I had already developed my own strong impressions of him, not just from speeches in the House and to the 1922 Committee, but also when he came to speak to our New Members' Dining Club – on which occasion he had strongly recommended Disraeli's *Sybil* and *Coningsby* as political reading ... [On 9 October 1961] I sorted out my best outfit, this time sapphire blue, to go and see the Prime Minister. The interview was short. Harold Macmillan charmingly greeted me and offered the expected appointment. I enthusiastically accepted. I wanted to begin as soon as possible and asked him how I should arrange things with the department. Characteristically, he said: 'Oh well, ring the Permanent Secretary and turn up at about 11 o'clock tomorrow morning, look around and come away. I shouldn't stay too long' (Margaret Thatcher, *The Path to Power* (HarperCollins, 1995), pp. 117–19).

against the deflation and unemployment of the 1930s which he had seen as MP for Stockton-on-Tees. It is said that when he was Chancellor of the Exchequer Treasury officials kept a tally of how many times he mentioned 'Stockton' each week. But history's lessons usually teach us what we want to learn. It was possible to take a very different view of the causes of war and of the historic achievements of capitalism. Things looked different from the perspective of Grantham [where Mrs Thatcher grew up in the 1920s, 1930s and 1940s] than from that of Stockton.[32]

Nearly twenty years later, as the values of Grantham (as Mrs Thatcher conceived of them) began to flow ever more powerfully through the somewhat resistant arteries and capillaries of Whitehall, a paper arrived in No. 10 crafted by Harold Macmillan that sought to thwart them head-on.

This was the most fascinating discovery in the 1980 No. 10 and Cabinet Office papers when they were displayed at the National Archives' then traditional 'press preview' in December 2010 of files about to be released under the Thirty-Year Rule.[33] Not only was their historic interest intrinsic to the politics of 1980; Macmillan's paper and the correspondence surrounding it in the Thatcher Archive preserved in Churchill College, Cambridge also shed fascinating light on Macmillan-the-modernizer of the early 1960s, and why, with his hero Disraeli, Macmillan had come to believe that Britain is 'a very difficult country to move . . . and one in which there is more disappointment to be looked for than success'.[34] It is worth considering this Macmillan–Thatcher debate for a moment as it is a revealing defence of his pursuit of modernity through a shift in economic policy versus hers at a time when, in the 10 Downing Street of Margaret Thatcher and the No. 11 of Geoffrey Howe, such a middle-way approach was deeply out of fashion. It also casts an intriguing light on what he thought he was attempting in the early Sixties.

Lack of 'movement' was a favourite theme of Macmillan's and it was visits to Chequers in his long twilight to dine with his Conservative successors that tended to bring it on. On 6 March 1971, for example, with Ted Heath the target, it was a general disquisition about the people's aversion to power:

The English people do not like power. They distrust power and fight it when it appears. It has always been so. They broke the power of the barons in the Middle Ages, they broke the power of the Crown under Charles I, then the landlords in the [1832] Reform Bill, then the press, then the middle class. Now it is the trade unions. It has all happened before, dear boy.[35]

It was at Chequers once more – dining this time with Mrs Thatcher in August 1980 – that he produced another burst of history-infused fatalism.[36] This time, though, the relative powerlessness of central government stemmed from a number of factors, wrote Macmillan in the memo he sent her after they had supped and talked: 'It must be admitted that the troubles of the last fifteen years are largely due to the refusal of the trades unions to accept any curb upon their monopoly position, and their determination to force up the wages in terms of money rates without regard to productivity.' (In the Churchill, Cambridge copy Mrs Thatcher has underlined this passage heavily, twice, using different pens, which indicates she read it more than once.)

In the summer of 1980, just over a year after taking office, the Thatcher government was faced by a dire fistful of economic indicators. Oil prices had effectively tripled during the course of 1979; inflation had peaked in May at 21.9 per cent; sterling was very high at $2.40 to the pound and hurting exports; interest rates were at 16 per cent, unemployment had just surged by 160,000 to 1.7 million and both public expenditure and money supply (the curbing of which were central to the economic strategy of Mrs Thatcher and her Chancellor of the Exchequer, Sir Geoffrey Howe), seemed beyond the government's control.[37]

To this darkening scene, Macmillan's eleven-page memorandum brought still further gloom and annotations from its recipient:

Unhappily, they [the Government] entered the campaign with apparently little knowledge of what powers they really have. They have little if any control of the wages paid either by central government or local government. The powerful bureaucratic system which has taken away the central powers of the Treasury over state employment and much reduced the power of Ministers over their own departments, makes it almost impossible for the Government to fix the wages of its own employees, since they are now controlled by a whole series of <u>commit-tees and mechanisms which have become rooted in the system</u>.[38]

Yet, the Thatcherite remedies of controlling the money supply and, if needs must, taking on the trades unions found no favour with Macmillan, who plainly still hankered for the tripartite institutional mechanisms embracing government, employers and trades unions that he prepared and implemented during *his* last burst of power (or powerlessness, as he would have thought of it during one of his glooms).

He poured scorn on excessive reliance upon monetarism:

> The so-called 'money supply' policy may be useful as a guide to what is happening <u>just as a speedometer is in a car</u>; but like a speedometer it cannot make the machine go faster or slower.

As for interest rates:

> Here in Britain a combination of <u>high Bank Rate</u> (to a point which would have been regarded as sheer usury in any other age) and the consequent attraction of foreign money (mostly in the form of hot money) into Britain, by rates higher than those prevailing in other countries and a corresponding increase in the <u>value of the pound</u> against <u>the dollar</u>, has seriously <u>increased the competitive difficulties of British exporting industry</u> without so <u>far producing any marked effect upon the inflation of prices</u>.[39]

It was in the last paragraphs of what by now had become a peroration rather than an economic memorandum that the old consensualist showed his true politico-philosophical colours and his hankering for remedies he sought to apply in the early 1960s. What was needed was 'a real campaign in favour of productivity':

> We should organise nationally, locally and industrially, possibly through the existing NEDDY's,* or possibly by some other organisation for the purpose ...
>
> It is by trying to switch the controversy on to productivity and the benefits in terms of wages, hours of work, holidays and the like that can

---

* Subgroups of the National Economic Development Council – which the Major government scrapped in the early 1990s (John Major, *The Autobiography* (HarperCollins, 1999), p. 667) – devoted to raising productivity in different sectors of the economy.

follow the adoption of modern methods, that we may hope to obtain by a return to 'consensus' politics, sneered at by some, but the essence of Tory democracy. Devisive [sic] politics in a democratic system are not likely to be applied for sufficient length of time to become effective even if such methods were desirable. Nor can permanent deflation be a credible solution to the threat of national and international recession.[40]

Macmillan, in short, was calling for a U-turn right across the Thatcher–Howe economic strategy *and* a return to the consensus politics the Prime Minister was convinced had brought Britain low.

The Treasury were asked to produce a point-by-point rebuttal and did so.[41] Advice was sought from Peter Thorneycroft, the Conservative Party chairman, who as Chancellor of the Exchequer had resigned from the Macmillan Cabinet in January 1958 (with his entire Treasury ministerial team) in protest at the Prime Minister's refusal to hold public expenditure at the previous year's level.[42] Lord Thorneycroft told Mrs Thatcher that if Macmillan went public with his thoughts, the 'doubts and cautionary notes that he quite properly inserts will be ignored; the similarity with the arguments of the Left will be stressed; the term consensus will be twisted from the Tory democracy theme of one nation to a compromise of principal [sic] and abandonment of purpose. My conclusion is that he should, if possible, be stopped from saying it.'[43]

There is nothing in either the National or the Thatcher archives to indicate that such an attempt was made – or that Macmillan received a letter of reply from Mrs Thatcher. But, for a moment, it was as if, with Labour in growing disarray after its 1979 defeat and soon to choose Michael Foot as its new leader in succession to Jim Callaghan, Harold Macmillan, the man who gave Mrs Thatcher her first ministerial job, had become the real Leader of the Opposition. Before October 1980 was out, both of them had decided to go public. Margaret Thatcher went first in what is probably her most memorable Party Conference speech and its flash of verbal defiance penned for her by her speechwriter, the playwright Ronnie Millar:

To those waiting with bated breath for that favourite media catchphrase, the 'U' turn, I have only one thing to say. You turn if you want to. The lady's not for turning.[44]

We knew at the time that Millar's adaptation of playwright Christopher Fry's title *The Lady's Not for Burning* was aimed at the so-called 'wets' in her Cabinet (Jim Prior, Ian Gilmour and others[45]). What we didn't know was that her conference speech of 10 October 1980 was a very public riposte to Macmillan's private August memorandum:

> No policy which puts at risk the defeat of inflation – however great its short-term attraction – can be right . . .
>
> If spending money like water was the answer to our country's problems, we would have no problems now. If ever a nation has spent, spent, spent and spent again, ours has. Today that dream is over.[46]

Four days later, though the country did not know it in such terms, the private Thatcher–Macmillan duel was resumed when the old man, in what was no doubt an interview previously arranged, went on BBC Television for one of his celebrated conversations with Robert McKenzie, the London School of Economics political scientist.

The full transcript is preserved in the Thatcher Archive complete with the Lady's underlinings. The interview is notable for its prescience about industrial strife to come:

> When the Chancellor says to me, as a businessman [Macmillan was still involved with the family publishing firm], 'All right I'm not to pay so much wages or I can't borrow from the banks', what will he do when the miners go on strike . . . ?[47]

On 13 November 1984 at the age of ninety, he delivered his maiden speech in the House of Lords as the Earl of Stockton on precisely this in the middle of what was by then a hugely embittered miners' strike: 'It breaks my heart to see what is happening in our country today. A terrible strike . . . by the best men in the world. They beat the Kaiser's army and they beat Hitler's army. They never gave in . . .'[48]

In his interview with Bob McKenzie, he was also in regretful old man mode: 'Well, these are dreams, they're old men's dreams . . . but they're the dreams that I have dreamt from the time the First War ended and the forty years I sat in the House of Commons and the long years I was a minister'[49].

Once again he used the 'speedometer' metaphor to downgrade the utility of monetarism. Once again he appealed for industrial peace and the old NEDC impulse shone through:

> Now supposing people, let's say the national boards of industries and the leaders of trade unions, why can't industry and the unions sit down and say, 'Boys, it's there, it's waiting for us if we'll get together, industry by industry, plant by plant, take the new technology . . .'

Then the veteran of the Somme appeared:

> Let us create a new concept of the co-operation of industry and trade unions, and workmen and masters, as they used to call them . . . They're in the same regiment. They would be welcome, a new deal, call it what you like . . .[50]

But it was precisely the breakdown of the postwar British New Deal over the years since Macmillan as Prime Minister had tried to shore it up with his combination of Tory paternalism and a dash of dirigisme that had created the politico-economic space that Margaret Thatcher and Geoffrey Howe were seeking to fill and which brought so much anguish to Macmillan, who, in his own idiosyncratic way, was as much the incarnation of that prototypical postwar British New Deal as Clem Attlee had been. Both Attlee and Macmillan, one suspects, saw Britain as a good regiment on a national scale.

Yet even now, in the brittle and grim economic and industrial circumstances of the autumn of 1980 Macmillan could not bring himself to recognize that the prescriptions of 1960–63 were, to borrow another phrase of his beloved Disraeli, 'exhausted volcanoes'.[51] Even in 1973, during a period of serious economic, industrial and political stress, when he published his final volume of memoirs, *At the End of the Day*, he portrayed the tripartite approach as an unqualified success:

> [T]his institution, now commonly known as 'Neddy', has become an important and valuable part of our national machinery. Moreover, it has been fruitful in every sense of the word. For not only has it been a source of much valuable discussion and action at the top level, but it has given birth to a large number of so-called 'little Neddys' which industry by industry have contributed much to the greater improvement of labour relations [this in the era of strikes and states of emergency

declared by the Heath government] as well as of productivity [the lack of which Macmillan saw as the heart of the 'British disease' in his interview by Bob McKenzie]. To Selwyn Lloyd, supported by his advisers in the Treasury, belongs the credit for this forward-looking scheme.[52]

This last sentence, too, is intriguing because it is usually forgotten that 'Neddy' – the National Economic Development Council (NEDC) – was a Selwyn Lloyd idea and, equally, that some senior Treasury officials, including the energetic Permanent Secretary, Sir Frank Lee, had real reservations about it in 1961–2 while the Chief Economic Adviser, Sir Alec Cairncross, thought the target of 4 per cent sustained growth per annum hopelessly unrealistic.

The great anatomist of what he called 'The Wasting of the British Economy', Sidney Pollard, traced the first impetus for 'Neddy' to the employers at the annual conference of what was then the Federation of British Industry (FBI) in November 1960 when, 'rather surprisingly', it passed a resolution calling for a plan for economic growth.[53] The internal Whitehall impetus was Lloyd's desire to do something positive and long term after his July 1961 deflationary measures, which were deeply disliked in the country and dented the standing of the Conservative government, finally taking the bloom off its golden three-figure majority election victory in October 1959 and placing it on a trajectory of electoral unpopularity from which it never fully recovered (even though the 1964 election was lost only by a whisker).[54]

That recurring curse upon postwar Chancellors and governments – pressure on sterling – with a loss of £100 million from the gold and dollar reserves in the second week of June 1961, a balance-of-payments gap of £80 million for the same month plus salary and wage increases touching 8 per cent while output and productivity were languishing around 3 per cent created an atmosphere of crisis in Whitehall and the Bank of England. The remedies the Treasury reached for were a recourse to the International Monetary Fund (IMF), a rise in bank rate to 7 per cent and a 'pay pause' for the public sector plus the ever vain hope that state income restraint would be contagious and spread to the private sector.[55] Altogether this represented a classic example of 'stop-go' economic policies which the Labour Party hung round the Conservatives' necks while promising that their approach to planning and growth would obviate the need for such inconsistencies if only the electorate would give them their chance. The economically literate and fluent Hugh Gaitskell was merciless on the hapless Lloyd, whom he regarded as an inept overseer of an economic policy that could only bring further relative economic decline as, in Gaitskell's words, 'it is not good enough to rescue the balance of payments at the expense of cutting back industrial expansion'.[56]

The mood music of British politics changed in the summer of 1961 and Macmillan sensed it as the gold and dollars were 'still flowing out of the reserves'[57] and Labour frontbenchers had their tails up even before Lloyd announced his measures in the Commons. Reflecting at Chequers after a rough week in Westminster, Macmillan wrote in his diary for 22 July 1961:

> . . . the HofC has become rather restless. I have agreed to answer at 3.15 – which means a quarter of an hour grilling at Question Time twice a week.* Under the old system, my questions were often partially reached or not at all.
>
> There was a stiff little debate on Tuesday, which gave the opposition a good chance. Gaitskell was very good, I thought, and both his professorial exposition and his waspish attack on me were in good style. Harold Wilson [Shadow Chancellor] was also very good. Maudling [President of the Board of Trade] and Selwyn Lloyd spoke – the former very effectively, the latter not so good. But he was hampered by the circumstances of the debate. In view of his statement next week, he could really say nothing.

Macmillan truly thought the pound was once more on the rim of devaluation:

> Altogether a bad week. The economic situation gets worse in the <u>short</u> term. It looks as if another £100 [million] will go from the reserves in July . . .

---

* This fifteen-minute 'grilling' on Tuesdays and Thursdays lasted until May 1997, when Tony Blair, on becoming Prime Minister, changed the practice to a single thirty-minute session on Wednesdays.

I fear that now sterling (being the weakest world currency) is taking all the strain of the rapidly worsening international situation [the Berlin crisis].[58]

The following day, after a poor night's sleep and a working lunch with Lloyd, his Chief Economic Adviser, Alec Cairncross, David Hubback (Lloyd's Principal Private Secretary), William Armstrong (the rising star in the Treasury then one of its Third Secretaries) and Lord Cromer (the new Governor of the Bank of England), a weary Macmillan placed on the page the exhausted reluctance of an expansionist economic temperament confronted by the need to deflate to appease unforgiving money markets, prop up a shaky world reserve currency and compensate for a resistant and relatively unproductive domestic economy:

> Selwyn has made good progress with his statement, but we are not very happy about the Government expenditure aspect. If we are to get our 'drawings' from the International Monetary Fund [$1.5 billion], we shall have to make – or pretend to make – large savings on Govt expenditure. This is (in the short as well as in the long run) more difficult than extra taxation. It is also very hard to achieve quickly ... But if the package is not good enough, the international usurers – bankers – will turn us down. Then sterling will go. (Whether this matters as much as we all think or not, I am not sure. It matters politically, because sterling has become a symbol. What really matters is that we should <u>not</u> add to demand by wage increases.)[59]

Three days later, the government got its measures through with a majority of 110 ('a triumph', wrote Macmillan) but not before he had endured twenty minutes of sustained barracking from Labour in the Commons Chamber and a biting wind-up speech by Gaitskell 'ending in a fierce (and rather witty) attack on me personally, and demanding my disappearance from the stage where an old actor had outstayed his welcome'.[60] Getting the July 1961 measures through the Commons may have been a parliamentary 'triumph' of a kind – but it took the gilt off Harold Macmillan's trademark having-it-so-good once and for all.

Sterling recovered as the 'usurers' moved in to buy it, and the trade gap began to narrow too. But Macmillan had by now come to have serious doubts about the postwar regime of fixed exchange rates (which were to last for another decade). Writing in the early 1970s, he recalled:

> I felt strongly that one of the disadvantages of a fixed currency exchange rate was the time lag and complexity of all the calculations. The rate now had become merely a measure. A floating rate would be a barometer and any weakness of the economy much more quickly detected by the market than by the Government statisticians. But this question, so often discussed, seemed to be beyond our power to decide unilaterally and still remains unresolved.[61]

It was in the wake of the July 1961 measures that Lloyd and the Treasury began to look in detail at a new peacetime version of tripartite government–industry–unions planning (the Attlee governments had tried with the Central Economic Planning Staff and the Economic Planning Board). It was an initiative that led to the creation of the National Economic Development Council, which, as Keith Middlemas put it, 'complemented earlier parts of a rather piecemeal set of running repairs to the postwar settlement . . .'.[62] Unfortunately for the would-be planners and long-term turners-round of the British economy in Whitehall, the mind of the British public and the British political weather was far more dominated by the short-term effects of Selwyn Lloyd's 'pay pause' than by possible changes to the hidden wiring of the UK's economic institutions. As Macmillan recognized, 'it was to lead us into great difficulties in detail'.[63]

The greatest 'difficulty' arose when the government applied the 'pay pause' guideline of 2–2.5 per cent for annual increases to the single most popular group of public sector workers – nurses – in early 1962. The offer of 2.5 per cent, made by the Minister of Health, Enoch Powell (the first time the bulk of the general public became aware of this extraordinary man) was rejected by the Royal College of Nursing on 13 March 1962, the day before the Conservatives suffered a shock in their dramatic loss of Orpington in the south-east London suburbs to the Liberals in probably the most significant by-election of the postwar years thus far (of which more shortly).[64]

The thinking that fed into the creation of the National Economic Development Council, however, was to represent the first flurries of an enduring politico-economic weather system that lasted for nearly twenty years – what David Marquand called the 'hands-on phase' of economic management[65] – practised by Conservative and Labour governments alike, first with a surge of new nationalizations in the Wilson governments, then a temporary dash of economic liberalism in the first two years of the Heath administration. It ended only with Margaret Thatcher's arrival in No. 10 and Sir Geoffrey Howe in No. 11 in 1979. That vintage showdown between Mrs Thatcher and Harold Macmillan in the summer and autumn of 1980 represented the clashing of the old weather system with the new across a cold and turbulent front.

But, as with all epochs, 1961–79 looks epochal only in retrospect. As Keith Middlemas, the biographer of 'Neddy',[66] noted, 'its symbolic importance to participants turned out, over the next ten years, to be very much greater than anyone in 1961–2 imagined except Lloyd, the FBI and George Woodcock [General Secretary of the Trades Union Congress], who saw particular advantage in a new avenue of access to economic ministers in anticipation of EEC entry'.[67] Woodcock, a quietly spoken, bushy-eyebrowed Lancastrian and son of a Catholic mill worker, possessed not only a first-class degree in Philosophy, Politics and Economics from Oxford but also a strong bent towards conciliation.[68] He was immensely keen on the unions moving from demonstrations to penetrating the corridors of power. 'We left Trafalgar Square a long time ago,' he said in 1963.[69]

Research institutes (the American import 'think-tank' had yet to permeate British political and scholarly language) had already shown quite an interest in the mechanics and performance of French indicative planning as established at General de Gaulle's invitation by Jean Monnet and the Commissariat au Plan in Paris,[70] with its tripartite 'Modernization Commissions' to tackle not just postwar recovery but the legacy of prewar decades of underinvestment. Anthony Sampson, an admirer of Monnet and connoisseur of UK institutions, writing in his first *Anatomy of Britain* in 1962, noted how 'after a long lapse' since the era of Sir Stafford Cripps and the Central Economic Planning Staff in the late 1940s, 'thoughts of planning seeped back in 1961', into Whitehall: 'In the course of 1960 and 1961 the French idea of a *Commissariat au Plan* – of industrialists and civil servants sitting together setting targets for economic growth – slowly filtered into Great George Street by way of the National Institute of Economic and Social Research.'[71]

The infiltration of the senior ranks of the Treasury was far from complete, however. Its top official from 1959 to 1962, Sir Frank Lee, was a profound believer in competition as the spur and something of a planning sceptic. But heart trouble kept him away from his and the Chancellor's office when Lloyd, within days of announcing the July 1961 measures, despatched a letter on 8 August asking the FBI and the TUC to join him in taking a five-year forward look at the British economy with a view to matching growth plans to available resources.[72] Yet as Samuel Brittan, the scholarly economic journalist with the best access to early-Sixties Whitehall, later wrote:

> Without Sir Frank Lee, NEDC would have remained a paper dream. He was ill in Paris during the July crisis; when he came back to London and found that the planning 'decision' had been taken, he spared no effort to make it work, whatever he might personally have thought about 'planning'. Lee was fully behind Lloyd's insistence, against the advice of many senior Treasury officials, that the NEDC office must be distinct from the Treasury if the unions were to have confidence in its independence.[73]

The unions were sceptical, too, fearing the proposed NEDC would be a backdoor way for Whitehall to draw them into incomes policy, and agreed to join only following 'the government's assurance to Woodcock and his colleagues that the NEDC would not be involved in either the creation or administration of incomes policy . . .'.[74] Woodcock became an enthusiast for 'Neddy', but, as Lloyd recorded in his diary note of the crucial meeting between the two of them sealing the NEDC deal on 11 January 1962, he

> began with a curious statement about the wages pause. He said that I would get no credit from 'history', the 'clever boys' including himself would still say how badly matters had been handled, but in fact I had by the wages pause performed a great public service. I really had concentrated public attention upon incomes policy. He had told the TUC this. He then repeated his thesis that the TUC were impotent and that I must not expect any help from them . . .

– though he did go on to say that NEDC would give the TUC an important bridgehead into Whitehall.[75]

Certain 'red lines', as they would be called today, were, however, drawn as part of getting industry, government and unions to sign up. The unions insisted that incomes policy be kept on one side; the Treasury that exchange rate policy (i.e. devaluation of the pound) would be off limits.[76] Generally speaking, the tough task Lloyd experienced in selling 'Neddy' showed that planning was not universally and naturally seen as an idea whose time had come in Britain, as opposed to France, whence the Treasury had despatched a team of officials in the autumn of 1961, led by Sir Edward Boyle, Financial Secretary to the Treasury, and Otto Clarke, for what Richard Thorpe has described as 'an eye-opener' visit to the Commissariat au Plan and the Ministry of Finance in Paris, encountering 'a sense of urgency totally absent in Britain'.[77]

The British team were hugely impressed by what they found. Clarke wrote up 'The Lessons of French Experience' for wider circulation in Whitehall. That note, to his credit, contained some important caveats (France was not alone in western Europe in experiencing rapid growth; it did not run a world currency as the UK did and would always devalue the franc rather than cut production). Clarke asked:

> To what extent is the French economic recovery attributable to 'Le Plan'? Not necessarily at all, for other war-shattered countries (Germany, Italy, Austria, Holland, Japan) have all had at least as great expansions of production (and without the devaluations of currency). But the consensus of opinion of the party (and indeed of the French themselves) was that 'Le Plan' had made a powerful contribution: without it, in the chaotic political background of the Fourth Republic, it was difficult to believe that a steady course of investment and growth could have been maintained: 'Le Plan' had provided a standard around which French business could rally.
>
> Moreover, the French (like the British) have institutions which are detrimental to growth, and without the strong pressure of 'Le Plan' these forces might well have prevailed . . . It is admitted, however, that this single-minded devotion to the expansion of production has been ranked above the fate of the franc. Such indifference would have been inadmissible for Britain . . .

THE PURSUIT OF MODERNITY

In his final assessment, Clarke cast aside the caveats:

> When all qualifications have been made, however, the fact remains that a tremendous achievement has been accomplished, and a great feat of economic and industrial statesmanship in associating all bodies of economic interest and opinion with the Government in a concerted effort to make good the effect of a generation's neglect of the French economy followed by the destruction of war, and to break through to a modern-minded and progressive economy and a rapidly increasing standard of living. From the British point of view, it is surely here that the lesson is to be learnt.

Sir Edward Boyle supplemented the Clarke memorandum with a note on 'French Planning' for Selwyn Lloyd. Boyle, a gentle, scholarly man of great charm, took his boss through the intellectual geography of his Cabinet colleagues, particularly the free marketers who did not care for dirigisme in either its French or putative British forms, what Boyle called the 'important matter of doctrine'. Clarke's report, said Boyle, points out that

> the French system does tend to restrict competition. This does not worry them, since there is little veneration among French economists or civil servants for the sacred texts of economic liberalism . . . But we should not forget, when considering the lessons of the French experience, that some of our ablest colleagues in the government (e.g. Maudling, Powell) really do believe in the doctrine which perplexes our friends on the continent. They regard the whole concept of 'planning to avoid waste of resources' as a heresy since – they would argue – the market is the only proper test of whether resources have or have not been wasted.

Boyle told Lloyd, 'I don't myself agree with this view; but I think it *is* true that a serious attempt at planning on the French model would constitute an important change in our economic policy – more than just a shift in emphasis.' Boyle confessed to being 'a moderate planner' who recognized 'that market forces may have an important part to play':

> Because one believes that planning could help, say, to remove obstacles to growth, one is not denying that economically sensible pricing policies in the basic industries are just as important as ever they were.

What one *is* denying is that the principles of competitive free enterprise, as revised by Keynes, contain, so to speak, all that is necessary for a country's economic salvation – this is the creed whose attractive power the French find hard to understand.

So, for Boyle,

the particular interest of the French experiment from the British point of view lies largely in the fact that its political and economic assumptions don't really fit in with either of the schools of thought which have been dominant in Britain up till now. The doctrine behind French planning can't be described as socialist doctrine but it's some way removed from liberal doctrine also; it is, one might say, neither Wilsonite nor Maudlingite. But it seems to me legitimate to question, after six sterling crises, within fourteen years, whether either of these two schools of thought has quite measured up to the job. And I think we ought at least to start from the presumption that the French experiences has *something* to teach us.[78]

The conclusions of the Boyle–Clarke mission to Paris were similar to those reached after a conference in London the previous spring organized jointly by the National Institute of Economic and Social Research (NIESR), Political and Economic Planning (PEP) and the Institut de Science Économique Appliquée. The 'Note on the Conference' by Christopher Dow (an ex-Treasury economist now directing the NIESR) pertinently contrasts the notions of economic planning in the era of Stafford Cripps in late-1940s Whitehall and the new susceptibility to the economic success story across the Channel in the early Sixties. 'The object of the conference', wrote Dow,

was to meet the widespread desire in this country to know more about the functioning of French economic planning. It is probably true to say that, until recently, there has been relatively little interest in this country in the French experiment since the early days of post-war reconstruction . . .

This lapse of interest must undoubtedly be accounted for in terms of our own political bias. We may very well have confused what the French were doing with what we once did and have since ceased to do. The long-drawn, detailed discussions with representatives of numerous industries had something in common with the way in which export targets were fixed during the reconstruction period in this country after the war.

In the late Forties, Dow continued, the word 'planning' was 'inextricably associated with the use of direct controls, and with a tone of voice that implied that the Government had a right to dictate, and industry a duty to obey. French economic planning has been done in a different spirit . . . Ideally, at least, it is a matter not of *directives* but of a voluntary co-ordination of plans in which all those party to it concur.' The real impulse for renewed British interest, however, was a technocrats' version of the 'Chipped White Cups of Dover' syndrome, or, as Dow put it, if 'the French system now calls for reappraisal on our part . . . it is not so much because of the methods used, as of the results obtained under it'.[79]

As Edward Boyle had reminded Lloyd, Macmillan's Cabinet was not exactly overflowing with true believers in the new tripartite planning idea. In fact, it would not have got through Cabinet (with only John Hare, the Minister of Labour, and Lord Hailsham, the Minister for Science, backing Lloyd[80]) if Macmillan had not exerted his prime ministerial authority on 21 September 1961:

> Cabinet at 11. We discussed the Chancellor of the Exchequer's letter on 'Planning', wh is to go to employers and T. Unions . . . A rather interesting and quite deep divergence of view between ministers, really corresponding to whether they had old Whig, Liberal, laisser-faire traditions, or Tory opinions, paternalists and not afraid of a little 'dirigisme'. The Economic Ctee of the Cabinet had rejected the Chancellor of the Exchequer's first draft. (He is abroad – in Vienna for the International Monetary Fund meetings etc.) But I got it more or less restored – having prepared a new draft of my own wh I think retained the vital points.[81]

The Conservative politician best equipped to mount a critique of Macmillan and Lloyd, Enoch Powell, the Minister of Health, was not a member of the Cabinet at this stage. He became so, while remaining at Health, after the great purge in the July 1962 'Night of the Long Knives'.[82] As soon as he was free of collective responsibility, after refusing to serve in the new Douglas-Home Cabinet in October 1963 (so with little more than a year in office under Macmillan), Powell turned his intellectual blowtorch on the entire notion of government-led planning and the feebleness of managements in allowing themselves to be drawn into what, to a free marketer like Powell, was the delusion that 'Neddy'-stimulated discussions should be allowed to set levels for prices and profits in the name of economic efficiency – a radical step for peacetime Britain. In an article in *New Society* in February 1964, Powell declared:

> A little nonsense now and then is not a bad thing. Where would we politicians be if we were not allowed to talk it sometimes? But non-sense in massive doses, solemnly swallowed by large and representative bodies of men, and commended, without a flicker of an eyelid[,] to the nation at large, is very dangerous indeed. It soon becomes respectable. Before long no one who aspires to be taken seriously can dare to question it in public.[83]

Powell believed that the tilt towards planning and Macmillan-style dirigisme was 'an axe laid at the root of a fundamental principle', as he told a Glasgow audience two months later. 'The fault is not that there is an excess of "Tory freedom", there is a deficiency.'[84]

Powell also made a practical point in the *Observer* just before Christmas 1963, arguing that by creating NEDC the Conservatives had forged a weapon which the natural party of planning – Labour – could use against them in the general election due in 1964.[85] This is exactly what Harold Wilson was by then doing as Leader of the Opposition after Hugh Gaitskell's tragic and unexpected death in January 1963. 'For years', Wilson declared in the autumn of 1963,

> we have called for an economic plan for Britain ... Now even the Conservatives have accepted the principle of economic planning ... Government leaders who fought previous elections on the slogan 'Conservative Freedom Works' are now said to be toying with a new phrase: 'Conservative Planning Works'.

Wilson, already the master of timing and the ironic put-down, concluded: 'Labour, of course, welcomes this deathbed conversion.'[86]

Wilson cited the NEDC target of 4 per cent sustained annual growth, a possibility Gaitskell had believed 'well within our grasp'.[87] Even those generally sympathetic to some kind of British economic planning might have thought this unduly optimistic, given the 2.5–3 per cent trajectory the UK economy had been achieving since Cripps, his planners and his incomes policy-makers were operating in the late 1940s. They would have been amazed if they had discovered that Selwyn Lloyd had been talked down from a 5 per cent target by his Chief Economic Adviser, Alec Cairncross. As Sir Alec recalled nearly thirty years later:

> I remember the day when Selwyn Lloyd proposed to me that we should say five per cent. I was horrified. I thought he's assuming that you can just do anything. You just say, as a government, 'We will make it five per cent' and it's five per cent. Well, it's not like that. And I got him to put it down at four per cent, which I still thought was going to be a bit high. And indeed it was a bit high.[88]*

Reviewing the UK's economic performance during the 1960s from the perspective of the early 1970s, Alec Cairncross recognized that the crucial links between targeting and wrenching the British economy above its natural growth rate had never been forged – indeed, they were not forgeable:

> Governments are constantly being admonished to go for a policy 'of sustained economic growth' as if it were open to them by some simple set of enactments to raise the rate of economic growth. Nobody is obliging enough to explain how. Is there something that Governments can do to improve output per man-hour in the average factory – something which remains a secret from the employers who stand to gain most from knowing?

---

* As Edmund Dell wrote: 'Such a target was beyond the foreseeable capacity of the economy.' Whatever successive governments – or NEDC – did or did not do, the Sixties saw UK growth rates at or near the previous trajectory (Edmund Dell, *The Chancellors: A History of the Chancellors of the Exchequer, 1945–90* (HarperCollins, 1996), p. 271): UK growth averaged 2.9 per cent a year between 1950 and 1964; it fell to an average of 2.6 per cent between 1964 and 1970 (Alec Cairncross, *The British Economy Since 1945*, 2nd edn (Blackwell, 1995), p. 155).

Cairncross proceeded to answer his own question:

> I believe that the direct influence of governments on economic growth
> is relatively modest and that the common belief to the contrary in this
> country has been actually pernicious, tempting governments into poli-
> cies which had the very reverse of the effects for which they were
> designed . . .[89]

Cairncross was not alone in his scepticism about growthmanship
in the Treasury of the early 1960s. Douglas Allen, who would later
become Permanent Secretary to both Labour's purpose-built growth
ministry, the Department of Economic Affairs, and the Treasury,
thought the same.

Speaking, as Lord Croham, on the BBC Radio 4 *Analysis* documentary 'From Clogs to Clogs?', which I made with Caroline Anstey
in 1991, he recalled the 1961–2 'doctrine' as

> a belief that you looked at what you believed was your past rate of
> expansion in the economy and said we've got to do better than that so
> we add a percentage. And that's the objective and, if we work on that
> basis and convince everybody we can sustain it, then investment will
> follow in behind it and perhaps the unions will comply with that and,
> therefore, the economy will expand.

But, for Croham, who worked in the Central Economic Planning
Staff in the late 1940s and retired from Whitehall as head of the
Home Civil Service in 1977, the fluid factors that result in economic
growth remain a mystery fifty years on from those nascent-NEDC
days,[90] as they did at the time: 'Well, of course, nobody really knows
why an economy expands. You can believe if you put more investment in the right places it will expand faster. But this idea of indicative
planning and taking a pre-achieved rate of something like two and a
half per cent and saying, "OK, we're now going for four or four and
a half", or whatever it was, is just a load of nonsense.'[91]

Yet to all the players in the NEDC, the Treasury (the Chancellor
of the Exchequer usually chaired it), TUC Congress House and
Federation of British Industries headquarters in 1961–2 as well as
Macmillan, it was plain that the existence of the Paris Commissariat
au Plan *had* coincided with a French economic miracle.

To Macmillan's credit, he knew 'Neddy' was a fragile thing as he told his Cabinet at the end of May 1962, in a unique tape-recorded opening soliloquy about the economic and political problems facing the government, that 'We have . . . the NEDC . . . it is a tender plant and we must be careful with it. Still the NEDC has decided whether 4 per cent gross [sic] per annum is what we ought to try to go for . . .' But, plainly, he had already succumbed to what Cairncross, Croham and Enoch Powell would see as one of the delusions of the early 1960s: 'It [four per cent growth] is not a thing you get by waiting, like a child that just grows as long as it eats enough . . .'[92] After the disastrous Orpington by-election result, Macmillan was attempting to nudge his Cabinet towards acceptance of a National Incomes Commission as another instrument of beneficial intervention to set alongside the National Economic Development Council.

Anthony Sampson caught best the combination of tentativeness and novelty of the NEDC in 1962 (it first met on 7 March with Lloyd in the chair). 'It is still too early', he wrote at the time,

> to assess the effects of Neddy: it is not intended to be such a close and powerful council as in France – where the technocrats of industry and the civil service work in harmony, without much trouble from the politicians or the chairmen. But the idea of planning appears to have come back to stay, and the consequences of this are enormous . . .

It would 'inevitably', thought Sampson, 'produce a new and powerful "Establishment" tending towards the French pattern' and it would transform the Treasury too, for '[p]lanning means urging expansion and optimism, staking claims for the future, producing a climate of growth and confidence, which is the antithesis of candle-ends [Gladstonian cheeseparing]'.[93]

Selwyn Lloyd sat down that March afternoon at No. 1 Bridge Street (just down the road from the Treasury) to tell the employers and the trade unions on the fledgling NEDC that their job was to 'seek agreement upon ways of improving economic performance, competitive power and efficiency, in other words to increase the rate of sound growth'.[94] But, as Lloyd spoke, Macmillan's fears that he was simply not up to the job of being a transformingly fluent modernizing Chancellor of the Exchequer were waxing. Within a few weeks,

Macmillan's Principal Private Secretary, Tim Bligh, was drawing up a list of those ministers the Prime Minister might wish to sack from his Cabinet and Lloyd (he was fifty-seven) was not among the group of over-55s (Butler, Home and Henry Brooke) that Macmillan 'would want to keep'.[95] It was already apparent inside the innermost circle of No. 10 that the pursuit of modernity would require political butchery and a touch of a (relative) youth policy in the Cabinet Room.

The months before the abattoir of the July 1962 reshuffle show Macmillan at his most ruthless and brutal. On Sunday 4 March 1962, as Lloyd's diary makes plain, Macmillan was giving him the impression over dinner at Birch Grove (they were discussing the outlines of Lloyd's forthcoming Budget) that he [Lloyd] could well be Macmillan's successor in No. 10:

> Talks about the future. He will have to decide six months before next election whether he will continue as PM or not – that means March 63 if election is autumn 63, or Oct 63 if election is May 64. If he is going to resign he must give his successor a chance. He would have to reconstruct the Government with people who were going to continue after the election – win or lose. Several would want to go – Charles Hill – Ernest Marples – Harold Watkinson – Jack Maclay – perhaps Alec Home – perhaps Hailsham – certainly Mills. He thought Eccles would probably go this July. He thought Thorneycroft might go. Soames, Hare, Brooke, self, Heath, Maudling, Erroll, Sandys would stay on [Macleod, curiously, is missing here]. Kilmuir would do what was wanted – he might stay on as Lord President. Butler would not stay on unless PM or prospect of it. I said, 'What about myself?' He said, 'You would have to stay on if PM'. I said I was not sure I wanted this. He talked again about his advice to the Queen to ask Home and Kilmuir for advice as to his successor. He was very good. He did not propose to write his memoirs unless he was bankrupt. [He eventually wrote *six* volumes though he was far from bankrupt.][96]

For all the cruelty involved when one eavesdrops retrospectively upon that March 1962 dinner, there is some evidence that Macmillan had for a time considered Lloyd to be a genuine successor. Lloyd did possess considerable qualities – a hard-working doggedness, loyalty to colleagues – but, sadly for him, flair, style and a way with words were not among them. Tom Caulcott, who joined Lloyd's Private Office in the Treasury as his number two Private Secretary in October 1961, wrote a private account of his dismissal as Chancellor in the days after his sacking. This is from its opening paragraph:

> From when I became his private secretary all the signs were that Selwyn Lloyd had a very close personal relationship with the Prime Minister, Harold Macmillan. It was not uncommon for them to have long private talks together besides the many official meetings ... which they both attended. My predecessor had told me that on journeys abroad which the Prime Minister had made he had written to the Queen to say who he recommended to be called on to form a government if he was killed (this is a standard practice) and named Selwyn Lloyd. I did not know if this had happened during my time with S. L., but we did see one minute from the P.M. in the Private Office in late 1961 which said that in the event of a war emergency two deputy prime ministers would be appointed, to be in different places, and that these two would be S.L. and R. A. Butler.[97]

Tom Caulcott goes on to record that: 'Forewarnings of a break in the close relationship between the P.M. and S.L. came over a period of some two months before 13 JULY 1962', the day Lloyd's sacking was made public:

> These were all small incidents in themselves. They range from reports of S.L. having been somewhat sharply interrupted by the P.M. at Cabinet, through remarks made by the P.M. to his private secretaries that S.L. never produced any new ideas, to the exclusion of S.L. from some talks at Chequers in late June 1962 when the next stage of the incomes policy was being planned – the ideas which led to the National Incomes Commission announced by the P.M. on 26 July 1962. But S.L. remained completely involved in all Government policy and if he had any feeling that he was losing the P.M.'s confidence he neither referred to it nor showed it by his actions. He did not know that the P.M. had decided to get rid of him. He was expecting to speak in the economic debate when the next stage of the incomes policy and the other measures which had been grouped together as the 'New Approach' were going to be announced. We were collecting material for him for that debate.[98]

We are eavesdropping here on the workings of that most sensitive and swift of instruments for transmitting both hard information and rumour – the Whitehall private office network.

Macmillan had intended that Lloyd would still be at the Treasury when the National Incomes Commission (inevitably christened 'Nicky', the twin of 'Neddy'*) was set up.

Originally, Macmillan had planned a major reshuffle at the end of the summer recess before Parliament gathered in the autumn of 1962 for its new session.[99] In early July he decided to bring it forward, possibly to get it over with before the next political season began. His Press Secretary, Harold Evans, wrote in his diary that in 'my note of the 7th [July] I recorded that it had been decided to go ahead with the reconstruction before the recess, and that at least six Cabinet Ministers would go. Selwyn Lloyd was at the centre of it . . .'[100] The previous day Macmillan had lunched with Rab Butler and the Chief Whip, Martin Redmayne. As Butler recalled in his memoir, *The Art of the Possible*: 'They had asked me what I would do if I were Prime Minister and forming a new government, since, said Macmillan, "That is virtually what I want to do now." I replied it would be easier for someone starting from scratch. On being cross-examined about the Treasury, I said I would make a change but we would miss the Chancellor from the government altogether.'[101]

On 8 July Macmillan penned a diary entry in which he placed his most unvarnished assessment (which corroborates what Tom Caulcott and David Hubback were picking up on the private secretaries' net):

> I am sure it is necessary to make the vital change at the Treasury. Selwyn – of whom I am very fond and who has become a true and loyal friend since I became P.M. seems to me to have lost his grip. He is, by nature, more of a staff officer than a commander [a big minus in Macmillan's vocabulary; he would later say the same of Ted Heath[102]]. But lately, he seems hardly to function in some vital matters – e.g. this Incomes Policy affair. The Pay Pause started a <u>year</u> ago, exactly. By the

---

* 'Nicky' was doomed from the start as the trade unions would have nothing to do with it. It set a norm of 2.5 per cent wage increase. It had no powers. All it could do was examine breaches after the event. This it did only four times before being abolished by the incoming Labour government in 1964.

end of this year, it was clear that it was to be succeeded by a more permanent policy. In spite of continual pressure from me, <u>nothing</u> at all was done, except long and fruitless discussions in Economic Policy Ctee and in Cabinet . . . and in despair wrote the new policy myself during the Whitsun holidays, with the help of two young men from the Cabinet Secretariat and Tim Bligh.[103]

What Macmillan did not record that day was the collateral impact on his thinking of terrible by-election performances by the Conservatives. Orpington had gone to the Liberals in March when Eric Lubbock switched a 14,000 Conservative majority in the 1959 election to a Liberal one of over 8,000. And in the very week of what was to be Lloyd's dismissal, Macmillan knew his party faced disaster in the Leicester North-East by-election (in the event the Conservative share of the vote fell from 48.1 per cent in 1959 to 24.2 per cent). The July 1961 measures contributed to a substantial weakening of the case for the Conservatives as skilled managers of the national economy. Also a factor was the strange, cumulatively perceptible feeling that the Conservatives had been around too long and were led by an increasingly weary Prime Minister.

Originally, the plan was for Macmillan to use a scheduled meeting with Lloyd in Admiralty House at 6 p.m. on Thursday 12 July (as the electors of Leicester North-East voted) to warn him that he would lose the Exchequer when the reshuffle was announced on the following Monday.[104] But the wrathful gods of politics and political gossip intervened.

On Wednesday 11 July Rab Butler attended a long-planned lunch with Lord Rothermere, proprietor of the *Daily Mail*, at Warwick House. As Lloyd's biographer, Richard Thorpe, puts it:

> In conversation with his host . . . Butler leaked details of Macmillan's long-term intentions. The front page of the *Daily Mail* next morning contained a story by the paper's political correspondent Walter Terry [who had been present at the lunch], headlined 'MAC'S MASTER PLAN'. Terry predicted that Butler, Lloyd and Macleod would be involved in an autumn Cabinet reshuffle, when 'Mr Lloyd may find himself in the House of Lords, as Lord Chancellor in place of Viscount Kilmuir'.[105]

Though inaccurate in several respects, Terry's story meant that Thursday 12 July was, in Harold Evans's words, 'when the button was pushed'[106] as rumours washed through Westminster, including that 'Rab has blabbed',[107] giving Evans a torrid time at that morning's daily briefing for the lobby correspondents.[108] Macmillan would later admit to his official biographer 'that he did the hatchet work clumsily'.[109] Alistair Horne's judgement is that '[c]oming on top of the cumulative effect of all the other stresses and pressures on him, the *Daily Mail* story had the effect of triggering off one of his rare losses of nerve, leading to a reflex reaction'.[110]

Poor Selwyn Lloyd seems to have had no inkling of the speed of his coming demise, let alone that there would be no Lord Chancellorship or any other Cabinet place for him, until late on the Thursday afternoon, as Tom Caulcott's note makes plain:

> On Thursday 12 July 1962 S.L. had an appointment to see the P.M. at 6 p.m. This appointment had been in the diary for over a week. I do not know when it was first made. D. F. Hubback . . . had reserved the time at the request of the P.M.'s office. There was no agenda, but this was not unusual. In fact there were some items which S.L. wanted to put to the P.M. including the proposal to repay the remainder of the I.M.F. Loan of July 1961. At some time after 4 p.m, T. J. Bligh, the P.M.'s Principal Private Secretary, came to our office. He went in to see S.L. and told him that when he saw the P.M. at 6 p.m. the P.M. would ask him to resign. This was the first I or S.L. knew of it. D. F. Hubback clearly had known in advance.[111]

Meanwhile, in Admiralty House, Macmillan was getting a terrible case of nerves: 'At P.Q.'s; visit from Nigerian Minister – Mr Njoku – meeting on Greater Malaysia – the fatal hour of 6pm, fixed for my interview with Selwyn, came.'[112]

Macmillan had no time during what Rab Butler called his 'Massacre of Glencoe'[113] to write up his diary. His record of his two days of bloodletting was penned in bed at Birch Grove on Saturday 14 July:

> I did my best – but it was a terribly difficult and emotional scene. It lasted ¾ hour. Naturally, I tried to persuade him of the need for a radical reconstruction on political grounds; that he had filled with

distinction the two highest posts – Foreign Sec and Chancellor of
Exr – and that (unless he aspired to leading the party, wh he had often
told me that he had not) now seemed the time for him to start a third
career [Lloyd was a lawyer by training] in business about which he
had often talked to me. But it was of no avail. I'm afraid that the truth
is that these events are always very bad and perh. the worst of all the
duties of a P.M. Selwyn refused a peerage; said he would stay in the
House and support his financial policy/ or, I suppose, criticise any
deviation from it.[114]

Lloyd, as Tom Caulcott recorded,

came back to the Treasury after the interview and he looked a broken
man. He got out the whisky and he, Hubback and I drank together.
He was most upset by the lack of warning. (We heard later that the
P.M. had said previously to his private secretaries that he would not
sack S.L. without a reasonable period of warning; but the leak in the
Daily Mail and evening papers of 12th July decided him to act at once
and announce the changes the next day). S.L. was not particularly
bitter in his complaints of the P.M. He had not been offered any other
government appointment.[115]

Macmillan was pretty broken-up, too, by that forty-five-minute
encounter in Admiralty House and his hope, expressed to Lloyd in
early March, that several of his Cabinet colleagues would be happy to
go proved plain wrong, not least because they had no warning of the
fate that awaited them. The Lord Chancellor, David Kilmuir, told
Macmillan that his cook would have been given greater notice.[116]

Enoch Powell, at his most mordant, would later say how as a non-
Cabinet minister attendee at Cabinet on 28 May 1962, hearing
Macmillan's soliloquy, post-Orpington, about the need for more intervention in general and an incomes policy in particular, 'I still relish
recalling how the heads which were to roll not long after nodded like
cuckoo-clocks in sycophantic approval.'[117] During a discussion on Cabinet government in 1990, Powell said working with Harold Macmillan
was 'like having a debate with Henry VIII in the chair. I always used,
in Macmillan's Cabinet, to imagine I was sitting in Henry VIII's council. I was conscious that he had the axe down by his chair.'[118]

That Friday, though he butchered six colleagues (with Lloyd that made seven – exactly one third of the Cabinet),* Macmillan was a highly anxious executioner – so nervous that Bligh prepared notes for him lest he dried up as, one by one, they trooped into the Cabinet Room:

Lord Mills – 10.15 a.m.
You are reconstructing your Cabinet and have to make a number of changes. You hope that after his many years of outstanding service to the country he will accept a Viscountcy [Macmillan underlined this].

Mr. Maclay – 10.30 a.m.
You are reconstructing your Cabinet and feel sure that he will agree that it would be right for you to appoint a new Secretary of State for Scotland (Mr. Michael Noble). You would like to recommend him for a CH [Companion of Honour] now and a Viscountcy later at a suitable time. ['Yes he agrees', Macmillan wrote by the CH. 'It's yours at any time', he scribbled next to the proposed Viscountcy].[119]

In the emotion of their sacking interview, Macmillan forgot to offer Lloyd the CH. Bligh rang him later and Lloyd said yes.[120] As the Liberal MP for North Devon, Jeremy Thorpe, biblically quipped of the political savagery over those two days in July: 'Greater love hath no man than this, that he lay down his friends for his life.'[121]

Butler, the triggerer, though he cannot have anticipated what was to happen over the next three days thanks to hints over lunch with Rothermere, was also a loser, though there is no admission of this – or of his indiscretion – in his memoirs. As his official biographer, Anthony Howard, disclosed, Butler had drafted a hand-written letter to Macmillan about the apparent loss of status involved in his losing the Home Office, even though he was to get the grand title of First Secretary of State as well as Minister in Charge of the Central Africa Office, as the Lobby were briefed, Macmillan giving him that most bitter of cups – the job of winding up the Central African Federation. His draft letter ended with a touch of what Howard called Rab's 'streak of self-pity' by

* The complete list of the victims was Lloyd, Kilmuir, Harold Watkinson (Defence), Charles Hill (Housing and Local Government), John Maclay (Scotland), David Eccles (Education) and Lord Mills (Minister without Portfolio).

declaring 'I ... think I shall be out on an African limb, as there has never yet been any clearly defined position for an undefined deputy.'*[122]

Butler behaved oddly throughout. At 10.30 the following Monday evening Harold Evans's phone rang in the Prime Minister's Press Office. It was Rab:

> His immediate purpose was not apparent but he began by saying, 'I haven't been in at all. I feel quite calm about it all because it *is* a revolution. I feel my neck all the time to see if it is still there.' But then, quickly, 'I do understand the Prime Minister's motives and I am behind him. I know why he got rid of Selwyn after six years. But it wasn't done properly. My two friends became too emotional.' After that, back to his own problems. 'I have had to find a room. I have no staff. I have had to do it all myself.'[123]

Very Rab.

Promotions went to Maudling (from colonies to the Treasury – the big winner); Powell (still Minister of Health but now with full Cabinet rank); Keith Joseph (Housing and Local Government); Edward Boyle (Education); Michael Noble (Scotland); Henry Brooke (from Chief Secretary to the Treasury to Home Office); Peter Thorneycroft (from Aviation to Defence); Reggie Manningham-Buller (from Attorney General to Lord Chancellor as Lord Dilhorne); Bill Deedes (to be Minister without Portfolio and responsible for press relations); John Boyd-Carpenter (from Pensions to Treasury Chief Secretary).

But the biggest loser was Macmillan himself. The July 1962 purge was seen as a mix of desperation, misjudgement and panic. He knew it straight away. On the Friday evening, Harold Evans popped into the Cabinet Room in Admiralty House to see him just before he left to brief the lobby journalists in the House of Commons Press Gallery. Macmillan was with the Cabinet Secretary, Sir Norman Brook: 'Of course, they will be saying I am an old man clinging like a limpet to power.'[124]

It was, in fact, Lloyd who had said this during their stressful conversation the previous evening, as he recorded:

> I said that we had frequently talked before about a government reconstruction at some stage but did not this sudden move savour of panic?

* This refers to Butler's appointment as First Secretary of State.

He said that the situation was desperate and something had to be done quickly. I said that I thought it was wrong psychologically to do it at this moment. I thought that if he intended a radical reconstruction he had much better wait until October. He said that the situation was too desperate for that. I said, 'Do you not think that they will say it is "the old man" who ought to go [Macmillan was 68]?' He said, 'Maybe.'[125]

On 13 July, Macmillan arrived 'absolutely exhausted' at Birch Grove and next morning read a scattering of the (largely hostile) daily newspapers. In bed that night in his mother's old bedroom, he wrote:

The dangers are

(a) A rally of extreme restrictionists to Selwyn. This has already happened with a bitter letter to Times from Nigel Birch.*
(b) Sense of 'panic' measures. It was unfortunate that Leicester by-election – where we were third, beaten by Liberal – was announced on Thursday night.
(c) Accusation agst me of 'disloyalty'. I have saved my skin by throwing my colleagues to the wolves. This will be pressed in spite of 6 years during wh I have been accused of just the opposite.
(d) More serious. Effect on market and sterling if the idea gets about that we are going to reverse engines and go in for a dangerously 'expansionist' policy [which is exactly what Macmillan and Maudling eventually did, as we shall see]. After discussion with Governor of the Bank, I got Maudling to issue a statement last night, to reassure in particular foreigners, etc. . . .[126]

There was another factor, which Macmillan did not itemize: very considerable sympathy among the Prime Minister's fellow Conservatives for Selwyn Lloyd as a wronged man, not least because he had not been offered another Cabinet post. The former Prime Minister Sir Anthony Eden, speaking at a Young Conservatives rally in his old constituency of Leamington Spa on 21 July, declared: 'I feel Mr

* Birch had resigned from the Treasury with Thorneycroft and Powell in January 1958. He wrote: 'For the second time the Prime Minister has got rid of a Chancellor of the Exchequer who tried to get expenditure under control. Once is more than enough' (*The Times*, 14 July 1962; Hennessy, *Having It So Good*, pp. 545–7).

Selwyn Lloyd has been harshly treated'; a remark which, naturally, the press picked up and which, Eden told Lloyd in a letter, was 'certainly received with remarkable enthusiasm by a crowd sitting out of doors in a cold gale of wind'.[127]

Macmillan was haunted, almost literally, by his dismissal of his Chancellor. Lloyd's marriage had broken up in the mid-1950s and Macmillan let him use Chequers when it was not needed for prime ministerial functions (Macmillan generally preferred to weekend at Birch Grove). Chequers became the permanent home of Lloyd's black Labrador, Sambo, looked after by Mrs Kathleen Hill, the curator of the PM's official country retreat. A fortnight after the Cabinet reshuffle, Macmillan summoned several of his ministers for a forum to discuss election strategy for a poll that might not be much more than a year away. As Macmillan

> sat on the terrace that balmy July evening, chatting expansively about the middle way ahead, other members of the entourage gradually became aware of the inquisitive presence of Sambo, walking along the line of the assembled company, vainly looking for his master. The dog eventually settled in front of Macmillan, gazing mournfully up at him. Those who were present never forgot the frisson that went through the gathering, nor the studied disregard with which Macmillan ignored the animal.[128]

Sambo stayed at Chequers, cared for by the devoted Mrs Hill, 'and became the founder of a Chequers dynasty of puppies. Eventually he was buried by the North lawn.'[129]

Macmillan could console himself that, with the butchery done, he had a Cabinet of younger modernizers at his disposal, Maudling at the Treasury in particular. (He noted on 17 July: 'short session of the new Cabinet 10.15–11. A curious feeling. It is very sad not to see David Kilmuir sitting opposite me, as for so long. Ld Home (For Sec) had taken his place. But there <u>was</u> a sense of freshness and interest.'[130])

It was to this still relatively new Cabinet that Macmillan unveiled his considered modernization strategy on Monday 29 October 1962, rather than preparing to inter them in their Third World War bunkers (Nikita Khrushchev had stood down over the Cuban missiles less than twenty-four hours earlier).[131] Those ministers who had heard his 28 May disquisition on 'the Orpingtonians' and 'the work-ing classes, as we are apt in this room to call them, but I suppose there's some new name for them now',[132]* would have found little to surprise them in the autumn version of Macmillan's springtime oral essay on the 'elements' in a modernizing blueprint.

It was certainly, by post-1979 standards, quite a left-wing pitch, built on a combination of state initiatives and public spending. 'If,' Macmil-lan had told them, 'we got the stability out of the general acceptance of the incomes policy ... some increase in government expenditure on the things we know are necessary – the housing, the slums, the universities, the schools – would follow.'[133] He meant it to be a big break with the past and that his ministers should realize this. They did: 'At 5pm the Cabinet met (with Ministers of Health [Powell], Power [Richard Wood] and PMG [Postmaster General, Reginald Bevins]) and listened to me expanding (for over an hour) my "Incomes Policy: A New Approach". They were exhausted, stupefied and temporarily silenced!'[134]

On 29 October Macmillan told his post-'Night of the Long Knives' Cabinet 'that great changes would be taking place in the next two decades in the pattern of population and industry' and that he 'would like to present them to his colleagues in the wider context of the mod-ernization of Britain' which 'had many aspects'.[135] Interestingly, he began with the government's own procedures and workload:

> First, there was the question whether the present machinery of Minis-terial Government was suitable for the conditions of to-day and the coming years. The burden on Ministers was becoming almost intoler-ably heavy, not merely in meeting the requirements of consultation as the basis for the collective responsibility of the Cabinet, but also in taking the growing volume of decisions which their Departments and the public expected them to take personally, and in facing the daily barrage of the press, radio and television.[136]

Early twenty-first-century eyes in Whitehall and Westminster, attuned to the demands of twenty-four-hour media, the internet and

---

* Certainly, Enoch Powell never forgot it: 'From that paper derived a series of socialist measures ... which were seen by him as the quid pro quo to the workers for co-operation in an inflation-free planned economy' (Enoch Powell, 'SuperWhig?', *Spectator*, 1 March 1980).

the 'blogosphere', would regard the Macmillan years as a lost age of media innocence and ease (especially before the unprecedented burst of press intrusion occasioned by the Profumo affair of 1963). But these things are relative. Macmillan was looking back to an era before what he called the 'hot, pitiless, probing eye' of television, in a speech in November 1961, drafted for him by Harold Evans, at the BBC's dinner to mark the twenty-fifth-anniversary of the official launch of BBC TV (still the nation's only channel). On top of his form, in his speech, which was televised live, the PM tackled a theme still familiar today in political conversations when he wondered aloud whether television's purpose was enlightenment or entertainment:

> I see no objection to making enlightenment as entertaining as possible. But it is not always easy on programmes on current affairs, for example. The entertainment formula in those programmes usually lies in what I believe are called 'confrontations' – clashes of personality combined with aggressive interviewing, which means that everybody should be as rude as possible within a short time to everybody else.[137]

And this at a time when, perhaps the young Robin Day apart, deference was still a power in the land, its media terrain included.

As for the burden upon ministers, early in his premiership Macmillan had commissioned a committee of privy counsellors chaired by Clem Attlee to look at it. Very little resulted of permanent value apart from the creation of the Chief Secretary post in the Treasury to relieve the Chancellor's load.[138] As he told the Cabinet on 29 October 1962, he was worried, too, about Parliament, both its procedures, which 'were designed for a less busy age', and 'the demands of [MPs'] constituencies'. Perhaps, he thought, the 'Government should . . . work out a plan to modernize their own machinery and that of Parliament, and seize the initiative in demonstrating that changes must be made to help the country to operate successfully in modern conditions'.[139]

Very little came of this either.* Indeed, the two parliamentary

---

* The most important procedural change in the continuous mechanisms of government on Macmillan's watch was the creation of the Public Expenditure Survey System following the Plowden Report of 1961. The brainchild of the brilliantly indefatigable Otto Clarke, it enabled Whitehall to plan its forward programmes on a five-year basis with funding uprated for rises in inflation. This was its Achilles

changes Macmillan did make that had the greatest enduring effect
were already agreed by the time he addressed the Cabinet at the end
of October 1962. The lesser of the two, as we have seen, was consenting to a fixed fifteen-minute period twice a week for Prime Minister's
Questions. The other, of far greater significance, was rescuing the
House of Lords from moribundity. The Conservative leader in the
Lords, 'Bobbety' Salisbury, had gravely warned a Cabinet Committee on Lords Reform, GEN 432, in February 1955 that the wholly
hereditary Upper House (the Law Lords and the Anglican Bishops
apart) needed 'a surgical operation' swiftly 'if the patient's life was to
be saved', or 'it would die through sheer lack of vitality'.[140]

The answer, as proposed by both Lord Palmerston and Walter Bagehot in the nineteenth century, was life peerages.[141] In *The English
Constitution* in 1867, Bagehot had famously written of the House of
Lords: 'Its danger is not in assassination, but atrophy; not abolition but
decline',[142] unless it could be transformed with the injection of a 'class
of respected revisers',[143] people with professional knowledge and experience. Ninety years after Bagehot's warning, the Macmillan government
acted upon this advice when Lord Home, Salisbury's successor as leader
in the Lords, introduced the Life Peerages Bill on 21 November 1957.
Not only would there be life peers, but women life peers. Taking them
'into a parliamentary embrace', said Lord Home, 'seemed to be only a
modest extension of the normal functions of a peer'.[144]

Labour had resisted the idea, not wishing to make the Lords more
effective and respectable. Macmillan called Gaitskell in for a chat
about it. The Labour leader was 'a little embarrassed – his party is
again divided by all this'.[145] Nevertheless, the Labour leadership
nominated life peers from the very first batch of fourteen (ten men
and four women*), who were announced on 24 July 1958. The Life

---

heel – though it endured for fifteen years before it gave way to cash planning and
cash limits before and during the economic crisis of 1976 (Peter Hennessy, *Whitehall*
(Pimlico, 2001), pp. 178–9).
* The most striking of the first creations were Barbara Wootton (as Baroness Wootton of Abinger), a great social scientist, economist and educator and friend of
Gaitskell's (Philip Williams, *Hugh Gaitskell* (Cape, 1979), p. 84); and Bob Boothby
(as Baron Boothby of Buchan and Rattray Head), Lady Dorothy Macmillan's lover
(though very few knew that at the time). 'Of course he must have it,' said Macmillan

Peerages Act 1958 'was to prove one of the most important legacies of the Macmillan government'.[146] Its cumulative effect has been to create that very house of 'respected revisers' Bagehot sought.[147]

It was his second modernizing theme that post-Cuba Monday morning in Admiralty House which Macmillan used to convey his latest version of the 'middle way' and consensus – 'that, in seeking a solution of the problem of population and employment, the choice did not simply lie between *laissez faire* and *dirigisme*. There was also the alternative of pragmatic compromise which was in line with the broad approach which the present Administration had inherited from their predecessors.' Not much could be done 'to reverse trends deriving from such fundamental forces as were drawing population towards the South-East' but '[i]t was out of the question to allow Scotland or the North-East or any large area to be abandoned to decay':

> The remedy did not lie in trying to preserve each individual commu-
> nity which had grown up for reasons long since irrelevant to modern
> conditions ... More imaginative changes and developments were
> required. The Highlands of Scotland, which had been the playground
> of the rich in the last century, might be developed into the playground
> of the masses, like the National Parks of North America. But the
> industrial belt in Scotland must remain industrial, in a modern and
> constructive form.[148]

Macmillan, to some derision, was shortly to despatch the ebullient Lord Halisham (who took to wearing a cloth cap for the purpose) to the North-East to see what could be done to revive the region ('the Opposition are very angry, so they must be afraid he may do some good'[149]).

His third modernizing theme that morning tackled the ever-present race between sunset and sunrise industries: 'The problem of indus-trial change tended at present to be viewed in terms of declining industries, such as the railways and shipbuilding. It was to these that

---

after Boothby had written in asking for a peerage, telling him he could have an hereditary one or a new life one, Boothby choosing the latter (Alistair Horne, *Mac-millan, 1957–1986* (Macmillan, 1989), p. 83; D. R. Thorpe, *Supermac: The Life of Harold Macmillan* (Chatto, 2010), pp. 419–20).

the Government gave most attention. It was important to put equal effort, investment and research into the industries that should grow in their place.'[150]

The paper on the 'Modernisation of Britain' Macmillan had circulated, by way of follow-up, to the Cabinet on 3 December 1962 is a disappointment partly because it was a minute to Maudling (Chancellor of the Exchequer) and Henry Brooke (Home Secretary) in their capacities as chairmen of respectively the Cabinet's Economic Affairs Committee and its Committee on Population and Employment. These two committees, taken together, were Macmillan's chosen instrument for co-ordinating modernization and what he called the 'more radical attack' that the stage now reached 'in our post-war history' required Britain to make 'upon the weaknesses of our economy, both productive and structural'.

'We face', he told his Cabinet, 'a situation in which the conditions of trade are becoming increasingly competitive and our commercial rivals increasingly better equipped to compete with us, while our own economy remains sluggish and "patchy".' Two things needed to be done:

(a) First, in order to enhance our competitive power and to ensure a level of exports commensurate with full employment at home, we have to increase our productivity by bringing our productive capacity into full use, by eliminating restrictive practices and by developing to the utmost the new methods which technology is bringing within our reach. Whatever the results of the Brussels negotiations [by this stage approaching their climax on Britain's application for EEC membership], this need is urgent. In or out of Europe, Britain needs to be brought up to date in almost every sphere of life.

(b) Second, we have to re-organise the structure of the island in such a way as to rectify the imbalance between south and north – between the 'rich' areas and the 'poor' areas, the over-employed regions and the under-employed regions – and redress the grave social anomalies which are created by this imbalance.

He urged his two modernization Cabinet committees to come up with ideas quickly as ingredients for 'the general theme of "The

Modernisation of Britain", which I should like to launch very early in the New Year'.[151] Macmillan, to his credit, had for all his growing fatigue, not lost his gownsman's instinct for thinking on quite a grand scale.

The diagnosis was candid, the philosophy a consensual mix of One Nation Disraelian Toryism with a dash of social democracy and *dirigiste* French planning– all nicely geared to UK entry into the EEC in about 1964 and a pleasing fourth general election victory on the way, achieved on the winning theme of caring modernization. This was the domestic and political equivalent of his 'Grand Design' for foreign policy, with which, of course, it was symbiotically linked. Had he pulled it off, Harold Macmillan would have gone down as one of the great British Prime Ministers – certainly up there with Clem Attlee and Margaret Thatcher in the postwar pantheon. But, as we shall see, December 1962 was just about the last moment Macmillan could have told himself it was all still possible.

What his government needed in the late autumn and early winter of 1962 was another way of encouraging the modernizing activities that were already underway, quite apart from the 'Neddy', the 'Nicky' and the beginnings of regional policy that the year had brought into being. The early Sixties balanced sunrises (civil nuclear power stations; motorways) and senescents to be rigorously restructured or invested in (railways;* hospital buildings; new universities; 'systems-built' housing) plus a dash of conservation (how to rid towns and cities of excessive traffic), though this last was seriously limited. If Macmillan had conducted an audit of this agenda in late 1962, it might have looked like this:

---

* It remains a mystery to me how, for example, Macmillan (a railwayman himself of a kind; he still possessed the free 'gold pass' as a former director of the Great Western pre-nationalization (Thorpe, *Supermac*, pp. 505–6)) could have refused to reprieve the magnificent Euston Arch despite the eloquent pleas of John Betjeman and a considerable level of pressure. Philip Hardwick's huge 1837 Doric Arch did not survive the mania for planning and modernization in its crassest form, being pulled down in late 1961 and early 1962 to make way for a new Euston Station that has remained unloved from that day to this and which, indeed, could have been built as the blot as it is without the Arch having to go. Betjeman had written in 1933 that if ever 'vandals' destroyed it 'it would seem as though the British constitution had collapsed' (cited ibid., p. 506).

CIVIL NUCLEAR POWER

The post-Suez 1957 plan to triple the still novel, two-year-old civil nuclear station building programme to between 5,000 and 6,000 megawatts by the end of 1965 was trimmed in 1960 to 5,000MW by the end of 1968, partly in recognition of problems encountered in the pace of construction.[152] It still remained a formidable undertaking on the rim of a new and, as it was almost universally regarded then, transforming, beneficial and economic (over the long-term) phenomenon. What is more, by the early Sixties a fast-breeder reactor programme was underway at Dounreay on the northern tip of mainland Scotland near Thurso in which uranium, it was hoped, could be used with such efficiency, thanks to the reuse of its fuel both U-238 and U-235 (compared to so-called 'once-through' reactors using mainly U-235),[153] that by the late 1970s the production of civil nuclear power would be transformed[154]* By the end of 1962, four Magnox nuclear reactors were feeding power into the UK National Grid (Calder Hall, 1956, the first in the world to do so; Chapelcross, 1959; Berkeley, 1962; Bradwell, 1962). Civil nuclear power, however, the shining hope of the Fifties, was, in fact, beginning to lose some of its radiance in the early Sixties.

MOTORWAYS

When in 1962 Ernest Marples, Minister of Transport, said his aim was for Britain to have a thousand miles of motorway by the early 1970s, a mere 150 miles existed.[155] Macmillan himself had opened the first stretch, the 8¼ miles of the Preston bypass in Lancashire, later to form part of the M6, on 5 December 1958 ('A great thing in itself,' he declared, 'but a finer thing as a symbol, as a token of what is to follow,' before, characteristically, quoting Robbie Burns to a chilled and no doubt baffled crowd: 'I'm now arrived thanks to the gods, thro' pathways rough and muddy'[156]).

* The dream was never realized in the UK; in the autumn of 2010 I witnessed the deconstruction and decontamination work inside the Dounreay sphere, once perhaps the most important British symbol of nuclear promise.

Here was a bit of planning and investment that delivered according to forecast and pretty well to budget:[157]

Britain's motorway network, 1958–72

Years	Miles finished	Cumulative total
1958	8	8
1959	65	73
1960	22	95
1961	40	135
1962	15	150
1963	49	199
1964	99	298
1965	57	355
1966	40	391
1967	72	473
1968	76	549
1969	50	599
1970	58	657
1971	133	789
1972	247	1036

Remarkably, the final motorway network looked very much like the 'Suggested Scheme of Motorways' produced in February 1942 by the Institution of Civil Engineers Post War National Development Committee at a time when in Europe only the King's enemies in Germany possessed them.[158]

UNIVERSITIES

By the early 1960s Britain's university student population had more than doubled from 50,000 to 118,000 since 1938–9, the last year of interwar peace, but the proportion of the eighteen-plus age group attending them was tiny, still only 4 per cent in 1962 (a fall from what was then the postwar peak of 4.2 per cent in 1959).[159] A mood was taking hold, however, that this represented another example of self-defeating British underinvestment in terms of skills and competitive power, a view shared by the energetic David Eccles at the Ministry of Education (one of those purged in July 1962).

In February 1961 Eccles appointed Professor Lionel Robbins, top-flight economist and one of the London School of Economics' greatest ever educators,[160] to review the range and content of higher-education provision in the UK (he was expected to recommend a big boost for science and technology courses, which he did). By the time he reported in October 1963, Macmillan had just been replaced by Sir Alec Douglas-Home (as he now became, having shed his Earldom to enable him to sit in the Commons).

But in late 1962, a great expansion was already planned. In 1959, the peak year, Sir Keith Murray, chairman of the University Grants Committee, had persuaded the government that the university population should grow to 175,000 by the late 1960s/early 1970s.[161] And in July 1961 the government sanctioned the building of seven new universities: Sussex (just outside Brighton); East Anglia (Norwich); York; Essex (just outside Colchester); Lancaster; Kent (in Canterbury); and Warwick (on the outskirts of Coventry).[162]

Universities were in vogue, students were a good thing and the state was going to give them all means-tested maintenance support and pay all their fees (as recommended by the Anderson Committee which reported in 1960[163]). It seemed, and, indeed it was, a golden age to be a don – all those new jobs – and a student – all those grants.

HOSPITALS

Over the first ten years of the National Health Service, not a single new hospital had been built; there had been extensions and improvements, but between 1948 and 1961, only £157 million had been spent on such capital works. Enoch Powell's arrival at the Ministry of Health began to change that. Powell deserves to be 'remembered as one of the few great Ministers of Health',[164] not least because of the hospital building programme he launched in January 1962 – a spend of £500 million over ten years to create ninety new hospitals and substantially improve another 134, together with a further 356 improvement schemes costing £100,000 or more.[165]

Powell's other great achievement was to begin a process of dramatic change which, with the aid of new drugs, was to rescue from the asylums considerable numbers of the mentally ill (who, Powell noted in his classic short book *Medicine and Politics*, had never had the public or the political support they deserved[166]). In March 1961 he used a speech to the National Association of Mental Health to announce a halving of mental patients in long-stay institutions to 75,000 by 1975, bringing to bear the power and imagery that he possessed in abundance (gifts that would lead to immense controversy when he applied them to immigration later in the decade). It is still remembered as the 'water-towers speech': 'There they stand, isolated, majestic, imperious, brooded over by the gigantic water-tower and chimney combined, rising unmistakable and daunting out of the countryside – the asylums which our forefathers built with such immense solidity.'[167]

HOUSING

If there is one area of retrospective consensus on postwar social policy it is that reaching for the sky as a way of helping solve the nation's housing shortage was a disaster. The term 'tower block' is, quite simply, code for the folly of planning and the indiscriminate break-up of community life based on back-street neighbourliness and extended family. The greatest *mea culpa* came from the lips of the young modernizer of 1962–4, and beneficiary of the July purge, Sir Keith Joseph. Even allowing for the fact that Joseph was temperamentally prone to anguished remorse, the degree of his regret when interviewed in November 1973 was striking: 'I was genuinely convinced I had a new answer. It was prefabrication and, Heaven help me, high blocks ... the best of intentions and the worst of results.'[168]

It was Joseph's predecessor at the Ministry of Housing, Duncan Sandys, who in 1955 changed the subsidy regime to local authorities to encourage them to build upward with unintended consequences that, to be fair to Sandys, would have been difficult to foresee. Until now, he told the Commons, all flats had received the same level of subsidy:

> Since construction, in practice, costs more as you go higher, the result has been that flats in low blocks have been more heavily subsidised in relation to costs than flats in high blocks. Apart from being inequitable, this has unintentionally influenced local authorities to concentrate on building blocks of three, four and five storeys, which, I believe, many honourable members would agree are most monotonous.[169]

If only they had stayed at 'three, four and five'; boredom would have been a price worth paying to avoid broken lifts and rubbish chutes, intimidating hallways and balconies, children unable to play outside in the eye line of their parents and, later, the rotting of the prefabricated materials and the 'concrete cancer' which eventually precipitated the demolition programmes that seriously got underway from the 1980s onwards, though the problems, indeed the perils, of living in tower blocks remained high in public consciousness well over half a century later.

But in the autumn of 1955 when Sandys changed the rules there was no dissent:

> From then on, the taller the block the bigger the subsidy in order to eliminate the financial advantages of erecting low-rise buildings. On such wonderfully egalitarian and aesthetic grounds, the explosion in high-rise was, almost unintentionally, launched. Within four years, the proportion of high-rise had risen five-fold to 15 per cent of the construction programme, and by 1966 it accounted for 26 per cent of all homes started.[170]

THE RAILWAYS

One word, a name, is all that it takes to revive memories of railways in the early Sixties – Beeching. The life of rail is still, well over fifty years later, divided between before Beeching and after Beeching. Examination of his March 1963 report, *The Reshaping of the Railways*, awaits in chapter 6. But, as Macmillan attempted to woo his Cabinet to across-the-board modernization in late 1962, two things were plain: the railways simply could not go on as they were; and Dr Richard Beeching, the physicist recruited from ICI to run the British Railways Board at a then astronomical salary of £24,000 (Cabinet ministers got £5,000),[171] had a brief to be ruthless and to cull and to substantially reduce British Railways' annual deficit, then running at £159 million.[172] For Anthony Sampson, publishing his first *Anatomy of Britain* in that year before *The Reshaping of the Railways*, Beeching was the very incarnation of the kind of new, technocratic, unsentimental man (Maidstone Grammar School; Imperial College, London) that laggardly Britain needed in abundance:

> I found Dr. Beeching one of the most reassuring of all the administrators I talked to. He approaches his vast problem – itself a kind of caricature of all Britain's problems – with the dispassionate expertise of a surgeon ... He is a big, relaxed man with a high dome, a bristle moustache and a slow gravelly voice ... The contrast with [Ernest] Marples [Minister of Transport], short and tense, is immediate but the two evidently fit together; there are some people who say that Marples' most important achievement was the hiring of Beeching.[173]

Beeching brought about the end of branch-line Britain. But, for romantics of a certain age (including the author), the great caesura was the passing of the steam engines, the product of the 1955 modernization plan, agreed by the British Transport Commission, Whitehall and the Cabinet, which outlined the end of our trainspotting world (and much more, given the aesthetic satisfactions of steam) with the progressive arrival of diesel and electric locomotives.[174] By the time Richard Beeching was wowing Anthony Sampson this was well underway.

During the great snow and protracted freeze of the winter of 1962–3, the old Great Western Class 2800s would steam past the playing fields of Marling School, Stroud, in drift-bound Gloucestershire before roaring up Sapperton Bank beyond Chalford to carry their South Walian coal through Swindon and on to London in a kind of last defiant service to a needy country. But going the other way were increasingly frequent and hugely depressing little clusters of dead locomotives being pulled by a single live one to the breakers' yards in Sharpness by the

Severn or Barry Island beyond Cardiff. It had to happen. Steam was labour intensive, uneconomic and deeply environmentally unfriendly. But those locomotives had life; they had individual characters, whereas their successor machines have neither. They left a psychological and poetic hole which the occasional breath of coalsmoke and the sound of a whistle at a preservation site can ease but never replace.*

One of my most vivid early-Sixties memories is of a drippingly wet August day in 1961 when, unable to walk in the Lake District Fells, my father drove me and my mother in our tiny black Austin A35 from Coniston, where we were staying, through Kendal to Tebay, where the line from Euston to Glasgow meets the northern uplands. Leaving Mum in the car (knitting, if I remember), we walked down past the railwaymen's terraces to the engine shed with its huge coaling tower.

To my surprise and delight, the driver of the waiting and very substantial tank engine on banker duty asked if we'd like to come up on the footplate. Tea was served, the colour of oxtail soup and of industrial strength, from an aluminium can kept close to the fire hole. I can taste it, heavily sugared, to this day and sense the wind and the rain lashing across the rails at the northern end of the shed.

The driver, who can't have been far off retirement, explained that the new Peak Class and other express diesels didn't need banking – so there was less to do these days. Steam locos still did, and you knew they were coming and required shoving if they sounded their whistles way down the Lune Valley. As if on cue, one did. A Black Five shot through Tebay station pulling a Birmingham–Glasgow express. The driver eased his Class 4 Fairbairn tank slowly into action (telling us that it was pointless to apply too much power too swiftly on wet rails as the younger drivers tended to do).

We caught up with the express some way up Shap, pushed it slowly

---

* We all carry our nostalgias. Steam is mine and I'm far from alone. Towards the end of his life in the early 1970s, the Benedictine monk and unmatched scholar of monasticism Dom David Knowles (see his *The Monastic Order in England* (Cambridge University Press, 1940), and *Christian Monasticism* (Weidenfeld & Nicolson, 1969)) was asked about the transient things in life he had once supposed to be permanent: 'with a rueful smile he observed that of all things in his world [he was born in 1896 and died in 1974] he had supposed the Latin Mass and the steam engine the most stable and lasting – and both were gone' (Christopher Brooke, in C. Brooke et al., *David Knowles Remembered* (Cambridge University Press, 1991), p. 25).

over the summit and ran back light to Tebay, where Dad and I made our farewells. I glowed for hours on the way back to Mrs Grizedale's at Coniston, over dinner and till bedtime. I would have glowed even more if I'd realized this would all be gone so quickly (though steam survived longest in the north-west, not finishing until summer 1968). I've been back in Tebay a couple of times. The station has gone. No sign of the remains of the shed or the coaling tower. The railwaymen's cottages survive. The M6 traffic roars its way north and south just up the hill from where the shed was. Deeply dull Virgin electric sets and cross-country diesels rush through periodically (the Pendolinos have a certain style but they can't match a Black Five let alone a Royal Scot or a Coronation).

The saddest photographic elegy for pre-modernization railway Britain for me was taken near the New England shed just north of Peterborough when my all-time favourite locos, the streamlined Gresley A4 Pacifics had given way to the huge Deltic diesels on the East Coast route to Edinburgh. There they waited, grey, grimy and neglected, until the metal-cutters were let loose on their exquisite exteriors. Such was the mania for modernization that not until as late as December 1960 was it decided *Mallard* (which had flashed down Stoke Bank between Grantham and Peterborough at 4.22 p.m. on Sunday 3 July 1938, briefly touching 126 miles per hour – her never-to-be-beaten world record) would be preserved.[175] And she can be viewed, glorious in her prewar blue livery, at the National Railway Museum in York). The 'Blue Streak', as the press christened her after her great triumph, *sans pareil*.[176]

In December 1960, when *Mallard*'s preservation order came through, there was another great British enterprise built on coal and steam that was about to make way, too. And here, in contrast to their attempts to modernize the economy, ministers in Whitehall really could determine outcomes and radical shifts.

4

Dash for the Exit

. . . one of the most profound changes in the history of the
world. The Romans never did anything like it . . . one of
the great moments . . .

Rab Butler on the end of the British Empire, 1983[1]

Historians have offered four main options for explaining the
end of empire. These may be put in the form of a cricketing
analogy. Either the British were bowled out (by nationalists
and freedom-fighters), or they were run out (by imperial overstretch and economic constraints), or they retired hurt
(because of a collapse of morale and 'failure of will'), or they
were booed off the field (by international criticism and especially United Nations clamour).

Ronald Hyam, 2006[2]

Has anybody ever thought of a more dignified way of getting
out of Empire?

Lord Charteris, Private Secretary to the Queen,
1952–77, on the Commonwealth[3]*, 1989*

It can be said that once Europe had shed her colonies, it
became a healthier and happier place. The same could not,
alas, be said of all her former colonial possessions.

Professor Sir Michael Howard, 2009[4]

He [Sir Richard Turnbull, penultimate Governor of Aden] told
me that when the British Empire finally sank beneath the waves
of history, it would leave behind it only two monuments: one

was the game of Association Football, the other was the
expression 'Fuck off'.

Denis Healey, Secretary of State for Defence,
1964–1970, 1989[5]

It is hard to imagine a proconsul of any other empire coining an imperial epitaph quite like that. In one sense, Turnbull was absolutely right.
The game of Association Football and that characteristically British
phrase 'Fuck off' adorn daily life in, some would say, a depressingly
natural way all over the former imperial possessions forty years and
more since the departing Sir Richard was photographed raising his
trilby in farewell salute to Aden's lance-carrying Federal Camel Corps
on 16 May 1967. It is near impossible now for all but a handful of
Brits to fathom the Turnbulls and their later imperial world – let alone
the countless colonial officials, soldiers, teachers, policemen and mis-
sionaries who went before them. As Denis Healey wrote:

> Such men were the last of Britain's proconsuls, a remarkable breed,
> who brought a degree of order and justice to millions of people who
> had known much less, but ultimately wanted much more. They do not
> deserve less respect because the tides of history have washed away so
> much of their achievements.[6]

Unscrambling the empire was just as vexing and time consuming
for Macmillan and his ministers as their attempts to prepare for the
geopolitical-economic imperatives of the late-twentieth and early
twenty-first centuries. The history student of today, looking back to
the early 1960s, appreciates in an instant the complications of the
Britain and Europe question. It is much more difficult to understand
why the problems of the Central African Federation (of Northern
Rhodesia, Southern Rhodesia and Nyasaland) took up so much
Whitehall time and caused such a degree of tension inside Macmillan's Cabinet. The loss of empire did not bite into the British psyche
in the way the 'psychodrama' of Europe[7] began to do in the Sixties
and with increasing powers to disturb throughout the following
decades. Perhaps we really were, as Bernard Porter described us,
'absent-minded imperialists'. Looking back forty years on from the

Macmillan and Douglas-Home governments' rush to decolonize, Porter reckoned:

> If the empire made so uneven and generally superficial an impression on British society and culture while it was a going concern, it follows that its dissolution did not need to have much of an impact either. This is borne out by the equanimity with which most Britons appeared to accept this fate in the post-World War II period, with only a small minority of Conservative zealots actively seeking to halt the process ... and with the single body dedicated to actually reversing it, the 'League of Empire Loyalists' (1954–67), being rightly regarded as a 'fringe' movement.[8]

There was, as Porter recognizes,[9] the notion of the Commonwealth (to which virtually all the released colonies and protectorates instantly signed up) to bring balm to bruised or even faintly regretful psyches. But had I been a politician or civil servant in the weeks and months after Macmillan's 'Wind of Change' speech in Cape Town on 3 February 1960, I would not have bet my pension on Britain's exit from the 'great game' of empire producing (Rhodesia apart) a sigh rather than a withdrawing squeal, if not a leonine roar. Perhaps this was due in part to the front benches of both political parties thinking by the early Sixties that the great game of territorial empire was now up, and withdrawal was the only viable policy. There was, for example, no equivalent of the fissures and fractiousness that the prospect of withdrawal from the European Union caused UK politics over half a century later.

Maybe the pursuit of affluence and modernity was bound to trump residual notions of civilizing missions or the more troublesome aspects of sustaining a world role, not to mention the relief of avoiding National Service in Malayan jungle, Kenyan bush or Cypriot backstreets. Philip Larkin certainly thought so by the end of the decade when he wrote 'Homage to a Government' in 1969 following the Wilson administration's decision to withdraw from east of Suez:

> Next year we are to bring the soldiers home
> For lack of money, and it is all right.
> Places they guarded, or kept orderly,
> Must guard themselves, and keep themselves orderly.

We want the money for ourselves at home
Instead of working. And this is all right.

It's hard to say who wanted it to happen,
But now it's been decided nobody minds.
The places are a long way off, not here,
Which is all right, and from what we hear
The soldiers there only made trouble happen.
Next year we shall be easier in our minds.

Next year we shall be living in a country
That brought its soldiers home for lack of money.
The statues will be standing in the same
Tree-muffled squares, and look nearly the same.
Our children will not know it's a different country.
All we can hope to leave them now is money.[10]

Shorn of empire, we *were* a 'different country', however little it bothered most of us, and the globe was a different place. For no other country had run a world system as large as Britain's at its imperial zenith and the dominions, colonies, protectorates and mandates were only part of it. This Ronald Hyam of Magdalene College, Cambridge made unforgettably plain in his introductory lecture to undergraduates in a chilly Mill Lane Lecture Theatre in January 1967. I am, I think, quoting him accurately as it is the most memorable opening stanza to a lecture I have ever heard in person:

It is very difficult for people of your age to appreciate the British Empire at its zenith. There is no shortage of clichés – a quarter of the earth's surface on which the sun never set – but they are as banal as they are misleading because they only give you a sense of the territorial expression of British power. A better test is this. If you were a chap almost anywhere in the world around 1904 and you went for a pee, you would point your cock at a piece of porcelain on which was written 'Shanks of Greenock'. [Pause] Not for nothing was Greenock called 'the arsehole of the British Empire'.

What better way could there be of illustrating the distinction between the 'formal' British Empire based on territory and the 'informal' empire of free trade?

The British Empire has been a begetter of historical debates on a suitably imperial scale. The 'Cambridge School', which shaped both Ronald Hyam and later myself, tended to disdain mega, all-embracing theories. As one of its high priests, Jack Gallagher, famously put it in his 1974 Ford Lectures at Oxford:

> All theories to explain the growth of imperialism have been failures. Here and there on the mountain of truth lie the frozen bodies of theorists, some still clutching their ice-picks, others gripping their hammers and sickles. All perished; and most of them because they believed they could find some single cause or factor which could satisfactorily explain imperialism's efflorescence in the later nineteenth century. We may expect a similar fate for those who want a monocausal explanation of its fall. They may climb hopefully, but they will not arrive.[11]

As Gallagher also noted, Britain's imperial 'collapse had its origins in small sparks eating their way through long historical fuses before the detonations began'.[12] The detonation on the Indian subcontinent was finally triggered by the Second World War; Suez was certainly one of the triggers for the explosions that led to the spate of disposals and independence ceremonies of the 1960s. But the debate continues about the most potent ingredients in the percussive mix.

Hyam, as we saw at the head of this chapter, preferred a metaphor drawn from *the* imperial sport, cricket.[13] Writing forty years after the early Sixties' rush to decolonize, he reckoned that

> [e]xcept for unregenerate Marxists and nationalist patriots, few historians think the violent assaults of freedom-fighters were decisive or can provide a sufficient overall explanation of imperial retreat. Equally, however, few would try to write out entirely nationalist protest in the broader sense. After all, not many states got independence without asking for it. The important question perhaps is how the British government arrived at the point where they were prepared to open the door to whoever knocked.[14]

Precisely. How was it that late-Fifties ambivalence about the pace and nature of decolonization had given way by 1964 to the wish, as Duncan Sandys put it, to avoid prolonging the UK's colonial obligations 'for a day longer than is necessary'? It was a shift that is still breathtaking to contemplate in terms of its speed and scope. It reminds me of another late imperial phenomenon – but a domestic one in this case. In British cinemas in the early Sixties it was still the practice, after the last film of the night, to play the National Anthem. Yet, every evening, without fail, as the credits rolled, it became the custom for even the more loyal of the Queen's subjects to dash for the exit. Though I did not realize it at the time, it was a metaphor for British policy across the world.

There is no doubt that British ministers had had enough. Territory was now an unarguable drag on rather than a multiplier of power for those who sought influence in the world. The romance of empire had gone – the plumage, the drum and trumpet certainly, but not entirely the Victorian residuals of the civilizing mission or the economic impulse. Also, *Churchill* had gone. The last great imperialist, during whose peacetime premiership not a single territory was granted independence. It was as if Macmillan and his Commonwealth and Colonial Secretaries wished to revert to a late-twentieth-century version of the empire of free trade, rather than territory, which dominated what Ronald Robinson and Jack Gallagher called the 'official mind' of imperialism before the 'Scramble for Africa' in the late nineteenth century.[15]

On top of this modified version of 'the imperialism of free trade'[16] lay the ever-pressing perspective of the global Cold War. As Macmillan had stressed in his 'Wind of Change' speech, preventing their former colonies from slipping into the communist bloc was – or should be – a primary purpose of the European decolonizers and a factor linking the old imperial powers in a common purpose with the United States, for all Washington's traditional distaste for other people's empires.

These linkages were manifested in the diary of Harold Evans, Macmillan's Press Secretary and himself an old Commonwealth Relations Office hand (which left him less than enthusiastic about the rapidity of the tilt to Europe[17]). His entry for 26 March 1960 records a conversation with Norman Brook about Macmillan's intention 'eventually to say indiscreetly in public what he has been saying discreetly in private e.g. the British as the Greeks in the Roman Empire of the Americans'.[18] A short time later, Macmillan thought aloud before Evans about the need 'for him to take an early opportunity to say something on the theory of the Commonwealth, not least on how to influence one's friends. He has no intention of being a Lord North [Prime Minister during the American War of Independence], though Gaitskell might like to play the role.'[19] Macmillan's wider 'Grand Design' plainly contained his own, early-Sixties version of Churchill's late-Forties and early-Fifties overlapping circles of US/UK 'special relationship', empire and Europe.

For all his eloquence, the mind of Macmillan was much harder to read than his words. For those without a Balliol training, such as the former engine driver and boxer Roy Welensky, Prime Minister of the Central African Federation, it could be infuriatingly Delphic. 'Harold Macmillan's mind', he wrote in his memoirs, 'was the most complicated I have encountered in my political life.'[20] Probably the only way to understand it was by appreciating Macmillan's one consistent purpose pushing through those formidable synapses – the desire to maximize British power and influence in the world, however adverse the circumstances. And the circumstances, in Africa especially, became increasingly testing in the early Sixties. How to organize a dignified dash for the exit without loss of trade and influence or serious setback in the Cold War?

Legend has it that the old bibliophile in No. 10 actually read Robinson and Gallagher's instant classic, *Africa and the Victorians*, when his family firm first published it in 1961, and that he 'never understood a word of it'.[21]* Nevertheless, there is a certain reverse symmetry between the Robinson and Gallagher analysis of the late nineteenth century (crises in Egypt and South Africa dragged reluctant Victorian statesmen into a scramble for territory to preserve the routes to India from local threats and rival colonialists[22]) and Macmillan's growing conviction that developments within Africa meant that its British portions could no longer be directly ruled from without.

Is there an analytical approach that might provide a model for the local pressures and their consequences which added so much to the stress of the fading men of empire in Whitehall? Paradoxically, it was Jack Gallagher, that magnificent scourge of theorists, who came up with the

---

* Though Richard Thorpe, his latest biographer, has been able to find no trace of the Prime Minister's having read it (conversation with Richard Thorpe, 14 April 2008).

most plausible – what he called 'international pressures' and 'domestic constraints' providing 'two jaws of the nutcracker', with 'local-colonial politics' providing the impetus to close it.[23] (Among imperial historians, this has become known as 'Gallagher's nutcracker'.)[24]

The Macmillan Cabinet Room in the early Sixties resounded to the sound of multiple nutcracking which, by the end of the decade (including the Douglas-Home and Wilson spells as imperial morticians), clocked up the remarkable tally of what we would nowadays call twenty-six independence packages from Cyprus in August 1960 to Fiji on 10 October 1970 (see table[25]).

The achievement of independence within the Commonwealth

Date		Territory	New name	Commonwealth status
1947	14 Aug.	Pakistan		Republic 1956; outside 1971–89
	15 Aug.	India		Republic 1949
1948	4 Jan.	Burma	Myanmar 1988	Outside
	4 Feb.	Ceylon	Sri Lanka 1972	Republic 1972
1956	1 Jan.	Sudan		Outside
1957	6 Mar.	Gold Coast (+ UK Trust Territory of Togoland)	Ghana	Republic 1960
	31 Aug.	Malaya	into Malaysia 1963	
1960	26 June	British Somaliland	into Somalia	Outside
	16 Aug.	Cyprus		Republic
	1 Oct.	Nigeria		Republic 1963
1961	27 Apr.	Sierra Leone		Republic 1971
	1 June	North Cameroons	into Nigeria	
	1 Oct.	South Cameroons	into Cameroun	Outside
			North and South reunited as United Republic of Cameroon, 1972, Republic of Cameroon, 1984	Joined 1995

Date		Territory	New name	Commonwealth status
	9 Dec.	Tanganyika	Tanzania (with Zanzibar) 1964	Republic 1962
1962	6 Aug.	Jamaica		
	31 Aug.	Trinidad and Tobago		Republic 1976
	9 Oct.	Uganda		Republic 1967
1963	16 Sept.	Singapore	joined Federation of Malaysia	Republic 1965, as separate state, seceding
	16 Sept.	North Borneo		
	16 Sept.	Sarawak	Sabah	
	10 Dec.	Zanzibar	Tanzania (with Tanganyika)	Republic 1964
	12 Dec.	Kenya		Republic 1964
1964	6 July	Nyasaland	Malawi	Republic 1966
	21 Sept.	Malta		Republic 1974
	24 Oct.	Northern Rhodesia	Zambia	Republic
1965	18 Feb	The Gambia		Republic 1970
1966	26 May	British Guiana	Guyana	Republic 1970
	30 Sept.	Bechuanaland	Botswana	Republic
	4 Oct.	Basutoland	Lesotho	Sovereign monarchy
	30 Nov.	Barbados		
1967	30 Nov.	Aden	into (South) Yemen	Outside
1968	12 Mar.	Mauritius		
	6 Sept.	Swaziland		Sovereign monarchy
1970	10 Oct.	Fiji		Outside 1987–98
1972	18 Apr.	East Pakistan	Seceding as Bangladesh	Republic
1973	10 July	Bahamas		
1974	17 Feb.	Grenada		
1976	28 June	Seychelles		Republic
1978	7 July	Solomon Islands		
	1 Oct.	Ellice Islands	Tuvalu	Special membership
	3 Nov.	Dominica		Republic

Date		Territory	New name	Commonwealth status
1979	22 Feb.	St Lucia		
	12 July	Gilbert Islands	Kiribati	Republic
	27 Oct.	St Vincent and Grenadines		
1980	18 Apr.	Southern Rhodesia	Zimbabwe	Republic
	30 July	New Hebrides	Vanuatu	
1981	21 Sept.	British Honduras	Belize (1973)	
	1 Nov.	Antigua and Barbuda		
1983	19 Sept.	St Christopher and Nevis	St Kitts-Nevis	

Not included: Protected States, nor former dependencies of Australia, New Zealand and South Africa; nor Hong Kong (where British rule ended in 1997 with retrocession to China).

Source: Ronald Hyam, *Britain's Declining Empire: The Road to Decolonisation, 1918–1968*, (Cambridge University Press, 2006), pp. 411–12.

Exiting from the colonies contributed powerfully to Macmillan's sense of fatigue, sometimes verging on self-pity, as his own personal strength and powers waned almost in tandem with those of the British Empire. 'What sufferings we go thro' to try to keep the Commonwealth together,' he wrote in his diary on 27 March 1963. 'Bed at 3 a.m. – slept badly.'[26] And there is a curious passage in his memoirs which reads almost as if it were written for a historian assessing his imperial and commonwealth policies forty or fifty years on:

Yet, if it is easy to see the errors which were made by the European leaders in Africa, it is equally proper to admit the faults of which we at home were no doubt guilty. What remains in my memory is the immense amount of time and trouble taken over the future of the African territories amidst so many other problems, internal and external, with which we, like every other Government, had to contend. If, as mortals, we could not command success, we might almost claim to have deserved it.[27]

The fate of Rhodesia/Zimbabwe alone should puncture any trace of excessive self-congratulation, as should the deeply bloodstained partition of India and Pakistan in 1947. It is comforting for some to think that, for the Brits, the relinquishing of their empire was something of a fine (if not finest) hour. Do Macmillan, his ministers, his officials and the shrinking tribe of departing governors and district commissioners deserve more than a tad of sympathy, as his memoir suggested? Could any other mere 'mortals' have done much better?

It must be remembered that dashing for the exit was not a pang-free experience for Macmillan. Quite apart from the exhausting slog of the casework of imperial disposal, which took a heavy toll on his ageing frame, Macmillan was at heart a rather reluctant undertaker of empire. After months of anxiety and effort expended on the Central African Federation, the forty-seventh anniversary of the outbreak of the Great War drew a revealing diary entry from him:

> August 4th
>
> . . . from which fatal date sprang all our troubles – the beginning of the end of Europe's supremacy, and the predominance of the white man in the world. From this date began the end of the old British Empire and the capture of the greatest Euro/Asian country – China – by the strange doctrines of a German Jew intellectual – Karl Marx [a slip of a tired pen? Russia, not China, straddles Europe and Asia]. Happily, we did not realise all this when we were young.[28]

Macmillan may or may not have read *Africa and the Victorians*, but he was Gallagher-like in his appreciation of the long historical fuses lit beneath imperial Britain which went off during his premiership.

Macmillan had slightly taken aback some of the British pressmen whom he had engaged in a kind of rolling conversation during the various stages of his 1960 tour of Africa. Anthony Sampson, for example, wrote in his memoir, *The Anatomist*, that Macmillan 'had a simplified view of Africa: it was, the Prime Minister said, like a lazy hippo which had suddenly been prodded'.[29] But, as Sampson recognized, the 'Wind of Change' speech had had a tonic effect on some of Africa's future leaders. Nelson Mandela, for example, thought the speech 'terrific' and, '[n]early forty years later Mandela, speaking in Westminster Hall, would recall Macmillan's courage in confronting "a stubborn and race-blind white oligarchy"'. The 1960 speech, Sampson wrote, 'had long repercussions in black Africa'.[30]

More immediately for Macmillan, Central Africa was the most explosive patch in 1961 – how to let the wind of change blow while preserving something multiracial in a new settlement. The presence of a substantial number of Europeans in the Rhodesias, Northern and Southern, meant that his political opponents within the Conservative Party, led by 'Bobbety' Salisbury, were especially exercised at what they saw as the prospect of imperial betrayal – and they could rely upon a widely read and sympathetic newspaper for support, Lord Beaverbrook's *Daily Express*, still then an influential and well-produced mass-circulation daily.

That the Central African question became critical in the early Sixties was not a surprise in Whitehall. In June 1959 the Cabinet Office had circulated a substantial forward look to where the continent of Africa might be in 1970, based upon an interdepartmental review conducted under the auspices of the Cabinet's Africa (Official) Committee chaired by Burke Trend.[31] This committee neatly encapsulated what Robinson and Gallagher famously described as 'the Official Mind of Imperialism'[32] as the British Empire, to nearly all intents and purposes, entered its last decade (though that this would be so was by no means plain to them in those warm months of the dazzling 1959 summer).

But the Trend Committee was prescient about the Central African Federation, in terms of both how much was riding on this six-year-old construct* and the consequences of what might happen if it fell apart (not until the early days of Mrs Thatcher's first government in April 1980 did Southern Rhodesia mutate into Zimbabwe, full independence and majority African rule[33]). Unscrambling Africa was bound to be truly trying where a substantial degree of white European settlement had occurred; in this respect Southern Rhodesia was especially vexing as it was 'a self-governing colony [since 1923] which took its present shape after conquest [by Cecil Rhodes in the 1880s and

* The Central African Federation consisted of Nyasaland and the two Rhodesias, North and South. It had been put in place in 1953 by the Churchill government as a multiracial entity that would, it was hoped, serve as a barrier against northward influence created by the apartheid government of South Africa, though the preponderance of power within the federation lay with the white settlers.

1890s], with an independent, strong, numerous and rapidly increasing European population' conjoined with two British protectorates in Northern Rhodesia and Nyasaland.

The Trend Committee described very precisely the dilemmas raised when this ramshackle structure began to feel the wind of change:

> The politically vocal part of the European population, unlike the Europeans in East Africa, are anxious for independence from United Kingdom control, although they are intensely loyal to the Commonwealth. The Africans in Northern Rhodesia and Nyasaland, on the other hand, look to the United Kingdom connexion to protect their interests against encroachment by local Europeans – although there is at the same time a rising pressure for universal adult franchise leading to African political control and independence.[34]

This was why the would-be sustainers of territorial empire in the early Fifties had come up with federation as 'a compromise between two different forms of possible association between three territorial units whose economies are uneven but to some extent complementary'. The Europeans saw this as a step to future Dominion status (as enjoyed by Canada, Australia, New Zealand and South Africa), 'but the Governments of the two Northern Territories preferred a looser type of association which promised economic advantage but did not imply political links'.[35]

What the Trend Committee called 'the compromise concept of Federation' enabled everyone involved, for a while, to read their own aspirations into the script of its future course, not least in Whitehall, where

> it was argued in its favour that it would bring economic and political benefits to the area as a whole and that, by promoting the development of multi-racial partnership based on 'civilized standards', it would prevent Southern Rhodesia from passing under the control of the Union of South Africa and would avoid a direct clash between a white-dominated Africa south of the Zambezi and a black-dominated Africa to the north.[36]

In other words, the Central African Federation was potentially the geopolitical pivot of the entire continent. The twentieth-century guardians of British power had grown up with the notions of the great exponent of geopolitics, Sir Halford Mackinder, who had a partiality for finding and expounding upon various global and regional locations around which power – and the projection of power – turned,[37] and these notions outlasted Mackinder's death in 1947. When the Central African Federation joined the list of geographical 'pivots', it placed a tectonic strain upon its fragile constitution that was up for review in 1960. The 'Federal experiment', as the Africa (Official) Committee called it, was also under considerable human stress as 'it is bedevilled by African fears of being dominated by local Europeans and by European fears of being submerged by an "uncivilized" African nationalism'.[38]

If the Federation's constitution failed to survive its coming test, the Trend Committee concluded, 'the picture grows darker' and the strain would become 'intolerable'. And here they did foresee what became the darkest stain on British imperial withdrawal since the massacres that accompanied the partition of India in 1947:

Confidence between the races will deteriorate sharply; there will be a grave risk that the Europeans will adopt increasingly restrictive policies; and in the end they may attempt to force the issue by declaring the Federation, or at least the two Rhodesias, fully independent under predominantly European Governments.[39]

The Africans would vigorously react in such circumstances 'by adopting the more extreme forms of resistance; and the white population will be compelled to resort to force in order to maintain their position – to the discredit of the United Kingdom, to the detriment of the Federation's economy, and to the embarrassment of the policy of moderation which we shall be trying to pursue in East Africa'. There was, too, a possibility of a break-up of the entire Federation, with Southern Rhodesia 'gradually' drifting 'into the orbit of the Union of South Africa' with 'Afrikaner racial policies' advancing 'northwards to the edge of the Zambezi, towards the heart of Central Africa'.[40] This is exactly what happened after Southern Rhodesia unilaterally declared independence in November 1965.

As Macmillan and his ministers contemplated the Federation in the aftermath of his 'Wind of Change' speech in Cape Town in February 1960, however, the imperial and geopolitical game was not up, and much was still to be played for in Central Africa. Indeed, in the home islands of empire, administrators were still hunting down and training a fair slice of the best males the British universities and playing fields could provide for service in its outposts across the seas, putting them through special programmes in the universities of Oxford, Cambridge and London before sending them off to their first postings abroad. These were known as the Devonshire courses, after a committee set up during the Second World War chaired by the eponymous duke, which in 1946 recommended their creation to help meet the changed and changing needs of the British Empire now its enemies had been seen off.[41] The commissioning of the Devonshire inquiry had been stimulated by Whitehall's ace recruiter for imperial service, Major Sir Ralph Furse. Furse had a certain idea of the characteristics required in a man for life in the colonies and in a cascade of quotations at the start of his memoir *Aucuparius: Recollections of a Recruiting Officer*[42] (published in 1962 just as dependency after colony was rushing through the exit) he quotes an Australian servant of empire, Lieutenant-Colonel Walter Crocker, twice in his support. In his *On Governing Colonies*,[43] Crocker began by paraphrasing Arnold Toynbee's *Study of History*:

> [F]or a régime of government to survive it must have charm for the governed. This is certainly true of empires. The handful of Europeans who exercise sway over millions must throw some charm over them. They must have the qualities of an authentic governing class – command, disinterestedness, fairness, and likeableness. These qualities can be found in most social groups in England – they do not depend on income alone – but they must be looked for and fostered.[44]

Crocker put the other side of his imperial ideal directly and pithily to Furse himself: 'The most dangerous man you can have in the Colonial Service is the clever cad.'[45]

In February 1943, Furse prepared a memorandum, 'The Case for Reform', to aid the finding and fostering of colonial servants while, no doubt, improving the chances of keeping clever cads out of the Colonial Service. Seventy years on, it is all too easy to parody Furse's summary of his paper, but its purpose was serious and it recognized the need for wider approaches to the recruitment of rulers, the manner of their ruling and their attitudes to the ruled themselves, in what was plainly seen as an enduring and developing enterprise rather than an imperial business likely to fold inside a generation or two:

Need of bold plans to meet probable post-war conditions . . .

The maintenance of contact between serving officers and informed public opinion not only on colonial affairs, but also on general questions of the day, and on such subjects as Economics, Welfare, etc. . . .

Training 'the whole man' instead of merely imparting professional knowledge.

The fortification of 'morale' and the breeding of confidence based on knowledge . . .

A fuller appreciation of the spiritual and artistic background of colonial peoples.

A better understanding of the educated native . . .

To cater for the special needs of a new type of white officer.[46]

Amazingly, the Devonshire courses ran from 1948 to 1969 (though by the end nearly all the members were from independent countries rather than the Colonial Service cadets, who dominated their first dozen years[47]).

The first Devonshire recruits were nearly all ex-National Servicemen and not all of them took the course entirely seriously, despite the high-minded intentions of Sir Ralph Furse and the Duke of Devonshire. Brian Wilson, who served in Hong Kong from 1948 to 1983, was part of the inaugural intake – a 'Course of Fun', he called it, with 'a relaxed group of over 100 lads, mostly wartime ex-Service, impatient to be done with lectures and to get on with the job in our respective territories. One humourless young man attending at Oxford who tried to press his Communist views on lecturers ceased to appear one day, and was presumed to have been quietly sacked. An amiable African on the course said he found the content unappealing and dropped out.'

Most of the course was shaped for those destined for Africa. Complaining that this was not much use for Hong Kong, special arrangements were made for the Hong Kong-bound 'to learn about the administration of a comparable waterfront community. This consisted of attending a meeting of the Stepney Borough Council which turned out to be a splendid slanging match between Councillors, vying with each other in invective and insults. The politest Councillor present was a West Indian.'[48]

The future district officers hit a spot of trouble when their courses required them to do a spell at the London School of Economics and they came across a group of local lefties

> almost all younger than ourselves, perhaps less mature and certainly more prone to silly ideas. Notice boards and corridors were plastered with posters on the lines of *Hands off Malaya*, *Down with Colonialism*, *Freedom for All*. The Devonshire men felt themselves a cut above this nonsense, believing that our job in our posted territory was to educate its people to their own eventual self-government.[49]

The LSE lefties, for their part, dubbed the Devonshire men the 'White Masters'.[50]

The Devonshire courses were originally eighteen months in duration. By the start of the 1960s it was down to a year, but the content was much the same: Colonial Government, Religion and Administration, Criminal Law, the Law of Evidence and Tort, Land Utilization, Problems of the British Empire, Land Tenure and Native Law, Imperial Economic History, Geography, Social Anthropology and Field Engineering[51] (this last course seems to have stuck in the minds of several Oxford Devonshires as its teacher, Mr Longland, used the University Parks to simulate the bush[52]).

My friend Michael Shaw still remembers how to lay cement in the hot tropics to avoid it cracking in the sun thanks to his Cambridge Devonshire 1958–9, and the lady with the long cigarette holder who came up from the School of Oriental and African Studies in London to teach him Swahili in the 'slightly decrepit rooms' in Petty Cury in Cambridge. The team picture of his Devonshire, taken in June 1959, has its Director, Hugh McCleary (an old Tanganyika hand) surrounded by fifty-seven young men – fifty-two white and five not.

The Gold Coast had already achieved independence as Ghana by the time Michael Shaw's cohort joined the course. Nonetheless, the Devonshires thought they had proper careers ahead of them in the Colonial Service. As the farewell telegram wishing him luck from the Devonshire staff in Cambridge reached him on board the *Rhodesia Castle* in the Royal Albert Docks in east London (where the City

Airport now operates) on 1 July 1959 he did not imagine he would be home again in three years. One of the first things the Deputy Governor of Tanganyika said to him after he docked in Dar es Salaam was, 'You've heard all this talk of independence. But I can tell you you have a job for a lifetime.'[53]

Shortly after, he began serving the Queen as District Officer number two in Dodoma, right in the middle of what is now Tanzania, primed by his Devonshire cement-laying and Swahili classes and such indispensable volumes as *Hints on the Preservation of Health in Tropical Countries* (which is particularly vivid on the temptations of alcohol as a solace for colonial solitariness). This still evocative handbook was produced by the Crown Agents for crown servants in hot climes complete with a warning inside the cover that 'A poisonous insecticidal solution has been used in binding this book.'[54]

By 1961 Michael Shaw was aide de camp to the extraordinary Sir Richard Turnbull, the last Governor of Tanganyika, the penultimate High Commissioner of Aden and later Denis Healey's interlocutor. On Saturday 22 July 1961, just five months before Tanganyika's independence, the East Africa Railways and Harbours Corporation based in Nairobi, Kenya, caught a photographic moment of the pure end of empire. No fewer than three governors (Sir Patrick Renison, Kenya; Sir Frederick Crawford, Uganda; and Turnbull, Tanganyika) are sitting aboard what looks like a huge trestle table with a canopy above it in the waters of Lake Victoria off Kisumu as Sir Patrick invites Lady Renison to commission RMS *Victoria*, the new mail steamer shipped over in pieces from Yarrow on the Clyde to ply the lake between all three British possessions. Michael Shaw, in pith helmet, watches over his boss as Turnbull stares myopically at the vessel towering over them. (The great man would never wear his glasses under the gubernatorial helmet as he feared it made him look like Groucho Marx![55]) After the ceremony, they all boarded the *Victoria*, which circumnavigated the lake clockwise, depositing each governor and his party in turn on their respective shore in a kind of waterborne imperial last bus home.

Did Michael Shaw and the other late Devonshires feel ever so slightly defrauded by what transpired over the next couple of years? 'Yes, because we thought that we had careers, and the sad thing is that we were doing things in terms of development in the late 1950s and early 1960s – setting up trading centres, building roads . . . All done on a shoestring. They were self-generating and the result of a reasonable level of honest and sensible government.' The end, when it came, was swift. 'It all accelerated so fast.' In 1962 he was back in Britain, and in 1963 he joined the Foreign Office. 'One left feeling thwarted,' although, forty years later, 'being able to go back and find that period out there remembered with respect as a period of good government' was pleasurable and the Tanzanians 'did not pitch at you for being part of that'.[56]

Tanganyika was different from the other East African colonies as it was a mandated territory, a former German colony taken after the Great War by the League of Nations and placed under the trusteeship of the British. It was, therefore, especially vulnerable to criticism at the United Nations (the successor organization to the League of Nations) should nationalist insurrection and subsequent repression occur. So a possible late-Sixties independence was brought forward to become an early-Sixties exit.[57]

In fact, no two colonies were alike in formation, history or (in the eyes of the colonizers) readiness for independence, which is why the Colonial Secretaryship of Iain Macleod is so central to any understanding of the dash to the exits. Macleod's political patron, Harold Macmillan, believed in the wake of his 1959 election victory that getting out of empire 'would need a Minister of great imagination, even genius . . . There was one man who seemed to me to possess the obvious qualities.'[58] And when he summoned him to No. 10, the old actor's sense of *comédie noire* was to the fore. 'Iain,' he said, 'I've got the worst job of all for you.'[59] In fact, the ambitious forty-six-year-old Macleod was terribly pleased. The Colonial Office in 1959 was a huge portfolio with high political visibility. And in Macleod, liberal instincts and a sense of personal drama were thoroughly mixed.[60] Africa on the brink of independence was for him the perfect stage. Macleod's elevation to the Colonial Secretaryship is one of those rare ministerial appointments of which one can assert that, because it was him or her, matters were as they became (premierships are another matter; among them the scene-shifters understandably have a higher batting average). For almost anyone else in Macmillan's post-1959-election Cabinet to have been given the job of imperial disposal, the process would have been different in both pace and tone (though Reggie Maudling, who replaced Macleod in the summer of 1961, turned out to be just as frantic a dasher for the door).

Alec Home, with his five-year experience as Commonwealth Secretary before moving to the Foreign Office in July 1960, had considerable doubts about his fellow Scot as the energetic winder-upper of empire. Recalling the early Sixties twenty-five years later, Home remembered: 'When I was in the Commonwealth Office and Macleod was in the Colonial Office he was always for galloping along with independence as fast as he could. I took the view that every year gained gave the countries a better chance when they became independent to be viable.' And, in a memorable and accurate summation, Home said 'I think that Macmillan was a wind of change man and Macleod was a gale of change man.'[61] For Macleod, as we shall see shortly, came increasingly to irritate and alarm his Prime Minister on matters African, not least because he seemed forever on the brink of resignation if Macmillan tried to reduce the wind speed.

Home later wrote of Macleod that he was 'the wrong man in the wrong place. His strength was shown in domestic politics where his brilliant oratory could be relied upon to leave his opponents speechless.'[62] It seems to have been Macleod's judgement of Patrice Lumumba, the very left-wing politician in the Congo who emerged to lead the new country amid the fast, bloody and chaotic Belgian withdrawal in 1960 (which deeply and understandably alarmed and scared the white settler groups in the British colonies of southern, central and eastern Africa), that triggered Home's most serious doubts about him as Colonial Secretary: 'He once told me – and clearly he believed it – that Lumumba was the greatest man in Africa. That indicated to me an alarming lack of judgement.'[63]

Macmillan was no fan of Lumumba either. On 10 July 1960 he wrote in his diary that the Congo

has fallen in chaos; murder, rape, intertribal warfare, mass flight of Europeans, etc. The Belgian Govt doesn't know quite what to do. The Prime Minister (Congolese) called Lumumba (or some such name) is a Communist and probably a Russian agent; the Premier of Katanga

[Moise Tshombe] (where the mineral wealth is) is a moderate and wants to be independent . . .[64]

Lumumba, who was shot by a political rival's troops early in 1961, was immortalized by the Soviet Union in the form of the Patrice Lumumba Friendship University in Moscow 'to provide higher education . . . for students from Africa, Asia and Latin America'. According to the former KGB archivist Vasili Mitrokhin, the 'University's first vice-rector and a number of its staff were KGB officers who used the student body as a recruiting ground for Third World agents'.[65] (However, Mitrokhin offers no evidence that Lumumba himself had been an instrument of the KGB.)

Whatever one thinks of Macleod's innate judgement and conviction that swift progression was necessary on decolonization, the dilemma he (or any alternative Colonial Secretary during this period) faced was truly vexing and stretching. The politics of it were local (on the spot in each colony or protectorate), international (US and UN in particular) and UK domestic (both inter- and intra-party in terms of general public opinion).

This last aspect marked Macleod's emergence as someone with an interest in colonial matters during the run-up to the election. Macleod was especially sensitive to the constantly fluctuating political calculation of electioneering and a great calibrator of mood-shifting questions. As the horrors of the Hola detention-camp atrocities (see below) unfolded in the early months of 1959, both he personally and his inbuilt electoral calculating machine were affected. At the end of May, Macleod wrote to Macmillan claiming that:

> Black Africa remains perhaps our most difficult problem so far as relations with the vital middle voters is [sic] concerned. It is the only one in which our policies are under severe criticism and for example the only one on which we are regularly defeated at the universities. Indeed the universities feel more strongly on this issue than on any other single matter.[66]*

---

* How strangely this reads today. Paradoxically, student opinion, as expressed through debating societies, seems to have had far more influence then than now. In the early Sixties there were but twenty-three universities with about 4 per cent of the eighteen-plus age group going to university (by 1970 it was 8.4 per cent). In 2018, it reached 50 per cent (Anthony Sampson, *Anatomy of Britain* (Hodder & Stoughton,

Hola was a camp in Kenya holding former Mau Mau members. On 3 March 1958 a massacre occurred when guards there beat dead eleven detainees, the brutality triggered by the Kenyans' refusal to undertake compulsory work. This caused Macmillan great difficulty politically and spurred Enoch Powell to his finest ever speech in the House of Commons ('We cannot say, "We will have African standards in Africa, Asian standards in Asia and perhaps British standards here at home. We have not that choice to make. We must be consistent with ourselves everywhere ... We cannot, we dare not, in Africa of all places, fall below our own high standards in the acceptance of responsibility'[67]).

As we have seen, Powell had resigned from the Macmillan government when the whole Treasury team quit in January 1958 over the Cabinet's unwillingness to trim public expenditure to the level they deemed necessary. But there were at least two members of the younger generation in Macmillan's Cabinet in the summer of 1959 who felt as strongly about Hola as Powell did. In a highly revealing interview in December 1967, Macleod told W. P. Kirkman, formerly *The Times*' Africa Correspondent and later Secretary of the Cambridge University Appointments Board:

> Everyone, of course, was shocked and horrified by what had happened, but two people's feelings, Quintin Hailsham and myself, went beyond that. I think we both felt outraged that such a thing could happen and for me this was the decisive moment when it became clear to me that we could no longer continue with the old methods of government in Africa and that meant inexorably a move towards African independence.[68]

His letter of May 1959 and recollections in 1969 illustrate two of the many sides of the Macleod character, also well captured by Anthony Sampson, who interviewed him for the first *Anatomy of Britain* in the early 1960s: 'He is a master of any kind of political manoeuvre. He is cool, calculating but not unemotional.' He was also, though a 'romantic Tory of the Disraelian kind', a man not at ease

---

1962), pp. 195–208; National Committee of Inquiry into Higher Education, *Report 6: Widening Participation in Higher Education for Students from Lower Socio-Economic Groups and Students with Disabilities* (HMSO, 1997), Table 1.1. I am grateful to Nicola Newson of the House of Lords Library for assistance with these figures).

with certain sections of his party (especially the more imperially minded of its layers): 'Macleod often shows signs of being restive with Conservatives: he talks with witty dislike of the "Deep South" – the right-wing strongholds along the south coast ... He sometimes talks of himself as being too left for his party.'[69]

The Conservative 'Deep Southerners' soon noticed the change of mind and pace in the Colonial Office after Macleod replaced Alan Lennox-Boyd, but, unsurprisingly, his officials noticed first. Macleod's biographer, Rob Shepherd, caught the exact moment in the autumn of 1959 when Macleod's emotion and reason were first converted into a defining policy and strategy:

> The precise moment at which Macleod's officials realized that this appointment heralded an about-turn in policy was never forgotten by those who witnessed it. No sooner had Macleod settled in, than he summoned his senior advisers, including Sir Hilton Poynton, the permanent secretary, Sir Leslie Monson, [an undersecretary in the Colonial Office] and 'Max' Webber,* the recently appointed head of the East Africa section, and asked them, 'What are we hoping to get out of this conference on Kenya?'
>
> His question was met by a long silence. It was finally broken by Webber, who had been anxious about the lack of discussion on strategy and who now suggested that the time had come for a breakthrough to African majority rule. Macleod simply nodded his assent, uttering not a single word. It was an historic moment. Macleod had signalled his radical intent and with it the end of Britain's African empire.[70]

It was a nod that changed the world. The problem of Hola-scarred Kenya was its stimulus.

It was also a nod that implied a near implacable ruthlessness on Macleod's part, both in the Cabinet Room in Downing Street and across a variety of colonial capitals. As he told W. P. Kirkman, 'I took the brutal, but I think practical view, that this was an omelette that you couldn't make without breaking eggs and you couldn't be friends with everybody.'[71]

---

* His real name was Fernley Webber and he ran the East Africa Department of the Colonial Office between 1958 and 1963.

The 'omelette' phrase is sometimes attributed to Lenin, as Macleod presumably knew when talking to Kirkman. (In fact, its origins lie in the mid-nineteenth century.[72]) And the eggs, Macleod was similarly convinced, had to be broken in every bit of Africa where the British Crown was sovereign, not just in the west where white settlement was very limited. As he explained to Kirkman:

[the] thing that seems to me odd was that this country generally – I don't just mean the Cabinet – or the Conservative Party or even parliament – had not grasped what seemed so blindingly simple a few years later, and that is that if you give independence in West Africa you cannot deny it in East Africa just because there is a white settler community there.[73]

West African independence was already underway by the time Macleod first sat at his desk, with Ghana (1957) a sovereign country and Nigeria (1960) imminent. There were other powerful undertows creating that rapid ebb tide of British territorial empire as the decades turned in addition to the symmetrical one outlined for Kirkman by Macleod. Writing in January 1964 in *The Spectator* (of which he was by then editor, having refused to serve in Douglas-Home's Cabinet the previous autumn), Macleod stressed the blood price that would have been paid by African and Brit alike had the UK tarried:

Were the countries fully ready for independence? Of course not. Nor was India [in 1947] and the bloodshed that followed the grant of independence there was incomparably worse than anything that has happened since to any country. Yet the decision of the Attlee Government was the only realistic one. Equally we could not possibly have held by force to our territories in Africa. We could not, with an enormous force engaged, even continue to hold the small island of Cyprus. General de Gaulle could not contain Algeria. The march of men towards their freedom can be guided, but not halted. Of course there were risks in moving quickly. But the risks of moving slower were far greater.[74]

This, in essence, was Macleod's riposte to Alec Home's relative caution.

Though Iain Macleod could not have known it when he inherited the still huge residual empire in 1959, its shrinking would, on his watch, turn out, on balance, to be a success story, and fifty years later the audit by Christopher Andrew seems just. As part of his examination of the secret elements of imperial withdrawal in his authorized history of MI5, Andrew reckoned: 'The post-war retreat from the greatest empire in world history without a single military defeat sets the British experience apart from the humiliations suffered by other European imperial powers. Britain's decolonization, unlike that of its main imperial rival, France, began before it was too late for an orderly withdrawal.'[75]

Macleod certainly was a realist. We do not know whether he was a student of Edmund Burke, but as Colonial Secretary he acted as if he had wholly absorbed Burke's line on Britain and American independence – 'not the least of the arts of diplomacy is to grant graciously what one no longer has the power to withhold'[76] – which, as Ronald Hyam noticed, became 'almost the guiding injunction for British decolonisation'.[77] Another part of Macleod's realism was a less than fastidious approach to the quality of democracy and due parliamentary process likely to prevail in the newly freed colonies. As he told a meeting of the Conservative Political Centre in October 1960:

> We should not be too disturbed if in the early years of independence some countries feel they need a stronger executive than we would find tolerable here. We should not despair if a new country builds its own traditions and makes its own mistakes. We cannot make them for them. Nor should we get too excited if they make disrespectful noises about us or our allies – it doesn't mean they've joined the Communist bloc.[78]

That last aside of Macleod's sounds like insouciance masking real anxiety.

Throughout the long haul of British withdrawal, preventing the communist bloc from filling the vacated political space with a red-tinged version of informal, if not territorial, empire was a constant preoccupation for the guardians of national security in Whitehall and the MI5 officers in the colonial capitals (the Security Service, not the Secret Intelligence Service, was responsible for such matters in empire days) together with the policemen of various colonial special branches.[79]

It is often forgotten that Harold Macmillan's famous 'Wind of Change' speech in Cape Town on 3 February 1960 pivoted on this very theme. Fearful of international communism, he told his audience:

> As I see it, the great issue in this second half of the twentieth century is whether the uncommitted peoples of Asia and Africa will swing to the East or to the West. Will they be drawn into the Communist camp? Or will the great experiments in self-government that are now being made in Asia and Africa, especially within the Commonwealth, prove so successful, and by their example so compelling, that the balance will come down in favour of freedom and order and justice?

'The struggle', Macmillan concluded gravely, 'is joined, and it is a struggle for the minds of men.'[80]

Macmillan certainly believed what he said in Cape Town in the speech of his life, both about the decolonizing wind of nationalism and the perils of Soviet and Chinese influence seeping in once the Europeans had departed. But his tone and thrust in its anti-communist passages reflected the welcome if paradoxical and somewhat concealed support he was getting on post-imperial policy from that great preacher against other people's versions of empire, the United States of America.

One of the prices paid for the folly of the invasion of Egypt in November 1956 was at the United Nations, where the 'British Empire was now not merely in the dock but reviled as a renegade'.[81] After Suez, as more and more freed ex-colonies joined the United Nations, Britain 'for the next fifteen years or so became Public Enemy Number One at the United Nations',[82] with the Americans conniving at the creation of various UN committees (the Committee of 17; later boosted to the Committee of 24) whose purpose was to hector the colonial powers into final retreats after the UN had passed Resolution 1514 in 1960 calling for universal colonial freedom.[83]

At the same time, Washington wanted a certain kind of unscrambling which, in practice, turned out to be very much the same kinds of departures and aftermaths Whitehall was seeking. Patrice Lumumba, and the possibility of more Lumumbas to follow in other territories, truly alarmed the Eisenhower administration: 'Eisenhower and Macmillan agreed that Lumumba must be removed or "fall into a river full of crocodiles" before he handed over the richest country in the region to Russian managers and technicians.'[84]

If it came to a choice, anti-communism would always trump anti-colonialism in the White House and the State Department. As the anatomizers of the special relationships involved in shedding empire, Roger Louis and Ronald Robinson, put it, 'For all the "holier than thou" attitudes of the Americans, the British and French empires were propped up in the democratic cause of saving the global free market from communist annexation,' and a common strategy was pursued of 'exchanging formal control for informal tutelage'.[85]

Though neither Eisenhower, Macmillan nor Macleod could have anticipated it, the very considerable efforts by the KGB after 1960 to penetrate and suborn the newly created post-imperial administrations in Africa led to immense irritation and frustration in Moscow (and KGB officers came to loathe African postings, much to the amusement of their SIS counterparts who rather relished African tours, not least because several of them were ex-district officers or commissioners[86]). When the KGB's archivist, Vasili Mitrokhin, was spirited out of Russia with his extraordinary hoard of document-derived notes, the Soviet failure in Africa became vividly apparent. As he and Christopher Andrew wrote:

> The former French and British colonies failed to live up to Khrushchev's expectations. Apart from Nkrumah [in Ghana], the only members of the first generation of African leaders to arouse the serious interest of the KGB were the Francophone Marxist dictators of Guinea and Mali, Ahmed Sékou Touré and Modibo Keïta. In all three cases, however, the [Moscow] Centre's hopes were dashed. As well as creating one-party states, Nkrumah, Touré and Keïta wrecked their countries' economies, leaving Moscow wondering whether to pour good money after bad to bail them out. The plentiful SIGINT generated by the KGB's attack on vulnerable African cipher systems doubtless enabled the Centre to follow the calamitous mismanagement of the Nkrumah, Touré and Keïta regimes in depressing detail.

The KGB, according to Andrew and Mitrokhin, 'became increasingly cynical at the Marxist rhetoric of some African leaders, which was often prompted, it believed, not by any real interest in following the Soviet example but chiefly – and sometimes simply – by the hope of securing Soviet economic aid'.[87] The Africans, like the masses generally, had proved a great disappointment to the Soviets.

Yet, at the time, it seemed to both Washington and Whitehall that the ending of west-European empires would offer quick and maybe permanent wins to those comradely imperiums run out of Moscow and Peking in the global game the Cold War required East and West to play. In fact, until Macmillan reshuffled him in the summer of 1961, Macleod had to play simultaneous chess (though bridge was *the* game of his life – and he played at international level[88]) on several colonial boards, some of which looked at various times as if they might burst into flames. His guile was great, his attention formidable, his hospitality forensic. The breakthroughs to eventual agreements would, as like as not, take place in his London flat in Knightsbridge's Hans Crescent behind Harrods, and later at 36 Sloane Court West in Chelsea, rather than around the huge conference table in the ornate Lancaster House, as Macleod and his wife, Eve, entertained the future leaders of independent Africa.[89]

Macleod's mercurial gifts were deployed not only across the continent of Africa but in the Whitehall jungle too, because other big players were involved, none of whom were 'gale of change' men. The most notable on a daily basis was the Commonwealth Secretary, Duncan Sandys. At moments of settler showdown or internal Whitehall crisis, Macmillan and his Foreign Secretary, were drawn in as well.

Reconstructing Macleod's multiple chess games across London and Africa is the stuff of several volumes and neither it nor the complicated geography of future voting patterns for the countries of the crumbling Central African Federation is to be repeated here. At its most testing, Northern Rhodesia seemed to be facing the Macmillan Cabinet with a *white* coup d'état against full majority rule of the kind that later vexed successive Labour and Conservative administrations between Southern Rhodesia's unilateral declaration of independence in November 1965 and its final mutation, after years of murderous civil war, into an independent Zimbabwe in 1980.

It is salutary to recall the Northern Rhodesian crisis of early 1961, as it is today scarcely remembered at all, crowded out of end-of-empire memory by the protracted agony of the Southern Rhodesian question. Macleod faced fierce resistance from his own backbenches, where the combative Central African Federation premier Roy Welensky had many supporters. Duncan Sandys, the Commonwealth Secretary and minister responsible for Southern Rhodesia, was more sympathetic to Welensky's claims for strong residual white representation in Northern Rhodesia and was just as tough and determined a politician as Macleod. Macmillan was forced to referee between the two and became increasingly irritated by Macleod's frequent resignation threats ('a daily event with Macleod', he wrote in his diary[90]). Kenneth Kaunda, the nationalist leader and first President of Zambia (as Northern Rhodesia became on eventual independence in 1964), threatened an 'explosion' of violence on a scale to dwarf Mau Mau in Kenya in the mid-Fifties if white domination continued.[91] Welensky at one stage appeared to be threatening a *white* coup d'état in Lusaka, the Northern Rhodesian capital.

Macleod took the threat of civil war seriously, as did Macmillan. It could be a government-wrecking event at home and a bloodbath in Central Africa, as he later recalled: 'I have no doubt at all that there would have been bloodshed, there would have been something of a "coup" by the Europeans in Northern Rhodesia supported by the Europeans in Southern Rhodesia. And the bloodshed that would have followed would have been appalling.'[92] In the end, a temporary deal was patched up – 50:50 representation – which Macleod sold to Kaunda in his Sloane Court flat in June 1961, suggesting that after a period of 'probation' in government, black majority rule would come in Lusaka.[93]

The Northern Rhodesian question quite wore Macmillan out. Macleod too had never worked so hard in his life – and, by way of reward, it almost certainly removed his chance of becoming Prime Minister one day when Lord Salisbury, friend of the Europeans in Africa generally and Welensky in particular, delivered upon Macleod one of the killer lines of postwar British political history. The House of Lords debated Central African policy on 7 March 1961, prompting Salisbury (who had resigned from the Macmillan Cabinet in 1957 partly over colonial policy) to talk about 'the miasma of mistrust' manifest among formerly loyal Europeans in the Central African Federation. He placed 'the main responsibility' for this at Macleod's feet. The Colonial Secretary, 'Bobbety' Salisbury declared, has 'adopted, especially in his relationship to the white communities of Africa, a most unhappy and an entirely wrong approach. He has been too clever by half.'[94]

It struck home. The press lit up. Salisbury's verbal barb branded Macleod's psyche. As his biographer put it: 'close friends had never seen him so upset . . . Salisbury's gibe, "too clever by half", stuck and was to do Macleod's reputation lasting damage.'[95] Macleod's combination of herbivorous policies defended in a carnivorous way allowed him to retain the affection – almost adulation – of a generation of progressive Conservatives to a degree unmatched by any centre-left Tory figure since. But, post-'Bobbety', he had no chance of carrying the Conservative right with him on the road to a Macleod premiership.

Macmillan, with immense relief, reshuffled him in the autumn of 1961 to become chairman of the Conservative Party, Leader of the House of Commons and Chancellor of the Duchy of Lancaster. He bade farewell to the colonial job and, in effect, delivered his riposte to Salisbury on the platform where he most excelled, at the Conservative Party Conference in Brighton on 11 October. For me, it remains the speech of his life. The small, bent figure, his body carried as if in constant pain (which it was), the round face, balding head – not the bearing and demeanour of a natural orator. Macleod, nevertheless, was matched only by Enoch Powell as a speaker among his generation of Conservatives. His great gift, as the newspaper columnist and connoisseur of Tory figures, Andrew Alexander, recalled, was 'to give the audience the impression he was taking everyone into his confidence'.[96]

Like all good orators, Macleod mixed grand sweep with educative detail – and educated he had been by his experience in the Colonial Office. For Macleod, 1959–61 represented a crash course in empire – until becoming Secretary of State he had never trodden on colonial turf.[97] He shared his insights with his party including those 'Deep Southerners' still far from reconciled with ending empire.[98] Macleod made his listeners in that seaside hall in the English 'Deep South' feel they were participants in a great historical moment – and participating in a way that did them and their country credit: 'You must be in no doubt that you are watching one of the great dramas of history, as so many countries thrust forwards through nationalism towards their independence.' It had 'fallen to me to be Colonial Secretary during two of the most tremendous years of advance the world has ever seen'. In 1945, 630 million people had lived in territories ruled by the British Crown; now the figure was 23 million.

He addressed the doubts and criticisms of those who simply could not see what they were living through as 'years of advance':

> We in this country have always understood the emergence of nationalism. If we look at the problems of Africa today . . . it is easy enough to point to a country and say, 'There in the Congo you can see what happens when there is inadequate preparation and you go too fast.' I agree. The Congo was a failure of inadequate preparation. But you must also look round the map of Africa and see the tragedies that can come if you go too slow. Of course the Congo events went too fast. There are other places in Africa where they have gone too slow.

And here he displayed his chief motivation and justification for his conduct of colonial policy and the swift imperial wind-up through which they were all living – 'confronted with this choice, as one would never hope to be, there is probably greater safety in going too fast than in going slow'.

There was, he continued, a touch of the circus about being Colonial Secretary but it was a circus constantly overshadowed by the possibility of tragedy:

> The tightrope of timing which the Colonial Secretary has to walk in every territory every week, sometimes almost every day, is the most difficult of all his tasks – how you try to reconcile the emerging nationalism of these counties with the need for the surest possible protection for the minority. As you walk this tightrope, you must realize that if you fall from it it will bring disaster and perhaps bloodshed to so many people to whom you stand in a position of trustee.

Macleod the spare-them-nothing realist gave way in his peroration to the Macleod who 'likes to depict himself as a romantic Tory of the Disraelian kind' with a special Scottish tang (he 'has even written a romantic play about the Hebrides',[99] wrote Sampson). He told the Conservative Party Conference:

> This is the last thing I shall say as Colonial Secretary . . . that I believe quite simply in the brotherhood of man – men of all races, of all colours, of all creeds. I think it is this that must be at the centre of our own thinking.

And now what lies ahead in this event? It is perhaps strange to an English and Welsh audience to quote the greatest of our Scottish native poets, but nobody has put this in simpler or finer words than Burns:

> It is coming yet for a' that,
> That man to man the whole world o'er,
> Shall brothers be for a' that.

And this is coming. There are foolish men who will deny it, but they will be swept away; but if we are wise then indeed the task of bringing these countries towards their destiny of free and equal partners and friends with us in the Commonwealth of Nations can be a task as exciting, as inspiring and as noble as the creation of empire itself.[100]

That oration in Brighton, blending reality, idealism, rhetoric and political bravery of the first order, was among the finest speeches of postwar British politics delivered by one of the greatest scene-shifters of the UK's geopolitics and place in the world since 1945.

Just occasionally, more than fifty years later, you hear an echo of it. For example, in a BBC Radio 4 documentary, *The Empire's Last Officers*, broadcast on 27 September 2010, John Smith, who in 1951 became a cadet in the Northern Nigerian Administration and later a highly thoughtful participant and connoisseur of our imperial withdrawal, after talking with great mutual warmth to an experienced Nigerian banker in Lagos with whom he had trained in the run-up to independence when they were both young, said, 'I believe firmly that if we'd tried to stay much longer relations could have become extremely embittered.' In an afterthought, which would also have intrigued Macleod (who died in 1970), Smith, when asked what it was like being a young district officer in his huge area of northern Nigeria, replied, 'It was a bit like going round the country with a feather duster.'

By the early twenty-first century, John Smith's cohort was dwindling fast. The remaining former guardians of empire stayed formidably well organized through their Overseas Service Pensioners' Association and kept in touch with each other and the latest literature on empire through *The Overseas Pensioner* magazine, which contains short pieces such as Norman Knight on 'Mongu: Where All the Flies Go in Winter Time', an extract from *Memories of a District Officer in Northern Rhodesia and of the War Years.* On the back cover of the October 2007 edition of the magazine, in which that extract featured,[101] is a colour picture of a young warrior with desert and rock in the background – 'A soldier of the Hadhrami Bedouin Legion, in undress uniform, Mukalla, Eastern Aden Protectorate, 1964 (with thanks to Michael Crouch, Aden Political Service, 1958–67)'.

In May 2008, when I spoke at their annual reunion lunch, which John Smith attended, there were some one hundred present – well and neatly dressed, their name and the colony or protectorate in which they served pinned to their jacket lapels or dresses. The oldest were in their nineties, the youngest in their fifties, usually with 'Hong Kong' on their badge, reflecting the last and most recent of the imperial disposals in 1997. Several of the men had the classic tropical-service look – taut-skinned, lean faces that had long been 'burnished in the sun' for the King Emperor or Her Majesty the Queen. Richard Turnbull's daughter was there too. They struck me as the last of the Romans.

By a curious and unforeseeable coincidence, the last gathering of the Overseas Service Pensioners' Association took place on polling day, 8 June 2017 – the general election triggered paradoxically by the turbulent political aftermath of the decision in June 2016 to leave the very European Union which was, in so many ways, intended to be the UK's geopolitical substitute for empire, the surrogate provider of its clout in the world.

There in the Connaught Rooms in Holborn gathered many pensioners and their extended families. The Prince of Wales came to deliver a thoughtful, warm and witty speech over pre-lunch drinks. As we waited for Prince Charles to arrive, Richard Lace, a district officer in Kenya when in his mid-twenties and later a Foreign and Commonwealth Office Minister, said to me: 'The empire dies today.' In a way, it did – quite unnoticed by the press, let alone the public preoccupied by the last hours of Theresa May's campaign to win a bigger majority with which she hoped to pave more effectively the parliamentary path to Brexit.

It is immensely difficult to conduct an audit of imperial exit. Did nothing become the Brits so much as the leaving of it? If I had been in that Brighton conference hall listening to Iain Macleod in October 1961 I would have been struck by how perilous the day-to-day withdrawal operations were, the considerable risks that were being taken in both the short term (more Congos) and the long term (the turning of a western flank in the Cold War by successful Soviet penetration). I would also, I think, have realized how psychologically important it was for the Brits to do it with dignity and in good order – to have a story we were not ashamed to tell ourselves in the years to come.

Macleod actually offered his hearers that day a first draft of the history he hoped was to come. He believed, he said,

> in what our grandfathers would have called the British Imperial mission. It is not yet completed. Since the world began, empires have grown and flourished and decayed, some into a sort of genteel obscurity, some leaving little heritage and culture behind them, some even no more than stones covered by sand. They are one with Nineveh and Tyre, but we are the only empire leaving behind us a coherent political scheme of development. We are the only people who, with all the hesitations and failures that there have been, are genuinely resolved on turning, to use Harold Macmillan's phrase, an empire into a commonwealth and a commonwealth into a family.[102]

When Macleod expressed that aspiration he already knew full well that a large-scale 'family' row was underway about British policy towards apartheid South Africa, which had left the Commonwealth the previous March after Macmillan had striven mightily but failed to persuade the South African premier, Hendrik Verwoerd, to make 'the smallest move towards an understanding of the views of his Commonwealth colleagues'.[103] The South African question was to poison intra-Commonwealth relations for a generation until Nelson Mandela was freed from prison in 1990 and the apartheid regime began to dismantle itself.

At home, the question of 'colour', as it was expressed in the early 1960s, began to rise up the barometer of political sensitivity when Commonwealth immigration continued to increase and anxieties, aroused during the Notting Hill and Nottingham riots of 1958, about the capacity and willingness of the host communities to absorb the newcomers in areas of particular concentration, showed no signs of abating. The empire coming home has left an immensely greater mark on British society and politics than the empire shed. And the early 1960s were turning points for both.

It is hard to recapture, half a century on, the sensibilities of the time. Even then, to view immigration as a 'problem' was thought by many – not just those on the centre left in their political views – as distasteful at best and racist at worst. Equally, it was part of the residual romance of empire, and the indivisibility of being a subject of the Crown (or Citizens of the United Kingdom and Colonies, as the British Nationality Act, 1948, dubbed them) in whichever part of the Crown's territories one was born or brought up, that led to a genuine resistance to categorize the Queen's subjects as first or second class or to place varying tariffs of restrictions on their rights as said subjects.

But the colonial governors and district commissioners were not the only ones dashing for the exits in the late Fifties and early Sixties. Noticeable proportions of the local populations were, too, from the West Indies in particular, and their travel plans reached right into the Cabinet Room and into Parliament. The Macmillan administration was very aware of the sensitivities aroused by even the possibility of controls upon coloured immigration; Whitehall began the mechanics of planning for it while ministers in public continued to deny that any such plans were being contemplated.[104] Whitehall, however, had shifted its opinion since the mid-1950s. Informal discouragement of immigration had failed. With the empire breaking up, fear of offending Commonwealth colonial opinion was also diminished since the question of controls had first swirled through the Cabinet and Cabinet committee meetings of the Attlee, Churchill, Eden and early Macmillan governments. And word was leaking out that, despite official denials, controls were on the way and a 'beat the ban' rush of immigration began to gather pace as 1961 unfolded:

Net Immigration from the New Commonwealth, 1959–61[105]

Year	West Indies	India	Pakistan	Others	Total
1959	16,400	2,950	850	1,400	21,600
1960	49,650	5,900	2,500	-350	57,700
1961	66,300	23,750	25,100	21,250	136,400

As thoughts about the desirability of control and its possible mechanics slogged their way through Whitehall working parties and Cabinet committees in the spring of 1961, Iain Macleod, as Colonial Secretary, was urging delay lest halting the flow from the Caribbean jeopardized the planned federation of the UK's colonies in the West Indies. He was, according to his biographer, 'the last minister to be persuaded of the need for some such action'.[106] In September the referendum on federation in the West Indies produced a 'no'. Another sensitivity was gone. In October, Macleod, as we have seen, was reshuffled from the Colonial Office to the leadership of the House of Commons and it fell to him to pilot the hugely contentious Commonwealth Immigrants Bill through Parliament.

Within weeks of delivering his 'brotherhood of man' oration to the Conservative Party Conference, Macleod was having to explain why a bill to curb immigration was in the Macmillan government's new Queen's Speech. The Labour leader, Hugh Gaitskell, who was passionately opposed to such legislation,[107] mercilessly pointed out the paradox in the House of Commons. Gaitskell cited Macleod's words at Brighton, acknowledged that the Leader of the House was 'a determined opponent of racial discrimination' but warned him that he would be 'watching him very closely' on the matter of curbing immigration.[108]

Macleod, to his credit, made no attempt to dissemble. He told Gaitskell, 'I detest the necessity for it in this country . . . but I believe it to be necessary.' In explaining why, he traced the mutation of opinion inside the Macmillan Cabinet and the degree to which the 1958 riots had lit a fuse:

> No one has been closer to this problem than myself, other than perhaps the Home Secretary [Rab Butler]. I have seen this when I was Minister of Labour [1955–9] grow from something about which no figures and no problem existed into a problem that flared into the headlines with race riots in this country, of all countries, and I have seen it when I was Colonial Secretary. I came to the conclusion in the spring of this year, looking at those figures, that it was no longer possible to avoid such legislation.[109]

But what did such legislation seek to do? In short, to curb 'coloured' immigration without seeming racist. This was impossible to accomplish when the government accepted that, in practice, border controls on the Irish Republic could not be applied in peacetime (they had been in the Second World War even though the Irish Free State was still technically a member of the Commonwealth). It left ministers highly vulnerable to attack from the Labour Party and gave the Macmillan administration some of its shakiest moments in Parliament.

Macmillan can be criticized for not giving the immigration question the attention it deserved. It struck his official biographer, Alistair Horne, having scoured his diaries, 'that Macmillan, when Prime Minister, devoted ten times as much attention to the problems of the Central African Federation as he did to the problem of Commonwealth immigration'.[110]

In fact, Macmillan's diary entry for 30 May 1961 captures this relative inattention and the nub of the private Cabinet motivations in reaching for a statute to curb the flow:

> A long Cabinet – 10.30–1 – this morning ... A long discussion on West Indian immigration into UK, wh is now becoming rather a serious problem. There seemed to be general agreement that we shall have to legislate in the autumn. Colonial Secretary [Macleod] (rather surprisingly) concurred. But we must keep a final decision till then and meanwhile ask Ld Chancellor [Kilmuir] and his Committee[111] (who have already done a lot of work) to go on preparing the necessary measures. There are a great many complications – not least of wh is Irish immigration.[112]

The primary instrument of control was to be a voucher system based on the value to the UK of a potential immigrant's skills. The scheme could be varied according to the condition and needs of the British economy. Applying it in a kind of variable geometry to a variety of passport holders – or would-be passport holders – was one of the vexing 'complications' to which Macmillan referred. It would bite on Commonwealth citizens born outside the UK and those who did not possess a Citizen of the UK or Colonies passport or a passport issued by the Republic of Ireland. The voucher scheme rested on these categories:

A: Those possessing a specific job offer from a UK employer.
B: Persons with skills or qualifications of use to the UK.
C: Unskilled workers.

The plan was to issue 10,000 vouchers per year for category C would-be immigrants (distributed on a first come, first served basis) and 20,800 per year for categories A and B combined.[113]

The Commonwealth Immigrants Bill was published, to uproar, when Parliament reassembled on 31 October. Butler, as Home Secretary the lead minister, had a torrid time throughout its passage. He recalled in his memoirs that

> the Labour Opposition, led by Hugh Gaitskell [whom Butler, unlike Macmillan, admired[114]], launched the most infuriated attack on the Bill, which they labelled as cruel and brutal anti-colour legislation. Indeed, had they persisted through the committee stage, which was taken on the floor of the House [as, at that time, were all bills of constitutional importance], we might not, in the view of Philip Allen [senior Home Office official], have got the measure through at all.[115]

Butler, like Macleod, was a reluctant controller. He had been 'gravely troubled by the Notting Hill riots in 1958'.[116] But he was a sensitive politician. He had believed in the 'open door' immigration policy of the Fifties, which

> Britain alone provided . . . for West Indians, as for all other Commonwealth peoples. We did so because we believed in the motto 'civis Britannicus sum' – that is to say, because the historic right of every Commonwealth subject, regardless of race or colour, freely to enter and stay in Britain was prized as one of the things which helped bind us together.[117]

But public attitudes had shifted and Butler moved with them:

> When public opinion on this issue was tested by the Gallup Poll as late as the summer of 1961, 21 per cent of people in this country still favoured the continuation of unrestricted entry. But by that date more than three times as many – 67 per cent – advocated the imposition of some restrictions. The motives of this decisive majority were doubtless mixed and not all were honourable; but in the circumstances of 1961 it was natural even for the liberal-minded to believe that immigrants could be integrated into our community with tolerance and without friction only if the potential size of the social difficulties involved was reduced.[118]

Listening now to both Macleod and Butler, one hears the sound of old instincts shed but decencies sustained. The Leader of the Opposition, however, was having none of it. Gaitskell was a child of empire and commonwealth at its most cerebral and high-minded. His father, Arthur, was a member of the fabled Indian Civil Service.[119] Gaitskell himself, had he been born a couple of generations earlier, would have made a great, reforming viceroy. The second reading of the Commonwealth Immigrants Bill drew from him one of the two greatest speeches of his life (the other was his anti-Common Market, 'thousand years of history' speech at the 1962 Labour Party Conference).

Butler had told the Commons that, under the British Nationality Act of 1948, 'a sizeable part of the entire population of the earth is at present legally entitled to come and stay in this already densely populated country. It amounts altogether to one-quarter of the population of the globe and at present there are no factors visible which might lead us to expect a reversal or even a modification of the immigration trend'.[120] Gaitskell countered that the question was not one of '50 million Indians' coming to Britain, it was about whether the Bill should be passed. The government did not know the true figures of immigration. These had waned as well as waxed in the past and 'with the Irish out all pretence has gone. It is a plain anti-Commonwealth Measure in theory and it is a plain anti-colour Measure in practice.'[121]

Gaitskell, who had a beautiful, penetrating though never ranting speaking voice, would have none of the breathing-space-to-permit-integration argument. Was the government 'seeking to combat social evils, by building more houses and enforcing laws against overcrowding, by using every educational means at their disposal to create tolerance and mutual understanding, and by emphasising to our own people the value of these immigrants and setting their face firmly against all forms of racial intolerance and discrimination?' Gaitskell implied they were not. Instead: 'They have yielded to the crudest clamour, "Keep them out".'[122]

What Gaitskell did not divulge, and few apart from his ministerial colleagues in the Attlee governments and a handful of officials in Whitehall knew, was that a special Cabinet committee, GEN 325, had sat between July 1950 and January 1951 to consider the then tiny flow of immigration from the empire and Commonwealth, partly because it was felt that the new welfare state might act as a magnet. The full Cabinet meeting on 22 February 1951 approved the committee's report, which warned that restrictions would harm intra-Commonwealth relations and instructed the Colonial Office to keep a close watch on the pace of immigration with a view to possible legislation to curb it.[123] As I wrote in an earlier volume in this series, if the existence and the work of GEN 325 had been known in the early 1960s it could have seriously embarrassed Gaitskell and his Labour colleagues. But '[n]ot a whisper of their work reached the public domain until their papers were released in January 1982'.[124]

For Macmillan, the parliamentary uproar over the Bill saw the Commons 'in so hysterical a mood' not seen 'since the days of Suez'.[125] In the privacy of his diary he described Gaitskell as 'the kind of cad that only a gentleman can be'.[126] Butler eventually steered the measure through. It received royal assent on 18 April 1962. The Commonwealth Immigrants Act came into force on 1 July the same year.

It was a moment of great significance in Britain's history, both imperial and domestic. 'Civis Britannicus sum' was gone – traded for a manageable flow of immigration, social peace and demographic integration. It did not turn out like that. What Butler called his 'labour permits . . . approximately halved the rate of net immigration'.[127] But by permitting so-called secondary immigration of dependants (allowing spouses, children and grandparents to join immigrants already in the UK and those permitted to enter by the new voucher scheme), the number of newcomers remained considerable and led to the Labour governments of 1964–70 modifying their 1961–2 stance and to the Conservative government of Ted Heath bringing forward another substantial piece of immigration legislation in the early 1970s. The immigration debate has remained a continuous factor, freighted with its own special sensibilities and anxieties, in British politics ever since. The cumulative change in the demographic make-up of the United Kingdom has been – and will always be – one of the great shifts in the history of Britain since 1945.

As already noted, the disposal of territorial empire has left scarcely a trace as the decades passed since that last, concentrated rush to withdraw, certainly in comparison with the empire coming *to* the UK in significant numbers. Occasionally, foreign statesmen allude to the loss of empire in order to get under the skin of the Brits. The tradition began while the last great handover was still underway. In December 1962 Dean Acheson, Harry Truman's Secretary of State (and a considerable Anglophile), famously told the young soldiers at West Point, the premier US military academy, that 'Great Britain has lost an empire and has not yet found a role'.[128] ('Always a conceited ass,' wrote Macmillan in his diary,[129] commenting later to a friend that Acheson was 'a nice man, but a kind of American caricature of an Englishman, and always overstates his case'.[130])

Former German Chancellor Helmut Kohl did the same some forty-seven years later at a conference to celebrate the twentieth anniversary of the fall of the Berlin Wall when, speaking of his old antagonist Margaret Thatcher in the company of Mikhail Gorbachev and George Bush Senior, he declared:

> Thatcher says the European Parliament should have no power because Westminster cannot surrender a single bit of its sovereignty. Her ideas are pre-Churchillian. She thinks the postwar era isn't over yet. She believes that history has been unjust. Germany is so rich and Britain has to fight for its survival. They won a war but lost an empire and their economy . . .[131]

Words such as those can still rankle in some British hearts and minds (including, it must be said, this author's).

Why? Because the drumbeats cannot be stilled that fast in a former great power possessing genuine global reach well within the lifetime of several million of us. A running theme of this book and its predecessors is the tracing of the residual great power impulse in its several forms. As I write, I have at hand the Cameron–Clegg coalition government's first National Security Strategy, *A Strong Britain in an Age of Uncertainty*. Its first act was to create its own version of Arthur Balfour's Committee of Imperial Defence, rather more tactfully called the National Security Council. And here, amid serious cuts to the budgets of the Armed Forces and the Diplomatic Service is its *cri de coeur*: 'The National Security Council has reached a clear conclusion that Britain's national interest requires us to reject any notion of the shrinkage of our influence.'[132] Perhaps, like Martin Luther addressing the Diet of Worms in 1521, successive sets of British politicians could do no other. As Jean Monnet put it, when asked about Britain's relative decline in the late 1970s, 'they have not suddenly stepped aside from history'.[133] We still haven't, and show no signs of doing so, Brexit notwithstanding.

5

The Missiles of October

I had the heebie-jeebies then all right. The Berlin crisis was
familiar pieces being played on the board. Cuba wasn't. It
was an entirely different game. I'm sure it was the closest we
came [to nuclear war].

> *Peter Hudson, former senior*
> *Ministry of Defence official, recalling*
> *October 1962 in 2007*[1]

I particularly remember that Sunday morning [28 October
1962]; Whitehall deserted, it was very quiet, rather a lovely
morning, and just walking in there to the Ministry of Defence
and thinking 'My God, I wonder whether this really is it.'

> *Peter Thorneycroft, Minister of*
> *Defence 1962–64*[2]

[A]ny real war *must* escalate into nuclear war.

> *Harold Macmillan, July 1961*[3]

[I]f the signal . . . had been received . . . [w]e would have done
it unhesitatingly. I really mean *unhesitatingly.*

> *Air Vice-Marshal Bobby Robson,*
> *Vulcan navigator at the time of*
> *the Cuban missile crisis, 2001*[4]

We were closer than most people knew during the Cuban crisis of 1962. As, every evening, I came back from work to visit
my wife in the nursing home, where she had given birth to
our youngest daughter, I kept looking into the cradle and

wondering whether I should not baptize the infant myself secretly, lest a disaster overtook us before we met again.

Lord Hailsham, Minister for Science and Technology
1959–64, writing in 1975[5]

From 1957, when Harold Macmillan acquired a substantial nuclear weapons capability with the RAF's V-force reaching operational strength, the spectrum of British defence stretched between two lines: its first line was intelligence; its last the Bomb. The Cuban missile crisis showed the world that the distance between them could be very short.

Macmillan himself knew this already. After an immensely secret review in Whitehall in 1961 of retaliation procedures should the Soviet Union launch a surprise bolt-from-the-blue nuclear attack,[6] the Prime Minister agreed that autumn (a year before Cuba) a grim little drill to increase the chances, were he to be wiped out by a pre-emptive strike, of a senior minister being available to authorize the deployment of the RAF's V-bombers over the Soviet Union and its satellites. With a macabre Shakespearean flourish, he informed the Cabinet Office of his decision:

I agree the following –

First Gravedigger	Mr Butler
Second Gravedigger	Mr Lloyd

HM 5/10/61.[7]

As General de Gaulle liked to say (quoting Nietzsche), 'the state is the coldest of monsters',[8] never more so than in its planning for the aftermath of a nuclear war, but at least the Brits – from the Prime Minister down – tried to inject a dash of private *comédie noire* into the whole grim business. In fact, alongside Macmillan's beyond-the-grave arrangements, a plan was put into place in the early Sixties for a means of communication from Whitehall's operation rooms to the prime ministerial Rolls-Royce should an intelligence warning be received of a likely Soviet attack that was so English – and so bizarre – that had it appeared in an Ealing Comedy it would have not been believed.

In the early 1960s, Whitehall's war planners became anxious that a surprise Russian attack on the UK, with but a few minutes' warning, would break the chain of political control over nuclear retaliation if the Prime Minister was on the road and out of reach of a telephone. A cunning (and cheap) plan was drawn up for an Automobile Association radio link – of the kind the AA used to communicate with its smart, brown-uniformed mechanics on motorbikes – would be used as the warning system. The idea was to use the AA radio system to alert the PM's driver, who would then get him to a phone box as fast as possible so he could ring into No. 10. The system ran from early 1962 until early 1970, when a proper car phone was installed.[9]

The AA link, conveniently installed in time for the Cuban missile crisis (when, as far as is known, it was not used), produced as exquisite an exchange of Whitehall letters as I have ever read. On 22 May 1962, Bryan Saunders, Private Secretary to the Minister of Works (whose responsibilities included the government car pool), wrote to his opposite number in Downing Street, Tim Bligh, to tell him that the AA radios 'have now been fitted in the three cars' earmarked for prime ministerial use. Saunders continued:

> I understand that if an emergency arose while the Prime Minister was on the road, the proposal is to use the radio to get him to a telephone. Perhaps we should see that our drivers are provided with four pennies [the sum needed in a GPO phone box before you could press Button A and get through] – I should hate to think of you trying to get change for sixpence from a bus conductor while those four minutes [the four-minute warning provided by RAF Fylingdales on the North Yorkshire Moors] were ticking by.[10]

Bligh, who was not one to be unduly alarmed by the prospect of a final few penniless minutes on earth, replied the following day:

> The first sentence of your . . . paragraph is correct. But a shortage of pennies should not present quite the difficulties which you envisage. Whilst it may be desirable, when motoring, to carry a few pennies in one's pocket, occasions do arise when by some misfortune or miscalculation they have been expended and one is penniless. In such cases, however, it is a simple matter to have the cost of any telephone call transferred by dialling 100 and requesting reversal of the charge, and this does not take any appreciable time.

Where US presidents and Soviet general secretaries (and, later, French presidents) had (and have) serving officers with them at all times carrying the nuclear retaliation codes and equipment to transmit them, British prime ministers in the Sixties had the AA and small change. As Bligh sensed a touch of risk about UK end-of-the-world procedures and was worried about the reverse charge call being put through, he had a fall-back in mind: 'We are considering the possibility of this office taking up membership of the AA – which would give our drivers keys to AA and RAC boxes throughout the country.'[11]

Macmillan's Shakespearean drollery and Bligh's sang froid apart, planning for the most perilous Cold War crises and a Third World War was an irredeemably grim business with the rolling Berlin crisis of 1958–62 adding a real-life edge to what the Strath Report of 1955 on H-bomb fallout described as events 'beyond the imagination' until they happened.[12] But imagine it the war planners had to, starting with the Padmore Report on 'Machinery of Government in War' which swiftly followed Strath's.[13]

Padmore effectively tore up the existing plans, including those implemented just before the Attlee government fell in 1951 for the central Third World War machine to be housed in old Second World War citadels in Westminster (a pair of 'Rotundas' codenamed SCOUT, close to Great Peter Street and Marsham Street).[14] The difficulty with SCOUT was that an H-bomb would entomb its occupants just before the flooding Thames drowned them.[15] From the Padmore plan, the Corsham bunker and a back-up near Kidderminster (never fully completed[16]) plus regional seats of government each headed by a senior minister were developed. Ordinary parliamentarians were not to have a country seat, though Padmore briefly thought of reviving the Second World War plan to pack them off to the Shakespeare Memorial Theatre in Stratford-upon-Avon.[17] In the event, Parliament, once it had passed the emergency legislation required for a Third World War, would cease to exist until the post-attack recovery phase when those members who had survived would be summoned by the Speaker (if he himself had survived) to the most suitable building that could be found.[18]

Once the Cold War was over the diplomat and former chairman of the Joint Intelligence Committee, Sir Rodric Braithwaite, said of preparing for the worst: 'It was inescapable, it was necessary *and* it was lunatic.'[19] It had to be done – and it was taken very seriously in White-hall right up to the end of the Cold War, even though the small groups who carried out the planning remained not just agnostic but deeply sceptical about what, if anything, would have worked after a thermo-nuclear assault.

The first big exercise of the post-Strath and Padmore provisions took place in April 1959 under the codename CLOUD DRAGON and the real-life Berlin and Cuba crises occurred in its shadow in the sense that its assumptions about the ferocity of nuclear attack, the extent of resulting destruction and what continuity of government was possible conditioned home defence thinking in the early Sixties.

CLOUD DRAGON assumed that East–West relations 'remained reasonably stable' between 1959 and 1964. The last months of 1964 and the early months of 1965 saw a serious deterioration, however, with a nuclear attack on the UK beginning 'soon after mid-day' on 25 April 1965.[20] The planners, seated in the calm of the Central Government War Room inside the North Rotunda in Westminster,[21] contemplated a devastated country. The Sheffield experience alone conveys the awfulness of the consequences:

> There was a 5 megaton ground burst to the north east of Sheffield which affected the whole of the city . . . Because of the high intensity of radioactivity fire fighting was impeded and widespread fires in Shef-field got out of hand. As a result, tens of thousands of homeless passed out of the city to the south in the first 48 hours. Life-saving operations continued to be seriously hampered by fall-out and by long hauls of ambulances to the south . . . Many casualties remain in the debris and there is little hope of their survival.[22]

The terrifying cold print of the might-have-been.

There is no evidence that Harold Macmillan read such reports as this, though he kept in touch with the construction and security of the alternative Central Government War Headquarters in the Cotswolds. In May 1963, for example, only a few months after the Cuban missile crisis, the Cabinet Secretary, Sir Burke Trend, briefed Macmillan on the waning of Corsham's security. The location of the bunker, he explained, 'must be presumed' to be 'a major intelligence objective' for the Russians and 'the espionage agents of the Soviet bloc in the United Kingdom will make a serious and continuous effort to obtain this information'. Indeed, MI5 had now reported 'the movements of a Soviet Naval Attaché in the neighbourhood of TURNSTILE in the last few days ... Whether or not the Russians have penetrated the main TURNSTILE secret, it seems probable they know of the existence of the extensive quarries in the TURNSTILE area and have assumed they would have a significant function in the event of a nuclear war.'[23]

The assistant naval attaché at the Soviet Embassy in the early 1960s was none other than Captain Eugene Ivanov, who shared the favours of Christine Keeler with John Profumo, Secretary of State for War, with such explosive consequences. Ivanov left for Moscow swiftly on 29 January 1963 after Stephen Ward, the society osteopath and close friend of Keeler's, warned him that the story might be about to break.[24] So the Russian attaché MI5 tailed from west London to Wiltshire in May 1963 is likely to have been Ivanov's successor in a post which, as in Ivanov's case, the Security Service knew was usually filled by a Russian military intelligence officer.[25]

Trend sought the Prime Minister's permission to investigate alternative locations for the last redoubt, some of which, he recognized, seemed 'at first sight fantastic' (which they were, including as they did 'Putting the central Government to sea – either above or below water'; 'Flying the central Government abroad – to (say) Canada'; 'Putting the central Government into a mobile column or columns of specially protected vehicles').[26] Advising Macmillan on Trend's brief, his Principal Private Secretary, Tim Bligh, wrote, 'The short point is that the hole in the ground near Bath must be regarded as known to Russia, and the alternative arrangements are based on locations near regional seats of government. And these themselves must be presumed to be amongst Soviet targets for the first wave of nuclear attack.'[27] Macmillan scrawled gloomily on Bligh's minute:

Yes. But whatever hole is
chosen will become known.
    H. M.[28]

Macmillan was prone to brooding on what he always called 'the nuclear', and contemplating being entombed in TURNSTILE must have been among the more lowering moments of his premiership.

In fact, in all his dealings with both Khrushchev and Kennedy, he never lost sight of two things: the unspeakable catastrophe of a war between East and West, which he believed would go nuclear very quickly; and the danger that world war would come through a combination of inadvertence and miscalculation as he was convinced it had in 1914. He carried in his pelvis the fragments of German ordnance that had felled him on the Somme at Ginchy near the Delville Wood on 15 September 1916 and which left him in 'recurrent pain' and with a shuffling gait until the end of his days seventy years on (just as the bullet through his hand at the Battle of Loos left him with a limp handshake).[29] At the time of Cuba, his mind was full of Barbara Tuchman's *The Guns of August*,[30] which his family firm had published that same year. It had, according to his official biographer, 'profoundly affected' him.[31] 'War pressed against every frontier,' wrote Mrs Tuchman:

> Suddenly dismayed, governments struggled and twisted to fend it off. It was no use. Agents at frontiers were reporting every cavalry patrol as a deployment to beat the mobilization gun. General staffs, goaded by their relentless timetables, were pounding the table for the signal to move lest their opponents gain an hour's head start. Appalled upon the brink, the chiefs of state who would be ultimately responsible for their country's fate attempted to back away but the pull of military schedules dragged them forward.[32]

In the early Sixties it might be East German border guards attempting to halt a Western military convoy on the autobahn from the Allied zones to Berlin, or incoming missiles – with but minutes, rather than an hour, to go – appearing on the screens in the Ballistic Missile Early Warning System installation at RAF Fylingdales, that would trigger it. Of all of this Macmillan was acutely aware even before he read Tuchman's vivid prose.

The Paris summit may have collapsed in disorder and indignity in May 1960, and with it the hopes of an early diplomatic solution to Berlin, but Macmillan never stopped seeking another international East–West conference, as he was to do in the fraught days of Cuba in October 1962 (to, one suspects, the passing irritation of Kennedy).

Not for nothing did Khrushchev call Berlin 'the testicles of the West', adding in his coarse way, 'Every time I want to make the West scream, I squeeze on Berlin.'[33] And this he did, with varying degrees of pressure, from the end of November 1958, when he suddenly announced that he intended to transfer responsibility for Berlin to the East German government and threatened unilateral action if the Western powers did not negotiate their withdrawal from the city within six months, right up to the Cuban missile crisis almost four years later.

To Macmillan's sustained anxiety about Berlin was added his frustration that it was the *Germans* for whom the West was having to risk everything. In a telegram of 23 June 1959 he let rip to Eisenhower about the wretchedness of it all:

> Perhaps I can add some general thoughts. We must maintain a public posture in which we can rally our people to resist a Russian attempt to impose their will by force. All the same, it would not be easy to persuade the British people that it was their duty to go to war in defence of West Berlin. After all, in my lifetime we have been dealt two nearly mortal blows by the Germans.
>
> People in this country will think it paradoxical, to use a mild term, to have to prepare for an even more horrible war in order to defend the liberties of people who have tried to destroy us twice in this century. Nevertheless, there is a double strain of idealism and realism in these islands to which I believe I could successfully appeal if we had first demonstrated that we have made every endeavour to put forward practical solutions and that the Russians were unwilling to accept any fair proposition.[34]

Macmillan's natural habit of thinking historically could as often embitter his political thought as enliven or enlighten it, and not just when dealing with Adenauer or the future of Germany. It sometimes embraced Europe's cause against America too, as during the week in August 1961 when he told Parliament Britain was applying for membership of the EEC. After briefing the lobby correspondents in their little tower room in the Palace of Westminster overlooking the Thames, his Press Secretary, Harold Evans, as we have seen, recorded in his diary that Macmillan insisted on my going down to his room and there I had a dissertation on European history – how ironical it was that this small peninsula attached to the land mass of Asia, thinking itself the hub of the universe, should now be utterly dependent on all the people it had driven overseas by persecution, punishment or poverty.[35]

But for American, Brit and European alike, Berlin, at peak moments of anxiety during its running crisis, really was the 'hub' of the Cold War universe as in August 1961 when Evans penned that entry.

For Macmillan himself, Berlin 'overshadows everything'[36] in 1961. The day he put that in his diary – 15 September – coincided with the decision as to which minister would go to what bunker if a Third World War came. In addition to designating Butler and Lloyd first and second 'gravediggers' should he himself be wiped out, Macmillan, in an especially grim period between the building of what became the Berlin Wall in the early hours of 13 August and the Soviets exploding the biggest H-bomb ever (fifty megatons dropped in the Arctic on the island of Novaia Zemlya on 30 October[37]), had to put together the final pieces of machinery of government for nuclear war and its aftermath. Only when the Cabinet Office's nuclear retaliation desk declassified the file forty-five years later did the few surviving ministers of the Macmillan government (the 'gravediggers' apart – who were all by then themselves dead) have an inkling of what was in store for them if Berlin had triggered war.

In London until the last minute would have been Macmillan, Butler (Home Secretary), Home (Foreign Secretary), Sandys (Commonwealth Secretary), Watkinson (Defence Secretary) and ten other ministers. Under the Cotswolds at BURLINGTON (it became TURNSTILE in 1963, shortly after Cuba) would be the Chancellor, Lloyd (to retaliate if Macmillan didn't make it), Macleod (Colonial Secretary), Maudling (President of the Board of Trade) plus eight more ministers. Eleven other Cabinet ministers would have headed a bunker apiece – Henry Brooke (Minister of Housing) in Wales near Brecon; Ernest Marples (Minister of Transport) in the north-west near Preston; Lord Hailsham (Lord President of the Council) in the south near Dover, and so on.[38]

The Cabinet Secretary, Sir Norman Brook, had also prepared plans for a half-way house emergency scheme if Berlin worsened.[39] He also warned:

We must be prepared for a lengthy period of fluctuating political tension with the possibility that, either suddenly or in the course of negotiations if they begin, a critical politico-military situation may develop. If such a situation arises urgent consideration will have to be given to the possibility of action – diplomatic, economic or military.[40]

Brook proposed an arrangement to bridge the gap between normal peacetime government and the strategic warning stage, '[at which] . . . point we might have to consider the possibility of a small War Cabinet'.[41] In these circumstances, the Prime Minister would preside over a Ministerial Committee on Berlin (himself, plus Butler, Home, Lloyd, Watkinson and Sandys)[42] with streamlined input from the Chiefs of Staff, the Joint Intelligence Committee and a special 'Berlin Room'.[43] In these circumstances, Brook explained, 'we shall not go underground or have executive decisions taken by "map rooms" [i.e. in BURLINGTON]. But the normal methods must be accelerated.'[44]

Throughout 1961 Macmillan was haunted by the possibility of Berlin suddenly going critical. His diaries are shot through with anxiety about war through miscalculation and laced with a constant desire for an East–West negotiation to take the sting out of the crisis:

. . . we may drift to disaster over Berlin – a terrible diplomatic defeat or (out of sheer incompetence) a nuclear war.

22 June 1961.[45]

If neither Kennedy nor de Gaulle will take a positive lead, I feel that I shall have to do so. We cannot just drift, or we shall drift to disaster.

23 September 1961.[46]

. . . all thinking people . . . know that we must have a negotiation and (with the cards we have) we cannot play the game too high.

25 September 1961.[47]

Khrushchev, in the course of a 6 hour speech at the Communist Party Congress threatened to blow up a 50 megaton and even a 100 megaton bomb. But, he said there was now no fixed date for the unilateral treaty with DDR [East Germany]. He was ready for negotiation.

19 October 1961.[48]

What worries me all the time is the possible parallel [with Munich, 1938]. Are we 'appeasing' Soviet Russia? Ought we to risk war? Is Khrushchev another Hitler? Myself, I am pretty happy about the answers to all these questions. Still, they pose themselves.

4 December 1961.[49]

As they have posed themselves subsequently to historians – some of whom have been highly critical of Macmillan.[50] Percy Cradock is right to suggest that Macmillan 'wanted negotiations at almost any price' and that he 'did not like the Germans and saw no reason to face nuclear war on behalf of Dr Adenauer's prejudices against the GDR'.[51] At the time, Macmillan knew that his deep urge for a diplomatic answer to Berlin was leading to accusations that he was 'the frailest of the four'[52] (Kennedy, de Gaulle and Adenauer being the other three). But Macmillan was not alone in Whitehall: his Cabinet was with him on Berlin. And he thought Adenauer and de Gaulle were posturing. Just after Kennedy's visit to London, in June 1961, on the way home from his bruising first encounter with Khrushchev in Vienna, which raised tensions considerably,[53] a despairing Macmillan ('everything is going wrong'[54]) poured his worries out in his diary at home in Birch Grove:

Khrushchev is determined to bring the issue to a head in the autumn . . . Faced with all this, and by no means encouraged by the reality (apart from the superficial success) of his visit to Paris, the President seemed rather stunned – baffled, wd perhaps be fairer. This was the real reason for his wish for a private talk . . .

I welcomed this. For I did not wish, if I called attention to some of the underlying realities of the Berlin problem, to be reported verbally and then misreported by hearsay, so that Americans wd think we were 'yellow' and French and Germans (who talk 'tough' but have no intention of doing anything about Berlin) could ride out on us . . . But certainly – so far as regards Russia – the prospects are pretty grim.[55]

So they were, for both sides were under real pressure.

Khrushchev's problem was a blend of three factors. After Sputnik in 1957, the 'missile gap' in favour of the Soviet Union (of which Kennedy had made much during his 1960 campaign for the presidency) became privately known in Washington to be not just a myth, but a reverse of the truth – the American 'Corona' satellite flights got underway in August 1960 and prime intelligence on Soviet rocket forces began to flow from Colonel Oleg Penkovsky of Russian military intelligence at much the same time. As a very senior member of the Secret Intelligence Service put it many years later, 'Penkovsky really did change the way we saw things. He solved many mysteries. We were quite wrong in our existing perceptions.'[56] Khrushchev did not know about Penkovsky until the KGB closed in on him in the second half of 1962 – but he, Khrushchev, knew his boastful public bragging about Soviet military superiority was pure bluff.

Khrushchev was under pressure, too, from his Warsaw Pact ally, the East German leader, Walter Ulbricht, and his rival for the leadership of world communism, Mao Tse-tung in China. Ulbricht wanted the Berlin problem sorted as thousands of his most skilled workers were flowing through the still-porous border from East Berlin to West. With the Sino-Soviet split developing, Mao was forever criticizing the Moscow leaders for excessive accommodation with the West.

What, from London's point of view, were 'the underlying realities of the Berlin problem', as Macmillan put it? British intelligence was well aware of the communist bloc influence on Khrushchev. Reporting in July 1960, a couple of months after the collapse of the Paris summit, the Joint Intelligence Committee wrote of 'Khrushchev's own lack of self-restraint when his vanity or innate combativeness are stirred', plus 'the Soviet inability to refrain from grasping at obvious gains; and the influence on Soviet action of the differences between Peking and Moscow'.[57] The JIC had known since the first Berlin crisis of 1948–9 of the special vulnerability of the Western sectors of the city. The Soviets could simply close off the land and waterway routes from West Germany with physical barriers, requiring the Western allies to shoot first if they tried to put a military convoy down one of the autobahn corridors – and they could do it at no notice without any advance warning to Western watchers.[58]

As the second Berlin crisis gathered pace in 1959, the Chiefs of Staff were reminded of this stark fact: 'The opportunities for physical obstruction are so great that the Soviets/GDR do not need to use force and may not do so.'[59] In July 1960 the JIC reinforced this assessment and alerted its readers to technological factors that would make the mounting of an airlift much more difficult this time. The Soviets, the JIC judged,

> would try to avoid opening fire first and might therefore allow the Allies to remove the first obstacles; but if the advance continued, and in the absence of negotiations, they would sooner or later have to oppose it with military force (which they could successfully do). The opposition would be likely to come from [GDR] conventional Forces . . . in the initial stages.
>
> Equally effective Soviet reaction is not immediately possible in the air, where more or less direct action against Allied aircraft offers the only reliable counter, although over a period of time ECM [electronic countermeasures] etc. could seriously hamper a full-scale airlift.[60]

His intelligence feed no doubt reinforced Macmillan's consistent view that who provided the border guards on the autobahns was not worth a Third World War and that a negotiated settlement was possible without global conflict or serious diplomatic defeat (though, of course, the question of the border guards was but the lightning conductor for the first-order confrontation over Berlin).

Eventually, a contingency anticipated by the JIC at the beginning of the crisis nullified much – but never all – of the venomous danger in which Berlin placed the world, though not without a final ratcheting up of tension and a dramatic tank-to-tank confrontation at Berlin's Checkpoint Charlie. That contingency was to become perhaps the most symbolic image of the Cold War – the Berlin Wall, thrown up at great speed in August 1961 and whose dismantling in November 1989 dramatically signified the end (or so it was assumed at the time) of Cold War confrontation. Two and a half years before it was built, the JIC anticipated the wall in a single sentence. 'They [the Soviets] will probably permit the [GDR] to seal off East Berlin from West Berlin to prevent the refugee exodus.'[61]

The early Sixties saw a second peak of Cold War hostility (the Suez crisis and the invasion of Hungary by the USSR in the autumn of 1956 were moments of great East–West peril rather than a prolonged period). The first phase grew during the late 1940s and reached its zenith in the first months of the Korean War in 1950. The Korean stalemate after mid-1951 and the armistice of 1953, following Stalin's death, showed, as had Stalin's own easing of the Berlin Blockade in June 1949, that the world could come back from the brink. The second phase – Berlin from the end of 1958 morphing into Cuba nearly four years later – was the more dangerous of the two because of the thermonuclear capabilities of both sides.

Many have argued that Berlin 1961 was more perilous than Cuba 1962. Paul Nitze, whose longevity within inner national-security circles in Washington lasted from the Truman White House to Reagan's, certainly thought so, believing the possibility of a direct armed clash to be greater in 1961 than in the following year.[62]

Tony Jay, an informed outsider who was editing the BBC Television *Tonight* programme at the time, still thinks so: 'I certainly felt much more worried about Berlin than I did about Cuba. I really did feel that the Russians could start annexing Western Europe by moving into West Berlin then into West Germany. Cuba was an island thousands of miles away. You couldn't do salami tactics with it whereas you could with Europe.'[63]

There could, therefore, be a long drawn-out choreography over Berlin (as Peter Hudson pointed out at the start of this chapter), whereas Cuba almost came out of the blue and went – like a tropical storm of fierce, electric force.

July–October 1961 felt as intense as anything that had been experienced since before the start of the Cold War. Kennedy was deeply shaken by Khrushchev's bullying, bluster and intransigence in Vienna in early June. 'I want peace, but if you want war that is your problem,' Khrushchev shouted, banging his fist on the table.[64] When he returned to Washington, after what Percy Cradock called 'his initiation in the painful rites of the Berlin club',[65] Kennedy ordered an urgent review of US options.[66]

Khrushchev did not table-bang with Macmillan directly at this stage. He contented himself with a particularly nasty outburst the following month when he ran into the British Ambassador to Moscow, Sir Frank Roberts, at the ballet. Khrushchev claimed that in a global nuclear war, the enormous United States and Soviet Union would survive but West Germany, France and the United Kingdom would 'perish' on 'the first day'. How many bombs would be needed to put the UK out of commission?' he asked Roberts. 'Six,' replied Roberts. Khrushchev then went into his ranting mode:

> he told the Ambassador that he had heard an anecdote about pessimists and optimists in Berlin; the pessimists thought that six bombs would be required to put the UK out of commission while the optimists felt that nine would be needed. Thus the UK Ambassador belonged to the category of pessimists. The Soviet General Staff, however, had earmarked several scores of bombs for use against the UK so that the Soviet Union had a higher opinion of the UK's resistance capacity that [sic] the UK itself.[67]

Since the Strath Report of 1955,[68] Whitehall's secret planning for what survival was possible had, in fact, been based on ten 10-megaton Russian H-bombs on the UK.

Optimists and pessimists. The terminology the early-Sixties Cold War crises has bequeathed us 'hawks' and 'doves',[69] and both lined up in the Washington of summer 1961 to press their analyses on Kennedy. There were also what a trio of Harvard analysts later described as 'owls', who reckoned that 'a major war would not arise from careful calculations but from organizational routines, malfunctions of machines or of minds, misperceptions, misunderstandings and mistakes'.[70] Macmillan was an 'owl' throughout both Berlin and Cuba.

Kennedy studied the range of hawkish, dovish and owlish papers presented to him on Berlin at the family home at Hyannis Port on Cape Cod over the weekend 22–23 July 1961. Two nights later, his broadcast to the American people contained elements of all three species of Cold War bird life. The New York Times billed the broadcast as Kennedy's 'second inaugural'[71] (in his first he had famously declared 'Let every nation know, whether it wishes us well or ill, that we shall pay any price, bear any burden, meet any hardship, support any friend, oppose any foe, in order to assure the survival and the success of liberty . . .'[72]).

For Kennedy – and the world – the stakes were high. And for the young President, still only seven months into his first term, the scars of Khrushchev's brutality were real. As Khrushchev warned his Presidium colleagues, he (Khrushchev) had deliberately set out to raise the stakes

over Berlin with that 'son of a bitch' Kennedy through a swift confrontation with the rookie President.[73] Now, on prime-time television
on a steamy Washington night, the rookie tried to put the Vienna
setback right.

It was a well-crafted speech. The United States could not abandon
its 'commitment to the two million free people' of Berlin. The city, 'a
tempting target' for the Russians because of its location, had 'now
become – as never before – the great testing place of Western courage
and will . . . We cannot and will not permit the Communists to drive
us out of Berlin, either gradually or by force.' There was some balm
for Macmillan when Kennedy declared, 'We will at all times be ready
to talk, if talk will help. But we must also be ready to resist with
force, if force is used upon us.' And in a phrase that was very Macmillanesque, Kennedy announced that, to ensure that the USA had 'a
wider choice than humiliation or all-out nuclear action',[74] he would
ask Congress to boost the US defence budget by $3.25 billion and to
increase the funding for civil defence (stimulating a surge of anxiety
across America[75]). Congress, moved by Kennedy's 'we seek peace; but
we shall not surrender', obliged.[76]

Khrushchev had deliberately invited John J. McCloy, Kennedy's
disarmament adviser, to his southern retreat at Pitsunda in the
Caucasus to receive his instant response to the President's speech.
'Kennedy has declared preliminary war on the Soviet Union,' he
shouted.[77] In Berlin the flood of refugees turned into a cataract as
the East Berliners came over the S Bahn and down through the
subway in droves.[78] McCloy left Pitsunda on 26 July, the very day
Khrushchev told his Ambassador to the GDR to tell Ulbricht that 'we
are approaching this question seriously and if this drags us into war,
there will be war'. He also told Ambassador Pervukhin to inform the
East German leader that 'we have to use the tension in international
relations now to circle Berlin in an iron ring' before the Americans
made their next move.[79]

The JIC's February 1959 prediction was about to come true.
Whitehall's strategic intelligence was sound but its tactical equivalent
did not predict the exact moment, because of the classic Berlin
problem – the Russians and East Germans could make their dispositions effectively out of nowhere. Kennedy, however, had anticipated

such a move nine days ahead of it happening. On 4 August, while walking in the White House's Rose Garden with Walt Rostow, his Special Assistant for National Security Affairs, he said:

> East Germany is hemorrhaging to death. The entire East bloc is in danger. He has to do something to stop this. Perhaps a wall. And there's not a damn thing we can do about it . . . I can get the alliance to move if he tries to do anything about West Berlin but not if he just does something about East Berlin.[80]

In the early hours of Sunday 13 August, when Kennedy was up in Hyannis Port and Macmillan asleep at Birch Grove (having just finished Trollope's Barchester series),[81] the construction of the wall began. The barbed wire and, within days, the breezeblocks were put in place just after Macmillan had been congratulating himself in his diary on the Americans' 'complete "volte face"' on negotiations with the Soviets over Berlin.[82] That Berlin August of 1961 remains one of the most vivid memories for all those who lived through the Cold War, whether or not they followed the minutiae of the crisis. The headlines and broadcasts over those later summer days – not least when the US Army sent 1,500 reinforcements down the Autobahn from West Germany (the Russians stopped them, counted them and let them through) – produced some really breathtaking moments. We felt, to borrow a phrase of P. D. James, as if we were subject to a kind of capricious 'arithmetic of survival'[83] completely beyond our control. Such events and the fears they induced were powerful recruiters for the Campaign for Nuclear Disarmament, as we shall see.

Macmillan reacted with a characteristic mixture of anxiety and sang froid. He left London for Yorkshire to take advantage of the new shooting season by slaughtering a few grouse at Swinton ('200 brace a day or so, wh with only 6 guns is good'[84]). After motoring on to Bolton Abbey in pursuit of further game, he penned a long entry in his diary about Berlin:

> A lot of telephoning, morning and evening, to Alec Home [Foreign Secretary] about the 'Berlin Crisis'. The East German authorities have shut down on all movement from East to West Berlin. The flood of refugees had reached such proportions – over 3000 a day – that they

were probably almost compelled to take this course. Partly because the West German elections are going on, and partly because the Americans have got very excited, the situation is tense and may become dangerous ...

The Americans wanted to issue a great and rather bombastic 'declaration', but this has now been shot down, partly by de Gaulle's irony and detachment, partly by our insistence on combining a willingness to negotiate with any declaratory reaffirmation of allied rights and obligations. The President sent me a message about sending more troops into Berlin. Militarily, this is nonsense. But I have agreed to send in a few armoured cars etc., as a gesture. I still feel that from Khrushchev's point of view, the Eastern German internal situation was beginning to crumble and something had to be done. But I also believe that he does not want to produce a situation wh may lead to war. The danger is, of course, that with both sides bluffing, disaster may come by mistake.[85]

Fears of 1914 again. And the tension continued to rise. Kennedy sent his Vice President, Lyndon Johnson, to Berlin along with the hero of the Berlin Air Lift, General Lucius Clay. The extra US troops who came down the autobahn were cheered in by West Berliners in scenes reminiscent of 1948–9.[86]

The coming weeks and months were among the most photogenic and photographed of the entire Cold War – the wall going up to replace the barbed wire; an East German policeman leaping over at the last minute; refugees rushing at it or being lowered or jumping from upper storeys of tall buildings which now became the border and whose windows would soon be bricked up; cleared zones filled with tank traps on the eastern side of the wall; and all but seven of the crossing points closed by the East Germans.

One of these – Checkpoint Charlie, between the US sector and East Berlin south of the Brandenburg Gate – became the scene of perhaps the most often shown film exhibit of the Cold War. At the end of October 1961, a senior US diplomat and his wife were refused entry to East Berlin to visit a theatre. Clay sent an armed detachment to get them through and then ten US tanks drove up fast to Checkpoint Charlie, the foremost halting suddenly and lurching at the stop-line. On 27 October 1961, Soviet tanks appeared. We learned later that their commander 'had a direct line to the Kremlin. Khrushchev told him that should the Americans use force, he must respond with force.' Kennedy, through a back channel, told Khrushchev that if his front tank withdrew, the first US tank would follow suit. After sixteen hours barrel-to-barrel, the lead Russian tank withdrew five yards. The American M-48 did the same.[87]

Macmillan thought the Checkpoint Charlie histrionics and brinkmanship absurd – and told Kennedy so. The Brits, in fact, had done a bit of low-key asserting themselves, however, within hours of the wall going up. On 13 August Sir Kit Steel, the Ambassador in Bonn, did it on his own initiative, as his Private Secretary, David Goodall, recalls:

> 'We'll take the Rolls and fly the flag,' he said. So he and his indomitable wife, with me in the front seat beside the driver, set off in the Rolls with the Union Flag flying bravely on the bonnet (and in pouring rain) for the East. Since the Ambassador was a stickler for old-fashioned proprieties, I was wearing a bowler hat. First we drove along Bernaeurstrasse . . . then proceeded to an improvised crossing point, where the East German border guards were plainly doubtful whether to let us through.
>
> But the flag, the grandeur of the car and the production of our British Military Government identity cards evidently persuaded them that it would be a mistake to stop us, so we drove on towards the shabby, run down centre of old Berlin. 'Now, David,' said the Ambassador, 'you must get out and walk' (i.e. to assert our physical presence). So I got out in the rain and promptly slipped on my back in the gutter, losing both my bowler hat and my dignity.[88]

Better, perhaps, losing a bowler than being fired on by a tank.

October 1961 ended with the standoff then stand-down at Checkpoint Charlie, particles of detritus from the Novaia Zemlya bomb spreading around the world, Khrushchev claiming he would double its size to a hundred megatons (which he never did),[89] and the erection of the grim, thirteen-foot-high wall in Berlin. The wall was, in its brutal way, progressively easing the crisis. Western rights of access to Berlin and within it were intact (David Goodall's bowler had served its purpose). But the people of East Berlin had been sacrificed to a wider peace. As Kennedy said to one of his aides: 'Why would Khrushchev put up a wall if he really intended to seize West Berlin? There wouldn't be any need of a wall if he occupied the whole city. This is his way out of his predicament. It's not a very nice solution, but a wall is a hell of a lot better than a war.'[90]

That autumn Khrushchev lifted his ultimatum from 1958 that a peace treaty be concluded for Germany completing the work left unfinished at the Potsdam conference of 1945. The Russian and American foreign ministers opened talks. But Macmillan did not get his conference to sort out Berlin and complete the work of the ruined Paris summit of 1960. In fact, though Macmillan did not know it, after the Kennedy–Khrushchev meeting in Vienna in June 1961, there would be no more four-power summits of the kind Macmillan craved. Although the Vienna meeting had been ghastly, the two superpowers would henceforth meet *à deux*. In the autumn of 1962 the Cuban missile crisis gave Macmillan a bit of great powerdom on the side – a last, fleeting part for the Old Greek in Whitehall playing up to the New Roman in Washington – but the automatic British place at the 'top table', as Churchill put it when he saw the British 'H' bomb as its guarantor,[91] was no longer there.

Berlin, mercifully, did not trigger a Third World War in the early Sixties, but it certainly stimulated the British to produce a fine set of films and novels with the 'testicles of the West' as its backdrop. As Louis Heren of *The Times* conveyed better than anyone, Berlin had a special allure: 'Isolation gave Berlin a sharp identity and enhanced its inner excitement.'[92] Louis, a Shadwell boy and the greatest of raconteurs, did not share Macmillan's irritation at the West having to defend *them*, of all people. Louis saw them as a rare genus – honorary cockneys:

West Berliners . . . probably had the world's lowest expectations and the highest score for survival. They were . . . largely ignored by the Bonn government because of its provincial meanness and dislike of cockneys. They knew their future would be decided by Washington and Moscow, and for reasons that had little to do with their well-being. They knew that the communications to the west . . . could be squeezed, blocked or cut. They also knew that theirs was no mean city. No wonder West Berliners were cockneys, aware that they would not get an even break but quick-witted and shrewd. They even spoke a German cockney, quick and abbreviated, sharp and mocking.[93]

For him, there could be no higher praise.

As a reporter in the late Fifties and early Sixties, 'Berlin,' Heren wrote, 'drew me like a magnet'.[94] So it did, too, some of the best spy novelists and film-makers. Just as early post-Second World War grimly battle-scarred Vienna was the star of Carol Reed's *The Third Man* in 1949,[95] two British classic novels swiftly resulted – John le Carré's *The Spy Who Came in from the Cold* (1963) and Len Deighton's *Funeral in Berlin* (1964). Both were made into cracking films by Paramount, with Richard Burton as Alec Leamas, the ageing SIS officer and agent runner in East Germany, in *The Spy Who Came in from the Cold* (1965), and Michael Caine as the brash operator Harry Palmer (a cockney character after Louis Heren's heart), in *Funeral in Berlin* (1966).

Deighton's *Funeral in Berlin* begins with Palmer calling on Robin Hallam, a Home Office official who deals with defectors, at his seedy flat in south-west London on an autumn Saturday morning: 'I walked up the steps where the sun was warming up a pint of Jersey and a banana-flavoured yoghurt. Tucked behind the bottles a *Daily Mail* peeped its headline "Berlin a new crisis?"'[96]

The following day he is flying over the

> parade ground of Europe [which] has always been that vast area of scrub and lonely villages that stretches eastwards from the Elbe – some say as far as the Urals. But halfway between the Elbe and the Oder, sitting at attention upon Brandenburg, is Prussia's major town – Berlin ... Nowhere does a grand bridge and a wide flow of water divide the city into two halves. Instead it is bricked-up buildings and sections of breeze block that bisect the city, ending suddenly and unpredictably like the lava flow of a cold-water Pompeii.[97]

Le Carré's *The Spy Who Came in from the Cold* begins and ends with the Berlin Wall as the last of Leamas's blown network of agents, Karl Riemeck, approaches one of the checkpoints that punctured it as Leamas watches from a West German police pillbox:

'A man . . .' the younger policeman whispered, 'with a bicycle'. Leamas picked up the binoculars.

It was Karl . . . Only the Vopo [East German People's Police] in the middle of the road [between] the line and safety . . . Then, totally unexpected, the searchlights went on, white and brilliant, catching Karl and holding him in their beam like a rabbit in the headlights of a car. There came the see-saw wail of a siren, the sound of orders wildly shouted. In front of Leamas the two policemen dropped to their knees, peering through the sandbagged slits, deftly flicking the rapid load on their automatic rifles . . .

The first shot seemed to thrust Karl forward, the second to pull him back. Somehow he was still moving, still on his bicycle, passing the sentry, and the sentry was still shooting at him. Then he sagged, rolled to the ground, and they heard quite clearly the clatter of the bike as it fell. Leamas hoped to God he was dead.[98]

The book ends at the Berlin Wall, too. Leamas and the woman he loves, Liz Gold, are coming back into the West from the East over the Wall. Liz is shot and falls back into the Soviet sector. George Smiley calls, 'Jump, Alec! Jump, man!' Leamas sees Liz lying dead at the bottom of the ladder. He slowly climbs down to die with her, 'glaring round like a blinded bull in the arena' as the shots ring out.[99]

Deighton set the end of *Funeral in Berlin* back in London, but the coldly magnetic city is its final thought. It is Armistice Sunday in November:

There is a sudden cannonade of artillery rumbling across the low cloud as Big Ben tolls eleven. Blancoed webbing and polished metal shine in the dull wintry light and there is a sudden flash of brandished trumpets. The notes of the Last Post crawl dolefully up the still thoroughfare as a thousand stand tensely silent.

Across the silent, wet street, a newspaper tumbles gently like an urban tumbleweed. It floats just buoyant on the wind, kisses a traffic sign, lightly dabs a slide trombone and plasters itself across army boots. The newspaper is rain-soaked to a dull yellow colour but the large headline is blunt and legible. 'Berlin – a new crisis?'[100]

The next big crisis was not to be *in* Berlin (though the Berlin problem was a part of it). In the autumn of 1962, the chilling alphabet of the Cold War suddenly moved on a notch from 'B' for Berlin to 'C' for Cuba, at which point P. D. James's 'arithmetic of survival' added up to almost certainly the most perilous crisis of the four decades of East–West confrontation.

Before analysing those dangerous days, what of the genuine world of espionage – the *permanent* confrontation of the Cold War? The early Sixties really were spy-soaked, not just in fiction.

It is easy to portray those years as ones of unredeemed failure, starting with the Berlin Wall, of which no tactical warning had been received by human or technical means (that is, neither from agents nor signals, electronic or satellite). Then there was the uncovering of a string of Soviet agents such as George Blake in MI6, John Vassall in the Admiralty, and the spy ring, run by the KGB 'illegal' Gordon Lonsdale at the Portland Underwater Detection Establishment.* That was certainly the public and press impression created by this string of scandals. In fact, in secret, British intelligence was for the first time in the Cold War beginning to enjoy a measure of real success against the Soviet bloc, leading to the exposure of both Blake and Lonsdale.

The Berlin 'failure' illustrated some of the endemic problems in procuring timely intelligence even when agents and systems were in place. Simon Case has described how, during successive Berlin crises (1948 for the blockade and 1953 for the riots in East Berlin), 'British and American intelligence did not have the sources to predict events; in 1961 the source existed, but the mechanics of espionage which involved the agent collecting and relaying information safely followed by assessment, source protection and distribution procedures, made it impossible to get the intelligence to the policy-makers in time.' As Case explains, the 'East German planning circle had been so tight that the opportunities to gather the crucial information were very slim. [Oleg] Penkovsky [a double agent in Moscow] learnt of the plans four days in advance, but had no means of getting the information to the West.'[101]

Penkovsky, a colonel in the Soviet military intelligence organization, the GRU, was the first top-flight agent the West ran in the Cold War. His speciality – rockets – struck his MI6 and CIA handlers (it was a joint operation) as a godsend, his intelligence confirming

* An 'illegal' is a super-secret Soviet agent, as distinct from a spy masquerading as a diplomat operating undercover out of the Russian Embassy or Trade Mission in London.

that no 'missile gap' existed in the Soviets' favour (quite the reverse) and providing a flood of information on weaponry and capability during the two years of maximum nuclear anxiety, 1961–2. In the course of a series of clandestine meetings in London and Paris when accompanying Soviet trade missions to the West, and snatched assignations with Janet Chisholm, wife of the Secret Intelligence Service Station Chief in Moscow, Penkovsky passed over photographed copies of more than 10,000 pages of documents during two years of operational life as a Western asset until his arrest on 22 October 1962 as the Cuban missile crisis approached its climax.[102]

Penkovsky was a driven man. His zeal to bring down the Soviet system he had come to loathe led him to plead with his MI6 and CIA handlers at his second meeting with them, in Room 360 of the Mount Royal Hotel near Hyde Park Corner on 21 April 1961, to let him have a small stock of tiny portable atomic weapons to blow up the Soviet leadership in Moscow. After all, he declared, 'If Hitler had destroyed our military command centres, he would have won the war.'[103] Wisely, the US and UK secret services took no notice; his MI6 handler was the shrewdest anti-Soviet operator of all, Harold Shergold. Shergold was well aware, as he reported to 'C', his SIS chief, Sir Dick White, that Penkovsky was unstable and craved eventual fame as 'the best spy in history'.[104] Shergold also knew how to distinguish between the reliability of things that Penkovsky understood at first hand, such as the capability of current Russian missiles and the future plans for Soviet rocket forces, and his often wild and rambling tittle-tattle about leading Moscow figures and the internal politics of the régime.

Penkovsky's product was given its own special codename and distributed on a strictly need-to-know basis in Whitehall. Neither the codename nor the product is yet declassified,[105] but Catherine Haddon has made a study of its impact on the Joint Intelligence Committee and its specialist groups on missiles (in July 1961, with Penkovsky in full spate, a new Missile Threat Co-ordination Committee was specially created[106]). She has detected a definite Penkovsky factor in the papers, which, with the yield from the first Corona satellite programme (which the US shared with the UK), removed a high degree of uncertainty that had previously existed about Soviet rocket capabilities. 'Despite the incomplete archive,' she writes, 'it is clear from the records available that the pace of missile-related intelligence intensified during 1961, and, combined with the richness of material from Penkovsky and American satellite imagery, this represented an important advance for UK intelligence.'[107]

Penkovsky's passion to spy verged on the messianic. He ran himself hard – and he took great risks. His handlers ran him hard, too – partly, one suspects, because they knew his occasionally reckless lack of trade-craft would at some point lead to his unmasking and it was important to milk him to the maximum before that happened. He was, briefly, the bringer of an intelligence feast to the West after years of famine. He also vindicated Shergold's insistence, when he had become SIS Controller Sov Bloc in the mid-Fifties, on abandoning the old system of networks (of the kind the fictional Alec Leamas ran), as they were immensely vulnerable to KGB penetration, and replacing them with the solo, high-grade, high-level agents nurtured and run with immense care and whose existence was known to but a handful in the secret world.[108] With such assets and a supply of well-placed defectors, British intelligence also had a far greater chance of discovering whether it was penetrated and by whom. It was one such Polish defector, handled by the CIA, Michael Goleniewski, who exposed Blake.[109]

Blake was summoned back to London from Berlin for interrogation by a team led by Shergold shortly before Shergold began to debrief Penkovsky in the Mount Royal Hotel. This must have offered SIS some private consolation, at least (because Blake, if he confessed, would go on trial and the country would know of this huge intelligence setback while remaining ignorant, naturally, of the secret triumph Penkovsky represented). In public, however, Blake could not be portrayed as anything other than a diplomat, a Foreign Office man, for, as Macmillan noted in his diary on 4 May 1961, after Blake's swift trial and sentencing

> . . . the case of George Blake – a traitor – has shocked the public. The L.C.J. [Lord Chief Justice, Lord Goddard] has passed a savage sentence – 42 years in prison! Naturally, we can say nothing. The public do not know and cannot be told that he belonged to MI6 – an organisation wh does not theoretically exist.[110]*

---

* Although Macmillan mentions Blake for the first time in his diary in early May 1961, he almost certainly had warning of his existence earlier.

On the basis of Goleniewski's information from inside Polish military intelligence, Shergold had been pretty certain from early 1961 that the MI6 mole was Blake.[111] SIS legend has Macmillan warning Kennedy of his coming exposure during their 'Grand Design' meeting in Washington in early April (' "C" 's nabbed a wrong 'un,' he is alleged to have said confidentially to a completely uncomprehending President).[112] Kennedy would soon have been aware of the immense damage caused by Blake. Legend also has it that his forty-two-year sentence reflected one year for every death of a Western agent he caused in the Soviet bloc. Blake denies this, but the number could have been far higher.[113]

In June 1950, Blake had been SIS's number two in the Seoul Embassy when North Korea invaded the South. Swiftly captured along with the rest of the diplomatic staff, he identified himself as an SIS officer and offered to work for the Russians while in captivity in the North in the autumn of 1951. The KGB's station chief in London, Nikolai Rodin, travelled to North Korea to prime him on how to operate once the war was over and Blake was back in London.[114] It was the reasons for his move towards betrayal in that North Korean prison camp that, according to Blake, caused him finally to confess to Harold Shergold and his team of interrogators in the SIS safe house in Carlton Terrace Gardens nearly a decade later. (It was the same house from whose balcony the newly returned Blake had been invited to witness the Coronation procession in June 1953.[115])

The SIS team, 'courteous' throughout, recalled Blake, made it plain they knew he was a Soviet agent and took him through a variety of indicators they possessed to this effect. Blake held out until

> whether by luck or by planning, they hit upon the right psychological approach . . . 'We know that you worked for the Soviets, but we understand why. While you were their prisoner in Korea, you were tortured and made to confess that you were a British intelligence officer. From then on you were blackmailed and had no choice but to collaborate with them.' . . .
>
> Suddenly I felt an upsurge of indignation and I wanted my interrogators to know that I had acted out of conviction, out of a belief in Communism, and not under duress or for financial gain.[116]

Privately, the SIS team had worried that Blake would not break and, without a confession, a conviction under Section 1 of the Official Secrets Act of 1911 would not be possible. SIS veterans recall that, almost as a last shot, Shergold said to Blake that he wondered how he, Blake, would proceed if he was conducting the examination in the same knowledge that the man under interrogation was guilty.[117] Whatever the sequence, the quiet attempt to appear to understand Blake worked.

Shergold took Blake home for the weekend to his cottage in the Sussex Weald. Blake made pancakes with Shergold's mother-in-law: 'The next three days had something surreal about them with everyone pretending that this was just an ordinary weekend party among friends. The only difference was that the house was surrounded by Special Branch Officers and, every time we went out for a walk, a police car drove slowly behind us. It . . . struck me as . . . endearingly English.'[118] So it was – and not the way the KGB treated Penkovsky when he was uncovered eighteen months later.[119]

Blake was a truly damaging 'wrong 'un'. It took a great deal of painstaking toil for SIS to trawl thorough all the papers that might have been compromised by him, and carefully grading the likelihood of his having seen them. 'Every file had red, amber or green on them,' an insider explained. 'Blake blew a lot of stuff all over the place.'[120] But, once the Cold War was over, what was thought to have been one of his technically most damaging betrayals turned out to be less so. Blake blew the Berlin tunnel, dug by the British and the Americans in 1955 to tap the cables used by the Soviet military in Berlin and East Germany. The Soviet authorities let the tapping continue until Khrushchev and the Soviet Premier, Nikolai Bulganin, were on their April 1956 visit to London, when they exposed it to cause maximum embarrassment.[121] Once Blake's treachery became known, it was seen as an unmitigated defeat for Western intelligence and the tapped traffic as a huge deception.

In fact, it turned out not to be so. In 1993 Sergei Kondrashev, Blake's controller in London, revealed that the KGB had merely told the Red Army and the GRU to take care of their telephone security. Apart from that, they let the military communications pour down that cable for fear of blowing their prize agent, Blake.[122] Western intelligence learned a very great deal about the Soviet forces in East Germany and Berlin from that traffic thanks to the KGB not caring about the Soviet military's secrets as much as they cared about their own.[123]

The appetite of both sides for intelligence on each other was huge and constant throughout the Cold War. In 1962, the JIC's Watch Lists ('Red' for a Soviet attack from a standing start; 'Amber' for a move west after a longer build-up) were permanent tasks for the intelligence world (seventeen indicators on the 'Red'; forty-seven on the 'Amber'), embracing a huge range of human, signals and electronic sources.[124] But, however good the flow, even during especially rich periods such as Penkovsky's span in 1961–2, there are real limits to intelligence. As Peter Freeman, a distinguished GCHQ official with long Cold War service, wrote (anonymously) in his first chapter on 'The Nature and Use of Intelligence' in the Butler Report of 2004:

> The most important limitation on intelligence is its incompleteness. Much ingenuity and effort is spent on making secret information difficult to acquire and hard to analyse. Although the intelligence process may overcome such barriers, intelligence seldom acquires the full story. In fact, it is often, when first acquired, sporadic and patchy, and even after analysis may still be at best inferential.[125]

It may also infer presciently and then lose sight of its insight as the years pass. Cuba was an example of this.

As early as 1957, as the research of my former student Alban Webb discovered, the JIC anticipated the possibility of a Cuban-style crisis. The Cabinet Office analysts thought the Soviet Union might 'be prepared in extreme cases to send "volunteer" formations' to a sympathetic country outside the Eastern bloc and that the Russians 'might well feel their policies and prestige would suffer a serious blow if they failed to respond to a request for help ... by making nuclear weapons available to [a] non-Communist power'.[126] This was two years before Fidel Castro's revolution in Cuba and part of an exercise to forecast hostilities short of global war up to 1965. But the JIC could not foresee the Castro phenomenon in 1957 any more than it could foretell Khrushchev's rush of blood by the Black Sea in May 1962 on a visit to Bulgaria, when he decided to put missiles into

Cuba.[127] For quite a while he had been deeply exercised by the presence of US Jupiter missiles in Turkey, and every time he holidayed by the Black Sea he would indulge in a little rant about them. He would give his guests a pair of binoculars and ask 'What do you see?' They would gaze across the water and see nothing. Khrushchev would grab the binoculars and cry: 'I see US missiles in Turkey, aimed at my dacha.'[128]

In this little holiday party-piece we find the trigger for the greatest and most analysed superpower confrontation of the postwar years – the Cuban missile crisis of October 1962. As John Lewis Gaddis, one of the finest Cold War-synthesizers, put it:

> No episode in the history of international relations has received such microscopic scrutiny from so many historians. Theorists have generalized exuberantly from this single event. Surviving participants have spent much of their lives reliving what they did during those critical thirteen days. And whether alive at the time or not yet born, almost everyone who knows anything about the last half of October 1962, regards it as the moment at which the world came closer than ever before, or since, to a nuclear conflagration.[129]

At the mere mention of Cuba and the date, memories still flare into life across the globe. Such a phenomenon carries its own historical danger in its very familiarity. Historians, as the French philosopher Raymond Aron liked to remark, have a duty to put back as much uncertainty into the past as we feel today about the future.[130] To a remarkable degree, Khrushchev's plan – more a grand design, as we shall see in a moment – remained remarkably secret remarkably long, given the amount of Soviet equipment and Russian troops already on the island by the time the CIA presented President Kennedy with the U-2 photographic reconnaissance showing unmistakable evidence of missile sites. This was on 16 October 1962, two days after the aircraft had overflown the San Cristóbal installations on the west of Cuba.[131]

It really was a war scare without warning. Britain, unlike the USA, retained an embassy in Havana, and an SIS station as part of it. The Ambassador, Herbert ('Bill') Marchant, caught this neatly in a telegram to Alec Home on 10 November 1962:

Any record of the story of these first two weeks of the Cuban crisis must necessarily read more like a wildly improbable sequel to [Graham Greene's] 'Our Man in Havana' than a Foreign Office despatch. Indeed I doubt whether a month ago any reputable publisher would have given a moment's consideration to a story in which Soviet Russia was to be credited with shipping some four dozen assorted giant missiles, each one longer than a cricket pitch, across the Atlantic to Cuba, where, Russian military technicians disguised as agricultural advisers would set them up in secret on launching sites – some of them just off the main road less than 50 miles from Havana. Certainly no publisher would have accepted a Chapter II in which less than a week later the same missiles were feverishly dismantled, packed up and re-shipped back across the Atlantic. Yet this in brief is precisely what seems to be happening.[132]

Nor could a publisher have anticipated just what a Tuchmanesque two weeks the crisis would represent. For what we now know about the near misses, especially under the waters of the Caribbean, has continued to chill the memory of the crisis since the 1990s.

Let us return for a moment to Nikita Khrushchev's dacha and his obsession with the newly placed US Jupiter missiles in Turkey, whose presence took the gloss off his holidays. Perhaps their greatest historical significance is that somewhere inside the synapses of the Soviet leader's brain, those rockets triggered an impulse that started to create a grand design in his mind – a dangerous and delusive urge, one might be tempted to conclude, whether one was a classically trained Balliol man in bed at Chequers over the New Year or a peasant-turned-Bolshevist in his holiday dacha beside the Black Sea. Deploying nuclear missiles on Cuba was to be the pivot of a daring attempt to tilt the balance of power and the Cold War permanently Russia's way, as we now know from Soviet archives mined by Aleksandr Fursenko and Timothy Naftali. Operation ANADYR (named after a Siberian river to give the impression it was an internal reinforcement exercise[133]) would, at a stroke, bring vast swathes of America within range of Soviet missiles, dramatically ameliorating their numerical inferiority. When the rockets were unveiled to the world *after* the November 1962 mid-term Congressional elections – as was the plan – Kennedy would be obliged to accept them as a fait accompli, together with a Soviet proposal to get the United Nations into West Berlin as an interim solution before the Allies got out, and a deal on the abolition of nuclear weapons testing in the atmosphere.[134]

ANADYR had too many moving parts. What was the fallback if Kennedy rumbled the plan and his administration simply refused to roll over? It is possible that if Anastas Mikoyan, the veteran diplomat, had been present at the Presidium meeting on 1 July 1962, his natural caution and scepticism would have enabled the plan to be properly scoped and tested. But he was absent.[135] A few days later, Fidel Castro's brother, Raúl, was in Moscow and the plot was hatched.

As Khrushchev's plan began to take shape in the Russian capital, Kennedy's mind in Washington was turning towards the appalling prospect of a nuclear war through miscalculation. This had nothing to do with CIA or National Security Agency warnings of Khrushchev's and Castro's intentions and everything to do with Barbara Tuchman's *The Guns of August*, which in July 1962 he too was reading. After absorbing Tuchman, Kennedy

> focused on a 1914 conversation between two German leaders. 'How did it all happen?' one asked. 'Ah,' the other replied, 'if only one knew.' Kennedy told his White House staff members, 'If this planet is ever ravaged by nuclear war – and if the survivors of that devastation can then endure the fire, poison, chaos and catastrophe – I do not want one of those survivors to ask another "How did it all happen?" and to receive the incredible reply: "Ah, if only one knew." '[136]

That same month, to help posterity know, he instructed a secret-service agent to install microphones and taping devices in the Cabinet Room, the Oval Office and the Library of the White House, though quite how he thought the tapes would survive a nuclear assault on Washington is hard to imagine unless the plan included their last-minute removal to the presidential nuclear bunker in the Appalachians. It is thanks to these tapes and the transatlantic scrambler phone transcripts in the National Archives that we can eavesdrop on the Kennedy–Macmillan conversations as the crisis deepened.

Given the intensity of US intelligence surveillance devoted to Cuba, it is remarkable how long it took Washington to realize what was happening. Charles de Gaulle found this aspect of the crisis as surprising as Khrushchev's initial strategy. During his Rambouillet conversation with Macmillan a month and half after the missile crisis, as de Zulueta recorded it, the General 'First of all ... had been astonished by Khrushchev's audaciousness in putting his bombers and his soldiers in Cuba and so risking a war. He had also been surprised at how bad the American intelligence had been.'[137]

Western intelligence had picked up the surge of shipping out of the Barents and Black seas in July, August and September 1962. It would have been hard to miss it (sixty-five ships sailed for Cuba in July, for example[138]). By the time the CIA's U-2 spy plane, overflying Cuba on 14 October, confirmed the existence of the medium-range ballistic missile (MRBM) launch sites near San Cristóbal, Khrushchev had completed a huge logistical amphibious operation, the largest of its kind in Soviet history,[139] a mere ninety miles off the coast of Florida.

Until those U-2 photographs reached Kennedy on 16 October, his administration, taking Soviet statements at face value, continued to believe that what war materiel was aboard those ships was for defensive purposes. By the time Kennedy threw a 'quarantine' around Cuba (he did not want to call it a blockade – which it was – because of associations with the two world wars) on 22 October, Khrushchev had managed to land on Cuba an astonishing 42,000 troops, 36 MRBMs, a squadron of nuclear bombers with six nuclear bombs in their inventory, 80 cruise missiles and 158 nuclear warheads.[140]

Mercifully, when the executive committee (Excomm) of Kennedy's National Security Council went into a series of crisis sessions from 16 October, they knew neither that the warheads were already there nor that the Soviet general in Cuba, Issa Pliyev, had authority to use the tactical nuclear weapons on US troops should they storm the beaches of Cuba. Robert McNamara, Kennedy's Defense Secretary, confirmed many years later that the risk of nuclear war over Cuba was 'far greater' than Excomm had realized at the time because they did not think authority to use the Luna tactical missiles could have been delegated to the Russian commander on the island.[141]

The UK government is generally seen as largely an observer of what was 'essentially a duel between Kennedy and Khrushchev', as

Sir Percy Cradock described Macmillan's position during the crisis.[142] Two American scholars, Ernest May and Philip Zelikow, who have processed the product of those hidden tape recorders in the White House, see the UK position differently, on account of Sir David Ormsby-Gore's ambassadorial sessions with Kennedy and Macmillan's transatlantic phone calls. 'It is,' they wrote '. . . obvious from these records that Macmillan and Ormsby-Gore became *de facto* members of Kennedy's Executive Committee.'[143]

When did the UK become involved in the crisis? By coincidence, senior figures from the British intelligence community were in Washington during its first week for a CIA conference on intelligence methods. The Agency's Deputy Director, Ray Cline, deceived them all week about the nature of the flap in Washington until a few hours before they left for home on Friday 19 October, when Kennedy permitted Cline to brief Sir Burke Trend, Deputy Secretary of the Cabinet, and Sir Kenneth Strong, Director of the Joint Intelligence Bureau:

> I misled them all week into thinking my preoccupation with business was about Berlin, not Cuba . . . My exercise in deception was totally successful because these British friends took several occasions with me during the week to argue with me that the Russians would never put missiles in Cuba because of the risk to their interests in Europe.[144]

It's very hard for even the best-primed people to understand the grand designs of others – though Trend and Strong would have no illusions about Khrushchev's impulsiveness.

Ormsby-Gore guessed that it was Cuba that same day, before word of Cline's conversation reached him. Macmillan recalled that Kennedy had spoken 'in guarded terms' to the British Ambassador: 'Although David Gore gave no details, he sensed that the alarm in the White House was "probably about missiles in Cuba". So the blow was destined to fall not in the East, but in the West – not in Germany, but in the Caribbean.'[145]

Macmillan did not allow Cuban anxieties to divert the flow of his weekend at Chequers over 20–21 October (though he slept badly on both nights). He pondered over the fate of the Central African Federation and Rab Butler's rather leisurely approach to 'the whole game'.

He talked to Heath about the progress of the Brussels negotiations, worked on his 'Modernisation of England policy' for the forthcoming Cabinet meeting on Tuesday and he took the Prime Minister of Uganda and the Duke of Devonshire for a walk in the Chilterns. At ten on the Sunday night 'I got a message from President Kennedy, giving a short account of the serious situation wh was developing between US and USSR over Cuba. I wd get a fuller account from the ambassador tomorrow.'[146]

Monday 22 October 1962 Macmillan dubbed 'The first day of the World Crisis!'[147] David Bruce, the hugely accomplished US Ambassador in London, brought Macmillan (by now back in Admiralty House, from where the UK end of the Cuban missile crisis would be handled) masses of material, including the U-2 photographs of the missile sites. Over the next few days, Gore in Washington and Kennedy, over both the teleprinter and the telephone, would supply updated reports and reflections in an almost constant stream.

Cuba was the making of Kennedy's reputation, and his gifts for pithiness with insight and for thinking aloud are very evident in records of the US–UK politico-military traffic of late October 1962. For example, in a message to Macmillan on that same Monday, Kennedy described the siting of missiles on Cuba as 'so deep a breach in the conventions of the international stalemate that if unchallenged it would deeply shake confidence in the United States'[148] (a phrase Macmillan repeated to his Cabinet, whom he kept fairly fully informed[149]). Khrushchev had meant Operation ANADYR to be the first of a series of steps that would shift the balance of the Cold War confrontation but had not anticipated the possibility of Kennedy's seeing it in such stark terms or its triggering (as Kennedy put it in the first of a string of telephone calls to Macmillan shortly after midnight on 22–23 October) an American countermove in the form of an 'escalation in a way that lessens the chance of a seizure of Berlin, or World War III'. 'Now,' Kennedy went on, 'we may not be able to prevent either, but at least we have served notice on him that we cannot accept the procedure and the actions which he carried out.'[150]

Kennedy's first conversation with Macmillan on the secure scrambled transatlantic line (which Macmillan was quite incapable of operating without de Zulueta's help[151]) took place shortly after he had addressed the American people and the world at 7 p.m. Washington time on the evening of 22 October. Kennedy spoke in his address about the missiles on Cuba as an addition 'to an already clear and present danger'. He was placing 'a strict quarantine' around Cuba to turn back any seaborne offensive military equipment en route for the island and calling on Khrushchev 'to halt and eliminate this clandestine, reckless and provocative threat to world peace'.[152]

From this moment on, the world held its breath. In the Kremlin, there was a sharp inhalation as the Presidium had not anticipated either that the missile sites would be discovered so soon, or the nature of Kennedy's response. Nor until 22 October did Soviet intelligence or the Russian leadership have any idea of the intense debate and contingency planning that had been preoccupying Kennedy's Excomm for six days. All the top military spy in Washington could tell the Kremlin was to expect a statement from Kennedy, which 'it is assumed . . . has to do with the possibility of new measures regarding Cuba or Berlin'.[153] Khrushchev lost grip of his grand design from that moment, and from then on three of the key Cold War capitals, Washington, London and Moscow, were engaged in a continuous and fraught recalibration of the possibilities of war and peace created by a Caribbean contingency for which, unlike Berlin, there was no elaborate preplanning. This was less a matter of Tuchmanesque transition-to-war planning, trapping the nuclear powers and tipping them over the brink, than a series of desperate, all-round attempts to keep away from it.

Khrushchev summoned his Presidium to a meeting ahead of Kennedy's televised address. Fursenko and Naftali call it 'arguably the most tense of Khrushchev's career'.[154] Even before he heard Kennedy's exact words, Khrushchev virtually admitted to his colleagues that Operation ANADYR was unravelling dangerously. 'The point is,' he said, 'we didn't want to unleash a war. All we wanted to do was to threaten them, to restrain them with regard to Cuba', as the American missile bases girdling the Soviet bloc 'have restrained us'.[155] The seasoned Anastas Mikoyan did not like what he was hearing, especially when Khrushchev touched on the command-and-control of the nuclear weapons on Cuba. He was appalled at the prospect of allowing Castro any say in their use and was alarmed at Khrushchev's policy of letting the Soviet commander on Cuba release the tacticals if there was a US invasion. 'Doesn't using these missiles mean the start of a thermonuclear war?' Khrushchev listened. In the event of an invasion, the short-range missiles could be launched against the beaches but only with conventional warheads. At 1.15 a.m. Moscow time on 23 October, the text of Kennedy's speech reached the Kremlin. Khrushchev immediately interpreted it as 'not a war against Cuba but some kind of ultimatum'.[156]

Tuesday 23 October was a day of high tension which all who lived through it will not forget. Would the Soviet freighters turn back? Publicly, the Kremlin suggested they would not, denouncing the US blockade as 'an act of aggression' and declaring that 'the Soviet Union cannot fail to reject the arbitrary demands of the United States'.[157]

Macmillan spent the day briefing his Cabinet on his conversations with Kennedy in the morning,[158] the Labour leader Hugh Gaitskell in the late afternoon (Gaitskell was accompanied by George Brown and Harold Wilson: 'They hadn't much to say. Brown was more robust than G. Wilson looked very shifty. Fortunately, they all distrust each other profoundly'[159]), and finally the Queen (she 'was naturally much interested in Cuba'[160]) before spending the evening, very tired, at supper with his confidante Ava Waverley.[161]

The always poised Philip de Zulueta reached home very late for a dinner party, after leaving a series of messages for his wife, Marie-Lou, who recalled: 'Philip finally arrived about ten. His face was a study. "I really am most desperately sorry, but we may be at war in the morning",' he told her.[162]

The US Navy blockade of Cuba was due to begin at 10 a.m. Washington time (2 p.m. London time) on 24 October. Macmillan woke at 6.30 a.m. and sought refuge in routine – finishing the red boxes he had been too tired to complete the night before:

> . . . the first clash will soon begin, if the Russian ships sail on. Not much from Russia yet, except words.[163]

Kennedy had not consulted Macmillan about the blockade. In fact, Whitehall thought it was illegal, as the Lord Chancellor, Lord Dilhorne, told the Cabinet on 25 October.[164] Macmillan dissembled on this in public, informing the House of Commons 'that this is not the moment to go into the niceties of international law'.[165]

He was to remain publicly supportive of Kennedy throughout while informing the President of his doubts and reservations in private. He was to Kennedy, perhaps, what Mikoyan was to Khrushchev – a purveyor of seasoned caution which, one suspects, irritated Kennedy but not to the point where the phone calls fell away. It was Macmillan's desire throughout the crisis for an East–West conference to ease the tension that worried his Ambassador, Ormsby-Gore, in Washington and the Foreign Office at home. The records ring to this theme, including the transcripts of his conversations with Kennedy and the telegrams that passed between them. Perhaps even more annoying to American ears was, as the CIA's Chester Cooper recorded after briefing Macmillan with Ambassador Bruce on 22 October, the Prime Minister's world-weary advice on how to live under a direct Soviet missile threat:

> [T]he British people, who have been living in the shadow of annihilation for the past many years, had somehow been able to live more or less normal lives and he felt that the Americans, now confronted with a similar situation would, after the initial shock, make a similar adjustment. 'Life goes on somehow.'[166]

Nonetheless, Kennedy seemed to place real value on his conversations and exchanges with Macmillan. Alec Home, who was by Macmillan's side virtually throughout the crisis, told me he reckoned the shared personal nuclear responsibility was a key element in their relationship – a kind of bonding of the button:

> Jack Kennedy, I always think, felt fairly lonely in carrying this responsibility and being the only man who could put his finger on the button ... Kennedy trusted Macmillan absolutely ... I think he was relieved that somebody else was in on the act.[167]

Home was talking in the context of Macmillan securing his Polaris deal at Nassau a few weeks after Cuba, but the judgement fits the missile crisis too.

It was on the day the US blockade of Cuba began that the special Kennedy–Macmillan relationship intensified. The President had not sought the Prime Minister's views about imposing the quarantine but, a few hours after the Soviet freighters began to turn back, Kennedy was on the phone asking Macmillan straight out the 64 thousand dollar question 'Should he take out Cuba?' I said I would like to think about this and send an answer (it's just like a revue called 'Beyond the Fringe' wh takes off the leading politicians) . . . Meanwhile the 'guilty' ships seem to be turning away. At least 3 or 4 have done so. We also know (from British Intelligence) that a number of Russian ships not so far on in the queue are returning via Baltic to Polish or Russian ports.[168]

Macmillan told Kennedy the turning round of the Soviet freighters 'is a great triumph for you'. As for the rest of us it was a huge relief but, as Macmillan knew full well, it was only a temporary one and he quickly put to Kennedy the most difficult question: 'How are you going to get the rockets out of Cuba? The ones that are there now?'[169]

It produced perhaps the most intriguing of all their exchanges, showing, among other things, how assiduous Macmillan was in infiltrating his conference-before-war theme into their conversations:

KENNEDY: Well, if we go through stage one . . . and if they respect our quarantine, then we've got this problem of the rockets on Cuba. And the last 24 hours' film shows that they are continuing to build those rockets, and then we're going to have to make the judgement as to whether we're going to invade Cuba, taking our chances, or whether we hold off and use Cuba as a sort of hostage in the matter of Berlin. Then any time he [Khrushchev] takes an action against Berlin, we take an action against Cuba. That's really the choice that we now have. What's your judgement?

MACMILLAN: Well, I would like to think about that. I think it is very important, because I suppose the world feels that we shall, sometime or other, [have] to have some sort of discussion with them. But we don't want to do that in such a way that he has all these cards in his hands.

KENNEDY: He has Cuba in his hands, but he doesn't have Berlin. If he takes Berlin, then we will take Cuba. If we take Cuba now, we have the problem of course of these missiles being fired, or a general missile firing, and we certainly will have the problem of Berlin being seized.

MACMILLAN: Yes, I agree with that. It needs thought. I see that he has made some proposal on the wireless in answer to Lord Russell

[Bertrand Russell had telegrammed Khrushchev on 23 October appealing to him 'not to be provoked by the unjustifiable action of the United States in Cuba'[170]] saying that he wants a summit meeting. Have you heard that?

KENNEDY: Yes, I saw that, but he said there would be no point in a summit if we continued our piratical actions. The implication was that he would be glad to talk, but not if we continued our quarantine or if we carry it out. He wasn't very precise . . . Then the Secretary General [of the United Nations, U Thant] has asked for a sort of cessation of our quarantine for 2 weeks, but we can't agree to that unless they would agree not to continue work on the missile bases.

MACMILLAN: Yes, I think that's quite right. But all the same, I think that he [Khrushchev] is a bit wondering what to do, don't you?[171]

Khrushchev certainly was wondering what to do, as we shall see in a moment. But just how great the consternation and debate were in the Kremlin neither Kennedy nor Macmillan could know. Even if the CIA or MI6 had a spy inside the Presidium (which they didn't), he would not have been able to meet his handlers to give anything approaching a real-time account of its deliberations. Penkovsky had been arrested on 22 October,[172] but even when operational he had not had access to human intelligence of this kind. However, the copious technical intelligence he had provided did mean that Western analysts knew precisely what kind of missiles were to be placed on those sites in Cuba.

In his conversation with Macmillan, Kennedy agreed that the Russians 'certainly have not been very precise in the last 24 hours' and then he put what Macmillan called, in the language of a contemporary US television quiz show, the aforementioned $64,000 question:

The question I would like to have you think about, Prime Minister, is this one. If they respect the quarantine, then we get the second stage of this problem, and work continues on the missiles. Do we then tell them that if they don't get the missiles out, that we're going to invade Cuba? He [Khrushchev] will then say that if we invade Cuba that there's going to be a general nuclear assault, and he will in any case grab Berlin. Or do we just let the nuclear work go on, figuring he won't ever dare fire them, and when he tries to grab Berlin, we then go into Cuba. That's what I'd like to have you think about.

Macmillan said he would.[173]

The nuclear clock was ticking – and the whole world knew it. Cuba was a very public crisis from the moment Kennedy made his television appearance on Monday 22 October until Moscow Radio announced on Sunday 28 October that the missiles were to be withdrawn from Cuba. For those six autumn days it really did feel as if a fuse had been lit.

Khrushchev knew it too. On Thursday 25 October he reconvened the Presidium to find a way out. He suggested a deal. He would withdraw the missiles from Cuba if Kennedy undertook not to invade Cuba. Operation ANADYR was no more. The grand design of using Cuba and Berlin to turn the Cold War tide against the West was abandoned. 'We can [still] defeat the USA from USSR territory,' he declared. 'We have succeeded in some things and not in others.' There was but a fleeting mention of Berlin.[174] If Sherlock Holmes had existed as a strategic analyst in 1962 he would, *Silver Blaze*-style, have treated Berlin as the mystery of the-dog-that-did-not-bark-in-the-night. The 'testicles of the West', so central to Macmillan and Kennedy's calculations, remained unsqueezed. Khrushchev appears not even to have contemplated doing so as ANADYR slipped from his grip.

Other mysteries remain. Did Khrushchev authorize the KGB station chief in Washington, Aleksandr Feklisov, to act as his back channel to Kennedy by floating the no invasion/no missiles trade to John Scali of the ABC news network over lunch on Friday 26 October? Scali, as Feklisov undoubtedly knew he would, passed on the message instantly to the US State Department.[175] The Feklisov–Scali contact was the first hint the West had of a change of tactic in the Kremlin – a recognition that turning their freighters round would not be sufficient.

Macmillan had spent the previous day, Thursday 25th, making a statement to the House of Commons in the morning about the crisis and briefing his Cabinet in the afternoon – 'I told the Cabinet about Cuba (wh they seem quite happy to leave to me and Alec Home)'[176] – before turning their thoughts to the modernization of Britain. At 6.30 he entertained the Westminster lobby correspondents for two hours

('The consumption of alcoholic refreshment was extraordinary'[177] –
no doubt several of them thought it quite possibly the last No. 10
party they would ever attend):

> President came on at 11 p.m. There was a much clearer picture now. U
> Thant had made his proposal of a 'ceasefire'. Of course, the Russians
> accepted, for they had everything to gain. Kennedy's answer was very
> ingenious. He referred to the major question – how to get rid of the
> rockets. But he wd agree to Ambassador [Adlai] Stevenson [at the
> UN] discussing it with U Thant in New York. 14 ships have turned
> round. 1 oil tanker stopped and was allowed to proceed. The Ameri-
> cans will not agree to call off the blockade on the unsupported word
> of the Russians. A short talk. We agreed to speak again tomorrow
> night.[178]

By the time they did, Kennedy had received a letter from Khrushchev containing the no invasion/no missiles offer. As Khrushchev's
message was still coming in that Friday evening in Washington, Dean
Rusk, Kennedy's Secretary of State, was briefing the UK, French and
West German ministers about the likely US timetable for destroying
the missile sites if preparations to make them ready did not cease.[179]
Ormsby-Gore concluded that the attack would come on Tuesday
30 October.[180]

Macmillan, as he wrote later in a long, catch-up diary entry on
4 November, was evermore worn out by the severity of the crisis, the
lack of sleep from staying up till the small hours to talk to Kennedy
on the phone and his age: ('At 68 I am not as resilient as when I was
a young officer. Yet this has been a battle, in which everything was at
stake') and the tension between 'the frightful desire to do something'
and 'the knowledge that not to do anything (except talk to the President and keep Europe and the Commonwealth calm and firm) was
prob the right answer'.[181]

The 'frightful desire to do something' continually broke through,
however. When he and Kennedy talked on the Friday night, Macmillan floated the idea of helping 'the Russians to save face . . . by our
undertaking to immobilise our Thor missiles which are here in England' while a conference was held to ease the crisis.

Kennedy replied:

> Sure, Prime Minister, let me send that over to the [State] Department. I
> think we don't want to have too many dismantlings. But it is possible that
> that proposal might help. They [the Soviets] might also insist on Greece,
> on Turkey, and Italy [Jupiter missiles were also stationed there] . . .

Macmillan could not 'see why they should ask for more, because
we have got 60 [Thor missiles, on RAF bases from East Anglia to
Yorkshire under dual-key US/UK control]. So that missile for missile,
you see, there wouldn't be as many as in Cuba'.[182]

In fact, the crisis was solved by a secret deal (of which Kennedy did
not inform Macmillan) whereby the US would withdraw its Jupiters
from Turkey after a decent interval if the Soviet Union removed its
own instantly from Cuba. The trade was achieved late on the evening
of Saturday 27 October when Bobby Kennedy, the US Attorney
General and the President's brother, paid a clandestine call on the
Russian Ambassador in Washington, Anatoly Dobrynin. To Khrushchev's immense credit, he kept this deal secret.

What really shook the analysts who pored over the entrails of the
Cuban missile crisis (and still do) was the rapidity with which it developed and the degree to which armed conflict might have arisen
through one side misreading – or wrongly anticipating – the actions
of the other, or by a refusal to contemplate abandoning a dangerous
posture once taken for reasons of pride. This last factor very much
concerned the Joint Intelligence Committee when it assessed 'First
Soviet Reactions to US Action and Intentions Concerning Cuba' on
Friday 26 October. Among the Soviets' 'primary reasons', the analysts, before hearing of Khrushchev's proposed deal, believed, was

> to safeguard what they have already established in Cuba and to reduce
> to a minimum the possible loss of face which might be caused by a
> failure to do so or to respond firmly. They probably believe that their
> installations already in Cuba provide additional leverage in any future
> negotiations on Berlin and other questions.[183]

A few weeks later, when the crisis was over, the JIC produced a paper
on 'Escalation', which it shared with the Americans and the Canadians,

examining 'the chances of avoiding global war once hostilities have broken out' as 'the side attacked could not give way, especially in the early
stages, without suffering a grave political reverse'.[184]

The JIC's analysts in the first weeks of November 1962 would have
had some knowledge of how fraught a day 27 October 1962 had
been. But not until the early 1990s, at the time of the thirtieth anniversary of the crisis when many of the relevant documents were
declassified, could they (if still alive) have appreciated just how close
the world came to war-through-inadvertence on what the Americans
came to call 'Black Saturday', which 'may well have been the closest
we have come to Armageddon'.[185]

What Kennedy, in particular, knew was alarming enough; Macmillan, too, though sadly he did not pen a diary for that extraordinary
day, which remains a blank between the last sentences of 26 October
('The situation is very obscure and dangerous. It's a trial of will.') and
the first of 28 October ('I am writing this in a state of exhaustion,
after being up all Friday and Saturday nights – to about 4 a.m.')[186]

Saturday the 27th was 'Missiles of October' day – the most Tuchmanesque moment of the entire Cold War. In perhaps the most gripping
passage of *The Guns of August*, Barbara Tuchman recreated the events
of another world-crisis Saturday – 1 August 1914; the day the German
ultimatum to Russia expired at noon – with brilliance and insight. The
afternoon lengthened. Reply came there none from Moscow. Theobald
von Bethmann-Hollweg, the German Chancellor, declared: 'If the iron
dice roll, may God help us.'[187] They did roll; just before five in the late
afternoon. On Saturday 27 October 1962, the nuclear dice came closer
to rolling than at any other time in the four decades of East–West confrontation and the missile crisis very nearly did take on a life of its own
even without a set of mobilization timetables to drive it.

Overnight on Friday 26th and Saturday 27th a U-2 spy plane
adapted with sensors to locate debris from Soviet nuclear tests took
off from Eielson Air Force Base in Alaska to fly to the North Pole and
back, safely away from Soviet airspace.[188] On the return leg, the
'northern lights' (the atmospheric phenomenon known as the aurora
borealis) affected its navigation equipment and the pilot, Captain
Charles Maultsby, strayed into Soviet airspace over the Chukotsk Peninsula in Siberia.[189] Soviet MiG-19s were scrambled to intercept the U-2

and US F-102s, carrying air-to-air nuclear missiles, were scrambled from Alaska to protect it. Mercifully, the F-102s reached Maultsby first and guided him back to base.[190] There was no way the Russians could tell what kind of U-2 it was – nuclear sniffer or photographic reconnaissance aircraft, the possible precursor of a nuclear strike by B-52 bombers.

Kennedy had moved his nuclear forces to Defence Condition [DEF-CON] 2 (one short of war) at 10 a.m. Washington time on Wednesday 24 October as the quarantining of Cuba came into force.[191] One in eight of their B-52s were now airborne at any one time.[192] The US Navy's nine Polaris submarines moved to their patrol areas within firing range of their Soviet targets.[193] The DEFCON-2 signal was uncoded. The Russians picked it up.[194] It was *not* the moment for a US spy plane to violate Soviet air space.

News of Maultsby's wanderings did not reach the Pentagon until early afternoon, causing Kennedy's Defense Secretary, Robert McNamara, to express 'sharp alarm about the danger of a war'.[195] According to his speechwriter, Ted Sorensen, Kennedy reacted by saying 'There's always some son of a bitch who doesn't get the message.' The President fully appreciated that the straying U-2 might have led Khrushchev to 'speculate that we were surveying targets for a pre-emptive nuclear strike'.[196]

It was a menacingly bad day for U-2s. Kennedy's Excomm was in late-afternoon session when news came in that a U-2, overflying Cuba, had been shot down and the pilot, Major Rudolf Anderson, killed. The transcript of the Excomm tape captures the moment vividly:

KENNEDY: Well now, this is much of an escalation by them, isn't it?

MCNAMARA: Yes, exactly. And this – this relates to the timing. I think we can defer an air attack on Cuba until Wednesday [31 October] or Thursday [1 November] but only if we continue our surveillance, and fire against anything that fires against a surveillance aircraft, and only if we maintain a tight blockade in this interim period. If we're willing to do those two things, I think we can defer the air attack until Wednesday or Thursday and take time to go to NATO.

KENNEDY: How do we explain the effect of this Khrushchev message of last night? And their decision [to shoot down US surveillance aircraft over Cuba], in view of their previous orders [to fire only if attacked], the change of orders? . . .

MCNAMARA: . . . I don't know how to interpret it.[197]

Only twenty-seven years later, during a conference in Moscow, was interpretation possible of the decision to launch a surface-to-air missile against Major Anderson's U-2:

> It is now clear that the order to fire was given by a subordinate commander in Cuba, unbeknownst to Moscow, where Khrushchev was urgently struggling to find a diplomatic resolution of the crisis . . . [it] was taken by Lieutenant General Grechko, the air defence commander, in consultation with the deputy-chief of Soviet forces, Lieutenant General Garbuz. The previous day, Fidel Castro had told General [Issa] Pliyev [commander of Soviet forces in Cuba] that his anti-aircraft batteries would open fire at low-level naval reconnaissance aircraft on Saturday morning.[198]

All the Soviet forces on the island were convinced a US attack was imminent. When the radar picked up the U-2, Grechko and Garbuz could not contact Pliyev and took the decision to fire themselves – way down the chain of command from Khrushchev in Moscow, whom Kennedy and McNamara were convinced had changed the rules of engagement.

After this revelation in 1989, most analysts would have plumped for the Grechko–Garbuz decision as the moment when the world came closest to an East–West nuclear war. We now know it was not the U-2s of 'Black Saturday' that brought the apocalypse closest but a near-miss underwater, shortly after Major Anderson had been shot down on 27 October 1962, of which *all* the protagonists were unaware apart from the crew of B-59, a Soviet Foxtrot-class diesel-electric submarine (an update on the earlier Zulu class)* armed with twenty-one conventional torpedoes and one nuclear torpedo capable of destroying a group of surface ships.[199]

The Foxtrots were noisy and had to surface at regular intervals to

---

* 'Foxtrot' and 'Zulu' were, respectively, NATO-assigned names for what the Soviets designated Project 641 and Project 611 patrol submarines.

recharge their batteries. The cautious and sensible Mikoyan had opposed their deployment to deep run the blockade, as had the Commander-in-Chief of the Soviet Navy, Admiral Sergei Gorshkov. They thought they had prevailed in the Presidium on 23 October but the order to turn back was not transmitted to the Foxtrots closing in on the shallow waters off Cuba.[200]

Their captains had written instructions not to fire their nuclear torpedoes without direct instructions from Moscow.[201] The US Navy sonars had little difficulty detecting the old and noisy Russian submarines and dropped grenades around those they discovered to force them to surface. Captain Valentin Savitsky spent several hours trying to shake off B-59's pursuers on 'Black Saturday'. Many years later, Vadim Orlov, his communications officer, described the moment when Cuba nearly went nuclear:

> [O]nly emergency light was functioning. The temperature in the compartments was 45–50C, up to 60C in the engine compartment. It was unbearably stuffy. The level of CO_2 in the air reached a critical practically deadly for people mark. One [of] the duty officers fainted and fell down. Then another one followed, then the third one ... They were falling like dominoes. But we were still holding on, trying to escape. We were suffering like this for about four hours.

The US Navy stepped up the pressure. The USS *Beale* began dropping depth charges:

> The Americans hit us with something stronger than the grenades – apparently with a practice depth bomb. We thought – that's it – the end.

It nearly was. For Savitsky lost it:

> After this attack, the totally exhausted Savitsky, who in addition to everything was not able to establish connection with the General Staff [in Moscow], became furious. He summoned the officer who was assigned to the nuclear torpedo, and ordered him to assemble it to battle readiness. 'Maybe the war has already started up there, while we are doing summersaults here' screamed emotional Valentin Grigorievich, trying to justify his order. 'We're going to blast them now! We will die, but we will sink them all. We will not disgrace our Navy.'[202]

Mercifully, after consulting his number two, Vasili Arkhipov, and the deputy political officer, Ivan Maslennikov, Savitsky calmed down and agreed to surface. Equally mercifully, as Len Scott put it, 'if the moment when Captain Savitsky was dissuaded from firing his nuclear torpedo was the moment when nuclear weapons came closest to being used, it took forty years for this to become known'. When Robert McNamara heard the story of *B-59* and the USS *Beale* at the fortieth-anniversary conference in Washington he said a nuclear attack on an American warship could easily have escalated into a full-scale East–West nuclear exchange.[203]

What about the UK's alert state on 'Black Saturday'? In the morning (London time), Macmillan finally reached a decision to raise it for the V-bombers. The shadow of those guns of August had been enveloping him for nearly five days. For on the evening of Monday 22nd, over a long-planned dinner in Admiralty House to mark the retirement of the US General Lauris Norstad as NATO's Supreme Allied Commander, Europe, Macmillan took his opportunity to engage in

> a private talk with General Norstad. Washington, in a rather panicky way, have been urging a NATO 'alert', with all that this implies (in our case Royal Proclamation and call-up of Reservists). I told him that we wd not repeat not agree at this stage. N agreed with this and said he thought NATO powers wd take the same view. I said that 'mobilisation' had sometimes caused war. Here it was absurd since the additional forces made available by 'Alert' had no military significance.[204]

In these circumstances it was the RAF's Vulcans, Victors and Valiants and the Thor missiles that mattered. Macmillan, of course, knew nothing of Captain Maultsby's problem with his flying instruments, Major Anderson had yet to take off and Captain Savitsky's increasing underwater anguish remained a secret of the deep. It was not until the morning of 'Black Saturday' that the Prime Minister summoned the Chief of the Air Staff, Sir Thomas Pike, to Admiralty House at eleven to inquire about 'the current alert posture of our forces', as Pike put it to his fellow chiefs when he briefed them that afternoon. Pike was treated to his own private dose of Tuchmanism. As he told his fellow chiefs:

The Prime Minister has been adamant that he did not consider the time was appropriate for any overt preparatory steps to be taken such as mobilisation. Moreover, he did not wish Bomber Command to be alerted, although he wished the force to be ready to take the appropriate steps should this become necessary. If the situation deteriorated further the Prime Minister intended calling a Cabinet meeting on the next afternoon [Sunday] at which the Chief of the Defence Staff [Lord Mountbatten] and the three chiefs of staff would be in attendance. At the moment, however, he did not wish the Chief of the Defence Staff to be brought back to London, since his intention was that matters should be played in as low a key as possible.[205]

It was as well for Macmillan's composure that he was unaware of what was actually happening on the RAF airfields that afternoon. As Sir Michael Quinlan, Sir Tom Pike's Private Secretary at the time, put it as a meeting of the RAF Historical Society in 2001,

in those days, ministers were far less apt to micro-manage affairs than they are today. Part of the reason for this is the focus that the modern media provides. If the Cuba crisis were happening now we would have the press outside every single airfield reporting on everything that was going on. In the 1960s ministers did not expect to be involved in the fine detail. The political guidance was 'Nothing overt please' and the military were largely left to get on with it.[206]*

---

* Macmillan was familiar with V-force readiness exercises. He had witnessed a practice 'scramble' at RAF Cottesmore in the late 1950s. Some splendid newsreel footage of this has survived. There he stands by the runway, bowler-hatted, umbrellaed and erect as a Guardsman as the klaxon sounds and the crews run to their aircraft (Rob Shepherd and I used the footage in our Widevision/Channel 4 production *What Has Become Of Us?*, transmitted on 18 December 1994). It was his practice to sign-off special, unannounced, Bomber Command exercises, which included the Thor missiles, when the Minister of Defence sought his permission. In the run-up to Cuba he sanctioned three, on 29 January 1961, 5 December 1961 and 8 March 1962 (TNA, PRO, PREM 11/3985, 'RAF Bomber Command Readiness Exercises'). In September 1962, the V-force had completed its annual autumn exercise, MICKY FINN, during which they practised dispersal to their war stations, involving about fifty airfields in all (TNA, PRO, AIR 24/2688, 'HQ Bomber Command October 1962. Post-Exercise Report on Exercise Mickey Finn II' and Squadron Leader Roy Brocklebank, 'Bomber Command 1960s: This Presentation Was TOP SECRET', paper delivered at Charterhouse School, 28 March 2008. It was later

As a result of Macmillan's conversation with the Chief of the Air Staff, the V-force and the Thor missiles were placed on Alert Condition 3 at one o'clock on the afternoon of Saturday 27 October,[207] the 'precautionary alert', which it held until 5 November. As the logbook of Headquarters No. 1 Group, Bomber Command at RAF Bawtry put it: 'All key personnel were required to remain on station and operations staff to be available at short notice. Although no generation of aircraft was ordered, some preparations were made to ensure rapid generation if necessary. All measures were unobtrusive.'[208]

On 1 February 1962, the V-force had implemented a Quick Reaction Alert system (QRA). There would henceforth around the clock be three bombers that could be airborne in a matter of minutes stationed on 'operational readiness platforms' (ORPs) at the end of the runway. On the afternoon of Sunday 28 October, their number was doubled to six.[209] Clive Richards, of the Ministry of Defence's Air Historical Branch, has found the revised alert condition instructions in October 1962, showing that three 'was a precautionary alert *only*, with aircraft generation beginning at Alert Condition 2' (which was never reached[210]), meeting, therefore, Macmillan's instructions to Pike.

But the memories of V-force crew on the ground indicate that the order played out rather differently. Air Vice-Marshal Michael Robinson, for example, will never forget it:

> As the commander of No. 100 Squadron at RAF Wittering, I sat with my crew in a Victor 2 bomber on that Saturday afternoon – the 27th – awaiting the next order from the Bomber Controller in our Headquarters at High Wycombe. The aircraft was loaded with its Yellow Sun MK2 [hydrogen bomb] and we had the Go-bag with all the necessary target and route instructions. At the time my immediate concern was, having checked the whole aircraft system to the nth degree, and then shut down the engines and all systems, would all the systems start up again correctly if we received either Readiness State Zero Two – start engines, or Scramble i.e. get airborne but under positive control to listen out to the appropriate coded message either to continue to our target or to return to base.[211]

published under the title 'World War III – The 1960's Version', in the *Journal of Navigation*, vol. 58, no. 3 (September 2005), pp. 341–7.

Air Vice-Marshal Robinson reckons that to reconstruct that afternoon, when, for him, 'a peak of the RAF's nuclear story was reached',[212] historians have to understand 'the essential difference between Readiness State One Five [fifteen minutes] which is aircraft/weapon generated but aircrew NOT IN COCKPIT, and Readiness State Zero Five [five minutes] – CREW IN COCKPIT. As far as I am concerned we were at Zero Five on that afternoon.'[213]

As for Macmillan's desired unobtrusiveness: the huge, white V-bombers were attention-seeking aircraft – once experienced never forgotten. When they overfly you, the world 'was filled with noise that you didn't so much hear as swim in', as Mark Ogilvie, who lived beneath the Vulcans' flight path in Lincolnshire, put it.[214] Even the sound of their taxiing to the end of the runway was unmistakable. And all the available aircraft crew at RAF Wittering were cockpit-ready 'for several hours before being ordered by the Bomber Controller to revert to Readiness 15'.[215] And, as Air Vice-Marshal Robinson recalls, RAF Wittering is beside one of the busiest north–south arterial routes: 'the whole of the QRA pan and the concentration of aircraft could be easily seen from a conveniently sited lay-by on the adjacent A1 road. Anyone observing from there could both *see* the aircraft and *hear* the changes in Readiness State as they were broadcast over the station Public Address System.'[216]

Might this have escaped Russian military intelligence? Air Vice-Marshal Robinson thinks not:

Whilst Macmillan directed that all activity was to be covert I doubt if the Soviet Embassy in London was unaware of what was happening at our V stations and Thor sites – there is nothing more overt than 59 Thor missiles in the erect launch position or numbers of V bombers concentrated at the downwind end of their airfields.[217]

Air Vice-Marshal Bobby Robson, whose Vulcan B-2 with its Yellow Sun Mark 2 loaded was on QRA as part of 44 Squadron at RAF Waddington a few miles north of Wittering beside the A15, has what he calls 'very eternal' memories of that day, including being four hours in the cockpit before returning to the aircrew's 'miserable cabin' to 'play Risk or Bridge when we weren't still in the aircraft or doing target study'. To say they remained at 'fifteen minutes is bollocks'. Back home in Woodhall Spa his wife Brenda was getting in the tinned food and evaporated milk.[218] There were no plans to protect wives and families, though some wives made private ones to get their children into the Pennines or to the Western Isles of Scotland if ever their husbands took off for real.[219]

Even now, veterans of the V-force find the hairs on their hands and arms rise if they hear the words the Bomber Controller would have used in a real, rather than an exercised, scramble.[220] While making *The Human Button* for BBC Radio 4 in 2008, my producer Richard Knight and I travelled to RAF Brize Norton to record a former navigator, Dr Robin Woolven, in the cramped rear of XH558, the one Vulcan then still flying – 'like sitting in a small cupboard and flying backwards', was how he described it, filled with the smell of oil, heat, electric boxes and blokes instantly recognizable to V-force crews.[221] While on the base we asked the control tower to recreate the 1960s 'Scramble' order for us. This is what the V-force crews would have heard had the world gone to war that Saturday afternoon in October, or at any time during the following days:

> Attention! Attention!
> This is the Bomber Controller for Bomb List Delta
> SCRAMBLE
> Authentication WHISKEY NINE JULIET
> E-Hour One Zero Zero Zero Zulu.

When Sir Tom Pike and his fellow Chiefs of Staff met in the Ministry of Defence that Saturday afternoon, they thought, on the basis of what Macmillan had told Pike of his Friday-night call from Kennedy, that war could very well come early the following week. The minute records Pike as saying:

> President Kennedy had communicated to the Prime Minster, the previous evening, that work on the missile sites in Cuba was being accelerated and it was impossible for the United States to accept this continued build-up. Accordingly, the President had asked the Acting Secretary-General of the United Nations [U Thant] for three assurances. These were, first, the cessation of the shipping of offensive weapons; second, the cessation of construction work on the missile

sites; third, the 'defusing' of the weapons already in Cuba. In addition, the President required a satisfactory verification system to be set up. The President had stated that unless he received these assurances within 48 hours [that is, by Sunday night London time] he would take action to destroy the rocket sites either by bombing, by invasion or by both.

It was understood that the United States invasion forces would be ready to operate by Monday, 29th October, but not before. The President had also stated that he would consult with the Tripartite nations [the occupying powers of West Germany and West Berlin, i.e. UK and France] before taking any definite action. However, the Prime Minister considered this might take the form of information rather than consultation.[222]

The chiefs soberly pondered what a US invasion of Cuba might mean. Being mole-less in Moscow, they did not know that Khrushchev, unlike Kennedy and Macmillan, did not see Berlin and Cuba as symbiotically linked in this instance. They thought Berlin indefensible and that this should be faced directly:

> One of the most likely Russian reactions to the United States' action [i.e. an invasion] over Cuba would be to occupy West Berlin. In view of the overwhelming force that they had available, this could be conducted with little warning. Moreover, Berlin was indefensive [sic] militarily and the forces there were in token strength only. Under these circumstances it would be useless to launch any of the ground access probes at present planned on a tripartite basis. The Prime Minister should be advised of this in order that he may urge the President to restrain General Norstad from undertaking any such operation.[223]

Also anticipating the Cabinet meeting (to which they would be summoned on the Sunday afternoon 'if the situation deteriorated further', as Pike reported Macmillan saying), the chiefs decided to point out that '[a]lthough there were certain measures which could be taken in a precautionary stage, and before any NATO Alert was declared, these had little military significance without the calling of general mobilisation'. For this reason they intended to press Macmillan and the Cabinet to put Bomber Command on Alert Condition 2:

It would be essential for Bomber Command to be alerted and dispersed as soon as the situation so warranted in order that its deterrent effect should be seen to remain credible. This measure would be the most effective that could be carried out short of general mobilisation, and would give political reassurance to the United States.[224]

The three chiefs drew up a brief for the absent Mountbatten based on their conclusions.

(a) Bomber Command should be alerted and dispersed in the event of positive indicators that the United States propose to operate against the Cuban mainland.

(b) The initial military measures that could be taken in a Precautionary Stage . . . would have little military significance and require a seven-day warning period to reach full effectiveness.

(c) Should the situation so warrant, mobilisation and associated measures must be taken in concert with other NATO nations under the NATO Alert System.

(d) In the event of the Russians occupying West Berlin, the United States President should be urged to restrain General Norstad from employing any of the tripartite ground access probes currently planned.[225]

Just how substantial was the UK's 'deterrent capacity' over the weekend of 27–28 October 1962? Of Bomber Command's 166 nuclear-capable aircraft, 'the Command could muster approximately 120 weapons-carrying aircraft capable of generation during October 1962'.[226] We know from Sir Kenneth 'Bing' Cross, Commander-in-Chief, Bomber Command, that 'without visible change 59 of the 60 [Thor] missiles had been made serviceable and ready simply by the use of the telephone'.[227] To 'Bing' Cross, in his Bomber Command bunker under the Chilterns at High Wycombe, would have fallen the decision to retaliate or not if Cuba had gone critical and Soviet missiles and bombers were on their way with the Prime Minister dead or out of reach and his two alternative decision-takers similarly uncontactable.[228] Just a couple of weeks before Cuba erupted, Macmillan had refreshed his plans for nuclear retaliation when he appointed Alec Home to replace Selwyn Lloyd (sacked as part of the 'Night of the Long Knives' in July) as alternative nuclear decision-taker. He told Home on 26 September 1962:

> I have been considering what arrangements should be made to ensure that in a time of grave international tension political authority, on behalf of the Government, will always be immediately available for the purposes of nuclear retaliation if this should be required.
>
> The decision to launch nuclear weapons is one of such gravity that it should clearly be taken by Ministers, or by the Prime Minister on behalf of the Government, if it is humanly possible to arrange this. But it is the essence of the strategic deterrent that it will be launched without fail if an enemy should attack us first with nuclear weapons, and modern developments have made it possible that the first warning of attack may be received only a few minutes before the missiles land.[229]

The famous four-minute warning, provided by the Ballistic Missile Early Warning System (BMEWS) inside its extraordinary golf balls at RAF Fylingdales on the North Yorkshire Moors, was still under construction at the time of Cuba and only became operational in 1963. In the autumn of 1962, warning would have come from existing BMEWS stations in Alaska and Greenland and from Manchester University's radio-astronomy installation at Jodrell Bank in Cheshire.[230]

Just what 'incoming' might Jodrell Bank have been expected to pick up had war come in October–November 1962? Whitehall's most recent attempt to estimate the Soviet Union's capacity to wreck the UK was still the 1955 Strath Report and its calculation that ten 10-megaton Russian H-bombs would, out of a mid-1950s population of 46 million, 'kill about 12 million people and seriously injure and disable 4 million others'. A more accurate estimate for an early 1960s nuclear assault is the Joint Intelligence Committee's November 1964 assessment for the Cabinet's Home Defence Committee that,

> should the Soviet Union strike first, the scale of attack would be currently some 330 nuclear weapons. Whilst some of these weapons would probably be of kiloton yield and many would be airburst, there is little doubt that this attack would cause even greater devastation than that set out in the Strath Report. An attack of this magnitude would cause the United Kingdom to cease to exist as a corporate political entity.[231]

While, unbeknownst to either of them, the missiles were on their way to Cuba, Macmillan told Home:

> Current arrangements provide that if a nuclear attack is delivered, or is known to have been launched, I am to be consulted immediately; but if this proves impossible, the competent military authority [Commander-in-Chief, RAF Bomber Command], if he is certain that an attack has in fact been made, has authority to order nuclear retaliation in the last resort without Ministerial authority. This is the only practicable arrangement in the event of a nuclear attack on this country in what would otherwise be normal conditions of peace – in other words, a 'bolt from the blue'. But a 'bolt from the blue', which implies the failure of the deterrent policy, and would clearly require immediate retaliation, is unlikely.

Macmillan went on to describe in uncanny detail the circumstances that might have prevailed if Khrushchev had not backed down at Sunday lunchtime and the Cabinet meeting for Sunday afternoon had taken place:

> A more likely situation would arise from an increase in international tension to the point where the Government would decide to institute the Precautionary Stage. At that stage it would be my duty (except for exceptional purposes such as international negotiations) to remain in London and to be immediately accessible myself at all times, as far as this is physically possible; and I should be in close touch with our other allies and with the military commanders of NATO and of our own services. Nevertheless, there would almost certainly be some occasions when I could not be reached for immediate consultation, for instance if I were moving by car from one place to another [Macmillan refrains from permitting Home access to the secret of the Automobile Association]; and I propose to nominate a Minister to act as my first Deputy, in London, for this purpose at such times.[232]

The other deputy was to go to the Corsham bunker, or BURLINGTON, as it was codenamed at the time of Cuba (it changed to TURNSTILE on 25 January 1963[233]). As Macmillan explained to Home:

There is also the possibility that London might be silenced before the necessary consultations could take place. I propose, therefore, to nominate another Minister as my second Deputy from among those who would go to the alternative headquarters of the central Government ... [He] will have no Parliamentary or other duties which will require him to move away from his communications there. He will be in continuous touch with developments in London and will know immediately if contact is broken that he has necessarily assumed responsibility.

I have decided to nominate you and Rab Butler (to whom I have sent a similar letter) as my Deputies for this purpose. I do not propose, until the Precautionary Stage is declared, to decide which will be first and which second Deputy (that is, which of you will remain in London and which will go to the alternative headquarters of the central Government).[234]

I once asked Alec Home, who became the primary nuclear retaliation decision-taker on assuming the premiership a year later in October 1963, if he could have pressed the button. He replied by telling me that the Soviet Union could never bank on a British Prime Minister *not* doing so if there were 'great hordes marching right across Europe and demolishing European civilization as we know it ... Terrible, isn't it, the thought; but reason, cold reason doesn't operate in those circumstances, quite often. And I'm not sure what cold reason would tell you, either, if they were on the march.'[235]

All the indicators suggest that, had Khrushchev not backed down, Sunday 28 October 1962 would have seen one of the most awesome and significant Cabinet meetings ever held, with Macmillan and his ministers having to decide (1) whether to raise the readiness of the V-force to Alert Condition 2; (2) whether to institute the Precautionary Stage and bring into operation all the elaborate plans of the Central Government War Book; (3) whether to begin the dispersal of Whitehall to the twelve regional seats of government and to BURLINGTON (this last at a very late stage in the precautionary period for fear of giving away its location*). Macmillan privately and alone

* Manning BURLINGTON was a matter of such extreme sensitivity that the Ministry of Works was ordered to wait until the last minute before 'Distributing

would have decided which nuclear deputy went where. My guess is that Butler would have gone to Corsham. Macmillan would have needed Home by his side in Admiralty House to help in the pursuit of preventive diplomacy until the last minutes when the helicopters would have whisked them away from Horse Guards Parade to the last redoubt under the Cotswolds to form a 'War Cabinet' as 'the supreme political authority . . . responsible for the conduct of the war worldwide'.[236]

The mind behind these end-of-the-world plans, Sir Norman Brook, the Cabinet Secretary, was not available to Macmillan over that Cuba weekend. He was off work ill. But his system was (almost) ready to go. The 'almost' in that sentence always comes to mind when I visit the Corsham bunker. Because of those firm instructions to the Ministry of Works *not* to set up the chairs and tables or put up the beds, there is still a pristine feel to the place with the furniture, the stationery, the little metal paperclip boxes all still stockpiled and ready to go just as they were on that late-October Sunday in 1962.

The weather was perfectly autumnal in both Washington and London that night as Bobby Kennedy put the Jupiters/Cuba deal to the Russian Ambassador. President Kennedy sent Excomm members home to see the families from whom Cuban demands had kept them for days. Robert McNamara recalled that 'as I left the White House and walked through the garden to my car to return to the Pentagon on that beautiful fall evening, I feared I might never live to see another Saturday night'.[237] As is evidenced by his epigraph to this chapter, his

---

furniture, stores and equipment and getting ready for use offices, dormitories, canteens and kitchens' and 'Erecting improvised signposts [underground in the quarry] to assist staffs to find their way about' (TNA, PRO, CAB 134/4259, MG (PT) (61) 8, 9, 1 September 1961, 'Interim Operational Orders for the Manning of BURLINGTON'). Not until the 'Precautionary Stage' gave way to the 'Destructive Phase' would BURLINGTON assume its 'control function' with 'London silenced', as Macmillan put it, for fear of signals emanating from the bunker giving its position away to Russian intelligence (TNA, PRO, CAB 21/4959, 'Sir Norman Brook: Miscellaneous Engagements and Personal Correspondence, 1961–1964', 'Cabinet Government', a private lecture to Home Office civil servants delivered by Brook on 26 June 1959, and TNA, PRO, CAB 134/4291, Annex to HDC (MG) (64) 20, 'ALUS Equipment on TURNSTILE Circuits').

opposite number, Peter Thorneycroft, felt exactly the same the following morning. So did I (though I *was* optimistic) as I set off with Hywel Thomas and other friends from Marling from the school hut in the Olchon Valley on the eastern rim of the Black Mountains for a long walk over Hay Bluff and Lord Hereford's Knob, thinking that if the world was going to end, this was as beautiful a spot as any in which to finish one's part in it.

It was certainly a better place to be than Khrushchev's dacha outside Moscow, to which the Presidium had been summoned late that Sunday morning. Even before the message from his Washington Embassy about the Jupiter deal had reached him, Khrushchev had decided to end the crisis and 'had actually dictated his concession speech, which was to take the form of a letter to the US President, before he knew of Kennedy's own concession'.[238] The shooting down of Major Anderson's U-2 had rattled him and he was seriously worried about Castro's state of mind – the Cuban leader had given the Soviet Ambassador in Havana a letter urging a nuclear war if that was the only way to preserve the honour of Cuba and the cause of socialism.[239] The 'no invasion' of Cuba pledge and the eventual dismantling of the Jupiters enabled Khrushchev to persuade himself that there had been real gains from Operation ANADYR, though not the geostrategic ones anticipated.

But botched – and hideously, dangerously botched – ANADYR had been. Even the last act was very nearly botched, too. Sergei Khrushchev, Nikita's son, has the story of the (sensible) decision to get Moscow Radio to broadcast his father's letter to Kennedy for reasons of speed almost collapsing into farce. Moscow Radio is alerted that an important message is coming and its most famous announcer, Levitan, is asked to come in to read it out. The official car carrying the message gets lost in the countryside between Khrushchev's dacha and the city, then it gets held up in traffic. Once inside Moscow Radio the messenger, Leonid Ilichev, gets stuck in the ancient lift. As it's a Sunday, there's no lift repairer in the building. Ilichev tries to push the letter through a crack in the lift doors, but its wax seals prevent it getting through and it tears. Finally the lift judders into life, completes its journey, Levitan broadcasts the letter – and the world is saved![240]

Back in Admiralty House, Macmillan, who had been considering on Saturday night and early Sunday morning summoning what his press secretary, Harold Evans, called 'a London summit meeting', to the consternation of Alec Home and his Foreign Office Permanent Secretary, Sir Harold Caccia (who thought this 'might be construed as the British being forced to crack'), finally plumped for what Evans saw as 'a mouselike message to Khrushchev, appealing to him to take the course proposed [in public] by Kennedy, and this went off at noon – just in time for us to be able to claim that it had anticipated Khrushchev's coming-in reply'.[241] I suspect Macmillan had not got over the summit-that-never-was in Paris in May 1960 in which another U-2 – the one overflying the Soviet Union from Pakistan to Norway and shot down just south of Moscow – played a pivotal part in its ruination. And, as we have seen, throughout the rolling Berlin crisis he had never concealed from either Eisenhower or Kennedy his desire for a conference to resolve it. To talk rather than mobilize was his first and natural instinct.

Macmillan, writing up his diary on the Sunday evening in a state of exhaustion, reckoned it was

> impossible to describe what has been happening in this hour by hour battle ... The <u>Turkey</u> offer of Khrushchev (to swap Cuban missile bases for Turkish) was very dangerous ... The press today ... were awful. It was like Munich ... All through Saturday night, the strain continued. This morning, I decided (Butler, Home, Thorneycroft and Heath agreeing) to send a message to Khrushchev. We <u>supported</u> the American demand that the missiles shd be taken out of Cuba. I appealed to him to do this, and then to turn to more constructive work – disarmament and the like. Our message was sent off at 12 noon. As we were finishing luncheon together, the news came (by radio) that the Russians had given in! First, they admit to the ballistic missiles (hitherto denied by Communists <u>and</u> doubted by all good fellow-travellers in every country). Then they said they would be 'packed up, crated and taken away' – a complete climb-down (<u>if</u> they keep their word).[242]

They did.

Instead of an afternoon considering declaring the Precautionary Stage and the readiness of the V-force, Macmillan, in Evans's words, 'flopped down in a chair by the tape machine, with Tim [Bligh], Philip de Zulueta and myself as audience. The captains and the kings [Butler, Home, Heath, Thorneycroft and Caccia] had departed and this was the No. 10 family.' Gazing round his room in Admiralty House, the old man told them: 'It's like a wedding when there is nothing left to do but drink the champagne and go to sleep.'[243]

When Hywel Thomas and I returned to Beili Bach from the northern escarpment of the Black Mountains late that afternoon and learned what had happened from friends who had not gone on the walk, we felt much the same (though we were beer boys rather than champagne men at the time).

When the Cabinet did meet at 10.30 on Monday 29 October, Macmillan's concern was less a Third World War than the view being put about by the Labour opposition that Britain had been a bystander in the crisis, which created a 'political dilemma' for the government:

> In fact we had played an active and helpful part in bringing matters to their present conclusion, but in public little had been said and the impression had been created that we had been playing a purely passive role. It would not be easy to correct this without revealing the degree of informal consultation which had taken place; but this might be embarrassing to President Kennedy and perhaps an irritation to other European leaders.[244]

The spectre of de Gaulle was already looming.

The rapidity, virulence and potentially fatal consequences of the crisis had thoroughly shaken Macmillan – as it had everyone else, from its instigator in Moscow and the responder in Washington to anyone in the world who cared to read the newspapers, listen to the radio or watch television. Fifteen years of Cold War had not prepared anyone for this. For Cuba had never been foreseen as a Cold War/hot war flashpoint except briefly and in a non-specific way by the Joint Intelligence Committee five years earlier. The handling of it, in Washington, London and Moscow, was, therefore, improvised – not so much a near war-by-timetable, more a case of busking on the brink. But the JIC and the UK's transition-to-war planners did learn from it. There was a substantial post-Cuba rethink, as we shall see shortly.

The first stab at it was made by the old classical scholar himself, craving a bit of peace and rest at Birch Grove over the weekend of 3–4 November with the V-force still on Alert Condition 3 and double the usual number of aircraft on QRA. As if anticipating the eyes of historians fifty years on, he wrote:

> The trouble about a first class crisis is that it is physically impossible to keep the diary going, just when it wd be really interesting! (The same thing happened during the Suez crisis.)
>
> It is now a week away – still difficult to realise. In Secretary [Dean] Rusk's words 'We looked into the mouth of the cannon. The Russians flinched.' (I don't think, myself, that it's as simple as that. All the same, the President was very firm and his will prevailed.)[245]

Apart from sending his noonday message to Khrushchev through diplomatic channels, which 'meant that it was not published till the very moment when the Russian <u>radio</u> message of "climb-down" came through', making it seem 'as if we had sent the telegram backing the horse <u>after</u> the race', Macmillan reckoned that 'we played our part perfectly. We were "in on" and took full part in (and almost responsibility for) every American move.'[246]

This was not true of the decision to impose a quarantine, but it is true that at a meeting of Kennedy's National Security Council on 23 October, 'Ormsby-Gore – acting entirely off his own bat and without referring back to Macmillan, but with his total support *ex post facto* – made a crucial suggestion. He recommended that the proposed "quarantine" of the US naval blockade be modified from 800 miles to 500 miles off the Cuban coast' to give Khrushchev longer to react. Kennedy accepted the idea.[247] And, as we have seen, Macmillan knew nothing of the Turkish Jupiters deal, which he thought a thoroughly bad idea when it was raised as a possibility.

In a similarly self-congratulatory vein, Macmillan told himself: 'Our complete calm helped to keep the Europeans calm (the French were anyway contemptuous; the Germans <u>very</u> frightened, tho' pretending to want firmness; the Italians windy; the Scandinavians rather sour as well as windy). But they <u>said</u> and <u>did</u> nothing to spoil the American playing of the hand.'[248]

Macmillan's contemporary insights served him well, however, when he asked himself '<u>Why did Khrushchev do the Cuban missiles?</u>'

He hoped to finish the job; go to the United Nations at the end of November; threaten about <u>Berlin</u>, and then reveal his Cuban strength, pointing out the 'soft under-belly' of U.S.A., 3 minutes warning instead of 15. (Of course, to us who face nearly 500 of these missiles in Russia trained on Europe, there is something slightly ironical about these 20–30 in Cuba. But, as I told the President, when one lives on Vesuvius, one takes little account of the risk of eruptions.')[249]

He had a point. A decade after Cuba the Americans had to come to terms with a direct and comprehensive threat to their homeland in the early 1970s when Admiral Gorshkov got into service his Delta submarines, whose missiles had a range of 4,000 miles.[250] These could target the bulk of the United States without even leaving their 'bastions' in the Barents Sea or the Sea of Okhotsk.[251] In 1962, however, Macmillan recognized that 'there is no comparison between the NATO and Warsaw Pact forces, which have faced each other for fifteen years or more in Europe, and the <u>sudden</u> introduction of missile threat into the Western hemisphere'. But the possibility of Cuba-induced horse-trading of nuclear missiles based in Europe Macmillan found alarming:

> The Turkey–Cuba deal wd have [of] course been greatly to the advantage of U.S. The Turkey base is useful but not vital. Cuba was vital. I suggested to [the] President that if anything of the kind was to be done, it wd be better done with our Thors. For British opinion could stand up; the Turks wd feel betrayed. (This offer, tho' it was not necessary, was useful.) However, it became clear on Saturday that anything like this deal wd do great injury to NATO.[252]

What really puzzled Macmillan was why Khrushchev 'in effect' threw in his hand on Sunday 28 October:

> This is the crucial question and [on] the answer much depends. Why did he not make some counter-move for instance, on Berlin? Will he make it quite soon? Or on Turkey, or Persia? This is, of course, still a mystery and every Ambassador and F.O. expert has a different theory. The general view is that he realised the Americans were serious and wd invade Cuba and capture it. (This they intended to do on Monday morning. The invasion was always timed for the Monday 29th. The

President told me earlier in the week about 23rd or 24th that the 'build-up' wd take a week from the day he made his speech – Monday 22nd). <u>This American invasion could not be stopped by conventional means</u>. Therefore the Russians wd have [had] to use nuclear, in a 'first fire' attack. This they would not face – and rightly. But if the Americans attacked, they wd do three things (i) destroy Castro and the Communist regime (ii) deal a great blow to Russian prestige (iii) capture the missiles. So, by his apparent 'cave-in', Khrushchev at least avoided all these disadvantages. On (i) Castro is going to be a tremendous nuisance. On (iii) the Russians will get back their missiles. On (ii) there is a loss of prestige, in the sense that the expensive little flutter has failed – but not so great a loss as an American invasion, which Russia could not or dare not prevent. So he decided to cut his losses.[253]

Not a bad assessment, given what Macmillan knew in early November 1962 – though he seriously underestimated the number of troops, believing there were 'some 10,000 Russian military personnel on the island', when, in fact, there were four times as many.

Macmillan depressed himself that Sunday at Birch Grove when he pondered the 'strategic lessons' of the Cuban missile crisis:

> May they not be that, under the cover of the terrible nuclear war, which nobody dares start, you can get away with anything you can do by <u>conventional</u> means?

Macmillan did not know about the Soviet tactical missiles on Cuba for use against an invading American force as it crossed the island's beaches. He continued:

> You can take Cuba. The enemy can only reply by all-out nuclear war. But this applies to Berlin. The Russians can take Berlin by conventional means. The Allies <u>cannot defend</u> or <u>re-capture</u> it by any conventional means. (The conclusion to be drawn is rather sinister.)

Indeed it was. And so was the sheer rawness and implicit brutality of nuclear deterrence. Only one thing was worse – if crude deterrence failed to trump all other factors. The real threat was a Captain Savitsky losing it at a moment of extreme international tension or war-through-inadvertence or by miscalculation. Macmillan had a sense of how close to the brink the world was in October 1962, even if he did not live long enough to learn of the anti-submarine warfare in the Caribbean on 'Black Saturday'.

He was full of praise for Kennedy's handling of the crisis, however, and compared his touch with that of the hapless Anthony Eden during Suez six years earlier:

> He [Kennedy] played a firm <u>military</u> game throughout – acting quickly and being ready to act <u>as soon as</u> mobilised. This was Eden's <u>fatal</u> mistake – in which we all share the responsibility. You cannot keep an 'army of invasion' hanging about. It must invade or disperse. President K did not bluster – but everyone knew that (if no other solution was found) there wd be an invasion ... He played the <u>United Nations</u> admirably. Eden tried to use the U.N. but Foster Dulles [US Secretary of State in 1956] really wrecked us there.[254]

Macmillan depressed himself still further by concluding his Birch Grove stocktake with the UK's domestic perception of his role. He was down, and '[e]ver since the end of the Cuba crisis I have <u>felt</u> very ill', he wrote on Monday 5 November. 'For after the lassitude of last week, I began on Friday to have continuous diarrhoea, wh is one of the symptoms. I managed to shoot on Saturday ... but it was bad yesterday and I went to bed after tea.'[255] His Labour critics had really got to him. He linked their arguments to one of his ruling passions – the desire to sustain the UK as a nuclear-tipped power:

> In the [House of Commons] debate on Tuesday (when Gaitskell took this line) and on Wednesday (when it was developed by Harold Wilson) the Opposition (supported by some of the press – esp. the 'columnists' and gossip writers) have been making out that the Americans not only failed to consult us, but have treated us with contempt; that the 'special relationship' no longer applies; that we have gained nothing from our position as a nuclear power; that America risked total war in a US/USSR quarrel without bothering about us <u>or</u> Europe. The reasons for this attitude are (a) ignorance of what really happened (b) desire to injure and denigrate me personally (c) argument agst deterrent (d) annoyance at the success – or comparative success of Cuba enterprise (e) shame – for they let it be known that they wd oppose force, or threat of force.[256]

Macmillan did not live, either, to see the publication of the Cuba tapes from Kennedy's Excomm or to read May and Zelikow's commentary depicting him as a kind of honorary member of it.

His fatigue and his stomach trouble that weekend at Birch Grove no doubt contributed to the tone of his perhaps not entirely cathartic diary entry:

> In fact, of course, the President and Rusk (and, above all, the President's 'Chef de Cabinet' [National Security Advisor], McGeorge Bundy) were in continuous touch with Alec Home and me. David Gore was all the time in and out of the White House. The whole episode was like a battle; and we in Admiralty House felt as if we were in the battle HQ. The teleprinter <u>and</u> the telephone (direct secret line to the White House) worked admirably – without a hitch.
>
> Actually, our secrets were almost too well kept; so this Opposition or critical line is rather dangerous. We are doing something to let the truth be known through judicious leaks. It will gradually seep through from Whitehall to London society and thence pretty generally. But it is rather a bore, and has some dangers. The British people must not feel themselves slighted.[257]

My own memory is that the British people felt relief, rather than slight. We had been to the brink and we had come back. You did not need to be a member of Macmillan's Admiralty House team or to have a place around the Joint Intelligence Committee table to appreciate the big picture or the enduring significance of Cuba. None of the previous Cold War crises had come anywhere near this one for plain and palpable public menace.

What did British intelligence make of it? At the time, the JIC had performed its customary role of trying to hose down the overanxious. During the crisis, its chairman, Sir Hugh Stephenson, and his analysts had provided a running commentary. They had no independent intelligence on the missile sites and the JIC assessment of 26 October of 'The Threat Posed by Soviet Missiles in Cuba' was, as they told their readers, 'based entirely on photographic evidence so far released to us by the US authorities'. On the crucial question of warheads, the JIC reported:

US position: Some sites which are probably for storing nuclear warheads are at present under construction.

Comment: We have no evidence on which to base a firm conclusion but we agree that these sites may be for the storing of nuclear warheads. Neither we nor the US authorities have any evidence on which to judge whether nuclear warheads have or have not reached Cuba.

. . . If all known sites are completed, we estimate that the overall Soviet initial launch capability against the US will have increased significantly by the end of 1962.[258]

Also on 26 October, the JIC assessed Khrushchev's reactions to the 'quarantine' and reckoned the 'Soviet response so far . . . has been relatively moderate'. They thought Khrushchev would play for time – attempting to complete the missile sites while making it politically more difficult (partly by mobilizing world opinion) for Kennedy to take additional action.[259]

The JIC's 'Black Saturday' assessment was remarkable for its coolness and its belief that nuclear war was unlikely even if the United States invaded Cuba. This was very much in line with their substantial paper of 9 February 1962 on 'The Likelihood of War with the Soviet Union up to 1966', in which the JIC judged Khrushchev and his Presidium to be well aware of the vulnerability of the Russian homeland to nuclear retaliation and 'therefore believe that the Soviet leaders, provided they remain rational, will not plan to initiate general nuclear war as a deliberate act of policy'.[260]

That February 1962 assessment did examine the danger of 'general nuclear war coming' through miscalculation of three kinds – the first of which fitted Cuba eight months later as did elements of the third – namely, if either

the Soviet Union or the West in some critical or tense situation were to make a false appreciation of what was considered by the other side to be intolerable; or the Soviet Union or the West were to believe wrongly that the other had weakened in its determination to use nuclear weapons if pressed too far; or either side were to fail accurately to foresee the consequences of the policies being pursued by a third party with which it was associated.[261]

So, on 'Black Saturday', by which time Khrushchev's Operation ANADYR had produced condition (a), did the JIC believe it would trigger general nuclear war if Kennedy responded by invading Cuba early the following week? It did not:

> We think that if . . . the Russians resort to arms it will be an effective military response, and we suggest that the most likely blow will be a tit-for-tat as nearly parallel as possible to the US action. It seems unlikely therefore that they will attack directly either US territory or the territory of any of the NATO powers. The closest parallel would appear to be a US base in some third country or an attack on some major US naval vessel. They might also attack Guantanamo [the US base on the eastern tip of Cuba] though they must expect that this would invite a full-scale US invasion of the island.[262]

What about the biggest tit-for-tat that so preoccupied Kennedy and Macmillan – Berlin for Cuba?

> We have considered the possibility of large-scale military action against Berlin but suggest that this is unlikely in view of the clear warning from the US that this would bring about a full confrontation. Indeed central to Soviet thinking in deciding upon their reply will be their fear of doing anything that might escalate into general nuclear war. Their overriding concern therefore is likely to be to limit their reply to the least dangerous possible place. Should the Russians make an attack such as we have suggested they would probably follow it up with clear indications that this went as far as they intended to go at the present stage.[263]

One wonders how different these assessments would have been if the JIC had been aware, as they wrote, of the tactical nuclear missiles, complete with warheads, on Cuba.

Along with several other parts of Whitehall's Cold War secret state, the JIC went in for quite a thorough inquest after Cuba. Their 'Black Saturday' assessment was 'UK Eyes Only' and not to be shown to the Americans, but its 14 November paper on 'Escalation' was, as we have seen, shared with the Canadians and the US. Its conclusion implied that after Cuba all sides were aware that inadvertent escalation, and the fear of loss of face once it was underway, were the great dangers, and that the terms of future deterrence had changed. The JIC reckoned: 'It is now the fear of global war arising through a process of escalation which constitutes the deterrent to limited aggression, rather than the fear of immediate massive retaliation.'[264]

In early December 1962, the JIC came commendably close to capturing the impulses which powered Operation ANADYR. In their 'Soviet Motives in Cuba' paper, the JIC's analysts believed

> that to have taken the risks involved Khrushchev was not simply actuated by the desire to seize the opportunity of turning a local situation to great advantage, but must have had specific and compelling motives for the action that he took. These may well have arisen from a concern that little Soviet progress had been made in the Cold War and that there had been no weakening in the West's determination to maintain the *status quo* in Berlin.
>
> We believe that Khrushchev probably considered it very important, both for the Communist cause and his personal position to try to obtain some lever against the West at this particular moment in the world's history. He may have concluded that by placing missiles with nuclear warheads 'in their own backyard', he could jolt the Americans out of what he considered an exaggerated confidence in their superior nuclear strike capability, and wake them up to the realities of the present nuclear confrontation.[265]

Looking back from the perspective of over fifty years, we can see that mutual deterrence prevailed. Fear of nuclear war on the part of both Khrushchev and Kennedy fuelled their respective scrambles for a method of de-escalation, a way out of what each knew was the most perilous confrontation the Soviet Union, the United States and the rest of the world had faced since the Cold War first chilled. But, as the JIC's assessments shortly before and shortly after the crisis implied, there were certain circumstances in which mutual deterrence might not work.

A few years later, the CND-supporting A. J. P. Taylor wrote his own piece of Tuchmanry, *War by Time-Table: How the First World War Began*. Cuba plainly provided his motive power, as his final paragraph indicated:

There is no mystery about the outbreak of the First World War. The deterrent failed to deter. This was to be expected sooner or later. A deterrent may work ninety-nine times out of a hundred. On the hundredth occasion it produces catastrophe. There is a contemporary moral here for those who would like to find one.[266]

This was, in fact, a view shared at the highest level in the Foreign Office during the last weeks of 1962 as the lessons of the missiles of October were pondered. Shortly after Khrushchev's climbdown, but before 'the ripples of the Cuba crisis had begun to die away',[267] Alec Home lunched with Iverach McDonald, foreign editor of *The Times*. Present also was Walter Lippmann, the legendary American commentator on international affairs, whose newspaper column on Thursday 25 October had actually suggested a Turkish Jupiters for Cuban missiles trade as a way to resolve the crisis (which was shown to Khrushchev either late on the Friday night or early on the Saturday morning[268]). Home warned them against excessive cheerfulness at the outcome of the autumn crisis: 'The chief frightening thing about it all is that Khrushchev could have miscalculated so badly. It could mean that he could blunder into war another time.'[269]

This was the spirit in which Whitehall conducted its 'Post-Cuba Review of War Book Planning', which Macmillan commissioned the Cabinet's Home Defence Committee to undertake 'in order', he explained to the new Cabinet Secretary, Sir Burke Trend (Brook retired in January 1963), 'to ensure that it was sufficiently flexible to enable us to act quickly and appropriately to a sudden emergency, in which we might have no more than two or three days' warning of the outbreak of war.'[270] A number of changes resulted, including a power whereby the Prime Minister could institute the Precautionary Stage without consulting the Cabinet.[271] The HDC also oversaw the drafting of an Emergency Powers (Defence) Bill, to be rushed through Parliament in the last hours of peace, that would pass their powers to a War Cabinet and the dozen ministers in charge of the twelve regional seats of government with drastic responsibilities involving life, death, money, food and property after an attack so 'as to amount to a voluntary abdication by Parliament of the whole of their functions for the period of the emergency'.[272] As we have seen, there was to be no bunker for MPs and peers.

While the Cabinet's Home Defence Committee absorbed the practical significance of Cuba in the deepest Whitehall secrecy, Stanley Kubrick pondered it in film, which led to his enduring classic and masterpiece *Dr Strangelove, or, How I Learned to Stop Worrying and Love the Bomb*, which was first screened in 1964.[273] But the Cuban missile crisis has never ceased to be good box office. Roger Donaldson's *Thirteen Days*, when it appeared in 2000 (2001 in the UK), grippingly portrayed Kennedy's handling of his military advisers on Excomm as they pressed for a swift air strike against the missile sites on Cuba.[274]

Strangelove is about a Third World War-by-accident caused by an insane Strategic Air Command General, Jack Ripper, sending his B-52s beyond their start lines to their targets in Russia and the failure of command-and-control systems when a near-wrecked aircraft, captained by the unforgettable Texan Major Kong (Slim Pickens), whose radio communications have been destroyed, drops its H-bomb (with a Stetsoned Kong riding it down like a bronco) on a Soviet missile base. The Soviets' fictional 'doomsday machine' on an island in the Arctic then proceeds to retaliate automatically. And, as the world ends, the sinister ex-Nazi scientific adviser Dr Strangelove (Peter Sellers) advises the US President (also Peter Sellers) to retreat to a deep mineshaft, with a surplus of beautiful women, to sit out the radiation while a new master race is bred below ground. The film is full of glorious one-liners, the best being the President's outburst as General Buck Turgidson (George C. Scott) wrestles with the Soviet Ambassador (Peter Bull) as he tries to take pictures of the Pentagon's 'Big Board'. 'Gentlemen!' he cries. 'You can't fight here. This is the War Room!'

Nearly forty years on from Cuba, I showed the by-now declassified JIC 'Red' and 'Amber' list of intelligence indicators from 1962, which constituted Whitehall's alert system for a Soviet attack from a standing start ('Red') and after a careful build-up ('Amber'), to a very seasoned retired SIS officer and the subject of 'Dr Strangelove' emerged quite naturally. The 'Red List' contained seventeen indicators. Number 11 gives the flavour:

Arrival of Soviet army specialist units in forward areas (especially missile, medical and interrogation units) and military personnel wearing rocket insignia.

The 'Amber List' ranged over forty-seven warning signs starting with:

Bringing units up to wartime strength and readiness through

(a) Recall of reserve personnel
(b) Postponement of demobilization of trained soldiers
(c) Cancellation of leave, confinement of troops at barracks, increase of security patrols in vital areas
(d) Reassignment to military duties of those units employed on civil projects.[275]

'It's frightfully difficult to put yourself in the context of 1962,' the retired MI6 man said. 'There was a very real feeling of threat. Any change [in the indicators] was bad news. It was a well-justified worry because [by 1963] we'd had Berlin, Hungary, Cuba. So this document must be seen in that context or it's unreal – it's "Dr Strangelove".' He paused and added: 'Neither side would allow themselves to believe that the other side were as frightened as they were,' and, he added, 'there were madmen on both sides'.[276]

Mercifully, one of the coolest and calmest of his MI6 colleagues, Gervase Cowell, a quiet, humorous and unassuming man, was on the end of the line in the Moscow Embassy's SIS station when the phone rang on 2 November, with the world's nerves still frayed and the RAF's V-bombers still on Alert Condition 3, and Oleg Penkovsky's prearranged signal of an imminent Soviet nuclear attack came down the line (three blows of breath, repeated in another phone call one minute later). Shortly before he died I asked Mr Cowell what he did on hearing those exhalations. The answer was nothing. He was sure Penkovsky had been captured and that his call signs and rendezvous locations had been extracted from him. Surprisingly, Cowell, a quiet, charming man whom I met a few times many years later, told neither his Ambassador, Sir Frank Roberts, nor his Chief back in London, Sir Dick White.[277] The incident was yet another 'what if?' of the Cuban missile crisis.*

* The 'what ifs?' of Cuba certainly left a permanent mark on Harold Macmillan. His grandson, Alexander (now Lord Stockton), who was staying with him and Lady Dorothy in Admiralty House during the crisis, recalled that 'Grandfather told me that as an old man he only had nightmares about two things: the trenches in the Great War and what would have happened if the Cuban missiles crisis had gone wrong' (conversation with Lord Stockton, 30 April 1998).

What *would* have happened is, in the words of the Strath Report of 1955, 'beyond the imagination'.[278] But Whitehall *had* tried to imagine it, in the context of two home-defence regions in the Midlands at least, in January 1961 in an exercise codenamed ACE HIGH. Over the weekend of 24–26 January 1961 at the Civil Defence Staff College in Sunningdale (later the Civil Service College), Whitehall departments, the police and the military tried to imagine the governmental consequences of an East–West war which erupted in 1965 after 'some months of worsening tension followed by a seven day precautionary period. The attack comprised 180 megatons ... delivered by manned aircraft and missiles in the compass of two hours on twenty main centres of population and ... missile sites and airfields.'[279]

For the purposes of the ACE HIGH 'Main Narrative', a Third World War broke out at eight o'clock on the morning of Saturday 18 September 1965 when 'nuclear weapons were delivered on or around deterrent bases by rockets and manned bombers, but our own nuclear strike force was successfully launched'.[280]

The run-up to Armageddon went like this:

SATURDAY 11 SEPTEMBER

Cabinet initiates the precautionary period and the government orders the manning of all regional seats of government, civil defence and other control centres 'on a wartime basis'.

MONDAY 13 SEPTEMBER

General mobilization announced and campaign launched through television, radio and the press, to convince the public of the need to take reasonable steps to preserve family life and to remain in their own homes apart from 'the 6 million people in priority classes [the elderly, the sick, women and children] from large cities', who were directed to reception centres and billets in safe areas.

Those remaining in the so-called 'Z' zones where 'high intensity' attacks are expected are urged to remain undercover in their own homes for 7 days and 'thereafter to obey strict regulations'.

'Many complied but some refused . . . except for some larger cities, there was no spontaneous mass evacuation. Problems were created in certain areas by substantial numbers of people who evacuated themselves from the larger cities. The tendency was to move westwards or into country districts . . . Many were living and sleeping in vehicles on the sides of roads.' Some panic buying and local shortages.

THURSDAY 16 SEPTEMBER

Emergency powers taken by the government, whose central core moves 'to its wartime location' (i.e. Corsham). Ministers appointed Regional Commissioners moved to their bunkers and 'were invested with all the powers of government except those specifically reserved, such as the control of the armed forces and external relations'.

SATURDAY 18 SEPTEMBER

After the launching of the V-bombers and the nuclear assault on their bases, between nine and eleven in the morning, the UK's main cities come under attack.

'The world situation is obscure and reports – mainly from neutral sources – have been conflicting. It appears that similar heavy attacks were launched upon Western Europe, North America and Western bases in the Middle and Far East.'

The estimated casualties from the Soviet assault (not including the anticipated victims of nuclear fallout) were 2 million dead in the UK as a whole, 4 million injured and a further 3 million homeless.

SUNDAY–MONDAY 19–20 SEPTEMBER

Hospitals in the undamaged and accessible areas are full and many injured are still held in forward medical aid units awaiting admission.

Considerable efforts have been made by the life-saving forces, where fallout permitted, and in some areas limited operations are still going on. It has not been possible, however, in most places to reach casualties near the main centres of damage. A high proportion of the life-saving forces, particularly in regions to the east and south, have exhausted their war emergency dose.

The grim story runs on through the 'Survival' phase in especial detail for the two test regions (based on the regional seats of government at Kidderminster and Nottingham) ranging through the problems of sustaining law and order, administering summary justice, trying to create self-helping communities based on the revival of cottage-industries until imports can start coming into repaired ports. The problem of money was considered. Should debts be written off? How were survivors to be registered? Could a system of rationing be imposed to govern the distribution of food from emergency stockpiles? Ditto coal? How could the BBC Wartime Broadcasting Service and the churches help sustain survivors' morale?[281]

ACE HIGH's narrative, though this is hard to believe, was more optimistic than other secret studies in its calculations of the arithmetic of ruin. For example, the Strath Report six years earlier had reckoned that if

> no preparations of any kind had been made in advance, a successful night attack on the main centres of population in this country with ten hydrogen bombs would, we estimate, kill about 12 million people and seriously injure or disable 4 million others – a total of about 16 million. Casualties on such a scale would be intolerable; they would mean the loss of nearly one third of the population; they would moreover include a disproportionate share of the skilled man-power on which our future would depend.[282]

ACE HIGH's scenario assumed that post-Strath preparations had succeeded, especially the successful evacuation of 6 million people. But even allowing for that, their working figures are, by Strath standards, optimistic.

A 1960 study of the 'Concept and Definitions of Breakdown', based on the experience of the mass conventional bombing of Germany and

Japan in the Second World War, suggested that the possibility of devolved government functions and tough emergency powers actually prevailing amid the irradiated rubble was highly questionable. The breakdown studies were conducted by the Joint Inter-Service Group for the Study of All-Out Warfare, or JIGSAW. As one of the team, the psychologist Dr Edgar Anstey, wrote in June 1960:

> [B]reakdown might be defined as occurring 'when the government of a country is no longer able to ensure that its orders are carried out'. This state of affairs could come about through breakdown of the machinery of control ... or through the mass of people becoming preoccupied with their own survival rather than the country's war effort and prepared to run the risk of being shot rather than to obey orders which would seem to them to involve unreasonable personal risk, in a word, through breakdown of morale.[283]

The JIGSAW team's subsequent finding in early 1963 really did render the ACE HIGH assumptions seriously questionable:

> About 30% destruction of a city renders the *whole* city population 'Ineffective' – i.e. wholly preoccupied with their own survival. The survivors would become a liability rather than an asset to the country.[284]

Also:

> A megaton delivery on a city such as Birmingham would also render 'ineffective' 50% of the population within a radius of about 20 miles, including e.g. Coventry, where the people would see, hear and smell what happened to Birmingham, and would either take to their cellars or get into their cars and drive to where they think they might be safe.[285]

The JIGSAWers concluded 'that a general collapse of the national structure of a country, which we call "Breakdown", occurs when about 50% of the population have been rendered ineffective'.[286] They based this calculation on the last months of the Second World War in Germany.[287] The planners took these exercises very seriously right up to the end of the Cold War.[288] But staring into the abyss – and beyond – was the grimmest kind of guesswork. Philip Allen, a senior Home Office civil servant (who later became its Permanent Secretary), sat on the Strath Committee and was earmarked, if Cuba had triggered a Third World War, 'to go with the Home Secretary' to his bunker 'and had a ticket of a particular colour' to secure access. Looking back on Cuba, 'I think for a time we did' fear that the two of them might have to go down their designated hole. Lord Allen admitted having 'a feeling that if it ever came to it, nothing would work quite in the way that one was planning. But, nevertheless, one simply had to plan.'[289] As a Foreign Office diplomat who played a part in the biennial UK/NATO transition-to-war exercises remarked, 'it all seemed horribly possible'.[290]

Reacting to the first serious batches of declassified material on what he called 'the British planning for Armageddon', Sir Rodric Braithwaite reckoned: 'Very serious and responsible people were doing just what they had to do. But they didn't seem to have been at all convinced that it had worked or that, if it had worked, it would have been worthwhile. They were all inescapably saddled with a hideous fantasy. There is no overtone of criticism at all in the foregoing. I don't see what else they could have done.'[291]

Living through the Cold War, one didn't need to be on the circulation lists for the Strath Report, ACE HIGH or the JIGSAW productions to know that properly defending the civilian population from thermonuclear bombardment would be impossible if deterrence failed and war came. And that feeling, the sense of what Rodric Braithwaite called 'hideous fantasy', was the Campaign for Nuclear Disarmament's strongest suit both before and after the Cuban missile crisis. That crisis, and the entering of the name 'Dr Strangelove' into the lexicon of the Cold War, would, it might be thought, have played powerfully into CND's hands. In fact, it was not as simple as that. Cuba marked a turning point in its fortunes as it did for what Kennedy called the 'conventions' of the East–West 'stalemate'.

CND was a remarkable institution whose methods changed the ecology of protest and took the instruments of pressure-grouping to new heights between its foundation in 1958 and the peak of CND Phase One in 1960 (it enjoyed a considerable revival during the Thatcher–Reagan years in the 1980s). In that year it captured the Labour Party Conference meeting in Scarborough for unilateral nuclear disarmament, though Hugh Gaitskell's impassioned fightback

('There are some of us . . . who will fight and fight and fight again to save the Party we love'[292]) from the conference platform in immediate response to the 1960 vote helped restore Labour to multilateralism one year later in Blackpool.[293]

In April 1960, too, unilateralist sentiment in the country as a whole reached its zenith if the Gallup Poll is a guide. In reply to the question 'What policy should Britain follow about nuclear weapons?' 33 per cent suggested the UK should give them up entirely; 27 per cent said pool them with NATO countries and rely mainly on US production; 24 per cent believed Britain should continue to manufacture its own nuclear weapons and 16 per cent had no opinion.[294] Early in 1960, CND calculated that its local groups had grown from 272 to 459 over the past year and, at Easter, its march from the Atomic Weapons Establishment at Aldermaston in Berkshire to London produced 'a four-mile column . . . ending as a Trafalgar Square crowd whose estimated size varied from 30,000 to 100,000'.[295]

Yet the much-ridiculed voluntary Civil Defence Corps, created by the Attlee government in 1948 to do for the Cold War what Air Raid Precautions had done during the Second World War, which as a Home Office-commissioned study privately admitted in 1960 was widely viewed as an 'anachronistic survival which has lingered on from the war',[296] numbered 357,000, of whom 170,000 were genuinely effective.[297] The corps had the numbers; CND had the image. And it had, in its early years, top-flight bearers of the message in the historian A. J. P. Taylor and the novelist J. B. Priestley. It had its logo, too, which swiftly went round the world and remains the global symbol of disarmament to this day. And it had youth and dash. The image of the Civil Defence Corps, often unfairly, was of a group of worthy men and women in blue battledress and berets who had to rely largely on government ministers as their trumpeters in public.

It was those same ministers – one in particular, Duncan Sandys – who had lit the blue touch-paper for CND's take-off in three key sentences in the 1957 Defence White Paper:

> It must be frankly recognised that there is at present no means of providing adequate protection for the people of this country against the consequences of an attack with nuclear weapons. Though in the event

of war, the fighter aircraft of the RAF would unquestionably take a heavy toll of enemy bombers, a proportion would inevitably get through. Even if it were only a dozen, they could with megaton [i.e. hydrogen] bombs inflict widespread devastation.[298]

By the time of the Sandys White Paper, the government had decided it could not afford both a shelter policy for the general public *and* a nuclear deterrent. It opted instead for the deterrent, as every government since has done.[299]

Whitehall's candour was CND's opportunity. And some turned it into an art form that anticipated *Dad's Army* (which was first broadcast in 1968[300]). Here is Christopher Booker writing in *The Guardian*'s 'Miscellany' column about his native Somerset on 18 July 1962:

> Perhaps some of you have observed the sorry plight of the civil defenders of Bath, Somerset. It seems that they lent twelve handbells, twelve special issue Civil Defence Handbells in fact, to the organisers of the local festival for their Venetian evening. And it now transpires that nine of these handbells have mysteriously disappeared. This apparently is little short of tragic for the civil defenders of Bath, since these were the very handbells that they intended to use to warn the citizens of nuclear attack.

What neither Booker nor the Civil Defence Corps realized in the summer of 1962 was that the Corsham bunker just up the A4 made them the target for the intensest of thermonuclear bombardments if and when BURLINGTON started operating.

As an organization, CND had its tensions, and its membership comprised a noticeably volatile coalition. By 1960 its followers had begun to take markedly different views about what kind of action anti-nuclear protest should take. Writing in 1964, Christopher Driver in his evocative study of CND Phase One, *The Disarmers*, reckoned the campaign was made up of six constituent parts into which, post-Cuba, the movement had once more begun to fragment. 'Driver's drivers', as they might be dubbed, were contrasting pairs of 'gradualists and radicals, constitutionalists and anarchists, power-manipulators and power-renouncers.'[301] In early 1960, a young American, Ralph Schoenman (who was to become Bertrand Russell's Private Secretary), did the rounds of the CND groups urging radical direct action, a kind of 'mass revolutionary civil disobedience', in Driver's words.[302]

Russell went with Schoenman, the Committee of 100 and the Direct Action Committee (the radical offshoots from CND); the clergyman most associated with CND's formation in 1958, Canon John Collins, stayed true to the original, purely peaceful approach. Russell and Collins fell out over tactics and strategy in the autumn of 1960 just as CND captured the Labour Party Conference. On 28 September 1960, Collins, following the leaking of the split to the *Evening Standard* (the plan had been to keep it quiet until after Labour had met in Scarborough), issued a statement that 'The CND is bound by conference decision to use legal and democratic methods of argument, persuasion and demonstration to achieve its aims, though, of course, we have sympathy and respect for individuals who feel bound by conscience to use illegal means and undergo imprisonment.'[303]

MI5, naturally, kept a close eye on CND, though the Security Service never treated it as a subversive organization (for example, the 1971 list of these – of both left and right – prepared for the Joint Intelligence Committee makes no mention of it[304]). MI5 did not brief Harold Macmillan on the human ingredients within CND until the spring of 1963, when yet another group of direct activists, the 'Spies for Peace', managed to penetrate the regional seat of government at Warren Row near Reading and produced a great splash to coincide with the Easter Aldermaston March.[305] (They later tried to penetrate Corsham, too, but failed to get sufficiently deep inside to confirm their suspicions that it housed the central Third World War bunker[306]).

MI5 reassured Macmillan that CND was not being run by communists:

> Since 1959 the Communist Party have participated in the Aldermaston marches and other demonstrations organised by the CND Direct Action Committee and the Committee of 100. This is not from the belief in the unilateralist cause but because the communists see in these movements a chance to embarrass the Government and weaken the NATO alliance. At the same time there is little evidence that the communists have succeeded in penetrating the movements to any great extent.[307]

The MI5 analysis coincided with Driver's:

Despite extensive early coverage by the *Daily Worker* the Communist Party as such did not begin to support CND systematically till 1959, and at the 1957 Labour Party Conference communist controlled [trade union] votes were actually cast against the unilateralist motion. By 1960 the position was reversed, and communist activity in unions on behalf of unilateralism, though probably not decisive in terms of votes, did give plausibility to Mr Gaitskell's outburst at Scarborough against 'pacifists, unilateralists and fellow-travellers'.[308]

In the aftermath of Cuba, the JIC produced a special paper on 'Anti-Nuclear Demonstrations at RAF Airfields in a Period of Tension'. 'In such a period', the JIC reported on 16 November 1962, 'there would undoubtedly be persons prepared to incite the public under the pretext of an anti-nuclear demonstration to prevent the operation of nuclear forces. The real point at issue is how effective they might be.'[309]

The JIC's analysts reckoned support for Committee of 100-style direct action had waned after the protest outside the US Air Force Base at Wethersfield in Essex on 9 December 1961. A few days earlier, Special Branch had raided the committee's headquarters and the homes of five of its workers. On 8 December they were charged under the Official Secrets Act and remanded on bail. On the day of action 5,000 people took part in the demonstrations at Wethersfield, RAF Brize Norton and RAF Ruislip.[310] MI5 believed (as was reflected in the JIC report of 16 November 1962) that the subsequent conviction and imprisonment of Michael Randle, Pat Pottle and four others 'and the failure of the "National Civil Disobedience Day" demonstrations marked the beginning of a decline in the Committee of 100's influence'.[311] Pottle and Randle achieved another kind of fame when in 1966 they helped spring George Blake from Wormwood Scrubs, where they had met while serving their eighteen-month sentences. As Blake wrote of them in his memoirs: 'It is true, that they in no way approved of what I had done – they condemned spying in general – and made no secret of this. But they thought the sentence I had been given vicious and inhuman . . . and had a great deal of sympathy for me.'[312]

The November 1962 JIC assessment reckoned that in a period of serious East–West tension, most Brits, including both nuclear disarmers and communists, would come to their senses:

> Since the Wethersfield demonstration support for the Committee of 100 has continuously declined, partly as a result of intrigues and partly because its more idealistic followers are shocked at the way it is being exploited for political purposes. If hostilities are imminent, natural loyalties will come into play and only a minority will be prepared to take active steps to impede the operation of the bases. A similar state of affairs will obtain in the Communist Party, which will lose much of its rank and file support.

There would remain a hardline hardcore, however:

> Those who continue to accept the party's discipline . . . can be expected to be particularly militant, stimulated not only by the desire to help Russia but by a belief that, when it comes to a real crisis, provided everything has been done to undermine their position, the imperialists will give in without a fight. It is reasonable to conclude, therefore, that, while the number of nuclear disarmers and Communists will be considerably reduced in a period of tension, there will be a militant rump which will try to be as obstructive as possible.[313]

British intelligence understood that there was a kind of Cold War flux in operation – and one driven not wholly by external events but by the nature of the British government's reaction to them too.

In its 1971 assessment of the security of the home base during 'a threat of general war', the JIC, drawing on 1960s experience, declared themselves 'particularly conscious of how much the situation in the United Kingdom could be affected by changes in apparently trivial circumstances or by events which have nothing to do with the crisis. The situation might be altered by anything ranging from an injudicious television programme to an evolution in social attitudes towards authority.' There could be 'a general feeling of "a plague on both your houses"'.[314]

Scepticism about the efficacy of civil defence was a supplementary factor here. For example, despite the downturn of its fortunes, CND managed very effectively to deride the contents of the Home Office's *Advising the Householder on Protection Against Nuclear Attack* when it was published in January 1963.[315] Thinking back to those living in potential Z areas (the most vulnerable to H-bomb attack), there is, for example, a terrible, hopeless poignancy, given the heat and blast that megaton weapons produce, in the booklet's paragraphs on the 'Fall-Out Room':

> To protect your family against fall-out, and so far as possible against heat and blast, you would need a fall-out room, stocked and fitted out as this booklet suggests . . .
>
> The penetration of the harmful radiations from fall-out is reduced by heavy and dense materials such as brick walls, concrete or hard-packed earth. You should try to get as much of this sort of material between yourself and the fall-out as possible.[316]

It's easy to see how reading that a few months after Cuba might inspire a degree of fatalism and 'a plague on both your houses'.

In fact, there was a good deal of the latter evident during the missile crisis. The philosopher Professor Sir Anthony Kenny, a future Master of Balliol College, Oxford and President of the British Academy, was a young Catholic curate in Liverpool at the time and found himself in a touch of trouble with some of his parishioners for delivering a sermon along those lines at the Church of the Sacred Heart in Hall Lane on the morning of Sunday 28 October. 'It looks as if I preached the sermon and Khrushchev instantly took the message as if carried by some celestial messenger,' Sir Anthony recalled over forty-six years later.[317]

As the JIC acknowledged in November 1962, 'crowds' were 'provoked in large centres of population' during Cuba.[318] On the evening of Tuesday 23 October, protestors very nearly succeeded in breaking into the US Embassy in Grosvenor Square. David Bruce, the American Ambassador, wrote in his diary:

> The Embassy sustained a massive assault this evening. About 2000 people had gathered in Grosvenor Square, amongst them tough elements probably belonging to the Communist Party. The manifestation was ostensibly the work of the Committee of One Hundred (Lord Russell's anti-bomb people). The crowd attempted to break through the plate glass doors of the ground floor, but were repulsed by the Police . . . Had the demonstrators succeeded in breaking in we might have had a nasty time.

Bruce told his Marines that 'under no circumstances are they to use pistols, even if attacked', though he added, 'I do, however, want to reconsider whether for the protection of the code room we should not, as a last resort, open fire.'[319]

The noise from Grosvenor Square reached Kennedy's Excomm in the White House:

> *Rusk*: The mobs [of protestors] that we simulated turned up in London instead of Havana. 2,000 people.
>
> *President Kennedy*: Surrounding the American Embassy?
>
> *Rusk*: Bertrand Russell's people stormed the embassy there. We haven't had any reports of them disarming Cuba.[320]

Cuba should have been CND's hour. But their neutralism failed to strike a widespread chord as, in its way, the JIC had anticipated. On 'Black Saturday', 27 October, the campaign's National Council met. Resolutions were passed urging the Macmillan government to declare its neutrality and insist on the ending of the American blockade of Cuba. The trade unions were asked to call a general strike if Cuba was attacked.[321]

Historians have traced CND's relative decline post-Cuba,[322] but it was already evident during the crisis. In London, a rally organized by the Committee of 100 took place on Saturday 27 October. CND held one on the Sunday. Only 5,000 people turned up each time.[323] Pat Arrowsmith, one of CND's most brilliant organizers, did the cause no good at all by fleeing to the West of Ireland with her fellow member of the Committee of 100, Wendy Butlin. Initially, their colleagues feared the two women might have been abducted, but, as Driver noted, 'Anxiety was soon allayed by a letter from the pair in *The Guardian* written from the West of Ireland where, they said, they had taken refuge on the assumption that nuclear war was about to break out and that this location represented the best chance in the British Isles of surviving the catastrophe. In the euphoric mood which came over Britain when the crisis was past, the two girls' behaviour seemed infinitely comic and caused the campaign some embarrassment.'[324]

One direct activist, however, could lay claim to having played an influential part in the missile crisis – Bertrand Russell, the ancient, brilliant if intemperate sage. At a CND Youth Rally on 15 April 1961, Russell, at the height of his row with Canon Collins about direct action, said:

> We used to call Hitler wicked for killing off the Jews, but Kennedy and Macmillan are much more wicked than Hitler ... We cannot obey the murderers. They are wicked, they are abominable. They are the wickedest people in the story of man and it is our duty to do what we can against them.

Such a judgement 'gave the more placid members of CND further pause'.[325]

To this day, doubts persist about Ralph Schoenman's influence on the nonagenarian pacifist, including his Cuba intervention when he sent telegrams to both Kennedy and Khrushchev. Absurdly exaggerated language was again in evidence and the difference in tone between the cable despatched to Washington and the one sent to Moscow extraordinary.

To Kennedy:

YOUR ACTION DESPERATE. THREAT TO HUMAN SUR-VIVAL. NO CONCEIVABLE JUSTIFICATION. CIVILISED MAN CONDEMNS IT. WE WILL NOT HAVE MASS MUR-DER. ULTIMATUM MEANS WAR. I DO NOT SPEAK FOR POWER BUT PLEAD FOR CIVILISED MAN. END THIS MADNESS.

To Khrushchev:

MAY I HUMBLY APPEAL FOR YOUR FURTHER HELP IN LOWERING THE TEMPERATURE DESPITE THE WORS-ENING SITUATION. YOUR CONTINUED FORBEARANCE IS OUR GREAT HOPE. WITH MY HIGH REGARDS AND SINCERE THANKS.[326]

This was not a pitch calculated to appeal to Middle England however great the anxieties as the Soviet freighters approached the quarantine line.

Russell, however, performed a vital service. His cable enabled Khrushchev to reply with a public message that Excomm discussed, as did Kennedy and Macmillan on the telephone. As Rusk reported to the meeting on the evening of 24 October:

> Mr Khrushchev did send a telegram to Bertrand Russell saying: 'The Soviet Union will take no rash actions, will not let itself be provoked by the unjustified actions of the United States. We will do everything which depends on us to prevent the launching of war.'[327]

On the phone later that evening, after the Soviet ships had started turning round, Macmillan used Khrushchev's reply, as we have seen, to further his [Macmillan's] desire for a summit:

> MACMILLAN: I see that he [Khrushchev] has made some proposal on the wireless in answer to Lord Russell saying that he wants a summit meeting. Have you heard that?
>
> KENNEDY: Yes, I saw that, but he said there would be no point in a summit if we continued our piratical actions. The implication was that he would be glad to talk, but not if we continued our quarantine or if we carry it out. He wasn't very precise.[328]

Adam Roberts, later Montague Burton Professor of International Relations at Oxford and President of the British Academy, was news editor of *Peace News* at the time and had a walk-on – or, more accurately, a ride-on – part in this drama on the evening of 24 October, that began while he was in Ralph Schoenman's Chelsea flat in pursuit of a story for his paper:

> My recollection is that I got to Schoenman's flat fairly late in the evening – say roughly 9 p.m. . . . . While I was there it transpired that a letter from Khrushchev addressed to Russell had to be delivered to him at his house at Penrhyndeudraeth in North Wales. I think that the existence of the letter had become known somewhat earlier in the day . . . I understood that it had come from the Soviet Embassy . . . I believe (though I didn't witness it) that the gist of the letter was conveyed . . . (by Ralph Schoenman) to Russell over the phone that day.
>   The question arose as to how to get the actual letter to Russell in his Welsh fastness. Because I had wheels, in the form of a Lambretta Li 125 Scooter, the letter in a brown sealed envelope was entrusted to me to take to Paddington, where I was in time to get it put into whatever overnight delivery service existed at the time. As I drove the scooter there I couldn't

help thinking that it was improbable that the entire future of world peace depended on me and my scooter. I remain as sceptical today.[329]

Roberts had real doubts about Schoenman:

Later it emerged that, as many of us had more than suspected at the time, Schoenman had acted in questionable ways during the Cuban missile crisis. On 24 January 1964 I interviewed a member of Russell's staff, Pat Pottle, who told me that some of Russell's initial telegrams had been sent by Schoenman while Russell was in bed asleep and knew nothing of the cable-sending till afterwards.[330]*

We don't know the details of Macmillan's Cuba-inspired nightmares that plagued him well into the 1980s, but, within weeks of Khrushchev's climbdown, he faced another and hugely unwelcome missile crisis. This time the cause lay in Washington, or, to be precise, the rocket ranges on which the US Air Force was testing Skybolt, the stand-off missile intended to keep the RAF's V-bombers in business. It wasn't working. As the former US Defense Secretary Robert McNamara put it to me very bluntly in 1990:

Skybolt. It was an absolute pile of junk . . . the development of which had been paid for 100% by the US – the British hadn't put in a dime – but they had an agreement that if we ever went forward with it, they would have a free ride.[331]

On 7 November 1962, just two days after the V-bombers came down from Alert Condition 3, the Kennedy administration decided to abandon Skybolt. When Macmillan became aware of the decision in early December, 'all hell broke loose', in McNamara's words.[332]

McNamara already had nuclear form with Macmillan. In June 1962 he had delivered a speech in Ann Arbor, Michigan, which was highly critical of smaller nuclear arsenals (i.e. those belonging – or

---

* Whatever the truth, Russell will have his place in the history of Cuba. We all sagged in the aftermath; not just CND. A schoolfriend, Giles Dolphin, told me only over forty years later of the nightmare Cuba gave him in the aftermath. In his dream, the missile crisis had tipped into war. We were standing outside the gym at Marling School with our friends when, suddenly, over Selsey Hill to the south, there was a huge vivid flash. I turned to Giles and said, 'Fuck! There goes Bristol' (where my sister Maureen was living) (conversation with Giles Dolphin, 19 September 2007).

soon to belong – to the UK and France), describing 'limited nuclear capabilities, operating independently' as 'dangerous, expensive, prone to obsolescence and lacking in credibility as a deterrent'.[333] Macmillan poured out his rage on the page of his diary for 19 June – which spilled over into an attack on US policy across several fronts:

> McNamara's foolish speech about nuclear arms has enraged the French and put us in a difficulty, wh the Opposition here will try to exploit. I shall have a chance to tell Rusk on Sunday what terrible damage the Americans are doing in every field in Europe. In NATO, all the allies are angry with the American proposal that we should buy rockets to the tune of umpteen million dollars, the [tactical] warheads to be under American control. It's a racket of the American industry. So far as the Common Market is concerned the Americans are (with the best intentions) doing our cause great harm. The more they tell the Germans, French etc., that they (U.S.A.) want Britain to be in, the more they incline these countries to keep us out. Finally, at a time when the dollar is weak and may, in due course, drag down the pound and bring all Western Capitalism into confusion, they go round the European capitals explaining their weakness and asking for help . . . It is rather sad, because the Americans (who are naïve and inexperienced) are up against centuries of diplomatic skill and finesse.[334]

Macmillan had believed this profoundly since his days with the Americans in wartime North Africa, when he famously outlined his 'Greeks and Romans' thesis to Dick Crossman, Director of Psychological Warfare in Algiers:

> We, my dear Crossman, are Greeks in the American empire. You will find the Americans much as the Greeks found the Romans – great, big, vulgar, bustling people, more vigorous than we are and also more idle, with more unspoiled virtues but also more corrupt. We must run A.F.H.Q. [Allied Forces Headquarters] as the Greek slaves ran the operations of the Emperor Claudius.[335]

Between Kennedy and McNamara's decision to cancel Skybolt and Macmillan hearing about it, his classical conceit had been further dented by perhaps the most polished American diplomat of the postwar years, Dean Acheson, who at West Point, the US military academy

19. Gaitskell and his would-be successors, George Brown and Harold Wilson, with Party General Secretary, Len Williams (*right*), on the Brighton seafront, 29 September 1962, during Party Conference week. The lady sketching appears oblivious to the future of Labour.

20. An anxious Macmillan at Nassau: determined to persuade Kennedy to part with Polaris missiles to keep the flag flying for Britain as a nuclear weapons state, 18–21 December 1962.

21. The Big Freeze bites: Piccadilly Circus, New Year's Eve 1962.

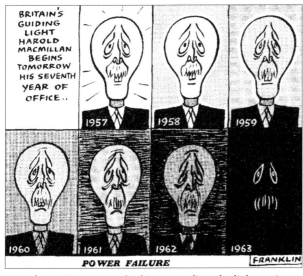

22. (*above*) From 'never had it so good' to the lights going out on 'Supermac', 9 January 1963.

23. (*right*) The General says 'Non': the histrionic pleasure of rejecting the UK's first application to join the EEC, Elysee Palace, 14 January 1963.

24. Intellectual modernity: the University of Sussex opens its doors, 18 October 1962. The new universities added greatly to the nation's stock of little grey cells.

25. (*right*) Students at Loughborough College of Advanced Technology at work on an RAF Hawker Hunter: the Robbins Report of 1963 sought to turn the CATs into universities and to boost science and technology across higher education.

26. A nearly empty M1 in Hertfordshire – when motorways were a novelty and a source of curiosity.

27. Brightly dawned the age of civil nuclear power: Calder Hall in Cumberland, 1962.

28. Enoch Powell, Minister of Health, unexpectedly demonstrates the value of vigorous exercise to his wife, Pam, and their two daughters, 23 January 1962.

29. Land of smokes no more? The cancerous properties of cigarettes made plain in a Ministry of Health poster, 12 June 1962.

30. Miss Turner, the Matron of St Thomas' Hospital, Central London, surveys the coming bounty of the ten-year hospital building programme, 22 January 1963.

31. New streets in the sky: Wickham House tower block on the Stifford Estate in Stepney built in 1962 welcomes the Queen on 18 July 1963.

32. The chic of the wire basket: enthusiastic shoppers sample the joys of self-service at a newly opened supermarket at Thurnscoe near Barnsley in 1963.

33. *Union of South Africa*, the final refurbished A4 Pacific to leave Doncaster Works, where it was built in the 1930s. On 24 October 1964 it was the last A4 to haul a passenger train from Kings Cross to the North.

34. (*right*) The axe-man cometh: Dr Richard Beeching launches his still controversial report on reshaping the railways, 27 March 1963.

35. (*below*) *Sir Nigel Gresley*, named after the designer of the A4, forlorn but still elegant in an Aberdeen siding, April 1966.

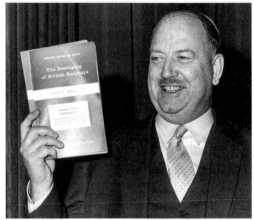

beside the Hudson River, on 5 December made his declaration that: 'Great Britain has lost an empire and has not yet found a role'.[336] Macmillan took the trouble to craft a careful reply (intended for publication) in response to a pained letter about Acheson from the PM's old wartime and early postwar political colleague, Lord Chandos, the former Oliver Lyttelton:

> I have only seen the various press reports of the speech. If these are accurate, in so far as he appeared to denigrate the resolution and will of Britain and the British people, Mr Acheson has fallen into an error wh has been made by quite a lot of people in the course of the last four hundred years, including Philip of Spain, Louis XIV, Napoleon, the Kaiser and Hitler. He also seems wholly to misunderstand the role of the Commonwealth in world affairs.
>
> In so far as he referred to Britain's 'attempts to play a separate power role [being] about to be played out' this would be acceptable if he had extended this concept to the United States and to every other nation in the Free World. This is [the] doctrine in interdependence . . .[337]

Interdependence was to be his theme when Skybolt crashed through the roof of Admiralty House and his life became dominated by the missiles of December.

On 9 December, Macmillan began talks with his defence advisers on 'what we ought to do if the Americans decide to drop it [Skybolt]'. The following day he realized they were. On 11 December he noted: 'Thorneycroft came in at 5 p.m. to report his talk with McNamara . . . It seems clear that the Americans mean to drop "Skybolt". There will be a great row in both countries. And it means a great battle with President Kennedy next week.'[338]

There was and it did.

The meeting at Nassau in the Bahamas had been fixed when Macmillan and Kennedy were on the telephone during the missile crisis and was intended to include a wide-ranging discussion of the state of the world post-Cuba.[339] But, as McNamara recalled in 1990 with feeling: 'the agenda for Nassau was totally scrapped and we didn't talk about a damn thing at Nassau except Skybolt and what to do to replace it in the British inventory'.[340] It has to be remembered that the matter of the UK deterrent and its sustenance was potentially a government-wrecking, first-order question for Macmillan. If he couldn't persuade the Americans to part with Polaris, his administration might fall. It is hard to remember now just how salient the nuclear question was in the early 1960s and how central it was in the minds of Macmillan and his ministers, to the sustenance of the UK's great powerdom and not just its Cold War posture.

Alec Home told me in 1988 that, when the RAF Comet flew out of Heathrow for the Bahamas on Monday 17 December 1962, 'I didn't think we would be successful . . . Jack Kennedy, and indeed the State Department and the Pentagon, were not at all keen on this [Polaris] deal, clearly, and from their point of view there was a lot to be said for keeping all the nuclear power in American hands, of course.' If Nassau had failed, he continued, 'we would have been in a very, very nasty position politically. I think that the government would probably have been beaten. It might well have been a case for an election, I would have thought.'[341] So, in the space of a few weeks, Macmillan shifted from fearing the arrival of Russian missiles that might very nearly destroy his country to worrying that withdrawal of American missiles could scupper his government.

How did Macmillan prevail? By pulling out all the stops and mobilizing every particle of his idea of playing Greek to Roman, summoning 'centuries of diplomatic skill and finesse' in what I think was the negotiation of his political lifetime. He also deployed every histrionic gift in his actor's armoury. As his indispensable note-taker, Philip de Zulueta, put it to me in 1988:

> He made a most moving and emotional speech, about the great losses and the great struggles for freedom and so on, and Britain was a resolute and determined ally, who was going to stand firm, and that it was very unreasonable for the United States not to assist her to do so . . . And it was all very well done indeed and very effective, and there wasn't a dry eye in the house. Splendid.[342]

In fact, as de Zulueta's note shows, the history-infused 'speech' was strung out over several days, and, as we shall see, it left both Kennedy and Macmillan (still feeling the effects of Cuba) quite exhausted.

Of the postwar premiers, Macmillan was second only to Churchill in his ability to fashion British history into a political-cum-rhetorical weapon. At his very first Nassau session with Kennedy in Kennedy's residence, the improbably named Bali-Hai at Lyford Cay, he passed on the admiration of the UK government for the manner in which the President had handled Cuba, and 'said he was sorry that the present talks which he had hoped would range over great world issues had now been overshadowed by the question of the SKYBOLT missile' which 'must be resolved' and then swiftly plunged into a history lesson on the Bomb. 'His memory of government perhaps went further back than that of anyone else in the room and he could recall the time during the war when Tube Alloys were being developed.'

He cleverly brought in the problem Kennedy and his people felt that Europe, France in particular, might pose to any solution for the demise of Skybolt. He 'was sure that the allied countries in Europe, and especially President de Gaulle, were quite aware of the historical background to this question':

> In the early days all the attention had been focussed upon the problem of actually making a bomb. This had originally been largely developed by British scientists and then, when France was occupied, Churchill and Roosevelt had agreed to transfer the work to the United States [Macmillan's dates were awry here; this did not happen until the summer of 1942] where the Hiroshima bomb had finally been produced. At that stage Britain and American had in a sense owned an equal share in the equity.[343]

Macmillan swept on, scooping up the regrettable McMahon Act when a Congress ignorant of the Churchill–Roosevelt agreements had cut off atomic collaboration; how 'harshly' President Eisenhower felt Britain had been treated; how collaboration had been restored in 1958; how he and Ike had discussed Skybolt and Polaris at Camp David in 1960 (and the President had given him a model of a Polaris submarine); how he had accepted the offer of Skybolt and now the time had come to 'switch from the lame horse, SKYBOLT, to what was now the favourite POLARIS'.[344]* It was beautifully done, in the grand manner.

---

* Whitehall, in fact, was well primed on Polaris. As early as May 1960, Rear Admiral Michael Le Fanu had prepared a very thorough study for the Controller of the Navy 'of how the Admiralty might best be organised to deal with a POLARIS

Kennedy was initially unmoved. He first tried to ease the UK team into accepting a combination of Skybolt (if it could be made to work, even though the US Air Force would not adopt it), the entirely unsuitable Hound Dog missile (it wouldn't fit the V-bombers) *or* a European-wide solution inside a NATO multilateral force. Macmillan wanted instead a small slice of America's top-of-the-range system with a UK capacity to deploy it, on its own judgement, if circumstances required it. In other words, for Macmillan, it had to be Polaris, but still with Ernie Bevin's 'Bloody Union Jack' on top of it.[345]

Macmillan admitted that in seeking Polaris,

> part of the reason was keeping up with the Joneses. But there was another reason. The world was not yet organized politically or economically in a way that took cognizance of the disappearance of national independence. In this age of transition there were great nations such as Britain, France and perhaps Germany, that felt they must have a means of defence which gave them the dignity and authority of being participants in this strange new game. There was yet another reason why the United Kingdom wished to acquire these weapons. The United Kingdom still had wide commitments overseas and must be able to use these weapons to defend itself. The defence could not of course be complete but would enable the United Kingdom, if threatened with nuclear attack, to make a significant counter threat. He was thinking of the threats made by Mr Khrushchev at the time of Suez.[346]

At every session, as the negotiation slogged on, Macmillan would return to the national theme, overlain with classical allusions of the classical scholar and the Guardsman:

> He had already taken his country a long way on the European road and if France accepted Britain would join the Common Market. It had been said that he was going against a thousand years of history

---

submarine programme' (TNA, PRO, ADM 1/27740, 'Admiralty Organisation for a Polaris Submarine Programme', 24 May 1960.) I am very grateful to James Jinks for drawing this file to my attention). JIGSAW had studied it, too, in the spring of 1960, and Group Captain Shelfoon pushed its claims elegiacally, praising Polaris as a 'secure' and 'quietly unobtrusive system' which is 'in every way compatible with the British character' (TNA, PRO, DEFE 10/402, SG (60) 39, 'A New Strategic Deterrent for the UK', A. F. Shelfoon, 17 June 1960).

by doing this. He would be going against it far more if he were to abandon Britain's independent power. Of course, if the whole of Europe were to regard itself as like the Kingdoms of Pontus and Bithynia impotent between the two [Roman] Empires [Western and Eastern] then they might ask why they should take any part in their defence.[347]

One imagines Kennedy may have struggled to comprehend those last references. Macmillan was quite happy for a British Polaris Force to be assigned to NATO in normal circumstances but the Royal Navy's submariners would not be content to be just part of a mixed-manned NATO multilateral force – 'they would not wish to feel that they had lost all connexion with their loyalty to their country'.[348] Perhaps Macmillan's greatest peroration came at the noon meeting in Bali-Hai on Thursday 20 December when he reverted to the Great War. It is, I suspect, the moment Philip de Zulueta recalled as not leaving 'a dry eye in the house'; his note captures the tired old man straining every grey cell and vocal cord in the service of his country:

... Britain needed some independent deterrent in order to give their voice a legitimate authority and strength in international councils. Whether the [Polaris] force was committed or assigned or dealt with under some other phrase, in fact it must be still capable of being used by the British Government when they wished.

This power would be exercised with the utmost sense of responsibility. But in the ordinary day-to-day diplomatic life and during periods of international stress people must know that the force could be used when the British Government regarded supreme national interests as involved. Unless this principle could be accepted he would prefer to drop the whole idea of the POLARIS system and find some other way.

He would go a very long way to tie the force to NATO but in the last resort he would have to say that it was as much part of Her Majesty's Government's forces as were the Brigade of Guards. The point was that if the Queen's Ministers gave orders Her troops would obey. If this great effort was to be made to maintain a British independent force it was to give Britain a standing in the world which her position and history commanded.[349]

In a final flourish, the veteran of the Somme linked his evergreen memories of the Great War with the still highly vivid immediate memory of Cuba that everyone in the room shared:

> When in the 1914 war his battalion had been nearly wiped out, the officers and men had fought not because of the 'entente cordiale' [with France] but because of their loyalty to King and country. At the time of Cuba when the President had rightly been so pleased by the steadfastness of his people they had not stood firm because of NATO but because of America.[350]

It was a tour de force – and it worked. The Cabinet, meeting under Butler in Admiralty House, had been kept fully informed and on 21 December accepted the assignment of the UK Polaris Force to NATO with its 'supreme national interests' proviso.[351] For his part, in the 'Agreed Joint Draft Statement on Nuclear Defence Systems', Kennedy accepted the 'supreme national interests' formula.[352] And Polaris was to be offered, too, to France and de Gaulle in an echo of the grand-design-that-never-was of the year before.

Many years later, the de Zuluetas dined with the Bundys at a mutual friend's. McGeorge ('Mac') Bundy had been with Kennedy throughout the Polaris negotiation. The conversation turned to Nassau. 'All I remember is that Macmillan won,' said Bundy.[353] McNamara told me in 1990 that not until they got to Nassau and Macmillan began the negotiation did Kennedy's people realize to what extent the deterrent was 'a very, very real political requirement in Britain . . . But it was a very, very, very difficult meeting and it shows how, I guess, naïve some of us in this country were, because certainly President Kennedy did not wish, nor did Dean Rusk nor I wish in *any* way to embarrass or weaken the British government. The reason was that we were allies and the British had played and were going to continue to play a very important role in our common defence and they felt they needed to maintain their nuclear deterrent.'[354]

Yet the victor of Nassau was far from sure he had won and spent a good part of the days between Christmas and New Year worrying about it. Macmillan's diary account of Nassau, written on 23 December when he was feeling 'absolutely exhausted' after an overnight flight, showed that he didn't entirely trust Kennedy, though he had come to appreciate McNamara:

The Americans pushed us very hard and may have 'out-smarted' us altogether. It is <u>very</u> hard to judge whether they speak the truth or not. But McNamara struck me as a man of integrity – much more reliable than President Kennedy, who makes the facts fit his arguments – or so it often seems. One of the unknown factors was, all through, how far the Americans were speaking the truth about Skybolt. A <u>very</u> successful test was made on the day <u>after</u> our conference ended. Did the President and McNamara know about this or did they expect another failure?

As for his own performance, Macmillan described the discussions as 'protracted and fiercely contested. They turned almost entirely on "independence" in national need. I had to pull out all the stops – adjourn; re-consider; refuse one draft and demand another etc. etc. Whether Parlt and the country will think we have done well or badly I cannot tell yet.' He could – should – have added General de Gaulle to that list. He stayed in bed all day until dinner the following day (Christmas Eve), recovering.[355]

Just after Christmas Macmillan received a not entirely reassuring letter from David Ormsby-Gore:

I am very sorry that I did not have an opportunity of saying goodbye before leaving the Bahamas. I had to dash ahead of the President on his plane because, as you know, it moves off the second he walks through the door . . .

The President was quite worn out by the exertions of the talks. He said that it was certainly the hardest working conference he had ever attended and he seemed delighted by the result . . .

However, some disillusionment set in soon after our arrival in Palm Beach. We watched the evening news bulletins together on television. These were uniformly superficial, critical and tended to concentrate on the alleged disagreements and ill-feeling which had developed between the two sides . . .

The next morning was, of course, worse. The President had had reports of the generally hostile reaction in London to the Bahamas Agreement and he was then confronted with the news of the first successful testing of Skybolt. He felt that the timing was appalling and that whoever was responsible in the Pentagon must be out of their minds. He told me he thought it was the first bad mistake that McNamara had ever made.[356]

Macmillan really wasn't sure the Nassau deal would hold. On the evening of 31 December he held an anxious meeting in Admiralty House with a small group of ministers and officials, including Dixon, who had come back from Paris. He wanted financial arrangements to be settled quickly and a down payment made for one or two Polaris missiles as it 'was important that it was manifest that some equipment was actually crossing the Atlantic'.[357] He had already commissioned a study of what could be done by UK industry if Kennedy pulled out. The answer, in mid-January, showed it would be hugely difficult and prohibitively expensive to go it alone – a UK Polaris would take ten years to produce and cost at least £200 million.[358]

At his New Year's Eve meeting, Macmillan had to put up with a mini-lecture from Ted Heath about the political price of Nassau. This foreshadowed Labour's reaction, especially once Harold Wilson became party leader after Gaitskell's death a few weeks later. Heath said

> that the Skybolt episode had brought before the public in a very clear manner the extent of our dependence on the United States. The same difficulty would be felt to apply to Polaris and until we actually had the missiles in our possession we would be at the mercy of the United States Government. For example, if there were some strong disagreement on important policy issues they might threaten to cancel the contract.[359]

The minutes suggest Heath kept his doubts to himself three days later when the full Cabinet, after being treated to a history lesson from Macmillan ('The nuclear weapon had been invented originally by British scientists ...') and a song of interdependence ('There was ... little attraction in a policy of complete independence ... [though] ... there were several compelling reasons for seeking to preserve a measure of independence as regards control over our nuclear deterrent'), formally approved the Nassau agreement.[360]

The day after Polaris's passage through Cabinet, de Zulueta briefed Macmillan on the far from smooth passage the Nassau Agreement had received in Paris, in the Élysée in particular. De Zulueta, prophetically, worried that, thanks to the Kennedy–Macmillan deal, 'the French will feel that we are so tied to the Americans in the defence field that we could never break away and will use this argument, disingenuously or not, to justify excluding us from the Six'.[361]

De Gaulle had summoned Dixon to see him two days earlier, on 2 January 1963. Dixon had tried to sell Nassau to the General ('The Bahamas arrangement was a good one because Polaris was cheaper and would be available sooner than if we tried to make a comparable device ourselves, the weapon was more sophisticated and would last longer, and we considered that under the arrangement our national interests were fully safeguarded'). De Gaulle was not impressed. As Dixon reported:

> He quite understood why the Prime Minister had concluded the arrangement at Nassau. Indeed he had the impression at Rambouillet that the Prime Minister's mind was turning from Skybolt to Polaris. France's position, however, was different from ours. In the first place they had not got any nuclear submarines nor a warhead suitable for a Polaris missile . . . Secondly, the geographical position of France was different from ours. Great Britain was still an island; France, and to an even greater extent Germany, was at the mercy of a sudden attack by the Soviet Union. In view of those dangers France must have complete control of her own 'force de dissuasion'. He was unmoved by my explanation that things did not happen this way nowadays.

De Gaulle was also very agitated by the idea of a NATO multilateral nuclear force, which would be an instrument for 'American control'. The report continued:

> The command structure, the habits of work, etc., would sap the will to act in a national way. The General went on to say that France would have no interest at all in assigning their Mirage IV bombers to NATO. He did not see why France should put her bombers under an American General. Finally, the General mumbled acidly that he quite understood why, with all our tradition, we had not found it possible to tell the Americans that the terms of their offer of nuclear help were unacceptable, and to turn instead to co-operation with European nuclear defence.

Dixon, shrewd as ever, sensed trouble ahead. Was the General thinking 'of making any public statement about French views in the near future?'

> He replied that he had no present intention of doing so. As I was leaving, he said, however, that he would no doubt be asked questions about Polaris at his press conference in about a week's time; he would be very prudent.[362]

He wasn't.

6

'Sixty-Three

The Sixties were a blur of sensations and excitements . . . The waters seemed to speed up, then froth up, then a tremendous fall over Niagara . . . We've shot Niagara when we get to the end of 1963.

Christopher Booker, Mile End Group
Masterclass, 15 January 2008[1]

1962 is over. It has been a <u>bad</u> year, both in Home and Foreign politics. The Govt's position is weak and there is a general view that the Socialists will win the General Election. The country is in a dissatisfied and petulant mood. My own popularity has gone down a lot. There is a wave of anti-European, <u>and</u> anti-American feeling. There is trouble about growing unemployment. The Press is, with scarcely an exception, hostile. The TV is critical. Altogether, we are at a low ebb. Can we recover in 1963 or 1964? I don't know. But I mean to have a good try.

Harold Macmillan, diary entry,
1 January 1963[2]

All our policies at home and abroad are in ruins . . . French domination of Europe is the new and alarming feature; our popularity as a Govt is rapidly declining. We have lost everything, except our courage and determination.

Harold Macmillan, diary entry, 28 January 1963
(following de Gaulle's veto of the UK
application for EEC membership)[3]

The Sleepers sleep at Audlem and Ambergate.
No passenger waits on Chittening platform or Cheslyn Hay.
No one departs, no one arrives
From Selby to Goole, from St Erth to St Ives.
They've all passed out of our lives.
On the Slow Train, on the Slow Train.

Michael Flanders and Donald Swann,
'The Slow Train', 1963[4]

Sexual intercourse began
In nineteen sixty-three
(Which was rather late for me) –
Between the end of the *Chatterley* ban
And the Beatles' first LP.

Philip Larkin, 'Annus Mirabilis', 1967[5]

There have been good performers in the last ten years. There
have been some good songs written. There have been some
interesting new waves. But no group has been so creative or
inventive or had such an impact on their generation as the
Beatles. They appeared in 1963 and started to split up in
1969, seven years of amazing creativity which saw the production of around 150 songs, songs the whole world sang, till
the next one came out.

Hunter Davies, 1978[6]

That thin wisp of tomorrow which can be guessed at and very
nearly grasped.

Fernand Braudel, 1995[7]

One of the many reasons for being eternally thankful that the Cuban
missile crisis did not trigger a global war that shattered the world in
late October or early November 1962 is that Cliff Richard did not
take the palm for the highest form of pop music that Britain was to
attain. If the five megatons of Russian nuclear weapons British intelligence thought likely to strike Liverpool had fallen, or the nine

megatons deemed possible on London and surrounding areas had dropped,[8] there would have been no Beatles and no Rolling Stones (and no 'Satisfaction', their number one hit of August to October 1965[9]). By the time Khrushchev backed down, the Beatles had only produced 'Love Me Do', which was released in early October 1962 and climbed with little fanfare to number seventeen in the charts just after Christmas – hardly enough to signify the transformation British pop music, or push it into its golden age (which, arguably, began a few months later when their third single, 'From Me To You', reached the top and stayed there between April and June 1963[10*]).

Unlike 1962, 1963 is not remembered for what didn't happen but is very much about what did. In the early twenty-first century there remains a remarkable and unusual mosaic of fragments that, in addition to the starburst of Beatlemania, still colour the collective memory, so vivid are some of its individual tiles:

- The Profumo affair (a scandal involving the eponymous War Minister and a beautiful young woman who also shared her favours with the assistant naval attaché in the Soviet Embassy).
- De Gaulle's veto of the first application for British membership of the European Economic Community.
- The Great Train Robbery.
- Macmillan's fall from the premiership amid chaotic scenes at the Conservative Party's annual conference and the unexpected succession of Alec Home (the human and procedural mechanics of which are still controversial today).
- The assassination of President Jack Kennedy.
- The growing clamour of the satire boom.

It was the year when young British adolescent males such as I, and great swathes of the population at large, realized that the Sixties *were* going to be different.

When a nation's mood music changes it is often a mixture of elegy and excitement – sometimes both in the same musical passage. The Beeching Report's death sentence on steam and branch line – the

---

* Their second single, 'Please Please Me', peaked at number two on the official UK chart, though reached the top on some others.

most elegiac coupling the Industrial Revolution produced – tinged with a bit of anticipated pleasure about faster, cleaner services in the trade-off between romance and efficiency. But romance inspires deep affection; you can admire – but never love – efficiency.

In cricket, the most wistful pastime ever invented by the Brits, the slow decline of the county game led to the eruption of the one-day contest with the first Gillette Cup series in 1963, which began to change both the nature and the metabolic rate of the summer game (and certainly led to an improvement in fielding).

Every year is a snapshot, and its portrait can be like the picture described as the 'decisive moment' by Henri Cartier-Bresson, the great French artist of the shutter, in his famous study of the camera-craft.[11] The way 1960s Britain smelt and sounded began to change during 1963 – a strange, stirring mixture of possibility and peril, the latter mitigated by a rising hope that some lessening of the rolling nuclear neurosis might result from the Cuban confrontation.

It felt like a beginning of the third phase of post-1945 British history. The age of austerity in the late Forties and early Fifties, then the age of easement, in terms of consumption patterns and standards of life, from the mid-Fifties through to the start of the Sixties. Historical shifts are so much easier to detect through the rear-view mirror than through the windscreen. Yet January 1963 was eventful and startling, certainly in the nation's politics. On the 14th de Gaulle delivered his veto during one of his theatrical and brilliantly staged press conferences in the Élysée Palace. Four days later, Hugh Gaitskell, the Labour leader, thought to be within touching distance of No. 10, died of lupus erythematosus, a then incurable immunological disease.[12]

Gaitskell's last great conference speech the previous September had rallied his party and the labour movement against a Britain signed up to Europe, shackled to the Treaty of Rome as it turned its back on his beloved Commonwealth. If federalism was the idea, Gaitskell declared, 'it does mean . . . the end of Britain as an independent European state . . . It means the end of a thousand years of history. You may say, "Let it end", but, my goodness, it is a decision that needs a little care and thought. And it does mean the end of the Commonwealth.'[13] Membership of a federal Europe was the political and emotional fault line for Hugh Gaitskell, to the intense regret of his acolytes on the centre right such as Roy Jenkins, who stood but did not applaud at the end of his friend's oration ('Charlie, all the wrong people are cheering,' Gaitskell's wife, Dora, said to Charles Pannell, Labour MP for Leeds West[14]).

In Paris, General de Gaulle had thought hard about what it meant. He would have none of it and, like Gaitskell, he too invoked Britain's deeper history. Gaitskell, in the Middlesex Hospital and in a very poor and sometimes rambling state,[15] probably did not know of developments in Paris. But the General had done his work for him and Britain would not be allowed, for another ten years, to turn its back (as Gaitskell would have seen it) on a millennium of its past.

As the quotations from his diary at the head of this chapter indicate, Macmillan was pessimistic and anxious on New Year's Day 1963, but by the middle of the month – thanks to de Gaulle – he was shattered. Had he not seen it coming? Or was it the suddenness and the brutality of it all that plunged him into despair? My own view is that whenever the crunch came and whatever the circumstances, de Gaulle would have thwarted Britain's accession to the European Economic Community, for the reasons he advanced to Macmillan during their sequence of bilateral conversations about the 'Grand Design' in 1961.

The General made his reasons continuously plain to his Ambassador to London, Geoffroy de Courcel, on the latter's regular visits to the Élysée Palace. Each time his boss summoned him, de Courcel would ask, 'Are you against Britain's entry to the EEC?' and each time the General replied that he 'hoped' Britain might 'one day' join the Community, provided she 'carried out certain transformations'.[16] These were, in essence, the diminution of the UK's Commonwealth and Atlanticist impulses and the growth of a more European frame of mind.

His biographer Jean Lacouture, the foreign editor of *Le Monde* between 1957 and 1975, makes much of de Gaulle's eloquent paean of praise for the way Britain governed itself and for the ethereal nature of its constitution in his great speech at Westminster Hall during the state visit of April 1960 ('Thus, lacking meticulously worked out constitutional texts, but by virtue of an unchallengeable general consent, you find the means on each occasion, to ensure the efficient functioning of democracy without incurring the excessive criticism of the ambitious, or the punctilious blame of purists'[17]). All this he had seen during his exile in the UK during the war. But he could never expunge from his memory the slights he was convinced he had received from Churchill and his ministers during those years. When he thought about Britain and her interests, he was torn between two conflicting emotions. Lacouture scanned them perfectly when he wrote: 'Charles de Gaulle did not like England. He admired her.'[18]

For all the consistency of de Gaulle's attitude towards Britain as a candidate for EEC membership, the US–UK 'special relationship' – and its crucial inner nuclear component – gave the General the perfect alibi for doing what he wished to do anyway and vetoing it, notwithstanding the recent floating of a Polaris possibility. In fact, Macmillan's last great bilateral with de Gaulle (and the final time the pair met[19]*) took place at Rambouillet just days before he flew to Nassau to prise Polaris from Kennedy to fill the gap left by the cancellation of Skybolt. The sixty-eight-year-old Macmillan was entering what was to be, with Rambouillet and Nassau, the most critical diplomatic phase of his premiership in a condition of very real mental and physical strain. With some justification a few weeks earlier, he had believed the world could be but a few days from the opening phases of a Third World War and had quickly commissioned a post-Cuba review of the UK's transition-to-war drills.[20]

Scholars have hovered over Rambouillet 15–16 December 1962 like vultures over carrion. Did de Gaulle think Macmillan had offered France some kind of nuclear partnership? During the opening session on the afternoon of Saturday 15 December, after a morning spent shooting on the estate (de Gaulle's naval officer son, Philippe, took part; the General didn't), Macmillan briefed de Gaulle on the UK attitude to possession of its own nuclear weapons and the 'position . . . of some embarrassment' the US had placed the UK in by cancelling Skybolt. Philip de Zulueta's note captured Macmillan's remarks:

> Of course once the [Skybolt] missiles had been delivered they could have been used independently. He would have to speak about this with

* Though Macmillan did attend his memorial service in Notre-Dame Cathedral on 12 November 1970 (Jean Lacouture, De Gaulle, The Ruler: 1945–1970 (Collins Harvill, 1991), p. 351).

President Kennedy. The Prime Minister was determined that so long as he was in power, Britain would maintain her independent deterrent and he would explain to the President that if he could obtain an adequate replacement he would be content, but otherwise Britain would have to make her own system; whether submarine or aerial. Of course this would cost a great deal of money and there might have to be corresponding changes in other defences.

This pre-echo of the Nassau negotiation was sandwiched between some vague thoughts about future co-operation – but no more than that:

> He had every sympathy with, and fully accepted, the French decision to become a nuclear power ... These nuclear forces were important for Britain as for France, because they were the symbol of independence and showed that the two countries were not just satellites. It was necessary all the same to discuss with the Allies how to organise such a force because it would be absurd to have an Alliance without plans for the joint use of its forces. The United Kingdom, for this reason, had an arrangement for the joint targeting of the V-bomber forces with the United States ... In addition, the United Kingdom of course had a plan of its own in case Britain was involved in a war without the United States. In the same way, France might have an independent nuclear capacity but nevertheless might have a joint plan for the use of this force with her Allies. The position would be rather like that in the First War when the armies under Haig and Joffre were national armies but planned together.

The two Great War veterans then engaged in a quick two-way chat, avoiding specifics, though Macmillan deftly (though probably unconvincingly, to de Gaulle's ears) slipped in a word or two about his dream of a united Europe:

> *President de Gaulle* said that he had been glad to hear what the Prime Minister said. He too felt that an independent nuclear force was necessary. Of course France's nuclear force would not be enormous, but nevertheless it would be very great. It would have the power to kill 20 million people and this was not to be despised because it would guarantee France against attack.

The Prime Minister suggested that bombers would not be sufficient to make this force credible. Submarines or some other form of missile propulsion would also be needed.

President de Gaulle agreed and explained that France was trying to make nuclear submarines, although they were of course less advanced than Britain.

The Prime Minister said that he felt there was no objection to countries co-operating to make these armaments, if they could then be bought outright . . . He felt that this was essential to avoid a position of dependence on the United States in this respect . . . this independence was essential, if it was ever to be possible to make the United Europe which was his dream. He was very glad that some co-operation had been possible between Britain and France in regard to the supersonic airliner [Concorde].

President de Gaulle said that there was co-operation, not only in the supersonic civil transport, but also in the space rocket programme. France had never refused to make joint arrangements with Britain in these respects.[21]

All very courteous, amicable and non-binding, but it was not deal-making conversation. The deal-talk Macmillan was seeking concentrated upon one area alone – Europe. It began as that winter Saturday afternoon deepened with the question of what kind of organization the EEC was (Macmillan thought it political; de Gaulle economic). Macmillan wanted the Brussels negotiations for British membership wound up soon; de Gaulle wanted delay ('Personally he had not found it at all surprising that the economic negotiations had not been very quick. Britain's entry would involve a complete change in the character and methods of the Common Market including the rules. He did not say that British membership was excluded, but the reality of the Common Market would be quite changed by Britain's entry'[22]).

The blow fell the next morning. According to the de Zulueta note, de Gaulle said of the EEC:

It was not possible for Britain to enter tomorrow and the General felt that the arrangements inside the Six might be too rigid for the United

Kingdom. The Prime Minister had said that unless agreement was reached at once it would never be reached but President de Gaulle's view was that the United Kingdom and the Prime Minister had embarked on a certain course which they would continue to follow. In the end agreement would be reached.

De Zulueta gives no hint of tears welling up in his master's eyes but his note conveys as much emotion as Whitehall training would allow:

> The Prime Minister said that he was astonished and deeply wounded by what President de Gaulle had said. Six months ago at Champs President de Gaulle had asked if Britain would ever be European ... He had expressed the fear that Britain's ties with the Commonwealth would make it too difficult for her to enter Europe. The Prime Minister had overcome those obstacles ...

Macmillan then tried all the historical ploys of which he was master (the missed opportunities of the 1930s; Churchill proposing Anglo-French union as France was about to fall in 1940):

> ... with nations as with individuals lost moments were seldom, if ever, recaptured. Once great decisions had been refused other paths were inevitably taken and the moment passed ... [Perhaps] Britain had better abandon her European ideas and make a life of her own.[23]

As we have seen, this kind of approach would work with Kennedy but now, the more wizened de Gaulle was quite unmoved. He admired Macmillan, plainly relished all the encounters at Champs, Birch Grove and Rambouillet and probably did feel some sympathy for him. But, throughout, British hopes rested in the General's hands, and that December morning, in the Château de Rambouillet, he crushed them.

Maurice Couve de Murville was not present when the blow fell but joined de Gaulle and Macmillan for the next session. Twenty years later he told Michael Charlton how the myth, on which we touched in chapter 2, had arisen:

> CHARLTON: Can you confirm one of the myths about the conference, that de Gaulle, when he saw Macmillan so crestfallen, quoted the words of the famous Edith Piaf song, 'Ne pleurez pas, Milord'?

COUVE DE MURVILLE: Oh no, no, no, he did not say that. No. But he used the words when he reported the meeting at our Council of Ministers, the French Cabinet ... he concluded by saying that, and that, after all, it was not tragic. Things were not ended for all time, altogether. And therefore 'ne pleurez pas, Milord!'[24]

De Murville, however, told Charlton that at Rambouillet, 'Macmillan was very sad and he almost broke down.'[25]

Both de Zulueta and de Murville expressed the view that after their Rambouillet encounter, Macmillan knew the centrepiece of his 'Grand Design' was in fragments:

DE ZULUETA: ... it was pretty clear to me, and I think to Mr Macmillan, that the General was against our going into the Common Market. I mean that I cannot say that I was particularly surprised when he gave his veto, although I was rather taken aback at the precise way in which it was done [during de Gaulle's press conference at the Élysée on 14 January 1963]. He was against it basically, I think, by then, and it was fairly obvious he was against it.[26]

De Murville concurred with de Zulueta's judgement when Michael Charlton suggested to him that 'Macmillan knew when he left Rambouillet that he'd been beaten? Defeated?'

COUVE DE MURVILLE: He knew, yes. Not beaten, but that things were in a deadlock. Because it was really finished.[27]

I suspect, Macmillan *did* know. But, as with most political animals, however shellacked by long experience – as Macmillan was – he allowed himself a dash of optimism when he wrote his diary back in No. 10 that Sunday evening:

The only glimmer of hope lies in the French unwillingness to be held up to all the world as having openly wrecked our entry and having never really tried to negotiate seriously.[28]

De Gaulle's sense of personal destiny, inseparable in his mind from the glory and destiny of France, removed any possibility of such a sense of shame. The conclusion of the Nassau deal on Polaris between Macmillan and Kennedy gave him the perfect peg on which to hang all the instincts on display at Rambouillet over that winter weekend.

Kennedy and Macmillan suspected in advance that the press conference scheduled for 14 January 1963 would produce a diplomatic firework display of a kind that only the General could ignite with his word power, his histrionics, his sense of history and of himself. De Gaulle relished these spectaculars and the Diplomatic Corps in Paris turned up as well as the journalists. Jean Lacouture was there to witness de Gaulle in action:

> That day, at the Élysée, the international press had been waiting expectantly for the first of his weekly press conferences [of 1963]. Over five hundred journalists and close on three hundred guests crowded into the Salle des Fêtes at the Élysée. The curtain moved and there he was. The ministers on one side, the 'entourage' on the other. We held our breath, knowing that in London and Washington Macmillan and Kennedy had been asked to be kept informed of the General's words as they came out, knowing that they, too, would probably be targets.[29]*

It took an agonizing quarter of an hour until the questioning reached Britain and Europe. De Gaulle was never less than statuesque but he tuned up the statesmanlike tone for the grand, set-piece reply, 'speaking' Lacouture noted 'rather more slowly than usual', in 'a serious, courteous tone of voice'. De Gaulle, in effect, put Philip de Zulueta's note of Rambouillet (which, of course, he had not seen) into the public domain and, in so doing, deprived Harold Macmillan of his place in the very top flight of British prime ministers. 'Britain', the General declared, 'is insular, maritime, bound up by its trade, its markets, its food supplies, with the most varied and often the most distant countries. Her activity is essentially industrial and commercial, not agricultural.'

Then, in the flight of one sentence, de Gaulle recaptured the essence

---

* We now know, thanks to Julian Jackson's biography of de Gaulle, that the cold brutality of the General that day was calculated and laced with *Schadenfreude*. He told an aide: 'This has dragged on long enough . . . We are going to have some fun' (Julian Jackson, *A Certain Idea of France: The Life of Charles de Gaulle* (Allen Lane, 2018), p. 591).

of his Westminster Hall address fifteen months earlier about the singularity of Britain and its institutions:

> She has, in all her work, very special, very original habits and traditions ... In short, the nature, structure, circumstances peculiar to England, are different from those of the other continentals ... How can Britain in the way that she lives, produces, trades be incorporated into the Common Market as it has been conceived and as it functions?

Now he readied himself to raise the spectre of creeping American power and what he saw as the inevitability of the UK becoming its intra-EEC distributor, if allowed in:

> It has to be admitted that the entry of Britain will completely alter the whole set of arrangements, understandings, compensations, rules that have already been drawn up between the Six, because all those states, like England, have very important peculiarities. So it is another Common Market that we would have to consider building and one that would be presented with all the problems of its economic relations, together with a host of other states, above all with the United States.
>
> It is predictable that the cohesion of all its members, which would soon be very large, very diverse, would not last for very long and that, in fact, it would seem like a colossal Atlantic community under American dependence and direction, and that is not at all what France wanted to do and is doing, which is a strictly European construction.

He returned to the special problem of Britain and laced it with a dash of 'ne pleurez pas, Milord':

> So, it is possible that one day Britain may sufficiently transform herself to become part of the European Community, without restriction and without reservation, and in that case the Six would open the door, and France would present no obstacle. If the Brussels negotiations did not succeed this time, there would be nothing to stop an agreement of association to be drawn up between the Common Market and Great Britain.
>
> Finally, it is very likely that the evolution peculiar to Britain and the evolution of the world are bringing the English towards the continent,

however long it may take. For my part, I readily believe it, and that is why, in my opinion, in any case, it will be a great honour for the British Prime Minister, my friend Harold Macmillan, and for his government, to have discerned so early, to have had the political courage to declare it and to have made the first steps in putting their country in the way that, one day, perhaps, will lead it to anchor itself to the continent.[30]

De Gaulle finished by pouring scorn on the American idea of a NATO multilateral nuclear force and declined the offer of Polaris for France made at Nassau. (This would not have surprised Macmillan. As the General had admitted at Rambouillet, France was nowhere near the stage needed in submarine design and construction to take the missiles.) How could one disentangle one's own nuclear capacity from a multilateral force 'in the unthinkable moments of the atomic apocalypse', he asked. No, said the General, 'we are keeping to the decision that we have made: to construct and, if necessary, to use our own atomic force'.[31]

Disappointment verging on despair almost overwhelmed Macmillan in the aftermath of that press conference, and the personal resentment he felt towards de Gaulle flowed down the transatlantic cable when he telephoned Kennedy:

> *Prime Minister*: Well, I think it's a very bad situation. I think this man has gone crazy – absolutely crazy.
>
> *President Kennedy*: Well, what do you think it is that's made him crazy?
>
> *Prime Minister*: He's simply inventing any means whatever to knock us out and the real simple thing is he wants to be the cock on a small dunghill instead of having two cocks on a larger one.[32]

In fact, de Gaulle's performance in the Salle des Fêtes was magnificent, deadly and mortal, both to Macmillan's hopes and to a dramatic shift in Britain's place in the world. No wonder the old man in No. 10 took it so badly and personally. It was, too, one of *the* great Cartier-Bresson decisive moments of the 1960s, though in the peculiar, almost perverse sense of being a *non*-turning point. From today's perspective, the emotional deficit many British people felt towards the European Community during the forty-six years of the UK's membership showed there was a good deal of psychological corroboration for de Gaulle's analysis.

At Chequers on 28 January, two weeks after the blow had fallen, Macmillan finally had time to reach for his diary. His pen scorched the page:

> On the <u>Brussels</u> front everything has been reduced to chaos by the extraordinary behaviour of de Gaulle. He gave a 'Press Conference' (with all the Corps Diplomatique present) to denounce Britain and oppose – on principle – her entry into the Common Market. Following the conference, which was in de Gaulle's most majestic and 'Louis Quatorze' style, the 'Goebbels' (M. Peyrefitte – Minister of Information) was putting round every kind of lie about us and about me. The reasons given for de G's sudden decision (of wh. not even Couve de Murville had been informed) are so diverse as to be ridiculous. The General's demarche to the world was followed by Couve de Murville going to Brussels to demand that the negotiations must now stop. This caused anger (but, alas, impotent anger) among the 5, who were just beginning to realise the real inwardness of French policy. De Gaulle is trying to <u>dominate</u> Europe. His idea is not a partnership, but a Napoleonic or a Louis XIV hegemony.[33]

Macmillan felt especially sorry for his negotiator in Brussels, Ted Heath, who had both excelled during the long, sloggy sessions and built a fine public reputation after years of enforced silence in the Whips' Office and an unspectacular spell as Minister of Labour. As the talks crashed around him in ruins in Brussels, Heath delivered a speech that combined epitaph with prediction and which its hearers never forgot. With a passion and an eloquence he could rarely muster later during his premiership, Heath declared:

> The end of the negotiations is a blow to the cause of the wider European unity for which we have been striving. We are a part of Europe, by geography, history, culture, tradition and civilisation ... There have been times in the history of Europe when it has been only too plain how European we are; and there have been many millions of

people who have been grateful for it. I say to my colleagues: they should have no fear. We in Britain are not going to turn our backs on the mainland of Europe or the countries of the Community.[34]

Ted Heath never did, and almost exactly ten years later, he led the United Kingdom into the European Community.*

For Macmillan, however, time was not an ally. There was no chance that he could try again. The consequences were profound both internationally and domestically as engineering Britain into the EEC before the next election was the pivot on which his foreign and home strategies turned. Matters were made worse because there was no fallback. As Sir Michael Fraser, *the* great backroom figure of Fifties, Sixties and Seventies party policymaking as Director of the Conservative Research Department, put it in an assessment that can hardly be bettered:

> Europe was to be our *deus ex machina*: it was to create a new contemporary political argument with insular socialism; dish the Liberals by stealing their clothes; give us something *new* after 12–13 years; act as a catalyst of modernization; give us a place in the international sun. It was Macmillan's ace and de Gaulle trumped it.[35]

De Gaulle's press conference marked the 'nemesis' of a national strategy.[36] January 1963 was the cruellest of months, illusions as exposed as the bare trees that stood out from the snowfields blanketing Britain in that most bitter of postwar winters.

Can Macmillan be faulted? Hadn't he given his all (and it was a formidable 'all') to try to ease the General onside? He had. But as Michael Fraser indicated to David Butler, he had prepared no fallback position. There lies among the files at Kew a fascinating, almost poignant piece of archive, a Prime Minister's Personal Note to Norman Brook dated 23 August 1962 replying to the Cabinet Secretary's paper on the reorganization of Whitehall 'if we become a member of the European Economic Community', a membership which would 'have

---

* Though late in life, he came to fear that the UK could turn its back on Europe, as he 'gloomily' confided to his Private Secretary, Michael McManus, on more than one occasion in 1999–2000 (e-mail from Michael McManus to the author, 6 November 2018).

a far-reaching effect on the policies and procedures of Whitehall as a whole'.[37] Macmillan's minute reveals the timetable he had in his mind ready for implementation once de Gaulle was persuaded, the big prize won and the shining path to yet another electoral triumph paved with European flagstones:

> I have read your paper. I think it right that steps should now be taken to consider what arrangements would be necessary if Britain becomes a member of the European Economic Community. There will of course be a number of stages before final ratification and full member-ship. The date for this might be at the earliest July, 1963, more likely January, 1964, or perhaps even July, 1964.[38]

The temptation of counterfactual history is ever present – if the push for the EEC had worked; if Macmillan's health had held up; if Jack Profumo's affair with Christine Keeler had remained under wraps. But 1963 was a year that underscores the great Macmillan line about the 'opposition of events'[39] and the feeling that comes to every reflective member of any political class at some time, that the gods of politics are among the most wrathful of deities.

Brook's summer 1962 planning for an intra-EEC UK rightly pointed out to Macmillan that membership would mean a cranking-up of Whitehall substantially beyond the Foreign Office and the economic ministries, which, under the leadership of Ted Heath, had been making the pace during the negotiations – 'if we enter the Community, we shall be involved in other matters – e.g., move-ment of population, level of social security payments, labour questions . . .'.[40]

Amid the ruins of late January/early February 1963, Brook's suc-cessor, Burke Trend, sought to get a grip on the questions facing a tired and distracted Prime Minister and his Cabinet with a memoran-dum for Macmillan on 'Machinery of Government in the Post-Brussels Period'. On 12 February 1963 he sent it to Tim Bligh, the Principal Private Secretary in No. 10, explaining that 'I have now sketched out . . . some of the issues which I think we must face, together with an indication of possible courses of action . . . I felt I ought not to wait any longer before putting on paper some of the questions that are beginning to be put to me.'[41]

The problem besetting the 'post-Brussels period', Trend told Macmillan, is that: 'We shall no longer have one clear and overriding objective, to which all the elements of our policy can be directed and, if necessary, subordinated. We shall have to evolve a new policy by a series of individual decisions on separate and often unrelated problems, both economic and politico-military, as they arise'. As cabinet secretaries tend to do after a crisis or a setback, Trend suggested a rejigging of the machinery of co-ordination overseen by a steering committee chaired by the Prime Minister; a kind of inner Cabinet that would not speak its name (Trend did not care for inner Cabinets and told Macmillan it 'would not be an executive committee'). He went on:

> The need for such a steering committee might prove to be only temporary; and we might dispense with it after a few months. But the collapse of the Brussels negotiations has left a momentary vacuum in our machinery for dealing with our external relations; and a small but powerful committee, able to provide a firm and clear lead to the normal inter-departmental work of Whitehall, might be the best way of filling it.

Trend broke the problem facing the EEC-excluded government into 'two distinct tasks':

(a) The functional control and stimulation of the economy.
(b) The physical planning of the country.[42]

– his way of capturing the Macmillan growth and modernization strategy.

Macmillan undertook to consider the Trend plan over the weekend at Chequers and instructed Bligh to arrange a meeting in Admiralty House on the Monday morning.[43] With Martin Redmayne, the Chief Whip, and Bligh also present, Macmillan and Trend duly met and decided upon 'a small steering group' consisting of Macmillan, Butler, Home (or Heath) to represent the Foreign Office and Maudling from the Treasury, which was to meet every other Tuesday, 'fitting in with the modernisation group on the home side'.[44]

Trend's repriming of the Cabinet machinery had its effect and it fitted neatly with Macmillan's old idea – economic growthmanship, as his diary entry for Thursday 21 February captures:

Motored early [from Chequers] to London. More snow, ice on the roads, and no sign yet of a real thaw [this wasn't to happen until March]. We were lucky that unemployment figure has remained under 900,000 – for all work on roads, building etc. has stopped for over two months . . .

Cabinet at 10.30. Long discussion on Central Africa – a gloomy outlook.

Meeting at 5pm with Butler, Home, Maudling and Heath to agree machinery for 'post-Brussels' political and economic policy. All went well.

7–10pm (dinner at Admiralty House). A very good talk with Maudling. We are in broad agreement on the general outline for Economic Recovery. We must face the risks in relation to sterling. If the nation will accept in practice (as well as in principle) need for a reasonable 'incomes policy' I believe we can have another 'go' without an inevitable 'stop'.[45]

Herein lay the ingredients of what became known as Reggie Maudling's 'dash for growth' – to go flat out for a long-term upward shift in the trajectory of expansion while being brave about the pressure on the balance of payments and probably the pound sterling, which would inevitably wear and tear the policy in its initial stages – of which more in a moment. By late February 1963 Macmillan and Maudling were having to learn how to deal with another ardent growth man, the new Labour leader, Harold Wilson, Gaitskell's successor. That same diary entry captures, in part, the new political weather system created by Wilson's leadership of the Opposition:

P.Q.s [parliamentary questions] went well. Wilson 'stuck his neck out' and I got a good reply. Our chaps seem in much better heart. Saw 1922 Executive [1922 Committee of Conservative backbenchers] and told them firmly that I had no intention of resigning or of having an election till 1964. Of course, if Govt were defeated in HoC, we wd resign; the Queen wd send for Wilson, who wd form a Govt and dissolve [Parliament] – and win. We must stick together and hold on. I think this lecture had a salutary effect.[46]

The era of 'the Two Harolds' – which left a flavourful memory even though it lasted but eight months – had begun. As Richard Thorpe put it, 'Gaitskell had been one of Westminster's clergymen; Macmillan and Wilson were both political bookies.'[47] The contest pitted actor against technocrat; downy old statesman against sharp stand-up comedian.

They were worthy opponents and connoisseurs of each other's styles. As Alistair Horne, Macmillan's official biographer put it, 'the two Harolds formed, to the end, a curious mutual admiration society for each other, based chiefly on parliamentary prowess'. For his part, Wilson told Horne: 'There was absolutely no malice. After we had savaged each other in the House, we would then meet for a drink . . . I think he liked my crack about his being "First in, first out" at Suez, and when he was moving in for the kill in the House he invariably kicked the table under the despatch box with his right foot. Such courteous intimations have become rare since then.'[48]

Macmillan had not warmed to Gaitskell, but seems genuinely to have been affected by his death. In one of his longest and most revealing catch-up diary entries – written at Chequers on 28 January and dealing with, among other things, the disaster of the de Gaulle veto – Macmillan wrote:

> Poor Hugh G. who has been ill for some weeks with a mysterious germ or virus, died on the night of Friday 18th . . . It is very sad – for altho' I did not find him a sympathetic character – he was a man of <u>high</u> quality and his death is a real loss to the nation. His successor is to be chosen soon. The candidates are Harold Wilson, [George] Brown, and [James] Callaghan. The first is able but dangerous. The second is a buffoon. The third is pretty good and wd be a respectable leader.

As so often in political diaries, tribute rapidly gives way to political calculation:

> It is not easy to estimate the effect of Gaitskell's death. (So far as the Gallup poll is concerned, it seems to have <u>increased</u> the Labour majority!!) Of course, he had become both experienced and respected. Wilson is the first, but not the second. Brown neither. He [Gaitskell] was the sort of upper-middle class leader which a party of the Left requires in <u>normal</u> times – Asquith or Attlee. He moved in many circles, and attracted the academic, the literary and the artistic, and (through his friendship with

Anne Fleming)* some of the 'smart' society of London. He was thought much of abroad in 'progressive circles' – both in America and (to a lesser extent since his anti-European market attitude) in Europe. He was a distinguished man, with considerable political courage – or at least, skill. He held his party together. His successor (with an election approaching) shd be able to do this easily.[49]

And so it proved.

Wilson took two ballots to get to the Labour leadership:

7 February 1963: Wilson 115 / Brown 88 / Callaghan 41
14 February 1963: Wilson 144 / Brown 103

The mercurial Brown, as embittered as another Brown would be forty years on about another's acquisition of the Labour scarlet, disappeared incommunicado for several days (to Scotland and a lochside retreat in Perthshire, as it turned out[50]). Brown had been Gaitskell's deputy, his considerable intelligence struggled alongside a high emotional charge which even a relatively small amount of drink could detonate.[51] But for that volatile combination, the succession to Gaitskell would have been his for the taking, not least because of his deep roots in the trade-union movement. The shrewdest of Labour figures, such as Ian Mikardo (the most accomplished bookmaker in the Labour movement), had long had their eye on Harold Wilson as a future winner – pretty well from the moment they entered Parliament together on Labour's high tide in 1945. For Wilson's BBC Radio 4 obituary, Mikardo said:

> I have no doubt, and I didn't have any doubt from the early days, that somewhere in a drawer in Wilson's residence there was a sheet of paper headed 'Way to the Top', and it listed all the things he was going to do in the sequence in which he was going to do them. That is the constant thread, the scarlet thread running through it all.[52]

Two of the words on Wilson's 'list' in February 1963 would have been 'science' and 'socialism'. With this fusion he would, he hoped,

---

* Even in the privacy of his diary Macmillan was careful not to mention Gaitskell's affair with the wife of the creator of James Bond; it's hard to believe he did not know about it.

propel himself into No. 10. Dick Crossman was his point man on this propulsive combination. Crossman, one of Wilson's campaign managers, in his diary entry for 8 February, reports Wilson telling him: 'One change I shall make is in the Party's view of science. The scientists, the technologists and their like felt excluded by the Gaitskell leadership, left out, not wanted. But if I get the job, I shall want to create an atmosphere where they all feel wanted in the Labour Party.' Crossman saw this as Wilson-as-Kennedy – 'the British equivalent of Kennedy's New Frontier, with a professional politician at the centre, hard-boiled, ruthless but with a basic inner drive and integrity, and round him a galaxy of talented, able and brilliant men'.[53]

This was the motive power of the Wilson pitch for the 1964 election, campaigning for which began the day he defeated Brown in the run-off. On one level, it reads like a clever mix of technocracy and political hyperbole. But there was substance to it as well as dash and it went to the heart of the longstanding concerns about Britain's society and the productive capacity of its economy – concerns that remain alive and unresolved in the second decade of the twenty-first century. As we shall see in chapter 7, it had the capacity to dazzle.

Macmillan did not intuit the scientific and technological angle of the Wilson trajectory but he got much of the rest right as he made his calculations of the new domestic political weather system generated by the rise of Wilson. 'Wilson got in fairly easily over poor Brown,' he wrote in his diary on 17 February. 'I'm afraid Brown lost the Welsh and Scottish Labour MPs who (tho' his natural supporters) are mostly "teetotal" and wd not vote for a drunkard.'[54] This tallies closely with the private assessment of Wilson's Shadow Foreign Secretary, Patrick Gordon Walker, who had thought of running himself but decided not to and nominated Brown (he hoped to be his deputy leader). The result of the first ballot, wrote Gordon Walker,

> showed that there had been a major defection among trade unionists and amongst many who had supported HG on personal grounds. The decisive thing was that GB was too unpredictable: that he drank too much and that we could not afford such a head man. He had personally affronted many people. He had a bunch of very loyal supporters.[55]

Macmillan recognized that the youthful Wilson could and would quickly accumulate a good deal of capital by exploiting the generational difference between the two of them, and his overall assessment of Conservative prospects was gloomy:

> Wilson is an able man – far more able than Brown. He is good in the House and in the country – and, I am told, on T.V. But he is a fundamentally dishonest – even 'crooked' man – almost of the '3 Card Trick' kind. This may, sooner or later, find him out – or, rather, be found out . . .
>
> The Gallup Poll has been very bad – 15% against the Party; as much against me. The collapse in Europe; the Polaris problem; above all, the economic setback and the *frightful* weather (still snow and frost and unemployment!) have caused a wave of depression in the Party in the H of Commons . . . 'Macmillan must go' is the cry. Faced with <u>Wilson</u> (47 or so) we must have a young man (Heath or Maudling). This line of approach leaves out poor Butler as well as me.

It was as if Macmillan realized that his place in the first rank of British prime ministers was now doomed and that what in the same passage he described as 'the pressure for a "sacrificial victim" in the person of the Leader (or Priest-King à la Frazer*) will begin to grow'. On this desire for change, he continued:

> there's something in it. We have had a run of bad luck. Once this starts everything seems to go wrong. Really, everything that wd have been passed over as a minor contretemps when things are good is elevated into a major crisis when things are bad. Nevertheless, apart from spite, this is mostly defeatism. If I were to resign <u>now</u>, it could be of no benefit to anyone. We *must* go on at least till May, perhaps to Oct 1964, in the hope that our economic measures will have produced their results. So we must stick it out.[56]

That freezing winter Sunday at Chequers Macmillan realized just how much was riding for him and his government on Maudling's

---

* A reference to Sir James Frazer, social anthropologist and ethnographer and author of the classic *The Golden Bough*. It describes the sacred grove at Nemi, twenty miles south-east of Rome, whose priest was succeeded by the person who slew him (J. G. Frazer, *The Golden Bough: A Study in Magic and Religion*, 3 volumes (Macmillan, 1890–1900), vol. 1, pp. 1–2).

'dash for growth'. Back there on 20 February he composed a note for his Chancellor of the Exchequer,[57] virtually inciting him to go for broke in his forthcoming Budget, urging him to think of 'the big stuff – the national plan [i.e. the NEDC targeting], the new approach, the expand or die' and to pump around £400 million into the economy.[58] (Treasury officials were advising somewhere around £250 million.)[59] In the end, the Maudling Budget of 3 April 1963 injected some £300 million.[60]

Macmillan was delighted. He purred with pleasure on 2 April as at Cabinet Maudling 'gave an outline of the main Budget proposals, in a masterly exposition – clear and convincing. After all the work we have done on it, the result is better than I had hoped.'[61] The following day he recorded in his diary:

> Budget. Chancellor of the Exr spoke from 3.30–5.15 – an admirable performance, which both in manner and in matter delighted the Govt benches and won reluctant admiration from the Opposition. Wilson's rather cheap sneers were not effective. The scene is set – expansion without inflation. Will Trades Unions play? It will depend on them.[62]

Events – and, later, history – were not kind to Maudling's attempt to break out from the multiple straightjackets of postwar economic and industrial realities. Edmund Dell, the Savonarola of post-1945 chancellorships, was in no doubt, in the mid-1990s, where the affable, intelligent yet languid Maudling sat in the dock alongside his peers: 'The best that can be said of it was that it was a hallucination. Maudling's 1963 Budget is the ultimate example of the effect of a combination of politics, ignorance, and hubris on economic management.'[63]

Maudling believed until his dying day that if Labour had not made such a fuss about the balance-of-payments deficit when Wilson took office in October 1964 and had held its nerve, the dash for growth would have begun to pay off in 1965. In his memoirs, Maudling acknowledges that his 1963 Budget 'was designed on an ambitious scale'. The idea, Maudling explained, was 'to range beyond the normal circumstances of revenue gathering and revenue dispensing to encourage a rate of development of the economy which could be sustained'.[64]

For a big man with a torpid manner, Maudling, in policy terms, was quite a chancer and he was constantly aided and abetted in this by nature's economic expansionist in No. 10 next door. Maudling drew up his growth plan with his eyes open. He knew its risks. The first was inflation. Though he saw 'spare capacity in the economy',[65] there was a danger that wages would rip. The second was the balance of payments. Maudling thought of floating the pound but it was too difficult for the UK to go it alone in the era of fixed exchange rates under the Bretton Woods system. He thought, too, of a two-tier interest rate system: one for home, one for abroad. The Treasury and the Bank of England told him this was not a runner because the UK was responsible for sterling as the world's second reserve currency.[66] Thus, wrote Maudling, in a very characteristic paragraph,

> we went for expansion, quite deliberately, with our eyes open, recognizing the dangers. The prize to be obtained, the prospect of expansion without inflation, the end of stop-go and a break-out from the constrictions of the past, was a glittering one. My policy has been described as a 'dash for freedom'. I think that is ascribing to me, rather unusually, an excess of energy and enthusiasm. In fact the whole policy was deliberate, calculated and coherent. No one could guarantee success, but the chances were high, and the alternatives were drab and depressing.[67]

Were they 'high'? Maudling and Macmillan were placing a good deal of faith in the National Economic Development Council improving the industrial atmosphere cumulatively and fairly swiftly and the National Incomes Commission operating 'a system whereby exceptions [to wage restraint] could be identified and the reasons why they could be treated as exceptions clearly defined' to avoid, in a voluntary, non-statutory fashion, a wages spiral (Macmillan described this approach to Maudling as the 'open air cure'[68]).

There were many optimistic assumptions in that strategy. It was very early days for both 'Neddy' and 'Nicky'. And there was no evidence that a new and more benign ecology in terms of industrial relations was about to envelop the UK in a warm front of co-operation. Sterling couldn't float to help take the strain (presumably because breaking out unilaterally from the Bretton Woods fixed-exchange regime would be too difficult). Nor, Maudling was advised, could the sterling balances be funded (effectively the reserves in the UK of the mainly

Commonwealth sterling area countries could be drawn on by them at any time). So all the restraints that had cramped his predecessors' room for manoeuvre during their chancellorships applied to Maudling too. But he was determined to grit his teeth as his dash for growth sucked in more imports and the balance of payments worsened because 'our calculation was that any strain on the balance of payments would be temporary and that we had adequate borrowing facilities to tide over any short-term difficulties'.[69]

In March 2011, Sir Samuel Brittan, the veteran economics commentator of the *Financial Times* (whose study of *The Treasury Under the Tories* has never been surpassed as an account of the Macmillan-Lloyd-Maudling era), reprised all the dashes for growth for his readers under the headline 'Yet Another Unprecedented Growth Strategy Means Politics as Usual'. Sir Samuel pointed out that the normal rate of growth of the UK economy has rarely varied, whatever wheezes and stimulants successive combinations in No. 10 and No. 11 Downing Street have applied to it:

> As for the longer term, taking boom and bust years together, the UK's annual growth of output per hour has never veered far from 2 per cent, leaving aside the post-war catch-up, until the recent worldwide crisis. This probably did mark a change. The statistical evidence so far is consistent either with a slowing down of the UK growth trend or with a once-and-for-all downward shift in levels after which the normal trend will be resumed.

'Either way,' Sir Samuel concluded, 'don't hold your breath.'[70]

After April 1963, Macmillan and Maudling did hold their breath; it was perhaps all they could do as the rest of the 'Grand Design' of 1961–2 was so much wreckage. In fact, much of the Sixties was devoted by politicians to quickening the natural biorhythm of the British economy as successive combinations of Premiers and Chancellors (and after 1964, Secretaries of State for Economic Affairs) pitted themselves against the rigidities and constrictions of the past, but the spectre of relative economic decline and industrial underperformance rarely left the Cabinet Room. It is, in fact, the most continuous and consistent haunter of all the peacetime administrations since Clem Attlee called on King George VI to kiss hands on the evening of 26 July 1945.

The April 1963 Budget was – and remains – one of the most significant of the great fiscal set-pieces of the postwar years. Reggie Maudling has left scarcely an imprint on the collective political memory of the first three post-1945 decades, yet in 1963 he cut quite a dash.* For all his apparent torpor, he had a formidable intellect, which he could switch on like a light if he thought the circumstances demanded it. And during his chancellorship he was seen as a coming young man who might well be the one in his generation (which included Ted Heath, Iain Macleod and Enoch Powell) to make it to the premiership.

He was a liberal Conservative, especially on Africa, as we have seen, though he was not wildly keen on the Common Market. He regarded de Gaulle's veto as 'a great disappointment, but not a disaster' and he said so publicly in the House of Commons.[71]

His private-office staff delighted in working with him. The drinks cupboard was always well stocked, and a fridge was brought in to take care of the gin and tonic; the atmosphere ever easy.[72] Derek Mitchell, who was his Principal Private Secretary at the time of the 1963 Budget, always found his political philosophy difficult to fathom. He told me in conversation later of the occasion when Reggie had accepted, somewhat reluctantly, an invitation to speak at the Master Cutler's feast in Sheffield. Amid the splendour of the Cutlers' Hall, he managed to conceal his boredom and got the speech out of the way as soon as he decently could. Pleading red boxes to be worked on (Derek knew this was a fib), he left the hall for his hotel and invited Derek up to his suite for a drink: 'Put the television on, Derek. Ah! *Come Dancing* – one of my favourites.' Derek poured and served the drinks. Reggie watched the TV set with rapt attention. These were the days when it was all white-tie-and-tails and tulle rather than catsuits. Finally, Reggie came out of his silent reverie.

'Do you know, Derek, this is what Conservatism is all about.'

Derek could never decide if this was a Reggie joke. 'If it wasn't,' he

* In contrast to his lacklustre Home Secretaryship in the Heath years and his resignation in July 1972 during a police investigation of the affairs of the corrupt and now bankrupt architect John Poulson, with whom Maudling had had business associations during the opposition years (Lewis Baston, *Reggie: The Life of Reginald Maudling* (Sutton, 2004), pp. 414–29).

said, with a beautiful smile, 'I find it rather depressing.' Maudling should have his place in the Conservative pantheon for that remark alone.

Even if there is now little or no public memory of Maudling and the April 1963 Budget, the Beeching Report of March 1963 is not forgotten. As Matthew Engel wrote forty-six years later, after taking a nationwide 'train journey to the soul of Britain', 1963 was 'the year when Britain finally and officially fell out of love with the railways ... the name Beeching still has instant recognition to generations unborn in the 1960s ... When I started telling people I was writing a book about Britain's railways, several just shrieked "Oh, Beeching!" as though no one and nothing else had ever happened.'[73] The name Beeching is as much a part of the Britain of the 1960s as Mick Jagger.

During the debate in the House of Commons on the 1955 modernization plan,[74] Enoch Powell described the search to find 'in our present railway system, as a sculpture is concealed in a block of marble, the railway system of the future which does pay and which corresponds to the economic needs of the country'.[75]* Richard Beeching was recruited to be that sculptor (though there was no trace of the artist inside that bulky, technocratic frame). It was a tough task for two reasons. The national railway system was chaotic, overextended and with a break-even point nowhere in sight. It was a mess, but a romantic mess. No other industry or its artefacts appealed so deeply to so many for so long. As Nicholas Whittaker put it in the prologue to his *Platform Souls*, trainspotting 'was our national hobby, as English as morris dancing and looked on with indulgence ... Railwaymen used to be our heroes, gritty working-class men with denim overalls and jaunty caps.'[76] But the special tug of the railway on the national emotions went beyond young lads at the end of platforms in

---

* Michelangelo's 'angel in marble' image was revived by *The Times* on the eve of the second anniversary of Disraeli's death, which was to be marked by the unveiling of a bronze sculpture by Mario Raggi in tribute to the great statesman and which still stands today in Parliament Square: 'In the inarticulate mass of the English populace which they [the Conservatives] held at arm's length [Disraeli] discerned the Conservative working man, as the sculptor perceives the angel imprisoned in a block of marble' (*The Times*, 18 April 1883).

gabardine macs (which had given way to the eponymous anorak before the combined effects of diesels locomotives and electrification ripped out the romance). It was the industry that personified steam, the releasing of the fossilized energy frozen in coal, that had transformed Britain's economy, its work and population patterns and brought virtually the whole country – urban and rural – within the sight, sound and smell of steam emitted from machines that have come closer than any others to possessing personalities.

Dr Beeching, however, seems to have felt none of this. His was the world of chemicals, which has inspired very few poems and even fewer chemical spotters. Indeed, as Anthony Sampson conveyed in his second anatomy of Britain, what he called the 'Beeching revolution . . . became a prototype or a symbol, of a new kind of ruthlessness in Britain. "Doing a Beeching" became a phrase for any drastic reassessment – even in the Church; and in the mood of 1963, after Britain's failure to enter the Common Market, the cold logic of Beeching served in some ways to provide some of that harsh reassessment that the Common Marketeers hoped would come from the continent.'[77] This is Beeching as the progenitor of a dash for efficiency alongside Maudling's dash for growth. He instantly became the epitome of the unsentimental, cost-benefit analyst, unafraid to rub people's noses in what he regarded as reality. Almost exactly forty-eight years after the publication of *The Reshaping of the Railways*,[78] I mentioned to that most courteous of parliamentarians, Tam Dalyell, that I was writing about Beeching; he said, with feeling: 'Bad man; as arrogant as hell. In all my forty-three years in the House of Commons, Beeching was the most arrogant of all.'[79] The memory of Beeching has an enduring motive power.

In fact, the name of the author of *The Reshaping of the Railways* ranks in shared memory alongside only one other of the great reformers, William Beveridge, nineteen years earlier, the difference being that Beveridge is remembered as a kind of secular saint and Beeching as a hobgoblin, just short of a devil. Despite five decades of demonization, I have a sneaking sympathy for Dr Beeching. Macmillan, speaking in the House of Commons on 10 March 1960, implicitly recognized the existing 1955 modernization plan (the replacement of steam by diesel and electric; new rolling stock; more efficient marshalling yards; improved signalling) was necessary but insufficient if that angel-in-marble of a railway system that paid its way was to be achieved. 'First,' the Prime Minister declared, 'the industry must be of a size and pattern suited to modern conditions and prospects. In particular, the railway system must be remodelled to meet current needs, and the modernisation plan must be adapted to this new shape.'[80]

Beeching began his report with that quotation and apologized for taking three years over his task, explaining that 'there had never before been any systematic assembly of a basis of information upon which planning could be founded, and without which the proper role of the railways in the transport system as a whole could not be determined. The collection of this information was itself a massive task' and took a year to complete.[81] This, justifiably, exposed the 1955 plan as an accumulation of wish lists drawn up by the British Transport Commission for the Ministry of Transport and the Treasury, all of whom were largely flying (or perhaps steaming) blind.

In setting out what he called 'The Nature of the Problem', Beeching began with a piece of contemporary economic history even his most severe critics could not gainsay:

> The railways emerged from the war at a fairly high level of activity, but in a poor physical state. They were able to pay their way, because road transport facilities were still limited, and they continued to do so until 1952. From then onwards, however, the surplus on operating account declined progressively. After 1953 it became too small to meet capital charges, after 1955 it disappeared and by 1960 the annual loss on operating account had risen to £67.7 million. This rose further to £86.9 million in 1961.[82]

In fact, the litany of British Railways' annual 'net operating revenue' from nationalization to Beeching look like this:[83]

1948	£23.8 million
1949	£10.6 million
1950	£25.2 million
1951	£33.3 million
1952	£38.7 million
1953	£34.6 million

1954   £16.4 million
1955   £ 1.8 million
1956   –£16.5 million
1957   –£27.1 million
1958   –£48.1 million
1959   –£42.0 million
1960   –£67.7 million
1961   –£86.9 million
1962   –£104.0 million
1963   –£81.6 million

Beeching now turned to the inadequacies of the 1955 approach when

a modernisation plan was embarked upon. It was a plan to modernise equipment, but it did not envisage any basic changes in the scope of railway services or in the general mode of operation of the railway system. It was expected that the substitution of electric and diesel haulage for steam, concentration of marshalling yards, reduction in number and increased mechanisation of goods depots, re-signalling, and the introduction of other modern equipment, would make the railways pay by reducing costs and attracting more traffic.[84]

Though Beeching did not allude to it directly, Ernest Marples's energetic arrival at the Ministry of Transport in October 1959 and Treasury anxieties about the lack of bite in the 1955 plan led to the creation of a Special Advisory Group (SAG) on the future of the British Transport Commission, chaired by Sir Ivan Stedeford of Tube Investments (Beeching was recruited from ICI to join the SAG), to take a tougher, sharper look at the problem.[85] In describing the nature of that problem Beeching stated in his report that, by 1960

it had become apparent that the effects of modernisation were neither so rapid nor so pronounced as had been forecast, that the downward trend in some railway traffics would persist, and the operating losses were likely to go on increasing unless radical changes were made . . . it was obvious, even before detailed investigation started, that neither modernisation nor more economical working could make the railways viable in their existing form, and that a reshaping of the whole pattern of the business would be necessary as well.[86]

This overall conclusion, too, was hard to avoid. The running of the railways flat out during the war, the less than brilliant management of them afterwards and the delusions of the 1955 modernization plan can all be placed on the charge sheet; but the main culprits were the lorry and the motorcar. Britain may have loved the romance of steam, but, as soon as circumstances allowed, Britons opted for more prosaic yet flexible and convenient forms of locomotion, either as traders or as private citizens, to conduct their business and their pleasure. And in an open society able to express its economic and personal preferences, it was both impossible and undesirable to prevent them. Nevertheless, the 'fact that the growth of new industries, more suited to road transport than rail, and the rising standard of living, expressed through increased car ownership, were important factors in the railways' decline did not prevent that decline from being presented as indicative of a national problem'.[87] Hence the talismanic property of the Beeching Report at the time and since.

What was the philosophy behind the Beeching approach and the remedies he so confidently proposed? Beeching was well aware of the factors that had made rail *the* technological pacemaker, the engine of economic growth and the transformer of society in the nineteenth century from the 1840s onwards, though he rather lacked the poetry the railways so easily inspire:

> Railways are distinguished by the provision and maintenance of a specialised route system for their own exclusive use. This gives rise to high fixed costs. On the other hand, the benefits which can be derived from the possession of this high cost route system are very great.
>
> Firstly, it permits the running of high capacity trains, which themselves have very low movement costs per unit carried. Secondly, it permits dense flows of traffic and, provided the flows are dense, the fixed costs per unit moved are also low. Thirdly, it permits safe, reliable, scheduled movements at high speed.[88]

For Beeching, the task was to reshape the railways, 'concentrating upon those parts of the traffic pattern which enable them to derive sufficient benefit from these three advantages to offset their unavoidable burden of high system cost' by prioritizing routes when dense flows are possible and developing them 'to the full'.[89]

What did the great cost-benefiteer come up with? A plan consisting of what he saw as fifteen 'strongly interdependent' elements which, if implemented in full and with vigour, should see 'much (though not necessarily all) of the Railways' deficit . . . eliminated by 1970':[90]

1. Discontinuance of many stopping passenger services.
2. Transfer of the modern [diesel] multiple unit stock displaced [by 1] to continuing services which are still steam locomotive hauled.
3. Closure of a high proportion of the total number of small stations to passenger traffic.
4. Selective improvement of inter-city passenger services and rationalisation of routes.
5. Damping down of seasonal peaks of passenger traffic and withdrawal of corridor coaching stock held for the purpose of covering them at present.
6. Co-ordination of suburban train and bus services and charges, in collaboration with municipal authorities, with the alternative of fare increases and possible closure of services.
7. Co-ordination of passenger parcels services with the Post Office.
8. Increase of block train movement of coal . . .
9. Reduction of the uneconomic freight traffic passing through small stations by closing them progressively . . .
10. Attraction of more siding-to-siding traffics . . . provision of time-tabled trains, of special stock, to meet customer requirements.
11. Study and development of a network of 'Liner Trains' [freight] services . . .
12. Concentration of freight sundries traffic upon about 100 main depots . . .
13. Rapid, progressive withdrawal of freight wagons over the next three years.
14. Continued replacement of steam by diesel locomotives for main line traction . . .
15. Rationalisation of the composition and use of the Railways' road cartage fleet.[91]

This was the configuration of Dr Beeching's railway 'angel-in-marble' of a system that would pay its way by 1970.

It was all very rational and practical; prosaic almost. Yet within forty or so pages of that recipe for profitability, the emotional and political dynamic was detonated inside Appendix 2 of the Beeching Report, in which he listed, one by one, the services, lines and the 2,363 stations and halts he wanted Marples and the Ministry of Transport to agree should be closed, as foreshadowed in item 3. It was these services, beginning with Glasgow Central–Carlisle (Local) and ending with Clapham Junction–Kensington Olympia, and these stations, from Abbey Town in England to Ynyslas in Wales,[92] that inspired Flanders and Swann to regretful and lyrical lament and led to a torrential outburst of complaint from the travelling public, some more persuasive than others.

For example, Willie Whitelaw, Conservative MP for Penrith and a future Deputy Prime Minister during the Thatcher years, a railway man by instinct and scion of the LNER, whose board his father had chaired, never forgot one constituent, a farmer whose land adjoined the Carlisle–Silloth line Beeching recommended for closure, complaining that if he could not see the mid-afternoon train he wouldn't know when it was time to return to his farmhouse for tea. The ever-affable Whitelaw urged him to buy a watch.[93] Macmillan had an equivalent memory. He recalled for his official biographer, 'Marples telling him of a railway service in Wales that was used by only one man: "If I gave him a Rolls Royce for life, we'd make £150,000, but there would be a terrible row in the press . . . !" '[94]

Beeching recommended a third of the railways' route mileage should go, with 266 services axed and 2,363 stations closed. He got his wish: 'Thirty-one per cent of the route mileage open to passengers in 1962 had closed by the end of 1973 and slightly more than half of this was achieved by the end of 1965.'[95] His was a report which touched every part of the United Kingdom and most communities, just as Beveridge entered every home (which is why the two documents left such imprints on the collective memory).

Despite such drastic chiselling, however, the angel of profitability inside the marble remained stubbornly unrevealed.

Beeching had a defence. His recommendations were not implemented as comprehensively or as vigorously as his report deemed necessary if sustained operating surpluses were to be achieved. However, as Chas Loft has pointed out, 'even if they had been, the railways would almost certainly have remained in serious financial difficulty. In 1972 Whitehall estimated that £115 million had been cut from railway operating costs in the four years to 1967 but that this had been largely consumed by increases in wages and other costs.'[96] Nor did the hoped-for level of development of freight services materialize. The motorway network, growing as the railways declined, plus the door-to-door convenience of ever larger lorries saw to that.

History as well as folk memory has been tough on Beeching. Matthew Engel had reduced the charge sheet to five as the fiftieth anniversary of *The Reshaping of the Railways* approached, which might be summarized as follows:

1. Profitability was not achievable either by 1970 or into the future.
2. Passenger traffic, not bulk freight, turned out to be the growth area.
3. Cities and towns were already beginning to choke with traffic in the early Sixties so urban closures were a mistake.
4. Beeching failed to anticipate some routes might become more important in the future.
5. Beeching had no sense whatever of a future in which fast, efficient long-distance railways could take on cars and planes and beat them.[97]

Beeching was not around to defend himself against posterity by 2009, when Engel's *Eleven Minutes Late* was published, but the fair-minded author did his best to give the Doctor his chance by exhuming a 1981 BBC television programme fittingly called *Hindsight*. He seemed quite unrepentant, though 'he was a far more relaxed figure, with his pension and his peerage: his accent had become less stilted, his hair less ludicrous, and he seemed altogether jollier'.[98] With some justification he said 'some of the excellent planning in my day has not been pursued with the rigour I would like'. He told his interviewer he wished more lines had closed; about half the surviving trunk routes should go. We needed only one line to Scotland: 'The East Coast route beyond Newcastle could be closed without any hardship to anyone except people in Berwick-upon-Tweed.' Did he mind posterity remembering him as a mad axeman? Not in the least, he said cheerily. 'Most people aren't remembered at all.'[99]

There was one railway story in 1963 that trumped even Beeching in terms of public attention. Crime is not intrinsically glamorous, quite the reverse, especially when violence is involved. But certain elements of those crimes acquire a patina of glamour because of the planning, the skill and the audacity in their making and committing. Such was the case of the Great Train Robbery, which took place beside and on the West Coast Main Line in the Buckinghamshire countryside during the small hours of 8 August 1963.

It was a story that had everything: a mastermind whose identity remains a mystery; an inside informant, known as 'The Ulsterman' (also officially undiscovered*), who told the gang exactly where on the Glasgow to Euston mail train was the high-value package (HVP) coach in which used banknotes were carried, presumably on their way to the Bank of England for destruction; a hideaway deep in the Oxfordshire countryside between Thame and Bicester; plus a cast of real-life characters who could quite easily (had most of them not been in jail) have auditioned for parts in *The Italian Job* a few years later. Then there was the swag: some 120 mailbags containing £2.6 million, a breathtaking sum in 1963, equivalent to about £50 million over half a century later.

Fifteen men, mainly from south London, to a high degree known to each other, were waiting for the mail train that summer night by Bridego Bridge near Linslade. Several of them became household names, especially the four who, for a time, got away – Charlie Wilson, Bruce Reynolds, Ronald 'Buster' Edwards and Ronnie Biggs, the last of whom reached Brazil and remained free, giving interviews to the press, until he gave himself up in 2001.

---

* In 2014, one of the gang, Douglas Gordon Goody, quiet, church-going, then eighty-five years old and living in Spain, identified 'The Ulsterman' as a Belfast-born postal worker from Islington, Patrick McKenna, to the immense surprise of his surviving family. As Mr McKenna was neither arrested nor tried, history can only record him as the *alleged* 'Ulsterman' (Tracy McVeigh, 'The Quiet Great Train Robber Reveals Identity of the Gang's Mystery Insider', *Observer*, 28 September 2014).

The train left Glasgow Central at 6.05 on the evening of 7 August, pulled by one of the heavy-duty workhorse diesels that emerged out of the 1955 modernization plan (no beautiful steam loco as in Harry Watt's 1936 masterpiece, *Night Mail* – which was filmed going the other way). At 12.30 a.m. on 8 August, two Land Rovers and an old army lorry set out from Leatherslade Farm near Oakley, over twenty-five miles to the west of Bridego Bridge. Shortly before three, they doctored the signals to bring the mail train to a halt at three minutes past three. It stopped short of the bridge. Driver Jack Mills tried to resist as masked men rushed into his cab. He later said in Court: 'I was struck on the back of the head four times, twice on the side of the head and I was severely bruised upon the upper part of my body and head . . . They had all got staves in their hands and one had a piece of iron piping.'[100] They forced him back on to his seat, threatening more violence if he didn't move the train down to the bridge and the waiting vehicles. The fifty-eight-year-old driver was off work until May 1964 and retired at the end of 1967, never a well man again.[101]

The impact when the news broke was immediate. I came down part of the West Coast Route the following night, from Glasgow Central to Stafford, on the way back from climbing with a school group in the Cuillins on the Isle of Skye. There was an eerie jumpiness about it, another element in what was developing into a strangely unsettling year.

Not just the British press but the world's media were fascinated by what at first sight was the perfect crime (if you put aside the brutal treatment of Jack Mills, which I did not). Some American papers took it as an illumination of the superiority of high-end British criminals compared with their own. ('How pallid our own crime syndicates are made to look, how wanting in imagination', *New York Times*; 'History's Greatest Robbery – There'll Always be an England', *Herald Tribune*).[102]

But the perfect crime it was not. The police found no fingerprints in either the diesel's cab or the HVP coach, but Leatherslade Farm, when the police discovered it on 12 August thanks to a suspicious local farm labourer, was liberally sprinkled with them. The gang had not cleaned up properly after themselves. There were empty mailbags and wrappers from the bundles of banknotes. There was even the

Monopoly Board on which the thieves had competed, reputedly using real money, before dispersing with their shares of the haul. The trial, when it came in early 1964, was to be a sensation. The Great Train Robbery is a story that continues to occupy a substantial place in the memory of the era. For years when I passed up or down on the West Coast Main Line between the Chiltern Hills and Bletchley I would think of it.

The early Sixties should be remembered not just for the railways but for another nationalized industry in a degree of trouble, civil nuclear power – even though, as we have seen, at the time it still seemed to be the very embodiment of pathfinding technology, of shining science laced with a promise of economic and industrial gains to come. It is not so remembered because, unlike Beeching, there was no single document published about it with ramifications that ran through every valley, glen or suburb where unprofitable branch lines were laid. Electricity certainly reached into virtually every home and farm in the UK by the early to mid-1960s but it did not directly engage the emotions in the way the railway industry did (unless there was a power cut). Nuclear-generated electricity did, however, capture the imagination at the time, with its prospect of clean, cheap and abundant energy in perpetuity. It represented perhaps the ultimate benign cycle on which a new industrial revolution might be based.

In the popular mind, atomic power for peaceful civil purposes really was a sunrise industry in which the UK was a world leader, the epitome of modernity in contrast to coal and the unmodernized railways, which were seen as senescent if not quite sunset industries.* But in the early Sixties, difficulties were already crowding in on the Macmillan government's appetite for civil nuclear power, in the corridors of Whitehall and the little-read minutes of the House of Commons Select Committee on the Nationalized Industries.

---

* Fifty years later, merely to utter the word 'Hinkley' is to arouse anxieties about whether the *French* designed and built pressurized water reactor is the best, the most viable and cost-effective way forward for the next generation of UK civil nuclear power stations and whether sufficient *Chinese* investment will be forthcoming to make it happen – a set of conjunctions unimaginable to any of the protagonists in the late-Fifties and early-Sixties nuclear debates.

In a debate on the trebling of the UK nuclear programme in April 1957, Reggie Maudling, the promising young Paymaster-General who reported to Macmillan directly on civil nuclear policy and the work of the Atomic Energy Authority, asked his fellow MPs 'if we cannot be optimistic about our nuclear advances what can we be optimistic about?'[103] It is painful now to read the early statements in Parliament as successive ministers succumbed to what that sage political observer Alan Watkins liked to call 'dawnism', a disease always ready to affect the occupational health of the political class. Indeed, there was a degree of international competition in nuclear hyperbole in the optimistic Fifties. Lewis Strauss, chairman of the US Atomic Energy Commission, declared in 1954: 'Our children will enjoy in their homes electrical energy too cheap to meter.'[104] In 1955 Geoffrey Lloyd, Minister of Fuel and Power in Churchill's last administration, seized upon civil nuclear power as giving the UK a chance to match past and lost industrial prowess:

> Here is new scope for our traditional genius ... for mixing a small proportion of imported materials with a large proportion of skill, ingenuity and inventiveness ... Our nuclear pioneers have now given us a second chance – to lead another industrial revolution in the second half of the twentieth century.

Lloyd delivered these words at a press conference on 15 February 1955 while launching the White Paper outlining the first UK civil nuclear programme.[105]

By the early 1960s some of the UK's nuclear pioneers were beginning to rue luminous predictions of the Lloyd – Maudling kind. Sir William Penney, one of three 'atomic knights' central to the story of both military and civil nuclear power (the other two being Sir John Cockcroft and Sir Christopher Hinton, of whom more shortly), told Anthony Sampson for his 1962 *Anatomy of Britain*: 'First they put us up on a pinnacle which was much too high then we went down into a hole which we never deserved: in five years they may regard us as quite a reasonable bunch of men.'[106]

At first glance, in the early 1960s there was still much to be Maudling-and-Lloyd-like about regarding the prospects for civil nuclear power – a story of technological improvements to come in a generational sequence.

The first 'Magnox' stations were already in operation at Calder Hall on the Cumberland coast and Chapelcross near Annan in Dumfriesshire in southern Scotland, generating civil electricity for the national grid alongside producing plutonium as necessary for the UK nuclear weapons programme. The Magnoxes acquired their name from the magnesium non-oxidizing cladding of the fuel rods.[107] Eight more were planned in England and Wales (Berkeley, Bradwell, Dungeness A, Hinckley Point A, Oldbury-on-Severn, Sizewell A, Trawsfynydd and Wylfa) and one in Scotland (Hunterston A on the Ayrshire coast southwest of Glasgow).

As Simon Taylor, historian of the UK's chequered civil nuclear history put it: 'The Magnoxes performed reliably and safely and were routinely referred to as "workhorses" over the next four decades' as contributors to the baseload of the national grid.[108] (Baseload generation is so-called to distinguish it from fluctuating intermittent sources such a solar, wind or wave power.) The likely successor generation to the Magnoxes – as, indeed, proved to be the case – the advanced gas-cooled reactors (AGRs), shared the same basic technology as the Magnoxes, 'but the design allowed for much higher gas temperatures and hence greater thermal efficiency'.[109] This was expected to be the technology for the Seventies and Eighties, by which time the prototype of fast-breeder reactors (FBRs) at the very top of Caithness in northern Scotland overlooking the Pentland Firth would have led to a fleet of them across the UK. The great promise of FBRs was that their use of highly enriched fuel (a blend of uranium and plutonium) meant they 'bred' more fissile material than they consumed, with obvious attractions in terms of resource use, cost and efficiency. The Dounreay Fast Reactor had gone critical in 1959.[110]

Beyond that lay the prospect of unlimited, clean nuclear energy produced by nuclear fusion once the civil nuclear scientists and engineers had matched the huge and dramatic step-change from fission to fusion, from atomic bombs to hydrogen bombs, that their military equivalents had managed in the 1950s in first the USA, then the Soviet Union followed by the United Kingdom. This was described pleasingly pithily as 'like putting the sun in a bottle' by Sir Walter Marshall, a great civil nuclear enthusiast and Chief Scientific Adviser to his Secretary of State at the Department of Energy, David Howell, in the early 1980s.[111] (Fusion, too, had had its own moment of dawn-ism in the late 1950s, as we shall shortly see.)

What mishap, then, set in motion the rollercoaster of expectation and esteem described by Bill Penney (an impressive, understated man, not given to exaggeration) in his conversation with Anthony Sampson but half-a-dozen years after the White Paper of 1955? Much of it had to do with the perilous combination of cost, timing and forecasting which has bedevilled so much of what the French call *grands projets*, where humility can be in short supply and hubris abundant. Never more so than in the field of nuclear energy.

To be fair to the framers of the founding 1955 White Paper, the document recognized that the costs of its ten-year programme for 1.5–2GW nuclear capacity might prove optimistic (much depended on income from the sale of plutonium to the Bomb-makers): 'The stakes are high but the final reward will be immeasurable.'[112] There was also much wishful thinking about possible export orders for nuclear plants. Only two were won: in 1961 to Tokaimura in Japan; in 1963 to Latina in Italy.[113]

In the post-Suez atmosphere of March 1957, the target was raised to between 5 and 6 GW by 1965[114] – the closure of the Suez Canal was read across into the disruption of Middle Eastern oil supplies to Europe, hence a rise in oil prices increasing the competitiveness of nuclear. In the event, the oil giants built bigger tankers and routed them round the Cape of Good Hope. In his memoirs Reggie Maudling was drolly ironic about the shakiness of the data with which he had to work when trebling the 1955 figures:

> Our plans were carefully laid on the best estimates available to us from public and private sources . . . The only trouble was that all the figures I gave turned out in the event to be wrong . . . We had been worried that there was a threat of a severe shortage of tankers in a few years' time . . . but when the plans came to fruition, the whole market position had changed and we virtually had tankers running out of our ears.[115]

In June 1960 the Macmillan government took a further plunge into the whirlpool of energy forecasting and nuclear build in another White Paper.[116] As Roger Williams, the geographer of postwar civil nuclear decision-making, expressed it: 'It was recognized in this short document both that there was no longer a case on fuel supply grounds for a rapid build-up in nuclear capacity, and that conventional generating costs were by this time about 25 per cent lower than those of nuclear plant.'[117] UK coal production was also improving. The decision this time was to amend the 1957 plans by building one station a year to reach a new target of 5GW by 1968. The estimated date for nuclear costs falling below conventional was now set for 1970.[118] It was never to be achieved. So much for 'too cheap to meter'.

There was a structural fault-line that vitiated civil nuclear decision-making in addition to the multiple uncertainties. Churchill, prodded by his personal scientific adviser, Frederick Lindemann ('The Prof'), had spun out nuclear matters from the Ministry of Supply into a new Atomic Energy Authority (AEA) in 1954 – part department, part independent agency – to run the R&D for both civil and military programmes. In 1957 electricity supply was reorganized into a Central Electricity Generating Board (CEGB) and the tough, tall engineer Sir Christopher Hinton moved out of the infrastructure side of the AEA to head it. Despite the intimacy of the nuclear world, the electricity-supply people had remarkably little influence within civil nuclear decision-taking until the early 1960s. This came to wider public attention when the House of Commons Select Committee on the Nationalized Industries inquiry into the electricity-supply industry brought the tensions between the AEA and the CEGB into the open in 1962–3.[119]

Hinton, who already had doubts about the commercial assumptions surrounding civil nuclear power when he arrived at the CEGB, was tersely acid about the AEA when giving evidence before the select committee. He was asked if he thought the AEA's R&D was shaped by the CEGB's needs and replied: 'I think that their activities are shaped by what they think our requirements ought to be.'[120]

Hinton had already shocked the AEA with an article published in the *Three Banks Review* in December 1961. In it he suggested that several advanced countries were pursuing their own reactor programmes and one of them might come up with a design better suited to UK needs than the products of British R&D. 'Ultimately,' Hinton declared, 'everyone connected with the development, design and construction of nuclear power plants must decide his research and development programme on the basis of what his customers find most economical and what he can develop and sell to give him a profit and them power at the lowest possible cost.'[121]

The government was sufficiently alarmed to set up an official Whitehall committee under the chairmanship of Sir Richard Powell, Permanent Secretary at the Board of Trade, to look at all aspects of UK reactor choice. Remarkably, 'this was the first forum in which representatives of the CEGB, the AEA, the Treasury and the Board of Trade had come together'.[122] Out of the Powell Committee came yet another nuclear White Paper in April 1964, in the last months of what was by now the Douglas-Home government.

Undoubtedly, the non-creative tension between the AEA and the CEGB, and its emergence into the public domain, contributed to the digging of the 'hole' in public perceptions that so worried Bill Penney. But the biggest shovel involved was wielded by the fusion debacle of 1958, Project Zeta, which first aroused and then truly dented public expectations. Its impact was all the greater because it involved the third of the great atomic knights, Sir John Cockcroft, Nobel Prize winner and, with Ernest Walton, first splitter of the atom in Cambridge's legendary Cavendish Laboratory in 1932.[123]

The generation of abundant power from the thermonuclear fusion of deuterium and tritium (light isotopes of hydrogen) to produce helium – releasing almost unimaginable energy in the process – had been a holy grail for nuclear scientists since the late 1930s,[124] and still is. Since the end of the Second World War, the USA, the UK and the Soviet Union had devoted considerable resources to its achievement. By late 1957 it appeared that Britain might be about to win the race. The scientists conducting Project Zeta at Harwell thought that some of the neutrons it was producing were of thermonuclear origin. On 9 September 1957 Sir Edwin Plowden, chairman of the Atomic Energy Authority, wrote to Macmillan informing him of this. It's intriguing to notice the high-level involvement of the Prime Minister. Plowden told Macmillan that Cockcroft, who headed the AEA's then huge research establishment at Harwell, believed that the likelihood that some of the neutrons were of a thermonuclear origin was high.[125] In fact, in their first internal report of 6 September 1957, the Zeta team were cautious, warning that 'at this stage, it is not possible to state whether or not the neutrons are of thermonuclear origin'.[126]

Already the press were getting a sniff of the thermonuclear from the Berkshire Downs. On 7 September the *Financial Times*, the most sober of all the national dailies, ran a story under the headline 'Harnessing H-Power for Industry. Harwell Experiments Successful', stating that Zeta had been producing neutrons since mid-August and claiming that 'some of these, UK scientists are confident, are due to the fusion of hydrogen atoms'.[127]

At a press conference at Harwell on 23 January 1958 the AEA's in-house historians Hendry and Lawson record that 'Cockcroft, to the astonishment of his colleagues, responded to a question that no one else would answer by saying that he was "90% certain" that some of the neutrons at least were of thermonuclear origin'.[128] The British press coverage was bursting with pride, and the story, naturally, girdled the globe.[129] Subsequent investigations showed that Cockcroft's 'statement was hardly justifiable, however, considering the uncertainties in the temperature measurements'.[130]*

The brief, Zeta-induced euphoria about fusion in 1958 did inspire a classic Macmillan moment. He was on a long tour of the Commonwealth when Cockcroft made his unfortunate '90% certain' remark. The New Zealand Prime Minister, Walter Nash, asked his visitor how Zeta worked. Macmillan, a scholar in sometimes unexpected areas, dredged from his memory the fact that deuterium can be extracted from the sea. The UK's High Commissioner in Wellington, Sir George Mallaby, caught the resulting exchange:

'Well', said Mr Macmillan, looking vaguely about him. 'You just take sea water and turn it into power.' Pausing for effect, Macmillan added, 'We are pretty good at sea water.'[131]

---

* On a human level, it's easy to see how the prospect of fusion can carry one away – especially if you visit the Joint European Torus at Culham and stand in the control room just a few feet away from where, for a few seconds, the torus had been the hottest place on the earth's surface when its ionized gases in the fusion-produced plasma reached 100 million degrees C and its director, Professor Steve Cowley, tells you that 'we will power the planet with fusion one day' (conversation with Professor Steve Cowley, Joint European Torus, Culham, 4 March 2016).

The unreliability of the Zeta story undoubtedly took the shine off the impression of British pre-eminence in civil nuclear matters. Coverage of such 'breakthrough' stories, as with 'miracle cure' medical ones, leaves a far deeper trace in the public memory than any revision of gigawattage in a government White Paper. It was a sad way for Cockcroft to complete his time at Harwell just before his planned move to Cambridge to become the founding Master of the new Churchill College.

One aspect of nuclear policy did brighten the gloom during Macmillan's last, rather searing months as Prime Minister in 1963. For any observer of leading figures in political or public life, let alone their biographers, a key question is 'What do you wish to be remembered for?' Certainly, in Macmillan's case it was another 1963 event – a matter of Cold War easement now almost entirely forgotten – the achievement of a Partial Test Ban Treaty for nuclear weapons agreed in July 1963, which prohibited future atmospheric testing by the nuclear states. Macmillan had been pressing for arms control in highly unpromising circumstances since 1959. For him, as his official biographer put it, it was the 'problem which overshadowed all others',[132] and, as he told his grandson, Alexander, one of the few things for which he hoped he would be remembered.[133]

Unlike Churchill, Macmillan was not given to tears. But when Kennedy rang him in Admiralty House on 25 July 1963 to say that he had withdrawn his last objection and the signing could go ahead in Moscow, Macmillan, stretched and exhausted by scandal, political strain and a government seemingly in terminal decline, was overcome. As he told his diary: 'I had to go out of the room. I went to tell D. [Dorothy] and burst into tears. I had prayed hard for this, night after night.'[134]

Macmillan's emissary at the Moscow talks was the Minister of Science, Lord Hailsham. Quintin Hailsham was a politician of mercurial brilliance – a Fellow of All Souls College, Oxford, and a classical scholar (his father had been a great educator and founder of the Regent Street Polytechnic as well as a senior politician), which many thought made him an odd choice (not a view I share) to head the new Ministry of Science Macmillan created after the 1959 general election.[135] He was also a lawyer and an old-fashioned Christian gentleman of great sensitivity that all too often in public perceptions was concealed beneath high-class political partisanship and bluster touching on hyperbole driven by a word power that could often carry him away. Anthony Sampson wrote in 1962 that Hailsham 'is one of the few men in cabinet who give the impression of passionate beliefs'.[136]

His relationship with Macmillan was not always easy. I sat with him in his back garden in Putney one late summer afternoon in 1975 interviewing him for a profile in *The Times* and he said, rather rue-fully when I asked him what he thought he would be remembered for: 'I won the 1959 election for Harold Macmillan whatever he said.'[137] In fact, making him Minister of Science was Macmillan's way of eas-ing Hailsham out of the party chairmanship in favour of Rab Butler after the election. On the Sunday after his victory Macmillan brooded over his new ministerial dispositions and was particularly revealing of his then view of Hailsham:

> My chief problem has been about the chairmanship of the Party. Ld Hailsham, with Ld Poole gone [from Conservative Central Office] (he has had to go back to business) is really not safe. After much effort and quite a lot of emotional scenes, we have at last got everything arranged. Butler is to be chairman of the Party and Hailsham is to be Ld Privy Seal and Minister for Science. He is in a very over-excited condition and keeps giving ridiculous 'press conferences' – but no doubt he will quieten down soon.[138]

Hailsham later thought that an element in his removal from the party chairmanship arose from Macmillan's mistaken view that he, Hailsham, was involved in a divorce case. 'He had', Hailsham wrote in his second volume of memoirs, 'misunderstood my role in an entirely private matrimonial matter in which I had been called as a witness. It was thoroughly unjust, wholly unfounded and to be influ-enced by it was very discreditable to him.'[139]

The Macmillan–Hailsham relationship was one of the most intriguing of the Macmillan era. The PM may have recoiled from Hailsham's volatility but he relished his flair and intelligence. At the time Hailsham was sent to Moscow to conduct a crucial Cold War nuclear renegotiation, he was also Macmillan's special envoy to the north-east of England, where, ebullient and flat-capped (he was a politician with an appetite for props), he toured the area between Tyne and Tees preaching economic regeneration – to the fury of Labour politicians who thought it one of their fiefdoms ('the opposition are very angry, so they must be afraid that he may do some good', purred Macmillan in his diary[140]).

Sending Hailsham to Moscow was risky. Many years later Macmillan deployed his sardonic side in a 1973 BBC television interview. He thought, he said, Hailsham might amuse Khrushchev: 'Of course, he is too boisterous, he could answer his jokes and so on, and he's very shrewd of course, and very determined',* and he had the back-up of a superb negotiator in the Moscow Embassy in the person of the British Ambassador, Sir Humphrey Trevelyan, and the ubiquitous Sir William Penney, once described by that great Whitehall-watching MP Tam Dalyell as 'the least flappable public person I have known'.[141] In fact, Macmillan was testing Hailsham for higher things – as a possible successor. When, as we shall see, political and personal mayhem followed Macmillan's decision to stand down in October 1963, Hailsham was, albeit briefly, his preferred candidate.

Even before the prostate trouble that precipitated his resignation, Macmillan had decided in early September that he would go before the 1964 general election. On 5 September he surveyed the prospects in his diary:

> I am beginning to feel that I haven't the strength and that perhaps another leader cd do what I did after Eden left. But it cannot be done by a pedestrian politician. It needs a man with vision and moral strength – Hailsham not Maudling. Yet the 'back-benchers' (poor fools) do not seem to have any idea, except a 'young man'. Admirable as Maudling is, I doubt if he cd revive our fortunes as well as Hailsham. (I sent H. to Moscow on purpose, to test his powers of negotiation etc. He did <u>very</u> well.)[142]

* Hailsham *did* amuse Khrushchev. At meetings Khrushchev would greet him with 'Here comes the Imperialist', to which Hailsham replied, 'Yes, an imperialist – but unfortunately without an empire' (Lord Hailsham, *A Sparrow's Flight: Memoirs* (Collins, 1990), p. 343).

Hailsham was a hereditary peer in the House of Lords. But the Peerage Bill was in its final stages in Parliament when Hailsham boarded the plane for Moscow, which allowed for the renunciation of hereditary titles. Inspired by the Tony Benn case (he had inherited his father's viscountcy in 1960 and fought tirelessly for the new legislation), it received royal assent on 31 July 1963. This made it possible for both Lords Home and Hailsham to signal their intention to resign their peerages the following autumn.

Hailsham returned from Moscow with presents from Khrushchev for Macmillan of caviar, crab meat and wine. Macmillan sent back a vase and some Stilton cheese. These were the last dealings Macmillan and Khrushchev were to have with each other.[143] It had wider symbolism too. Macmillan had stiffened every sinew of national influence to keep the UK at the highest of the world's top tables alongside the two superpowers. Now in his sad political twilight, as Hailsham noted later, it was 'the last time that Britain appeared in international negotiations as a great power'.[144]

This last hurrah came for Macmillan but nine months after the Cuban crisis, when the missiles might well have flown. It was a fitting end for a very nuclear premiership that would soon be concluded. As Hailsham wrote in his memoirs:

> [I]f nothing else stood to his credit, Harold Macmillan's influence in bringing about the . . . partial Test Ban Treaty would entitle him to be treated as one of the great benefactors of this generation . . . [He] saw that the time was ripe and the parties were willing.[145]

But in the collective memory, even among the 'attentive public',[146] Macmillan's 1963 is overwhelmingly associated with the Profumo affair. It was – and remains – a lightning conductor of a story that has everything, touching as it does multiple fascinations, phobias and national obsessions reviving in neon lights all the realities and fantasies that swirl around that mythical but potent creature – the British Establishment at play, at politics and in bed. It even had a dash of the high Cold War, involving as it did an assistant naval attaché at the Russian Embassy. As Lord Denning, Master of the Rolls and the Bench's prose-master general, whom Macmillan asked to investigate the affair, expressed it nearly thirty years later: 'It had all the ingredients in which the public like to revel: scandal, sex, spies and security.'[147]*

As so often with dramatic political storms, there was already in the Profumo months of 1963 an existing climate shaped by scandal, sex and spies and security – Lord Denning's fissile quartet – into which it erupted. It was created partly by the case of John Vassall, a gay Admiralty clerk in the Moscow Embassy who had been sexually compromised in 1955, then blackmailed by Russian intelligence into passing over naval secrets.[148] Before Vassall, the conviction of George Blake and the breaking of the so-called Portland spy ring, run from the outside by the Soviet 'illegal' 'Gordon Lonsdale' (his real name was Konon Molody) inside the Admiralty's Underwater Detection Establishment, had caused the government serious anxiety about Soviet penetration and led to Macmillan commissioning a review of 'security procedures in the public service' led by the leading inquirer-of-the-day, Lord Radcliffe,[149] in May 1961.

Radcliffe reported in April 1962 and recommended a serious tightening up of procedures, especially of the so-called 'positive vetting' (now known as 'developed vetting') for those engaged in secret work.[150] The Radcliffe Report gave a public already sensitized to Cold War espionage a vivid primer on the scale and relentlessness of the Russian intelligence effort against the UK:

> The evidence we heard satisfies us that to-day much the most serious source of danger lies in the intelligence services of the Soviet *bloc* . . . These services must be envisaged as steadily at work in this country collecting information for intelligence purposes and trying to break through our screen of protective security to get at the secrets we wish

---

* I must, at the outset, declare an interest, not, heaven forbid, as a participant (1963 was O-level year at my grammar school in Stroud and how we learned as the summer and early autumn unfolded of many things tailor-made to inflame young adolescent minds). But Jack Profumo and I became friends in the 1980s when I joined the Attlee Foundation as a fellow Trustee. I was honoured to deliver a eulogy for Jack in the Great Hall in the Mile End Road when he was made an Honorary Fellow of Queen Mary, University of London, in recognition of his service to the East End of London, when he joined Toynbee Hall after his resignation from the House of Commons. I liked him. I admired him. I respected him. He had charm, wit, intelligence and great generosity of spirit.

to preserve. In this work they are prepared to employ all the most up-to-date resources of espionage and they look for useful agents or instruments wherever skill or occasion presents an opportunity ... Nor should the instruments of the Russian Intelligence Service be envisaged as selected either necessarily or essentially on ideological grounds. Any form of sympathy and compulsion that can be laid hold of will serve its turn and among these compulsions fear, pressure and mercenary motives are as strong as any other.[151]

The Macmillan government accepted the Radcliffe Committee's recommendations in their entirety and tightened up the 'positive vetting' system.[152]

Amid this swirling perception of the KGB and GRU (Russian military intelligence) officers and agents attempting to use a cocktail of ideology, sex, money and blackmail to suborn the Queen's subjects, the Vassall case added yet another potent ingredient to the Profumo affair when it erupted: it had envenomed the press against both the Macmillan government and the Prime Minister personally. Two journalists, Brendan Mulholland of the *Daily Mail* and Reginald Foster of the *Daily Sketch*, had been imprisoned on 7 March 1963 for refusing to disclose the sources of stories they had written about the Vassall case.[153] The Vassall affair had also led to the unjustified resignation of Tam Galbraith, undersecretary at the Scottish Office, who had earlier been Civil Lord of the Admiralty, where Vassall had served as his Private Secretary (leading to absolutely unjustified insinuations that there had been a homosexual relationship between the two of them; he quickly rejoined the government after a tribunal into the Vassall case had cleared him).

Relations were unquestionably strained between the Macmillan administration and the press when the House of Commons began to debate the imprisonment of Mulholland and Foster on 21 March 1963 on the instructions of the High Court for failing to give the Vassal Tribunal their sources. By the end of the debate about the jailed journalists the public phase of the Profumo affair had begun – injected by a quartet of Labour MPs, including two members of the party's Shadow Cabinet, Dick Crossman and Barbara Castle, under the protection of parliamentary privilege. Mrs Castle referred to the disappearance of a model, Christine Keeler, who had failed to appear as a prosecution witness at the Old Bailey trial of a West Indian, John Edgecombe, who was accused of shooting her because of her alleged preference for another man, 'Lucky' Gordon. It was Reggie Paget, a maverick Labour MP, who introduced into the debate the name of the War Minister, John Profumo. The fourth Labour MP involved was George Wigg, an army veteran who liked to portray himself as the squaddies' friend in the Commons and who had clashed seriously with Profumo in the chamber in the past.[154]

For Crossman, as he recorded in his diary, 'the real interest of the affair is the hostility between the press and the Government, which makes the press willing to leap at anything. A secondary interest is the sleaziness of those Tories who get mixed up with this kind of society.'[155] Later in the debate, Harold Wilson made what Crossman (an ally of the leader of the Opposition) described as 'a long speech . . . brilliantly defining press freedom and has since made three further speeches, using the occasion to put Labour formally on the side of the press against the Government. By doing so, he has done more for our public relations than Gaitskell ever did in his whole leadership.'[156]

The following morning, Profumo came down from the War Office to the House of Commons to deny any impropriety and to threaten to sue anyone who repeated the previous day's allegations outside Parliament.[157] And so began the opening public steps towards what Valerie Profumo (the actress Valerie Hobson – unforgettable star, alongside Alec Guinness, in the 1949 Ealing Comedy *Kind Hearts and Coronets*) would later describe to their son as 'the Great Fall' of 1963.[158]

The private story had begun much earlier, on a summer Saturday night, 8 July 1961, alongside the river beneath Cliveden, the mansion owned by the Astor family, where the chalk of the Chilterns is punctured by the Thames in what geomorphologists call a 'Water Gap' carved by the meltwater of the last ice age. Here the scene was set for what is still the most evocative political scandal of the postwar years.

Still the best setter of that scene is Tom Denning, whose inquiry has left him almost as legendary as Jack Profumo himself. Denning was much celebrated among his legal peers for his vividly crafted paragraphs and for his style, which was that of a natural storyteller. His famous report of September 1963 is a special mix of thriller and morality tale. It sold like a bestseller, too. As Denning proudly recalled in his 1992 Introduction to the Pimlico edition of his report: 'My report was published as a Blue Book [as official government publications were often called in those days] on Thursday 26 September 1963. Nothing like it had ever been seen before. Nor since.' Denning proudly quoted *The Times*' report the following day:

SALE OF 4,000 COPIES IN 1 HOUR

An orderly queue of about 1,000 stretched from the Stationery Office retail bookshop in Kingsway well into Drury Lane when the shop opened at 12.30 am today for the first sale to the public of the Denning report. It was stated that more than 4,000 copies were sold by 1.30 am.

From that day to his death in 1999 Lord Denning possessed star quality as a summarizer, an evoker of mood, a dispenser of analysis and judgement and wielder of a pen so potent that is has stimulated a degree of reaction almost as pungent as his own prose.

Here is the opening of Denning's 1992 summary of the 114 pages that brought him immortality in the autumn of 1963:

The Profumo affair was a sensation which captured the attention of the world.* It arose out of a trifling incident in the summer of 1961. Mr John Profumo, the Secretary of State for War, had been at a weekend party at Lord Astor's great house at Cliveden. The guests went down to the swimming pool. One of the girls had taken off her bathing costume and bathed naked – and seized a towel to hide herself. All a piece of fun in which nobody saw any harm.

The sentences are short, vivid but to the point. It's almost the judicial equivalent of a policeman reading from his notebook in court.

* My friend and room-mate at *The Times*, Roger Berthoud, was the *Evening Standard*'s man in Paris during the Profumo summer. He heard indirectly through his contacts that General de Gaulle was fascinated by it and read the British newspapers avidly throughout. One day he looked up from the papers and said to an aide: 'That'll teach the English for trying to behave like Frenchmen.'

Denning, by the way, spoke in what was usually called a rich Hampshire burr, a sound rarely heard on the early postwar bench (though it was made famous in the cricketing commentary box by that poet among journalists, John Arlott). Next, Denning introduces Stephen Ward, a man of some charm, an osteopath and a portrait painter with society clients – to some a fascinator who was made a scapegoat for the whole affair and who was driven by 'Establishment' hypocrisy to suicide; to others, including, one suspects, Denning himself, a moral swamp of the first order, with dodgy connections to Russian intelligence:

> One of the guests that evening was Stephen Ward, a friend of Lord Astor with a cottage nearby. He brought with him two others as his own guests. One of them was Captain Ivanov, the Russian Naval Attaché. The other was Christine Keeler, an attractive 19-year-old. John Profumo took a fancy to her. He visited her at her flat in Wimpole Mews in London. He wrote a letter to her starting with 'Darling'. Captain Ivanov also took a fancy to her and also visited her at her flat in Wimpole Mews.
>
> Such was the setting of a school for scandal. Politicians saw John Profumo as a security risk and made the most of it. Others saw him as a moral risk, lowering the standards of polite society. Newspapers saw it as a headline story to fascinate their readers.

It was also a matter of truth-telling in Parliament. Denning once more:

> The conduct of Mr Profumo was raised in the House of Commons on 22 March 1963, when Mr Profumo made a personal statement to the House. It had been drafted for him by five Ministers at 4am [the Profumos had only just arrived home jet-lagged from holiday]. In it, he said 'There was no impropriety whatsoever in my acquaintanceship with Miss Keeler.'[159]

Macmillan's account in his diary for 22 March 1963 carries, in retrospect, much revealing freight – not least his own sensitivity to matters of the bedroom, given his own longstanding cuckolding by Bob Boothby as well as his disdain for this particular slice of society. Referring to the debate in which Crossman, Wigg, Castle and Paget had launched the Profumo affair upon Parliament and the public, Macmillan wrote:

> Later in the debate . . . attacks were made on a Minister . . . alleged to [be] mixed up in a rather squalid criminal case about a black man who shot a 'model'. 'Model' is the word wh. is nowadays used to describe a rather better class of prostitute . . . It has been widely rumoured for some time that a Mr Ward (an osteopath, suspected of being a pimp) had this girl in his string and that Bill Astor was mixed up with the affair (having given this Mr Ward a cottage at Cliveden) . . . The girl who should have appeared in the trial of the black man – another lover – for attempted murder, has disappeared. Bill Astor has also left the country.[160]

'Cliveden' was a word already resonant in British political vocabulary as the place where appeasers consorted in the 1930s, and the brilliant leftist journalist Claud Cockburn had coined 'the Cliveden set' in his interwar paper *The Week*, and it stuck.[161] Macmillan, consistent in his anti-appeasement, scribbled an aside judging: 'The old "Cliveden" set was disastrous politically. The new "Cliveden" set is said to be equally disastrous morally.'[162]

The next passage of the diary also drips with distaste but has no whiff of the deluge to come for Profumo, the government and the Conservative Party, or for Macmillan's personal fortunes:

> All this gossip, grossly exaggerated no doubt if not altogether untrue, has been circulating in the lobbies and the clubs for some months.

In fact, the old man appears to think he had cauterized the affair:

> Conferences were held in the middle of last night and early this morning and I was asked to approve a 'personal' statement after the House met (at 11am) today. I went thro' the text with the Attorney General [Sir John Hobson; no relation to Mrs Profumo] and went to the House to give Profumo my support. His statement was clear and pretty convincing.[163]

Macmillan, rightly, has been criticized for not confronting Profumo personally. But, as his biographer Richard Thorpe put it, 'he did not feel that it would be productive. A gentleman had given his word; it would reflect badly if that word was not believed. The truth is that such a meeting would have been difficult for Macmillan, painful and embarrassing, and he ducked it.'[164]

Just how embarrassed Macmillan was by what he conceived of Jack Profumo's world seeps through the paragraphs of the diary he wrote that day:

> Profumo has behaved foolishly and indiscreetly, but not wickedly. His wife (Valerie Hobson) is very nice and sensible. Of course, these people live in a raffish, theatrical, bohemian society where no one really knows anyone and everyone is 'darling'. But Profumo does not seem to have realised that we have – in public life – to observe different standards from those prevalent today in many circles.[165]

Macmillan's weary, disapproving remarks did not, however, prove to be the coda of the story of the minister and the model. Far from it. As Lord Denning described it in his early-1990s recitative:

> But the story would not die. On 5 June 1963 Mr Profumo confessed. He wrote to the Prime Minister admitting that his statement to the House was not true and that having misled the House he could not remain a member of the administration.
>
> His resignation gave rise to a political storm. It raged so hard that the Prime Minister ... asked me to make an inquiry into the whole affair. I made it in three months and reported in September 1963. But in those three months the story grew day by day. Rumours abounded of the conduct of members of the Government. Quite half of them were said to be guilty of sexual abnormalities and perversions.[166]

Denning was right. The story acquired a second set of legs – of a Heinz-like 57 varieties of nooky-in-high-places, which came with an extra frisson: a free cocktail of 'Establishment' hypocrisy. Britain was no longer in the 1950s. This is why the Profumo affair is a locus classicus not just for political historians but for social and cultural historians as well.

Before turning to the enduring significance of the Profumo summer and the Denning autumn of 1963, what about that other area where fantasists and others love to frisk – the secret world of Whitehall's security and intelligence agencies? How much did they know, how soon did they know and to whom did they tell it and when?

MI5's first attempt in early 1961 to fathom Stephen Ward, who was of interest to the Security Service because of his connection to Ivanov (number two naval attaché in the Kensington Embassy; in reality a GRU intelligence officer), was laced with Ealing Comedy of the mistaken-identity variety. Stephen Ward had aroused their interest because they had heard that a man of that name had been in increasing contact with Ivanov, to whom he boasted about his society connections. 'The Special Branch [of the Metropolitan Police, which dealt with espionage and subversion]', Christopher Andrew writes, 'initially directed the [Security] Service to another Stephen Ward, who, on being summoned to a meeting with a D1 operations officer who used the alias "Keith Wood" on 29 May [1961], said "that there must have been some mistake since he had never met a Russian in his life . . . He was at present engaged in writing a history of the Durham Light Infantry".' He was offered a cup of coffee and an apology.[167]

Another member of MI5 put 'Wood' on the right track: '[T]he information was that Ward was a difficult sort of person, inclined to be against the government. This attitude stemmed from the war years, when the Army refused to recognize his American medical degree. At some time or other Ward had been declared a bankrupt and he is also believed to have been involved in a call-girl racket.'[168]

'Wood' met Ward on 8 June 1961 and was able to make his own assessment of the man, noting: 'Ward, who has an attractive personality and who talks well, was completely open about his association with Ivanov. Despite the fact that some of his political ideas are certainly peculiar and are exploitable by the Russians, I do not think he is of security interest.'[169] There the matter might have rested but for the frisson one suspects Ward experienced from contact with the secret world: he invited 'Wood' to lunch on 12 July 1961 just four days after the frolicsome weekend at Cliveden where Jack Profumo was first attracted by the undoubted beauty of Christine Keeler.

Ward, according to Christopher Andrew, wished to give 'Wood' the benefit of his views about Soviet policy. 'Wood', naturally, was more keen to know about the goings on at Cliveden. Profumo's presence at a party with Ivanov and Ward understandably 'caused some anxiety in Leconfield House [MI5's Mayfair headquarters in Curzon Street]'. MI5's director general, Sir Roger Hollis, contacted Sir Norman Brook, the Cabinet Secretary, and suggested he speak to Profumo about Ward and Ivanov.[170]

Brook called on Profumo on 9 August 1961. The Cabinet Secretary warned the War Minister that Ward might be interested, as Denning put it in his report, 'in picking up scraps of information and passing them onto Captain Ivanov'.[171] Profumo expressed gratitude for the warning. 'Neither the Security Service nor Sir Norman Brook', Denning concluded, 'had any doubts of Mr Profumo. They did not know he was having an affair with Christine Keeler and had no reason to suspect it.' Brook even asked Profumo whether, in Denning's words, it was 'possible to do anything to persuade Ivanov to help us [Hollis had suggested this]. But Mr Profumo thought that he ought to keep well away from it.'[172] Profumo acted on Brook's warning and broke off contact with Ward.

He also began to break off his relationship with Keeler, Denning surmising that

> Mr Profumo thought that the Security Service must have got knowledge of his affair with Christine Keeler: and that the real object of Sir Norman's call on him (though not expressed) was politely to indicate that his assignations with Christine Keeler should cease.

They had arranged to meet the next night, 10 August. After seeing the Cabinet Secretary Profumo wrote what afterwards became the famous 'Darling' letter to Keeler saying they could not now meet ('Alas something's blown up tomorrow night'), finishing: 'Please take great care of yourself and don't run away. Love J'.[173]

Denning concluded that the 'Darling' letter, 'if not the end, was the beginning of the end of the association between Mr Profumo and Christine Keeler. He may have seen her a few times more but that was all. It meant also that he stopped seeing Stephen Ward. Sir Norman Brook's talk had had its effect.'[174]

When the story eventually erupted in Parliament, the Labour Party took the high road of opposition – deliberately concentrating in Parliament and in interviews on the security aspect rather than the still 'alleged' affair between Profumo and Keeler.[175] And it remains a key question: did anything reach Ivanov and Russian intelligence because of the Profumo–Keeler relationship at a tense moment in the Cold War?

Multiple voices suggest not. In old age, Jack Profumo was asked by his son, the novelist David Profumo, if Keeler had tried to discuss defence matters with him? 'Never,' he replied. 'To start with, she wasn't trained enough to be able to make an approach. If she had been trying to do it, she would have chosen a moment for some pillow talk. And there was never *any* of that.'[176]

Lord Denning did not believe there had been a security risk. Assessing MI5's performance in his report he wrote:

> Once they [the Security Service] came to the conclusion that there was no security risk in the matter, but only moral misbehaviour in a Minister, they were under no duty to report it to anyone. They did come to that conclusion. They came to it honestly and reasonably and I do not think they should be found at fault.[177]

MI5's authorized historian, Christopher Andrew, writing in 2009, declared that 'Denning's Report vindicated the role of the Security Service. His judgment, though challenged by numerous conspiracy theorists, has stood the test of time.'[178]

Ivanov, a drunk and a womanizer – hardly the cream of the GRU crop (his boorish behaviour led the British government to ask the Soviet authorities to send him home; which they did, as we have seen, in January 1963) – did ask Ward, probably during the fateful Cliveden weekend in July 1961, to try to extract from his influential friends any information about US plans to give West Germany atomic weapons. Denning pursued this in his inquiry, reporting:

> Stephen Ward said to me (and here I believed him), 'Quite honestly, nobody in their right senses would have asked somebody like Christine Keeler to obtain any information of that sort from Mr Profumo – he would have jumped out of his skin.' If said at all by Stephen Ward, it was, I believe not said seriously expecting her to act on it. I am quite satisfied that she never acted on it. She told me, and I believed her, that she never asked Mr Profumo for the information. Mr Profumo was

also clear that she never asked him, and I am quite sure that he would not have told her if she had asked him.[179]

Yet as so often with causes célèbres that touch the secret world, loose ends still trail from the security aspects of the Profumo affair. Unknown to UK intelligence at the time, the United States had a (still) unidentified agent inside the KGB Residency within the Soviet Embassy in London in the early 1960s. The GRU station was housed separately. Rivalry rather than co-operation between the two services was often the norm.

This was a particularly intriguing revelation and 'what if?' in Professor Andrew's *The Defence of the Realm*. As he reports it:

> On 14 June 1963, nine days after Profumo's resignation, the agent reported overhearing a Soviet intelligence officer say that 'the Russians had in fact received a lot of useful information from Profumo from Christine Keeler, with whom Ivanov had established contact, and in whose apartment Ivanov had even been able to lay on eavesdropping operations at the appropriate times'.[180]

This is highly unlikely. The Keeler–Profumo trysts were too few for 'a lot' of anything to be transmitted, even if you disagree (which I do not) with what the protagonists said and Lord Denning judged about the security/pillow-talk question. Professor Andrew does not believe it either:

> Though the double agent did not realize it, the Soviet intelligence officer's boast was based on deeply improbable speculation rather than reliable intelligence. Ivanov was a GRU officer and it is highly unlikely that detailed reports on his operations would have been sent to the KGB residency where the double agent was stationed.[181]

The agent's report did reach Robert Kennedy, US Attorney General, but it is not known if he passed it on to his brother, the President.

Knowledge of that report did not reach British intelligence until 1966, by which time Macmillan was long gone, Profumo doing philanthropic work in the East End of London and Christine Keeler the subject of 'Where are they now?' columns in the newspapers. The MI5 archive contains the 1966 despatch from the Security Service's liaison officer in the British Embassy in Washington, outlining the June 1963 agent report:

> I imagine that if it had reached us [in 1963], it would have been diffi-
> cult to do other than to accept that it had emanated from a genuine
> source who had proved reliable in the past, even though our own
> material gave us no reason to believe that there had been security
> breaches as a result of Profumo's infatuation with Keeler, and the
> latter's involvement with Ivanov.[182]

As Professor Andrew drily comments: 'If the contents of the double agent's report had been mentioned by Denning in 1963, the conspiracy theorists would have had a field day.'[183]

Another bizarre aspect of the story is the degree to which the Foreign Office in the months between the Cliveden weekend in 1961 and the outing of Jack Profumo in 1963 did *not* keep Ward at arm's length as advised by MI5. Ward saw himself as an important back-channel between the Soviets and the British government about the possible calling of an international conference in London to ease the tension, and during the Cuban missile crisis, as his watcher 'Keith Wood' put it: 'Without our knowledge Ward was used by the Foreign Office ... to pass off-the-record information to the Russian embassy.'[184]

Once Profumo's confession to the Commons and resignation from the government on 5 June raised what Denning called its 'political storm',[185] summer 1963 became the season in which anything was believable, including to those in 10 Downing Street. For a time Macmillan began to wonder if he and his government were the victims of a special operation by the Soviets to destabilize them. He summoned the SIS chief Sir Dick White, who had headed MI5 until 1956. The old PM had much more faith in White than he did in Hollis, his replacement at MI5.

Dick White did not believe there was a Soviet plot, but on 17 June 1963 a joint SIS–MI5 working party was established 'to look into the possibility that the Russian Intelligence Service had a hand in staging the Profumo affair in order to discredit Her Majesty's Government'. (The result of this inquiry has not been declassified, but it is safe to assume that no such plot was uncovered. If it had been it would surely have found a prominent place in the authorized history.)[186] Less than a week later, Macmillan wrote to the Queen to apologize for the 'terrible behaviour' of Her Majesty's former Secretary of State for War ('I had of course no idea of the strange underworld in which other people, alas, besides Mr Profumo have allowed themselves to become entrapped'). He told the Queen that he had started 'to suspect in all these wild accusations against many people, Ministers and others, something in the nature of a plot to destroy the established system'.[187] The creation of the SIS–MI5 group may explain a cryptic entry in Macmillan's diary for 21 July 1963:

> For[eign] Sec [Home] discussed security and I went over to dine later at Dorneywood [the Foreign Secretary's residence in Buckinghamshire]. 'C' [White] came to dinner and we had a long and valuable talk. I am terribly worried about certain possible developments, wh. will have a shattering effect.[188]

It took some time for the MI5–SIS working party to complete its work. By the time it reported that there was no such Soviet plot, Macmillan had gone and Alec Home was PM.[189]

It needs a political anthropologist to anatomize the behaviour of the British political tribes and their press observers in the summer and autumn of 1963 and a touch of social anthropology to do the same for the British people that induced such a mood of *Schadenfreude* in Charles de Gaulle's Élysée Palace and such avid attention in the White House, where there were plenty of customers for Ambassador David Bruce's shrewd and vivid reports from the US Embassy in London. On 18 June, the day following the Profumo debate in the Commons, he predicted that Macmillan would survive long enough for President Kennedy's visit to Europe and the UK at the end of June, but 'his replacement cannot be too long delayed'. The old man was now 'an electoral liability'.[190]

We do not know if Harold Macmillan was familiar with Enoch Powell's law of political failure (of which more in a moment), but Powell certainly unnerved him. Though he promoted Powell to full Cabinet rank as Minister of Health after the 'Night of the Long Knives', Macmillan did not warm to his fellow classical scholar. The feeling was reciprocated. Alec Home recorded in his memoirs that:

One morning I came into the Cabinet Room rather early and found the Cabinet Secretary, Sir Norman Brook . . . changing all our places. I asked him what had happened – 'Had there been a shuffle? – or had one of us died in the night?' 'Oh no,' said Sir Norman, 'it's nothing like that. The Prime Minister cannot stand Enoch Powell's steely and accusing eye looking at him across the table any more, and I've had to move him down the side.'[191]

Powell was a Grade I listed romantic about Parliament ('Take Parliament out of the history of England and that history itself becomes meaningless'[192]), but utterly realistic about the nature of politics:

All political lives, unless they are cut off in midstream at a happy juncture, end in failure because that is the nature of politics and of human affairs.[193]

Powell wrote those words in his 1977 biography of Joe Chamberlain, but they fit Harold Macmillan between June and October 1963 to perfection. During his long retirement, when discussing the endgame of his premiership with his official biographer, Alistair Horne, he cried out: 'It was a wounding thing, oh it was . . .'[194]

At the end of May, shortly before taking a few days' rest in his beloved Highlands of Scotland with Lady Dorothy, Macmillan confided, as was his custom, his worries to his diary. On 30 May, it was security in two forms:

The first is not too bad but may become a nuisance. It concerns Philby, once employed by F.O. [for 'F.O.' read 'Secret Intelligence Service'] (in war and immediately after) who was suspected of being the 'Third Man' who gave the tip-off to Burgess and Maclean . . . some months ago he disappeared [from Beirut where he was a correspondent of the *Observer* newspaper], leaving his wife and children. She has now come to England . . . His disappearance caused a flurry but the press (since dog does not eat dog) kept fairly quiet. We now know that he (Philby) is in Russia. When this news comes out (if it does) there will be a new row.[195]

Macmillan's assessment of Philby's flight from Beirut to Moscow is surprising. Philby had done immense harm to SIS not just through the cataract of secret information he had passed to the Russians over twelve years in the secret world (including the crucial US–UK intelligence relations role in the Washington Embassy at the height of the early Cold War) but in terms of morale and self-confidence after he had been eased out of MI6 in 1951.[196] Burke Trend's Philby file, not declassified until 2017, showed a high level of concern, including within No. 10, about the handling of the re-eruption of the Philby affair.[197]

After Philby, Macmillan's second worry – inevitably – was Profumo:

> The second matter is more serious. The case of Mr Ward (who got Profumo into trouble) is being pursued actively by Harold Wilson, Wigg and one or two of that ilk. Wilson has sent me some so-called evidence that Ward was a spy or agent of the Russians. (The security people do not believe this, but believe he was a pimp, not a spy). Wilson came to see me on a fishing expedition on Monday. He is clearly not going to leave this alone. He hopes, under pretence of security, to rake up a 'sex' scandal, and to involve ministers, and members of 'the upper classes' in a tremendous row, wh. will injure the 'establishment'. Wilson, himself a blackmailing type, is <u>absolutely</u> untrustworthy. No one has ever trusted him without being betrayed. (This is the line of Gaitskell's friends including his widow.) I have asked the Lord Chancellor [Dilhorne] to look into all the available evidence about the Ward case and advise me about what, if anything, should be done.[198]

That done, Macmillan and his wife then set off for their Whitsun break in Scotland. Perhaps without realizing it, Macmillan, by commissioning Dilhorne's inquiry, had fired the starting-gun for the explosive phase of the Profumo affair.

On 31 May Jack and Valerie Profumo also set off for a short holiday, in Venice. As their son wrote forty-three years later in his family memoir:

> They stayed at the Cipriani, which (rather strangely to me, all things considered) remained their favourite hotel thereafter. Before they left my father had been given yet another opportunity to indicate whether the Dilhorne inquiry might discover any flaws in his [March 1963]

statement [to the House of Commons], but he had held his ground. Knowing that he would be questioned the following week, he realised he had to confess to his wife during their Italian sojourn.[199]

In his old age, Profumo recalled for his son the moment he came clean with his wife over a Bellini cocktail before dinner on their first night in the Cipriani:

> By that time it was perfectly clear to me that it was no good me covering it up any more, because the goose was cooked so to speak. She was very good about it. I just owned up. She said, 'Well, I don't know what the history of all this is, but from what you tell me now you are a hot potato so you ought to go back and make the best of it. Don't go on like this. We had better get back.'*

The Profumos returned on Whit Sunday, 'avoiding the air route which would have attracted obvious attention. It was a desperate homecoming.'[200]

It was a desperate homecoming for Harold Macmillan, too. He and his wife were staying with friends at Ardchattan Priory near Oban when 'I was told by telephone that Profumo had admitted that he had lied to me, to the House, and to the courts', wrote Macmillan in a long catch-up entry in his diary on 7 July. 'Altho' we managed to finish our Scottish holiday and go to Iona and Gleneagles as planned, from the day I got back until now (when there is a slight pause) there has been a serious and at times dangerous crisis, wh. seemed likely to involve the fall of the Govt as well as my resignation.'[201]

The heady cocktail of sex, secrecy and scandal served up by the Profumo affair was profoundly distasteful to Macmillan. That phone call to Oban from No. 10 plunged him into the worst pit of his political life – and he knew it. In that same diary entry he wrote: 'I do not remember ever having been under such a sense of personal strain. Even Suez was "clean" – about war and politics. This was all "dirt".'[202]

Apart from all the obvious factors, Macmillan recoiled from speaking of sexual matters. Everyone, including the American Ambassador,

* David Profumo adds a filial touch here ('Somehow I doubt this is a verbatim recollection of the exchange, but in his nineties my father preferred not to revisit this scene too closely').

David Bruce, knew, as his widow, Evangeline, told Alistair Horne, 'that sex was a "forbidden subject"'[203] with Harold Macmillan (though how many people knew about Lady Dorothy's longstanding affair with Lord Boothby at that time is unknowable – certainly the public did not).

In June 1963, Macmillan was sixty-nine years old. He had been in the Cabinet since October 1951 and Prime Minister since January 1957. He was worn out. His sympathetic official biographer reckoned:

> Perhaps if it had happened at a time when Macmillan had possessed more ebullient vigour, in the confident years between 1959 and 1961, he might have weathered the Profumo storm more successfully. As it was, coming in the wake of so many other misfortunes and reverses, he never quite got over it. To colleagues, he suddenly seemed older and more alone, and never regained his former deftness. It may well also have exacerbated the illness that finally drove him from office only weeks later.[204]

Macmillan was prone to placing quite regular glooms in his diaries about his health and/or the burden of prime ministerial office. But, as Horne indicates, he does seem to have suffered a lessening of vitality from mid-1961. In June that year, after being examined by his doctor, Sir John Richardson, he recorded: 'I have no more "élan vital!" I am finished! In other words, I ought to have a month's holiday. As it is, I am to have four days, starting tomorrow evening.'[205]

The Profumo affair sapped him mightily – physically, psychologically and, one suspects, spiritually too. His cherished 'Uncle Harold' old-man act was catching up with him and becoming a reality. At the heart of his long catch-up diary entry on 7 July is the great Profumo debate in the House of Commons on 17 June when Parliament reassembled after the Whitsun Recess:

> I got back to London on June 10th . . . MPs were already in London, holding meetings etc. Every part of the Profumo story . . . was used agst the Govt by an exultant press, getting its own back after Vassall. The Times was awful – what has since been called a 'Haylier than thou' attitude which was really nauseating.[206]

The pun referred to Sir William Haley, the austere, greatly respected editor of *The Times*, who had written a leading article in the 11 June edition of the paper under the headline

IT *IS* A MORAL ISSUE

> Eleven years of Conservative rule have brought the nation psychologic-ally . . . to a low ebb . . . The Prime Minister and his colleagues can cling together and be still there a year hence. They will have to do more than that to justify themselves.*

The pressure and criticism were relentless on the beleaguered old man in Downing Street:

> Day after day the attack developed, chiefly on me – old, incompetent, worn out. In the debate (on June 17) I had to tell the whole story – from Feb 1 (when Profumo denied and continued to deny any but the most perfunctory acquaintance with Ward and Miss Keeler) to his confession. I had to defend the police, the security service, and civil service, and myself. Meanwhile the Parliamentary Party were under-going one of those attacks of hysteria wh. seize men from time to time. In the end, 27 of our Conservatives 'abstained' – that is, not only the usual malcontents . . . but a lot of worthy people, who had been swept away by the wave of emotion and indignation.[207]

For Macmillan, usually a master performer in the chamber, the debate was pure torment. Alec Home said later it was 'the only time I remember him worsted – he so fundamentally hated the whole thing'.[208]

Anthony Sampson, biographer of Macmillan as well as anatomist of Britain, wrote that 'Macmillan left the House looking bowed and dispirited'.[209] How could it have been otherwise? Norman Shrapnel, the *Manchester Guardian*'s sketch writer, witnessed the Profumo debate from the Parliamentary Press Gallery, and asked later of Mac-millan's performance, '[H]ow could it have been good?' Macmillan

---

* Haley – and that leading article – were still spoken of with awe when I joined *The Times* eleven years later in June 1974.

(one of the very finest political actors of the postwar years) 'was being given the casting choice of fool or knave. He could admit either a culpable knowledge or a hardly less culpable ignorance.'[210]

Shrapnel wrote it up as if he were a theatre critic:

> There was only one way to play it, and Mac needed no one to tell him what it was. 'I have been deceived, grossly deceived,' he quavered like some Restoration cuckold appalled to find himself in such a revival. It must have been the most humiliating role of his career and he played it like a trouper . . . The dreadful lines even acquired a certain dignity. They never told him: that was the theme and the refrain. He was sinned against, not sinning, unless it was culpable to be unaware of the things that went on in the sophisticated world. The idea that an officer and a gentleman, a colleague, a Secretary of State, should misconduct himself with a girl no better than she should be, and then lie about it to the House of Commons, was simply outside the comprehension of the circles he was accustomed to moving in – circles, his listeners must have been beginning to feel, of a high-minded innocence rarely found in these wicked times.[211]

Shrapnel then noticed something only a seasoned gallery observer would have picked up and it was highly revealing of each of the 'two Harolds'. Macmillan

> maundered on, shuffling along his high wire, winning admiration at least from those who recognized technique when they saw it. But why was he extending his ordeal by going on so long? He was waiting for the one thing that could save him. He knew what that was, and Harold Wilson knew too; but not all the back-benchers were equally acute, and so Wilson had to take precautions.

What could have 'saved' Macmillan?

> This pathetic, sub-Lear, wronged-old-man act might win a little pity, but you don't hold your team together, still less win elections, on that commodity. What he needed from his glum followers was not their pity but active sympathy, and to get that he knew he had to be seen fighting. Like many another patrician, Macmillan was adept at the rough stuff, given half a chance.

But what was there to fight? Nothing – unless the Opposition back-benchers, scenting the kill at last, were foolish enough to start baiting him. It was what Macmillan hoped for and Wilson feared, so much so that he had put out preliminary warnings. They kept quiet, and the orchestrated silence . . . showed what a deadly weapon it can be . . . It was cruel.[212]

Some on his own side twisted the knife in Macmillan too. Nigel Birch, who had resigned from the Treasury with Peter Thorneycroft and Enoch Powell in January 1958, turned to poetry, to Robert Browning's 'The Lost Leader', for his weapon:

> . . . let him never come back to us!
> There would be doubt, hesitation and pain.
> Forced praise on our part – the glimmer of twilight,
> Never glad confident morning again![213]

Birch was not alone in his party in wishing for a new leader.

Harold Wilson, for his part, was still in the 'glad confident morning' of his leadership of the Labour Party. He was forensic in the Profumo debate and continued to eschew the morality line of attack. Dick Crossman thought 'Macmillan's speech was very long and very effective, though very plaintive', but that Wilson had 'made an absolutely magnificent speech, the best I've ever heard him make, better than I thought possible. It was really annihilating, a classical prosecution speech, with weight and self-control.'[214]

Wilson, speaking before Macmillan, did, in fact, make a passing reference to morality (the Profumo disclosures had 'shocked the moral conscience of the nation') but made security the point of his spear, saying of Macmillan:

> After the Vassall case he felt that he could not stand another serious security case involving a Ministerial resignation, and he gambled desperately and hoped that nothing would ever come out. For political reasons he was gambling with national security. I think that is why he was at such pains to demonstrate to me his unflappability and his unconcern.[215]

This was very effective but it was unfair; Macmillan believed Profumo's denials and realized the truth only when he took that phone call in Oban.

In his speech Macmillan did 'confess frankly to the House that, in considering what I should do, the Vassall case, and the effect it had on [Mr Galbraith], was certainly in my mind'.[216] And he did not conceal from the Commons the 'deep, bitter and lasting wound' Profumo's deception had inflicted on him – 'I find it difficult to tell the House what a blow it has been to me, for it seems to have undermined one of the very foundations upon which political life must be conducted.'[217]

The crux of Macmillan's speech was his appeal for a measure of understanding:

> My colleagues have been deceived, and I have been deceived, grossly deceived – and the House has been deceived – but we have not been parties to deception, and I claim that upon a fair view of the facts as I have set them out I am entitled to the sympathetic understanding and confidence of the House and of the country.[218]

He won the division on 17 June but the Government's majority was down from its usual nineties to sixty-nine. The Chief Whip, Martin Redmayne, had warned him it might fall to forty. If it had he would have contemplated resignation.[219] As for the public, they were both deeply riveted by the cataract of revelations and profoundly unimpressed by Macmillan.

'It was the low ebb of the Macmillan administration,' wrote his official biographer, citing polling data. Only 23 per cent of voters, according to Gallup, believed Macmillan should stay on as Prime Minister. His ratings slumped against Wilson's (35 per cent to 54 per cent). After the Profumo debate, Macmillan, as was his custom, repaired to the House of Commons Smoking Room; 'only two people joined him there – his son-in-law, Julian Amery and his son, Maurice. Not one of his Cabinet colleagues went to speak to him.'[220]

Four days later, Lord Denning was sent for. It was a risk Macmillan plainly felt he had to take. He hoped that the resulting report 'will clear the ministers and make people a little ashamed of their behaviour, partly by the blackmailing statements of the "call girls", partly by the stories started by or given to the press, and partly (I have no doubt) by Soviet agents exploiting the position, more than half the Cabinet were being accused of perversion, homosexuality and the like'. But he equally recognized that when Denning reported political turbulence would return generated by 'something unpleasant about this or that minister being revealed by Lord Denning'.[221]

Waiting-for-Denning produced a summer of titillation and trepidation from the Prime Minister down, to his Cabinet, the Profumos, several men and women in Whitehall and the secret world and quite a swathe of the British people. On 3 July Stephen Ward was committed for trial accused of living on the earnings of prostitution, the women concerned being Christine Keeler and Marilyn 'Mandy' Rice-Davies (who was to leave a very definite trace on the public's memory). The media frenzy grew exponentially – as did the rumours of hanky-panky in high places of almost eighteenth-century proportions as the witnesses began to slip through obscure Whitehall doors en route to Lord Denning's office. Over the three months of his inquiry, he later wrote, 'the story grew day by day. Rumours abounded of the conduct of members of the Government. Quite half of them were said to be guilty of sexual abnormalities and perversions.'[222] The Profumo affair had turned into a mixture of morality play, psychodrama and a treatise on the nature of that elusive but oft cited phenomenon, the 'British Establishment', and has remained so to this day.*

There was indeed a paradoxical and grimly fascinating symmetry to the 'British Establishment' aspect of the Profumo affair. Just as Harold Macmillan was coming to believe there was a Russian-devised plot at work to bring it down, Stephen Ward was convinced that same Establishment was at work to destroy him when he was arrested on 8 June. Richard Davenport-Hines, who published a vivid reconstruction of the era and the event in 2013, describes Ward's arrest as simply 'an act of political revenge',[223] citing the lawyer Louis Blom-Cooper

---

* It has also given us one of the pawkiest and oft-quoted one-liners of the postwar years, delivered by Mandy Rice-Davies and here is how it is preserved in the first edition (1996) of *The Oxford Dictionary of Political Quotations*, edited by Antony Jay:

Mandy Rice-Davies 1944 –
English courtesan
at the [court appearance]*of Stephen Ward, 29 June 1963, on being told that Lord Astor claimed that her allegations, concerning himself and his house parties at Cliveden were untrue:*
'He would, wouldn't he?' (p. 304).

(on his way to QCdom and a legal career of great repute) on how this was so. Blom-Cooper had written in 1964:

> [T]he established order went into battle against this man, whose sole offence was a nonconformity in sexual matters that met with the same kind of relentless reaction from the prosecuting authorities that characterized the prosecution of *Lady Chatterley's Lover.*
>
> Dr. Ward's arrest and removal to police custody, the refusal to grant him bail until the start of the committal proceedings, the refusal to allow him to organize from prison the sale of his paintings, his committal to the Old Bailey for trial rather than to Quarter Sessions, his trial before a High Court Judge rather than before the Recorder of London or the Common Sergeant – all these things betokened a sense of persecution, even if each event was by itself, but not cumulatively, explicable to those versed in legal procedure.[224]

On 30 July, as his trial reached its final stage, Ward took an overdose of barbiturates 'and was found in a deep coma'.[225] He died on 3 August, three days after his conviction, achieving thereby a special kind of immortality in the popular memory of the extraordinary summer of 1963, eclipsed only by Profumo and Keeler themselves.

The Profumo affair was one of those rare occasions when politics and matters of state fuse with society and culture in a hybrid that becomes greater than the sum of its parts. It was – and remains – symbolized by what a veteran Whitehall friend of mine calls '*the* photograph of the 1960s' – Lewis Morley's 1963 study of a naked Christine Keeler straddling a chair of contemporary design, head held in both hands and tilted seductively. It makes the perfect contrast with stills of the bowler-hatted, pinstripe-suited and briefcase-carrying Lord Denning, for whose findings the nation waited as the dramatis personae of the story that had everything made their clandestine way into his office. The rumour mills ground fiercely on as several parts of the Establishment sank further into their summer of anguished anticipation and for a time it seemed that anyone was prepared to believe anything of anybody.

Would we ever know exactly what they said to him courtesy of the transcripts of the evidence sessions Denning's stenographers made? There was a time when I thought it unlikely, for during a debate on public records in the House of Lords that I was covering from the press gallery for *The Times* on 20 April 1977, I heard Lord Denning in his unmistakable voice say:

> Some years ago I had to conduct an inquiry into the Profumo incident. Some very secret records containing all sorts of indiscretions were made. Should these records be kept, or not? The key answer to that was that the evidence was given in confidence. I assured everyone who gave evidence before me that such evidence was completely confidential and would not be disclosed.

Were copies made?

> Only one copy was kept and many people would have liked to read it. A year or two later I was asked whether even that one copy could be destroyed. A good case was put forward for destroying it. The information had been given in confidence and, therefore, the question was raised as to whether it would not be a breach of faith for such records to be disclosed later – even 30, 40 or 50 years later.

Denning, the natural storyteller, could not resist build-up then crescendo. He told their lordships:

> The answer is that the confidence is being maintained; the records of the Profumo inquiry have been destroyed and the information is only in my head and I am forgetting it all now.[226]

But, as I discovered later, the Profumo transcripts had *not* been destroyed. At least one, probably two, Cabinet Secretaries had decided otherwise, for they had survived in one of the most secret archives in Whitehall and the secret state generally – the Cabinet Secretary's Miscellaneous Files in the Cabinet Office. In late 2013 I put down a parliamentary question asking 'whether the files of the 1963 Denning Inquiry into the Profumo affair have been selected for permanent preservation with a view to eventual release at the National Archives'. Lord Wallace of Saltaire, the House of Lords spokesman for the Cabinet Office, replied on 9 December 2013: 'I can confirm that the Denning Inquiry papers held by the Cabinet Office have been selected for permanent preservation.'[227]

The original embargo was a hundred years – so we could expect Lord Denning's, or rather, his witnesses's 'all sorts of indiscretions' in

January 2064. That tariff has subsequently been reduced. After an intervention by the Advisory Council on National Records and Archives, it was lessened in 2016 to 1 January 2048. 'This date', Baroness Chisholm of Owlpen told me in a Cabinet Office written answer, 'reflects the fact that individuals mentioned in the Denning files are still alive, and Lord Denning gave assurances to those from whom he took evidence that the papers would never be published'.[228] I shall be a hundred years old when those files are opened at Kew. I shall have to step-up my exercise régime.

'Establishment' – 'there was a word', wrote John Lawton, novelist supreme of contemporary British history, in his *Old Flames*, 'at the heart of the mystery, buried so deep in the unwritten English code it was impossible to define and much of the time impossible to discern'.[229] In 1963 Macmillan was, as we have seen, both its protector against subversion and plot and its epicentre. The Profumo affair had parched his spirit and siphoned his remaining zest for the job of Prime Minister. But he felt he could not retire till Denning had reported.

By early September he was back from holiday with Lord Swinton in North Yorkshire. Just before he set out south he brooded on what was to come:

> I rather shrink from going back, out of the clean Yorkshire air, into Whitehall and its fog. Naturally, what I decide must depend partly on the date of publication and the content of the Denning report.[230]

On 5 September he wrote:

> My mind is beginning to be clearer about my own position. I must stay to deal with Ld Denning's report and the debate in Parl . . . But I cannot go on to an election and lead in it. I am beginning to feel that I haven't the strength and that perhaps another leader cd do what I did after Eden left.[231]

Earlier, Macmillan had written intriguingly:

> Ld D is going to find it rather difficult to draw the line between becoming a censor of morals and a protector of national security.[232]

I suspect that 'Ld D' felt no such difficulty himself. Fellow lawyers knew that there was always a well-thumbed Bible next to his pile of legal documents. As Denning himself put it: 'Although religion, law and morals can be separated, they are nevertheless still very much dependent on one another.'[233]

Two large pools of anticipation accumulated as Denning inquired. Firstly, a political pool – what would his report do to Macmillan? Would he have to resign? Might the government fall, bringing with it a swift autumn election? Or stagger on until the autumn of 1964, by which time the Parliament Act would require the dissolution of the 1959 Parliament?

The second pool was brimming with rumour and filled by a growing public fascination with the revelations of the Ward trial and the rumours sweeping the press and the country about who was doing what to whom in the bedrooms (and even the dining rooms) of a certain kind of society. In 1963, Britain was still shockable. Deference, too, was in the dock.

Occasionally, the two pools would touch each other. Lord Hailsham had a gift for analysing the flow. During a BBC Television interview on 13 June, Hailsham, with considerable force (he also possessed a gift for histrionic outrage), declared: 'A great party is not to be brought down because of a squalid affair between a woman of easy virtue and a proved liar.' Many years later, during a BBC Radio 4 discussion on Politics and the English language, I raised this outburst with Lord Hailsham. His reply was moving: 'I wish I were as good a man as I now know Jack Profumo to be.' I sent a warning to Profumo urging him to listen to the programme (which was prerecorded). He replied that Quintin Hailsham had already said much the same thing to him in private.

Hailsham thought Macmillan had a made a grievous mistake in commissioning Denning. In his memoir he described it as 'a ghastly error and should never be repeated . . . They [such inquiries] should never be indulged in to satisfy public prurience or salacity nor simply to enquire into allegations into the private sexual lives of public figures unless genuine questions of security are involved.'[234] Hailsham was, I suspect, one of the few members of the Cabinet with a good idea of how Tom Denning's style would play out in the pages of his report: many among those, like him, with long experience of the Bar were well familiar with its singularities before its publication.[235]

There was plenty in the Denning Report for the more inflamed readers: 'The Man in the Mask' who allegedly served naked diners wearing only a waitress's pinny.[236] (This was pretty devastating stuff for a schoolboy to read; it simply did not accord with what I knew of dining practices in mid-Gloucestershire at the time.) Then there was 'The Man Without a Head' in a photo allegedly in Ward's possession relating to the Duchess of Argyll's divorce case.[237] But in terms of high politics, rather than low life in high places, it was Denning's section on the responsibility of ministers that was most keenly awaited – not least by the 'wounded' old man in 10 Downing Street. The key paragraphs were 284 to 286 on 'The Ministers':

> What is their responsibility, if any? The case is reduced to this: there were persistent rumours about Mr Profumo, the crux of which was that he had an *immoral* association with Christine Keeler. The Ministers knew that this was the crux of the matter, for it was the point on which they concentrated their attentions. If these rumours were affecting the confidence which Parliament reposed in Mr Profumo or the Government, then it was for the Prime Minister and his colleagues to deal with it. The Prime Minister did not himself see Mr Profumo but he left it to the Chief Whip and the Law Officers. These ministers inquired of Mr Profumo whether there was any impropriety in his association with Christine Keeler. He repeatedly assured them that there was no impropriety, and in the end they were satisfied that he was telling the truth. And, on being told by them, the Prime Minister was satisfied too.

There followed from Denning's pen the balm for which the PM and his minsters had, no doubt, been hoping: 'All were clearly acting with the utmost honesty and good faith: their integrity is beyond question.'

Parliament, however (Denning advised), might care to look at two aspects: should the ministers have asked Profumo specifically if he *in fact* had committed adultery; and should they have made further inquiries?'

The final paragraph, 286, returned to criticize, but relatively mildly:

> Nevertheless, the fact remains that the conduct of Mr Profumo was such as to create, amongst an influential section of the people, a *reasonable belief* that he had committed adultery with *such* a woman in *such* circumstances as the case discloses. It was the responsibility of

the Prime Minister and his colleagues, and of them only, to deal with this situation: and they did not succeed in doing so.

This was not government-toppling stuff.

The mood lifted in No. 10. Macmillan believed paragraph 284 'has had a great effect. All day long [on 26 September] came messages of congratulation'. 'I feel somehow', he wrote in his diary, 'that the tide is turning and that the people as a whole will support me.'[238]

Within Macmillan's tired and ageing frame there lurked a considerable capacity for recovery. He had shown buoyancy even in the depths of the Profumo summer in the House of Commons when he announced the securing of the Partial Test Ban Treaty.*

In the very chamber that had so recently tortured him during the debate following Profumo's resignation, he put on what turned out to be one last bravura performance in which he drew on every fibre of his long experience of adversity, from the Somme to Khrushchev. Norman Shrapnel witnessed the scene from the Press Gallery. 'It came at 11 o'clock on 26 July 1963 when Macmillan stalked into the crowded House to make a statement', Shrapnel wrote, and continued:

> Nerves were more than usually raw; we were at the end of a bad-tempered day near the end of a gruelling session. The Profumo disaster was five weeks behind . . . it looked as if getting rid of the Government would be a humane act . . .
>
> Yet what happened? Far from shambling off as quietly as a fallen star decently should, here was Supermac making one last triumphal appearance . . .
>
> So the man they had been calling the Lost Leader was now, for one last night, the Conquering Hero . . . All the Tories, and some Labour men too, were on their feet and cheering.

The old actor had for one night regained his mastery of the House of Commons. Shrapnel described how

> Mac made the most of every heady moment. He walked slowly along the Treasury [i.e. Front] bench, past his cheering ministerial colleagues – the survivors and successors of his notorious sacrificial orgy not so many

---

* See pp. 361–3 above.

months before [the 'Night of the Long Knives' of July 1962] ... Then, reaching the Speaker's Chair, he did an unheard of thing. Instead of disappearing from view behind the Chair in the conventional way, he turned and bowed to his ecstatic audience. He bowed again, and the cheers re-echoed.

Shrapnel said of the man and his performance that Macmillan 'understood, if anybody did, the art of serious political acting'.[239]

But for all the satisfaction of the Test Ban and the relief that Denning's report was not a demolition ball, the primary question remained for Macmillan: should he go or should he stay? On 20 September he drove to Buckingham Palace for his weekly audience with the Queen. (He had received his copy of the Denning Report three days earlier, though it was six days away from publication.) Macmillan had decided to warn the Queen what he planned to say at the forthcoming Conservative Party Conference in Blackpool in the traditional leader's address. He opened by reporting on the 'very satisfactory state of the Economy':

> [W]ith production *rising* and unemployment *falling* (contrary to the usual autumnal pattern), I then told her of my plans of announcing on October 12th that I would *not* have an Election this year and that I would *not* lead Party at Election. This would involve a change in January or February. The Queen expressed her full understanding. But I thought she was very distressed, partly (perhaps) at the thought of losing a P.M. to whom she has become accustomed, but chiefly (no doubt) because of all the difficulties about a successor in which the Crown will be much involved.

Prophetic words between head of state and head of government. But then the Queen engaged in a stunning flight of foresight, as her Prime Minister recorded:

> We discussed at some length the various possibilities. She feels the great importance of maintaining the [personal royal] prerogative [of appointing a Prime Minister] intact. After all, if she asked someone to form a government and he failed, what harm was done? It often, indeed at one time almost invariably, happened in the first half of the 19th century. Of course, it would be much better for everything to go smoothly, as in my case ...[240]

President Kennedy's weekend visit to Birch Grove on 29–30 June on the way back from delivering his triumphant 'Ich Bin Ein Berliner' speech in Germany had really perked up the PM. (It was the last time they were to meet.) Macmillan was deeply affected by Kennedy's assassination less than five months later. Carlyn Wyndham (later Baroness Chisholm of Owlpen, who answered my question about the Denning files on the Profumo affair) actually brought the old man the news of Kennedy's death as a young girl when, on 22 November, Macmillan was recuperating with her parents, John and Pamela Wyndham, at Petworth House in Sussex after his resignation:

> I was in The White Library at Petworth with my mother, father and Harold. I was still too young to have dinner with them so when they were at home always spent a couple of hours with them between tea and dinner.
>
> The house phone rang. I answered it. It was Nanny, who asked me to tell my parents that President Kennedy had been assassinated. I put the phone down turned around and gave the message. Harold was sitting in an armchair next to the fire and next to me. He started to cry very quietly and I remember hugging him for quite some time and holding his hand.[241]

After Kennedy's death in Dallas the Birch Grove weekend at the end of June 1963 took on an elegiac quality in Macmillan's memory, comparable perhaps to his lifelong sense of loss over his friends killed on the Great War battlefields. Richard Thorpe wrote that '[i]n later years Macmillan looked back over these few days with much emotion and could not recall them without his eyes misting over. It was like a country house weekend.'[242] Macmillan himself described relationships between his and the President's entourages in much the same terms: 'After all we were friends and many of us intimate friends; and the whole atmosphere was that of a country house party, to which had been added a garden party and a dance . . .' Jackie Kennedy later wrote that she and her husband had been determined to make a great effort to cheer up a Profumo-beset Harold and Lady Dorothy.[243] Local families and schoolchildren greeted the arrival of the President's helicopter and mingled with the dazzling Kennedys. About 100 CND supporters turned up.

On Sunday morning, Philip de Zulueta, himself a Catholic, took the President to Mass at nearby Forest Row. As de Zulueta later recalled, on the way to the church the President asked him about the level of political 'unrest' engendered by the Profumo affair: 'He inquired if the nuclear test ban treaty would be of assistance to the Prime Minister. I said that it would be of some assistance electorally but that the fundamental point was the state of the economy.' But, as Alistair Horne added, 'perhaps what disappointed Kennedy most in his Birch Grove visit was to find his friend, whom he had come so genuinely to respect, beneath all the flippancy seeming so disconsolate, so fatigued and so lacking in new ideas'.

For Macmillan, the 'visit ended far too soon'.[244] After lunch the helicopter came to carry the Kennedys the short distance to Gatwick and the waiting Air Force One. As part of a tribute to the slain President, Macmillan penned a poignant retrospective description of their departure:

> Hatless, with his brisk step and combining that indescribable look of a boy on holiday with the dignity of a President and Commander-in-Chief, he walked across the garden to the machine. We stood and waved. I can see the helicopter now, sailing down the valley above the heavily laden, lush foliage of oaks and beech at the end of June. He was gone. Alas, I was never to see my friend again. Before those leaves had turned and fallen he was snatched by an assassin's bullet from the service of his own country and the whole world.[245]

The tonic effect of the Kennedy visit and the securing of the Test Ban Treaty did give a fillip to Macmillan psychologically – and the opinion polls improved too. By early August the Conservatives had recovered from a mid-July 20 per cent behind Labour to a mere 6 per cent.[246] In the big 7 July catch-up entry in his diary, Macmillan acknowledged his vacillation about retirement and promised himself he would make 'time to take stock of the position and make my decision calmly and quietly'.[247]

Macmillan then went through a self-induced diary of indecision:

> 20 *September*. Tells the Queen he will announce at the Conservative Party conference his intention to retire in January 1964.

30 September. Tells Lord Swinton of his intention to retire and that Hailsham would be the best choice to succeed him.

6 October. Tells his son, Maurice, that he was now considering staying for two or three more years.

7 October. Tim Bligh tells him Cabinet opinion now wishes him to stay on.

That evening, after dining with Butler, Home, Dilhorne and Sandys, Macmillan went to bed set on telling his Cabinet the following morning that he would carry on. He rang Edward Ford, the number two Private Secretary at Buckingham Palace, asking him to inform the Queen accordingly.[248]

In the middle of the night Macmillan suffered an acute problem with his prostate. He was patched up sufficiently to chair Cabinet at ten (restoration work completed, they were once more meeting in No. 10 Downing Street, having vacated Admiralty House). Though plainly in serious discomfort (his spasms were so intense that he had to leave the Cabinet Room twice during the three-hour meeting), he asked his colleagues if they thought he should carry on through the general election and withdrew so that they could think about it.

His diary picks up the story:

At 12.45 Mr [Alec] Badenoch [urologist and surgeon] came. He re-inserted the instrument and drained the bladder. After consultation with Dr K-L [King-Lewis; Sir John Richardson, his usual physician, was on holiday in the Lake District], he told me that the cause was inflammation of the prostate gland (by either a benign or malignant tumour) and that it wd have to be dealt with.[249]

It is extraordinary how compulsive diary-writing can be. Macmillan, despite the pain and the drama, managed to write all this up on the same day:

I heard (at about 1.30) from Chief Whip [Redmayne] that the Cabinet had (with one exception) agreed to back me to the full if I decided to go on through the General Election (the exception was 'Aristides' [austere Athenian statesman] – Enoch Powell, who thought I ought to resign).[250]

Character can emerge in vivid form at moments of crisis: the Cabinet meeting of 8 October was plainly one of them.

Rab Butler, as he told Alistair Horne, offered Macmillan a Valium.[251] Quintin Hailsham, as Enoch Powell later recalled, declared (as Macmillan made one of his painful excursions from the Cabinet Room), 'Prime Minister, wherever you go, you know our hearts go with you.' Powell scribbled a note to his neighbour at the Cabinet Table, Bill Deedes, 'to the effect that I had never heard a more effective coup de grâce'. As for 'Aristides' himself, his retrospective judgement was that:

> You lose the public, you lose the press, you lose the party in the House, but the men whose heads you can cut off before breakfast you lose last. The most difficult operation there is for a Cabinet itself is to depose a Prime Minister.[252]

Macmillan somehow got through the rest of the day. His doctors met at four. He was to go to the King Edward's Hospital for Officers for an operation. He managed an appearance at a staff party to celebrate the reoccupation of No. 10 before leaving for 'Sister Agnes' (as the hospital is informally known) 'in excruciating pain'[253] at 9 p.m. The BBC ran the news within the hour. The starting gun had been fired for one of the most fevered passages of postwar political history.

Much argument subsequently ensued about whether or not Macmillan's resignation was finally precipitated by his belief that he had a malignant cancer. Richard Thorpe, for his 2010 biography of Macmillan, makes use of a memorandum drawn up by David Badenoch, the son of Macmillan's surgeon, after conversations with his father:

> By the time of the resignation, the histology of the prostate was known to be benign – a fact that was discussed with Macmillan well before his resignation. At no time was Macmillan led to believe that he had cancer of the prostate by AWB [Alec Badenoch], and even if he had a cancer, it would not have been a cause on its own to resign from office with immediate effect . . . He [Macmillan] stated to AWB that the illness 'came as manna from heaven – an act of God'.[254]

Macmillan's operation was to take place on Thursday 10 October. On Wednesday 9 October he made his political and constitutional dispositions:

1. Letter for Alec [Home] to read out on Friday [to the conference in his capacity as President of the National Union of Conservative Associations], wh makes it clear that altho' I had decided to go on through the Election, this was now impossible.
2. Approval of this letter by the Queen . . .
   Wrote up the diary. Read Bible (Samuel 1) . . .

10 October
Operation performed successfully. I did not remember having been taken from my room and the operating theatre.

It was all over by 1 pm.

But I remember little about the rest of the day, or the next day . . .[255]

The Conservative Party, on the other hand, has not forgotten from those days to this; nor have those who watched events unfold through the newspapers or on the television screen. (The Hennessy family had, at last, acquired a second-hand television, although it worked none too well in the dip on the Cotswolds in which we resided.) For Blackpool '63 turned out to be a classic example of the politics of the roulette wheel with all the caprice, the cruelty and the disappointments that go with it.

For Harold Macmillan there was something in his political demise of the fall of David Lloyd George forty-one years earlier as described by Lord Beaverbrook: 'the mists gathered, other banners were unfurled, night fell'.[256] The first banner to be unfurled was that of Lord Hailsham; the Knight of the Thistle banner of Alec Home was still very much concealed by the gathered mists. As Hailsham recalled:

On the Monday [7 October] I was summoned to Downing Street by the Prime Minister. I had not the smallest inkling of what was to take place. He told me, formally, that he wished me to succeed him, and gave me to understand that he expected to retire about Christmas. He certainly then had no more suspicion than I that, before the end of the week, events were going to overtake him.

397

Hailsham admits in his memoir that his 'recollection of the exact sequence of events is distinctly hazy', but

> I do remember being almost struck dumb with surprise at the content of our conversation and do not remember a thing that I said. I was not due to visit Blackpool until the Tuesday evening ... I was due to address the annual Conservative Political Centre meeting on the Wednesday evening.[257]

The gods of politics are cruel creatures (not that Hailsham, a devout Christian, would have had any belief in them). That conference speech was the occasion of both his fiftieth birthday and his downfall as a contender for the succession. On the Wednesday afternoon, as he recalled it:

> The pot suddenly came to the boil ... Maurice Macmillan and Julian Amery (Harold's son-in-law) came suddenly, down from the sickroom in London. Harold had taken a turn for the worse and was going to resign at once before the conference had ended. Their joint message was clear and was conveyed straight from Harold himself. 'You must act at once,' said Julian.[258]

Hailsham decided to do just that. He would announce his intention to disclaim his peerage when replying to the vote of thanks at the end of his speech that night in the Empress Ballroom, Blackpool. He went to warn Rab Butler in his suite at the Imperial Hotel: 'He was not pleased and tried to dissuade me.'[259]

The result that night was a shot of electricity that transformed the Conservative Party Conference. Though he was one of nature's political showmen, even Hailsham was surprised by what he had unleashed in indicating that Lord Hailsham would soon be transmuted into Mr Quintin Hogg:

> The prepared speech which I delivered for a totally different situation did not go down either particularly well or particularly badly. But when I came to reply to the vote of thanks, totally impromptu, and at the very end made my decision known, the effect was one of the most dramatic in my lifetime. The whole audience, and the platform, went mad, standing, cheering and waving in the full light of national television.[260]

I remember it having quite an effect in Bell Court, Nympsfield too, as we watched the flickering picture on that raddled old TV.

Randolph Churchill, the ebullient son of Winston, rushed round Blackpool distributing 'QH' badges, to Hailsham's regret ('too like the Republican and Democratic Conventions in the United States'[261]) and to Rab Butler's disgust ('Randolph . . . had returned from America with hundreds of badges marked Q for Quintin. He came up to my room and obligingly handed me some for my wife, myself and friends. These I consigned to the waste-paper basket'[262]).

Poor Rab was appalled by the unfolding drama and, no doubt, the seeping away of his last chance of No. 10. Writing eight years later in *The Art of the Possible*, Butler reckoned:

> It would have been better for him [Macmillan] and for everyone else if the decision had been taken at a less preposterous time. Less harm would have been done to the Conservative Party, and dignity, which was altogether lost during the ensuing days, might have been preserved. However, nobody seemed to share my views, least of all Macmillan, who was by then so anxious to support Hailsham that he was not thinking, or probably even informed, of loyalty from me.[263]

Hailsham, whose memoirs read as painfully in their Blackpoolian passages as do Butler's, sought out Home in the aftermath of throwing his peer's coronet into the ring to urge him not to do likewise. Hailsham told his old schoolfriend 'I did not think that it was at all a good idea for him to stand . . . I did not think his understanding and knowledge of home affairs was adequate . . . he was not best pleased. He reminded me that he had been Minister of State in the Scottish Office. "That," I replied, "is not enough. They would skittle you out in six months." '[264]

Hailsham certainly had momentum after his moment in the Empress Ballroom that placed him briefly at the centre of British political attention. In that week of bizarre volatility, perhaps the most surprising aspect – then and in retrospect – is that 'Q' for Quintin was brought down by a baby – his own, Kate. The Hailshams' domestic arrangements were such that Lady Hailsham, who had been asked to come to Blackpool after his meeting with Butler, had to bring Kate with her.

In a paragraph of his memoirs that burns with regret laced with a sense of injustice Hailsham records:

> Some odious people subsequently tried to make out that I did this only to advertise my candidature, and I am sorry to say that this abominable calumny was fed by my detractors to Harold in the nursing home [and] duly appeared in his diary . . . The case was quite the contrary. There are times when a man needs his wife by his side, and this was emphatically one of them.[265]

Hailsham was right about Macmillan recoiling from what he heard of the conduct of Hailsham in Blackpool. After a disturbed night in 'Sister Agnes' on 13–14 October, Macmillan surveyed the strange scenes he had triggered. He still plainly pined for the Hailsham premiership that would not now happen ('He belongs <u>both</u> to this strange modern world of space and science <u>and</u> to the great past – of classical learning and Christian life'[266]). But both Dilhorne, the Lord Chancellor, and Redmayne, the Chief Whip, had come to his bedside to tell him Hailsham was fading as the premier-in-waiting:

> Both these are, in principle, 'Hoggites' but they feel rather upset at the rather undignified behaviour of Hogg and his supporters at Blackpool. It wasn't easy for him, since wherever he appeared he was surrounded by mobs of enthusiastic supporters. But it was thought that he need not have paraded the baby and the baby food in the hotel quite so blatantly or talked so much at large. This is said (both by L.C. and C. Whip) to be turning 'respectable' people away from Hogg. Nor need he have talked so much about his giving up his peerage and going into the H of Commons at this stage. After all, I was not yet politically dead – certainly not buried.[267]

This was truly rich coming from Macmillan. After all, he had despatched his son and his son-in-law to tell Hailsham to get on with it, and in his diary entry for 9 October had written: 'If *Hailsham* is to be a competitor, he must at once give up his peerage and find a constituency.'[268]

After being briefed by Dilhorne and Redmayne, five days later Macmillan concluded: 'So Hogg (who really had the game in his hand) had almost thrown it away. But the movement against Hogg . . . had not gone to Butler or Maudling, but to Home.'[269]

It was emotionally and politically easy for Macmillan to segue to a
Home succession. He had long had a special regard for his qualities.
On their return from negotiating the purchase of Polaris missiles
from the USA with President Kennedy at Nassau in December 1962,
Macmillan had told the Queen that 'Alec Home is steel painted as
wood'.[270]

It was around this time that Home read a prescient article in the
New Statesman by Anthony Howard speculating on the possibility
of succession by Hailsham or himself to Macmillan if the peerages
legislation received royal assent and contemplated the possibility
seriously.[271] Yet at Macmillan's painful and poignant Cabinet on 8
October, Alec Home told his colleagues he was not interested in succeeding Macmillan and had offered to join Dilhorne in sounding out
opinion as to who should.[272] Enoch Powell, who, with Iain Macleod,
would refuse to join the Douglas-Home government, took this as a
pledge not to run.[273] Perhaps his Cabinet colleagues were seeing the
wood not the steel. But Alec Home was the straightest of men. I don't
think he intended to run for No. 10 until later in the week, or that he
was dissembling when he told James Margach of the *Sunday Times*:
'Oh, they must find someone else, once they get away from this Blackpool hothouse. Even if they can't agree on Rab or Quintin there must
be someone else. But please, please, not me!'[274]

But by the Saturday of that hot-house week, 12 October, the steel was
shining through the wood and it pierced his friend Rab Butler like a
rapier. Butler was due to give the closing speech to the Party Conference
that afternoon in Macmillan's place – a golden chance to shine, particularly as Maudling had bored the hall with his rather leaden economics
speech earlier in the week. Home, by contrast, had wowed them with
his on foreign affairs, but this did not worry Butler that Saturday morning as he put the final touches to his speech in his suite in the Imperial
Hotel. Recalling the day when he realized, in retrospect, that the premiership was slipping away from him (as it had done in 1957, and,
possibly, in 1953 when Churchill suffered a stroke and Eden was in the
United States for medical treatment), he wrote in his memoir:

> We had frequent opportunities for meeting the Homes, who had the
> next-door set of rooms. He told us on more than one occasion that he

could not himself contemplate coming down from the House of Lords and denuding it of himself as well as its leader [Hailsham]. He appeared to Mollie and me to stick to that view during the Conference until the Saturday when he told us he was consulting his doctor.[275]

Home delivered his shaft over lunch at the Imperial, with their wives present, ahead of Butler's afternoon speech. As Richard Thorpe, official biographer of both Home and Macmillan, described the scene:

> During the lunch, Home dropped a bombshell. He casually mentioned that he was seeing his doctor in London the next week. Surprisingly, Butler did not immediately grasp the significance of the remark and asked him why. 'Because I have been approached about the possibility of my becoming the leader of the Conservative Party,' replied Home. Stunned and devastated, Butler unsurprisingly failed to rouse the Tories.[276]

It might be dubbed, in the phraseology of the Conservative Party, the lunch of the long knives. Rab quietly captured the shock and the hurt in *The Art of the Possible*:

> It became clear to me at Blackpool that there was considerable support for Alec, partly because he made a good speech on foreign policy, partly because he took the chair at my [Saturday afternoon] meeting as President of the National Union, and partly because of lobbying by back-benchers, who saw him as the best compromise candidate. His wife, Elizabeth, had told Mollie that they did not really get the view that it was coming their way until the next week: but, in fact, it was.

Rab Butler had taken 'great pains' with his end-of-conference speech.[277] It paraded all his virtues as a master painter of policy on a wide canvas, including a passage of great, long-term significance – to do for higher education, building on the Robbins Report, what his 1944 Education Act had done for secondary schooling (seven new universities, a big push on technological education and a 'higher education for every boy and girl in the land who can benefit from it'[278]).

Poor Rab! All that speech is remembered for is its failure to arouse. In June 1963, John Morrison, chairman of the Conservative back-benchers' 1922 Committee, had told him 'the chaps won't have you'.[279]

On the afternoon of Saturday 12 October it became plain that the activists wouldn't have him either. He was a great provider of service to the state, but he did not fire them up. Rab – competent, decent, humane – will forever be one of the great might-have-beens of the UK premiership – along with Denis Healey and Michael Heseltine.

Against this background, this classic illustration of the caprice of politics, Macmillan's scouters of opinion had to divine who the party would have. Controversy has sizzled from that week to this about how they did it and who emerged.

In fact, in his quiet, undemonstrative fashion, it was Selwyn Lloyd who played a significant part in paving Home's road to the premiership in Autumn 1963. As Thorpe puts it: 'He was prominent among those who pressed Home to stand; he had influence with the rank-and-file delegates; and he had influence with Martin Redmayne, the Chief Whip.'[280]

The most vivid account of Lloyd furthering Home's cause comes from the pen of Jonathan Aitken, Lloyd's godson and himself a future Cabinet minister. Aitken was then a twenty-one-year-old undergraduate at Oxford; he was also a great-nephew of the incomparable, much-mimicked Lord Beaverbrook, a Canadian newspaper proprietor of the most buccaneering kind, owner of the *Daily Express* and the *Evening Standard*, both of which provided an insatiable market for political intrigue and gossip at the highest level. Aitken was, in addition to his studies, serving as Lloyd's 'gofer, chauffeur and amateur private secretary'.[281] He was with his godfather in Blackpool when Conservative politics turned Sicilian:

> Knowing how much my Uncle Max loved keeping up with the news, I made it my business to telephone him every evening from my hotel room in Blackpool. I gave him many tit-bits of gossip about the conference which he passed on to his editors, usually with instructions that I should be paid ten or twenty pounds for providing such 'excellent information'. These colourful details, many of which ended up in the Londoner's Diary column of the *Evening Standard*, were nothing to the big secret I became privy to before the Conservative party decamped from Blackpool. For while the conference delegates and the newspapers (especially the *Daily Express*) were whipping up a frenzy

of excitement over the two-horse leadership race between R. A. Butler and Quintin Hailsham, behind closed doors the magic circle of decision-makers had decided that they would prefer to back a dark horse – the Fourteenth Earl of Home.

Jonathan Aitken presents Lloyd as 'a key figure in this king-making process', as his godfather was quietly and characteristically unobtrusively very well placed:

> He carried great weight in the party as a former Foreign Secretary, Chancellor of the Exchequer and chairman of a current inquiry into [Conservative] Central Office reorganization. He disliked Butler, mistrusted Hailsham and had a high regard for Alec Home who had been his successor at the Foreign Office. He persuaded other key figures of his view that Home was the man to back, among them Martyn [sic] Redmayne, the Chief Whip, and John Morrison, the chairman of the 1922 Committee. With the support of these and other grandees a Home bandwagon began quietly rolling.[282]

At first Uncle Max, on the other end of the phone at his Surrey country seat in Cherkley, would have none of it.

'That sea air in Blackpool's infected your brain. Ya talking balls.'

But 'the Beaver' was intrigued by his nephew's inside line and summoned him to Cherkley: 'By this time I had gleaned more intelligence from Selwyn Lloyd about the growing support for Home.'[283] Beaverbrook remained sceptical but nonetheless used his nephew to wind up Derek Marks, the legendary political editor of the *Daily Express* over the telephone:

> 'Mr Marks I have here in my study at Cherkley a bright young man . . . He is the President of the Oxford University Conservative Association. He tells me that the new Prime Minister is gonna be the Earl of Home. Whaddya say about that?'

Marks, as Aitken recalled, 'told his proprietor in vernacular language that Oxford was the home of lost causes'.[284] A similar conversation took place with Randolph Churchill, who was preparing a piece for the *Evening Standard* and remained convinced the prize would go to Hailsham. At the last moment, the *Daily Express* picked up the surge for Home and, as Aitken recalled, 'ran it ahead of the competition under the headline "HOME IS HOME AND DRY". So the *Express* had a good scoop for which I was sent a cheque for one hundred pounds. With that, and my winnings from the bookies, I was once again living like a king' in Oxford.[285]

There were some who distrusted the succession process at the time, most notably Enoch Powell, that most principled, prickly and least biddable of politicians, and the only one who thought Macmillan should go at the 8 October Cabinet meeting. Shortly after the Conservatives' war of succession, Powell wrote it up in a memorandum entitled 'Narrative of the events of 8–19 October 1963 as known to me directly', which he made available to his biographer Simon Heffer.

Dilhorne summoned a succession of Cabinet ministers to his small back room in the Imperial on Friday 11 October, the day before Powell's choice, Butler, felt the Home steel. Powell recorded that: 'I began by ruling out Lord Hailsham as lacking the self-control, stability, patience and prudence which was essential to a Prime Minister, and I stated flatly that I wouldn't serve under him.' Dilhorne indicated that Macmillan favoured Hailsham. Powell said he had no personal objections to Home, 'but I could not conceive that it would be a wise or even a practicable operation'. He was, quite simply, in favour of Butler. Years later, Powell told me it was because Butler 'believed in the institutions' (this plainly trumped his almost romantic view of the virtues of hereditary aristocracy).

The reason he gave Dilhorne at the time had a characteristically Enochian touch. Butler

> would unite and represent the talent and youth on the Treasury bench: I believed (as I had believed in January 1957) that if given the opportunity he would soon appeal to the public; and while he and Mr Macmillan were approximately equal in duplicity, there was in Mr Butler what I had never discerned in Mr Macmillan, an ultimate substratum of faith in things which I myself believed in.[286]

Powell recorded Dilhorne as saying Macmillan believed Butler 'lacked decision in a crisis and was liable to be suddenly deserted by willpower'. Simon Heffer adds: 'Dilhorne and Powell then argued about Home, whom Dilhorne persisted in saying was Powell's second preference: Powell had to impress upon the notoriously unintellectual Lord Chancellor that that was not at all what he had said.'[287]

When Dilhorne's tally of results from his canvassing of Cabinet opinion was published in the second volume of Alistair Horne's life of Macmillan in 1989, Powell's doubts were reinforced. There is a consensus among political historians that the Education Minister, Sir Edward Boyle, was wrongly placed in the Home column.[288] It's Iain Macleod's name appearing in the same list of Home supporters that has exercised politicians and scholars alike. How could Macleod, who, with Powell, declined to serve in Alec Home's government, have been dubbed a Home supporter by Dilhorne? Wasn't he a Butler man through and through? Hadn't Butler told him he would be Chancellor of the Exchequer in a Butler government? Hadn't he expected to succeed Butler when the time came?[289]

There are those who detect the ace poker player he was in Macleod's activities in the great war of succession – and suspect that he had plumped for Home in his chat with Dilhorne as part of a highly cunning strategy – that he underestimated Home's support in the Cabinet, and voted for Home to block Hailsham in order that he (Macleod) could emerge at the last minute as the deadlock-breaking candidate.[290] Macleod, sadly, kept no record of his session with Dilhorne.

Rob Shepherd, Macleod's biographer, believes: 'The evidence that Dilhorne got it wrong is compelling.'[291] Powell, too, thought it 'inconceivable' that Macleod voted for Home. Butler said he was 'not at all surprised' to hear that Macleod had opted for Home, as 'Macleod was very shifty, much more than you think.' Macmillan, true to character, said, 'Well, you know ... Macleod was a Highlander!'[292]

Who knows? As Home shimmered his way towards the premiership Macleod was among the most active of the Cabinet ministers who tried to block him in the last stretch at the famous 'midnight meeting' at Enoch Powell's house on the night of Thursday–Friday 17–18 October. By this stage, Macmillan, misled or not by Dilhorne's canvass, was well advanced in crafting his advice to the Queen on whom she should send for. On the morning of 17 October, Dilhorne waited on Macmillan in hospital, with his Parliamentary Private

Secretary, Knox Cunningham, taking the note. This was the Dilhorne tally of the Cabinet. Alec Home is recorded as not voting. Everyone else did:

Those whose first choice is *R. A. Butler*
  R. A. Butler
  Henry Brooke
  Enoch Powell

Those whose first choice is *Alec Home*
  Deedes
  Boyle
  Soames
  Hare
  Macleod
  Heath
  Sandys
  Marples
  Myself
  Noble

Those whose first choice is *Quintin*
  Quintin
  Thorneycroft

Those whose first choice is *Maudling*
  Maudling
  Boyd-Carpenter
  Erroll
  Joseph[293]

Home, according to Redmayne's canvass, led MPs' preferences 'but not by much'. Those who knew him best in the House of Lords were two to one for Home. The constituencies were 60 per cent for Hailsham, 40 per cent for Butler.[294]

Macmillan was worn out by his duty as a gatherer and transmitter of views about his successor on 17 October:

But after 6, the work began and I dictated memorandum for the Queen (shd she ask my advice) and also signed a formal letter of resignation.

> We finished at midnight! Tim Bligh has set up an office in the hospital
> and two typists from No. 10 have been here all day.[295]

It was worth waiting for a classic Macmillan piece of work –
written as if it were a prime piece of contemporary history complete
with character vignettes. Macmillan removed the other runners, one by
one, before deftly steering his sovereign towards Alec Home, whom
the Queen knew very well. As her former Private Secretary Martin
Charteris told the Queen's biographer Ben Pimlott over thirty years
later: ' "Rab" wasn't her cup of tea. When she got the advice to call
Alec she thought "Thank God". She loved Alec – he was an old
friend. They talked about dogs and shooting together. They were
both Scottish landowners, the same sort of people, like school
friends.' Lord Charteris made it plain that the constitution prevails
over personal preference in Buckingham Palace. 'We all understood
that Alec could not form a government unless "Rab" agreed to serve,
and, if not, the Queen would have to call for "Rab".'[296]

Macmillan did not give Rab the most glowing reference in his
advice to the monarch in the paragraphs in which he compares the
claims of Butler and Hailsham:

> On the one side, long experience, devoted service to the Party, abso-
> lute integrity of character, great political skill, and the moral and
> intellectual inspiration of the Conservative Party after the 1945 col-
> lapse. On the other hand, Lord Hailsham, a man of the highest
> moral standing, keen churchmanship, strong opinions, a great orator,
> a fine public performer, able to enthuse in a way that recalls some of
> the older leaders in the past, and perhaps the most favoured election
> winner.

After awarding Butler and Hailsham their respective palms, the
old man cast them both into the dust:

> Nevertheless it soon emerged that there were very strong opponents of
> each. There were those for instance who thought that Mr Butler with
> all his qualities was a dreary figure who would lead the Party to in-
> evitable defeat or to a worse defeat than was necessary. These sections
> included not only members of the House of Commons but strong

sections in the Party Organisation. On the other side there were those who thought that Lord Hailsham, in spite of his great qualities, was somewhat unpredictable. This included the more old fashioned people who are shocked at the gimmicks and the inescapable advertising which play an important role in political life.

At this point Macmillan injected a rather chatty tone for a head of government advising his monarch on the solemn business of exercising her personal royal prerogative of appointing a Prime Minister: '(Incidentally there is nothing new in this because I have heard, all through my life, the same criticism of Sir Winston Churchill from the days of Sidney Street with his coats, hats, cigars, romper suits and all the rest of it.)' After this aside, Macmillan finished off Hailsham:

> But apart from this question of taste I think there is a real sense of alarm lest under the tremendous stress of world politics Lord Hailsham would not be able to remain sufficiently calm to handle the kind of situation which only too frequently arises.

The blade is suddenly sheathed and the prime ministerial hand rearranges itself ready to stroke at the first mention of Alec Home:

> When we come to the position of Lord Home it is noticeable that apart from being the first choice of very large groups as set out earlier he seems to be the second choice of everybody. Nobody is against him . . .

(At this point Macmillan's critics in the Cabinet, had they had sight of this super-sensitive document, would have accused him of misleading his sovereign about the degree of support for Home.)

> . . . and indeed everyone seems to think he has all the qualities except the great disadvantage of being a 'right down regular peer'.

(Ditto.)

> . . . This seems to be the only fear expressed by anyone.

(Ditto.)

> Cabinet colleagues would work loyally under Lord Home as their chief. Members of Parliament would feel that they were efficiently and

strongly led, organised bodies of the Party who already have a deep respect for Lord Home as representing qualities, which although often derided are still admired, would rally round him.

Macmillan even paraded the two sides of the Cold War as if they too were Home men: ('It will be an advantage that he is already so well known and liked by the main figures, including Mr Gromyko and Mr Khrushchev, as well as Mr Rusk and President Kennedy.')

Macmillan rounded off his memorandum with a nod to the constitutional niceties. Many years later Lord Charteris made the distinction between 'capital "A" advice' from a Prime Minister, which the monarch has to take, and 'lower case "a" advice where it touches upon her personal prerogatives, including the appointment of a Prime Minister', which she does not.[297] In October 1963 she did ask Macmillan for advice on the Conservative succession:

> Your Majesty has asked for my advice. I thought it right to prepare myself against this possibility and hence set out my thoughts on paper in this memorandum. Your Majesty may care to have a copy for the Royal Records and I will keep a copy. I think in the present circumstances this is a wise course to take in order to safeguard Your Majesty's position.
>
> *October 17, 1963*[298]

The silky words and assumptions of that memo were being roughed up at the very time Macmillan was dictating them to his secretary, as Stop-Home ministers made their way to Enoch Powell's house in Belgravia, forcing Macmillan the following morning to dictate an addition to it.

On this frantic, penultimate day of the war of Tory succession, the political journalists were ahead of the Cabinet ministers in picking up Macmillan's powerful tilt towards Home. In mid-afternoon, William Rees-Mogg of the *Sunday Times* rang Iain Macleod to tell him Home was going to be Macmillan's recommendation.[299] Macleod alerted Powell. The word burnt its way rapidly through the political tinder. Hailsham began to work the telephone from his home in Putney. Powell and Macleod rang Home. As Macleod later recalled in a famous article in the *Spectator* magazine (which he was now editing) in January 1964, reviewing Randolph Churchill's book on the events of October 1963 in toughly critical terms for being pro-Macmillan (his critique introduced the term 'magic circle' into the political lexicon):

> I spoke first. I told him there was no one in the party for whom I had more admiration and respect; that if he had been in the House of Commons he could perhaps have been the first choice; but I felt that those giving advice had grossly underestimated the difficulties of presenting the situation in a convincing way to the modern Tory Party. Unlike Hailsham, he was not a reluctant peer, and we were now proposing to admit that after twelve years of Tory government no one amongst the 363 members of the party in the House of Commons was acceptable as Prime Minister.[300]

Powell did not record what he himself said.

Powell had been torn away by the rapidly swirling events from his daughter Jennifer's birthday party, and when ministers began to arrive chez Powell in South Eaton Place for the late-night Stop-Home meeting they found the place filled with balloons.[301] Simon Heffer describes the increasingly rococo Belgravia scene:

> As well as Powell, Macleod and [Toby] Aldington [deputy chairman of the Conservative Party] there were Maudling, in black tie after dinner – fetched from a neighbouring street by Pam Powell as his telephone was permanently engaged – and [Frederick] Erroll. While the conclave continued, Pam Powell and Beryl Maudling went out to buy the first editions of the newspapers at a railway station. The meeting did not remain secret for long. Maudling had foolishly given his daughter Powell's telephone number in case anyone wanted him. It was recognised by the journalist Henry Fairlie, who put two and two together. A picket of pressmen arrived within minutes, and stayed outside until long after the new Prime Minister was in office. The photographers were in time to record the arrival of Redmayne, invited by the ministers to hear their views and relay them to Macmillan.[302]

Redmayne tried to persuade them to accept Home. They countered by arguing that, as Hailsham and Maudling had both agreed to serve under Butler, Rab was plainly the one to go to the Palace. Redmayne left, agreeing to convey their views to Macmillan. Aldington rang the Queen's Private Secretary, Sir Michael Adeane, to brief him on the meeting.

Powell rang Butler in the early hours of 18 October in what has become known as the 'loaded revolver' conversation (Powell's phrase). All Butler had to do was fire it and the premiership would be his. 'Thank you for telling me,' said Rab. 'The Prime Minister must be told.'[303]

Macmillan was briefed by Redmayne at 8.30 in the morning in his hospital bed. So began what he described as 'A terrible day and very bad for me. The doctors protest, but I cd see no way of shuffling out of my duty.'

That duty, plainly, in the old man's eyes was to head off the revolt by getting Home to the Palace as quickly as possible. Though Macmillan could 'hardly hold a pen', he wrote up this extraordinary day in his diary that night. His duty, in his eyes, was to ensure above all that Butler did not make it to No. 10. He wrote of Redmayne's briefing:

> It seems that the news that the general choice favoured Home got out last night (leaked by someone). Meetings were organised by Powell, who got Macleod to help him. Erroll and Maudling were brought in, Hailsham came too [he didn't; he was contacted by phone]. Also Butler was approached. The idea was an organised revolt by all the unsuccessful candidates – Butler, Hailsham, Maudling and Macleod – against Home. Considering their intense rivalry with each other during recent weeks, there was something rather 18th century about this . . . and somewhat distasteful.

> Home rang Macmillan

> and felt somewhat aggrieved. He had only been asked to come forward as a compromise candidate, for unity. He felt like withdrawing. I urged him not to do so.

Macmillan had somehow convinced himself that if the Queen sent for Butler, the Conservative government and party would face meltdown; this was an absurdly apocalyptic view – had he succeeded Butler would have been an exceptionally well-primed premier.

Macmillan wrote:

> If we give in to this intrigue, there wd be chaos. Butler wd fail to form
> a Govt; even if given another chance (for the Queen might then send
> for Wilson) no one else wd succeed. We shd have a Wilson Govt; a
> dissolution [of Parliament]; and our party without even a nominal
> leader.

Reading the Macmillan diary over half a century on, there is an
almost panicky air to that entry. How could Macmillan be so sure
that Butler could *not* form an administration if the Queen invited
him to try and that Home could? Why should she send for Wilson if
there was a stalemate? The Conservatives still possessed a big majority in the House of Commons. According to Macmillan's diary, 'the
Chief Whip [Redmayne] (and Tim [Bligh]) took the same view'.

The outcome pivoted around this moment:

> This was a most critical moment, but I decided to go on. My letter of
> resignation was sent and delivered to Palace at 9.30am ... So ended
> my premiership.[304]

Not quite. Macmillan had to prepare for the Queen's visit later that
morning to hear his advice on the succession. His first task was to
dictate the aforementioned addendum to his bladework of the previous day, taking into account what Redmayne had told him of the
midnight meeting at Enoch Powell's:

> Since obtaining the reports from the four sources to which I have
> referred and compiling this memorandum on the night of October 17,
> I have this morning received accounts of movements among certain
> Ministers to oppose the choice of Lord Home. It remains the fact that
> out of the Cabinet Ministers, not less than ten when asked who they
> would like to succeed me in the event of my resignation answered the
> question, Lord Home. One or two of these may of course now be
> changing their position; but this is the information which the Lord
> Chancellor gave me yesterday. I would judge that what is happening
> is that the rival forces of the defeated parties (if I may use such an
> expression) that is of Mr Butler and Lord Hailsham are now trying
> to join together in a last-minute agreement amongst themselves to

support Mr Butler. I still do not think that this alters the immediate situation . . .[305]

These last words are remarkable. If Hailsham and Butler, Maudling, Macleod and Powell all refused to serve under Home he would fail to form a government. The 'situation' was 'altered' and the question was would Rab pull the trigger of the revolver that had been handed to him. As Martin Charteris indicated to Ben Pimlott, the Queen would have sent for Butler if fire he had. And the conclusion of that last sentence reveals exactly how the 'situation' had been 'altered':

> . . . although it may of course affect Lord Home's success in forming an Administration should Your Majesty entrust him with the task.

Here Macmillan, ill and exhausted though he may have been, dug deep into nineteenth-century history (the precedent was Queen Victoria and Lord Aberdeen in 1852[306]) (a) to find a constitutional way out for the Queen, and (b) to get his man into 10 Downing Street:

> After all there is nothing unusual in a Minister having to take soundings and enter into negotiations before an Administration can be successfully formed, and there is nothing that is reported in today's newspapers as a result of last night's efforts by certain ministers to alter the advice which I have given to Your Majesty. If Lord Home fails to form an Administration likely to command the support of the House of Commons, he will no doubt report this to Your Majesty and Your Majesty can then entrust the commission to other hands.
>
> *October 18, 1963*[307]

His constitutional draftsmanship done, Macmillan had to prepare himself to meet his sovereign, insisting on wearing a white silk shirt for the audience. When the Queen arrived at 11 a.m., accompanied by Adeane, she found her Prime Minister waiting in the King Edward VII Board Room, the shiny shirt gleaming from beneath one of his old brown pullovers. Mercifully the attached bottle into which his bile drained was out of sight. He was, as he wrote later, 'in great discomfort'.

The head of state and (for another hour or so) the head of government were both visibly moved. Many years later he painted the scene for his official biographer:

> She said, very kindly, 'What are you going to do?' And I said, 'Well I am afraid I can't go on.' And she was very upset . . . Then said, 'Have you any advice to give me?' And I said, 'Ma'am, do you wish me to give any advice?' And she said 'Yes, I do' . . . So then I said 'Well, since you ask for it, Ma'am, I have, with the help of Mr Bligh, prepared it all, and here it is.' And I just handed her over my manuscript . . . then I read it to her, I think . . .[308]

The Queen agreed with Macmillan that Home was best placed to command the widest support and thanked him. In another bizarre twist, the No. 10 staff had placed Macmillan's memorandum in a huge white envelope for Adeane to convey back to the Palace. Macmillan thought it made the short and stocky Adeane look like the Frog Footman in *Alice in Wonderland*.

Exhausted, the old man returned to bed and dozed off, only to be woken by a Post Office engineer removing his scrambler telephone: 'I said: Hell, I was Prime Minister two hours ago, you might leave it a bit. No, he said, that's the rule. So that was the end of my power.'[309] Such are the practicalities of the British constitution at work.

Across at the Palace, the Frog Footman contacted Alec Home and invited him to call on the Queen. He arrived at 12.15 p.m. The Queen asked him to try to form an Administration. He agreed to do so and took the short car journey to No. 10. He saw Butler first. Rab declined to pull the trigger of the revolver the midnight men had given him. Instead, he reserved his position, although he made no pledge to serve under Home. But the war of succession was as good as over. That evening Home met with Hailsham, Butler and Maudling together. Hailsham agreed to serve under him. The following morning, Friday 19 October, Maudling agreed to carry on as Chancellor of the Exchequer. Butler agreed to go to the Foreign Office. Powell and Macleod held out. Alec Home went to the Palace to kiss hands and accept the Queen's commission.

When the news reached The Hirsel, the Douglas-Homes' house in the Borders, the Dowager Countess said of her son: 'So good of Alec to do Prime Minister.'[310]

It was indeed, for he was instantly pitted against a most formidable opponent already buoyed aloft by a triumphant Party Conference at Scarborough and a coruscating leader's speech.

The arguments still rage about whether or not Macmillan manipulated the result; whether or not the Queen should have accepted his advice (Very difficult for her not to, even though it was advice with a little 'a', unless she decided she could not trust her outgoing PM. Even then, how could she conduct her own canvass of Cabinet and Conservative Party opinion?) The way Macmillan constructed his memorandum of advice for the monarch, especially his depiction of the characters of the contenders, plainly reflected his far-from-detached personal views.

In a strange piece of political symmetry that became apparent only much later, the two Conservative leaders to come who were already in the House of Commons in 1963 – Ted Heath and Margaret Thatcher – agreed with Macmillan and the Queen. Heath was Home's number two at the Foreign Office. As he wrote in his memoirs:

> I had supported Alec from the outset. It is sometimes suggested that I helped to engineer Alec Douglas-Home's path to No. 10 for entirely selfish reasons because I knew that he would lose the election and prove to be only a stop-gap, enabling me to become leader ... of course it is true that, had a younger candidate from my own generation, such as Reggie Maudling, succeeded Macmillan in 1963, it would obviously have become impossible for me to become leader when I did [in 1965]. But politics is an unpredictable business, and it would have been madness for me to assume anything about the longer-term at that stage.[311]

Mrs Thatcher, then a junior minister at Pensions and National Insurance, told the Whips, 'that she preferred RAB', but 'I was then asked my view of Alec. "Is it constitutionally possible?" I asked. Assured that it was, I did not hesitate. I replied, "Then I am strongly in favour of Alec." ' Her authorized biographer, Charles Moore, notes that she retained a high regard for Home: 'She always referred to him as "Alec", while never referring to Macmillan as "Harold".'[312]

Alec Home was not a greasy-pole climber or a man of destiny whose life could be fulfilled only by achieving the highest office. Harold Wilson, however, was unabashed in his ambition to succeed his new opponent as the next incumbent of No. 10 Downing Street.

The year 1963 was one of those that morph into an evocative date in its own right, with successive and very public dramas and casts of characters to match, biting into the national collective memory. Yet there is always a dash of hidden history that emerges only many years later. The choicest for me in 1963 has to do with a nuclear moment, though not one freighted with the intense peril of 1962's Cuban missile crisis. It is an episode worth waiting for nonetheless – and a very British one at that. It was that great cricket-loving Whitehall intellectual Michael Quinlan, then a high-flying young civil servant in the Air Ministry, who related it to me.

It took place during the final over of the Lord's Test, England vs West Indies on Tuesday 25 June 1963 – a scene older cricket lovers will never forget. In a gathering gloom the very fast Wes Hall was bowling to David Allen of Gloucestershire while Kent's Colin Cowdrey stood with his broken arm in plaster at the other end. The result trembled on the brink: it could be an England win, a West Indies win, a tie or a draw. It took longer than four minutes to complete that over, Michael explained, and during it every screen in the RAF's operations room in Whitehall was switched from the new Ballistic Missile Early Warning System on Fylingdales Moor in North Yorkshire onto the Lord's Test. The Russians could have had us retaliation free! As for the Test match, it was a draw.*

---

* Hennessy, *The Secret State: Preparing for the Worst 1945–2010* (Penguin, 2010), p. xxv.

7

Tweedy Aristocrat, Gritty Meritocrat

[A]s every year goes by the claim [for Wilson] to be by far the most brilliant Leader of the Opposition becomes more clearly established. But, in fact, he used the House of Commons very effectively as a platform. It's very important for a Leader of the Opposition to establish at least equality of performance with the Prime Minister of the day. Harold took on Harold Macmillan in his declining days and certainly was his equal. Then he took on Sir Alec Douglas-Home and, quite frankly, he beat him on virtually every occasion; and so he established himself very clearly as the obvious leader, the dominant personality in the House of Commons and then backed it up at the same time with a nationwide campaign.

Peter Shore recalling 1963–4 in 1992[1]

I don't think I ever actually got them out. It was purely a chance remark at lunch because Kenneth Harris [*Observer* journalist] said to me 'Do you think you could be Prime Minister?' and I said, 'I really don't think so because I have to do all my economics with matchsticks.' But it stuck, of course. Harold Wilson wasn't going to miss something like that [chuckling].

Lord Home of the Hirsel recalling 1963 in 1989[2]

The Douglas-Home–Wilson counterpoint was short-lived, but a collector's item in the long history of political central casting. It seemed at times to include every element of the British fixations with class, background, accent, style, drapery. It even had glasses – Sir Alec's

TWEEDY ARISTOCRAT, GRITTY MERITOCRAT

half-moons were a source of parody and derision. It was, in cricketing terms, a showdown between Gentlemen and Players, only a year after the eponymous annual match had been abandoned for ever at Lords.

Alec Home, though 'born to rule', as one of the sneers of the time put it, certainly had neither expected the premiership nor trained himself for it. Harold Wilson had. As Ian Mikardo, a fellow Bevanite who arrived in Parliament on the same Labour high tide in 1945, expressed it in Wilson's BBC Radio 4 obituary, *The Scarlet Thread*:

> I have no doubt, and I didn't have any doubt since the early days, that somewhere in the drawer in the Wilson's residence there was a sheet of paper headed 'Way to the Top', and it listed all the things he was going to do in the sequence in which he was going to do them. That is the constant thread, the scarlet thread running through it all.[3]

Hugh Gaitskell's unexpected death in January 1963 suddenly presented Harold Wilson, the classic scholarship boy, with his ultimate examination paper (his preparation at Oxford for Schools had been legendary[4]). It was comprehensive and sustained when it came to the first paper of his political finals – winning the Labour leadership in 1963. His overall First would depend on winning the forthcoming battle for No. 10. Would the scarlet thread reach the front door of No. 10?

It was Alec Home's misfortune to acquire the keys not just in the semi-chaotic and certainly politically neuralgic circumstances of the 1963 Conservative Party Conference and after, but in the very month that Harold Wilson had reached the peak of his political life so far with one of the finest – perhaps *the* finest – speech he was ever to deliver. What has gone down in British political history as his 'white heat' speech to the Labour Party Conference in session at Scarborough on 1 October 1963 made Harold Wilson the playmaker of UK politics. I still regard his oration at Scarborough that early autumn day by the sea as the signature speech of Harold Wilson's long span in British politics, from his arrival in the House of Commons as MP for Ormskirk in July 1945 to his resignation as Prime Minister in April 1976. It drew on the planning experience of the Attlee era, on the lost opportunities of what Wilson saw as the locust years of Conservative administrations since, and above all the promise of technological transformation to come – if only government could be placed in the hands of a new generation with the future in their bones who would propel the British economy up the league tables of economic performance and GDP per head and keep it there.

At its core lay the need to 'industrialize our science', as one witness put it to a House of Lords inquiry in 2017 on the eve of the publication of the ninth industrial strategy since 1945.[5] In his account of the Labour government of 1964–70, Wilson described how he intended to get this right should he win the election (which could be a year away at most) by creating a new Ministry of Technology. One of the tasks of Mintech (as it was inevitably dubbed when it came to pass)

> would be to speed the application of new scientific methods to industrial production. This had been the main theme of my speech at Labour's Scarborough conference in October 1963, which had attracted considerable attention. Britain had always been good in the scientific laboratory, but all too often the results of fundamental research had been clothed with the necessary know-how only by foreign industrialists . . .
>
> During the war some of our major inventions – such as jet propulsion, radar and other electronic developments, and antibiotics – had been handed over to the United States under the lend-lease arrangements from 1941 to 1945 and developed there – to the point where, in some cases, we were paying royalties on what were essentially British inventions or discoveries. The process had continued apace after the war and I decided something must be done about it.[6]

Doing something about it began to take its initial shape on the Yorkshire coast in the small hours of 1 October 1963.

Wilson had left drafting late, even though the speech had been a while in the making. With the help of his Shadow Minister for Education and Science, Dick Crossman, Wilson had been cultivating scientists, several of whom were enthused by his approach.[7] But, like so many politicians, Wilson needed an imminent deadline to reach for his rhetorical heights. (Churchill and Macmillan were exceptions, both able to draft coruscating oratory well in advance of its delivery.)

Crossman, who relished 'his tremendous performance', records in his diary that Wilson 'had been up until half past three in the morning and later told me he was so tired when he started that it was quite a pleasure to wake himself up by speaking. He spoke beautifully, completely collectedly, carrying the whole conference with him.'[8]

Wilson's words that morning flowed hot, bright and glowing like molten steel. If words could transform an economy, these were the ones, crafted into a final crescendo, that would have halted and reversed the country's long and dispiriting relative decline:

> In all our plans for the future, we are re-defining and we are re-stating our socialism in terms of the scientific revolution. But that revolution cannot become a reality unless we are prepared to make far-reaching changes in economic and social attitudes which permeate our whole system of society.

Then there was the passage that will forever be associated with his name and his first early-Sixties flowering as the country's leading political speaker:

> The Britain that is going to be forged in the white heat of this revolution will be no place for restrictive practices or for outdated methods on either side of industry . . . In the Cabinet room and the boardroom alike those charged with the control of our own affairs must be ready to think and speak the language of our scientific age.[9]

The impact of his speech in that Scarborough hall was extraordinary, and all the more potent for being unexpected. Even Tam Dalyell, who was very close to Crossman, had anticipated (as he told me everyone else did too) that Wilson would concentrate on attacking Macmillan and his government. Instead they heard this brilliant, constructive speech that captivated and inspired.

Dalyell had been elected MP for West Lothian at a by-election the previous year. An Etonian by schooling, a schoolteacher by profession, a historian and an economist by degree, he had a deep interest in science and had helped Crossman to gather the scientific minds at no fewer than thirty-four meetings in 1963–4.[10] He subsequently believed that Wilson's white heat was genuinely felt in the ballot boxes on 15 October 1964. He told me in early 2016, when we were talking about the centenary of Harold Wilson's birth:

It was my view in 1963/64, and remains my considered view now, that Harold's speech – remember his *first* as party leader – was worth twenty-five to thirty Labour seats in October 1964. This was also the view of friends of mine elected in 1964 – Joel Barnett, Terry Boston, Colin Jackson and Merlyn Rees, to name but a few.

In other words, that Wilson owed his slim majority of four a year later to the power of his Scarborough speech.

Part of his listeners' rapture was due to Wilson's skilful grafting of his novel modernity theme to ancient class grievances in a way that also chimed with the anti-Establishment tocsin that was ringing out across early-Sixties Britain. And the Labour activists would have noted instantly the homage paid to Nye Bevan's 'commanding heights' image in the opening sentence:

> For the commanding heights of British industry to be controlled today by men whose only claim is their aristocratic connection or the power of inherited wealth or speculative finance is as irrelevant to the twentieth century as would be the continued purchase of commissions in the armed forces by lordly amateurs. At the very time that even the MCC has abolished the distinction between amateurs and professionals, in science and industry we are content to remain a nation of Gentlemen in a world of Players.

Here he made a neat segue way into Britain's place in the world – a reframing of great powerdom that today is less remembered:

> For those of us who have studied the formidable Soviet challenge in the education of scientists and technologists, and, above all, in the ruthless application of scientific techniques in Soviet industry, know that our future lies not in military strength alone but in the efforts, the sacrifices and above all the energies which a free people can mobilise for the future greatness of our country. Because we are democrats, we reject the methods which communist countries are deploying in applying the results of scientific research to industrial life. But because we care deeply about the future of Britain, we must use all the resources of democratic planning, all the latent and underdeveloped energies and skills of our people, to ensure Britain's standing in the world.[11]

With 'white heat', Harold Wilson had not only found a theme with which to unite his party – a new signature tune to eclipse the rows over nationalization and the Bomb that had vexed previous Labour Party Conferences since their election defeat in 1959 – but had also discovered political mercury, a pool of quicksilver that could shimmer and flow into those places Labour rhetoric tended not to reach. This was immediately evident in the press section of the Scarborough Ballroom, as Wilson's biographer, Ben Pimlott, brings out: 'Conference as a whole expressed its delight [both] during the speech and when it ended. In the press compound, Alan Watkins had to restrain Charles Douglas-Home [Alec's nephew, who was working for the *Daily Express*] from applauding.'[12]

At Scarborough, Wilson seized his moment, found his voice and set his personal and national presence on a new and upward trajectory. He scored its boundaries wider and deeper in a series of follow-up speeches in the first months of 1964. Taken together with Scarborough, they were a claim to power from a prime minister and government-in-waiting and were recognized as such at the time (Penguin quickly gathered them up and published them as a 'Penguin Special'[13]).

Wilson delivered the first of his Scarborough sequels at a Sunday rally in Birmingham Town Hall on 19 January 1964 under the head-line 'A New Britain'. Over fifty years later once can still sense its power, but also its overstretch, an overclaiming, however admirable his aspiration, that could only doom any government he led to relative failure, so high a bar had he set with his statement that 'Labour wants to . . . bring the entire nation into a working partnership with the state.'[14] He described a Labour-governed nation exhibiting a high and admirable level of civic virtue with 'every home, every club, every pub its own Parliament-in-miniature thrashing out the issues of the day'.[15]

Wilson was a connoisseur of Gladstonian politics (at Oxford he had won the Gladstone Prize in 1936 for an essay on 'The State and the Railways 1823–63'[16]). Those 'New Britain' speeches in the great halls of the big cities were Wilson's version of the Grand Old Man's Midlothian campaign of 1879 (a breathtaking thirty speeches in two weeks[17]). As Dick Crossman said of the Scarborough speech in his diary: 'he had provided the revision of Socialism and its application to modern times which Gaitskell and Crosland had tried and completely failed to do. Harold had achieved it'.[18]

Re-reading those speeches now, one can detect three target audiences: the electorate as a whole (their government-in-waiting character); the Labour Party itself and its ever-lurking centrifugal tendencies; and the rising meritocracy, humanities trained and scientifically literate alike, of whom, with his feel for history, his economics and his statistical agility, he was the incarnation. As Peter Clarke caught it, Wilson 'was the first major leader to represent the new ruling class – an upwardly mobile Oxbridge meritocracy recruited through provincial grammar schools – which was to take over during the next twenty-five years producing Heath as well as Healey, Jenkins as well as Thatcher'.[19]

Read together, as they should be, the three early 1964 speeches, together with Scarborough, represent the most impressive political oratory of the age, the rhetorical fulcrum of Sixties politics. Quite apart from their content, they have a distinctive linguistic feel. They are peppered, for example, with the words 'purpose' and 'purposive' to the point where those words became Wilson's verbal tics. Planning, he told his Birmingham audience, was all about 'purposive expansion'.[20] Labour believed in it, knew how to do it. Macmillan's 'Neddy' showed the Conservatives were late and only partial converts to the key ingredient that would fire up a British economy languishing in the wake of its competitors. Labour was about 'economic purpose, social purpose, world purpose'.[21]

What was needed, he said in his next speech, on 'Labour's Economic Policy' at the beautiful Brangwyn Hall in Swansea on Saturday 25 January 1964, was a new approach to economic planning.[22] Industry, and the mobilization of science for industrial purposes, would provide the motive power. 'Finance must be the index, not the determinant of economic strength.'[23] All depended 'on what we turn out from our factories, mines and farms, our laboratories and our drawing offices'.[24] This was still a Britain imagined as a producing and manufacturing nation above all. Services do not get a mention. Problems with the pound sterling in an era of fixed exchange rates – a deep and persistent problem for Labour as soon as they took office and a shadow hanging over virtually all the years in power thereafter – are dealt with in a similar way. 'The key to a strong pound', Wilson told his audience in the Brangwyn Hall, 'lies not in Britain's finances but in the nation's industry.'[25] Whitehall would be reshaped to help forge the New Britain. There would be a new senior 'Minister of Economic Planning'[26] and a new 'Ministry of Technology to expand civil research and make it more purposive'.[27]

There were those in Whitehall itself who were impressed by Wilson's pitch for office on 'a growth ticket' (or to be more precise, a greater growth ticket, as the Conservatives were also portraying themselves as economic expansionists), as Peter Jenkins, star political columnist for the *Guardian* and later the *Independent*, would put it in his reflections on the politics of the Sixties.[28] Robin Butler had joined the Treasury in 1961. He would serve Harold Wilson in the mid-1970s as his Economic Affairs Private Secretary in No. 10 and rise eventually to be Cabinet Secretary and head of the Home Civil Service. He told me many years later that the 'white heat' speech had 'turned me on. There was a feeling that we were being overtaken by those we had defeated in the war; that there was something moribund about the country; too much relying on old stock and old capital.' Butler was also struck by Wilson's character: 'Harold was a more accessible intellectual. He wasn't in an ivory tower like Gaitskell.'[29]

Wilson rounded off his prospectus for government in Swansea with more detail of Labour's big idea: 'The problems we are facing underline the need for effective economic planning covering industrial policy, financial policy, and the application of science to British industry. This is why we have been thinking in terms of a Minister of Economic Planning . . . to ensure that an effective plan is worked out for production, exports, imports, capital investment, and industrial training and technological research. What Neddy has begun, this Ministry must carry through to completion, with effective powers for the job.'[30]

It was a pitch for the intrusion of very considerable state power – a shot of such magnitude that it could only have come from a man who had witnessed a home front successfully mobilized between 1939 and 1945. Yet there was more to it than that. In Swansea, in perhaps the most prescient passage of his 'New Britain' speeches, he concentrated on the human cost of what was then described as automation:

For socialism for us means humanizing what can so easily become a harsh, even brutal, technological revolution . . . Socialism in our New Britain will provide that leavening we never had in the first Industrial Revolution.[31]

That humanizing, that leavening, remains a problem of the first order over half a century later. That night Wilson suggested that each new peak in production brought about by the spread of automation 'is marked by a higher and higher level of unemployment'.[32] What he did not foresee was the growth of service industries that would fill the place left by those jobs made technologically redundant by the power and reach of the computer, robotics and, increasingly, artificial intelligence. Wilson did have a sense of what the great Austrian-born Harvard economist Joseph Schumpeter had described twenty years earlier as the 'creative destruction' that technology-fuelled capitalism could wreak.[33] It was as if Wilson's idea of planning was devoted to boosting the 'creative' part of that juxtaposition while curbing its 'destructive' properties. In Schumpeter's classic *Capitalism, Socialism and Democracy* of 1942, there is a vivid line on Karl Marx that could apply to Harold Wilson at his best: 'The cold metal of economic history is in Marx's pages immersed in such a wealth of steaming phrases as to acquire a temperature not naturally its own.'[34]

Wilson was skilled, too, at capturing the long sweeps of history and integrating them into his speeches. His theme in the Usher Hall, Edinburgh, on 21 March 1964, for example, was directly anti-declinist. 'A First-Class Nation' was how he entitled his text: 'We reject this doctrine of inevitable second-class status, of inevitable decline, of increasing dependence.'[35]

He skilfully linked this theme with a key aspect of the Macmillan years – their approach to the Common Market and a UK entry into the European Economic Community. The Conservatives, he declared, 'have really given up hope. They are reconciled to a second-class industrial status because the one avenue of escape on which they placed total reliance failed them. For a year and a half they maintained that there was no future for Britain except as part of a wider European industrial complex . . . [that] . . . Britain is nothing without Europe.'[36]

Running through all the signature speeches was another distinctive Wilsonian scarlet thread; his version of class warfare – what one might call the weaponizing of meritocracy into a bullet to fire at the heart of privilege. Here he is in full cry in the Usher Hall:

> The Labour Party, Mr Chairman, reject this grovelling, this defeatist doctrine of humiliating impotence. We reject the dismal tones of friends abroad who say that we have lost our way in the world, that our flame is burning low, that we have nothing to offer except the memories and nostalgia of a faded imperial grandeur, or the feudal glories of our tourist attractions, or our ancient monuments in Scotland – and in the Cabinet. We think we have more to offer.[37]

He could rarely resist a touch of class-tinged stand-up even when striving, as he was in all the New Britain speeches, to behave as a prime minister-in-waiting.

Alec Home was a sitting target, a gift from the political gods, a tethered and tweedy aristocrat helpless before the taunts of the gritty meritocrat. Or was he? Home rather got the better of the first exchange in the days following his succession to the premiership. On hearing that Home had accepted the Queen's commission to form a government Wilson contemptuously, but perhaps inevitably, said 'after half a century of democratic advance . . . the whole process has ground to a halt with a 14th Earl'.[38] A few days later, on 21 October 1963, Home found the perfect retort, surprisingly on television, a medium in which he did not naturally thrive. As the chroniclers of Wilson's rise, Anthony Howard and Richard West, recorded:

> Looking the opposite of a staid and stuffy aristocrat – once or twice his face even broke into an urchin smile – he put up the performance of the handsome confident cricketer that he had been in his youth. Even the fast-ball questions (Butler's disappointment, Macleod's and Powell's withdrawal, his own self-confessed ignorance of economics) were dealt with crisply and neatly, and he eventually brought off a full on-drive in the direction of the Leader of the Opposition. Asked whether a 14th Earl was not especially vulnerable to attack by the Labour Party he replied reflectively: 'I suppose Mr Wilson is really, when you come to think of it, the 14th Mr Wilson. I don't see why

criticism should centre on this. Are we to say that all men are equal except peers?' It was a boundary stroke.[39]

So it was. But it didn't deter Wilson from littering his subsequent big city speeches with his version of the ever-powerful British obsession with class and status, which he interwove with his 'white heat' crusade, melding the two in a crucible of outrage. In his setting-out-his-stall speech in Birmingham Town Hall, for example, he quickly swung into his favourite aria:

> We are living in the jet-age but we are governed by an Edwardian establishment mentality. Over the British people lies the chill frost of Tory leadership. They freeze initiative and petrify imagination. They cling to privilege and power for the few, shutting the gates on the many. Tory society is a *closed* society, in which birth and wealth have priority, in which the master-and-servant, landlord-and-tenant mentality is predominant. The Tories have proved that they are incapable of mobilizing Britain to take full advantage of the scientific breakthrough. Their approach and methods are fifty years out of date.[40]

Labour, he went on, would replace that closed society with an open one 'in which brains will take precedence over blue-blood, and craftsmanship will be more important than caste'. The Birmingham audience was then treated to perhaps his most cherished trope. Election year, he declared, brought with it a 'chance to sweep away the grouse-moor conception of Tory leadership and refit Britain with a new image, a new confidence'.[41]

It was the archetype of Alan Watkins's 'dawnism'. It was a dreadful oversimplification – men in labs in white coats prevailing over men in tweeds slaughtering fur and feather on bleak moorlands with retainers beating their way through the bracken – but, for Wilson, it worked. Not only did it fit in with his great Scarborough theme, it also enthused his activists, whose metabolic rate rose pleasurably when privilege was excoriated and the traditional class enemy duffed-up. It made for great political theatre – which now meant television – too. Once the general election campaign was underway in September 1964, Wilson would wait until the red light of the BBC or ITN cameras lit up to indicate he was being beamed live into the evening news bulletin, then turn to look directly into the camera to deliver the message of the night. Very often it was denunciation of the Conservatives, laced with future hope if only the electorate did the right thing. As Lord Poole, who ran the 1964 campaign for the Conservatives, said: 'He's the only really competent political TV performer this country has produced.'[42]

Despite his boss's stylish '14th Mr Wilson' shot to the boundary, Poole could never have contemplated saying the same about Alec Home. Nor would Home himself, especially after encountering an especially candid make-up lady preparing him for a television studio in which he was due to perform. It left such a mark on him that he recorded the exchange in his memoir, *The Way the Wind Blows*:

> In 1963 I had an unpromising start when I was being made up for some Prime Ministerial performance; for my conversation with the young lady who was applying the powder and tan went like this:
>
> Q. Can you not make me look better than I do on television?
> A. No.
> Q. Why not?
> A. Because you have a head like a skull.
> Q. Does not everyone have a head like a skull?
> A. No.
>
> So that was that. The best that I could do for the cartoonist was my half-moon spectacles. Elizabeth [Lady Home] always said that they lost me the 1964 election. So one cannot win.[43]

It was his gift for such self-deprecation – always cheerfully expressed – that made Alec Home, among many other qualities, so likeable, even if it was not a vote winner.

There was a steely side to Alec Home, too, as Harold Macmillan acknowledged when he described him as 'steel painted as wood'. Despite his initial hesitation, he ran a determined final lap in the October 1963 leadership race and entered No. 10 with no illusions about the toughness of the task he faced. 'The fourth and last year of a Parliament is not the ideal time to take over the leadership of a Party and a Government,' he later wrote.[44] And he keenly felt the refusal of Enoch Powell and Iain Macleod to serve under him. He remained convinced for the rest of his life that he lost the 1964 election the day they spurned him: 'Had these two pulled their weight, I have no doubt at all that our short-head defeat would have been converted into a narrow victory.'[45]

Alec Home was Prime Minister for just under a year – 362 days, to be precise; from 19 October 1963 to 16 October 1964. It was a premiership played out in the shadow of the coming general election. His true colours and mettle and, to some extent, his capabilities never became appreciated by the country he led out of a sense of duty rather than ambition. His tenure in Downing Street is remembered, if at all, for only one reform, the abolition of resale price maintenance, which would soon have a profound and cumulative effect upon the retail trade and the domestic economy of the UK.

His first task was to shape his Cabinet. It was noticeably more a matter of continuity than of change. The only striking appointment was restorative rather than innovative, giving Selwyn Lloyd, the principal victim of Macmillan's 'Night of the Long Knives', a place at the Cabinet table once more as Lord Privy Seal and Leader of the House of Commons.

Many years after the political butchery of July 1962, Alec Home told me that he thought Macmillan was never the same prime minister again after wielding the knife.[46] He thought Lloyd had been badly treated. As he said at Lloyd's funeral in the Wirral, he found Selwyn a man who knew 'a time to keep silence, and a time to speak ... He never courted the crowd – he shunned it. He never tried the showmanship of oratory – he disdained it. He was content to be himself – a nice, good, companionable and compassionate man.'[47] In other words, Lloyd and Home were kindred spirits (my judgement, not Home's).

Selwyn Lloyd was on a high on the morning of Saturday 19 October 1963 when at 7.45 he arrived at No. 10 to be told by Home that he wanted him back in the Cabinet. After a day of gentlemanly haggling the two agreed he should lead the House of Commons as Lord Privy Seal. At a Privy Council meeting on Monday 21 October to swear in the new Cabinet, the Queen, Lloyd recalled in his diary, was 'full of smiles. Michael Adeane said that she had told him she was very pleased that I was coming back.' (The Duke of Edinburgh, one the other hand, met Lloyd in a Palace corridor and delivered a characteristic line: 'What they haven't brought you back again, have they?')[48] Thanks to

Alec Home, Selwyn Lloyd had an enjoyable Indian summer on the government front bench. When he dined with Macmillan at the House of Commons the following spring, Macmillan noticed that Lloyd 'has perked up a lot and seems to have no grievance'.[49]

The same could not be said for the serial loser in the events of October 1963, Rab Butler. Lloyd's diary picked up Butler's plangency at that same swearing-in ceremony on 21 October: 'He is very anxious that everyone should say that he has done the right thing.'[50] His time as Foreign Secretary was a rather sad and distinctly unperky coda to a career of great political and public service.

In later years Alec Home used to say it would probably have been better if Butler had succeeded Macmillan; he said it once to me over lunch, during which he was explaining that people are happier if the figure expected to get the job does so.[51] He said the same to his official biographer, Richard Thorpe, who rightly judged that the

> question of whether Rab Butler would have won the 1964 election is one of the great conundrums of postwar political history. Harold Wilson believed that he would have done so.* Rab Butler's great advantage as Prime Minister in 1963 would have been the lack of controversies that dogged Alec Home, who later believed that, as the public had seen Rab Butler as the heir apparent, it might have been better in the end for him to have had the job. Anyone else was seen in some sense as an 'unnatural' successor.[52]

The controversies that most hurt Alec Home during his premiership were intra-party ones when the two Cabinet ministers who would not serve under him, Iain Macleod and Enoch Powell, turned their pens into swords – Macleod in plain sight; Powell under an easily penetrated camouflage. Both of them had initially picked up their writing instruments as part of the rising generation of young Conservative MPs who had entered Parliament in the 1950 or 1951 general elections to argue the case for a more selective and targeted approach to welfare in their pamphlet *The Social Services: Needs and Means*, published in early 1952.[53]

Just over ten years on from their early 'One Nation' days, their

---

* He said this to Richard Thorpe in conversation on 13 November 1981.

targets were not the needy but their closest neighbours in the Conservative Party. In the immediate aftermath of Blackpool, Macleod and Powell had agreed to keep mum about their reasons for refusing to serve under Alec Home. It was the account of *The Fight for the Tory Leadership*, published by the mercurial and combative journalist and would-be politician Randolph Churchill in January 1964, that caused Macleod to put aside all restraint and to use his new position as editor of the *Spectator* to publish perhaps the most famous book review in British political history (at 4,000 words it was certainly one of the longest) under the headline 'The Tory Leadership' in the 17 January edition of the magazine.

Macleod mattered. Not only had he shone as a very young Health Minister in the early 1950s, his place in political history was already assured as the gale-of-change Colonial Secretary who had quickened the bringing of independence to large parts of Africa as described in chapter 4. Even more than that, he was the very talisman of progressive Conservatism for the coming and rising generation of Tories. He was a spell-binder on the political platform, his hunched posture adding physical emphasis to the bite and clarity of his words (as, in a curious way, did his slightly raffish taste for gambling and his participation in international bridge tournaments). Nearly half a century after his death in 1970, the Macleod glow still shines in the memory and the words of some very substantial Conservative figures: in the spring of 2017 Michael Heseltine said about him: 'He represented One Nation Conservatism with a voice that echoed through every corner of the land. He exuded strength in the power of his voice and his personal impact . . . He left a mark on his generation'[54] – and, indeed, on several generations to come.

That enduring mark was made partly by the two words in Macleod's book review that instantly took their place in the enduring lexicon of British political language – 'magic circle'. The term even has its own entry in the *Dictionary of National Biography*.[55] The thrust of Macleod's argument was that a 'magic circle' of old Etonians had fixed the succession for one of their own, that 'from the first day of his premiership to the last, Macmillan was determined that Butler, although incomparably the best qualified of the contenders, should not succeed him'. In Macleod's view, Butler possessed 'the priceless quality of being able to do any job better than you think he will'. And to round off his denunciation of the 'magic circle', Macleod claimed that Randolph Churchill's book was the 'trailer' for the 'screen play' memoirs of the magician-in-chief himself, Harold Macmillan.[56]

The arch-fixer shrugged off the Macleod attack with studied (perhaps feigned) insouciance about the Old Etonian claim, but the outgoing PM nonetheless realized how damaging Macleod's piece really was in an election year. Macleod, he wrote in his diary,

> has fairly put the 'cat among the pigeons'. His article is very cleverly written on the whole . . . But the really damaging part of his attack is on the alleged determination of the small inner ring (Macmillan; Redmayne; Manningham-Buller etc.) to have an Etonian! This, of course, just suits the press today, most of which loves to attack Eton and the 'aristocracy'. It's all great nonsense, but it touches off the curious 'inverted snobbery' emotion wh is very strong today.[57]

Far from laying a deep, anti-Butler plot, Macmillan, recalling, no doubt, that his prostate had struck just after his decision to soldier on to fight the 1964 general election, noted ruefully that 'had it not been for my illness, I shd now be Prime Minister myself'.[58]

The two politicians most damaged by the 'magic circle' article were Alec Home and Macleod himself. Home rang Macmillan for advice: 'I thought he wd be wise to ignore the whole thing. Controversies of this kind (not principles but gossip and personalities) are like fires. They must be fanned if they are to burn.'[59] But Home was genuinely seared by the heat of Macleod's philippic and his wounds did not heal. Interestingly enough, as Macleod's *Spectator* piece recalled, relations between the two men had been very civil when Macleod refused to serve in October 1963 (his two conversations, wrote Macleod, 'were very friendly but brief').

As Richard Thorpe explained, Home was 'deeply saddened, not for his own reputation or feelings, but by what he considered irreparable damage to the Conservatives' success in the election'. It was not the 'magic circle' passage that disturbed Home most but what Thorpe called

> a less regarded point towards the end of the article: 'we have confessed that the Tory Party could not find a Prime Minister in the House of Commons at all' . . . Alec Home regarded the Macleod article as a

crucial contribution to the Tory defeat at the election, and on the day he resigned as Prime Minister he was to be seen pacing the drawing-room floor of Selwyn Lloyd's flat in Buckingham Gate, blaming the defeat on Macleod in language those who were present had not heard him use before.

In fact, in 1990 Home told Thorpe that he (in Thorpe's words) 'believed it was the single most important factor in the party's narrow defeat in the general election of October 1964'[60] (an interesting thought – but, in my judgement, the most potent element influencing the outcome was the warmth of Wilson's 'white heat' approach). Home already had a suspicion about what might be lurking in Macleod's brain, which was well known for its prowess in political calculation. It had been seeded when Macleod and Powell came to tell him why they would not join his administration:

> The reason which they gave to me was that they did not believe that a man with my social background could win a General Election for the Conservative Party at that time in the twentieth century. I said that I thought they were wrong; but that if that was their reason for declining to serve I could only accept it and be sorry. I had a feeling that at the back of their minds was the calculation that, although we might lose in 1964, the next opportunity would not be long and that then we should win under another leader. But in politics one cannot do such clever mathematical sums and hope that events will conform. When a General Election comes it is necessary to fight flat out to win.[61]

Macleod's 'magic circle' article was undoubtedly a calculated act, but there is evidence that it was a misjudged one. Macleod simply did not anticipate the degree of animus his words would arouse. As Rob Shepherd, Macleod's biographer, wrote thirty years later, 'the depth of hostility that it provoked towards him caused him to confess privately to close colleagues that he thought it had ended his political career'.[62] His friend and fellow liberal Conservative Humphry Berkeley remembered that Macleod had told him over lunch at the White Tower that

> [h]e couldn't bear to be near the House of Commons – he was being shunned by everybody. And there was a period of two or three weeks when he didn't go to the House of Commons. I said to him: 'Look, you

can't abandon us.' He replied: 'I can't bear that smoking-room.' So I said: 'OK, after a ten o'clock vote we'll go and have a drink there.' We went and had a drink there and were cut by every single person in the room.[63]

But, in the longer run, Macleod's 'magic circle' phrase changed the rules and, thereby, the faces of the Conservative leadership for ever. Once Alec Home had lost the general election, he commissioned a change in election procedures for the party leader. Whether or not a 'magic circle' had been in operation, and I think it had in the sense of there being a strong anti-Butler animus at work which Macmillan used to powerful effect, in future there would be no more such cabals. Instead, votes would prevail – those cast by members of the Conservative Parliamentary Party.[64] As Ted Heath once told me, without that rule change he could never have expected to lead his party and, therefore, form a government.[65] The same can be said of Margaret Thatcher, John Major and Theresa May (though perhaps not of David Cameron). Macleod's article had lit a fuse that changed his party for ever.

Enoch Powell wanted to change things too, but he sought a politico-economic restoration not a sociological revolution – a return to free-market principles and a reversal of what he regarded as the semi-socialist whiggery of the Macmillan legacy. Powell at this stage in his political life had not achieved an equivalent resonance to Macleod either within his party or beyond. That would have to wait for another four years until his fissile speech on immigration policy in Birmingham in April 1968. Very few political connoisseurs, for example, would have picked up his extraordinary speech on St George's Eve in April 1961 to the City of London branch of the Royal Society of St George, which his biographer Simon Heffer regards as the leitmotif oration of his political life[66] – his notion of Englishness and the policies that flow from a living past:

> From this continuous life of a united people in its island home spring, as from the soil of England, all that is peculiar in the gifts and achievements of the English nation, its laws, its literature, its freedom, its self-discipline. All its impact on the outer world – in earlier colonies, in later *Pax Britannica*, in government and law giving, in commerce and in thought – has flowed from impulses generated here.

And what went into the making of these 'impulses'? Powell enumerated them in a combination of language and image that would – or should – have secured the place of this scholar romantic in postwar British political history even if he had not turbo-charged the immigration debate in the late 1960s. His words were delivered with an intensity heightened by the rise and fall of his voice that made him sound a little like an air-raid siren with a Birmingham accent:

> Backwards travels our gaze, beyond the grenadiers and the philosophers of the eighteenth century, beyond the pikemen and the preachers of the seventeenth, back through the brash adventurous days of the first Elizabeth and the hard materialism of the Tudors, and there at last we find them, or seem to find them, in many a village church, beneath the tall tracery of a perpendicular East window and the coffered ceiling of the chantry chapel.
>
> From brass and stone, from line and effigy, their eyes look out at us, as we gaze into them, as if we would win some answer from their inscrutable silence. 'Tell us what it is that binds us together; show us the clue that leads through a thousand years; whisper to us the secret of this charmed life of England, that we in our time may know how to hold it fast.'[67]

Three years later, free of office (he was Minister of Health when he addressed the Society of St George), his intervention took inscrutability to melodramatic heights, even though it was addressed to the hard practicalities of political economy rather than the ethereal elements of people and nation.

Powell's intervention was prompted by the austere and bookish editor of *The Times*, Sir William Haley (the bête noire of Macmillan at Profumo-time). Haley asked Powell to write a series of pieces on the current condition of Conservatism. Powell agreed on the condition that his authorship would be concealed by anonymity. As Simon Heffer wrote in his 1998 biography of Powell:

> Haley did not let him down. Corrections to the articles were handled by Haley himself, from his home and not from his office. Powell and his wife drove to Haley's home in Blackheath after dark to deliver the articles; and the typescripts were destroyed afterwards. When Powell

was paid it was in cash, so no transaction went through the newspaper's accounts. The secret has remained safe to this day.[68]

Thus, the wartime brigadier in military intelligence carried out his clandestine operation by night in the south-eastern suburbs of London. His articles were published under the by-line 'A Conservative'. But you didn't need to have worked at Bletchley Park to decode their authorship. Each piece was laced with Enochian threnodies, some of them a pure match in style and content of his St George's Eve peroration three years earlier. No other leading Conservative of the day could have sculpted a paragraph like this:

> National pride, call it patriotism, has always been the mainspring of the Conservative Party, long before England awoke one morning to find that her factories and fleets had won an Empire. Has the Conservative Party of today the courage and the candour to base its patriotism on Britain's reality not her dreams?

Powell's critique ran over three days – 1–3 April 1964 – under the strapline 'A PARTY IN SEARCH OF A PATTERN'.[69] The first instalment, headlined 'From the Years of Protest to the Years of Disasters', tore into those Tory consensus-seekers who had reacted to the Conservative defeat in the 1945 election by moving too close to Labour's thinking on welfare and the economy in order to bring the party back from the political 'wilderness'. Particularly galling, I suspect, for those who had sat beside him in Macmillan's government during what 'A Conservative' called the 'year of disasters 1962–63' was this passage:

> The Common Market negotiations had failed; but the Party remained committed to whatever the implications had been ... The Prime Minister-making operation of October placed at the head of the party someone politically neutral, unidentified with any recognisable strand of Conservative thought. The cry of 'modernisation' took on a shriller note, and now the Cabinet contained a bigger proportion of technocrats. Ministers who would be doing for doing's sake.

The second article, 'The Field Where the Biggest Failures Lie', reasserted the claims of a free-market Conservatism against what Powell regarded as a disastrous pursuit of economic and industrial intervention:

Embarrassment . . . is inherent in the recent series of policies, virtually all originating in the present parliament, where economic advantage is claimed as the object and the result of intervention, or at least guidance, by public authority. The location of industry policy and the regional development plans . . . the gradual approach to the planning of growth by NEDC [the National Economic Development Council] and of incomes by the NIC [National Incomes Commission] – these and similar policies . . . represent a shift in policy as definite as it is recent. The difficulty is to reconcile it with the conviction of a party which bases itself, and must base itself, on the belief that economic ends are best achieved by the mechanism of competitive enterprise.

Powell concluded that the 'dilemma has to be resolved, and to be seen to be resolved. It can only be resolved one way'. It was – or began to be – fifteen years later when Margaret Thatcher entered No. 10 in the spring of 1979.

Powell's final arrow, aimed at what he saw as the delusions of contemporary Conservatism, struck at the heart of the whole notion of the Commonwealth. The old empire hand who had fallen in love with British India had turned dyspeptic sceptic and now sought, as the headline of article three declared: 'Patriotism Based on Reality Not on Dreams'.

It's difficult now to convey just how much the Commonwealth mattered to a country attempting a grand-scale shedding of territorial empire with as much dignity as possible. The idea of Commonwealth was crucial to that dignity and to having a good story to tell about both exit and aftermath. Powell spared neither right nor left – including Wilson's and Labour's stress on the Commonwealth in terms both of international politics and of trade (a widely shared view that is hard to recall over half a century on):

The Commonwealth has really become a gigantic farce. Most people, including most Conservatives, know this, and in their hearts they despise the politicians who keep the farce going.

Nor did Powell spare the still considerable string of British military bases across the world – the 'expensive and delusory souvenirs' of an empire in which he had believed and a Commonwealth in which he did not. Powell always seemed to regard the Commonwealth as a valueless psychological comfort blanket for imperium lost.

Powell's triptych of articles was merciless, and unmistakably Enoch. Macmillan knew who it was straightaway and he did not care for it one bit:

> The Times is publishing a series of 3 articles on 'Conservatism since the War'. Two have appeared and one is to be published tomorrow. They are vicious and defeatist, written by an old-fashioned Liberal. The general view is that the author is Enoch Powell. I don't think they will do great damage, but it is all part of Sir W. Haley's rancour against us all.[70]

Whatever Macmillan thought, Powell's articles certainly did not help in an election year. They served as a tocsin of dissent, a critique of consensual orthodoxy of the mixed economy/welfare state post-war settlement, whose sounds would get louder and louder as the economic underpinnings of the British New Deal progressively crumbled. Margaret Thatcher would later write: 'Undoubtedly Enoch was our finest intellect.'[71] She thought Powell and Macleod were wrong not to serve under Home, whom she supported,[72] but over the decades of her path to No. 10, she absorbed his critique of state intervention in the economy.

I suspect Alec Home listened, too, to one aspect of the Enochian critique in particular. Like Powell, Home was not a believer in the big state and he craved a more streamlined Whitehall and Cabinet system; he told me during a conversation in 1985 that, had he won the 1964 election, he would have invited Powell back into the Cabinet and unleashed him upon the reform of Whitehall.[73] What a titanic clash that would have been! (I discovered later from Powell that Home had never mentioned this to him.)

So in 1964 Powell's critique from the right created a pincer movement with Harold Wilson's modernist attack entering from the other flank, leaving the Douglas-Home government apparently wallowing in a state of entropic decay. Or did it? There was one member of the class of 1950 who was energetically pursuing a course designed to demonstrate precisely the opposite at the very time that Powell and Macleod were plunging their nibs into the administration's flesh – Alec Home's President of the Board of Trade, Ted Heath. And his instrument was not a pen but the price tags of goods in the shops. Heath was determined to abolish resale price maintenance (RPM), which he did, in the teeth of Cabinet doubts, so giving a powerful and sustained stimulus to the consumer revolution we have been living through ever since.

RPM was the arrangement whereby the price of any individual good was kept the same across all retail outlets, from the traditional open-all-hours corner shop to the spreading supermarket sector. The Board of Trade had waited for years for a minister to tackle this particular restrictive practice, but cornershop Britain had a 'there'll-always-be-an-England' quality to it. And behind every counter, so the party managers thought, there lurked a natural Conservative voter and, quite often, a pillar of the local Conservative Association.

But when Heath was sent to the Board of Trade, the man and the hour were met. As so often in reforming bursts, there was a trigger – or triggers, in the case of RPM in 1964. The Labour MP John Stonehouse was putting through a private members' bill in the House of Commons to abolish it, and the supermarkets were finding a way of undermining it by giving their customers trading stamps which could be used for future purchases.* I suspect that Alec Home himself was a stranger to the supermarket trolley and did not warm to the finer points of pricing policy. But his support was crucial for Heath as the Cabinet was loaded with doubters about the wisdom of abolishing RPM in an election year. In a conversation in 1985, I asked Alec Home about it:

> Ted Heath was very keen and nobody else was very much. I thought it was right and therefore we went ahead. It probably cost us seats at the general election. That was a clear case where the Bill was right and the timing was wrong. But I didn't feel I could overrule Ted Heath on this particular occasion because he was essentially right on what the Bill proposed ... It certainly lost us quite a lot of Conservative votes. But then if a thing is so patently right ... you have to take the decision and risk it.[74]

* The Green Shield Stamp was very much an artefact of Sixties Britain and led to some funny, if blasphemous graffiti ('Jesus Saves – Green Shield Stamps', is one I recall in particular).

An even greater risk would have been Ted Heath resigning over RPM. With Macleod and Powell refusing to serve, to have lost Heath would have been immensely damaging.

In his memoirs Heath admits that when the resistance to RPM abolition was at its height on the Conservative backbenches in April 1964, '[a]lthough I did not threaten to do so, I was close to resigning at that point, and I believe Alec and the party recognized that'.[75] He always looked back on RPM abolition as 'one of the most satisfying successes of my ministerial career' and, to his credit, he came to admit that he 'underestimated the need for thrashing this question out among ourselves at an early stage. If we had enjoyed the luxury of more time before the next general election, we could undoubtedly have placated almost all of the opposition to RPM abolition.'[76]

Though Heath never headed the Treasury, he can claim to have been as influential in the long term as any Chancellor of the Exchequer if judged by the criterion of how and where we shop. The abolition of RPM, together with the coming of the motorway network and the out-of-town shopping centre led Britain from corner shop and the occasional tiny high-street supermarket to the hypermarket and the shopping mall.

Heath's conduct of RPM reform displayed the range of qualities that later marked his premiership – the mixture of high purpose and attention to detail laced with stubbornness and a certain lack of sympathetic warmth to those who disagreed with him or who worried about aspects of modernization. Of the class of 1950, Macleod was the inspiration, Powell the romantic and Heath the technocrat.

There was a fourth member of the cohort who was absolutely crucial to the electoral fortunes of the Douglas-Home government – Reggie Maudling, the Chancellor of the Exchequer, who was a mixture of sharp intelligence, apparent indolence and abundant affability. Could the reflation over which he presided – the 'Maudling boom' – create a tide that would carry the Conservatives back once more into office as Macmillan's consumer boom had done so successfully in 1959?

Maudling had no time for Powell's free-market alternative. He thought privately that Powell 'talked utter balls' on economics but sent him jolly thank-you notes when Powell put copies of his speeches in the post. In January 1964, a particularly Enochian denunciation of the 'hocus pocus' of incomes policy in a speech to the National Liberal Forum received the following reply:

My dear Enoch

Many thanks for sending me a copy of your full text. I'm sure your intention, as you say, was helpful: unfortunately our friends in the press have not taken it so! But that is not unusual.

Reggy.[77]

Not one sliver of the Powell analysis fitted Maudling's push for growth, which rested above all on a surge in public spending and a willingness to ride out the balance-of-payments difficulties. As his top official economic adviser in the Treasury, Alec Cairncross, later wrote, Maudling

> took risks with the balance of payments in the hope of a breakthrough in economic growth in which we had little faith; and delayed – in the end abandoned – action of any kind to check an obvious boom in 1964, comforting himself with the thought that, if necessary, the pound could be allowed to float, and ensuring that the alternatives of import quotas and an import surcharge were given careful study.[78]

As Chancellor, Maudling had a mission to spring the UK from its 'strait-jacket' of balance-of-payments problems that placed unnerving pressure on the pound in an era of fixed exchange rates and locked successive governments into dispiriting cycles of stop-go policies in which spasms of growth were followed by deflations.[79] He defended his cause right up until his sad death from cirrhosis of the liver in February 1979, aged only sixty-one.

In 1978, he recalled his 1963–4 strategy with the kind of self-ironic drollery that appealed to so many of his colleagues:

> So we went for expansion, quite deliberately, with our eyes open, recognizing the dangers. The prize to be obtained, the prospect of expansion without inflation, the end of stop-go and a break-out from the constrictions of the past, was a glittering one. My policy has been described as a 'dash for freedom'. I think that is ascribing to me,

rather unusually, an excess of energy and enthusiasm. In fact the whole policy was deliberate, calculated and coherent. No one could guarantee success, but the chances were high, and the alternatives were drab and depressing.[80]

The deliberately expansionary budget of April 1963 was based on a reduction in income tax and a large increase in public expenditure in pursuit of the NEDC's agreed target of 4 per cent annual growth in GDP. The Treasury's Public Expenditure White Paper of December 1963 laid out a 17.5 per cent increase in spending between the financial years 1963–4 and 1967–8,[81] which all depended, if crisis was to be avoided, on that historically very high rate of growth being sustained over the coming five years.

Given the perspective of hindsight – or even at the time – it is difficult not to sympathize with the doubters within the Treasury about the practicality of the dash for growth, for all the attraction of bursting out of the straitjacket and Maudling's affable persuasiveness. As that connoisseur of postwar Chancellors, Edmund Dell, later wrote: 'The best that could be said of it was that it was an hallucination. Maudling's 1963 Budget is the ultimate example of the effect of a combination of politics, ignorance, and hubris on economic management.'[82] A besetting problem – and a near perpetual temptation – for UK governments is to plan for the consumption of the fruits of growth before it has happened.

The Maudling 'dash for growth' left scars on the Treasury. Roy Jenkins, whose chancellorship spanned 1968–70, judged that Treasury officials 'became in my view somewhat obsessed by 1964 guilt'. His Permanent Secretary, the direct and astringent Sir Douglas Allen, blamed his predecessor, Sir William Armstrong, for having, in Jenkins's words, 'behaved weakly in his restraint of Maudling in the spring and summer of that pre-election splurge and balance of payments disaster, and he was determined not to repeat this fault in his 1970 dealings with me'.[83]

In the first Prime Minister of his chancellorship, Macmillan, Maudling had a bone-bred expansionist. In his second he had a man far from at home with public-expenditure surveys and growth forecasts, though the two men got on well. In his memoirs, Maudling offers a shrewd sketch of Home and his appeal to the Conservative Party's male membership, who, as Maudling expressed it, 'regarded him as the sort of man they would like to be themselves: a good athlete; not brilliant but intelligent; a man of charm, integrity and balance', adding, revealingly, that he 'was good at taking advice, he delegated and I believe, though I am biased, he was pursuing the right economic policy'.[84] Maudling's dash for growth and the fear of a deteriorating balance of payments in the autumn of 1964 did cause some headaches – for Home over the timing of the election and a monster one for Harold Wilson and Jim Callaghan, Maudling's successor in the Treasury, in the form of an £800 million balance-of-payments deficit.

What did Alec Home achieve in the field in which he had made his name – foreign affairs? Deep in the Cold War secret state and, therefore, visible to only a tiny number of people, he oversaw the running-in of the refinements from the post-Cuba review of the procedures for the transition to a Third World War. Having replaced Selwyn Lloyd on his sacking in 1962 as one of Macmillan's two alternative nuclear decision-takers (the first being Rab Butler), he was already privy to the most daunting drills of all, involving nuclear retaliation. He inherited the new arrangement whereby in a fast-moving emergency, the Prime Minister could make the decision to move to the Precautionary Stage without consulting the Cabinet.[85] In line with the practice begun by Macmillan in 1961, Home had to put his mind to the choice of his own nuclear deputies.

For a naturally decisive man it took him a while. On Christmas Eve, always a moment for a last-minute catching-up of unfinished business, Sir Burke Trend, the Cabinet Secretary, sent him a gentle reminder:

> You may remember that I mentioned to you a short time ago that it would be desirable that you should approve the appointment of two Ministerial Deputies to yourself, who would be empowered to authorise nuclear retaliation if, at the critical moment, you were not available. You said that you would like to reflect further about this; and if you have the opportunity to do so during the holiday, we could then arrange for the necessary instructions to be sent to the selected ministers early in the New Year.

Trend helpfully suggested those to whom the special nuclear responsibility might fall:

> You will recall that Mr Macmillan, when Prime Minister, appointed yourself and Mr Butler as his Deputies for this purpose. I am not sure, however, that the choice need necessarily be determined by seniority; and you may think it would be appropriate to appoint Mr Butler and either Mr Heath or Mr Selwyn Lloyd or Mr Thorneycroft [who remained as Minister of Defence through the Macmillan–Home transition].

Trend added a rider:

> On present plans one of the two Deputies would remain with you in London, while the other would proceed to a separate location from which nuclear retaliation could be authorised even if London were destroyed. It would be convenient if, when you have selected the two Deputies, you would indicate the role which you would like each of them to fill.[86]

Alec Home did decide over Christmas and replied to Trend's minute on New Year's Eve:

> Butler and Thorneycroft. A word please about the roles. Do we want a third Deputy if Thorneycroft is tied to Defence H.Q. and occupied with its problems?[87]

Not until April 1964 was it finally resolved. Thorneycroft was thought likely to be too preoccupied with defence operational matters at such a critical moment. So Butler would stay with the Prime Minister in London and Selwyn Lloyd would be despatched to the RAF Bomber Command bunker in High Wycombe rather than to TURNSTILE in the Cotswolds, which, as we have seen, it was thought Russian intelligence had rumbled.[88] No doubt, if the Cold War had shown signs of flaring up in the early months of 1964, the dispositions would have been made more swiftly. It didn't – though the Douglas-Home government did face its own crisis.

It had to do with buses, not missiles. Leyland buses were built in Lancashire, and some of them were destined for export to the streets of Havana. President Johnson became fixated on this breach, as he saw it, of the trade embargo with Castro's Cuba. Home and LBJ had had the briefest of meetings after President Kennedy's funeral in

November and had agreed to talk again in Washington in February.[89]
In the meantime, the Leyland contract (which was in place before the
missile crisis) came up for renewal in early January 1964. It was
announced that it would run for another five years, supplying $10 mil-
lion worth of buses (with an option for a further 1,000 of them
thereafter) and $1 million worth of spare parts.

LBJ hit the phone to convey the warmth of his feelings about
this to the Prime Minister. Home drolly replied that buses did not
exactly pose a nuclear threat to the United States. A month later
Home and Butler set off for Washington anticipating a further
presidential eruption of the legendary LBJ kind. When they met in the
White House, the Prime Minister, firmly if emolliently, told the President that for him 'to go to the House of Commons and say that the
government was taking steps to restrict trade would bring about a
strong anti-American feeling, and that would be a very bad thing'.[90]

But it was poor Rab Butler on his visit to Washington in May 1964
who had the President unleash both barrels on him over what were
becoming the most politically charged buses in the long history of
motor transport. Rab Butler liked creating little scenes around himself and was a keen if somewhat detached observer of such scenes
created by others. In the White House that morning he found rich
pickings:

> The meeting took place in a small study with only President Johnson,
> McGeorge Bundy [his National Security Advisor], David Harlech
> [formerly Ormsby-Gore] (who still felt deeply the loss of Kennedy, but
> whose value in Washington was as great as ever) and myself. Dean
> [Rusk, Secretary of State] only attended for a few minutes and had
> shown previously great unwillingness to come.

With good reason. He knew only too well what was about to happen. Butler, at his most feline, resumes the story:

> The President launched immediately into Cuba trade. He explained
> that [Richard] Nixon or some other Republican opponent would take
> full advantage of the fact that he, LBJ, was giving me coffee and I was
> trading with Castro. He besought me to send the bill for the Leyland

buses and other items to his ranch in Texas and he would pay the account. Alternatively I was to invoice the material to Bundy and he would pay up. After he had been going on somewhat violently for five minutes a telephone flashed. Disregarding us, he spoke firmly into the receiver for a long stretch of time, apparently giving instructions to a political boss to get something through the Senate or the House. He kept using the expression 'fix him' or 'send him to me and I will see him whoever I am with and whatever I am doing'. This call took up quite a part of the interview and revealed the man's intense political preoccupation.

Rab Butler was not really built to deal with a man like LBJ. 'I believe', he wrote in his memoir, 'that he never let up at all and that politics was his hobby and his life.'[91]

David Harlech wrote in his valedictory despatch from Washington two years later that Johnson was 'one of the most egotistical men I have met. His political talents are undoubtedly of a high order and his "populist" approach to the problems of his country is in tune with the broad traditional instinct of Americans – certainly more so than the slightly sceptical, highly sophisticated and almost aristocratic approach of President Kennedy.' Harlech added intriguingly: 'The thought of the impression he would make in a *tête-à-tête* with General de Gaulle is too horrendous to contemplate.'[92] One thing is sure: he would not have disrupted a conversation with the titan of the Élysée to take a telephone call.

The great political uncertainty of the spring of 1964 for domestic politics was not the future of the Leyland order (which was delivered) but the timing of the general election. Among the first Home consulted was Harold Macmillan, magician of the 1959 victory – a move both kindly and shrewd that, no doubt, brought the old man a measure of consolation in his retirement. Home told his ex-chief that there were some in the Cabinet such as Maudling and the Minister of Agriculture, Christopher Soames, who wished for a June election. His own instincts were for October. So were Macmillan's. On 1 April the veteran operator sent his successor a memorandum fleshing out the case for October:

1. I have thought further about the questions which we discussed on March 26th.

2. The Budget is an instrument of policy. It should be the servant and not the master.

3. If there is to be an election in *June*, there should be a standstill Budget (except for minor adjustments) – and that is no *increase* and no revision of taxation.

4. If the election is to be in *October*, increases in tobacco and spirits are tolerable. Beer is doubtful. No betting tax.

5. *Date of Election*. I am coming more and more a partisan for October and for the following reasons:

   a) The Party in Parliament has been thoroughly upset by RPM. This reacts on the constituencies.

   b) Since the Bill cannot be carried till the middle of May, this confusion will injuriously affect a June election.

   c) It is always an advantage to an *opposition* to have Parliament in session. It is therefore an advantage to the Government to have an interval between the end of Parliament and the Election. This was proved in 1959.

   d) The decision will ultimately be on almost Presidential lines. Therefore, the longer Wilson has to become i) a bore ii) mistrusted as a crook, the better.

   e) *After* a summer holiday, the mood of the people is better. It was in 1959.

6. *Against* this is the argument 'You are hanging on to the bitter end etc.'. But I think you could meet this (at least to some extent) by a clear and simple statement of intentions in April.[93]

Home talked to Butler and other colleagues. On 9 April he made the announcement. It was to be October. Selwyn Lloyd pencilled it into his diary – 15 October 1964.[94] So it was.

Macmillan's use of the words 'on almost Presidential lines' was telling. In 1962–3 there was a flowering of the debate about prime ministerial government gradually usurping collective Cabinet government and a growing presidentialism in the conduct of political competition with John Mackintosh (then a professor and later a

448

Labour MP) pushing the prime ministerial line,[95] as did the Shadow Education Minister, Dick Crossman, in his celebrated 'Introduction' to the new Fontana edition of Walter Bagehot's 1867 classic, *The English Constitution*.[96]

Wilson, whose whole life seemed in some respects a preparation for an assault on Downing Street, may have fitted into this frame. Alec Home, a most reluctant premier, certainly did not. The essential Home came out, I think, in a conversation I had many years later with Derek Mitchell, who had succeeded Tim Bligh as his Principal Private Secretary in No. 10. 'He was', said Mitchell, 'extraordinarily kind and courteous. He had ... a sort of aristocrat's genuine ease in sizing people up, making them comfortable and generally inspiring affection.'

Mitchell explained:

People also liked the high degree of informality. The girls in the Garden Room [the Downing Street secretaries] liked the fact that there'd be a grandchild parked outside in a pram ... And in the flat where he and Elizabeth almost camped out during the week, one saw the flowers that had been brought down from Scotland, the suitcase that lay on the floor, opened but not unpacked, ready for the lid to be closed again on Friday evening when they retired, with some obvious relief, back to the country where they liked to be.[97]

Chance gave me an opportunity to ask Alec Home about this when, with my BBC Radio 4 producer, I was waiting for the taxi to take us back from The Hirsel to Berwick-upon-Tweed railway station after recording an interview in the spring of 1989. Alec Home pointed out a magnolia and invited me to admire it (which I did), explaining that it was flowering for the first time in twenty-five years. I seized the moment.

HENNESSY: You love it here don't you?
HOME: Yes.
HENNESSY: You don't like being away from here do you?
HOME: No.
HENNESSY: You never really wanted to be Prime Minister did you?
HOME: Terrible intrusion in one's private life.[98]

No doubt he did not want to lose the premiership when he did, as his hard words about Macleod in Selwyn Lloyd's flat attest. But I believed absolutely what he said to me nearly twenty-five years later. Certainly Harold Wilson would never have thought that, let alone said it. The 1964 general election was indeed to be a contest between a gentleman and a player.

8

Wisps of Tomorrow

We must not day-dream of affluence unless we are seriously determined to create it. It will not come by itself . . . Although we could probably muddle through the next ten years by making minor adjustments as we go along, I believe we shall be running into great danger if we do not use the first part of this period to study most carefully the various possibilities of automation and its implications and to decide on a course of action which would lead to the smoothest possible transition into this age of plenty.

> *Sir Leon Bagrit, 'The Age of Automation',*
> *BBC Reith Lectures, 1964*[1]

. . . the right of the individual to live his private life free from the intolerant prejudices of others or the arrogant interference of the state and the police.

> *Roy Jenkins, on the 'seven great issues of*
> *today and tomorrow', 1959*[2]

The press, the public, the political parties, were full of enthusiasm for higher education, especially university education.

> *John Carswell on the aftermath of*
> *the 1963 Robbins Report*[3]

So dazzling is the memory of Harold Wilson's 1963 Scarborough Party Conference speech, and so fickle other collective political memories, virtually nobody can recall that at the centre of Rab Butler's unrousing speech to his own party's conference in Blackpool on

Saturday 12 October 1963 lay a heartfelt passage about the party's policies for the general election of 1964:

> A first feature of this programme is a new and exciting break-through on the educational front. For on the future of education not only the efficiency of our society but the fulfilment of our ideals depends. In the nineteenth century a Conservative government completed the process of making primary education free and compulsory for all. In 1944 I played my part in opening the doors of secondary education to all. Now a fresh challenge and opportunity await us. Already seven new universities are being created, and plans are in hand to increase substantially the capacity of existing universities, colleges of advanced technology and teacher training colleges. These programmes will be developed, in the light of the Robbins Committee Report. Our aim is higher education for every boy and girl in the land who can benefit from it.[4]

Robbins was one of the master reports of the twentieth century and a great liberal document, which sought to do for the life of the mind in the UK what the Beveridge Report had set out to do for the well-being of its physical bodies twenty-one years earlier, and is often seen as the progenitor of the new 'plateglass' universities (to distinguish them from the existing 'red bricks' and the ancient 'ivy-clads').

The septet of new universities Butler mentioned at Blackpool are now very much a familiar part of the intellectual landscape and have contributed mightily to the stock of knowledge: Sussex; York; Lancaster; Warwick; Essex; Kent and East Anglia (the University of Stirling was added later, as was Coleraine). As Butler indicated, the Macmillan and Douglas-Home governments, in addition to the new foundations that came to life in the 1960s, accepted, too, the Robbins proposals for an expansion of student numbers within all university institutions old and new.

Both of the scientific and scholarly inquiries the Macmillan government commissioned in 1961–2 as part of its modernization-of-Britain theme reported in the first days of the Douglas-Home premiership and they are worth looking at in tandem. Robbins was essentially about human capital as the age cohorts shaped by Rab Butler's secondary-education-for-all 1944 statute reached university and college age. The other, the Trend Report on 'Organization of Civil Science', was the first look at how the state should structure itself as both the provider and patron of scientific research and development since the path-breaking 1918 Haldane Report commissioned by Lloyd George during the Great War.[5]

Both Robbins and Trend, from their different angles, revisited the 1946 Barlow Report on scientific manpower. As did Harold Wilson at Scarborough, all three touched upon a persistent failure of the UK to industrialize its science – a problem that continues to preoccupy Whitehall and Westminster to this day.

There is a pronounced and enduring choreography about the inquiries that provide a recitative to the grand opera of British central government defence reviews – now called strategic defence and security reviews – industrial strategies, to which R&D in science and technology is integral, being the most prominent. If you strip away the reference to the British Empire and, by implication, to Josef Stalin's Soviet Union, the opening paragraph of the Barlow Report, for example, would serve quite comfortably as the nose of an inquiry over seventy years on. It certainly fitted the early 1960s in which Trend and Robbins were reporting:

> We do not think it is necessary to preface our report by stating at length the case for developing our scientific resources. Never before has the importance of science been more widely recognised or so many hopes of future progress and welfare founded upon the scientist. By way of introduction, therefore, we confine ourselves to pointing out that least of all nations can Great Britain afford to neglect whatever benefits the scientist can confer upon her. If we are to maintain our position in the world and restore and improve our standard of living, we have no alternative but to strive for that scientific achievement without which our trade will wither, our colonial Empire will remain undeveloped and our lives and freedom will be at the mercy of a potential aggressor.[6]

Barlow, a senior civil servant and Second Secretary to the Treasury, had a lustrous team at his side, including the great physicist Sir Edward Appleton and the zoologist Solly Zuckerman as members and C. P. Snow advising. And his committee had impact. The doubling of trained scientists emerging each year from 2,500 to 5,000 was achieved in four years, though the recommendation that two or three new UK institutions of the calibre of Caltech and MIT in the USA be instituted was not followed through.[7]

Burke Trend, another Treasury Second Secretary when appointed to his committee, a classicist with an acute sense of the importance of science, sought to reform, revamp and reinvigorate the machinery of central government to bring greater coherence and verve to both government ministries and the state-financed research councils.[8] The committee's recommendations, when set alongside those of Robbins, which urged a rapid rise in science and technology places in higher education (74,000 by 1967; 174,000 by 1980[9]), created a moment when far more than a whiff of change seemed possible. In science writer Tom Wilkie's words, 'for the first time since the Great War, it looked as if the UK might truly equip itself as a modern industrial nation'.[10]

The Robbins Report was – and remains – an inspiring document. Lionel Robbins, a great LSE economist who had served with distinction in the War Cabinet Office's Economic Section in the 1940s, was a man of considerable physical presence with a powerful, leonine face topped by a striking array of silver hair. His own chapter on 'Aims and Principles' blended both the beauty and utility of the life of the mind. Written in an age before the poetry of university life had been crowded out by the plumbing,[11] fifty years later the Robbins Report seems closer to Cardinal John Henry Newman's *Idea of a University** than it does to today's almost entirely utilitarian approaches to tertiary education.[12]

Robbins recognized that the prime purpose of his inquiry was that

> seventeen years after the passing of the great Education Act of 1944, which inaugurated momentous changes in the organisation of education

---

* Newman's *Idea of a University* was first published in 1873 and was effectively a compilation of two earlier works: *Discourses on the Scope and Nature of University Education*, published in 1852, which comprised ten lectures designed to prepare the ground for the creation of the Catholic University of Ireland; and a second work, *Lectures and Essays on University Subjects*, a collection of lectures and articles that Newman wrote as the founding president of the university, which was published in 1859.

in the schools, we have been asked to consider whether changes of a like order of magnitude are needed at a higher level.[13]

They undoubtedly were. He continued with the following caveat:

[W]hile emphasising that there is no betrayal of values when institutions of higher education teach what will be of some practical use, we must postulate that what is taught should be taught in such a way as to promote the general powers of the mind. The aim should be to produce not mere specialists but rather cultivated men and women.[14]

Add this to the 1960 recommendation of the Anderson Committee that university grants (fees and a means-tested measure of maintenance) should be available to all would-be students possessing two A-levels and the offer of a university place,[15] and a golden patch of higher education beckoned – not least because all the main political parties signed up to the Robbins nostrums. The Conservative manifesto for the 1964 election, *Prosperity with a Purpose*, declared: 'There will be places for 100,000 extra students by 1968, and for a steadily growing number after that.'[16] *Let's Go with Labour for the New Britain* promised a 'massive expansion in higher, further and university education'.[17] The Liberals *Think for Yourself – Vote Liberal*, pledged the party 'to double full time places in higher education in the next 10 years'.[18]

In addition to these political promises, part of the offering of the early Sixties was the growing prospect of what we now dub the third industrial revolution. The first had been based on coal and steam power; the second founded upon electricity and the internal combustion engine; the third would come from automation and computing. This stemmed not only from Wilson's Scarborough speech or Trend and Robbins; it involved prophets of the future such as Sir Leon Bagrit of Elliott Automation, whose 1964 BBC Reith Lectures I devoured in the pages of *The Listener* as a sixth-former. Bagrit executed a series of imaginative leaps of considerable gymnastic proportions and invited his listeners and readers (Penguin quickly published the lectures as a Pelican paperback) to follow. Reading *The Age of Automation* once more after a long gap, one is struck by its predictive power as well as some significant changes in society, economy and industry that have not happened (though some still might). 'Our main problem', Bagrit said, 'in the successful application of automation is one of imagination . . .'[19]

In a particularly vivid and prophetic paragraph, Bagrit captured both the possibility of a dramatic miniaturization of computing hardware *and* an internet (although he did not call it that) which could link every electronic device to a cornucopia of knowledge:

> A whole range of new possibilities is being opened up by the development of extremely small computers, using micro-circuitry developed for communication systems in confined spaces, such as in aircraft or missiles. The enormous reduction in size that has taken place during recent years can be illustrated, perhaps, by saying that, whereas the computer of 1950 needed a large room to contain it, the 1964 model is down to the dimensions of a suitcase: by 1974 the normal computer will be no bigger than a packet of a hundred cigarettes.

Then followed the internet prophecy:

> In civilian life this kind of computer clearly has great advantages. It is now possible to envisage personal computers small enough to be taken around in one's car, or even in one's pocket. They could be plugged into a national computer grid, to provide individual inquirers with almost unlimited information.[20]

The only thing awry in that forecast of the developments that were to change the world from the early 1990s was the *international*, rather than national, nature of what Bagrit called 'grids'.

His prophecies on work, wealth and leisure in an age of plenty were, on the other hand, excessively optimistic: 'I am assuming that an avalanche of leisure cannot arrive overnight. A working week of 15 hours may take 50 years to arrive,' i.e. by 2014 or thereabouts (and we're still waiting). But Bagrit's was an enticing and generous vision of a Britain where only a third of the population need work to keep everyone else in abundance,[21] and those who did not work could retire at fifty-five on generous pensions provided by a welfare state replete with resources.[22] Politics, too, would be transformed – though not tranquil:

If we pursue automation technology, the centre of our social problems
will shift to the distribution of the riches we have found ourselves
capable of creating . . . there will be a great deal of argument.[23]

The transition to an age where scarcity was no more would not be
easy, Bagrit acknowledged. Society would need to be trained and
retrained for perhaps even three jobs during a working life.[24] Individuals would need gentle help on how to use their leisure. Education
would need to be transformed, as would the capacity of the state
(Bagrit urged a powerful co-ordinating Minister for Modernization
at senior Cabinet level[25]).*

The 1964 Reith Lectures fitted the mood of the times in portraying
paradise delayed, not least in terms of individual possibilities for
fulfilment – a kind of full enjoyment policy to come. There were,
however, some gratifications arriving in 1964 that had an almost
instant impact on society – especially upon the children of the early
postwar generation. British cultural historians, for example, will lin-
ger long on the first day of that year. As Richard Weight, explained,
it was the launch day

> of the longest-running British pop show, *Top of the Pops*. In a symbol
> of British secularism, the show was first broadcast from a disused
> church in Rusholme, Manchester, with the Beatles singing 'I Want to
> Hold Your Hand' and the [Rolling] Stones (first on the programme) 'I
> Wanna Be Your Man'. Facing less media competition in a smaller
> country than the United States, *TOTP* collected the nation's youth
> around family TV sets in a weekly act of communion.[26]

Bill Cotton Jr (son of Billy Cotton, bandleader and racing driver),
the BBC's Head of Light Entertainment, had finally persuaded the
Corporation that the flowering of early-Sixties British pop music

---

* A more immediate economic prospect, though little noticed at the time, was the
promise of succour from the sea in the form of North Sea oil. In May 1964 the government ratified the UN Continental Shelf Convention, which gave the UK
sovereignty over its continental shelf to a depth of 200 metres. This reached to what
would become the bonanza-laden Forties Field, 110 miles out in the North Sea to the
east of the Moray Firth. In September 1964 the Ministry of Fuel and Power issued
the first exploration licences (James Bamberg, *British Petroleum and Global Oil,
1950–1975: The Challenge of Nationalism* (Cambridge University Press, 2000), p. 199).

deserved its own bespoke programme.[27] It was an instant and enduring success. It showed that, in the right circumstances, music can be the swiftest form of cultural transformation and, in this case, a national one too with a UK-wide transfusion into the bloodstream of shared national entertainment. Other aspects of early-Sixties cultural change may have taken longer to acquire such a geographical reach, but the impact of the new wave of music was instant and powerful.

Top of the Pops did not come out of the blue to change the galaxy of British pop culture. A new constellation was already forming in the early Sixties and much of its dazzle was created by the television producer Jack Good. His obituarist Richard Williams wrote of him that '[b]eyond a flair for spotting dramatic potential, Good had what the music industry would call great ears'.[28] Those who benefited from the acuteness of Jack Good's hearing equipment pre-*Top of the Pops* were the young Cliff Richard and shows such as *Six-Five Special* on the BBC and *Oh Boy!* on ITV.

This aural and visual effect combined quickly touched another great institution of popular culture and widespread public attention – association football. Thanks to the efforts of Cotton and Good and, above all, the singers and the songwriters involved, the recitative from the terraces that accompanied matches played every Saturday in those temples of mass participation quite literally changed its tunes. As the librettist of football chants, Adrian Thrills, put it in his study of the genre, *You're Not Singing Anymore*, 'the sounds of the terraces were about to blossom into what was undoubtedly their golden age . . . The full flowering of the football anthem coincided with the pop boom of the early Sixties.'[29]

Terrace pop, as it might be called, became a national phenomenon but, fittingly, Liverpool was its epicentre – to be precise, the sacred Spion Kop Terrace at Anfield, which then held 28,000 devotees of Liverpool FC buoyed up by the full glory of Bill Shankly's era as the club's manager.[30] As Thrills explained, in the first years of the 1960s: 'The Kop started to express themselves with passionate versions of pop hits such as "She Loves You" by the Beatles, "I Like It" by Freddie and the Dreamers, and "Anyone Who Had a Heart" by Cilla Black. "You'll Never Walk Alone", the song that was to become their anthem, was written by Rodgers and Hammerstein for the musical *Carousel*, but adopted by the Kop after Gerry and the Pace-makers charted with the track in 1963.'[31]

The early Sixties was the explosive, buccaneering phase of another entertainment phenomenon, the package holiday (which also pos-sessed its own anthem in 'Summer Holiday', recorded in 1963 by Cliff Richard and the Shadows as part of the soundtrack to the film of the same name in which they starred[32]). The pioneering phase had begun modestly enough in 1949 when a young Reuters journalist, Vladimir Raitz, offered an all-in holiday for £32.10s, including a flight to Corsica, tented accommodation by the beach in Calvi and as much unrationed food as you could eat with generous quantities of wine to lubricate it.[33]

Raitz later co-wrote a book with Roger Bray called *Flight to the Sun* about this new and, as it turned out, lasting form of British activ-ity.[34] The figures tell only part of the story. In 1959 about 2.25 million Brits took a foreign holiday, though only one in eight went to Spain (which would swiftly become the magnet destination). By 1967 the figure was 5 million[35] and the small fishing villages of the Spanish Costas such as Benidorm were well on the way to permanent trans-formation to vast pleasure lands. Raitz and Bray likened it to the pioneering days of the Wild West: 'For the travel industry and its customers, the decade of the Beatles and the Rolling Stones was not unlike that brief period when the American West hovered between lawlessness and the arrival of the US Marshal. The difference was that along the Spanish Costas the cowboys were more real than mythological.'[36]

As the rush to the sun quickened, British seaside resorts, both great and small, fell further and further behind. Over the decade of the 1960s, the number of people holidaying in the UK rose by 20 per cent but the quantity taking holidays abroad leapt by 230 per cent, includ-ing growing numbers of young people (up to 20 per cent by 1966).[37] There was a sour note in the reaction to this of Eric Croft, director and secretary of the British Hotels and Restaurants Association. He thought there was an element of snobbery in it stemming from 'the fashionable habit of keeping up with the Joneses. It is much more impressive to be able to talk of the *pension* we found at some Medi-terranean resort with an unpronounceable name, where sanitation does not exist, and where a visit to the chemist is almost a daily necessity, than to admit to having had a grand holiday at a boarding house, with good English food, at one of our seaside resorts.'[38]

But not only did the package holiday add to the freedoms of many whose sole previous experience of foreign travel (if they were male) had usually been in the King's or Queen's uniform, it added to their experience of food, too, however wholesome those big boarding-house breakfasts might be. Italian cafés had been a staple provider in many a high street in early postwar Britain but in the 1960s it was the former British Empire where a reverse takeover of the British stomach gathered pace in an ever-wider diversity of provision with, for example, the import of 'tandoor – clay ovens – for dry-roasting of yoghurt-marinated and spiced chicken'.[39] The tastes acquired on package holidays abroad, not least in Greece and Cyprus, added to what the historian of the British table, Christopher Driver, called the 'collision of food worlds in Britain [which] opened literally insular British cooks and eaters to the influences and materials of at least three major culinary civilizations: Chinese, Indian and Middle Eastern'[40] – a huge and cumulative addition to the joys of life and taste.

Every generation redefines its enjoyments or discovers new ones. In the early Sixties, however, there was the beginning of a significant step towards a pleasure lost for those who regarded smoking as a release, or, in some cases, a craving that verged on necessity. On Ash Wednesday 1962 (fittingly enough) the Royal College of Physicians launched its report *Smoking and Health*,[41] 'the first official report specifying the dangers of smoking'.[42]

It rested on the research conducted by Richard Doll and Austin Bradford ('Tony') Hill in the late 1940s and early 1950s, supported by the Medical Research Council, which produced one of the most significant pieces of epidemiology since the Second World War. It resulted in a celebrated article in the *British Medical Journal* of 30 September 1950 entitled 'Smoking and Carcinoma of the Lung: Preliminary Report',[43] containing what Doll's biographer, Conrad Keating, has described as 'the now classic observation'[44] that 'smoking is a factor, and an important factor, in the production of carcinoma of the lung'.[45]

The Chief Medical Officer at the Ministry of Health, George God-ber, frustrated by the lack of interest in Whitehall about the dangers of smoking, sought to project the epidemiological research to a wider public. He later told Keating: 'We wanted to come up with a plan to offset the influence of the commercial sector in trying to keep people smoking after the scientific breakthrough brought about by Doll and Hill.'[46] In 1958 Godber found a sympathetic ear in the new president of the Royal College of Physicians, Robert Platt, an enthusiast for preventative medicine. The report was ready by the summer of 1961 and was approved by the Royal College in July that year. The physicians decided to take a risk and print 10,000 copies. They were sold out in days. The publication *Smoking and Health* had instant impact and gave Doll and Hill's research the megaphone it needed. Smoking and the risk of lung cancer was planted firmly in the public's consciousness for evermore. In the UK smoking fell by 12.5 per cent in a year. But addiction is stubborn, and the consumption of cigarettes did not significantly fall again until the 1970s.[47]

There was another medico-scientific breakthrough that will be forever associated with the early Sixties, connected not with death but with birth. It swiftly became known as the Pill. As with smoking, medical research on this form of contraception had been considerable in the early postwar years:[48] in 1951 researchers in the United States established that the compound norethisterone inhibited ovulation.[49] In 1957, norethynodrel was given approval by the US Food and Drug Administration as a 'menstrual regulator' and in 1959 it was cleared for use as an oral contraceptive.[50]

This was not a breakthrough without medical anxiety, however. As the historian of medicine Roy Porter put it:

> The amount of oestrogen contained in 'the pill' was arbitrary and women were seriously overdosed from the first. By 1961, adverse side-effects were being reported – thrombosis, phlebitis, migraine and jaundice, and in 1969 the UK Committee on the Safety of Medicines advised doctors to prescribe oral contraceptives with no more than fifty microgrammes of oestrogen.

There were concerns especially for couples who were part of the Catholic community in which I had been raised. But the breakthrough also brought a sense of liberation to many women. Lara Marks, historian of the contraceptive pill, records a particularly vivid conversation during which she was told by one of her interviewees: 'I can still remember that feeling of elation, you know, it was marvellous! It was like winning the pools!'[51]

Another terse addition to the language of early-Sixties anxiety was 'drugs' – literally a whiff of change to come – and successive generations have grown up in the shadow of those who, for whatever reasons, seek solace or stimulation in chemical consolations. Traditionally, successive UK governments had treated drug abuse as a medical/psychiatric problem, though steps had been taken to deal with the use of opium and cocaine in the interwar years.

The early Sixties saw the beginnings of change in both the pattern of drug use among the young and growing official anxieties about the problem. As the historian of UK drugs policy Richard Weight put it:

> From the opium dens of Edwardian London to the cocaine clubs of the jazz age, recreational drug use was largely confined to the Bohemian artistic circles and the Bright Young Things of the leisured upper classes. Between the 1920s and the 1950s it became more widespread among the British middle classes than historians have previously supposed. And public consciousness of the pleasures and perils of drug taking became correspondingly greater. However, it's not until the emergence of Britain's first youth culture – the cosmopolitan, aspirational Mod movement starting in 1959 . . . that recreational drug use became widespread among working class youth.[52]

The amphetamine Benzedrine was the 'drug of choice' for those Mods who used ('Bennies', they called them) along with Drinamyl (or 'Purple Hearts'). This new world of tablet consumption fused with the old liquid world of alcohol and 'the two cultures collided in the growing number of pubs where dealers sold their wares'.[53]

The Douglas-Home government responded to rising anxiety about amphetamines by framing the Drugs (Prevention of Misuse) Act of 1964, which, reflecting worries about growing cannabis use, made it illegal to set-up premises in which it could be smoked. Other drugs were added (LSD in 1966, for example) and the number of controlled substances in Britain rose from thirty-three in 1950 to 106 in 1970.[54]

Another aspect – a nasty and violent if a fringe one – of the Mod phenomenon captured public attention in the early 1960s. It was highly visible and telegenic compared with the largely concealed world of drug taking – the 1964 disturbances on the Brighton seashore in confrontations between Mods and Rockers: two tribes divided by their drapery, their taste in music and their choice of motorcycle. The fighting possessed the drama of a showdown. Parka-clad Mods would ride their Italian motor scooters into the town in search of the beaches on which to fight with no thought for families enjoying seaside picnics on a May Bank Holiday.

The public recoiled from this thousand-strong invasion and seventy-five charges were brought in the courts. It led to much anguished debate – as did the repeat in Margate a year later – about disaffection among young working-class males and the condition of society and senses of morality in general.[55]

Harold Macmillan famously told the journalist Henry Fairlie in 1963: 'If people want a sense of purpose, they should get it from their archbishops. They should not hope to receive it from their politicians.'[56] The mainstream Christian churches, however, were having what the sociologist of religion Grace Davie calls 'a bumpy ride in the 1960s'.[57]

Attendance at the Sunday services of the Established Church of England was continuing the slow decline that had been in evidence since 1945 (figures for England only):

1945	2,989,704
1950	2,958,840
1955	2,894,710
1960	2,861,887
1965	2,682,187[58]

By contrast, the Catholic Church was enjoying a steady rise in Sunday Mass worshippers thanks to immigration from the Republic of Ireland and, to some extent, the new Commonwealth – as well as a steady flow of often celebrity converts such as the actor Alec Guinness. In 1959 converts to Catholicism were running at 15,794 a year; in 1958, 3,771 Roman Catholics went the other way.[59] The figures below are for the whole of the UK.[60]

1945   3,036,826
1950   3,557,059
1955   3,926,830
1960   4,495,157
1965   4,875,825

Pew statistics, of course, are only part of the story. The internal spiritual, doctrinal and liturgical lives of the churches are crucial, and both the Anglicans and the Catholics were in a degree of ferment.

Macmillan had taken great delight in appointing the warm, scholarly Michael Ramsey to Canterbury in 1961 in succession to Geoffrey Fisher, against Fisher's advice. Many years later I heard the gist of the Macmillan–Fisher exchange in January 1961 in No. 10 from Victor Stock, Ramsey's former chaplain (Macmillan had told Ramsey, who had told Stock):

> FISHER: I have come to give some advice about my successor. Whoever you choose, on no account must it be Michael Ramsey, the Archbishop of York. Dr Ramsey is a theologian, a scholar and a man of prayer. Therefore, he is entirely unsuitable as Archbishop of Canterbury. I have known him all my life. I was his Headmaster at Repton.

> MACMILLAN: Thank you, Your Grace, for your kind advice. You may have been Dr Ramsey's headmaster but you were not mine.

Shortly after, Macmillan picked up the phone and rang Ramsey in Bishopthorpe Palace to read him the letter he proposed to send the Queen nominating him as Cantuar.[61]

Archbishops of Canterbury are the spiritual leaders of a denomination that, with its rich intertwining of history, geography and a wide variety of theological strands and styles, lives and breathes perpetually in a condition of tension that is part of the price for its wonderful eclecticism. It was early in the Ramsey years that the Church of England found itself handling a new debate with a very modern tang.

This was provided by another learned figure, the New Testament scholar Dr John Robinson, the suffragan Bishop of Woolwich whose *Honest to God*[62] caused an immediate stir when it was published in 1963. Its questioning of traditional notions of God and prayer eventually won it the extraordinary sale of 3.5 million copies, but at a cost to Robinson, who was accused by some of atheism, heresy even.[63] Canon Eric James, a fellow priest in the Southwark diocese, later recalled that 'people were ... knocked over by his idea that "their image of God must go" '.[64] In 1969 Robinson returned to Cambridge as Dean of Chapel at Trinity College.

In the Catholic Church the ferment in the early 1960s came from the very top in the warm and open person of Pope John XXIII, who had succeeded Pius XII on the seat of St Peter in 1958. No world leader has ever begun so brilliantly as when the new Pope asked parents all over the globe to give their children a kiss from the Pope. He planted a very special kiss on his own church by calling for 'a new Pentecost' and summoning the Second Vatican Council in Rome (the first had sat in 1869–70). He spoke of his desire for *aggiornamento* (a new beginning). Sadly he presided over only its first session, 1962–3, and the task of completing the Council's work fell to his successor, Paul VI.[65] John XXIII had a great impact on my generation of UK Catholics and Vatican II continues to be the template against which many of us test our thinking. It also left an enduring change in not just vernacular language replacing Latin at Mass but the involvement of the laity in the church.

In the UK, possibilities for a new age of secular reform and improvement were in the air across a wide range of individual freedoms and rights that went into making from the mid-Sixties onwards what my research student Matthew Cooper has called 'the rise of the equality state'.[66] The equality state never had a Beveridge to be its champion, and its configurations are more easily defined in retrospect, but their cumulative reshaping of UK society and its norms were no less potent for that.

In some ways, the new equality state tackled the gaps in the Beveridgian welfare state while recognizing three new 'giants', in addition to Beveridge's five, that had to be tackled on the road to social justice: the rights and place of women (including equal pay – wittily dubbed as 'the oldest pay claim in history'[67]), the needs of immigrants and their integration into UK society, and tackling the persistent pockets of poverty in society. One could also include greater equality of sexual preferences with the legislation of homosexual relations between consenting adults in the late Sixties. These needs were apparent enough by the early part of the decade, but if there was to be legislation for them, it would have to be a coincidence of a reform-minded government in power and a 'liberal hour' mood among the public.

It would also require a broadening in the definitions of freedom within which the British system of politics and government operated from political and legal rights, through welfare rights to more positive rights not to be discriminated against on grounds of gender, ethnicity or sexual preference. These from the mid to late 1960s began to shift the boundaries between the state and the public and private spheres in a mixture of state power extensions in coverage of individual behaviour (making discriminatory behaviour towards others illegal) and a withdrawal of state power (from, for example, the bedrooms of individuals and their private sexual behaviour).

The spread of comprehensive education might be seen as one of the new equalities – certainly by those who lacked enthusiasm for the selection at the age of eleven which shaped the tripartite system laid down by the 1944 Education Act. It is associated above all with Anthony Crosland's tenure as Secretary of State for Education, 1965–7, but, as the biographer of the welfare state, Nick Timmins, has pointed out, it was already underway to a degree not appreciated before the change of government in 1964. He wrote of Sir Edward Boyle, that most gentle, liberal and scholarly of Conservatives, who had been given the Education Ministry by Macmillan in July 1962 after the despatch of David Eccles in the 'Night of the Long Knives':

> What struck Boyle when he arrived was how far the comprehensive idea had progressed. No fewer than 90 of the 146 [local] education authorities had either gone comprehensive or had plans to do so, in whole or in part. Since many of these were not Labour controlled, their plans, he concluded, 'could not simply be written off as politically motivated' . . . As Boyle later put it, the notion that comprehensive reorganisation started with [Crosland] . . . is 'one of the historical myths . . . It didn't. It started a number of years before.'[68]

Driving this was the quality and inherent *inequality* of the provision in secondary modern schools (though there were plenty of glowing exceptions). As the social policy analyst David Donnison put it, the move towards comprehensive schools was less of a vote in favour of comprehensives, more a huge rejection of secondary moderns.[69]

The debate about ending selection and introducing a comprehensive system so dominated the politico-educational debate that a crucial gap in the implementation of Rab Butler's 1944 Act is often overlooked – its technical-education provision. This fell between the ministries of Education and Labour and relied on the local authorities providing part-time education in 'county colleges' up to the age of eighteen. It did not happen. 'Technical schools', wrote Timmins, 'left in the hands of local authorities to organise, never took off: at most they educated 2 per cent of the school population.'[70]

It was nearly one hundred years since Matthew Arnold, poet, scholar and education inspector, had prepared a paper for the 1868 Parliamentary Commission on Endowed Schools following a visit to Prussia to see its technical high schools at work. Arnold's account had considerable impact on the Commissioners. This section from their final report should have been carved on the desks of every education minister from that day to this:

> [W]e are bound to add that our evidence appears to show that our industrial classes have not even that basis of sound general education on which alone technical education can rest . . . In fact, our deficiency is not merely a deficiency in technical instruction, but . . . in general intelligence, and unless we remedy this want we shall gradually but surely find that our undeniable superiority in wealth and perhaps in energy will not save us from decline.[71]

A paragraph of great resonance and real prescience apart from the implication of lesser intelligence in the 'industrial classes'. Technical education was a wind of change that never blew.

Decline: sense of, fear of, anticipation of – for all the hopes and glories of the kinder, gentler Britain gradually created in the postwar years, a depressing threnody of relative decline also accompanied them. As the twentieth anniversary of VE Day approached, with the bulk of the remaining empire moving into independence and the question of Britain and Europe lurking in its ever unsettling way and having suffered two very public international humiliations within seven years (the Suez crisis of 1956 and de Gaulle's 'Non' of 1963), this might have been the moment to take a long, hard look at Britain's place in the world in all its aspects – hard, soft and every other kind of power in between. Britain was navigating – or seeking to navigate – through several squalls that together formed a very considerable wind of change. It should not have been beyond the wit of the early-Sixties generations at Westminster and in Whitehall, like a sculptor discerning a statue in a piece of marble, to have designed, from all the raw material bequeathed by the past, a sensible and viable overseas and defence policy that reflected new realities. But it is awfully difficult for any generation to face up to big, baffling and overlapping anxieties, especially in a country that just five decades earlier had been a highly potent prewar playmaker in the world's financial and industrial markets and a formidable operator with an unequalled military presence around the globe.

One aspect of the UK's instruments of influence – its nuclear deterrent – was going to be a live question in the coming general election. But the impulse to remain what a shrewd American observer, Stryker McGuire (*Newsweek*'s man in London) called 'a pocket superpower'[72] was genuinely widespread. Even the foreign and defence policy dissenters in the Campaign for Nuclear Disarmament were part of this, as one of their more dazzling luminaries, the historian A. J. P. Taylor, made plain in his memoirs:

> We thought that Great Britain was still a great power whose example would affect the rest of the world. Ironically we were the last Imperialists. If Great Britain renounced nuclear weapons without waiting for international agreement, we should light such a candle as would never be put out. Alas this was not true. No one cared in the slightest whether Great Britain had the bomb or did not have the bomb.[73]

The capacity to move in a world that, at least to some extent, hangs on UK thoughts, actions and wishes, in a strange way united a wide swathe of people across the left–right spectrum. They shared an appetite for influence that was difficult to slake. A once formidable international player, engaged in a rolling and never more than partial adjustment to often unpalatable realities, can be subject to mood swings. There is also a constant danger of disappointment. Thirty years later, Douglas Hurd, a highly historically minded Foreign and

Commonwealth Secretary, famously described for a Chatham House audience some of the ingredients 'which have allowed Britain to punch above its weight in the world'.[74] This led his friend and Cabinet colleague William Waldegrave to retort: 'If you punch above your weight you place yourself in danger of being knocked out.'[75]

In fact, it was David Hannay who first coined the 'punching' metaphor when UK Ambassador to the United Nations, in a despatch to Douglas Hurd in early 1991 shortly after arriving in New York to be our man on the Security Council. Hannay described the UK and France as 'both boxing a bit above their weight, which demands a good deal of ingenuity and fleetness of foot if it is to be done successfully'.[76]

Hannay, who also served in Brussels as the UK's Permanent Representative to the European Communities (he was cutting his diplomatic teeth in the Kabul Embassy in the early 1960s), is an accomplished calibrator of British influence across the multiple floating exchange rates of the world's diplomatic markets. In the last days of 2017 – during another period of considerable anguish about our place in the world – he offered the MPs on the House of Commons Foreign Affairs Select Committee's inquiry into 'The UK's influence in the UN', a new metaphor-cum-performance indicator that he called 'the trepidation index: do people mind about trampling on your toes more than on someone else's toes? If they don't mind trampling on your toes as much as they do on someone else's, you are going to lose influence.'[77] The hope of sustaining, perhaps even enhancing, British influence in the world was the fuel that propelled the push to join the EEC. Geoffrey Howe, a consistent pro-European, caught this very well when he turned to quoting Archimedes to explain it: 'Give me a place on which to stand and I shall move the world' was how Geoffrey put it to me in more than one conversation.[78]

David Hannay's 'trepidation index' works both ways. The homespun version was the fear that a serious slippage in UK influence was either underway or a growing possibility. Very few felt that this might be the time to cut a more modest dash in the world. Macmillan reflected this in one of his state-of-the-nation letters to the Queen, shortly before successfully steering the government's policy on EEC membership through his party's annual conference in Llandudno in October 1962. 'The Conservative Party', he told the sovereign, 'are being asked, and I think will agree, to turn their minds from the old Imperialism which no longer has its old power, to a new concept of Britain's ability to influence the world.'[79]

The Queen, naturally, was fully aware of the geopolitical shifts underway in her kingdom's relationships with the rest of the world. Victoria was the queen of raised Union Jacks round the globe; Elizabeth, though only a decade into her reign, was already the monarch of lowered flags. By the early 1960s, the Queen's performance as constitutional monarch was already established as world class. She remained box office both at home and abroad. She was, however, still only in the first phase of building her extraordinary set of special personal relationships with the new Commonwealth presidents and prime ministers of the nascent independent nations that emerged from the UK's dash for the exit.

To the relief of some of her advisers, several of the candy-floss elements of the 'new Elizabethanry' of a decade before had fallen away.[80] As her biographer Ben Pimlott wrote of the Queen, in the early 1960s she 'fulfilled her role impeccably, avoided spontaneous gestures or remarks (in contrast to her sometimes pilloried husband), gave away little of what she actually thought and offered no hostages to fortune. She remained popular, admired, fêted wherever she went.'[81]

It was as if she had followed de Gaulle's advice when on his state visit in April 1960 she had asked him what he thought her role should be amid the uncertainties facing her country. The General replied by saying: 'In that station to which God has called you, be who you are Madam.'[82] That is exactly what she had done and would continue to do.

Yet, as the 1959 Parliament moved further into its twilight and the shadow of the coming general election loomed larger, a delicate constitutional question lurked. Might the result produce a new Parliament without an overall majority and the narrowest of gaps between the two major parties? Might her personal prerogatives have to be called upon for the second time in twelve months?

9

The 8.15 from Lime Street

Those who are satisfied should stay with the Tories. We need men with fire in their belly and humanity in their hearts. The choice we offer ... is between standing still, clinging to the tired philosophy of a day that is gone, or moving forward in partnership and unity to a just society, to a dynamic, expanding, confident, and, above all, purposive new Britain.

Harold Wilson, Empire Pool, Wembley,
12 September 1964[1]

The Britain that I have seen bears no relation to the picture painted by Labour leaders of a country which is selfish, gloomy and stagnant. I have found people confident, buoyant and self-reliant ... As Foreign Secretary and now as Prime Minister, I know that the world is still a dangerous place. It is just at this moment when France and China are becoming nuclear powers, that the socialists would propose to discard all control by a British government over Britain's nuclear arm ...

Sir Alec Douglas-Home's final election
broadcast, 13 October 1964[2]

We're running neck and neck. I'll be very surprised if there's much in it – say twenty seats either way. But things might start slipping in the last few days ... they won't slip towards us.

Rab Butler to George Gale of the Daily Express,
9 October 1964[3]

We're a Conservative country that votes Labour from time
to time.

Reginald Maudling at his count in Barnet after
leaving an election-night party at the
Savoy Hotel, 15–16 October 1964[4]

Most politicians possess what a Whitehall friend of mine calls a
front-of-house persona and a back-of-house persona (he was talking
about Margaret Thatcher, who was an exception to this, being exactly
the same in her views in private as in public).[5] This aspect of Harold
Wilson as prime minister-in-waiting during the summer of 1964 was
brought out quite strongly when, fifty-three years later, a document
written in July of that year reached the National Archives from the
Cabinet Secretaries' super-secret cupboard.

The file in question contained a 'Secret and Personal' note from the
head of the Home Civil Service, Sir Laurence Helsby, to the Cabinet
Secretary, Sir Burke Trend. Dated 28 July 1964, it covered the contents of a conversation between Helsby and Wilson about his plans
for the machinery of government if Labour won the election.*

The encounter had begun with the staffing at No. 10, particularly
the appointment earlier that year of Derek Mitchell to succeed Tim
Bligh as Principal Private Secretary. Helsby reported to Trend:

> In talking about No. 10 Wilson said that he had been cross when
> Mitchell was appointed, but that his irritation had stemmed largely
> from the postponement of the Election – about which he was cross
> quite independently. He thought that the post of Principal Private Sec-
> retary was essentially personal to the particular Prime Minister and
> 'his people' had told him that the precedents suggested that the right

---

* Wilson prided himself on being a former Cabinet Office insider from his time as a
member of the War Cabinet secretariat between 1941 and 1943. Two weeks before
announcing his surprise resignation in March 1976, he gave me an interview for a
profile of the Cabinet Office as an institution for *The Times*. With pride he could
quote the serial number of a particular paper he had prepared for the Secretary of
the War Cabinet, Sir Edward Bridges. His memory and recall were legendary, and he
plainly enjoyed displaying them before the young man from *The Times* (who enjoyed
it too).

course would be to make a change pretty soon after he arrived at 10 Downing Street. He said, however, that he understood quite clearly that Mitchell was absolutely first class: in particular Douglas Jay had assured him of this. I said that Mitchell's appointment was made entirely on my recommendation and not as a matter of the Prime Minister's personal selection; and my recommendation had been based on my judgement of the best man available to serve whoever was Prime Minister over the next few years.[6]

Mitchell stayed – though he was to have some furious encounters with Mrs Marcia Williams, Wilson's personal and political secretary. It is the next section of Helsby's note, headlined 'Economic Affairs', where the front-of-house/back-of-house contrast shines through, between Wilson the old Whitehall hand and guileful manager of political colleagues in private. Public Wilson, as we have seen, stressed the importance of a growth-minded Department of Economic Affairs as a counterweight to the Treasury. Listen to the private Wilson on the DEA and George Brown:

Wilson made it clear at the outset that the proposal to set up a Ministry of Economic Affairs was intended as a solution of a personal problem. He spoke quite frankly of George Brown's position: for health and other reasons he did not expect him to survive long in this position.

A reference, no doubt, to Brown's drink problem.[7] 'He was,' Helsby continued, 'however, committed to giving him this Department and he would have some such title as First Secretary of State – but *not* Deputy Prime Minister.'

What about the reach and power of the DEA? Helsby went on:

The impression I received was of an experiment of a kind which Wilson regarded as non-essential. He fully recognised that the Department would have no executive powers and he thought that it should be a very small Department. Its primary job would be co-ordination and the provision of a home for some of the work of NEDC [National Economic Development Council].

Wilson showed a great sense of the importance of the Treasury's function and emphasised that it was essential to keep the Treasury strong.[8]

This is exactly the way the power flows played out until the DEA was finally abolished in 1969.[9]

In the same batch of releases from the Cabinet Secretaries' hottest files were two other government-in-waiting documents dealing with the secret state and how much to tell incoming ministers about it, given their inexperience as a result of not holding office since 1951.

The first, dated 30 September 1964 and classified 'TOP SECRET AND STRICTLY PERSONAL', is from Sir Charles Cunningham, Permanent Secretary at the Home Office, to Trend:

> Thank you for your letter of 25th September, about your discussions with 'C' [Sir Dick White, Chief of the Secret Intelligence Service] of the question how far, if there is a change of Government, incoming Ministers should be informed of the details of certain highly secret operations.
>
> So far as the Security Service is concerned, I entirely agree with the view that we must tell the new Home Secretary frankly what we are doing. I agree also that it would be helpful, if there is a change of administration, for the outgoing Prime Minister to talk to his successor about the Security Service as well as about M.I.6. My guess, however, is that the work of the Security Service, at any rate in the first instance, would be most usefully discussed with any new Home Secretary; and thereafter it would no doubt be convenient if Roger Hollis were to put the new Prime Minister also in the picture.[10]

Hollis, the director-general of MI5, wrote to Trend the following day pointing out that the Denning Report had made the Security Service 'sufficiently known', adding 'I will certainly be talking to the new Home Secretary about the scope of our work and the particular authorisations which the Home Secretary gives to us, and it may be that the Home Secretary will think that I should later see the Prime Minister.'[11] To modern eyes it seems odd that senior figures in the secret state should even contemplate whether their responsible ministers should or should not know about the clandestine work of the secret agencies.

Sir Frank Soskice, who became Home Secretary a few weeks later, had himself been part of the secret world during the Second World War, when he had served as a Special Operations Executive lawyer.

Thanks to the Whitehall 'need to know' principle, that, of course, did not mean he was au fait with other parts of the hidden state. Knowledge of MI6 was a greater problem as not until 1994 was the existence in peacetime of the Secret Intelligence Service avowed with the passage of the Intelligence Services Bill through Parliament. Wilson had been a Cabinet minister under Attlee but he had never sat on the small Cabinet committees Attlee had used to authorize special operations. When Macmillan invited Wilson to Downing Street in July 1963 to discuss the flight of Kim Philby from Beirut to Moscow he discovered that Wilson 'had never heard of C'.[12]

The days before the 1964 general election were especially poignant for Winston Churchill, who had presided over the secret state during its finest hours and was the most avid customer of its intelligence product. He had decided not to stand for re-election in Woodford. Arthur Bottomley, who would become Commonwealth Secretary in the first Wilson government, once told me that he and his fellow Labour MPs thought that Churchill, silent and brooding in his regular place on the Conservative benches, might be hoping to die in the chamber he loved so much. All general elections are historically significant, but everyone knew that there would be a special quality about the 1964 campaign because, for the first time since 1898, Winston Churchill would not be 'heard on the hustings'. Churchill's departure from Parliament was marked on 29 July with a resolution of appreciation passed by the House of Commons, though, sadly, it seems as if Churchill himself had little idea of what was going on.[13]

The 1964 general election was the first in the UK to be truly televised: 'Ninety per cent of homes now had television compared to 70% in 1959.'[14] This was another reason why the televisually adept Harold Wilson was thought to be the maker of the political weather in summer and early autumn 1964. He had scarcely put a foot wrong since his 'white heat' conference speech at Scarborough. Geoffrey Goodman was assigned by the *Daily Mirror* to follow Wilson throughout the 1964 election campaign as he had been to their joint hero, Aneurin Bevan, in what was to be his last contest.* In his

---

* Bevan died of cancer in July 1960 aged only sixty-two – 'like a great tree hacked down, wantonly, in full leaf', wrote his friend and biographer Michael Foot (Michael Foot, *Aneurin Bevan, 1897–1960*, abridged by Brian Brivati (Gollancz, 1997), p. 592).

memoir, *From Bevan to Blair*, Goodman links the two in a way that no other observer has. Bevan was broody and tired in their late-night sessions sipping whisky on the campaign trail. He felt, as Shadow Foreign Secretary, wrote Goodman, 'isolated among the party leadership; a lone figure fighting to hold aloft a belief in socialist values and a terrible fear that the cornerstones on which his philosophy was based were being eroded'.[15]

Goodman at such moments worried about Bevan's health, even though 'Nye was in full spate' earlier in the evening as at Corwen in North Wales where he delivered a distinct pre-echo of Wilson's great theme of 1963–4:

> He spoke about Britain living in a shrinking world; of technology and the rapid march of communications; of the complexities facing all politicians trying to work in a political and social climate of ever-widening cycles of change ... And the phrase – still scribbled in my notebook – with which he summed it up: 'We are moving into a world in which smaller and smaller men are strutting across narrower and narrower stages.'[16]

Geoffrey Goodman loved Nye Bevan. Once I asked him why. 'Because he made you think your dreams were possible,' Geoffrey replied.

Goodman did not love Harold Wilson but was impressed by him and 'we gradually built up a kind of friendship':

> To this day I am still amazed at the way Wilson stood up to the rigours of that campaign. For the journalists covering the 1964 Wilson election tour – touching pretty well every corner of the country – it was utterly exhausting, crazy, requiring a novel ... to provide anything like a worthwhile description and absolutely riveting.[17]

The political journalists found it very difficult to accommodate the growing imperium of television with its very different deadlines:

> It was a considerable daily headache – except for Harold Wilson, who quickly adapted himself and his entourage to the new requirements and was well ahead of game plan in his handling of this new monster of intrusiveness, television. His speeches were timed to perfection. He

knew precisely when, and how, to pitch his crowning remarks to achieve maximum impact on the TV screen.[18]

The Conservatives knew how good Wilson's performance was, both on the boards and on the screen. The mastermind of the Conservative campaign, Lord Poole, later said of Wilson: 'He's the only really competent political TV performer this country has produced.'[19] A young Jonathan Aitken had the job of crafting speeches for both Alec Douglas-Home and Selwyn Lloyd designed to appeal to 'the youth vote'. It was swiftly plain that Wilson was already successfully siphoning this particular electoral stream. Conservative Central Office despatched Aitken to witness Wilson in action and to report back on his deficiencies. It produced one of the finest accounts of Wilson in his oratorical prime: 'Instead of discerning weaknesses in the Leader of the Opposition's armour, I could only report his enormous strengths. For Wilson was master of one of the great art forms of election campaigning that was still alive and well in the 1960s – dominating a big crowd at a public meeting.'[20]

Aitken travelled to Ipswich to witness Wilson performing before an audience of 2,000 in the open air, including nests of hecklers off whom Wilson fed with delight.* Aitken recalled how he

> took his opponents head on from the start, declaring himself amazed at the discovery of 'a human species I thought was extinct – the Tory working man' . . . Interrupters were crushed like ants under a giant's heel. After a succession of such squashing, Wilson took a sip from a glass of water. The pause allowed the shout, 'Getting tired, are you?' Back came the instant riposte: 'No, it's the Tories who are tired – and ever since Profumo we know what's been tiring them!'
>
> After the rubbishing of hecklers came the rubbishing of Tory ministers. My boss, Selwyn Lloyd, came under fire for the wage restraint policy known as the 'pay pause', which he had introduced as Chancellor. It had been relaxed by the new Prime Minister. 'Oh well, the one thing the Tories can plan is an election boom,' said Wilson. 'Old

---

* Political legend has it that Wilson was only worsted once by a heckler during the 1964 campaign, during a speech in the naval dockyard town of Chatham: Wilson: 'Why do I stress the importance of a strong Royal Navy?' Heckler: 'Because you're in effing Chatham, that's why.'

celluloid put the brakes on the economy then the Fourteenth Earl puts his foot on the accelerator. They make a fine couple. I call 'em Stop-Go and Son' [*Steptoe and Son* was in its comedic prime on BBC TV in 1964] . . . It was rousing election rhetoric and even Conservative Central Office's secret agent could scarce forbear to cheer the Labour leader for providing such wonderful entertainment.[21]

Aitken returned to London thinking Wilson 'would win the election easily'.

Elections are always difficult to read. There is a dash of quantum physics about them – they are a mix of waves and particles. Sometimes (1945, 1966, 1979, 1997) the electorate votes for a serious squirt of social democracy or liberal capitalism, but usually it wants a sensible fusion of both and looks to Westminster and Whitehall to broker it.

What were the waves and particles of the general election of 1964? In the grand sweep of post-1945 British politics and political economy, it has a particular significance as the first example of what Peter Riddell calls the 'declinist general election'.[22] Wilson set out his stall firmly and powerfully as the man to halt and then reverse the UK's deep-set relative economic decline (Ted Heath did the same in 1970 and Margaret Thatcher in 1979).

Labour's manifesto, *Let's Go with Labour for the New Britain*, drafted by the vivid pen of Peter Shore, is suffused with the counter-decline theme. The section headed 'A modern economy' distils it, blending the themes Wilson had delivered from platform after podium since his Scarborough speech:

> The aims are simple enough: we want full employment; a faster rate of industrial expansion; a sensible distribution of labour throughout the country; an end to the present chaos in traffic and transport; a brake on rising prices and a solution to our balance of payments problems.
>
> As the past thirteen years [since the Conservatives regained power in 1951] have shown, none of these aims will be achieved by leaving the economy to look after itself. They will only be secured by a deliberate and massive effort to modernise the economy; to change its structure and to develop with all possible speed the advanced technology and the new science-based industries with which our future lies. In short, they will only be achieved by socialist planning.[23]

The 1964 Labour manifesto, one of the most distinctive of the postwar decades, caught skilfully the electorate's desire both for what Ralf Dahrendorf called 'a better yesterday' (he was speaking about the nascent Social Democratic Party in the early 1980s[24]) and the appetite for a distinctive upward leap in the trajectory of economic production and productivity.

In the summer and autumn of 1964, both main parties pitched in this way, though Labour's brio and Shore's word power took the palm. Here is how the Conservatives' *Prosperity with a Purpose* did battle with Labour over who could plan and grow best. Under 'An expanding economy', it laid out first how far a new Conservative government would aim to raise the rate of economic expansion combined with a retrospective justification of Maudling's dash for growth:

> We shall give first priority to our policy for economic growth, so that Britain's national wealth can expand by a steady 4 per cent a year. We recognise that this involves a high level of imports, and we are prepared to draw on our [gold and dollar] reserves whilst our exports, both visible and invisible, achieve a balance with them ... But the long-term problem of the balance of payments can only be solved by bringing our trading economy to the highest pitch of competitiveness and modern efficiency.[25]

The manifesto acknowledged both the Conservative Party's almost social democratic adoption since 1959 of planning, and a divergence from the Labour Party on its instruments:

> We have set up the National Economic Development Council, bringing together Government, management and unions in a co-operative venture to improve our economic performance ...
>
> NEDC gives reality to the democratic concept of planning by partnership. In contemporary politics the argument is not for or against planning. All human activity involves planning. The question is: how is the planning to be done? By consent or by compulsion? The Labour Party's policy of extended state ownership and centralised control would be economically disastrous and incompatible with the opportunities of a free society.[26]

Labour did see what its manifesto called 'a vital contribution' needed from the nationalized industries – not least to its proposed national plan – through expansion of existing corporations and new ones through the renationalization of steel and the bringing of water supply into full public ownership.[27]

Another theme where the two main parties were at odds was secondary education, though both promised university expansion along Robbins Report lines. Comprehensive education was an unequivocal Labour pledge combined with a promise to raise the school-leaving age from fifteen to sixteen: 'Labour will get rid of the segregation of children into separate schools caused by 11-plus selection: secondary education will be reorganised along comprehensive lines.'[28] On secondary schools, the Conservative manifesto also pledged a raising of the leaving age to sixteen but was silent on comprehensive education.[29]

Often it's the silences in the manifestos that are the most revealing. *Let's Go with Labour . . .* made no mention of the changes that were to come – especially after the 1966 general election when Labour acquired a huge ninety-seven-seat majority – on social reform, which the second Wilson government either legislated for directly or allowed individual backbenchers parliamentary time to get their bills through (homosexual law reform; legalizing abortion) plus other measures embraced by 'the rise of the equality state'.[30]

The Labour manifesto did, however, have a strong section on 'Commonwealth immigration', which was rising up the UK's political agenda. The manifesto had a real sense of the serious problems to come unless action was taken:

> As the centre of a great Commonwealth of 700 million people, linked to us by ties of history and common interest, Britain faces the three great problems of poverty, rapidly rising population and racial conflict.
>
> By herself Britain cannot, of course, solve these problems; but more than any other advanced country of the West, we have the greatest opportunity and the greatest incentive to tackle them. We believe that the Commonwealth has a major part to play in grappling with the terrible inequalities that separate the developed and underdeveloped nations and the white and coloured races.
>
> That is why a Labour Government will legislate against racial discrimination and incitement in public places and give special help to

local authorities in areas where immigrants have settled. Labour accepts that the number of immigrants entering the United Kingdom must be limited. Until a satisfactory agreement covering this can be negotiated with the Commonwealth a Labour Government will retain immigration control.[31]

The Conservative Party manifesto was silent on race relations legislation.

On the great geopolitical shifts of early-Sixties Britain – the withdrawal from territorial empire and the tilt towards Europe – the two manifestos both have the air of an interim assessment of a story that was still unfolding. The consensus between the two main parties about the need to decolonise is striking not least because of the contrast with the pro- and anti-European cleavage *within* the parties that was present in 1964 and remains so to this day – Europe as *the* great disrupter question of postwar British politics.

First the Labour interpretation, which is headlined 'The end of colonialism':

When World War II unleashed the demand throughout Asia and Africa for the end of colonialism, Britain's first response was an act of creative statesmanship. The Labour Government, headed by Clement Attlee, granted full and complete independence to India, Pakistan and Ceylon [now Sri Lanka], and thereby began the process of transforming a white colonial empire into a multiracial Commonwealth. No nobler transformation is recorded in the story of the human race.

The implication here was that this noblest of transformations was a Labour one. The manifesto continued:

So long as they were in Opposition, the Conservatives denounced this policy as socialist scuttle. Faced with responsibility, however, in 1951 they were compelled very largely to accept it. But the leadership they should have given was vitiated by the Suez fiasco and the equivocal attitude to African demands for independence, and the promises which they made – and have been forced to break – to the settlers.

After the sideswipe at Suez came the Euro-virus:

How little they were able to transfer their faith and enthusiasm from the old Empire to the new Commonwealth was shown when Harold Macmillan and Alec Douglas-Home both declared there was no future for Britain outside the Common Market and expressed themselves ready to accept terms of entry to the Common Market that would have excluded our Commonwealth partners, broken our special trade links with them, and forced us to treat them as third-class nations.

And as for the EEC, a Wilson government would not be applying:

Though we shall seek to achieve closer links with our European neighbours, the Labour Party is convinced that the first responsibility of a British Government is still to the Commonwealth.[32]

– though apply the Wilson government did, in 1967.

The equivalent paragraphs in the Conservative manifesto must have been painful to write only eighteen months since General de Gaulle brought to nothing that huge investment of time, energy and political capital in the UK-EEC negotiations of 1961–3:

Entry into the European Economic Community is not open to us in existing circumstances, and no question of fresh negotiations can arise at present. We shall work, with our EFTA partners, through the Council of Europe, and through the Western European Union, for the closest possible relations with the Six consistent with our Commonwealth ties.[33]

Following this rather forlorn passage is a much perkier one on 'The role of the Commonwealth':

The [Commonwealth] Prime Ministers' Conference this summer reflected the vigour and increased the strength of the modern Commonwealth. In a few weeks' time it [the Commonwealth] will comprise 20 nations, 13 of whom will have achieved their independence since the Conservatives took office.

This historic evolution is now reaching its final stage. Of our remaining dependencies many are well on the road to sovereignty. A number have multi-racial populations presenting special problems. Others are too small to bear the burden of separate statehood.

36. True Brit: Colin Cowdrey of Kent and England, his broken arm in plaster, comes to the wicket to join David Allen, of Gloucestershire and England, during the last over of the England v West Indies Test Match at Lords, 25 June 1963.

37. (*below*) Every screen in the RAF operations room in Whitehall connected to the new Ballistic Missile Early Warning System on Fylingdales Moor in North Yorkshire, was tuned to the Lords Test as the game could end in an England win, a West Indies win, a tie or a draw. 'The Russians could have had us cost free.'

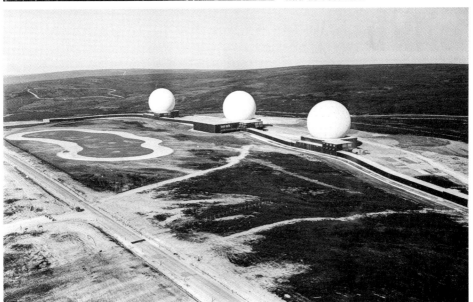

38. The most famous fall from political grace in the post-war years: John Profumo on 18 June 1963.

39. The fascinators of the hour: Christine Keeler (*left*) and Mandy Rice-Davies take a break during the trial of Stephen Ward, 22 July 1963.

40. Man of morals: the bowler-hatted Lord Denning comes up from rural Hampshire to examine the entrails of the Profumo affair, 16 September 1963.

41. (*below*) Denning's best-selling report was published on 17 September 1963 inspiring a media frenzy.

42. *Beyond the Fringe*: a new age of satire is unleashed by Alan Bennett, Peter Cook, a pointing Jonathan Miller and a seated Dudley Moore.

43. Beauty and the Beatles: Dusty Springfield joins the Fab Four on *Top Gear* and on the front cover of the *Radio Times*, 11 July 1964.

44. Culture shock: the Mods invade Eastbourne, Easter 1964.

45. Harold Wilson conjurs up the 'white heat' of the technological revolution for the 1963 Labour Party Conference in Scarborough, 1 October (the young Tony Benn leaning forward on the left).

THE BBC REITH LECTURES 1964

SIR LEON BAGRIT

THE AGE OF AUTOMATION

46. Sir Leon Bagrit forecasts an age of abundance, a surplus of leisure and a kind of internet.

47. Prince Philip, Duke of Edinburgh, a life-long advocate of technological progress, visits the Marconi Wireless Telegraphy Company, Chelmsford, 11 December 1962.

48. Rab Butler takes the polite applause of the Conservative Party Conference in Blackpool after an underwhelming speech with Iain Macleod on his left and his rivals Alec Home and Quintin Hailsham to his right, 12 October 1963.

49. The Queen, accompanied by her Private Secretary, Sir Michael Adeane, calls on Macmillan in the King Edward VII's Hospital for Officers, to hear his advice on his successor as Prime Minister, 18 October 1963.

50. A pensive Sir Alec Douglas-Home takes a tea break during the Kinross and West Perthshire by-election which returned him to the House of Commons on 8 November 1963 after he had renounced his peerage.

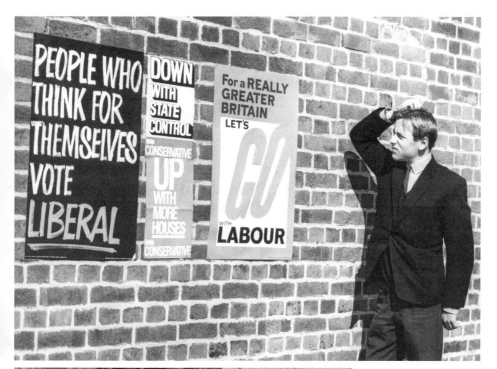

51. (*above*) Spoilt for choice: an elector contemplates the destination of his vote.

52. Recovered from his prostate trouble, Harold Macmillan tries his old magic one last time on 12 May 1964 at a by-election in Devizes.

53. Harold Wilson arrives at Euston Station on the 8.15 from Liverpool Lime Street to electoral victory, 16 October 1964.

54. A premier-in-waiting greets a gold-standard Prime Minister, Clement Attlee, on the steps of Labour Party Headquarters in Transport House on the afternoon of 16 October 1964.

In each case we shall work for a fair and practical solution which will protect the interests of the people concerned.[34]

In that last paragraph lay the hint of serious trouble to come in Southern Rhodesia, which announced a white-dominated unilateral declaration of independence just a year later and did not make the shift from Rhodesia to Zimbabwe until 1980.

There was another big theme exerting its own special irradiated glow through the 1964 campaign – what Macmillan called 'the nuclear' and most people 'the Bomb'. The public positions of both main parties appeared to offer a real choice on the UK's future as a nuclear power. Here is Labour's manifesto prospectus carried under the headline of 'Tory nuclear pretence':

> The Nassau agreement to buy Polaris know-how and Polaris missiles from the USA will add nothing to the deterrent strength of the western alliance, and it will mean utter dependence on the US for their supply. Nor is it true that all this costly defence expenditure will produce an 'independent British deterrent'. It will not be independent and it will not be British and it will not deter. Its possession will impress neither friend nor potential foe . . . We shall propose the re-negotiation of the Nassau agreement.

A Labour government would be concerned about nuclear proliferation

> and will put forward constructive proposals for integrating all NATO's nuclear weapons under effective political control so that all the partners in the alliance have a proper share in their deployment and control.[35]

The Conservatives, with Douglas-Home very much the stalwart voice in expressing the policy, were determined to make this a distinguishing issue between themselves and Labour. Under the heading 'Defence and deterrence', the Conservative manifesto sought to make it a playmaker policy in their attempt to keep Labour out of the Cabinet Room:

> Over 90 per cent of our defence effort is devoted to conventional arms. But in the nuclear age no money spent on increasing the size or

improving the conventional equipment of our forces could by itself secure the defence of these islands. The only effective defence is the certainty in the mind of any enemy that there is no prize he could win by our defeat which could compensate him for the destruction he would suffer in the process. Conservatives do not accept the view that we could never be threatened on our own, or that an enemy will always assume we shall have allies rushing to our side.

Britain must in the ultimate resort have independently controlled nuclear power to deter an aggressor. We possess this power today. Only under a Conservative Government will we possess it in the future.[36]

Clem Attlee appeared on Labour's final election broadcast to dismiss the idea that Britain's influence in the world depended on its nuclear weapons. But the Wilson government kept them. Nearly a quarter of a century later, I was genuinely surprised to discover that Alec Home was *not* surprised that his successor had carried on with Polaris. In 1988, Home told me that he 'had always found, in dealing with Harold Wilson on security matters, that he was reliable in terms of the national interest'. As a result, Home continued,

> in spite of the manifesto, in spite of what he said during the election campaign, I didn't think he'd be able to bring himself to cancel it [Polaris] when he understood the facts. There are quite a lot of facts the Leader of the Opposition doesn't have. When he got into government I thought he would carry on the programme, so it didn't worry me unduly.[37]

In 1995, after Alec Home had died, I discovered in a newly declassified 1964 file what I think was perhaps a contributory factor in his assessment of Wilson's likely policy. It was a note in Douglas-Home's No. 10 papers of a meeting on nuclear matters between Denis Healey, Labour's Shadow Defence Secretary and the incumbent Defence Secretary, Peter Thorneycroft, on 3 February 1964. The two men talked on a privy councillor basis. During their conversation Healey had sounded Thorneycroft out on the idea of keeping the Royal Navy's Polaris force and pooling it with US Polaris boats as an Atlantic Nuclear Force assigned to NATO – the idea, in fact, with which Labour ran for a while once in office.[38]

A question that was by the end of the Sixties to become significant was immigration from the so-called 'New Commonwealth' nations (though India and Pakistan were not that 'new' by 1964). It was the Smethwick constituency in Birmingham, where the sitting MP was the Shadow Foreign Secretary, Patrick Gordon Walker, which provided the lightning conductor for the 1964 election debate on immigration.

The party leaderships were very careful in the language they used during the campaign, but the Conservative candidate, Peter Griffiths, a local primary school headmaster, had already helped remove the Labour council from office, aided in part by the immigration question.[39] On the hustings, Griffiths proposed a halt to immigration for five years and the deportation of immigrants with a criminal record or who were unemployed on a long-term basis.

The campaign is remembered for the coarseness of some of the language used. Griffiths himself did not deploy the slogan 'If you want a nigger for a neighbour, vote Labour', but declined to condemn those who did, asserting that such words were 'a manifestation of popular feeling'.[40] Against the prevailing Labour tide, Gordon Walker went down to defeat in Smethwick on a swing of 7.2 per cent to the Conservatives.[41] During the House of Commons debate on Labour's first Queen's Speech, Wilson denounced Griffiths, declaring that he 'will serve his time ... [in the Commons] ... as a Parliamentary leper'.[42]

General elections always cause outbreaks of political neuralgia induced by heightened political sensitivity. In 1964, a vivid example was a long-forgotten Midlands motor components firm, Hardy Spicer. On 29 September, with the contest in full swing, the news broke that over 200 inspectors had gone on strike at the Birmingham factory – action which, if prolonged, could bring a high proportion of the UK's motor manufacturing to a halt. This unmissably raised the question of excessive trade union power, which could only redound to the disadvantage of the Labour Party.[43] The news coincided with an opinion poll showing a spurt in Tory fortunes and a Conservative lead of 2.9 per cent – as reported in the early edition of the *Daily Mail* on 1 October, which Wilson read at home in Hampstead Garden Suburb the previous evening before retiring for the night.[44]

At the Labour press conference the following morning, Wilson compounded his difficulties and astonished his advisers by the way he tried to turn the Hardy Spicer strike to Labour's advantage:

> I am bound to say that some of us are getting a little suspicious about the fact that in every general election a dispute suddenly blows up in a firm whose production affects a large section of the motor-car industry. We are waiting daily and expectantly for news from British Oxygen where there were sudden disputes both in the 1959 and 1955 elections . . . This sort of thing, happening election after election, is a matter which cannot be left where it is. The Labour Government intends to hold an inquiry with full powers, to get at the facts in any dispute which occurs in this general election.[45]

The attendant press were taken aback, the Conservatives exultant.

Word of Wilson's remarks reached Reggie Maudling before the Conservative Party's morning press conference across Smith Square in Central Office. It enabled him to prepare what the seasoned political commentator Bernard Levin used to call a well-rehearsed spontaneity. Tony Howard and/or Richard West, co-authors of *The Making of the Prime Minister*, witnessed the scene as the affable Maudling turned on the sarcasm:

> Although Maudling had already heard Wilson's charge before the Conservative press conference opened, he managed to give a show of complete surprise when the point was raised by a reporter. 'I must say that's a rum one,' he said with a great grin. 'Tory shop stewards going round sabotaging Mr Wilson's election! Really!!'[46]

Alec Douglas-Home perked up that day. He even enjoyed the heckling, which rather plagued him on his election tours, according to an aide.[47]

Yet the gods of politics were with Wilson. A saviour appeared in the person of the chairman of Hardy Spicer, Herbert Hill, an affable man with a patrician air and quite unschooled in the ways of public relations. The day after Wilson's misjudgement at Labour's morning press conference, he unleashed his thoughts in a way that changed the political climate once more. Summoning the press to Hardy Spicer's Mayfair office, he said:

They are people who are not of very high intelligence. If they were, they would understand the issues involved here economically. I feel very much that they are 'poor dears' and am very sad for them. They are our workers for whom we strive and whose welfare we seek to promote. They are a lot of misguided people.[48]

A journalist who saw Wilson that afternoon found a much-relieved Labour leader: 'It was the only time I've ever seen Wilson really laughing. He just couldn't stop all through the interview.'[49]

That evening Herbert Hill issued a writ against Harold Wilson, thereafter enabling Labour to refuse the discuss Hardy Spicer as the matter was sub judice. Yet political friend and political foe alike were amazed that Wilson had made such a hash of it. One of his aides told the Nuffield election cartographers David Butler and Tony King that Wilson had, in the end, 'scored a boundary through the slips; but he never should have made the stroke'.[50] Maudling told Howard and West later that 'what really annoyed me about it was that it was the only time when we really got Wilson rattled. I'll never know why he did it: quite out of character for him to make a mistake like that.'[51]

Another election 'particle' that caused a real stir had no lighter side, for it involved a blowback from the Profumo affair. It was a heckler who lit the blue touch paper that was Quintin Hogg, as Lord Hailsham had now become, Secretary of State for Education and Science, at a meeting in Plymouth on the evening of 6 October 1964.

Hogg's theme was ideals in public life. He had just begun to refute Wilson's assertion that Macmillan 'debauched the standards of public life' when a young heckler pounced with, 'What about Profumo?' Hogg erupted. As the report in the following morning's *Times* put it:

Mr Hogg snatched his glasses from his face and retorted: 'If you can tell me there are no adulterers on the front bench of the Labour Party you can talk to me about Profumo.' At this point other hecklers stood up and joined in the shouting, bellowing 'Profumo, Profumo.' Mr Hogg shouted: 'If you cannot tell me that, you had better not dabble your fingers in filth. If you cannot tell me that, you had better keep your mouths shut because that sort of filth should be kept out of public life. So let us have no more filth of that kind.'

It took several minutes before the noise subsided and Mr Hogg was able to resume the theme of his speech. At Plymouth station before he left on the midnight sleeper for London, Mr Hogg said: 'I do not regret one word I said. I have always thought these things should be kept out of politics. But I thought it was necessary to give a salutary lesson to the foolish young man who chose to taunt me with the Profumo affair. Everyone knows that these sort of things are not the monopoly of any one party.'[52]

By the time Hogg found his way to his berth on the Paddington sleeper, the impact of his Plymouth eruption had reached the Birmingham Bull Ring, where Wilson was performing. Geoffrey Goodman wrote later that it was the only moment in the campaign when Wilson's guard dropped. The news of Hogg's words reached the press table in the Bull Ring and a note was passed up to the platform for Wilson's attention:

> In mid-flow he glanced at it and pushed it aside. There was no pause or falter. But later back in his hotel room there were scenes of panic, even hysteria. Mrs Williams was in tears. Wilson sat in a corner of his room, silent. Mary Wilson was white-faced. News of this was brought to me, waiting downstairs [in the Albany Hotel], by an old friend and former [journalistic] colleague, Alfred Richman, who was part of the Wilson entourage.

There was talk of legal action, as a way of stopping the newspapers running the story. But, by 'the early hours the pot had stopped boiling, though only just. Wilson went to bed, calmed by Mary whose presence and demeanour that night was a source of great strength to her husband and, without a doubt, a crucial factor in a night of crisis.'[53]

The following morning, the eighty-one-year-old Clem Attlee, that gold standard Prime Minister, sat at the typewriter in his flat in the Temple and tapped out a statement which Harold Wilson had asked him to make (Attlee delivered it at a meeting in Southall later that day[54]). It was an intervention that did not waste a word:

> It is time he grew up. He should know that when he has met with a rude interjection he does not lose his temper. He made a very unseemly

remark. Mr Hogg acted like a schoolboy. He made general accusations against the Labour frontbench without a shadow of justification.
The man is a Cabinet Minister. He was nearly leader of his party and
he ought not to say this kind of thing. In fact, members of the Labour
Party have scrupulously refrained from making political capital out of
the unfortunate moral lapses of a certain Tory minister.[55]

This was a pure Major Attlee-like dismissal of bad form.

Quintin Hogg's combative ebullience was very much part of his
character. Another senior Cabinet minister who ran true to form during the election campaign was the Foreign Secretary, Rab Butler. He
left his intervention until the very end and, even now, it is not possible
to be sure that it was wholly deliberate – which in a way is fitting for
a politician who took ambiguity to stratospheric heights.

The great Butler indiscretion took place on a train on the East
Coast Main Line two days after Hogg's 'adulterers' moment in Plymouth. Part of it may have had to do with Butler's (justified) feeling
that – in contrast to all previous postwar general elections – he had
been sidelined during the campaign. The *Daily Express*, among
others, had noticed this and sent their top political commentator,
George Gale, in pursuit of the elusive Rab.

Rab was due to speak in Teesside on the evening of 8 October
1964. Gale joined him on the 2.15 from King's Cross to Darlington
on the understanding that he would leave Rab on his own for a while
to work on his Foreign Office red boxes in his reserved compartment.
After about an hour, Gale joined him. Butler, no doubt, should have
made it plain whether or not he was speaking attributably before
Gale led him skilfully into indiscretion by suggesting that the election, though the polls suggested the outcome would be very close,
might slip away from the Conservatives in the last days. Rab later
claimed he thought he was speaking off the record.[56]

The story, strangely hidden away on an inside page of the *Daily
Express* the following morning, contained remarks from Butler that,
as his official biographer, Anthony Howard, put it, 'to anyone who
knew Rab had a ring of total authenticity'.[57] Gale knew his man.
'Matured indiscretions', dropped from Butler's lips, 'like ripened fruit
from apple trees':

How was the election going? 'Very close. We're running neck and neck. I'll be very surprised if there's much in it, say twenty seats either way. But things might start slipping in the last few days.' Slipping away? 'Yes, they won't slip towards us.' What of the Tory campaign so far? 'Alec has done very well. Possibly he has spent too much time outside London' ... And what of Sir Alec's praise for the young, dynamic Edward Heath? 'That's interesting ... I think Alec's a bit bored by him – not as a Minister of course.'[58]

That interview was the second shock wave in two days to hit Conservative Central Office. A senior Tory official told Howard and West: 'Hogg's outburst on adultery was greeted in Central Office next morning with rage and dismay. But people weren't as angry as they were about Rab's remarks to George Gale.'[59]

Meanwhile, the other future Conservative Prime Minister, Margaret Thatcher, was defending her seat in Finchley against John Pardoe for the Liberals, who was thought to be in with a chance. (In the event he came second, reducing Mrs Thatcher's 1959 majority from 16,260 to 8,802.) Bernard Donoughue was at a meeting in Hampstead Garden Suburb when she was asked 'What is the purpose of life?' At the time Donoughue did not record her reply,[60] but when I asked him about it fifty-three years later, he said: 'Sadly cannot precisely remember. But think along the lines of working hard to do good. My main recollection was of her throwing her raincoat back over her shoulder and Denis catching it. Role for life.'[61]

The campaign of 1964 was thus a particularly flavourful general election, but it ended on a rather jaded note. Wilson did not shine at his eve-of-poll meeting on his own turf in the magnificent setting of St George's Hall in Liverpool. In his prime, he played the political game with true flair, but sometimes flair players fail to rise to the occasion. The Douglas-Homes returned to his constituency of Kinross and West Perthshire to stay overnight in Culdees Castle, a dramatic contrast to urban Liverpool, on the eve of a poll he thought privately was, as Butler had forecast, likely to slip away from the Conservatives. His wife Elizabeth told him the next day: 'It isn't the end of the world if we lose.'[62]

Back in Liverpool, Wilson may for once have been weary and low on electricity but the atmosphere in St George's Hall was not. Wilson's 'was a dull and tired performance', but, according to Anthony Howard and Richard West:

> There was nothing dull about the audience or the immense hall itself, with its brown quartz pillars topped with Corinthian gilt, and its marble statues of Gladstone and other Victorian statesmen. But Wilson arrived late and Frank Cousins, the union leader, grew more and more tedious as he played for time in an introductory oration. It was not until 9.05 that Wilson came on to the platform and the immense audience rose to sing, in its mass Liverpudlian accents: 'For He's a Jolly Good Fellow – and so say all of uzz.'[63]

And Wilson's formidable televisual instincts were still sharp:

> 'Comrades and friends,' Wilson began, using the word 'comrades' for almost the first time since his left-wing days in the 'fifties. For the next five minutes he kept looking continuously at his watch to judge the exact moment – 9.16 – when he was due to appear on a live ITN newscast. 'He'll be saying the bit about people,' said one of the party's TV experts, and sure enough at 9.16 sharp, Wilson paused and began to read out in a loud Churchillian tone: 'We care for people; they care for profit. We care about opportunity; they are preoccupied with inheritance and conserving inheritance. They are concerned with the retention of power; we are concerned to exercise power democratically for the benefit of our people as individuals and our people as families.'[64]

He delivered another carefully prepared line at 9.24 when the light on the BBC camera showed he was being beamed live into their news bulletin, this time calling for a crusade.

According to Howard and West: 'The best part of the evening came after the meeting was over. A jostling crowd of 2,000 Liverpudlians marched through the city centre accompanying Harold and Mary Wilson back to the Adelphi Hotel.' And in a nod to the Beatles' 'She Loves You', they 'chanted Wilson's name and "Yeah, yeah, yeah"'.[65]

The Wilsons repaired to Suite 100 in the huge hotel built to house the passengers of Cunard et al. between disembarking from the boat trains at nearby Lime Street Station and boarding their liners waiting at the huge berths of Liverpool docks the following morning. The press were invited in for a party. At this stage Wilson had a jolly relationship with many of them and the journalists reciprocated – they had bought gifts for the Wilsons (John Betjeman's poems for Mary; *The Cricketer's Companion* and the *Footballer's Companion* for Harold together with a copy of Anthony Trollope's *The Prime Minister*): 'Referring to Harold Macmillan in his speech of thanks, Wilson said that he would be the second Prime Minister in the last three "to sleep with a Trollope beside the bed".'[66]

Uncertainty lurked in Suite 100 of the Adelphi, however. The final polls pointed to a Labour victory, but they were well within the margin of error (Gallup gave Labour a lead of 3.5 per cent; NOP 3.1 per cent[67]). Just after the polls closed, so too late to be an influence on the result, news began to come in from Moscow that Khrushchev had been deposed by a 'troika' of Alexei Kosygin, Leonid Brezhnev, and Anastas Mikoyan.[68]

Wilson was a railway buff and had a faint obsession with old Bradshaw timetables, as Roy Jenkins (who had a similar passion[69]) later noticed. On the evening of 15 October 1964, railway timetables became part of the nerves:

> Even at this late hour they had not finally chosen the train [on which to travel to Euston the next morning]. There was a contingency booking on the 8.15 from Lime Street, to Euston, due in at 12.10. But Wilson was firm that he would not travel down on this early train if things went badly. 'If we lose we'll have all the time in the world. You can come with me on the 10.15 – and bring the brandy.' He was planning, in case of defeat, to spend the whole week-end on the golf course. As the result grew more and more close and uncertain, it was the choice of train which seemed to Wilson a cause of almost neurotic anxiety.[70]

It was to be a night and an early morning of uncertainty and anxiety for Wilson, punctuated by a burst of euphoria at his greatly increased majority in his Huyton constituency (trebled to nearly 20,000). Just after 3 a.m., back in the Adelphi from his count, he finally decided that it would be the 8.15 from Lime Street. It was to be the strangest of political rail journeys. In those days, transistor radios would not work on moving trains, leading to frantic tuning-in at every stop on the way. At 10.30, somewhere north of Nuneaton, Wilson the statistician got out his slide rule and calculated his destiny: 'It's no good. We shan't make it . . . We've lost by one seat.'[71]

Understandably, Wilson got snappy with the press on board; especially with the photographers, who tried to capture him eating sausages, bacon and sauté potatoes with his beloved HP Sauce.[72] The train then arrived late, at 12.25 p.m. Wilson refused to make a statement to the TV reporters gathered at Euston. By 12.45 he was back at Transport House, where he told a press conference: 'It's still too early to comment on the result.'[73]

In fact, it was to be another two hours before Wilson realized the great prize of the premiership would be his. At 2.47 the Brecon and Radnor result took Labour to the magic tally of 315 seats.[74] Just before 3.30 Sir Alec went to Buckingham Palace to tender his resignation to the Queen.[75] He left quietly and on foot through the Privy Purse Door, close by the Queen's Private Secretary's office.[76] At 3.50 the telephone rang in Transport House. A call for Mr Wilson from the Private Secretary, Sir Michael Adeane: 'Would it be convenient for you to come round and see Her Majesty?'[77]

It had been a remarkably close-run thing. The final result was Labour 317 seats (44.1 per cent of votes cast); Conservatives 304 (43.4 per cent); Liberals 9 (11.2 per cent). An overall Labour majority of four on a turnout of 77.1 per cent.[78]

Between the Brecon and Radnor declaration and Adeane's call to Wilson, a little farce had broken out in Transport House of the ludicrous back-of-stairs kind that sometimes becomes part of an event's history. Geoffrey Goodman witnessed it. Wilson was in the process of changing from a lounge suit to a morning suit for his visit to the Palace, assisted by Alf Richman. Richman noticed Wilson's striped trousers were held aloft by a pair of red braces:

'Harold, you can't wear *them*. It's not the thing.'

'Why not? They're perfectly good braces.'

'You simply can't do that. You must have proper black braces to go with the rest of the outfit.'

'But I haven't got another pair of braces. These are all I have – unless either of you two can lend me a pair.'[79]

Richman rushed off to a nearby department store, purchased a pair of black braces and attached them to Wilson's trousers just in time for him to stand on the steps of Transport House at 3.58 p.m., with Clem Attlee beside him, before getting into the car with his wife Mary and their twenty-year-old son Robin for the short drive to the Palace. The Queen was spared the socialist braces. But had a new kind of British socialism come to kiss hands in the person of her new Prime Minister? He had fire in his belly, humanity in his heart and technocracy in his mind. Would it be enough? Would there be an age of Harold Wilson? For all the minuscule size of the Labour majority, it was a moment brimming with possibility.

Epilogue: A Certain Idea of Britain

The state is an important instrument; hence the struggle to control it. But it is an instrument, and nothing more. Fools will use it, when they can, for foolish ends, and criminals for criminal ends. Sensible and decent men will use it for ends which are decent and sensible, and will know how to keep fools and criminals in their place.

R. H. Tawney, 1944[1]

A family with the wrong members in control – that, perhaps, is as near as one can come to describing England in a phrase.

George Orwell, 1941[2]

The British were the only people who went through both world wars from beginning to end. Yet they remained a peaceful and civilized people, tolerant, patient and generous. Traditional values lost much of their force, other values took their place. Imperial greatness was on the way out; the welfare state was on the way in. The British Empire declined; the condition of the people improved. Few now sang 'Land of Hope and Glory'. Few even sang 'England Arise'. England had risen all the same.

A. J. P. Taylor on 1945 and after, 1965[3]

I have always felt a part of Taylor's 'risen' Britain. That – to borrow from General de Gaulle – is my 'certain idea' of Britain. It was an earlier and even more troublesome Frenchman, Napoleon Bonaparte, who is said to have declared that to understand a man or woman in their maturity you must think of the world as it was when they were twenty.[4] I was nearly eighteen at the time of the October 1964 general election. Does Napoleon's law apply to me? I think very largely that it does. If you put to one side the possibility that a Third World War and thermonuclear exchange could have put an end to *any* idea of Britain as we had known it, the years of my early postwar formation were tinged with a sense of progress and the optimism that goes with such a feeling. We experienced, in varying degrees, the first warmth of a mass-consumption society, especially once all rationing ended in 1954, and the accumulating improvements in health, education and welfare engendered by the reforms of the postwar settlement during the late war and early postwar years.

The instrument of the state, in Tawney's terms, seemed to be in the hands of those in both the big political parties who believed in the full employment/welfare state nostrums of Keynes and Beveridge and of those who carried with them the intense, shared experience of the Second World War, whether lived on the battlefronts or the home front. The state-as-provider had quickly come to seem the natural supplier not just of health, education and welfare but of basic national infrastructure, too. I can remember wondering in 1962 why the state hadn't put in place a motorway-building programme much earlier in the postwar years. Motorways were then a thing of fascination and anticipated pleasure, especially when the M6 began to string itself ever closer towards the Lake District. Almost everywhere my adolescent mind looked there was progress to be found: an economic growth plan in NEDC (what we would now term an industrial strategy); plans for a fistful of new universities plus grants and fees for all who could acquire the right A levels; a new hospital building programme; Empire into Commonwealth and, perhaps, a Britain in Europe, a new field on which to display our statecraft and slake our thirst for exerting influence beyond our shores.

The standard model of UK politics after the war very much reflected these optimisms. What do I mean by the standard model? For any country, the answer to that question is to be found partly in the nature of its political competition. In all the general elections during which I have been breathing (starting in 1950) it has, in essence, inside the UK been a tussle between liberal (small 'l') capitalism – the best mechanism, to my mind, that the world has yet developed for economic growth and innovation – and social democracy – the best instrument humankind has yet produced for a higher degree of wealth redistribution and social justice. This was the political model that underpinned and reflected the postwar British New Deal.

The electorate, of course, wishes for the benefits of each to different degrees at different times and it is the job of Westminster and Whitehall to try to engineer this benign fusion for them. Sometimes this has strains of wishing for that 'better yesterday'. It is not a particularly heroic programme for a political society, but it is a benign one, for happy and safe is the country where that is the political ecology and where an exemplary constitutional monarch consistently contributes to a sense of stability. It also encourages a political culture whose characteristics may include sometimes crude and partisan exchanges, but which can also draw on deep pools of civility and tolerance. It would be a matter of anxiety if this model were to break down, as it may be in the early stages of doing (though not, mercifully, the constitutional monarchy).

It was the remarkable John Buchan, statesman, scholar and thriller writer (most famously author of *The Thirty-Nine Steps*[5]), who wrote in his memoir of 1940 (the year he died): 'in the cycle to which we belong we can only see a fraction of the curve'.[6]

The arc I had been part of for nearly eighteen years in 1964 reflected the development of what the American political and constitutional historian Philip Bobbitt would later call 'the constitutional industrial state' that had begun to form in the late nineteenth century. 'The watermark of any particular constitutional order', wrote Bobbitt, 'is its claim to legitimacy . . . Give us power, the nation state said, and we will improve your material well-being.'[7] The political competition stimulated by the forthcoming general election of 1964 was, I think, the high point of that 'watermark' for the UK nation, as both main parties pressed their claim to be best placed to stimulate and then sustain 4 per cent economic growth per year and to use most wisely its productive dividend for improved health, education and welfare.

Some mysteries remain about that dash for growth. Why, for example, did the Conservatives, like Labour, look to the French model of indicative planning rather than to the social market approach that had helped give Adenauer's West Germany an even higher rate of expansion than de Gaulle's France? David Howell, with his fellow Bow Groupers, did read *Prosperity Through Competition*, the social market testimony of Ludwig Erhard, Adenauer's Finance Minister and key architect of the West German 'economic miracle'.[8] Many years later, David told me that none of Macmillan's chancellors (Derick Heathcoat-Amory; Selwyn Lloyd; Reggie Maudling) showed the slightest interest in it.[9] For Macmillan himself, Germany was most unlikely to be a model for anything, given what he described as the 'incredible wickedness' of Germany in 1914 and 1939, which meant that 'Europe has twice pulled itself to pieces in a single generation', as he put it in a private and intensely melancholic letter to his friend Robert Menzies in February 1962.[10]

Other economic and industrial aspects of Buchan's arc in Britain from 1945 to 1964 are in no way mysterious to the eyes of later generations. For example, every industrial strategy since the war has attempted to tackle three key, deeply persistent and interrelated problems: low UK productivity compared with our main competitors, a shortage of technical education and skills among the UK workforce and an inability to fully industrialize or commercialize the country's considerable prowess as a scientific and a research and development nation. The 1944 Education Act produced formidable change but its technical educational provision never took off. The framers of the thinking that produced the National Economic Development Council would have every sympathy with those who crafted the 2017 version of industrial strategy.

Yet those first postwar decades do – and did – have a touch of gold around them, even though UK growth rates lagged behind those of West Germany and France. French economists called them 'the thirty glorious years' (ending with the oil shocks in the early to mid 1970s). More recent American economic historians have characterized the first two-and-a-half decades as 'the Great Leap Forward':[11] the Princeton economist Robert Gordon argues that the great technical breakthroughs of the second industrial revolution of the late nineteenth century did not reach their maximum effect in terms of 'total factor productivity' until the years after 1945, boosted by wartime innovation and stimulated still further by the rise of a mass-consumption society whose ingredients were electricity, cars, telephones, running water and sewerage, improved infrastructure generally plus the spread of mass higher education.[12] Gordon was writing about the United States (where, of course, overall consumption and living standards were much higher), but his analysis fits early postwar Britain apart from mass higher education, which the UK reached only in the late 1980s and early 1990s. This delayed bonus from late-nineteenth-century technological breakthroughs powerfully shaped the nature of the UK's standard model of politics and the liberal capitalism/social democracy tussle at the heart of it. It enabled the UK version of Bobbitt's 'constitutional industrial state' to make generous offers to its people compared with past political eras.

The Second World War had also laid down a new psychological path along which subsequent socioeconomic progress could march. It was another US economic historian, Robert Higgs, who caught this best: 'The war economy . . . broke the back of pessimistic expectations almost everybody had come to hold during the seemingly endless depression.'[13] This too was as true of the UK as it was of the US: it was very significant that the UK's key postwar templates – the Beveridge Report of 1942, the Keynes-infused full employment White Paper of 1944, the Butler Act of the same year and the creation of the National Health Service in 1948 – were all pessimism breakers. From 1949, NATO provided another, geopolitically speaking. Later I would add Empire into Commonwealth and the exemplary constitutional monarchy of Elizabeth II to that list. They provided the seven flags around which the post-1945 UK could rally. Embroider them on a single generational banner of shared aspiration and the effect is truly lustrous. That banner remains central to my certain idea of Britain. Our postwar approach to political economy, welfare and education and international affairs may have possessed a certain 'ramshackle' quality, but it had its distinctive pillars too which underpinned its relative optimism about incremental improvement and our notions of the kind of country we both were and were going to be.

Eventual EEC entry in 1973 could be seen, both at the time and retrospectively, as completing the postwar settlement by resolving the unfinished business of the UK's relationship with Europe. Hence the force of Sir Nicholas Soames (Churchill's grandson) crying out to me over a Westminster car park as Parliament and the country ground towards Brexit: 'It's the end of the postwar settlement!' (Churchills have a feel for epochs). For some, however, EEC entry was a step too far for an ancient country whose intense feel for its sovereignty had helped it to stand alone magnificently in 1940–41, just thirty years earlier. Whatever becomes of the UK post-Brexit, historical debate will feed deep on the pros and cons of the strange life of European Britain 1973–2019 and the Brexit debate will morph into a fight over yesterday.

Returning to the early postwar era, these were the years before the notion of affluence acquired a double edge. The centre left in the UK was profoundly influenced by J. K. Galbraith's *The Affluent Society*,[14] first published in 1958, with its contrast in the USA between private affluence and public squalor. Along with the home grown *The Future of Socialism* by Anthony Crosland, published in 1956,[15] it enlivened the case for more and better public provision. Avner Offer, an Oxford economic historian and early twenty-first century anatomist of affluence in the UK and the US, contrasts the early postwar era of improved consumption with what he called 'The challenge of affluence' that influenced later attitudes and which, perhaps, makes it harder to recall the previous notions of the concept. 'During the postwar years', he wrote in 2006, 'household appliances were the magic boxes of affluence. Those appliances (like radio and television) that provided sensual arousal diffused very rapidly almost regardless of income.'[16] This was the early age of affluence, too, which 'liberated most people [in the USA and the UK] (though never all of them) from the anxieties of subsistence'.[17]

But, at some point, probably in the 1970s in the UK, the price of affluence became of greater and wider concern. In my first twenty years of life, the concern was to boost the nation's nutritional intake; later, obesity-related anxieties took hold. As Avner Offer expressed it in *The Challenge of Affluence*: 'An emergent problem of substance abuse is associated with pre-processed foods where easy exposure to arousal has altered the body shape of the population, and is beginning to threaten to undo some of the public health achievements of previous decades.'[18]

There is also a besetting problem with a rising tide of affluence – it does not flow evenly across the land, producing resentment and a sharp sense of unfairness. Geoffrey Moorhouse, a *Guardian* feature writer and a grammar-school boy from Bury in Lancashire, captured this vividly in 1963–4 when he set out to depict 'The Other England' and to contrast it with what he called 'the Golden Circle' of London and the south-east (already moving towards becoming a city state within a nation, a process that has become more pronounced with every decade since Moorhouse wrote his Penguin Special).[19]

Overall the children of the early postwar years were provided for better than ever before. Quite apart from the collective security afforded us by the 1949 North Atlantic Treaty and the avoidance of a Third World War, we had more free healthcare, education and welfare pumped into us than any previous generation. Of this I was certainly aware in the early 1960s, no doubt overlain with an ambiguous sense also of being part of a rising meritocracy. These, as well as a sense of history, were the ties of both affection and loyalty that bound me to the country of my birth.

There is a particularly beautiful and telling line that R. H. Tawney crafted for a newspaper article after he had returned home from soldiering on the Western Front in early 1917: 'Only those institutions are loved which touch the imagination,' he wrote.[20]

A nation is more than simply its institutions, but they are an essential part of it. And they, the personalities and power of our history which make my country – in all its moods, through all its fluctuating fortunes – have continuously touched my deepest imagination and shaped, as I have attempted to explain, my certain idea of Britain. If I can be sure of one thing in these fluid times, I am *certain* that they will continue to do so, arousing love and fascination in equal measure.

Chronology

	17	Summit ends in disarray as Khrushchev walks out over U-2 incident.
	19–31	Macmillan privately accepts that UK must join the European Economic Community (EEC) in order to maintain its influence in Europe and the wider world.
June	1	Macmillan circulates a list of questions on the pros and cons of UK membership of the EEC to a group of top officials.
	20	Cabinet agrees to purchase the US Skybolt stand-off missile for the RAF's V-force.
	23	Bank rate increased from 5 per cent to 6 per cent.
	26	British Somaliland gains independence as Somalia.
	29	House of Commons votes against the legalization of homosexual acts.
July	6	Bevan dies at the age of sixty-two. Top officials complete *The Six and the Seven Report*, replying to Macmillan's UK/EEC questions.
	13	Cabinet discusses *The Six and the Seven Report*. Agrees to 'seek a . . . mutually satisfactory arrangement between the EEC and EFTA'.
	27	Derick Heathcoat-Amory resigns as Chancellor of the Exchequer and is replaced by Selwyn Lloyd. Home replaces Lloyd as Foreign Secretary. Edward Heath becomes Lord Privy Seal. Christopher Soames becomes Agriculture Secretary. Enoch Powell becomes Health Secretary. Duncan Sandys becomes Commonwealth Secretary.
August	12	Unofficial shipping strike begins.
	16	Cyprus becomes independent.
	24	Shipping strike ends.
September	15	Cabinet approves US use of Holy Loch for its Polaris submarines.
October	1	Nigeria becomes independent.
	27	Bank rate reduced from 6 per cent to 5.5 per cent.
November	8	Kennedy elected President of the United States.
December	8	Bank rate reduced to 5 per cent.
	22	Ernest Marples, Minister of Transport, informs Macmillan that he intends to appoint Dr Richard Beeching of ICI as chairman of the British Transport Commission.

1961

January	6	Macmillan completes his 'Grand Design' document 'to deal with the economic, political and defence problems of the Free World!'
	21–22	Macmillan unveils 'Grand Design' at Chequers to a small group of senior ministers.
February	28–29	Macmillan–de Gaulle meeting at Rambouillet.
March	5	West German Deutschmark revalued by 5 per cent.
April	12	Russian Yuri Gagarin becomes first man in space.
	17	Budget. Surtax threshold raised from £2,000 to £5,000. Profits tax increased. New 10 per cent tax on television advertising.
	20	Macmillan tells Cabinet a decision has to be taken on UK policy toward the EEC.
	26	Cabinet supports the idea that UK should apply for EEC membership subject to the final terms of entry.
	27	Sierra Leone becomes independent.
May	31	South Africa leaves the Commonwealth.
June	1	New British Railways Board formed, with Dr Beeching in the chair.
	17–18	Cabinet conference at Chequers on UK and EEC.
	28	Lloyd circulates Cabinet paper warning of economic difficulties and urging wage controls and spending cuts.
July	20	Plowden Report on control of public expenditure published.
	21–24	Cabinet decides to apply for UK membership of the EEC conditional on final terms of entry.
	25	Lloyd raises bank rate from 5 per cent to 7 per cent and introduces emergency economic measures, including spending cuts and a 'pay pause' until the end of March 1962. Announcement of the tripartite National Economic Development Council.
	28–29	Macmillan and Cabinet Secretary Norman Brook institute planning for the machinery of government should tension in Berlin tip into war.

	31	Macmillan informs the House of Commons that the UK intends formally to apply for EEC membership.
August	2	Macmillan presents the government's case on EEC membership in the House of Commons.
	4	International Monetary Fund announces support for the pound sterling. House of Commons approves EEC application by 313 votes to 4.
	9	First UK application made to join the EEC.
	13	East Germans start building a wall in Berlin to prevent population fleeing west.
September	1	Soviet Union resumes nuclear testing in the atmosphere.
	25	National Economic Development Council launched.
	26	EEC Council of Ministers accepts UK request for negotiations.
October	5	Bank rate reduced to 6.5 per cent.
	10	Lead negotiator, Ted Heath, outlines UK case for EEC membership at a meeting of EEC states in Paris.
November	2	Bank rate reduced to 6 per cent.
	8–9	Negotiations begin; EEC and UK agree experts should start work on problems of common external tariff if UK were to join.
December	9	Tanganyika becomes independent as Tanzania.

1962

January	14	EEC agrees the principles of a Common Agricultural Policy.
February	1	White Paper on Incomes Policy sets out a 2.5 per cent norm for pay rises.
March	7	First meeting of the National Economic Development Council. Bank rate reduced to 5.5 per cent.
	14	Orpington by-election. Liberals overturn a formerly safe Conservative majority by over 7,000 votes.
	22	Bank rate reduced to 5 per cent.
April	1	'Pay pause' ends.

	9	Budget: profits tax increased by 2.5 per cent; confectionery tax on sweets, ice cream and soft drinks.
	26	Bank rate reduced to 4.5 per cent.
May	8	After a two-month impasse, UK–EEC negotiations resume in Brussels on the basis of reports from experts.
	28	Macmillan leads a discussion in Cabinet on 'the Orpingtonians' and presses the case for incomes policy and increased state spending.
June	2–3	Macmillan meets de Gaulle at Château de Champs.
July	13	Macmillan sacks a third of his Cabinet in the 'Night of the Long Knives'. Maudling replaces Lloyd as Chancellor of the Exchequer.
	26	National Economic Development Council sets 4 per cent annual growth target for the UK economy. National Incomes Commission announced by Macmillan.
	30	EEC's Common Agricultural Policy comes into being.
August	6	Jamaica gains independence.
	31	Trinidad and Tobago gains independence.
September	10–19	Commonwealth Prime Ministers' Conference in London discusses Commonwealth concerns about UK's decision to apply for EEC membership.
October	3	Hugh Gaitskell tells the Labour Party Conference that UK membership of the EEC would mean 'the end of a thousand years of history'.
	8	EEC negotiations resume in Brussels after summer break.
	9	Uganda gains its independence.
	16	Cuban missile crisis begins.
	22	Kennedy broadcasts on Cuba crisis.
	27	Macmillan places V-bomber force on Alert Condition 3 (fifteen minutes' readiness).
	28	Khrushchev backs down over Cuba.
November	5	Alert Condition 3 ends.
	14	Joint Intelligence Committee produces a paper on the danger of war through unintended escalation.
December	3	Macmillan circulates Cabinet paper on 'The Modernisation of Britain'.

	11	Kennedy administration announces the cancellation of the Skybolt missile.
	15–16	Macmillan meets de Gaulle at Rambouillet.
	18–21	Macmillan meets Kennedy at Nassau and secures a deal to purchase Polaris missiles for the Royal Navy.
	19–20	Brussels negotiations deadlocked over agricultural questions.
	26	Severe snowstorms begin a freeze that lasts until March.

1963

January	3	Cabinet authorizes purchase of Polaris missiles.
	14	De Gaulle vetoes the UK's application for EEC membership during a press conference in the Élysée Palace.
	15–18	Heath meets EEC ministers in Brussels.
	18	Gaitskell dies.
	28	Macmillan notes in his diary: 'All our policies at home and abroad are in ruins.'
	28–29	Final Brussels ministerial meeting ends in acrimony.
February	4	Macmillan warned of allegations about the private life of his Secretary of State for War, John Profumo.
	6	National Economic Development Council approves 4 per cent growth target.
	7	Result of the first ballot of Labour leadership election declared: Wilson 115; Brown 88; Callaghan 41.
	14	Result of second ballot declared: Wilson 144; Brown 103. Harold Wilson becomes Leader of the Opposition.
March	27	Beeching Report, *The Reshaping of the Railways*, published.
April	3	Maudling unveils an expansionary Budget: income tax cut; public spending and investment incentives increased.
June	5	Profumo resigns from Government and Parliament.
July	25	Partial Test Ban Treaty signed in Moscow.
August	12	Lord Poole, Conservative Party chairman, informs Macmillan that the parliamentary party would like a change of leadership.
September	16	Singapore, North Borneo and Sarawak gain independence and create Federation of Malaysia.

	17	Macmillan receives advance copy of Denning's report
	26	Lord Denning publishes his report on the Profumo affair.
	20	Macmillan informs the Queen that he does not wish to fight the next general election and that it will be delayed until 1964.
October	1	Harold Wilson delivers 'white heat' of technology speech at Labour Party Conference in Scarborough.
	7	Macmillan changes his mind and decides to stay on until after the general election. Suffers pain in the night due to prostate trouble.
	8	Macmillan shares with the Cabinet his intention to carry on. Enters hospital.
	10	Macmillan undergoes operation.
	10–12	Conservative Party Conference meets amid intense speculation about the leadership.
	17	Macmillan decides to back Home and prepares a memorandum for the Queen.
	18	Macmillan resigns. Queen sends for Home and asks him to try to form an administration. Macleod and Powell decline to serve under Home.
	19	Home calls on the Queen to tell her that he can form an administration. Queen appoints him Prime Minister.
	20	Butler appointed Foreign Secretary; Heath, President of the Board of Trade; Lloyd rejoins the Cabinet as Lord Privy Seal.
		Robbins Report on Higher Education published.
November	8	Sir Alec Douglas-Home wins by-election in Kinross and West Perthshire.
December	12	Kenya becomes independent.
		Treasury Public Expenditure White Paper proposes increase of 17.5 per cent in public spending between the financial years 1963–4 and 1967–8.

1964

January	14–15	Cabinet divided over abolition of resale price maintenance proposed by Heath.
February	27	Maudling increases Bank rate to 5 per cent.

April	14	Budget. Maudling places additional duties on alcohol and tobacco.
	15	Heath puts pressure on Douglas-Home to resist more Conservative backbench amendments on Resale Price Maintenance Bill.
May	11	UK government ratifies UN Convention on the Continental Shelf.
July	6	Nyasaland becomes independent.
September	11	Labour launches its manifesto, *Let's Go with Labour for the New Britain.*
	15	Douglas-Home calls on the Queen at Balmoral. Parliament to be dissolved on 25 September and general election held on 15 October.
		Liberals launch manifesto, *Think for Yourself.*
	18	Conservatives launch their manifesto, *Prosperity with a Purpose.*
	21	Malta becomes independent.
		UK government auctions blocks of North Sea for oil development.
October	15	News reaches London that Khrushchev had been deposed in Moscow.
	15–16	Labour returned with an overall majority of four.
	16	China explodes its first atomic device, in Sinkiang Province.
		Douglas-Home resigns.
		Wilson appointed Prime Minister.
	24	Northern Rhodesia becomes independent as Zambia.

Notes

PRELUDE

1. At the Royal Institute of British Architects in London on 12 June 2007.
2. I am very grateful to Bettina and Paul Mack for hosting a very jolly lunch at Bell Court on 14 August 2007, when I pooled early-Sixties Cotswold memories with Michael and Tessa Watts, Rose Westwood, Winnie Morgan, Mary Wooldridge and Tony Wooldridge.
3. *The Denning Report*, Cmnd 2152 (HMSO, 1963). It was reprinted, with a new introduction by Lord Denning, as *The Denning Report: The Profumo Affair* (Pimlico, 1992).
4. Glyn Daniel, *Some Small Harvest* (Thames & Hudson, 1986), pp. 90, 340.
5. J. V. Smith, *It All Began With Moses* (Choir Press, 1999), p. 19.
6. The Chiefs of Staff were warned that the signals traffic pouring out of the bunker once it was operational would give away its location to the Russians 'within a day or so at the outside' and they would drop a nuclear weapon on it causing a level of destruction that would block the entrances and exits. The National Archives (TNA), Public Record Office (PRO), DEFE 5/136, 'Chiefs of Staff Committee Memoranda, 20 February–28 May 1963', Annex to COS 96/63, 'United Kingdom Commanders-in-Chief Committee. Terms of Reference'. See also Peter Hennessy, *The Prime Minister: The Office and Its Holders Since 1945* (Penguin, 2004), pp. 133–4.
7. TNA, PRO, PREM 11/5222, 'Central Government in War', Brook to Macmillan, 12 May 1959.
8. TNA, PRO, CAB 21/4135, 'STOCKWELL – Chiefs of Staff Presentation, August–September 1960'.
9. Chapman Pincher, 'Britain Gets a Chain of H-Forts', *Daily Express*, 28 December 1959.
10. TNA, PRO, CAB 21/4135, Bishop to Bligh and Bligh to Bishop, 29 December 1959.
11. Ibid., 'D. Notice: 14.1.60', 'Underground Operational Centres'.

12. TNA, PRO, CAB 21/4135, 'STOCKWELL – Chiefs of Staff Presentation'.
13. TNA, PRO, CAB 21/6081, 'Machinery of Government in War: BURLINGTON; Ministerial Nominations', Cunningham to Brook, 10 August 1961.
14. Ibid., Bishop to Macmillan, 5 October 1961.
15. Ibid., Bishop to Brook, 12 September 1962.
16. The drills are preserved in TNA, PRO, WO 32/20122.
17. Ibid., 'First Information Slip'.
18. Ibid., 'GHQ UKLF Equipment for Prestocking at BURLINGTON', 18 October 1961.
19. Conversation with Peter Hudson, 16 August 2007.
20. TNA, PRO, PREM 11/5222, Orme to Bligh, 18 August 1959. Plus the attachment on 'OPERATION "VISITATION"'. I am grateful to James Waller for alerting me to the release of this file. Waller to Hennessy, 14 June 2007.
21. Private information.
22. Peter Hennessy, *The Secret State: Whitehall and the Cold War* (Penguin, 2003), pp. 166–7.
23. Conversation with Macmillan's grandson, Lord Stockton, 30 April 1998.
24. *Dr Strangelove, or, How I Learned to Stop Worrying and Love the Bomb* (Columbia Pictures, 1964).
25. Conversation with Peter Hudson, 16 August 2007.
26. Private information.
27. Private information.
28. Churchill used the words in his 'Finest Hour' speech on 18 June 1940. Brian MacArthur (ed.), *The Penguin Book of Twentieth-Century Speeches* (Viking, 1992), pp. 188–9.
29. I am very grateful to Wing Commander Steve Rover-Parkes and Andy Quinn, JSCU Mines Manager, for showing me, my students and Sir Kevin Tebbit (former Permanent Secretary, Ministry of Defence), around 'Site 3' on 19 June 2006.

OVERTURE: FROM ROMANS TO ITALIANS

1. Michael Howard, *Liberation or Catastrophe? Reflections on the History of the Twentieth Century* (Hambledon Continuum, 2007), p. 28.
2. Conversation with Sir Michael Howard, 7 January 2008.
3. Raymond Aron, *On War: Atomic Weapons and Global Diplomacy* (1956; published in Britain by Secker and Warburg, 1958).

4. Frisch's article is reproduced in John Carey (ed.), *The Faber Book of Science* (Faber & Faber, 1995), pp. 403–12, as 'Otto Frisch Explains Atomic Particles'.

5. Ronald W. Clark, *The Greatest Power on Earth: The Story of Nuclear Fission* (Sidgwick & Jackson, 1980), pp. 45–7, 159–63. See also Jeremy Bernstein, *Nuclear Weapons: What You Need to Know* (Cambridge University Press, 2008), pp. 46–7, 80–87.

6. Ibid., pp. 89–95. The original Frisch–Peierls 'Memorandum on the Properties of a Radioactive "Super-Bomb"' and 'On the Construction of a "Super-Bomb" Based on a Nuclear Chain Reaction in Uranium' can be found at the National Archives, Public Record Office, in AB 1/210. It is reproduced in Peter Hennessy, *Cabinets and the Bomb* (British Academy/Oxford University Press, 2007), pp. 24–30.

7. Rachel Carson, *Silent Spring* (Houghton Mifflin, 1962; Penguin Classics edn, 2000).

8. John Carey in Carey (ed.), *The Faber Book of Science*, p. 345.

9. Conversation with Bob Marshall-Andrews, 16 August 2009.

10. Carson, *Silent Spring*, pp. 22–3. For Carson's influence on Kennedy see ibid., Linda Lear, 'Afterword', p. 259. See also Linda Lear, *Rachel Carson: Witness for Nature* (Allen Lane, The Penguin Press, 1998); for the Communist Manifesto see Karl Marx and Friedrich Engels, *The Communist Manifesto* (Penguin Classics edn, 2002), p. 219.

11. John Kenneth Galbraith, *The World Economy Since the Wars: A Personal View* (Sinclair-Stevenson, 1994), pp. 172–3.

12. Peter Hennessy, *Never Again: Britain 1945–51* (Penguin, 2006), pp. 390–403.

13. The phrase is from David Reynolds. See his *Britannia Overruled: British Policy and World Power in the 20th Century* (Longman, 1991), p. 202.

14. As outlined to Lord Franks when Ambassador in Washington in 1948. See Peter Hennessy, *Having It So Good: Britain in the Fifties* (Penguin, 2007), p. 279.

15. Douglas Hurd and Edward Young, *Choose Your Weapons: The British Foreign Secretary; 200 Years of Argument, Success and Failure* (Weidenfeld & Nicolson, 2010), p. 346.

16. P. G. Wodehouse, 'Preface' to 'Joy in the Morning' as reproduced in *The Jeeves Omnibus*, vol. 2 (Hutchinson, 1990), p. 215.

17. Bob Morris was talking to students taking the 'Hidden Wiring' option of the MA in Twentieth Century History at Queen Mary, University of London on 24 March 2010.

18. Richard Cockett, *Thinking the Unthinkable: Think-Tanks and the Economic Counter-Revolution, 1931–1983* (HarperCollins, 1994).
19. James Barr, *The Bow Group: A History* (Politico's, 2001).
20. Simon Heffer, *Like the Roman: The Life of Enoch Powell* (Weidenfeld & Nicolson, 1998), see especially chapters 8 and 9.
21. Tony Judt, *Ill Fares the Land* (Penguin Press, 2010), reviewed in 'Social Democracy: A Plea for Liberalism', *The Economist*, 3 April 2010, p. 78.
22. Judt, *Ill Fares the Land*, p. 4.
23. Enoch Powell, *Freedom and Reality* (Batsford, 1969), p. 252. Mr Powell's paper on 'History as Myth' was delivered at Trinity College, Dublin on 13 November 1964. I am grateful to Paul Coupar-Hennessy for bringing it to my attention.

CHAPTER 1: THE CHIPPED WHITE CUPS OF DOVER

1. Michael Young, *The Chipped White Cups of Dover: A Discussion of the Possibility of a New Progressive Party* (Unit 2, 1960), p. 4.
2. Michael Shanks, *The Stagnant Society: A Warning* (Penguin, 1961), p. 232.
3. Anthony Sampson, *Anatomy of Britain* (Hodder & Stoughton, 1962), p. 634.
4. Henry Fairlie, 'On the Comforts of Anger', in the 'Suicide of a Nation?' special edition, edited by Arthur Koestler, of *Encounter*, no. 118 (July 1963), pp. 10, 13.
5. Dr Paul Addison, author of *The Road to 1945* (Cape, 1975), speaking during questions after his Gresham College Lecture on Clement Attlee, 27 October 2005.
6. A phrase he liked to use. See *The Chipped White Cups of Dover*, p. 6.
7. Conversation with Michael Young, 24 March 1994, for the Widevision Productions/Channel 4 series, *What Has Become of Us?*, transmitted on 18 December 1994.
8. Hennessy, *The Secret State*, plate 20 between pp. 148 and 149.
9. Young, *The Chipped White Cups of Dover*, p. 4.
10. Iain Dale (ed.), *Labour Party General Election Manifestos, 1900–1997* (Routledge/Politico's, 2000), pp. 49–60. Michael Young delivered his distillation of the 1945 manifesto in conversation with me on 24 March 1994.
11. My former student, Dr Matthew Grant, helpfully lists them in his 'Historians, the Penguin Specials and the "State-of-the-Nation" Literature, 1958–64', *Contemporary British History*, vol. 17, no. 3 (Autumn 2003), pp. 50–52.

12. Arnold. J. Toynbee, *A Study of History* (Oxford University Press, 1948), pp. 108–9.
13. Robin Denniston, 'Anthony Sampson: Author of "Anatomy of Britain" and Biographer of Mandela', *The Independent*, 21 December 2004.
14. For the author's notion of the 'British New Deal' see Hennessy, *Having It So Good*, chapter 1.
15. Fairlie, 'On the Comforts of Anger', p. 10.
16. Arthur Koestler, 'Introduction: The Lion and the Ostrich', *Encounter*, July 1963, p. 7.
17. Mary Douglas, *The Lele of the Kasai* (Oxford University Press, 1963).
18. Michael Shanks, 'The Comforts of Stagnation', *Encounter*, July 1963, p. 31.
19. Elizabeth Young, 'Against the Stream', ibid., pp. 105–6.
20. Arthur Koestler, *Arrow in the Blue* (Collins/Hamish Hamilton, 1952).
21. Arthur Koestler, *Bricks to Babel: Selected Writings with Author's Comments* (Picador, 1982), p. 571.
22. Ibid.
23. Ibid., p. 572.
24. Ibid., pp. 572–3.
25. Peter Hennessy, *Whitehall* (Pimlico, 2001), p. 352.
26. Shanks, *The Stagnant Society*, p. 199.
27. Grant, 'Historians, the Penguin Specials and the "State-of-the-Nation" Literature, 1958–64', p. 49.
28. Colin Robinson (ed.), *A Conversation with Harris and Seldon* (Institute of Economic Affairs, 2001), p. 25.
29. Ibid.
30. Hennessy, *Having It So Good*, pp. 210–11.
31. Norman Macrae, *Sunshades in October: An Analysis of the Main Mistakes in British Economic Policy Since the Mid Nineteen Fifties* (Allen & Unwin, 1963), p. 15.
32. Fernand Braudel, *A History of Civilizations* (Penguin, 1995), p. xxxviii.
33. Macrae, *Sunshades in October*, p. 179.
34. Ibid., p. 177.
35. Koestler, *Bricks to Babel*, p. 573.
36. Shanks, 'The Comforts of Stagnation', pp. 35–6.
37. *I'm All Right Jack* (Charter Film Productions, 1959).
38. David (now Lord) Puttnam was speaking on *Movies with a Message*, Part 2, 'I'm All Right Jack', which he presented on BBC Radio 4 on 8 January 2006.
39. Ibid. for this and the discussion that follows.

40. A long-time staple of our conversations.
41. Puttnam, *Movies with a Message.*
42. Ibid.
43. Dominic Sandbrook, *Never Had It So Good: A History of Britain from Suez to the Beatles* (Little, Brown, 2005), p. 327.
44. 'The Blood Donor' was broadcast on 23 June 1961. I am very grateful to my friend and guide since Cambridge days, Peter Riddell, for pointing out that *Hancock's Half Hour* on BBC TV should have featured in my *Having It So Good.* He was quite right. I hereby make belated amends.
45. Philip Oakes, *The Entertainers: Tony Hancock* (Woburn-Futura, 1975), p. 40.
46. Christopher Booker, *The Neophiliacs: A Study of the Revolution in English Life in the Fifties and Sixties* (Collins, 1969), p. 165.
47. Humphrey Carpenter, *That Was Satire That Was: The Satire Boom of the 1960s* (Gollancz, 2000), p. 107.
48. Ibid., p. 1.
49. Harry Thompson, *Peter Cook: A Biography* (Sceptre, 1997), p. 97.
50. Morgan Daniels, 'Scarcely Felt or Seen? British Government and the 1960s Satire Boom', unpublished undergraduate thesis, Department of History, Queen Mary, University of London, 2007, p. 3.
51. Ibid., p. 109.
52. Hennessy, *Having It So Good*, pp. 571–2.
53. From the CD *The Complete Beyond the Fringe* (EMI, 1996).
54. Malcolm Muggeridge, 'England, Whose England?', *Encounter*, July 1963, p. 14.
55. Conversation with Kathleen and Tam Dalyell, 7 September 2007.
56. John Carswell, *Government and the Universities in Britain: Programme and Performance, 1960–1980* (Cambridge University Press, 1985), Appendix 1, p. 172.
57. Addison, *The Road to 1945.* Dr Addison reviews the 'consensus debate' in 'Epilogue: The Road to 1945 revisited', which concludes the revised edition of the book published by Pimlico in 1994, pp. 279–92.
58. I am very grateful to Dr Addison for sending me his diary extract. Addison to Hennessy, 22 May 2007.
59. Carpenter, *That Was Satire That Was*, pp. 113–14.
60. Macmillan diaries (unpublished), Western Manuscripts Department, Bodleian Library, University of Oxford, entry for 2 February 1962.

61. Peter Catterall (ed.), *The Macmillan Diaries*, vol. 2: *Prime Minister and After, 1957–1966* (Pan Books edition, 2014), diary entry for 3 February 1962, p. 447.
62. Harold Evans, *Downing Street Diary: The Macmillan Years 1957/63* (Hodder, 1981), p. 183, diary entry for 4 February 1962.
63. Conversation with Paul Addison, 19 June 2007.
64. Hennessy, *Having It So Good*, p. 543.

CHAPTER 2: GRAND DESIGN

1. Anthony Sampson, *Macmillan: A Study in Ambiguity* (Allen Lane, The Penguin Press, 1967), p. 171.
2. Booker, *The Neophiliacs*, p. 148.
3. Macmillan diaries (unpublished), entry for 30 December 1960; Catterall (ed.), *The Macmillan Diaries*, vol. 2, p. 353, diary entry for 4 January 1961; ibid., p. 354, diary entry for 6 January 1961.
4. Macmillan diaries (unpublished), diary entry for 23 December 1960.
5. Ibid., diary entry for 23 January 1961.
6. Catterall (ed.), *The Macmillan Diaries*, vol. 2, p. 351, diary entry for 1 January 1961.
7. Ibid., p. 347, diary entry for 28 December 1960.
8. TNA, PRO, PREM 11/3325, 'Memorandum by Prime Minister on Future UK Political and Economic Policy: Meeting of Ministers at Chequers, 22 Jan. 1961', 'Memorandum by the Prime Minister', 'HM, December 29th 1960 to January 3rd, 1961'.
9. Catterall (ed.), *The Macmillan Diaries*, vol. 2, p. 339, diary entry for 30 November 1960.
10. Ibid., p. 335, diary entry for 11 November 1960.
11. Alistair Horne, *Macmillan, 1957–1986* (Macmillan, 1989), p. 283.
12. Ibid., p. 284.
13. Ibid.
14. TNA, PRO, PREM 11/3325, 'Memorandum by the Prime Minister'.
15. Ibid.
16. TNA, PRO, CAB 129/100, C (60) 35, 29 February 1960, 'Future Policy Study, 1960–1970', 'Note by the Prime Minister'. See also Hennessy, *Having It So Good*, pp. 574–95.
17. TNA, PRO, PREM 11/3325, 'Memorandum by the Prime Minister'.
18. Ibid.
19. Ibid.

20. Percy Cradock, *Know Your Enemy: How the Joint Intelligence Committee Saw the World* (John Murray, 2002), p. 171. See his chapter 8 on the Sino-Soviet dispute, pp. 161–78.
21. TNA, PRO, PREM 11/3325, 'Memorandum by the Prime Minister'.
22. Ibid.
23. Ibid.
24. Ibid.
25. Ibid.
26. Ibid.
27. Ibid.
28. Ibid.
29. Ibid.
30. Ibid.
31. Horne, *Macmillan, 1957–1986*, p. 32.
32. TNA, PRO, PREM 11/3325, 'Memorandum by the Prime Minister'.
33. Macmillan diaries (unpublished), diary entry for 8 May 1957.
34. Jean Lacouture, *De Gaulle, The Ruler: 1945–1970* (Collins Harvill, 1991), p. 215.
35. TNA, PRO, PREM 11/3325, 'Memorandum by the Prime Minister'.
36. Alistair Horne, *Macmillan, 1894–1956* (Macmillan, 1989), pp. 167–75.
37. TNA, PRO, PREM 11/3325, 'Memorandum by the Prime Minister'.
38. Ibid.
39. TNA, PRO, PREM 11/3322, 'Meeting Between Prime Minister and General de Gaulle, Rambouillet, 27–29 January 1961: Record of Discussions'. De Gaulle to Macmillan, 26 December 1960.
40. TNA, PRO, PREM 11/3325, 'Memorandum by the Prime Minister'.
41. Ibid. (emphasis in original).
42. André Malraux, *Fallen Oaks: Conversations with de Gaulle* (Hamish Hamilton, 1972), p. 47.
43. Lacouture, *De Gaulle*, p. 421.
44. TNA, PRO, PREM 11/3325, 'Memorandum by the Prime Minister'.
45. Lacouture, *De Gaulle*, chapter 31, 'The Nuclear "I"', pp. 413–33.
46. Ibid., p. 433.
47. TNA, PRO, CAB 158/32, JIC (58) 52, 'France – Nuclear Weapon Capability', 1 May 1958; CAB 158/38, JIC (59) 76, 'Development of Nuclear Capability by Fourth Countries – UK Views', 23 October 1959; CAB 158/38, JIC (59) 84, 'The Nuclear Capability of Fourth Countries by 1970', 23 October 1959.
48. Lacouture, *De Gaulle*, p. 416; Charles de Gaulle, *Memoirs of Hope: Renewal 1958–62* (Weidenfeld & Nicolson, 1971), p. 215.

49. TNA, PRO, PREM 11/3325, 'Memorandum by the Prime Minister' (emphasis in original).
50. Hennessy, *Cabinets and the Bomb*, p. 48.
51. TNA, PRO, PREM 11/3325, 'Memorandum by the Prime Minister'.
52. Ibid.
53. TNA, PRO, PREM 11/2990, 'Points Discussed with General De Gaulle at Rambouillet on March 12 and 13, 1960'.
54. TNA, PRO, PREM 11/3325, 'Memorandum by the Prime Minister'.
55. Lorna Arnold, *Britain and the H-Bomb* (Palgrave Macmillan, 2001), p. 200.
56. TNA, PRO, PREM 11/3325, 'Memorandum by the Prime Minister'.
57. Ibid.
58. Ibid.
59. Ibid.
60. Ibid.
61. Ibid., Brook to Macmillan, 20 January 1961.
62. Ibid.
63. Catterall (ed.), *The Macmillan Diaries*, vol. 2, p. 357, diary entry for 23 January 1961; see also Macmillan diaries (unpublished), diary entry for 23 January 1961.
64. TNA, PRO, PREM 11/3325, Brook to Macmillan, 20 January 1961.
65. TNA, PRO, PREM 11/3322, Prime Minister's Personal Minute no. M.38/61, Macmillan to Home, Lloyd and Watkinson, 26 January 1961.
66. Ibid., 'Sketch of Discussions with President de Gaulle'.
67. De Gaulle, *Memoirs of Hope*, pp. 210–11.
68. Macmillan diaries (unpublished), diary entry for 29 January 1961.
69. TNA, PRO, PREM 11/3322, 'Record of a Conversation Between President de Gaulle and the Prime Minister After Luncheon on Saturday January 28, 1961', 'HM, January 28, 1961'.
70. J. R. Seeley, *The Expansion of England* (Cambridge University Press, 1883).
71. Private information.
72. TNA, PRO, PREM 11/3322, 'Record of a Conversation Between President de Gaulle and the Prime Minister in the Marble Room at Rambouillet at 2.30 p.m. on Saturday, January 28, 1961'.
73. Ibid.
74. General de Gaulle, *War Memoirs: Unity 1942–1944* (Weidenfeld & Nicolson, 1959), p. 227.
75. TNA, PRO, PREM 11/3322, 'Record of a Conversation Between President de Gaulle and the Prime Minister in the Marble Room at Rambouillet at 2.30 p.m. on Saturday, January 28, 1961'.

76. De Gaulle, *Memoirs of Hope*, p. 188.
77. TNA, PRO, PREM 11/3322, 'Record of a Conversation Between President de Gaulle and the Prime Minister in the Marble Room at Rambouillet at 2.30 p.m. on Saturday, January 28, 1961'.
78. Ibid.
79. Ibid.
80. Ibid., 'Record of a Conversation at Rambouillet Between President de Gaulle and the Prime Minister in the Marble Room at Rambouillet at 5.30 p.m. on Saturday, January 28, 1961'.
81. Macmillan diaries (unpublished), diary entry for 29 January 1961.
82. Howard, *Liberation or Catastrophe?*, p. 163. Sir Michael's 'Britain, France and the Making of Europe' was read to the Institut Français pour Relations Internationales in 1995.
83. Ibid., p. 171.
84. TNA, PRO, PREM 11/3322, 'Record of a Conversation Between the Prime Minister and President de Gaulle in the Marble Room at Rambouillet at 11 a.m. on Sunday, January 29, 1961'.
85. Ibid., 'Record of a Conversation Between the Prime Minister and President de Gaulle in the Marble Room at Rambouillet at 2.45 p.m. on Sunday, 29 January, 1961'.
86. Ibid.
87. Macmillan diaries (unpublished), diary entry for 29 January 1961.
88. Catterall (ed.), *The Macmillan Diaries*, vol. 2, p. 358, diary entry for 29 January 1961; see also Macmillan diaries (unpublished), diary entry for 29 January 1961.
89. TNA, PRO, PREM 11/3322, Macmillan to Adenauer, 31 January 1961.
90. Ibid., Macmillan to Kennedy, 1 February 1961.
91. Ibid., Kennedy to Macmillan, 7 February 1961.
92. Catterall (ed.), *The Macmillan Diaries*, vol. 2, p. 368, diary entry for 26 March 1961.
93. Horne, *Macmillan, 1957–1986*, p. 280.
94. BBC1, 6 June 1972.
95. Conversation with Lord Greenhill.
96. Catterall (ed.), *The Macmillan Diaries*, vol. 2, pp. 368–9, diary entry for 26 March 1961.
97. *Foreign Relations of the United States*, vol. 13: *1961–1963* (USGPO, 1994), p. 1033.
98. TNA, PRO, PREM 11/3311, Brook to Members of the Cabinet, 17 April 1961. The summary is called 'Outline of Memorandum' and dated 15 April 1961.

99. TNA, PRO, CAB 129/105, C (61) 54, 'Washington Talks: Note by the Secretary of the Cabinet', 13 April 1961.
100. Michael Charlton, *The Price of Victory* (BBC Books, 1983), pp. 246–7.
101. Ibid., p. 247.
102. Ibid., p. 248.
103. TNA, PRO, CAB 129/105, C (61) 54, W (61), 1st Meeting, 5 April 1961.
104. Charlton, *The Price of Victory*, p. 247.
105. *Foreign Relations of the United States*, vol. 13: *1961–1963*, no. 3, 'Discussions with Prime Minister Macmillan, 12 April 1961'.
106. Catterall (ed.), *The Macmillan Diaries*, vol. 2, p. 372, diary entry for 8 April 1961.
107. Charlton, *The Price of Victory*, p. 265.
108. Ibid.
109. Ibid.
110. TNA, PRO, CAB 128/35 Part 1, CC (61), 22nd conclusions, 20 April 1961.
111. Hennessy, *Having It So Good*, pp. 612–13.
112. TNA, PRO, CAB 128/35, CC (61), 42nd conclusions, 21 July 1961.
113. Macmillan diaries (unpublished), diary entry for 20 April 1961.
114. TNA, PRO, CAB 128/35 Part 1, CC (61), 22nd conclusions, 20 April 1961.
115. Philip Williams, *Hugh Gaitskell* (Cape, 1979), p. 729.
116. Lewis Baston, *Reggie: The Life of Reginald Maudling* (Sutton, 2004), pp. 139–40.
117. TNA, PRO, CAB 128/35 Part 1, CC (61), 22nd conclusions, 20 April 1961.
118. Ibid.
119. Hennessy, *Having It So Good*, p. 285.
120. TNA, PRO, CAB 128/35 Part 1, CC (61), 22nd conclusions, 20 April 1961.
121. Alan S. Milward, *The United Kingdom and the European Community*, vol. 1: *The Rise and Fall of a National Strategy 1945–1963* (Frank Cass, 2002), p. 344.
122. TNA, PRO, FO 371/150369, 'EEC Relations with UK', Kilmuir to Heath, 14 December 1960.
123. The full NATO Treaty is reproduced in Nicholas Henderson, *The Birth of NATO* (Weidenfeld & Nicolson, 1982), Appendix B, pp. 119–22.
124. TNA, PRO, FO 371/150369, Kilmuir to Heath, 14 December 1960.

125. TNA, PRO, CAB 195/19, CC (61), 22nd conclusions, 20 April 1961.

126. Ibid.

127. Catterall (ed.), *The Macmillan Diaries*, vol. 2, p. 377, diary entry for 26 April 1961.

128. TNA, PRO, CAB 128/35, Part 1, CC (61), 24th Conclusions, 26 April 1961.

129. Ibid.

130. Catterall (ed.), *The Macmillan Diaries*, vol. 2, p. 492, diary entry for 21 August 1962.

131. TNA, PRO, CAB 128/35, Part 1, CC (61), 24th Conclusions, 26 April 1961.

132. Ibid.

133. Ibid.

134. Edward Heath, *The Course of My Life* (Hodder, 1998), pp. 208–9.

135. TNA, PRO, CAB 128/35, Part 1, CC (61), 24th Conclusions, 26 April 1961.

136. Ibid.

137. Hennessy, *The Prime Minister*, p. 251.

138. TNA, PRO, CAB 128/35, Part 1, CC (61), 24th Conclusions, 26 April 1961.

139. Heath, *The Course of My Life*, p. 203.

140. TNA, PRO, CAB 128/35, Part 1, CC (61), 24th Conclusions, 26 April 1961.

141. Ibid.

142. TNA, PRO, PREM 11/3311, 'Position of France in Western Alliance: "The Grand Design"; Discussions and Correspondence Between Prime Minister and President Kennedy', Macmillan to Kennedy, 28 April 1961.

143. Ibid., Kennedy to Macmillan, 8 May 1961.

144. Ibid., Macmillan to Kennedy, 15 May 1961.

145. Catterall (ed.), *The Macmillan Diaries*, vol. 2, p. 391, diary entry for 11 June 1961.

146. Evans, *Downing Street Diary*, pp. 156–7, diary entry for 6 August 1961.

147. Catterall (ed.), *The Macmillan Diaries*, vol. 2, p. 393, diary entry for 18 June 1961.

148. TNA, PRO, CAB 128/35, Part 1, CC (61), 35th Conclusions, 22 June 1961.

149. PRO, CAB 128/35, Part 2, CC (61), 42nd Conclusions, 21 July 1961.

150. Ibid.

151. *Pointing the Way* was the title of his volume of memoirs covering 1959–61 (Macmillan, 1972).

152. PRO, CAB 128/35, Part 2, CC (61), 42nd Conclusions, 21 July 1961.

153. Catterall (ed.), *The Macmillan Diaries*, vol. 2, p. 399, diary entry for 22 July 1961.
154. PRO, CAB 128/35, Part 2, CC (61), 44th Conclusions, 27 July 1961.
155. Ibid.
156. House of Commons *Official Report*, 31 July 1961, col. 928.
157. Ibid., cols. 929–30.
158. Ibid., col. 930.
159. Ibid., col. 931.
160. Ibid., col. 933.
161. Ibid.
162. Ibid., cols. 934–5.
163. Ibid., cols. 936–7.
164. Ibid., col. 936.
165. Ibid., col. 940.
166. Catterall (ed.), *The Macmillan Diaries*, vol. 2, pp. 402, 404, diary entry for 5 August 1961; see also Macmillan diaries (unpublished), diary entry for 5 August 1961.
167. House of Commons *Official Report*, 2 August 1961, cols. 1480–81.
168. Hugo Young, *This Blessed Plot: Britain and Europe from Churchill to Blair* (Macmillan, 1998), p. 338.
169. House of Commons *Official Report*, 2 August 1961, col. 1481.
170. House of Commons *Official Report*, 2 August 1961, col. 1482.
171. Ibid., cols. 1489–90.
172. Ibid., cols. 1490–91.
173. Ibid., col. 1491.
174. Ibid., cols. 1501–2.
175. Ibid., col. 1511.
176. Ibid., cols. 1512–13.
177. House of Commons *Official Report*, 3 August 1961, cols. 1651–2.
178. Catterall (ed.), *The Macmillan Diaries*, vol. 2, p. 403, diary entry for 5 August 1961.
179. House of Commons *Official Report*, 3 August 1961, col. 1658.
180. Heath, *The Course of My Life*, p. 211.
181. House of Commons *Official Report*, 3 August 1961, col. 1674.
182. House of Commons *Official Report*, 2 August 1961, col. 1494.
183. House of Commons *Official Report*, 3 August 1961, col. 1753.
184. Hennessy, *Having It So Good*, p. 452.
185. House of Commons *Official Report*, 31 July 1961, col. 938.
186. House of Commons *Official Report*, 3 August 1961, cols. 1781–6; Horne, *Macmillan, 1957–1986*, pp. 260–61.

187. House of Commons *Official Report*, 2 August 1961, col. 1492.
188. Roy Jenkins, *Gladstone* (Macmillan, 1995), p. 525.
189. Conversation with Sir Michael Palliser, 18 September 2008.
190. Ibid.
191. Conversation with Lord Wilson of Dinton, 2 October 2008. He originally advanced his 'anaesthetic' interpretation to my MA students at Queen Mary during a session on Cabinet Government.
192. Harold Macmillan, *At the End of the Day: 1961–63* (Macmillan, 1973), p. 27.
193. Macmillan diaries (unpublished), diary entry for 12 October 1961.
194. Catterall (ed.), *The Macmillan Diaries*, vol. 2, p. 419, diary entry for 13 October 1961.
195. Macmillan, *At the End of the Day*, p. 31.
196. Young, *This Blessed Plot*, p. 130.
197. TNA, PRO, PREM 11/3338, 'Meeting Between Prime Minister and General de Gaulle: Discussions Held at Birch Grove, 24–26 Nov 1961', de Zulueta to Macmillan, 17 November 1961.
198. Ibid., Pierson Dixon, 'General de Gaulle. His Views on Europe and Berlin', 16 November 1961.
199. Ibid.
200. Horne, *Macmillan, 1957–1986*, p. 315.
201. Catterall (ed.), *The Macmillan Diaries*, vol. 2, p. 429, diary entry for 25 November 1961.
202. TNA, PRO, PREM 11/3338, 'Visit of President de Gaulle to Birch Grove House, November 24–26, 1961'.
203. Ibid.
204. Ibid.
205. Ibid.
206. Ibid.
207. Macmillan diaries (unpublished), diary entry for 26 November 1961.
208. Sir David Goodall to Peter Hennessy, 29 September 2008.
209. Heath, *The Course of My Life*, p. 211.
210. Ibid.
211. Charlton, *The Price of Victory*, p. 271.
212. TNA, PRO, PREM 11/3559, unsigned and untitled report, 23 July 1961.
213. Heath, *The Course of My Life*, p. 225.
214. Nora Beloff, *The General Says No* (Penguin, 1963), p. 116.
215. Heath, *The Course of My Life*, p. 214.
216. Beloff, *The General Says No*, p. 120.
217. Heath, *The Course of My Life*, p. 216.

218. Ibid., p. 220.
219. Beloff, *The General Says No*, p. 144.
220. TNA, PRO, PREM 11/3775, 'Meeting Between Prime Minister and President de Gaulle, Chateau de Champs, 2–3 June 1962', 'Record of a Conversation at the Chateau de Champs at 5.50 p.m. on Saturday, June 2, 1962'.
221. Horne, *Macmillan, 1957–1986*, p. 328.
222. TNA, PRO, PREM 11/3775, 'Record of a Meeting at the Chateau de Champs at 10.30 a.m. on Sunday, June 3, 1962'.
223. Ibid.
224. Ibid.
225. Ibid., 'Record of a Conversation at the Chateau de Champs at 5.50 p.m. on Saturday, June 2, 1962'.
226. Ibid., Dixon, Paris to the Foreign Office, 23 May 1962.
227. Catterall (ed.), *The Macmillan Diaries*, vol. 2, p. 473, diary entry for 27 May 1962.
228. Ibid., p. 475, diary entry for 3 June 1962.
229. TNA, PRO, PREM 11/4272, 'UK Application to Join EEC: Discussions on Possible Machinery of Government Changes; Cabinet Secretary Wrote to Prime Minister', Brook to Macmillan, 23 August 1962.
230. Ibid., 'Common Market: Responsibility for Our Relations with the Community as Members', August 1962.
231. Ibid., Brook to Macmillan, 23 August 1962.
232. Catterall (ed.), *The Macmillan Diaries*, vol. 2, p. 494, diary entry for 3 September 1962.
233. Charlton, *The Price of Victory*, pp. 253–4.
234. Catterall (ed.), *The Macmillan Diaries*, vol. 2, p. 494, diary entry for 5 September 1962.
235. Ibid., p. 496, diary entry for 12 September 1962.
236. Williams, *Hugh Gaitskell*, pp. 728–9.
237. Horne, *Macmillan, 1957–1986*, p. 355.
238. Ibid.
239. Charlton, *The Price of Victory*, p. 278.
240. Milward, *The Rise and Fall of a National Strategy*, p. 395.
241. Catterall (ed.), *The Macmillan Diaries*, vol. 2, p. 499, diary entry for 22 September 1962.
242. Williams, *Hugh Gaitskell*, p. 729.
243. Evans, *Downing Street Diary*, entry for 22 September 1962, p. 218.
244. Catterall (ed.), *The Macmillan Diaries*, vol. 2, p. 505, diary entry for 11 October 1962.

245. Sampson, *Macmillan*, pp. 217–18.
246. TNA, PRO, PREM 11/4230, 'Record of a Conversation at Rambouillet at 3.45 p.m. on Saturday, December 15, 1962'.
247. Ibid., 'Points on Which the Prime Minister Could Draw in Discussion with General de Gaulle. UK/EEC Negotiations', Pierson Dixon, 14 December 1962.
248. Ibid., de Zulueta to Macmillan, 30 November 1962.
249. Charlton, *The Price of Victory*, pp. 293–4.
250. Catterall (ed.), *The Macmillan Diaries*, vol. 2, p. 526, diary entry for 16 December 1962; see also Macmillan diaries (unpublished), diary entry for 16 December 1962.

CHAPTER 3: THE PURSUIT OF MODERNITY

1. Conversation with Tom Caulcott, 2 April 2009.
2. Catterall (ed.), *The Macmillan Diaries*, vol. 2, p. 482, diary entry for 8 July 1962.
3. TNA, PRO, PREM 11/4520, 'Town and Country Planning', 'Cabinet, October 25th, Modernising Britain'. I am grateful to Dr Chas Loft for drawing my attention to this file.
4. TNA, PRO, CAB 128/36, CC (62) 63, item 4.
5. Lord Keynes, 'Overseas Financial Policy in Stage III', 3 April 1945, circulated to the War Cabinet on 15 May by Sir John Anderson, Chancellor of the Exchequer, as WP (45) 301, TNA, PRO, CAB 66/65.
6. Austin Robinson, 'A Personal View', in Milo Keynes (ed.), *Essays on John Maynard Keynes* (Cambridge University Press, 1975), p. 20.
7. Quoted in David Hubback, 'Sir Richard Clarke, 1910–1975: A Most Unusual Civil Servant', *Public Policy and Administration*, vol. 3, no. 1 (Spring, 1988), p. 19.
8. TNA, PRO, T 267/7, R. W. B. Clarke, 'Foreword', to Treasury Historical Memorandum no. 5, 'The Government and Wages, 1945–1960', July 1962, p. 1.
9. Edmund Dell, *The Chancellors: A History of the Chancellors of the Exchequer, 1945–90* (HarperCollins, 1996), pp. 258–9.
10. D. R. Thorpe, *Selwyn Lloyd* (Cape, 1989), pp. 310–11.
11. Macmillan quotes the letter in *Pointing the Way, 1959–1961* (Macmillan, 1972), p. 234.
12. Ibid., pp. 234–5.
13. TNA, PRO, CAB 129/100, FP (60) 1, 'Future Policy Study, 1960–1970', 24 February 1960. See also Hennessy, *Having It So Good*, pp. 576–95.

14. TNA, PRO, CAB 129/102, Part I, C (60) 107, 'The Six and the Seven: The Long-Term Objective', 6 July 1960. See also Hennessy, *Having It So Good*, pp. 613–19.
15. 'Elisabeth Kübler-Ross', Obituary, *The Times*, 2 September 2004.
16. J. M. Keynes, *Essays in Persuasion* (Macmillan, 1931).
17. J. M. Keynes, *Essays in Persuasion* (Royal Economic Society/Macmillan, 1972), pp. 325–6.
18. Iain de Weymarn to Mervyn King, 7 April 2009.
19. David Coleman, 'Population', in A. H. Halsey (ed.), *British Social Trends Since 1900: A Guide to the Changing Social Structure of Britain* (Macmillan, 1988), p. 104.
20. Iain de Weymarn to Peter Hennessy, 22 April 2009.
21. TNA, PRO, CAB 129/100, FP (60) 1, 'Future Policy Study, 1960–1970', 24 February 1960.
22. TNA, PRO, CAB 129/102, Part I, C (60) 107, 'The Six and the Seven: The Long-Term Objective', 6 July 1960.
23. Harold Macmillan, *Winds of Change: 1914–1939* (Macmillan, 1966), p. 366.
24. Keith Middlemas, *Power, Competition and the State*, vol. 2: *Threats to the Postwar Settlement: Britain, 1961–74* (Macmillan, 1990), pp. 23–56.
25. David S. Landes, *The Unbound Prometheus: Technological Change and Industrial Development in Western Europe from 1750 to the Present* (Cambridge University Press, 1969), p. 497.
26. Barry Eichengreen, *The European Economy Since 1945: Coordinated Capitalism and Beyond* (Princeton University Press, 2007), pp. 72, 95.
27. Heath, *The Course of My Life*, p. 184.
28. Harold Macmillan, *Riding the Storm, 1956–1959* (Macmillan, 1971), p. 54.
29. David Landes, *The Wealth and Poverty of Nations* (Abacus, 1999), p. 470.
30. Dell, *The Chancellors*, p. 258.
31. John Turner, *Macmillan* (Longman, 1994), pp. 274–5.
32. Margaret Thatcher, *The Path to Power* (HarperCollins, 1995), p. 118.
33. They were the chief element in Sanchia Berg's 'package' on the BBC Radio 4 *Today* programme on 30 December 2010. See also Martin Kettle, 'What Harold Macmillan Could Teach David Cameron', *Guardian*, 31 December 2010.
34. H. M. Hyndman, *The Record of an Adventurous Life* (Macmillan, 1911), p. 224.
35. Heath, *The Course of My Life*, p. 462.

36. Mark Pattison to Margaret Thatcher, 20 August 1980, The Margaret Thatcher Archive Trust, THCR 1-5-11, 'Macmillan Memorandum on Economic Affairs, 8-10/1980', Churchill College, Cambridge.

37. Dell, *The Chancellors*, pp. 470–72.

38. THCR 1-5-11, 'Memorandum. From: the Rt. Hon. Harold Macmillan, O.M.', 20 August 1980.

39. Ibid.

40. Ibid.

41. THCR 1-5-11, Tolkien to Lankester, 3 October 1980.

42. Hennessy, *Having It So Good*, pp. 545–53.

43. THCR 1-5-11, Thorneycroft to Thatcher, 12 September 1980.

44. Iain Dale (ed.), *Margaret Thatcher in Her Own Words* (Biteback, 2010), p. 118.

45. Hugo Young, *One of Us: A Biography of Margaret Thatcher* (Macmillan, 1989), pp. 208–9.

46. Dale (ed.), *Margaret Thatcher in Her Own Words*, pp. 113 and 116.

47. BBC 1 Television, 'The Way Ahead', 14 October 1980.

48. Horne, *Macmillan, 1957–1986*, p. 626.

49. BBC 1, 'The Way Ahead'.

50. Ibid.

51. Disraeli was speaking of the ministers in Gladstone's Liberal Government in a speech in Manchester on 3 April 1872. Antony Jay (ed.), *The Oxford Dictionary of Political Quotations* (Oxford University Press, 1996), p. 119.

52. Macmillan, *At the End of the Day*, p. 37.

53. Sidney Pollard, *The Wasting of the British Economy*, 2nd edn (Croom Helm, 1984), p. 43.

54. David Butler, *British General Elections Since 1945* (Blackwell, 1989), p. 19.

55. Thorpe, *Selwyn Lloyd*, pp. 325–6.

56. House of Commons *Official Report*, 7 November 1961, col. 810.

57. Macmillan, *Pointing the Way*, p. 375.

58. Catterall (ed.), *The Macmillan Diaries*, vol. 2, pp. 399–400, diary entry for 22 July 1961; see also Macmillan diaries (unpublished), diary entry for 22 July 1961.

59. Catterall (ed.), *The Macmillan Diaries*, vol. 2, p. 400, diary entry for 23 July 1961; see also Macmillan diaries (unpublished), diary entry for 23 July 1961.

60. Macmillan diaries (unpublished), diary entry for 27 July 1961.

61. Macmillan, *Pointing the Way*, p. 378.

62. Middlemas, *Power, Competition and the State*, vol. 2, p. 28.
63. Macmillan, *Pointing the Way*, p. 377.
64. Robert Shepherd, *Enoch Powell: A Biography* (Hutchinson, 1996), pp. 238–9.
65. David Marquand, *The Unprincipled Society: New Demands and Old Politics* (Cape, 1988), p. 46.
66. Keith Middlemas, *Industry, Unions and Government: Twenty-One Years of the National Economic Development Office* (Macmillan, 1983).
67. Middlemas, *Power, Competition and the State*, vol. 2, p. 39.
68. Sampson, *Anatomy of Britain*, pp. 566–7.
69. Ibid., p. 595.
70. Jean Monnet, *Memoirs* (Collins, 1978), pp. 232–63.
71. Sampson, *Anatomy of Britain*, pp. 280–81.
72. Thorpe, *Selwyn Lloyd*, p. 327.
73. Samuel Brittan, *The Treasury Under the Tories* (Penguin, 1964), p. 222.
74. Robert Taylor, *The Trade Union Question in British Politics: Government and the Unions Since 1945* (Blackwell, 1993), pp. 112–13.
75. Quoted in Thorpe, *Selwyn Lloyd*, p. 328.
76. Ibid., p. 331.
77. Ibid., p. 329.
78. TNA, PRO, T 325/72, 'Economic Growth, French and British Economic Planning and National Economic Development Council (NEDC) Briefing and Reports of Discussions', 'Planning: The Lessons of French Experience. Note by Mr R. W. B. Clarke', 2 November 1961; Boyle to Lloyd, 6 November 1961. The visit to Paris had taken place on 19–20 October 1961. I am very grateful to Mark Wilkins for alerting me to this file and for several valuable conversations on the general theme of this chapter.
79. J. C. R. Dow, 'Economic Planning in France', *Planning*, vol. 27, no. 454 (14 August 1961), p. 208.
80. Thorpe, *Selwyn Lloyd*, p. 327.
81. Catterall (ed.), *The Macmillan Diaries*, vol. 2, pp. 412–13, diary entry for 21 September 1961; see also Macmillan diaries (unpublished), diary entry for 21 September 1961.
82. Heffer, *Like the Roman*, pp. 287–8.
83. 'The Irresistible Market' first appeared in *New Society* on 6 February 1964. It is reproduced in Rex Collings (ed.), *Reflections of a Statesman: The Writings and Speeches of Enoch Powell* (Bellew, 1991), pp. 541–6.
84. Cited in Heffer, *Like the Roman*, p. 349.

85. Ibid., p. 346; *Observer*, 22 December 1963.
86. Quoted in Ben Pimlott, *Harold Wilson* (HarperCollins, 2016), p. 277.
87. Williams, *Hugh Gaitskell*, p. 672.
88. Peter Hennessy and Caroline Anstey, 'From Clogs to Clogs? Britain's Relative Economic Decline Since 1851', Strathclyde/*Analysis* Papers on Government and Politics no. 3 (Department of Government, University of Strathclyde, 1991), pp. 42–3.
89. Alec Cairncross, 'Economic Growth', *Economics*, no. 9 (1971–2), p. 149; Alec Cairncross, *Essays in Economic Management* (George Allen & Unwin, 1971), p. 21.
90. Conversations with Lord Croham on several occasions.
91. Hennessy and Anstey, 'From Clogs to Clogs?', p. 37.
92. TNA, PRO, PREM 11/3930, 'Remarks Made by Prime Minister at Cabinet on 28 May 1962'.
93. Sampson, *Anatomy of Britain*, pp. 281–2.
94. Ibid., p. 331.
95. TNA, PRO, PREM 5/374, 'Ministerial Appointments. Ministry of Harold Macmillan (Conservative), Part 6', Bligh to Macmillan, 19 April 1962.
96. Quoted in Thorpe, *Selwyn Lloyd*, p. 332.
97. The nuclear deputies minutes can be found in TNA, PRO, CAB 21/6081, 'Machinery of Government in War: BURLINGTON; Ministerial Nominations', Macmillan to Butler and Lloyd, 18 October 1961, Annexes 1 and 2. For the background see Hennessy, *The Secret State*, pp. 277–83.
98. 'The Dismissal of Selwyn Lloyd Chancellor of the Exchequer 12th and 13th July 1962', T. H. Caulcott, 28 July 1962. I am very grateful to Tom Caulcott for making this fascinating record available to me.
99. D. R. Thorpe, *Supermac: The Life of Harold Macmillan* (Chatto, 2010), p. 521.
100. Evans, *Downing Street Diary*, p. 204.
101. Lord Butler, *The Art of the Possible* (Hamish Hamilton, 1971), p. 233.
102. Horne, *Macmillan, 1957–1986*, p. 242.
103. Catterall (ed.), *The Macmillan Diaries*, vol. 2, p. 481, diary entry for 8 July 1962.
104. Evans, *Downing Street Diary*, p. 204.
105. Thorpe, *Selwyn Lloyd*, pp. 339–40.
106. Evans, *Downing Street Diary*, p. 204.
107. Horne, *Macmillan, 1957–1986*, p. 342.
108. Evans, *Downing Street Diary*, p. 204.

NOTES

109. Horne, *Macmillan, 1957–1986*, p. 342.

110. Ibid., pp. 342–3.

111. Caulcott, 'The Dismissal of Selwyn Lloyd'.

112. Catterall (ed.), *The Macmillan Diaries*, vol. 2, p. 483, diary entry for 14 July 1962.

113. Butler, *The Art of the Possible*, p. 234.

114. Catterall (ed.), *The Macmillan Diaries*, vol. 2, p. 483, diary entry for 14 July 1962.

115. Caulcott, 'The Dismissal of Selwyn Lloyd'.

116. Thorpe, *Supermac*, pp. 522–3.

117. Enoch Powell, 'SuperWhig?', *Spectator*, 1 March 1980.

118. Peter Hennessy and Caroline Anstey, 'Diminished Responsibility?' Strathclyde/*Analysis* Papers no. 2 (Department of Government, University of Strathclyde, 1991), p. 6.

119. TNA, PRO, PREM 5/374, Bligh to Macmillan, 13 July 1962.

120. Catterall (ed.), *The Macmillan Diaries*, vol. 2, p. 484, diary entry for 14 July 1962.

121. Jay (ed.), *The Oxford Dictionary of Political Quotations*, p. 364.

122. Anthony Howard, *RAB: The Life of R. A. Butler* (Cape, 1987), p. 292.

123. Evans, *Downing Street Diary*, p. 209.

124. Ibid., p. 207.

125. Cited in Thorpe, *Selwyn Lloyd*, p. 342.

126. Catterall (ed.), *The Macmillan Diaries*, vol. 2, p. 485, diary entry for 14 July 1962.

127. Thorpe, *Selwyn Lloyd*, p. 356.

128. Thorpe, *Supermac*, p. 525.

129. Thorpe, *Selwyn Lloyd*, p. 357.

130. Catterall (ed.), *The Macmillan Diaries*, vol. 2, p. 486, diary entry for 17 July 1962.

131. For which minister would have gone to which bunker see Hennessy, *The Secret State*, pp. 281–3.

132. TNA, PRO, PREM 11/3930, 'Remarks Made by Prime Minister at Cabinet on 28 May 1962'.

133. Ibid.

134. Macmillan diaries (unpublished), diary entry for 28 May 1962.

135. TNA, PRO, CAB 128/36, CC (62) 63rd Conclusions, 29 October 1962.

136. Ibid.

137. Michael Cockerell, *Live from No. 10: The Inside Story of Prime Ministers and Television* (Faber & Faber 1998), pp. 78–9. See also Evans, *Downing Street Diary*, p. 170.

138. See TNA, PRO, PREM 11/2351, 'The Burden on Ministers', Brook to Macmillan, 20 February 1957; CAB 130/137, GEN 616, 1st Meeting, 31 October 1957. Peter Hennessy, *The Hidden Wiring: Unearthing the British Constitution* (Gollancz, 1995), chapter 7, pp. 161–78.
139. TNA, PRO, CAB 128/36, CC (62) 63.
140. TNA, PRO, CAB 130/86, Cabinet House of Lords Reform Committee, GEN 432, 3rd Meeting, 10 February 1955.
141. Walter Bagehot, *The English Constitution* (1867; Fontana edn, 1963), p. 144.
142. Ibid., p. 149.
143. Ibid., p. 137.
144. House of Lords *Official Report*, 30 October 1957, col. 590.
145. Macmillan diaries (unpublished), diary entry for 2 April 1958.
146. Thorpe, *Supermac*, pp. 418–19.
147. I made this one of the themes of my maiden speech in the House of Lords: House of Lords *Official Report*, 3 December 2010, cols. 1706–9.
148. TNA, PRO, CAB 128/36, CC (62) 63.
149. Catterall (ed.), *The Macmillan Diaries*, vol. 2, p. 534, diary entry for 11 January 1963.
150. TNA, PRO, CAB 128/36, CC (62) 63.
151. TNA, PRO, CAB 129/111, C (62) 201, 'Modernisation of Britain', 3 December 1962.
152. Roger Williams, *The Nuclear Power Decisions: British Policies 1953–1978* (Croom Helm, 1980), pp. 84, 334.
153. David J. C. MacKay, *Sustainable Energy – Without the Hot Air* (UIT Cambridge, 2009), p. 163.
154. Williams, *The Nuclear Power Decisions*, p. 44; Walter C. Patterson, *Nuclear Power* (Penguin, 1976), p. 77; William A. Patterson, *50 Years of Dounreay* (North of Scotland Newspapers, 2008).
155. Sir Peter Baldwin and Robert Baldwin (eds.), *The Motorway Achievement*, vol. 1: *The British Motorway System: Visualisation, Policy and Administration* (Motorway Archive Trust and Thomas Telford Ltd, 2004), p. 183.
156. Thorpe, *Supermac*, p. 418.
157. Baldwin and Baldwin (eds.), *The Motorway Achievement*, vol. 1, pp. 182–3. The table, although accurately reproduced, contains errors, so should be regarded as indicative rather than definitive.
158. Ibid., p. 144.
159. A. H. Halsey, 'Higher Education', in Halsey (ed.), *British Social Trends Since 1900*, p. 270.

160. Ralf Dahrendorf, *A History of the London School of Economics and Political Science 1895–1995* (Oxford University Press, 1995), pp. 213–15.

161. Nicholas Timmins, *The Five Giants: A Biography of the Welfare State*, new edn (HarperCollins, 2001), p. 200; see also Carswell, *Government and the Universities in Britain*.

162. Timmins, *The Five Giants*, p. 200.

163. *Grants to Students*, Cmnd 1051 (HMSO, 1960).

164. Timmins, *The Five Giants*, p. 208.

165. *A Hospital Plan for England and Wales*, Cmnd 1604 (HMSO, 1962).

166. Enoch Powell, *Medicine and Politics* (Pitman Medical, 1976).

167. Timmins, *The Five Giants*, p. 211.

168. *The Guardian*, 12 November 1973.

169. House of Commons *Official Report*, 17 November 1955.

170. Timmins, *The Five Giants*, p. 185.

171. Matthew Engel, *Eleven Minutes Late: A Train Journey to the Soul of Britain* (Macmillan, 2009), p. 215.

172. Horne, *Macmillan, 1957–1986*, p. 251.

173. Sampson, *Anatomy of Britain*, p. 544.

174. *A Plan for the Modernisation and Re-equipment of British Railways* (British Transport Commission/HMSO, 1955).

175. Don Hale, *Mallard: How the 'Blue Streak' Broke the World Speed Record* (Aurum, 2008), p. 159.

176. Ibid., p. 149.

CHAPTER 4: DASH FOR THE EXIT

1. Charlton, *The Price of Victory*, p. 258.

2. Ronald Hyam, *Britain's Declining Empire: The Road to Decolonisation, 1918–1968* (Cambridge University Press, 2006), p. xiii.

3. Conversation with Lord Charteris, 13 March 1989.

4. Michael Howard, *War in European History* (Oxford University Press, 2009 edn), p. 140.

5. Denis Healey, *The Time of My Life* (Michael Joseph, 1989), p. 283.

6. Ibid., pp. 283–4.

7. Conversation with Chris Patten, 9 May 2004.

8. Bernard Porter, *The Absent-Minded Imperialists: Empire, Society and Culture in Britain* (Oxford University Press, 2007), p. 318.

9. Ibid., p. 319.

10. Philip Larkin, *High Windows* (Faber & Faber, 1974), p. 29.

11. John Gallagher, *The Decline, Revival and Fall of the British Empire* (Cambridge University Press, 1982), p. 74.

12. Ibid., p. 73.

13. Hyam, *Britain's Declining Empire*, p. xiii.

14. Ibid.

15. Ronald Robinson and John Gallagher with Alice Denny, *Africa and the Victorians: The Official Mind of Imperialism* (Macmillan, 1961).

16. John Gallagher and Ronald Robinson, 'The Imperialism of Free Trade', *Economic History Review*, 2nd series, vol. 6, no. 1 (1953), pp. 1–15. For the article's impact see John Darwin, 'John Andrew Gallagher, 1919–1980', *Proceedings of the British Academy: Biographical Memoirs of Fellows VI* (British Academy/Oxford University Press, 2008), pp. 57–78, and Ronald Hyam, 'The Oxford and Cambridge Imperial History Professoriate, 1919–1981: Robinson and Gallagher and Their Predecessors', in Ronald Hyam, *Understanding the British Empire* (Cambridge University Press, 2010), p. 520.

17. Evans, *Downing Street Diary*, p. 150, diary entry for 16 July 1961.

18. Ibid., p. 111.

19. Ibid., p. 112.

20. Roy Welensky, *4000 Days* (Collins, 1964), p. 361.

21. Hyam, *Understanding the British Empire*, p. 521.

22. Robinson and Gallagher, *Africa and the Victorians*, esp. chapters 1 and 15.

23. Gallagher, *The Decline, Revival and Fall of the British Empire*, pp. 73–4, 94–9, 149–53.

24. Hyam, 'The Oxford and Cambridge Imperial History Professoriate'.

25. Hyam, *Britain's Declining Empire*, pp. 411–12.

26. Catterall (ed.), *The Macmillan Diaries*, vol. 2, p. 555, diary entry for 27 March 1963; see also Macmillan diaries (unpublished), diary entry for 27 March 1963.

27. Macmillan, *At the End of the Day*, p. 332.

28. Catterall (ed.), *The Macmillan Diaries*, vol. 2, pp. 404–5, diary entry for 4 August 1961.

29. Anthony Sampson, *The Anatomist: The Autobiography of Anthony Sampson* (Politico's, 2008), p. 93.

30. Ibid., p. 94.

31. TNA, PRO, CAB 134/1355, AF (59) 28 (Final), 'Africa: The Next Ten Years', May 1959 (circulated 3 June 1959).

32. It was the subtitle of their classic *Africa and the Victorians*.

33. Brian Lapping, *The End of Empire* (Granada, 1985), pp. 532–3.

34. TNA, PRO, CAB 134/1355, AF (59) 28 (Final), 'Africa: The Next Ten Years'.

35. Ibid.

36. Ibid.

37. See Gerry Kearns, *Geopolitics and Empire: The Legacy of Halford Mackinder* (Oxford University Press, 2009).

38. TNA, PRO, CAB 134/1355, AF (59) 28 (Final), 'Africa: The Next Ten Years'.

39. Ibid.

40. Ibid.

41. *Post-War Training for the Colonial Office*, Colonial no. 198 (HMSO, 1946).

42. Ralph Furse, *Aucuparius: Recollections of a Recruiting Officer* (Oxford University Press, 1962).

43. W. R. Crocker, *On Governing Colonies* (George Allen & Unwin, 1947).

44. Ibid., p. 132.

45. Crocker is quoted between p. v and p. 1 of Furse, *Aucuparius*.

46. Ibid., Appendix 3, pp. 316–17.

47. Anthony Kirk-Greene, *Britain's Imperial Administrators, 1858–1966* (Macmillan, 2000), p. 135.

48. B. D. Wilson, 'A course of Fun (the first Devonshire)', in David Le Breton (ed.), *I Remember It Well: Fifty Years of Colonial Service Personal Reminiscences* (Librario, 2010), p. 25.

49. Ibid., pp. 25–6.

50. R. E. N. Smith, 'Checking the Books', in Le Breton (ed.), *I Remember It Well*, p. 28.

51. Le Breton (ed.), *I Remember It Well*, pp. 21–9.

52. Ibid., p. 23.

53. Conversation with Michael Shaw, 9 August 2010.

54. *Hints on the Preservation of Health in Tropical Countries* (The Crown Agents for Overseas Governments and Administrators, 1957). The section on booze can be found on p. 33.

55. Conversation with Michael Shaw, 9 August 2010.

56. Ibid.

57. Hyam, *Britain's Declining Empire*, p. 277.

58. Macmillan, *Pointing the Way*, p. 19.

59. Iain Macleod interviewed by W. P. Kirkman, 29 December 1967, and cited in Robert Shepherd, *Iain Macleod: A Biography* (Hutchinson, 1994), p. 151.

60. Ibid., pp. 151–2.

61. Brian Lapping, *End of Empire* (St Martin's Press, 1985), p. 484.
62. Lord Home, *The Way the Wind Blows* (Collins, 1976), p. 186.
63. Ibid.
64. Catterall (ed.), *The Macmillan Diaries*, vol. 2, pp. 313–14, diary entry for 10 July 1960.
65. Christopher Andrew and Vasili Mitrokhin, *The Mitrokhin Archive II: The KGB and the World* (Allen Lane, 2005), p. 432.
66. TNA, PRO, PREM 11/2583, 'Memorandum by Sir David Stirling on Policy for East and Central Africa: Ministerial Discussions', Macleod to Macmillan, 25 May 1959.
67. House of Commons *Official Report*, 27 July 1959, cols. 234–7.
68. Quoted in Shepherd, *Iain Macleod*, p. 159.
69. Sampson, *Anatomy of Britain*, p. 83.
70. Shepherd, *Iain Macleod*, p. 168.
71. Ibid., p. 187.
72. Elizabeth Knowles (ed.), *The Oxford Dictionary of Phrase and Fable* (Oxford University Press, 2005), p. 509.
73. Quoted in Shepherd, *Iain Macleod*, p. 162.
74. Iain Macleod, 'Trouble in Africa', *Spectator*, 31 January 1964.
75. Christopher Andrew, *The Defence of the Realm: The Authorized History of MI5* (Allen Lane, 2009), p. 442.
76. Edmund Burke, 'On Conciliation with America', reproduced in W. M. Elofson with John A. Woods (eds.), *The Writings and Speeches of Edmund Burke*, vol. 3: *Party, Parliament and the American War, 1774–1780* (Clarendon Press, 1996), pp. 105–69.
77. Hyam, *Understanding the British Empire*, fn. 115, pp. 63–4.
78. Iain Macleod, 'One World', The Conservative Political Centre, 13 October 1960, cited in Shepherd, *Iain Macleod*, p. 257.
79. Calder Walton, 'British Intelligence and Threats to National Security, c. 1941–1951', unpublished PhD thesis, Faculty of History, University of Cambridge, 2006, chapter 6, 'The Empire Strikes Back', pp. 270–328. See also Andrew, *The Defence of the Realm*, chapters 7 and 8, pp. 442–82.
80. Harold Macmillan, Cape Town, 3 February 1960, reproduced in MacArthur (ed.), *The Penguin Book of Twentieth-Century Speeches*, pp. 288–93.
81. Wm Roger Louis, *Ends of British Imperialism: The Scramble for Empire, Suez and Decolonization* (I. B. Tauris, 2006), p. 695.
82. Ibid., p. 696.
83. Ibid., pp. 700–702.

84. Wm Roger Louis and Ronald Robinson, 'The Imperialism of Decolonization', reproduced ibid., pp. 451–502. This quotation is taken from p. 497.
85. Ibid., p. 500.
86. Private information.
87. Andrew and Mitrokhin, *The Mitrokhin Archive II: The KGB and the World*, p. 428.
88. Shepherd, *Iain Macleod*, pp. 19–24.
89. Ibid., p. 165.
90. Catterall (ed.), *The Macmillan Diaries*, vol. 2, p. 396, diary entry for 22 June 1961.
91. Shepherd, *Iain Macleod*, p. 220; Lapping, *End of Empire*, p. 488.
92. Reproduced from the Kirkman interview in Shepherd, *Iain Macleod*, p. 219.
93. Ibid., pp. 232–3.
94. House of Lords *Official Report*, 7 March 1961, cols. 306–7.
95. Shepherd, *Iain Macleod*, pp. 226–7.
96. Conversation with Andrew Alexander, 10 November 2010.
97. Shepherd, *Iain Macleod*, p. 154.
98. Sampson, *Anatomy of Britain*, p. 83.
99. Ibid.
100. Shepherd, *Iain Macleod*, pp. 253–5.
101. *The Overseas Pensioner*, no. 94 (October 2007), p. 44.
102. Shepherd, *Iain Macleod*, pp. 254–5.
103. House of Commons *Official Report*, 22 March 1961, col. 445.
104. Randall Hansen, *Citizenship and Immigration in Post-war Britain: The Institutional Origins of a Multicultural Nation* (Oxford University Press, 2000), pp. 100–105.
105. Zig Layton-Henry, *The Politics of Immigration: Immigration, 'Race' and 'Race' Relations in Post-war Britain* (Blackwell, 1992), p. 13.
106. Shepherd, *Iain Macleod*, p. 109.
107. Williams, *Hugh Gaitskell*, pp. 676–9.
108. House of Commons *Official Report*, 31 October 1961, col. 28.
109. House of Commons *Official Report*, 7 November 1961, col. 926.
110. Horne, *Macmillan, 1957–1986*, p. 423.
111. The papers of the Cabinet's Commonwealth Migrants Committee can be found in TNA, PRO, CAB 134/1469.
112. Catterall (ed.), *The Macmillan Diaries*, vol. 2, p. 385, diary entry for 30 May 1961.

113. I am indebted to Randall Hansen for his portrait of the entrails of the scheme. See his *Citizenship and Immigration*, pp. 109–11.
114. Butler, *The Art of the Possible*, p. 154.
115. Ibid., pp. 206–7.
116. Ibid., p. 206.
117. Ibid., p. 205.
118. Ibid., pp. 205–6.
119. Williams, *Hugh Gaitskell*, p. 4; David Gilmour, *The Ruling Caste: Imperial Lives in the Victorian Raj* (John Murray, 2005).
120. House of Commons *Official Report*, 16 November 1961, col. 687.
121. Ibid., cols. 792–803.
122. Ibid.
123. For GEN 325 see TNA, PRO, CAB 130/61; CAB 128/19, CM (51) 15th Conclusions.
124. Hennessy, *Never Again*, p. 442.
125. Horne, *Macmillan, 1957–1986*, p. 423.
126. Catterall (ed.), *The Macmillan Diaries*, vol. 2, p. 428, diary entry for 22 November 1961.
127. Butler, *The Art of the Possible*, p. 206.
128. Jay (ed.), *The Oxford Dictionary of Political Quotations*, p. 1.
129. Catterall (ed.), *The Macmillan Diaries*, vol. 2, p. 523, diary entry for 7 December 1962.
130. Horne, *Macmillan, 1957–1986*, p. 672, fn. 4.
131. Roger Boyes, 'Thatcher Out in the Cold as Grand Old Men Relive Collapse of the Berlin Wall', *The Times*, 2 November 2009.
132. *A Strong Britain in an Age of Uncertainty: The National Security Strategy*, Cm 7953 (Stationery Office, October 2010), pp. 9–10.
133. Monnet, *Memoirs*, p. 451.

CHAPTER 5: THE MISSILES OF OCTOBER

1. Conversation with Peter Hudson, 16 August 2007.
2. Lord Thorneycroft, Oral History Transcript, John F. Kennedy Presidential Library, Boston, Massachusetts. The interview took place in 1966.
3. TNA, PRO, PREM 11/3815, 'Emergency arrangements in event of a major crisis in Berlin', Prime Minister's Personal Minute, M243 A/61, Macmillan to Brook, 29 July 1961.
4. Conversation with Air Vice-Marshal Bobby Robson, 26 July 2001.
5. Lord Hailsham, *The Door Wherein I Went* (Collins, 1975), p. 215.
6. Hennessy, *The Secret State*, pp. 155–62.

7. TNA, PRO, CAB 21/6081, 'Machinery of Government in War: BURLINGTON; Ministerial Nominations', Macmillan to Bishop, 6 October 1961.

8. On 18 June 1949, de Gaulle said to General Leclerc: '[D]ressaient devant nous les intérêts des États qui sont, comme le dit Nietzsche "les monstres plus froids des monstres froids".' Conversation with Professor Julian Jackson, 17 September 2007.

9. TNA, PRO, PREM 13/3086, 'CARS. Installation of Radio-Telephone in Prime Minister's Car', Halls to Allen, 15 March 1970.

10. TNA, PRO, PREM 11/5223, 'Machinery of Government in War: Plans for the Central Nucleus (including STOCKWELL/BURLING-TON); Nuclear Retaliation Procedures; Exercises; Part 2', Saunders to Bligh, 22 May 1962.

11. Ibid., Bligh to Saunders, 23 May 1962.

12. TNA, PRO, CAB 134/940, HDC (55) 3, 'The Defence Implications of Fall-Out from a Hydrogen Bomb: Report by a Group of Officials', 8 March 1955; Hennessy, *The Secret State*, pp. 121–2.

13. TNA, PRO, CAB 21/4117/1, 'Machinery of Government in War: General Policy', 'Report by a Working Party of Officials', 4 July 1955.

14. TNA, PRO, CAB 21/4117/1, 'Machinery of Government in War: General Policy', Mallaby to Brook, 22 November 1951; Hewison to Brook, 3 August 1951.

15. TNA, PRO, CAB 21/4117/1, 'Machinery of Government in War'.

16. Its early codenames were MACADAM and then QUADRANGLE. See TNA, PRO, CAB 21/4153, 'Machinery of Government in War: QUADRANGLE', 30 December 1960.

17. TNA, PRO, CAB 21/4117/1, 'Machinery of Government in War'.

18. TNA, PRO, CAB 21/4144, 'Machinery of Government in War: General Policy', Padmore to Darracott, 9 May 1957.

19. Conversation with Sir Rodric Braithwaite, 18 April 2002.

20. TNA, PRO, CAB 21/4198, 'Machinery of Government in War: Exercise CLOUD DRAGON II (1960)', undated.

21. TNA, PRO, CAB 21/4144, 'Machinery of Government in War: General Policy', 'Exercise "CLOUD DRAGON"', 30 January 1959.

22. TNA, PRO, CAB 21/4198, 'Central Government War Room: Report on Exercise "CLOUD DRAGON"'.

23. TNA, PRO, PREM 11/5224, 'Machinery of Government in War; Part 3', Trend to Macmillan, 28 May 1963.

24. *The Denning Report: The Profumo Affair*, p. 86.

25. Ibid., p. 7.

26. TNA, PRO, PREM 11/5224, 'Machinery of Government in War; Part 3', Trend to Macmillan, 28 May 1963.
27. Ibid., Bligh to Macmillan, 29 May 1963.
28. Ibid.
29. Horne, *Macmillan, 1894–1956*, pp. 44–6.
30. Barbara W. Tuchman, *The Guns of August* (Macmillan, 1962).
31. Horne, *Macmillan, 1957–1986*, p. 383.
32. Tuchman, *The Guns of August*, p. 72.
33. Jeremy Isaacs and Taylor Downing, *Cold War* (Bantam, 1998), p. 171.
34. TNA, PRO, PREM 11/2686, 'Discussions on Possible Summit Meeting: Part 14', Macmillan to Eisenhower, 23 June 1959.
35. Evans, *Downing Street Diary*, pp. 156–7, diary entry for 6 August 1961.
36. Macmillan diaries (unpublished), diary entry for 15 September 1961.
37. Isaacs and Downing, *Cold War*, p. 233.
38. TNA, PRO, CAB 21/6081, 'Machinery of Government in War: BURLINGTON; Ministerial Nominations', Brook to Macmillan, 13 September 1961; Bishop to Macmillan, 15 September 1961; Bishop to Brook, 6 October 1961.
39. Ibid., Bishop to Brook, 6 October 1961.
40. TNA, PRO, PREM 11/3815, 'Organisation of Government to Deal with a Crisis in Berlin: Memorandum by the Secretary of the Cabinet', September 1961.
41. Ibid., Brook to Lee, 25 August 1961.
42. Ibid.
43. Ibid.
44. Ibid.
45. Catterall (ed.), *The Macmillan Diaries*, vol. 2, p. 397, diary entry for 22 June 1961.
46. Macmillan diaries (unpublished), diary entry for 23 September 1961.
47. Ibid., diary entry for 25 September 1961.
48. Catterall (ed.), *The Macmillan Diaries*, vol. 2, p. 420, diary entry for 19 October 1961.
49. Ibid., pp. 432–3, diary entry for 4 December 1961.
50. See especially John Gearson, *Harold Macmillan and the Berlin Wall Crisis, 1958–1962* (Macmillan, 1998).
51. Cradock, *Know Your Enemy*, pp. 145–6.
52. Ibid., p. 145.
53. Isaacs and Downing, *Cold War*, pp. 172–3.
54. Catterall (ed.), *The Macmillan Diaries*, vol. 2, p. 389, diary entry for 11 June 1961.

55. Ibid.
56. Private information. See also Len Scott, *The Cuban Missile Crisis and the Threat of Nuclear War: Lessons from History* (Continuum, 2007), pp. 8–15.
57. TNA, PRO, CAB 158/40, JIC (60) 49, 'Soviet Intentions in the Second Half of 1960', 14 July 1960.
58. Hennessy, *The Secret State*, pp. 25–6.
59. TNA, PRO, DEFE 6/56, JP (59) 68, Final, 27 May 1959, 'Berlin Contingency Planning: Report by the Joint Planning Staff'.
60. TNA, PRO, CAB 158/40, JIC (60) 40, 'Soviet and East German Reactions to Military Measures Foreseen in Berlin Contingency Planning', 6 July 1960.
61. TNA, PRO, CAB 158/35, JIC (59) 17, 'An Assessment of Soviet Policy Regarding Berlin', 5 February 1959.
62. Paul Nitze, *From Hiroshima to Glasnost: At the Center of Decision* (Grove Weidenfeld, 1989), p. 205.
63. Conversation with Sir Antony Jay, 24 April 2008.
64. Isaacs and Downing, *Cold War*, p. 173.
65. Cradock, *Know Your Enemy*, p. 151.
66. Isaacs and Downing, *Cold War*, pp. 173–4.
67. TNA, PRO, FO 371/160546, 'Soviet Attitudes Towards Peace Treaty and Status of Berlin', Hood to Samuel, 17 August 1961. My former research student, Catherine Haddon, uncovered the file in 2002 that first revealed this bizarrely menacing encounter.
68. TNA, PRO, CAB 134/940, HDC (55) 3, 8 March 1955.
69. Scott, *The Cuban Missile Crisis and the Threat of Nuclear War*, p. 6.
70. G. T. Allison, A. Carnesale and J. S. Nye Jr (eds.), *Hawks, Doves and Owls: An Agenda for Avoiding Nuclear War* (Norton, 1985), p. 210.
71. James Reston, 'Kennedy to Speak on Berlin Tonight', *New York Times*, 25 July 1961.
72. MacArthur (ed.), *The Penguin Book of Twentieth-Century Speeches*, p. 301.
73. Aleksandr Fursenko and Timothy Naftali, *Khrushchev's Cold War: The Inside Story of an American Adversary* (Norton, 2006), pp. 355–66.
74. Robert Dallek, *John F. Kennedy: An Unfinished Life 1917–1963* (Allen Lane, 2003), pp. 423–4.
75. Isaacs and Downing, *Cold War*, p. 174.
76. Dallek, *John F. Kennedy*, p. 424.
77. Fursenko and Naftali, *Khrushchev's Cold War*, p. 377.
78. Isaacs and Downing, *Cold War*, p. 174.

79. Fursenko and Naftali, *Khrushchev's Cold War*, p. 377.
80. Dallek, *John F. Kennedy*, p. 425.
81. Macmillan diaries (unpublished), diary entry for 12 August 1961.
82. Catterall (ed.), *The Macmillan Diaries*, vol. 2, p. 405, diary entry for 13 August 1961.
83. P. D. James, *Original Sin* (1994) in P. D. James, *An Adam Dalgliesh Omnibus* (Faber & Faber 2008), p. 164. It refers to her character Gabriel Dauntsey's time in RAF Bomber Command during the Second World War.
84. Macmillan diaries (unpublished), diary entry for 19 August 1961.
85. Catterall (ed.), *The Macmillan Diaries*, vol. 2, p. 407, diary entry for 19 August 1961; see also Macmillan diaries (unpublished), diary entry for 19 August 1961.
86. Isaacs and Downing, *Cold War*, p. 180.
87. Ibid., p. 182.
88. Horne, *Macmillan, 1957–1986*, p. 314; Sir David Goodall to Peter Hennessy, 29 September 2008.
89. Isaacs and Downing, *Cold War*, p. 233.
90. Dallek, *John F. Kennedy*, p. 426.
91. Peter Hennessy, *Muddling Through: Power, Politics and the Quality of Government in Postwar Britain* (Gollancz, 1996), p. 106.
92. Louis Heren, *Growing Up on The Times* (Hamish Hamilton, 1978), p. 226.
93. Ibid.
94. Ibid.
95. *The Third Man*, British Lion Film Corporation, 1949.
96. Len Deighton, *Funeral in Berlin* (Cape, 1964), p. 3.
97. Ibid., p. 19.
98. John le Carré, *The Spy Who Came in from the Cold* (Gollancz, 1963), pp. 11–12.
99. Ibid., pp. 221–2.
100. Deighton, *Funeral in Berlin*, p. 304.
101. Simon Case, 'The Joint Intelligence Committee and the German Question, 1947–61', unpublished PhD thesis, Department of History, Queen Mary, University of London, 2008, p. 272. For Penkovsky and the Berlin Wall see Jerrold. L. Schecter and Peter S. Deriabin, *The Spy Who Saved the World* (Brassey's, 1992), p. 226.
102. Schecter and Deriabin, *The Spy Who Saved the World*, p. 3.
103. Ibid., p. 102.
104. Tom Bower, *The Perfect English Spy: Sir Dick White and the Secret War 1935–90* (Heinemann, 1995), pp. 274–5.

105. Private information.

106. TNA, PRO, CAB 182/11, JIC (MT) (61) Revised, 'Terms of Reference for the Missile Threat Co-ordination Working Party', 7 July 1961.

107. Catherine Haddon, 'Union Jacks and Red Stars on Them: UK Intelligence, the Soviet Nuclear Threat and British Nuclear Weapons Policy, 1945–1970', unpublished PhD thesis, Department of History, Queen Mary, University of London, 2008, p. 230; Catherine Haddon, 'Hidden Voices: Oleg Penkovsky and British Cold War Diplomacy, 1961–62', unpublished MA thesis, Department of History, Queen Mary, University of London, 2002.

108. For the Shergold-inspired SIS rethink see Hennessy, *Having It So Good*, pp. 317–18.

109. Christopher Andrew and Oleg Gordievsky, *KGB: The Inside Story* (Hodder, 1990), p. 364.

110. Catterall (ed.), *The Macmillan Diaries*, vol. 2, p. 380, diary entry for 4 May 1961.

111. Bower, *The Perfect English Spy*, p. 259.

112. Private information.

113. Michael Smith, *The Spying Game: The Secret History of British Espionage* (Politico's, 2003), p. 225; Ben Macintyre, *A Spy Among Friends: Kim Philby and the Great Betrayal* (Bloomsbury, 2014), p. 234.

114. Christopher Andrew and Vasili Mitrokhin, *The Mitrokhin Archive: The KGB in Europe and the West* (Penguin, 1999), p. 520. For Blake's denial see George Blake, *No Other Choice* (Cape, 1990), p. 207.

115. Ibid., p. 5.

116. Ibid., p. 198.

117. Private information.

118. Blake, *No Other Choice*, p. 199.

119. Schecter and Deriabin, *The Spy Who Saved the World*, pp. 353–73.

120. Private information.

121. David Stafford, *Spies Beneath Berlin* (John Murray, 2003).

122. Ibid., pp. 187–8.

123. Private information.

124. They are listed in Hennessy, *The Secret State*, pp. 6–11, and can be found in TNA, PRO, CAB 158/45, Part 1, JIC (62) 21.

125. *Review of Intelligence on Weapons of Mass Destruction: Report of a Committee of Privy Counsellors*, HC 898 (Stationery Office, 2004), p. 14.

126. TNA, PRO, CAB 158/29, JIC (57) 62, 'The Possibility of Hostilities Short of Global War up to 1965', 20 September 1957. Alban Webb's work is contained in 'An Analysis of the Joint Intelligence Committee's

Assessment of the Soviet Threat and Input into the Cuban Missile Crisis and Its Aftermath', unpublished undergraduate research dissertation, Department of History, Queen Mary, University of London, 2001.

127. John Lewis Gaddis, *We Now Know: Rethinking Cold War History* (Oxford University Press, 1997), pp. 264–5.

128. Ibid., p. 264.

129. Ibid., p. 260.

130. Franciszek Draus (ed.), *History, Truth, Liberty: Selected Writings of Raymond Aron* (University of Chicago Press, 1985), pp. 336–7. Aron's 'Max Weber and Modern Social Science' was published in 1959 as his introduction to an edition of two Weber lectures, 'Science as a Vocation' and 'Politics as a Vocation', both originally published in 1918–19.

131. Isaacs and Downing, *Cold War*, p. 213.

132. I am very grateful to Professor Len Scott for bringing this despatch to my attention. TNA, PRO, FO 371/162408, 'Blockade by US', Marchant to Home, 10 November 1962.

133. Fursenko and Naftali, *Khrushchev's Cold War*, p. 451.

134. Ibid., pp. 438–64.

135. Ibid., pp. 443–4.

136. Dallek, *John. F. Kennedy*, p. 505.

137. TNA, PRO, PREM 11/4230, 'Visit of Prime Minister to France: Record of Discussions with General de Gaulle, Rambouillet, 15 and 16 Dec 1962', 'Record of a Conversation at Rambouillet at 3.45 p.m. on Saturday, December 15, 1962'.

138. Isaacs and Downing, *Cold War*, p. 213.

139. Gaddis, *We Now Know*, p. 267.

140. Scott, *The Cuban Missile Crisis and the Threat of Nuclear War*, p. 38.

141. Ibid., p. 85.

142. Cradock, *Know Your Enemy*, p. 179.

143. Ernest R. May and Philip D. Zelikow (eds.), *The Kennedy Tapes: Inside the White House During the Cuban Missile Crisis* (Harvard University Press, 1997), p. 692.

144. Richard Deacon, *'C': A Biography of Sir Maurice Oldfield* (Futura, 1984), p. 135.

145. Macmillan, *At the End of the Day*, p. 150.

146. Catterall (ed.), *The Macmillan Diaries*, vol. 2, p. 508, diary entries for 20 and 21 October 1962.

147. Ibid., diary entry for 22 October 1962.

148. TNA, PRO, PREM 11/3689, 'Situation in Cuba: part 2', Kennedy to Macmillan, 22 October 1962.

149. TNA, PRO, CAB 128/36, CC (62) 61st Conclusions, 23 October 1962. See also Hennessy, *The Prime Minister*, pp. 126–7.
150. TNA, PRO, PREM 11/3689, 'Record of a Conversation Between the Prime Minister and President Kennedy at 12.30 a.m. on Tuesday, 23 October 1962'.
151. Hennessy, *The Prime Minister*, p. 123.
152. *Public Papers of President John F. Kennedy 1962* (US Government Printing Office, 1964), pp. 806–9.
153. Fursenko and Naftali, *Khrushchev's Cold War*, p. 466.
154. Ibid., p. 468.
155. Ibid., p. 469.
156. Ibid., pp. 471–4.
157. Isaacs and Downing, *Cold War*, p. 221.
158. TNA, PRO, CAB 128/36, CC (62) 61, 23 October 1962.
159. Macmillan diaries (unpublished), diary entry for 23 October 1962.
160. Ibid.
161. Ibid. For Macmillan's relationship with Ava Waverley see Horne, *Macmillan, 1957–1986*, p. 168.
162. Conversation with Lady de Zulueta, 2 December 2008.
163. Catterall (ed.), *The Macmillan Diaries*, vol. 2, p. 511, diary entry for 24 October 1962.
164. TNA, PRO, CAB 129/11, CC (62) 70, 'Cuba', memorandum by the Lord Chancellor, 25 October 1962.
165. House of Commons *Official Report*, 25 October 1962, col. 1060.
166. Sherman Kent, 'The Cuban Missile Crisis of 1962: Presenting the Photographic Evidence Abroad', *Studies in Intelligence*, 10/2 (Spring, 1972), pp. 22–3.
167. Hennessy, *Muddling Through*, p. 112.
168. Catterall (ed.), *The Macmillan Diaries*, vol. 2, pp. 511–12, diary entry for 24 October 1962.
169. TNA, PRO, PREM 11/3690, 'Record of a Telephone Message Between the Prime Minister and President Kennedy, 24 October 1962'.
170. Bertrand Russell, *Unarmed Victory* (Penguin, 1963), pp. 31–2.
171. TNA, PRO, PREM 11/3690, 'Record of a Telephone Message Between the Prime Minister and President Kennedy, 24 October 1962'.
172. Schecter and Deriabin, *The Spy Who Saved the World*, pp. 346–7.
173. TNA, PRO, PREM 11/3690, 'Record of a Telephone Message Between the Prime Minister and President Kennedy, 24 October 1962'.
174. Fursenko and Naftali, *Khrushchev's Cold War*, p. 483.
175. Ibid., pp. 484–5.

176. Catterall (ed.), *The Macmillan Diaries*, vol. 2, p. 512, diary entry for 25 October 1962.
177. Ibid.
178. Ibid; see also Macmillan diaries (unpublished), diary entry for 25 October 1962.
179. L. V. Scott, *Macmillan, Kennedy and the Cuban Missile Crisis: Political, Military and Intelligence Aspects* (Macmillan, 1999), p. 155.
180. Ibid., p. 156.
181. Catterall (ed.), *The Macmillan Diaries*, vol. 2, p. 514, diary entry for 4 November 1962.
182. TNA, PRO, PREM 11/3690, 'Record of a Telephone Message Between the Prime Minister and President Kennedy, 26 October 1962'.
183. TNA, PRO, CAB 158/47, JIC (62) 97, 'First Soviet Reactions to US Action and Intentions Concerning Cuba'.
184. TNA, PRO, CAB 158/47, JIC (62) 70 (Final) (E), 'Escalation', 14 November 1962.
185. Scott, *Macmillan, Kennedy and the Cuban Missile Crisis*, p. 159.
186. Catterall (ed.), *The Macmillan Diaries*, vol. 2, p. 513, diary entry for 28 October 1962; Macmillan diaries (unpublished), diary entry for 26 October 1962.
187. Tuchman, *The Guns of August*, p. 74.
188. Kennedy letter to Khrushchev, 29 October 1962, reproduced in May and Zelikow (eds.), *The Kennedy Tapes*, pp. 636–7.
189. Scott, *The Cuban Missile Crisis and the Threat of Nuclear War*, p. 71.
190. Ibid., pp. 71, 80, 100, 120, 147–8.
191. Scott, *The Cuban Missile Crisis and the Threat of Nuclear War*, p. 134.
192. Ibid., pp. 1–2.
193. Sherry Sontag and Christopher Drew with Annette Lawrence Drew, *Blind Man's Bluff: The Untold Story of Cold War Submarine Espionage* (Arrow, 1998), p. 45.
194. Scott, *The Cuban Missile Crisis and the Threat of Nuclear War*, p. 85.
195. May and Zelikow (eds.), *The Kennedy Tapes*, p. 519.
196. Ted Sorensen, *Kennedy* (Hodder, 1965), p. 789.
197. May and Zelikow (eds.), *The Kennedy Tapes*, p. 571.
198. Scott, *The Cuban Missile Crisis and the Threat of Nuclear War*, pp. 91–2.
199. Ibid., p. 101.
200. Fursenko and Naftali, *Khrushchev's Cold War*, pp. 478–80.
201. Scott, *The Cuban Missile Crisis and the Threat of Nuclear War*, p. 104.
202. Quoted in Scott, *The Cuban Missile Crisis and the Threat of Nuclear War*, p. 105.

203. Ibid., p. 156; Tim Reid, 'Soviet Submariner "Saved the World" in Cuban Crisis', *The Times*, 14 October 2002.
204. Catterall (ed.), *The Macmillan Diaries*, vol. 2, p. 510, diary entry for 22 October 1962.
205. TNA, PRO, DEFE 32/7, 'Record of a Conversation Between the Chief of the Air Staff, the First Sea Lord and the Chief of the Imperial General Staff in the Ministry of Defence at 14.30 on Saturday 27th October 1962'.
206. Sir Michael was speaking at the RAF Historical Society's seminar on 'The RAF and Nuclear Weapons' which is recorded in *RAF Historical Society Journal*, no. 26 (2001).
207. TNA, PRO, AIR 25/173, 'Operation Record Book, Headquarters No. 1 Group, October 1962'.
208. Ibid.
209. Ibid.
210. Clive Richards, 'RAF Bomber Command and the Cuban Missile Crisis', *RAF Historical Society Journal*, no. 42 (2008), pp. 34–6.
211. Air Vice-Marshal Michael Robinson to Peter Hennessy, 2 December 2007.
212. Air Vice-Marshal Michael Robinson, 'Summary of the Previous RAFHS Seminar on the Origin and Development of the British Nuclear Deterrent 1945–60', *RAF Historical Society Journal*, no. 26 (2001), p. 15.
213. Robinson to Hennessy, 2 December 2007.
214. Mark Ogilvie to Peter Hennessy, 10 December 2008.
215. Robinson to Hennessy, 2 December 2007.
216. Robinson, 'Summary of the Previous RAFHS Seminar . . .', p. 15.
217. Robinson to Hennessy, 2 December 2007.
218. Conversation with Air Vice-Marshal Bobby Robson, 14 December 2008.
219. Theresa Brookes speaking in *The Human Button*, first broadcast on BBC Radio 4, 2 December 2008.
220. Squadron Leader Roy Brocklebank speaking in *The Human Button*. The Bomber Controller's 'Scramble' instruction is reproduced in his paper 'Bomber Command 1960s: This Presentation Was TOP SECRET', paper delivered at Charterhouse School, 28 March 2008. It was later published under the title 'World War III – The 1960's Version', in the *Journal of Navigation*, vol. 58, no. 3 (September 2005), pp. 341–7.
221. Dr Robin Woolven speaking in *The Human Button*.
222. TNA, PRO, DEFE 32/7, 'Record of a Conversation Between the Chief of the Air Staff, the First Sea Lord and the Chief of the Imperial General Staff in the Ministry of Defence at 14.30 on Saturday 27th October 1962'.

223. Ibid.
224. Ibid.
225. Ibid., 'Annex Brief for the Chief of the Defence Staff'.
226. Richards, 'RAF Bomber Command and the Cuban Missile Crisis', p. 29.
227. TNA, PRO, AIR 24/2689, 'Minutes of the Commander-in-Chief's Conference of Group, Station and Squadron Commanders Held at RAF North Luffenham on 14th and 15th November 1962'.
228. For Cross's instructions in this eventuality see TNA, PRO, AIR 8/2238, 'Operational Readiness of Bomber Command, 1958–61', Hudleston to Cross, 11 August 1959, and DEFE 25/49, GEN 743/10 (Revise), 'Nuclear Retaliation Procedures. Report from the Working Group', 23 January 1962. For Macmillan's nomination of Butler and Home as his retaliation deputies see CAB 21/6081, 'Machinery of Government in War: BURLINGTON; Ministerial Nominations', Macmillan to Butler, 26 September 1962, and Macmillan to Home, 26 September 1962.
229. Ibid., Macmillan to Home, 26 September 1962.
230. Scott, *Macmillan, Kennedy and the Cuban Missile Crisis*, pp. 64–5, and Jaya Narain, 'Soviets Tried to Make Me Defect Says the Jodrell Bank Genius', *Daily Mail*, 22 November 2008.
231. For the Strath Report see TNA, PRO, CAB 134/940, HDC (55) 3, 'The Defence Implications of Fall-Out from a Hydrogen Bomb: Report by a Group of Officials', 8 March 1955. For the 1964 assessment see CAB 134/4291, HDC (MG) (64) 24, 12 November 1964, 'Possible Course of War after a Nuclear Exchange'.
232. TNA, PRO, CAB 21/6081, Macmillan to Home, 26 September 1962.
233. TNA, PRO, CAB 134/4290, HDC (MG) (63) 1.
234. TNA, PRO, CAB 21/6081, Macmillan to Home, 26 September 1962.
235. Hennessy, *Muddling Through*, p. 129.
236. TNA, PRO, CAB 134/4290, HDC (MG) (63) 11, 22 July 1963, 'The Report of the Working Party on the Military Functions of Central Government in War'.
237. Robert S. McNamara, *Blundering into Disaster: Surviving the First Century of the Nuclear Age* (Bloomsbury, 1987), p. 11.
238. Fursenko and Naftali, *Khrushchev's Cold War*, p. 490.
239. Ibid.
240. Sergei Khrushchev, *Nikita Khrushchev and the Creation of a Superpower* (Pennsylvania State University Press, 2000), pp. xvi–xvii. I am very grateful to my friend and colleague Professor Cathy Merridale for bringing this story to my attention.

241. Evans, *Downing Street Diary*, pp. 225–6, diary entry for 28 October 1962.
242. Catterall (ed.), *The Macmillan Diaries*, vol. 2, pp. 513–14, diary entry for 28 October 1962.
243. Evans, *Downing Street Diary*, p. 224, diary entry for 28 October 1962.
244. TNA, PRO, CAB 128/36, CC (62) 63rd Conclusions, 29 October 1962.
245. Macmillan diaries (unpublished), diary entry for 4 November 1962.
246. Ibid.
247. Horne, *Macmillan, 1957–1986*, p. 369.
248. Catterall (ed.), *The Macmillan Diaries*, vol. 2, pp. 514–15, diary entry for 4 November 1962.
249. Ibid., p. 515.
250. Sontag and Drew, *Blind Man's Bluff*, p. 176.
251. Jim Ring, *We Come Unseen: The Untold Story of Britain's Cold War Submariners* (John Murray, 2001), p. 129.
252. Catterall (ed.), *The Macmillan Diaries*, vol. 2, p. 516, diary entry for 4 November 1962.
253. Ibid.; see also Macmillan diaries (unpublished), diary entry for 4 November 1962.
254. Catterall (ed.), *The Macmillan Diaries*, vol. 2, p. 517, diary entry for 4 November 1962.
255. Macmillan diaries (unpublished), diary entry for 5 November 1962.
256. Catterall (ed.), *The Macmillan Diaries*, vol. 2, pp. 517–18, diary entry for 4 November 1962.
257. Ibid., p. 518; see also Macmillan diaries (unpublished), diary entry for 4 November 1962.
258. TNA, PRO, CAB 158/47, JIC (62) 93, 'The Threat Posed by Soviet Missiles in Cuba', 26 October 1962.
259. Ibid., JIC (62) 97, 'First Soviet Reactions to US Action and Intentions Concerning Cuba', 26 October 1962.
260. TNA, PRO, CAB 158/47, JIC (62) 10, 'The Likelihood of War with the Soviet Union up to 1966', 9 February 1962.
261. Ibid.
262. TNA, PRO, CAB 158/47, JIC (62) 99, 'Possible Soviet Response to a US Decision to Bomb or Invade Cuba', 27 October 1962.
263. Ibid.
264. Ibid., JIC (62) 70 (Final) (E), 'Escalation', 14 November 1962.
265. Ibid., JIC (62) 101 (Final), 6 December 1962, 'Soviet Motives in Cuba'.
266. A. J. P. Taylor, *War by Time-Table: How the First World War Began* (Macdonald, 1969), p. 121.

267. Iverach McDonald, *A Man of The Times: Talks and Travels in a Disrupted World* (Hamish Hamilton, 1976), p. 184.
268. Fursenko and Naftali, *Khrushchev's Cold War*, pp. 487–8.
269. McDonald, *A Man of The Times*, p. 184.
270. TNA, PRO, DEFE 13/321, 'Government War Book 1963–1964', Trend to Thorneycroft, 21 May 1963.
271. Ibid., 'Review of Government War Book Planning in the Light of the Cuba Crisis', Cabinet Office, 20 May 1963.
272. Ibid. The draft bill is appended to the review as Annex B.
273. Cinema Club, VHS CC8168; DVD (Sony Pictures Home Entertainment, ASIN: B000053W4Z, 2002).
274. Hollywood Pictures Home Entertainment Beacon Pictures, DVD 21/ D888414.
275. TNA, PRO, CAB 158/45, Part 1, JIC (62) 21, 'Indicators of Sino-Soviet Bloc Preparations for Early War', 26 February 1962.
276. Private information.
277. Private information. See Mr Cowell's obituary, 'Gervase Cowell: An Honourable Expulsion from Moscow', *The Times*, 8 May 2000.
278. TNA, PRO, CAB 134/940, HDC (55) 3.
279. TNA, PRO, LAB 12/1019, 'Central Government Study: Regional Seats of Government'. Central Government Study, January, 1961. ' "ACE HIGH". Report'.
280. Ibid., 'Central Government Study, "ACE HIGH", Exercise Situation September 1965, Main Narrative'.
281. Ibid., ' "ACE HIGH" Report'.
282. TNA, PRO, CAB 134/940, HDC (55) 3.
283. TNA, PRO, DEFE 10/402, 'Study Group', 1960, SG (60) 35, 'Note on the Concept and Definitions of Breakdown', 10 June 1960.
284. Ibid., SG (60) 13, 'Likely Effects of Nuclear Weapons on the People and Economy of a Country', 'Hypothesis I', E. Anstey, 20 May 1963.
285. Ibid., SG (60) 56, 'Birmingham Study', W. G. Weeks, 6 September 1960; SG (60) 13, 'Likely Effects of Nuclear Weapons on the People and Economy of a Country', 'Hypothesis II', E. Anstey, 20 May 1963.
286. Ibid., SG (63) 13, 'Likely Effects of Nuclear Weapons on the People and Economy of a Country', 'Hypothesis III', E. Anstey, 20 May 1963.
287. Ibid., SG (60) 36, 'Effects of Damage on a Nation', A. G. McDonald, 13 June 1960.
288. Private information.
289. Interview with Lord Allen of Abbeydale, 31 May 1994, for the Widevision/Channel 4 production *What Has Become of Us?*, transmitted 18 December 1994.

290. Conversation with Lord Janvrin of Chalford Hill, 28 January 2009.
291. Letter from Sir Rodric Braithwaite to the author, 16 November 2001.
292. Jay (ed.), *The Oxford Dictionary of Political Quotations*, p. 145.
293. Christopher Driver, *The Disarmers: A Study in Protest* (Hodder & Stoughton, 1964), pp. 94–7.
294. Ibid., p. 94.
295. Ibid., p. 93.
296. TNA, PRO, CAB 21/4762, 'Motivational Factors and Recruitment to the Civil Defence Corps', report by Market Research Department, F. C. Pritchard, Wood and Partners Ltd, October 1960.
297. Matthew Grant, *After the Bomb: Civil Defence and Nuclear War in Cold War Britain, 1945–68* (Ashgate, 2009), p. 166.
298. *Defence: Outline of Future Policy*, Cmnd 124 (HMSO, 1957).
299. Hennessy, *The Secret State*, pp. 147–9.
300. Hilary Kingsley and Geoff Tibballs, *Box of Delights: The Golden Years of Television* (Macmillan, 1989), pp. 98–9.
301. Driver, *The Disarmers*, p. 238.
302. Ibid., p. 242.
303. Ibid., p. 113.
304. TNA, PRO, CAB 186/8, JIC (A) (71) 16, 'The Security of the United Kingdom Base in a Situation Leading to a Threat of General War', 23 March 1971.
305. Grant, *After the Bomb*, pp. 177–8.
306. Ibid., p. 178; Hennessy, *The Secret State*, pp. 102–3.
307. TNA, PRO, PREM 11/4285, 'Development of Nuclear Disarmament Movement: Memorandum by the Home Office'.
308. Driver, *The Disarmers*, p. 72.
309. TNA, PRO, CAB 158/47, JIC (62) 104.
310. Driver, *The Disarmers*, p. 124.
311. TNA, PRO, PREM 11/4285, 'Development of Nuclear Disarmament Movement'.
312. Blake, *No Other Choice*, p. 223.
313. TNA, PRO, CAB 158/47, JIC (62) 104.
314. TNA, PRO, CAB 186/8, JIC (A) (71) 16.
315. Grant, *After the Bomb*, pp. 217–18.
316. *Civil Defence Handbook No. 10: Advising the Householder on Protection Against Nuclear Attack* (HMSO, 1963), p. 7.
317. Conversation with Sir Anthony Kenny, 3 February 2009. See also his *A Path from Rome* (Sidgwick & Jackson, 1985), pp. 169–90.
318. TNA, PRO, CAB 158/47, JIC (62) 104.

319. Extract from David Bruce's diary for 23 and 24 October 1962, reproduced in Scott, *Macmillan, Kennedy and the Cuban Missile Crisis*, pp. 87–8.

320. May and Zelikow, *The Kennedy Tapes*, p. 333.

321. Scott, *Macmillan, Kennedy and the Cuban Missile Crisis*, p. 88.

322. Richard Taylor, *Against the Bomb: The British Peace Movement, 1958–65* (Oxford University Press, 1988); Grant, *After the Bomb*, pp. 173–4, 175–6, 185–6, 187, 191.

323. Scott, *Macmillan, Kennedy and the Cuban Missile Crisis*, p. 88.

324. Driver, *The Disarmers*, p. 146.

325. Ibid., p. 120.

326. Ibid., p. 143.

327. May and Zelikow, *The Kennedy Tapes*, p. 369.

328. TNA, PRO, PREM 11/3690, 'Record of a Telephone Message Between the Prime Minister and President Kennedy, 24 October 1962'.

329. Letter from Professor Sir Adam Roberts to the author, 8 January 2009.

330. Ibid.

331. Peter Hennessy and Caroline Anstey, *Moneybags and Brains: The Anglo-American 'Special Relationship' Since 1945* (BBC Radio 4 Analysis/Department of Government, University of Strathclyde, 1990), p. 11.

332. Ibid.

333. Lawrence Freedman, *Britain and Nuclear Weapons* (Papermac, 1980), p. 13.

334. Catterall (ed.), *The Macmillan Diaries*, vol. 2, pp. 478–9, diary entry for 19 June 1962.

335. Horne, *Macmillan, 1894–1956*, p. 160.

336. Jay (ed.), *The Oxford Dictionary of Political Quotations*, p. 1.

337. Macmillan diaries (unpublished), diary entry for 7 December 1962.

338. Ibid., diary entry for 9 December 1962; Catterall (ed.), *The Macmillan Diaries*, vol. 2, pp. 524–5, diary entries for 10 and 11 December 1962.

339. TNA, PRO, PREM 11/4229, 'Prime Minister's Talks with President Kennedy and Mr Diefenbaker in the Bahamas, December 18–22, 1962', 'Introduction'.

340. Hennessy and Anstey, *Moneybags and Brains*, p. 11.

341. Hennessy, *Muddling Through*, pp. 111–12.

342. Ibid.

343. TNA, PRO, PREM 11/4229, 'Record of a Meeting Held at Bali-Hai, The Bahamas, at 9.50 a.m. on Wednesday, December 19, 1962'.

344. Ibid.

345. For Bevin and the Union Jack see Hennessy, *Cabinets and the Bomb*, p. 48.

346. TNA, PRO, PREM 11/4229, 'Record of a Meeting Held at Bali-Hai, The Bahamas, on Thursday, December 20, 1962'. For Khrushchev's, or, more accurately, Bulganin's threats at the time of Suez see Hennessy, *Having It So Good*, p. 445.

347. TNA, PRO, PREM 11/4229, 9.50 a.m. session on 20 December 1962.

348. TNA, PRO, PREM 11/4229, 4.30 p.m. session on 19 December 1962.

349. Ibid., noon session on 20 December 1962.

350. Ibid.

351. TNA, PRO, CAB 128/36, Part 2, CC (62) 76th Conclusions, 21 December 1962.

352. TNA, PRO, PREM 11/4229, Annex II.

353. Conversation with Lady de Zulueta, 2 December 2008.

354. Hennessy and Anstey, *Moneybags and Brains*, pp. 11–12.

355. Catterall (ed.), *The Macmillan Diaries*, vol. 2, p. 527, diary entry for 23 December 1962; Macmillan diaries (unpublished), diary entry for 24 December 1962.

356. TNA, PRO, PREM 11/4147, Ormsby-Gore to Macmillan, 28 December 1962.

357. Ibid., 'Record of a Meeting at Admiralty House at 6.00 p.m. on Monday, December 31, 1962'.

358. TNA, PRO, PREM 11/4148, Amery to Thorneycroft, 15 January 1963; Thorneycroft to Amery, 28 January 1963.

359. TNA, PRO, PREM 11/4147, 'Record of a Meeting at Admiralty House at 6.00 p.m. on Monday, December 31, 1962'.

360. TNA, PRO, CAB 128/37, CC (63) 1st Conclusions, 3 January 1963.

361. TNA, PRO, PREM 11/4147, de Zulueta to Macmillan, 4 January 1963.

362. TNA, PRO, PREM 11/4147, Dixon to Foreign Office, no. 2, 2 January 1963.

CHAPTER 6: 'SIXTY-THREE

1. The session took place at Queen Mary, University of London.

2. Catterall (ed.), *The Macmillan Diaries*, vol. 2, p. 533, diary entry for 1 January 1963.

3. Ibid., p. 539, diary entry for 28 January 1963.

4. Quoted in full as the epigraph to Jeffrey Richards and John M. Mackenzie, *The Railway Station: A Social History* (Oxford University Press, 1986).

5. Philip Larkin, 'Annus Mirabilis', in Anthony Thwaite (ed.), *Philip Larkin: Collected Poems* (Faber & Faber, 2003), p. 146.

6. Hunter Davies, *The Beatles: The Authorized Biography* (Granada, 1978), 'Introduction to the 1978 Edition', p. 9.
7. Braudel, *A History of Civilizations*, pp. xxxvii–xxxviii.
8. TNA, PRO, DEFE 4/224, 'Nuclear Targets in the United Kingdom. Assumptions for Planning', COS 1929/2/11/67.
9. *British Hit Singles*, 16th edn (Guinness World Records, 2003), p. 397.
10. Ibid., p. 75.
11. Henri Cartier-Bresson, *The Decisive Moment* (Simon & Schuster, 1952).
12. Williams, *Hugh Gaitskell*, pp. 760–63.
13. MacArthur (ed.), *The Penguin Book of Twentieth-Century Speeches*, pp. 322–5.
14. Roy Jenkins, *A Life at the Centre* (Macmillan, 1991), pp. 145–6.
15. Williams, *Hugh Gaitskell*, p. 762.
16. De Courcel was speaking at University College London on 24 November 1982. He is quoted in Lacouture, *De Gaulle*, p. 351.
17. Ibid., p. 352.
18. Ibid., p. 351.
19. Horne, *Macmillan, 1957–1986*, p. 432.
20. Hennessy, *The Secret State*, p. 202.
21. TNA, PRO, PREM 11/4230, 'Visit of Prime Minister to France: Record of Discussions with General De Gaulle, Rambouillet, 15 and 16 Dec. 1962', 'Visit of the Prime Minister to Château de Rambouillet, December 15–16, 1962'.
22. Ibid.
23. Ibid.
24. Charlton, *The Price of Victory*, pp. 293–4.
25. Ibid., p. 293.
26. Ibid., p. 291.
27. Ibid., p. 294.
28. Catterall (ed.), *The Macmillan Diaries*, vol. 2, p. 526, diary entry for 16 December 1962.
29. Lacouture, *De Gaulle*, p. 358.
30. Julian Jackson, *A Certain Idea of France: The Life of Charles de Gaulle* (Allen Lane, 2018), pp. 358–9.
31. Lacouture, *De Gaulle*, p. 359.
32. Horne, *Macmillan, 1957–1986*, p. 446.
33. Catterall (ed.), *The Macmillan Diaries*, vol. 2, p. 536, diary entry for 28 January 1963.
34. Heath, *The Course of My Life*, p. 235.
35. Quoted in Thorpe, *Supermac*, p. 537.

36. Milward, *The Rise and Fall of a National Strategy*, p. 8.

37. TNA, PRO, PREM 11/4272, 'UK Application to Join EEC: Discussions on Possible Machinery of Government Changes; Cabinet Secretary Wrote to Prime Minister', Brook to Macmillan, 23 August 1962.

38. Ibid., Macmillan to Brook, 23 August 1962.

39. This was the formulation of his famous 'events, dear boy, events' he used to Professor David Dilks, who helped Macmillan with his memoirs.

40. TNA, PRO, PREM 11/4272, Brook to Macmillan, 23 August 1962.

41. Ibid., Trend to Bligh, 12 February 1963.

42. Ibid., Trend, 'Machinery of Government in the Post-Brussels Period'.

43. Ibid., Macmillan to Bligh, 14 February 1963.

44. Ibid., Bligh's 'Note for the Record' of a meeting on Monday 18 February 1963 on 'Machinery of Government Post-Brussels Period'.

45. Catterall (ed.), *The Macmillan Diaries*, vol. 2, p. 542, diary entry for 21 February 1963; see also Macmillan diaries (unpublished), diary entry for 21 February 1963.

46. Catterall (ed.), *The Macmillan Diaries*, vol. 2, p. 542, diary entry for 21 February 1963; see also Macmillan diaries (unpublished), diary entry for 21 February 1963.

47. Thorpe, *Supermac*, p. 537.

48. Horne, *Macmillan, 1957–1986*, pp. 155, 157.

49. Catterall (ed.), *The Macmillan Diaries*, vol. 2, pp. 537–8, diary entry for 28 January 1963.

50. Anthony Howard and Richard West, *The Making of the Prime Minister* (Cape, 1965), p. 35.

51. Peter Paterson, *Tired and Emotional: The Life of Lord George-Brown* (Chatto & Windus, 1993).

52. Hennessy, *Muddling Through*, p. 247.

53. Janet Morgan (ed.), *The Backbench Diaries of Richard Crossman* (Hamish Hamilton and Cape, 1981), p. 972.

54. Catterall (ed.), *The Macmillan Diaries*, vol. 2, p. 541, diary entry for 17 February 1963.

55. Robert Pearce (ed.), *Patrick Gordon Walker: Political Diaries 1932–1971* (Historians' Press, 1991), p. 277.

56. Catterall (ed.), *The Macmillan Diaries*, vol. 2, p. 541, diary entry for 17 February 1963; see also Macmillan diaries (unpublished), diary entry for 17 February 1963.

57. TNA, PRO, PREM 11/4202, 'Budget 1963: Discussions and Correspondence Between Prime Minister and Chancellor of the Exchequer', Macmillan to Maudling, 20 February 1963.

58. Ibid.
59. Baston, *Reggie*, p. 192.
60. TNA, PRO, PREM 11/4202, 'Budget 1963: Discussions and Correspondence Between Prime Minister and Chancellor of the Exchequer', Macmillan to Maudling, 20 February 1963.
61. Macmillan diaries (unpublished), diary entry for 2 April 1963.
62. Ibid., diary entry for 3 April 1963.
63. Dell, *The Chancellors*, p. 292.
64. Reginald Maudling, *Memoirs* (Sidgwick & Jackson, 1978), p. 112.
65. Ibid., p. 114.
66. Ibid., p. 116.
67. Ibid.
68. Ibid., p. 114.
69. Ibid., pp. 114–15.
70. Samuel Brittan, 'Yet Another Unprecedented Growth Strategy Means Politics as Usual', *Financial Times*, 18 March 2011.
71. House of Commons *Official Report*, 12 February 1963, col. 1242.
72. Baston, *Reggie*, p. 183.
73. Engel, *Eleven Minutes Late*, p. 212.
74. *A Plan for the Modernisation and Re-equipment of British Railways*.
75. House of Commons *Official Report*, 3 February 1955, col. 1328.
76. Nicholas Whittaker, *Platform Souls: The Trainspotter as Twentieth-Century Hero* (Gollancz, 1995), pp. 11, 14.
77. Sampson, *Anatomy of Britain*, p. 583.
78. *The Reshaping of the Railways* (the Beeching Report) (HMSO, March 1963).
79. Conversation with Tam Dalyell, 15 April 2011.
80. House of Commons *Official Report*, 10 March 1960, col. 643.
81. *The Reshaping of the Railways*, p. 1.
82. Ibid., p. 3.
83. Terence Gourvish, *British Railways 1948–73: A Business History* (Cambridge University Press, 1986), pp. 93, 175, 397.
84. *The Reshaping of the Railways*, p. 3.
85. Charles Loft, *Government, the Railways and the Modernization of Britain: Beeching's Last Trains* (Routledge, 2006), pp. 72–5.
86. *The Reshaping of the Railways*, p. 3.
87. Loft, *Government, the Railways and the Modernization of Britain*, p. 14.
88. *The Reshaping of the Railways*, p. 4.

89. Ibid., pp. 4–5.
90. Ibid., p. 60.
91. Ibid., pp. 59–60.
92. Ibid., pp. 102–28.
93. Loft, *Government, the Railways and the Modernization of Britain*, pp. 1–2.
94. Horne, *Macmillan, 1957–1986*, p. 251.
95. Loft, *Government, the Railways and the Modernization of Britain*, p. 3.
96. Ibid., p. 6.
97. Based on Engel, *Eleven Minutes Late*, pp. 222–4.
98. Ibid., p. 224.
99. Ibid.
100. Peter Guttridge, *The Great Train Robbery* (The National Archives, 2008), p. 21. I have drawn heavily on Mr Guttridge's account, which is based in large part upon the files relating to the robbery in The National Archives.
101. Ibid., pp. 102–3.
102. Ibid., pp. 6–7.
103. House of Commons *Official Report*, 30 April 1957, col. 42.
104. Lewis Strauss, speech delivered to the National Association of Science Writers, New York, 16 September 1954. See Fred R. Shapiro (ed.), *The Yale Book of Quotations* (Yale University Press, 2006), p. 737.
105. Quoted in Simon Taylor, *The Rise and Fall of Nuclear Power in Britain: A History* (UIT Cambridge, 2016), p. 10; *A Programme of Nuclear Power*, Cmd 9389 (HMSO, February 1955).
106. Sampson, *Anatomy of Britain*, p. 521.
107. Maxwell Irvine, *Nuclear Power: A Very Short Introduction* (Oxford University Press, 2011), p. 31.
108. Taylor, *The Rise and Fall of Nuclear Power in Britain*, p. 15.
109. Irvine, *Nuclear Power*, p. 37.
110. Ibid., pp. 40–42.
111. Conversation with Lord Howell of Guildford, 12 September 2016.
112. *A Programme of Nuclear Power*.
113. Irvine, *Nuclear Power*, p. 34.
114. *Capital Investment in the Coal, Gas and Electricity Industries*, Cmnd 132 (HMSO, March 1957).
115. Maudling, *Memoirs*, p. 66.
116. *The Nuclear Power Programme*, Cmnd 1083 (HMSO, June 1960).
117. Williams, *The Nuclear Power Decisions*, p. 67.

118. Ibid., p. 68.

119. Ibid., p. 93.

120. Ibid., p. 94.

121. Sir Christopher Hinton, 'Nuclear Power', *Three Banks Review* (December 1961), p. 18.

122. Williams, *The Nuclear Power Decisions*, p. 97.

123. *Oxford Dictionary of Science* (Oxford University Press, 2010 edn), p. 174.

124. J. Hendry and J. D. Lawson, *Fusion Research in the UK, 1945–1960* (AEA Technology/HMSO, 1993), p. 1. See also Daniel Clery, *A Piece of the Sun: The Quest for Fusion Energy* (Duckworth, 2013), pp. 64–71.

125. TNA, PRO, AB 6/1994, 'Controlled Thermonuclear Reactions Work by UKAEA', Plowden to Macmillan, 9 September 1957.

126. Hendry and Lawson, *Fusion Research in the UK*, p. 44.

127. Cited ibid., p. 45.

128. Ibid., p. 51.

129. Ibid., p. 52.

130. Ibid., p. 53.

131. Sir George Mallaby, *From My Level: Unwritten Minutes* (Hutchinson, 1965), p. 67.

132. Horne, *Macmillan, 1957–1986*, p. 504.

133. Conversation with Lord Stockton, 13 April 2011.

134. Catterall (ed.), *The Macmillan Diaries*, vol. 2, p. 582, diary entry for 27 July 1963.

135. Sampson, *Anatomy of Britain*, p. 527.

136. Ibid.

137. The profile appeared as 'Lord Hailsham: Memoirs of a Genuine Eccentric', on 6 October 1975.

138. Catterall (ed.), *The Macmillan Diaries*, vol. 2, p. 252, diary entry for 18 October 1959.

139. Lord Hailsham, *A Sparrow's Flight: Memoirs* (Collins, 1990), p. 324.

140. Catterall (ed.), *The Macmillan Diaries*, vol. 2, p. 534, diary entry for 11 January 1963.

141. Horne, *Macmillan, 1957–1986*, pp. 511–12; letter from Tam Dalyell, 28 August 2016.

142. Catterall (ed.), *The Macmillan Diaries*, vol. 2, pp. 589–90, diary entry for 5 September 1963.

143. Horne, *Macmillan, 1957–1986*, p. 523.

144. Hailsham, *The Door Wherein I Went*, p. 219.

145. Ibid., p. 217.

146. Gabriel Almond, *The American People and Foreign Policy* (Harcourt, Brace, 1950), p. 138.
147. Lord Denning in his 'Introduction' to *The Denning Report: The Profumo Affair* (Pimlico, 1992), the edition of his 1963 report reissued, p. vi.
148. Andrew, *The Defence of the Realm*, pp. 398, 492–3.
149. See Hennessy, *Whitehall*, pp. 565–8.
150. *Security Procedures in the Public Service*, Cmnd 1681 (HMSO, April 1962).
151. Ibid., p. 1.
152. Ibid., p. iii.
153. Thorpe, *Supermac*, p. 540.
154. House of Commons *Official Report*, 21 March 1963.
155. Morgan (ed.), *The Backbench Diaries of Richard Crossman*, p. 989, diary entry for 27 March 1963.
156. Ibid., pp. 989–90.
157. House of Commons *Official Report*, 22 March 1963.
158. David Profumo, *Bringing the House Down: A Family Memoir* (John Murray, 2006), p. 5.
159. Lord Denning, 'Introduction', *The Denning Report: The Profumo Affair*, p. v.
160. Catterall (ed.), *The Macmillan Diaries*, vol. 2, p. 552, diary entry for 22 March 1963.
161. Claud Cockburn, *I, Claud* (Penguin, 1967), p. 179.
162. Catterall (ed.), *The Macmillan Diaries*, vol. 2, p. 552, diary entry for 22 March 1963.
163. Ibid.
164. Thorpe, *Supermac*, p. 542.
165. Catterall (ed.), *The Macmillan Diaries*, vol. 2, pp. 552–3, diary entry for 22 March 1963.
166. Denning, 'Introduction', *The Denning Report: The Profumo Affair*, p. 5.
167. Andrew, *The Defence of the Realm*, p. 495.
168. Ibid.
169. Ibid., pp. 495–6.
170. Ibid., p. 496.
171. *Denning Report*, Cmnd 2152, paragraph 33.
172. Ibid., paragraphs 33 and 34.
173. Ibid., paragraphs 35 and 36.
174. Ibid., paragraph 37.
175. Morgan (ed.), *The Backbench Diaries of Richard Crossman*, pp. 989–95.

176. Profumo, *Bringing the House Down*, p. 164.
177. *Denning Report*, Cmnd 2152, paragraph 283.
178. Andrew, *The Defence of the Realm*, p. 499.
179. *Denning Report*, Cmnd 2152, paragraph 32.
180. Andrew, *The Defence of the Realm*, p. 499.
181. Ibid., pp. 499–500.
182. Ibid.
183. Ibid., p. 500.
184. Ibid., pp. 496–7.
185. Denning, 'Introduction', *The Denning Report: The Profumo Affair*, p. v.
186. Andrew, *The Defence of the Realm*, p. 500.
187. Horne, *Macmillan, 1957–1986*, pp. 485–6.
188. Catterall (ed.), *The Macmillan Diaries*, vol. 2, p. 579, diary entry for 21 July 1963.
189. Andrew, *The Defence of the Realm*, p. 500.
190. Thorpe, *Supermac*, p. 546.
191. Home, *The Way the Wind Blows*, p. 192.
192. In conversation with Robin Day on BBC TV, broadcast 4 February 1979.
193. Enoch Powell, *Joseph Chamberlain* (Thames & Hudson, 1977), p. 151.
194. Horne, *Macmillan, 1957–1986*, p. 496.
195. Catterall (ed.), *The Macmillan Diaries*, vol. 2, p. 569, diary entry for 30 May 1963.
196. Private information. See also, Macintyre, *A Spy Among Friends*, p. 269.
197. TNA, PRO, CAB 301/269, 'The Disappearance of Harold Adrian Russell "Kim" Philby, Former Member of the Foreign Service, January 1963'.
198. Catterall (ed.), *The Macmillan Diaries*, vol. 2, p. 569, diary entry for 30 May 1963.
199. Profumo, *Bringing the House Down*, p. 188.
200. Ibid.
201. Catterall (ed.), *The Macmillan Diaries*, vol. 2, pp. 570–71, diary entry for 7 July 1963.
202. Ibid.
203. Horne, *Macmillan, 1957–1986*, p. 494.
204. Ibid., p. 496.
205. Catterall (ed.), *The Macmillan Diaries*, vol. 2, p. 395, diary entry for 21 June 1961.
206. Ibid., p. 571, diary entry for 7 July 1963.
207. Ibid.
208. Horne, *Macmillan, 1957–1986*, p. 484.

209. Sampson, *Macmillan*, p. 246.
210. Norman Shrapnel, *The Performers: Politics as Theatre* (Constable, 1978), p. 30.
211. Ibid.
212. Ibid., pp. 30–31.
213. House of Commons *Official Report*, 17 June 1963, col. 99.
214. Morgan (ed.), *The Backbench Diaries of Richard Crossman*, p. 1001, diary entry for 22 June 1963.
215. House of Commons *Official Report*, 17 June 1963, cols. 34–41.
216. Ibid., col. 62.
217. Ibid., cols. 54, 56.
218. Ibid., col. 77.
219. Horne, *Macmillan, 1957–1986*, p. 483.
220. Ibid., p. 484.
221. Catterall (ed.), *The Macmillan Diaries*, vol. 2, p. 572, diary entry for 7 July 1963.
222. Denning, 'Introduction', *The Denning Report: The Profumo Affair*, p. v.
223. Richard Davenport-Hines, *An English Affair: Sex, Class and Power in the Age of Profumo* (HarperPress, 2013), p. 294.
224. Louis Blom-Cooper, 'Prostitution: A Socio-Legal Comment on the Case of Dr. Ward', *British Journal of Sociology*, vol. 15, no. 1 (March 1964), p. 65.
225. Davenport-Hines, *An English Affair*, p. 325.
226. House of Lords *Official Report*, 20 April 1977, cols. 193–4.
227. House of Lords *Official Report*, Written Answer, 9 December 2013, cols. 111–12.
228. House of Lords *Official Report*, Written Answer, 13 September 2016. See also Patrick Kidd, *TMS* (The Times Diary), 'Better Late Than Never', *The Times*, 15 September 2016.
229. John Lawton, *Old Flames* (Weidenfeld & Nicolson, 1996), p. 85.
230. Catterall (ed.), *The Macmillan Diaries*, vol. 2, p. 588, diary entry for 29 August 1963.
231. Ibid., pp. 589–90, diary entry for 5 September 1963.
232. Ibid., p. 574, diary entry for 23 July 1963.
233. Iris Freeman, *Lord Denning: A Life* (Hutchinson, 1993), pp. 213–14.
234. Hailsham, *A Sparrow's Flight*, p. 332.
235. See Sir Martin Nourse's 'Law and Literature: The Contribution of Lord Denning', chairman's inaugural lecture, Lincoln's Inn Denning Society, 17 November 2003. I am grateful to Simon Brown, Lord Brown of Eaton Under Heywood, for bringing this to my attention.

236. *Denning Report*, Cmnd 2152, paras 319–28.
237. Ibid., paras 330–35.
238. Catterall (ed.), *The Macmillan Diaries*, vol. 2, p. 599, diary entry for 27 September 1963.
239. Shrapnel, *The Performers*, pp. 26–7.
240. Macmillan's diary entry for 20 September 1963, reproduced in Horne, *Macmillan, 1957–1986*, p. 533.
241. Carlyn Chisholm to Peter Hennessy, 7 October 2016.
242. Thorpe, *Supermac*, p. 554.
243. Horne, *Macmillan, 1957–1986*, p. 514.
244. Ibid., pp. 516–17.
245. Ibid., p. 517.
246. Thorpe, *Supermac*, p. 556.
247. Catterall (ed.), *The Macmillan Diaries*, vol. 2, p. 575, diary entry for 7 July 1963.
248. Thorpe, *Supermac*, pp. 558–9.
249. Catterall (ed.), *The Macmillan Diaries*, vol. 2, p. 603, diary entry for 8 October 1963.
250. Ibid., p. 604.
251. Horne, *Macmillan, 1957–1986*, p. 321.
252. Heffer, *Like the Roman*, p. 320.
253. Catterall (ed.), *The Macmillan Diaries*, vol. 2, p. 604, diary entry for 8 October 1963.
254. Thorpe, *Supermac*, pp. 565–6.
255. Catterall (ed.), *The Macmillan Diaries*, vol. 2, pp. 604–5, diary entries for 9 and 10 October 1963.
256. Lord Beaverbrook, *Men and Power, 1917–1918* (Hutchinson, 1956), p. 345.
257. Hailsham, *A Sparrow's Flight*, p. 350.
258. Ibid., p. 352.
259. Ibid.
260. Ibid., p. 353.
261. Ibid.
262. Butler, *The Art of the Possible*, p. 242.
263. Ibid.
264. Ibid., pp. 351–2.
265. Hailsham, *A Sparrow's Flight*, p. 354.
266. Catterall (ed.), *The Macmillan Diaries*, vol. 2, p. 607, diary entry for 14 October 1963.
267. Ibid., p. 608.

268. Ibid., p. 605, diary entry for 9 October 1963.
269. Ibid., p. 606, diary entry for 14 October 1963.
270. Quoted by Richard Thorpe while delivering his paper on 'Alec Douglas-Home: The Underrated Prime Minister' to the Twentieth Century British History Seminar, Institute of Historical Research, 9 October 1996.
271. D. R. Thorpe, *Alec Douglas-Home* (Sinclair Stevenson, 1996), p. 289.
272. Thorpe, *Supermac*, p. 560.
273. Ibid., footnote to p. 560.
274. James Margach, *The Abuse of Power: The War Between Downing Street and the Media from Lloyd George to James Callaghan* (W. H. Allen, 1978), p. 129.
275. Butler, *The Art of the Possible*, p. 243.
276. Thorpe, *Supermac*, p. 565.
277. Butler, *The Art of the Possible*, p. 243.
278. Ibid., p. 244.
279. Thorpe, *Supermac*, p. 548.
280. Thorpe, *Selwyn Lloyd*, p. 374.
281. Jonathan Aitken, *Heroes and Contemporaries* (Continuum, 2006), p. 14.
282. Ibid., pp. 14–15.
283. Ibid., pp. 15–16.
284. Ibid., p. 16.
285. Ibid., p. 18.
286. Heffer, *Like the Roman*, pp. 323–4.
287. Ibid.
288. Shepherd, *Iain Macleod*, pp. 326–7.
289. Ibid., pp. 310–20.
290. Ibid., p. 320.
291. Ibid., p. 326.
292. Horne, *Macmillan, 1957–1986*, p. 562.
293. Ibid., pp. 560–61.
294. Ibid., p. 559.
295. Catterall (ed.), *The Macmillan Diaries*, vol. 2, pp. 609–10, diary entry for 17 October 1963.
296. Ben Pimlott, *The Queen: A Biography of Elizabeth II* (HarperCollins, 1996), pp. 332–3.
297. Hennessy, *The Prime Minister*, p. 266.
298. Thorpe, *Supermac*, p. 626.
299. Shepherd, *Iain Macleod*, p. 328.
300. Ibid., p. 330. Macleod's *Spectator* article appeared on 17 January 1964.

301. Heffer, *Like the Roman*, p. 327.
302. Ibid., pp. 327–8.
303. Ibid., p. 328.
304. Catterall (ed.), *The Macmillan Diaries*, vol. 2, p. 611, diary entry for 18 October 1963.
305. Thorpe, *Supermac*, p. 626.
306. Hennessy, *The Prime Minister*, p. 29.
307. Thorpe, *Supermac*, p. 626.
308. Horne, *Macmillan, 1957–1986*, p. 565.
309. Ibid., p. 566.
310. I have the story from Michael Ancram, the Marquess of Lothian, whose mother was friend and neighbour to the Dowager Countess of Home. Conversation with Michael Ancram, 13 September 2016.
311. Heath, *The Course of My Life*, pp. 256, 269.
312. Charles Moore, *Margaret Thatcher: The Authorized Biography*, vol. 1: *Not for Turning* (Allen Lane, 2013), p. 168.

CHAPTER 7: TWEEDY ARISTOCRAT, GRITTY MERITOCRAT

1. Quoted in Hennessy, *Muddling Through*, p. 249.
2. Lord Home interviewed by the author on the BBC Radio 3 *Premiership* series broadcast on 4 October 1989.
3. Ian Mikardo interviewed for *The Scarlet Thread*, BBC Radio 4.
4. Pimlott, *Harold Wilson*, chapter 3, pp. 37–59.
5. Evidence from Dr Steedman to the Lords Committee: House of Lords Select Committee on Science and Technology, Oral Evidence, 10 January 2017. For the eight previous industrial strategies since 1945 see House of Lords *Official Report*, 29 November 2016, cols. 160–62; House of Lords *Official Report*, 23 January 2017, col. 473. For the 2017 marque see *Industrial Strategy: Building a Britain Fit for the Future*, Cm 9528 (Stationery Office, November 2017).
6. Harold Wilson, *The Labour Government, 1964–1970: A Personal Record* (Weidenfeld and Michael Joseph, 1971), p. 8.
7. Morgan (ed.), *The Backbench Diaries of Richard Crossman*, pp. 983–4, diary entry for 5 March 1963.
8. Ibid., p. 1026, diary entry for 8 October 1963.
9. The meat of the 'white heat' speech is preserved in MacArthur (ed.), *The Penguin Book of Twentieth-Century Speeches*, pp. 336–8. It can be read in full in *Labour's Plan for Science* (Labour Party, 1963).

10. Tam Dalyell, *The Importance of Being Awkward* (Birlinn, 2011), pp. 94–6.
11. *Labour's Plan for Science*, p. 7.
12. Pimlott, *Harold Wilson*, p. 305.
13. Harold Wilson, *The New Britain: Labour's Plan Outlined by Harold Wilson. Selected Speeches 1964* (Penguin Special, 1964).
14. Ibid., p. 10.
15. Ibid., p. 12.
16. Pimlott, *Harold Wilson*, p. 54.
17. Peter Clarke, *A Question of Leadership: Gladstone to Thatcher* (Hamish Hamilton, 1991), p. 30.
18. Morgan (ed.), *The Backbench Diaries of Richard Crossman*, p. 1026, diary entry for 8 October 1963.
19. Clarke, *A Question of Leadership*, p. 258.
20. Wilson, *The New Britain*, p. 16.
21. Ibid., p. 21.
22. Ibid., p. 36.
23. Ibid., p. 30.
24. Ibid., p. 23.
25. Ibid., p. 30.
26. Ibid., p. 36.
27. Ibid., p. 33.
28. Peter Jenkins, *Mrs Thatcher's Revolution: The Ending of the Socialist Era* (Cape, 1987), p. 10.
29. Conversation with Lord Butler of Brockwell, 21 February 2017.
30. Wilson, *The New Britain*, p. 36.
31. Ibid.
32. Ibid.
33. Joseph A. Schumpeter, *Capitalism, Socialism and Democracy*, 4th edn (Allen & Unwin, 1952, first published 1942), p. 83.
34. Ibid.
35. Wilson, *The New Britain*, p. 47.
36. Ibid., p. 43.
37. Ibid., p. 44.
38. Kenneth Young, *Sir Alec Douglas-Home* (Dent, 1970), pp. 173–4.
39. Howard and West, *The Making of the Prime Minister*, pp. 94–5.
40. Wilson, *The New Britain*, p. 9.
41. Ibid., p. 10.
42. Howard and West, *The Making of the Prime Minister*, p. 198.
43. Home, *The Way the Wind Blows*, p. 203.

44. Ibid., p. 188.
45. Ibid., p. 186.
46. We were discussing the proofs of the second volume of Alistair Horne's biography of Macmillan, which I had carried with me to Lord Home's house in the Borders, The Hirsel, before undertaking a BBC Radio interview. Conversation with Lord Home, 8 May 1989.
47. Thorpe, *Selwyn Lloyd*, p. 436.
48. Ibid., p. 383.
49. Catterall (ed.), *The Macmillan Diaries*, vol. 2, p. 633, diary entry for 25 April 1964.
50. Thorpe, *Selwyn Lloyd*, p. 383.
51. Conversation with Lord Home, 8 May 1989.
52. Thorpe, *Alec Douglas-Home*, p. 319.
53. Shepherd, *Iain Macleod*, pp. 67–8.
54. Conversation with Lord Heseltine, 9 April 2017.
55. Jay (ed.), *The Oxford Dictionary of Political Quotations*, p. 242; Richard Thorpe, 'Magic Circle', *Oxford Dictionary of National Biography* online, article published 19 May 2011.
56. Iain Macleod, 'The Tory Leadership', *Spectator*, 17 January 1964.
57. Catterall (ed.), *The Macmillan Diaries*, vol. 2, pp. 624–5, diary entry for 18 January 1964.
58. Ibid., p. 625, diary entry for 19 January 1964.
59. Ibid.
60. Thorpe, *Alec Douglas-Home*, p. 344; Thorpe, 'Magic Circle'.
61. Home, *The Way the Wind Blows*, p. 184.
62. Shepherd, *Iain Macleod*, p. 358.
63. Quoted ibid., p. 365.
64. Home, *The Way the Wind Blows*, p. 221.
65. Hennessy, *Muddling Through*, p. 268.
66. Heffer, *Like the Roman*, p. 534.
67. Powell's speech to the Royal Society of St George is reproduced in Enoch Powell, *Freedom and Reality*, ed. John Wood (Elliot Right Way Books, 1969), pp. 337–41.
68. Heffer, *Like the Roman*, p. 351.
69. *The Times*, 1–3 April 1964.
70. Catterall (ed.), *The Macmillan Diaries*, vol. 2, pp. 631, diary entry for 2 April 1964.
71. Thatcher, *The Path to Power*, p. 144.
72. Ibid., p. 129.
73. Peter Hennessy, *Cabinet* (Blackwell, 1986), p. 168.

74. Quoted ibid., p. 66. Conversation with Lord Home, 6 February 1985.
75. Heath, *The Course of My Life*, p. 263.
76. Ibid.
77. Baston, *Reggie*, p. 222.
78. Quoted in Dell, *The Chancellors*, p. 302.
79. Maudling, *Memoirs*, p. 115.
80. Ibid., p. 116.
81. Baston, *Reggie*, p. 224.
82. Dell, *The Chancellors*, p. 292.
83. Jenkins, *A Life at the Centre*, p. 291.
84. Maudling, *Memoirs*, p. 130.
85. Hennessy, *The Secret State*, p. 202; TNA, PRO, DEFE 12/321, 'Review of Government War Book Planning in the Light of the Cuba Crisis'.
86. Hennessy, *The Secret State*, p. 286; TNA, PRO, CAB 21/6081, 'Machinery of Government in War: BURLINGTON; Ministerial Nominations', Trend to Douglas-Home, 24 December 1963.
87. TNA, PRO, CAB 21/6081, Bligh to Trend, 31 December 1963.
88. Hennessy, *The Secret State*, p. 287.
89. Thorpe, *Alec Douglas-Home*, p. 339.
90. Ibid., p. 348.
91. Butler, *The Art of the Possible*, p. 256.
92. Matthew Parris and Andrew Bryson, *Parting Shots* (Viking, 2010), pp. 92–3. The Harlech valedictory telegram was despatched in March 1965.
93. The Macmillan memorandum is reproduced in Thorpe, *Alec Douglas-Home*, p. 354.
94. Ibid., p. 355.
95. John P. Mackintosh, *The British Cabinet* (Stevens, 1962).
96. R. H. S. Crossman, 'Introduction' to Bagehot, *The English Constitution*, pp. 1–57.
97. Hennessy, *Muddling Through*, p. 236.
98. Conversation with Lord Home, 8 May 1989.

CHAPTER 8: WISPS OF TOMORROW

1. Leon Bagrit, *The Age of Automation* (Penguin, 1965), p. 89.
2. Jenkins, *A Life at the Centre*, p. 130.
3. Carswell, *Government and the Universities in Britain*, p. 52.
4. Butler, *The Art of the Possible*, p. 244.
5. Ministry of Reconstruction, *Report of the Machinery of Government Committee*, Cd 9230 (HMSO, 1918).

6. *Scientific Man-Power: Report of a Committee Appointed by the Lord President of the Council*, Cmd 6824 (HMSO, May 1946).

7. Tom Wilkie, *British Science and Politics Since 1945* (Blackwell/Institute of Contemporary British History, 1991), p. 49.

8. *Committee of Enquiry into the Organisation of Civil Science*, Cmnd 2171 (HMSO, October 1963).

9. Committee on Higher Education, *Higher Education*, Cmnd 2154 (HMSO, October 1963).

10. Wilkie, *British Science and Politics Since 1945*, p. 68.

11. To borrow the distinction drawn by Lord Smith of Clifton, Trevor Smith, the political scientist who has used it frequently in conversations with the author.

12. Stefan Collini, *Speaking of Universities* (Verso, 2017), p. 64.

13. *Higher Education*, p. 5.

14. Ibid., p. 6.

15. *Grants to Students*, Cmnd 1051.

16. Iain Dale (ed.), *Conservative Party General Election Manifestos, 1900–1997* (Politico's/Routledge, 2000), p. 154.

17. Dale (ed.), *Labour Party General Election Manifestos*, p. 115.

18. Iain Dale (ed.), *Liberal Party General Election Manifestos, 1900–1997* (Politico's/Routledge, 2000), p. 114.

19. Bagrit, *The Age of Automation*, p. 38.

20. Ibid., p. 33.

21. Ibid., p. 83.

22. Ibid., p. 82.

23. Ibid.

24. Ibid., p. 74.

25. Ibid., p. 51.

26. Richard Weight, *MOD! A Very British Style* (Bodley Head, 2013), p. 114.

27. Ibid.

28. Richard Williams, 'Jack Good. Visionary Producer Who Led a Revolution in the Coverage of Popular Music on Television', *Guardian*, 2 October 2017.

29. Adrian Thrills, *You're Not Singing Anymore: A Riotous Celebration of Football Chants and the Culture that Spawned Them* (Ebury Press, 1998), pp. 29–30.

30. In 2017 the club created *Liverpool Sound*, a fascinating film of how the leading chant-makers among their fanbase set about their craft.

31. Thrills, *You're Not Singing Anymore*, p. 31.

32. Phil Hardy and Dave Laing, *The Faber Companion to 20th Century Popular Music* (Faber & Faber, 1990), p. 668.

33. Charles Woodley, *Flying to the Sun: A History of Britain's Holiday Airlines* (The History Press, 2016), pp. 7–10.

34. Roger Bray and Vladimir Raitz, *Flight to the Sun: The Story of the Holiday Revolution* (Continuum, 2001).

35. Ibid., pp. 81–2.

36. Ibid., p. 80.

37. Ibid., p. 81.

38. Ibid.

39. Christopher Driver, *The British at Table, 1940–1980* (Chatto & Windos and Hogarth Press, 1983), p. 83.

40. Ibid., p. 73.

41. The Royal College of Physicians, *Smoking and Health* (Pitman Medical, 1962).

42. Conrad Keating, *Smoking Kills: The Revolutionary Life of Richard Doll* (Signal, 2009), p. 88.

43. Richard Doll and A. Bradford Hill, 'Smoking and Carcinoma of the Lung: Preliminary Report', *British Medical Journal*, vol. 2, no. 4682 (1950), pp. 739–48.

44. Keating, *Smoking Kills*, p. 89.

45. Doll and Hill, 'Smoking and Carcinoma of the Lung', p. 746.

46. Keating, *Smoking Kills*, p. 229.

47. Ibid.

48. Lara V. Marks, *Sexual Chemistry: A History of the Contraceptive Pill* (Yale University Press, 2001). See especially chapter 8, 'A Dream Come True', pp. 138–57.

49. Roy Porter, *The Greatest Benefit to Mankind: A Medical History of Humanity from Antiquity to the Present* (HarperCollins, 1997), p. 569.

50. This and the following ibid., p. 570.

51. Ibid.; Marks, *Sexual Chemistry*, p. 194.

52. Richard Weight to Peter Hennessy, November 2017. I am hugely grateful to Dr Weight for his briefings on drug use and public policy and for insights into his thinking ahead of the publication of his *Pleasure Island: Drugs and the British* (Oxford University Press, forthcoming).

53. Weight to the author, November 2017.

54. Weight to the author, September 2017.

55. Weight, *MOD!*, pp. 213–17.

56. Henry Fairlie, *The Life of Politics* (Methuen, 1968), p. 16. Macmillan's view is expressed in a footnote on that page.

57. Grace Davie, *Religion in Britain Since 1945: Believing Without Belonging* (Institute of Contemporary British History/Blackwell, 1994), p. 33.
58. Halsey (ed.), *British Social Trends Since 1900*, p. 524.
59. Sampson, *Anatomy of Britain*, p. 176.
60. Halsey (ed.), *British Social Trends Since 1900*, p. 524.
61. Hennessy, *The Prime Minister*, p. 250.
62. John A. T. Robinson, *Honest to God* (SCM Press, 1963).
63. John Bowker (ed.), *The Oxford Dictionary of World Religions* (Oxford University Press, 1997), p. 821.
64. Quoted in Monica Furlong, *C of E: The State It's In* (Hodder, 2000), p. 115.
65. Bowker (ed.), *The Oxford Dictionary of World Religions*, p. 1017.
66. Matthew Cooper, 'The Labour Governments 1964–1970 and the Other Equalities', unpublished PhD thesis (University of London, 2013), p. iii.
67. Ibid., p. 203.
68. Timmins, *The Five Giants*, pp. 239–40.
69. Ibid., p. 239.
70. Ibid., p. 99.
71. *Report of the Endowed Schools Commission*, House of Commons, 1868, vol. 28, part 1, pp. 79–80.
72. Peter Hennessy, *Distilling the Frenzy: Writing the History of One's Own Times* (Biteback, 2013), p. 26.
73. A. J. P. Taylor, *A Personal History* (Hamish Hamilton, 1983), p. 227.
74. Jay (ed.), *The Oxford Dictionary of Political Quotations*, p. 185. Lord Hurd delivered his remark on 3 February 1993.
75. Conversation with Lord Waldegrave of North Hill, 27 July 2011.
76. David Hannay, *Britain's Quest for a Role: A Diplomatic Memoir from Europe to the UN* (I. B. Tauris, 2013), p. 182.
77. House of Commons Foreign Affairs Select Committee, Oral Evidence, 'The UK's Influence in the UN', 19 December 2017, Question 24, HC 675.
78. *The Oxford Dictionary of Quotations*, 2nd edn (Oxford University Press, 1968), p. 14. The version given is: 'Give me but one firm spot on which to stand, and I will move the earth.'
79. Macmillan to the Queen, 7 October 1962. Quoted from the Macmillan Archives in Horne, *Macmillan, 1957–1986*, p. 358.
80. Private information.
81. Ben Pimlott, *The Queen: Elizabeth and the Monarchy*, Golden Jubilee edn (HarperCollins, 2002), p. 314.
82. Lacouture, *De Gaulle*, p. 352.

CHAPTER 9: THE 8.15 FROM LIME STREET

1. D. E. Butler and Anthony King, *The British General Election of 1964* (Macmillan, 1965), p. 110.
2. Ibid., p. 126.
3. George Gale, 'On Tour Yesterday, the Man on the Edge of Things', *Daily Express*, 9 October 1964.
4. Howard and West, *The Making of the Prime Minister*, p. 230.
5. Private information.
6. TNA, PRO, CAB 301/194, 'Views of Harold Wilson (as Leader of the Opposition and Later Prime Minister) on the Machinery of Government', Helsby to Trend, 28 July 1964.
7. Paterson, *Tired and Emotional*.
8. TNA, PRO, CAB 301/194, Helsby to Trend, 28 July 1964.
9. Hennessy, *Whitehall*, pp. 182–8.
10. TNA, PRO, CAB 301/204, 'Briefing of Ministers in an Incoming Administration', Cunningham to Trend, 30 September 1964.
11. Ibid., Hollis to Trend, 1 October 1964.
12. Catterall (ed.), *The Macmillan Diaries*, vol. 2, p. 575, diary entry for 11 July 1963.
13. Butler and King, *The British General Election of 1964*, p. 120; Thorpe, *Alec Douglas-Home*, p. 361.
14. Butler and King, *The British General Election of 1964*, p. 156.
15. Geoffrey Goodman, *From Bevan to Blair: Fifty Years Reporting from the Political Front Line* (Pluto Press, 2003), p. 80.
16. Ibid., p. 83.
17. Ibid., pp. 106–7.
18. Ibid., p. 107.
19. Howard and West, *The Making of the Prime Minister*, p. 198.
20. Aitken, *Heroes and Contemporaries*, pp. 73–4.
21. Ibid., pp. 74–5.
22. Peter Riddell and I first talked about this in the 1980s. We reprised the theme once more in conversation on 6 August 2017.
23. Dale (ed.), *Labour Party General Election Manifestos*, p. 109.
24. A phrase he used on several occasions, including in conversation with the author.
25. Dale (ed.), *Conservative Party General Election Manifestos*, p. 147.
26. Ibid., p. 148.
27. Dale (ed.), *Labour Party General Election Manifestos*, p. 110.

28. Ibid., pp. 114–15.
29. Dale (ed.), *Conservative Party General Election Manifestos*, p. 153.
30. It is one of the themes of Cooper, 'The Labour Governments 1964–1970 and the Other Equalities'.
31. Dale (ed.), *Labour Party General Election Manifestos*, p. 120.
32. Ibid., pp. 119–20.
33. Dale (ed.), *Conservative Party General Election Manifestos*, p. 145.
34. Ibid., p. 146.
35. Dale (ed.), *Labour Party General Election Manifestos*, pp. 123–4.
36. Dale (ed.), *Conservative Party General Election Manifestos*, p. 145.
37. Hennessy, *Muddling Through*, p. 114.
38. TNA, PRO, PREM 11/4733, 'Talks on Defence Policy with Members of HM Opposition', Thorneycroft to Douglas-Home, 3 February 1964.
39. Butler and King, *The British General Election of 1964*, pp. 354, 364.
40. Ibid., p. 354.
41. Ibid., p. 291.
42. Pimlott, *Harold Wilson*, p. 355.
43. Howard and West, *The Making of the Prime Minister*, p. 173.
44. Ibid., p. 148.
45. Ibid., p. 177.
46. Ibid.
47. Ibid.
48. Ibid., p. 180.
49. Ibid.
50. Butler and King, *The British General Election of 1964*, p. 116.
51. Howard and West, *The Making of the Prime Minister*, p. 180.
52. Quoted ibid., p. 190.
53. Goodman, *From Bevan to Blair*, pp. 107–8.
54. Howard and West, *The Making of the Prime Minister*, p. 192.
55. Butler and King, *The British General Election of 1964*, p. 120.
56. Howard and West, *The Making of the Prime Minister*, p. 196.
57. Howard, *RAB*, p. 334.
58. Ibid.
59. Ibid.
60. Butler and King, *The British General Election of 1964*, p. 250.
61. E-mail from Bernard Donoughue, 10 August 2017.
62. Thorpe, *Alec Douglas-Home*, p. 372.
63. Howard and West, *The Making of the Prime Minister*, p. 222.
64. Ibid., pp. 222–3.
65. Ibid., p. 223.

66. Ibid., p. 227.
67. Butler and King, *The British General Election of 1964*, p. 208.
68. Pimlott, *Harold Wilson*, p. 317.
69. Hennessy, *Muddling Through*, p. 255.
70. Howard and West, *The Making of the Prime Minister*, p. 227.
71. Ibid., pp. 225, 234–5.
72. Ibid., pp. 234–5.
73. Ibid., p. 235.
74. Butler and King, *The British General Election of 1964*, p. 289.
75. Howard and West, *The Making of the Prime Minister*, p. 237.
76. Private information.
77. Howard and West, *The Making of the Prime Minister*, p. 237.
78. Butler and King, *The British General Election of 1964*, p. 303.
79. Goodman, *From Bevan to Blair*, p. 109.

EPILOGUE: A CERTAIN IDEA OF BRITAIN

1. 'We Mean Freedom', Fabian Society Lecture, 1944, reproduced in R. H. Tawney, *The Attack and Other Papers* (Allen & Unwin, 1953), p. 97.
2. George Orwell, *The Lion and the Unicorn: Socialism and the English Genius* (Secker & Warburg, 1941), reproduced in Peter Davison (ed.), *Orwell's England* (Penguin, 2001), p. 264.
3. A. J. P. Taylor, *English History 1914–1945* (Oxford University Press, 1965), p. 600.
4. Cited in D. R. Thorpe, *Eden: The Life and Times of Anthony Eden, First Earl of Avon, 1897–1977* (Chatto & Windus, 2003), p. 3.
5. John Buchan, *The Thirty-Nine Steps*. This first appeared as a serial in *Blackwood's Magazine* in August–September 1915, before being published in book form by William Blackwood & Sons in October.
6. John Buchan, *Memory Hold-the-Door* (Hodder & Stoughton, 1940), p. 277.
7. Philip Bobbitt, *The Garments of Court and Palace: Machiavelli and the World That He Made* (Atlantic, 2013), pp. 155–6.
8. Ludwig Erhard, *Prosperity Through Competition: The Economics of the German Miracle by Its Creator* (Thames & Hudson, 1958).
9. Conversation with Lord Howell of Guildford, 11 October 2017; e-mail from David Howell, 15 September 2017.
10. TNA, PRO, PREM 11/3644, Macmillan to Menzies, 'Secret and Personal', 8 February 1962.

11. Robert J. Gordon, *The Rise and Fall of American Growth: The US Standard of Living Since the Civil War* (Princeton University Press, 2016), p. 538.
12. Ibid., pp. 533–65.
13. Robert Higgs, 'Wartime Prosperity? A Reassessment of the US Economy in the 1940s', *Journal of Economic History*, vol. 52, no. 1 (March 1992), p. 57.
14. J. K. Galbraith, *The Affluent Society* (Hamish Hamilton, 1958).
15. C. A. R. Crosland, *The Future of Socialism* (Jonathan Cape, 1956).
16. Avner Offer, *The Challenge of Affluence: Self-Control and Well-Being in the United States and Britain Since 1950* (Oxford University Press, 2006), p. 360.
17. Ibid., p. 357.
18. Ibid., p. 359.
19. Geoffrey Moorhouse, *Britain in the Sixties: The Other England* (Penguin Special, 1964). See especially chapter 2, 'The Great Divide'.
20. It is reproduced in Tawney, *The Attack and Other Papers*, p. 34.

Index

and the Cuban missile crisis 221,
224–9, 251, 253–5, 259–61,
280–82, 285–9
a danger to France and Germany
315
Europe as a same size economic
unit 96, 118
exploding of biggest H-bomb 228
failure in Africa 204–5, 211
and a French nuclear deterrent 114
industrial advance of 40
and intelligence effort against UK
364, 445
and Kim Philby 378
and nuclear power 355
and nuclear war 233–5, 275, 304
output per worker 77
and Patrice Lumumba 198, 203
plan for 'volunteer formations'
247
politico-military threat of 41
and the Profumo affair 225, 371,
375, 378, 385
repression in 12
and thermonuclear fusion 358
and Third World War planning
8–9
Spain 459
Special Advisory Group on the
future of the British Transport
Commission 346
Special Branch 371
Spectator, The 201
'Spies for Peace' 298
Sputnik 1, 230
Spy Who Came in from the Cold,
The (le Carré) 240–41
stagflation 126
Stalin, Josef 233
steam engines 175–7

Stedeford, Ivan 346
Steel, Christopher 109, 238
Stephenson, Hugh 284
Stepney Borough Council 193–4
sterling area 340–41
sterling exchange rate 142–3
Stevenson, Adlai 260
Stock, Victor 464
Stockton, Alexander 290
Stockton, Earl of see Macmillan,
Harold
STOCKWELL see Central
Government War HQ
(alternative), Cotswolds
Stonehouse, John 440
Strath Report (1955) 223–4, 234,
273, 291, 293–5
Strauss, Franz Josef 48
Strauss, Lewis 354
Strong, Kenneth 252
Study of History (Toynbee) 192
Suez crisis (1956) 19, 100, 182, 356,
468, 481
'Suggested Scheme of Motorways'
(1942) 171
Summer Holiday (film) 459
Sunshades in October (Macrae) 24
Swann, Donald 318, 349
Swinton, Lord 388, 395

Tanzania (Tanganyika) 195–6
Tawney, R. H. 495–6, 501
Taylor, A. J. P. 287–8, 296, 468, 495
Taylor, Simon 355
Tebay station and engine shed 176–7
Technical education 467
terrace pop 458
Terry, Walter 157–8
Test Ban Treaty conference 53, 57,
62, 66